The Great Conversation
VOLUME II: Descartes through Heidegger

The Great Conversation
Second Edition

VOLUME II: Descartes through Heidegger

NORMAN MELCHERT
Lehigh University

Mayfield Publishing Company
Mountain View, California
London • Toronto

Library of Congress Cataloging-in-Publication Data

Melchert, Norman.
The great conversation : a historical introduction to philosophy / Norman Melchert. — 2nd ed.
       p.   cm.
   Includes bibliographical references and indexes.
   Contents: v. 1. Pre-Socratics through Descartes — v. 2. Descartes through Heidegger.
   ISBN 1-55934-476-8 (v. 1 : pbk.). — ISBN 1-55934-477-6 (v. 2 : pbk.)
   1. Philosophy—Introductions.   2. Philosophy—History.   I. Title.
[BD21.M43   1995]
190—dc20   94-34907
                                                          CIP

Manufactured in the United States of America
10 9 8 7 6 5 4 3   2   1

Mayfield Publishing Company
1280 Villa Street
Mountain View, California 94041

Sponsoring editor, James Bull; *production editor,* Merlyn Holmes; *copyeditor,* Sally Peyrefitte; *text designer,* Gary Head; *cover designer,* Jeanne M. Schreiber; *manufacturing manager,* Aimee Rutter. The text was set in 10.5/12 Berkeley Old Style by G & S Typesetters and printed on 45# Glatfelter Restorecote by R.R. Donnelley & Sons Co.

Cover: *The Great Metaphysician,* 1917, by Giorgio de Chirico. Oil on canvas, 41⅛ x 27½″. The Museum of Modern Art, New York. The Philip L. Goodwin Collection. Photograph © 1995 The Museum of Modern Art, New York. De Chirico's painting reflects the image of metaphysics we find in many philosophers since Nietzsche.

Text and photo credits appear on page 649, which constitutes a continuation of the copyright page.

 This book is printed on acid-free, recycled paper.

Contents
VOLUME II: Descartes through Heidegger

Brief Contents to Companion Volume
Pre-Socratics through Descartes

A Word to Instructors

The second edition of *The Great Conversation* is available in two paperback volumes as well as in the complete hardback book. This is Volume II. It contains slightly more than half the contents of the whole, from a transitional chapter dealing with the Renaissance period to treatments of Wittgenstein and Heidegger. Volume I begins with the pre-Socratics and ends with Descartes. Two chapters overlap the volumes: that transitional medieval-to-modern chapter and the chapter containing Descartes' *Meditations*. Both volumes are appropriate as core texts for introductory philosophy courses; they could also be used in history of philosophy course sequences.

This second edition incorporates many changes aimed at greater clarity and ease of reading. The larger of these changes are listed below:

- An entirely new chapter, one on Nietzsche, has been added.
- Each chapter contains two sets of questions for student use: "Basic Questions" aimed at promoting mastery of a philosopher's views, and more advanced questions "For Further Thought."
- The book remains a selective history rather than a compendium of a little bit of everything. In this edition, however, at least some important philosophers who do not get a full dis-

cussion are represented by brief "snapshot" treatments of their thought. These philosophers are Pythagoras, Bacon, Locke, Berkeley, Spinoza, Leibniz, Schopenhauer, James, Russell, and Sartre.
- A discussion of the rights of women, focusing on the work of Mary Wollstonecraft and John Stuart Mill, has been added.
- To emphasize the fact that philosophy is written by human beings and does not drop full-blown from the sky, the book now includes pictures of many of the philosophers.
- There are brief new treatments of Zeno's paradoxes and Gaunilo's objection to Anselm's argument.
- The section on Kierkegaard's treatment of despair and the self has been substantially expanded.

The book continues to represent major philosophers through extensive quotations set in a fairly rich cultural and intellectual context. The "story" of how our thinking about fundamental matters developed from its beginnings to very recent times is still informed by the metaphor of a conversation. And the interactive character of that conversation is still made concrete by an extensive number of cross-references, both within the text and in footnotes. The three complete

---

NOTE: In this second volume, you will find some cross-references that reach back to the first volume, so there will be references to page numbers that do not exist within the scope of the book. I trust this will be neither confusing nor excessively frustrating.

works included—Plato's *Euthyphro* and *Apology* and Descartes' *Meditations*—remain cornerstones of the book.

Reactions to the first edition confirm my own feeling that this dynamic, connected, conversational approach to philosophy is an excellent way to bring beginning students into that conversation.

Acknowledgments

I wish to thank all those users of the first edition of this book, instructors and students alike, who offered comments and suggestions for improvement. I hope they will find that their counsel has had the effect they hoped for. The continued philosophical stimulation from my colleagues in the faculty seminar at Lehigh University has been invaluable. But to my own students I owe a special debt of gratitude for their excitement and enthusiasm in response to this great conversation.

The second edition, like the first, has benefited greatly from the careful and creative editing of Sally Peyrefitte. And Marianne Napravnik remains a steadfast support and friend in the often complex business of book writing. I also wish to thank the publisher's readers: James Fieser, Christopher Newport University; Michael Henry, St. John's University; Raymond Herbenick, University of Dayton; Don Porter, College of San Mateo; Merrill Ring, California State University, Fullerton; J. Wesley Robbins, Indiana University, South Bend; and Anita Silvers, San Francisco State University.

Books, like philosophies, are written by persons, not minds. We all have personal debts which are greater than mere words can express. Mine continue to be greatest to my wife, Novi.

A Word to Students

Before a dinner one night, I recounted the story of Socrates to a small group of professors—scientists and engineers. I told them about the oracle that had declared there was no one wiser than Socrates, about his perplexity on hearing this, and about his determination to discover what the oracle might have meant. I explained how Socrates doggedly interrogated his fellow citizens, trying to find someone wiser than he, with negative results: how he found that people did not seem to know what justice really was, or courage, or piety, or beauty. Worst of all, I said, he discovered that nearly all claimed to know a lot about such things; so they *thought* they knew things they didn't truly know. I told them that Socrates concluded that he *was* wiser than they, at least in one sense: that he did not claim to know what he actually did not know. And I explained that the hostility Socrates generated among those he questioned—and often publicly embarrassed—was one of the factors that led to his death at their hands.

The response of the professors was to ask, "Is this true, or are you making it up?" I was astonished. This story, I thought, was a part of our history that every educated person must surely know. But on reflection I realized that I was being naive. Why should they have known this? And why should they be expected to have a sense of the significance of Socrates for our age? Where in their largely scientific education would it have turned up?

What is true for these highly intelligent and technically proficient professors is true as well for most of us, including most college students. Ours is a particularly unhistorical age. It is the spirit of the times to be interested in the latest products, not only of our advancing technologies, but also of our writers and thinkers and perhaps especially of our moviemakers and musical performers. Paying attention only to the present, however, is like hearing just snatches of a conversation. Its meaning is unclear, and one is likely to give it an interpretation that it will not bear. For we *are* engaged in a conversation, one that reaches back to earliest times and that, barring catastrophe, will be carried on beyond us.

The topics in that conversation include some of the deepest and most persistent concerns of our species. What sort of creatures are we? What kind of world do we inhabit? What, if anything, can we know to be true? How should we behave and live? There are lots of opinions about these matters. But there is a particular way of addressing them that we have come to call "philosophy." Socrates is, we might say, the patron saint of those who ask these questions and seek to answer them in that way. What way is that? We would not be wrong to call it "rational." But to appreciate what that means, we have to follow the participants in this great conversation as they struggle with these deep and difficult issues.

This book is designed to help its readers understand some of the major milestones in this conversation. Since it is partly through this history that we have become who we are—as individuals and as members of a culture—an acquaintance with this conversation helps us to understand ourselves, our times, and our human nature. And it should make current conversations bearing on these topics more meaningful.

I take the metaphor of a conversation quite seriously. So we will eavesdrop, as it were, on Democritus as he tries to solve a problem posed for him by Parmenides. We will follow Aristotle as he criticizes his teacher, Plato. We will take note while Descartes tries to put philosophy on firm foundations—something he thinks none of his predecessors had managed to do. And we will try to understand Nietzsche's view that this whole conversation tells us more about the philosophers themselves than it tells us about reality. I will represent this ongoing debate sympathetically and *internally,* trying to refrain from imposing my own evaluations as much as possible. But I will take pains to point out the relevance of one thinker's arguments to those of another.

One of my convictions about philosophy is that it is *interactive.* When making a claim or constructing an argument, a philosopher nearly always has other philosophers in mind. That is what makes a conversation. One of the best ways to grasp the significance of an argument is to see what it is an argument *against,* as well as what it is an argument *for.* So we need to see what other views our thinker is objecting to, correcting, or elaborating on.

To help you get a feel for this conversational context, I include a large number of cross-references in the text. Taking the little time required to follow up these references will help you to understand what a philosopher thinks is at stake and why it matters that we get it right. A philosopher is someone who cares deeply about the right answer to some fundamental problem, who feels intensely the importance of some question. To understand philosophy, you need to identify these questions and feel their urgency. Pursuing these cross-references should help you do just that. I hope you will get the feeling of joining a conversation in progress and finding that a first-rate discussion is going on.

Pursuing the cross-references will also help you to avoid a mistaken impression that many newcomers to philosophy get: that this is hard-to-understand talk about something very abstract.

Philosophy is never (well, hardly ever) that. Philosophers write about the most concrete things there are—about us and our lives and the world we live in. What they write *is* sometimes hard to understand. But because they write about real issues that make a difference in our lives, it is worth the effort required to understand them.

Since philosophy is interactive, you should also pose your own questions to these thinkers. I hope that you will be not just an observer of this conversation, but a participant. One of my own teachers, a little white-haired man with a thick German accent, used to say, "Whether you will philosophize or won't philosophize, you *must* philosophize." He meant by this that we all work out answers to these questions in the living of our lives. And if this is true, surely we are wise to listen to Socrates, who tells us that, for a human being, the unexamined life is not worth living. Philosophy offers you an opportunity to improve your own present views about important matters by comparing your views with some of the best that humans have thought through the ages.

There are two stages in this process. The first stage is *understanding.* This requires that you not react too quickly to what you read on the basis of your own present views. Before you say that some philosopher's opinions are "obviously" wrong or that his arguments are absurd, make an effort at sympathetic appreciation; try to feel what it would be like to "inhabit" a world in which such views make good sense. In short, first try to see things from the philosopher's point of view, however strange it may seem to you. At the end of each chapter you will find some "Basic Questions" to help you in your quest for understanding. There is also a glossary of key words and their definitions at the back of the book. The first appearance in the text of each glossary entry is set in **boldface** type.

The second stage is *evaluation,* in which you try to reach some reasoned judgment of your own about the matter at hand. One of the best ways to do this is to write something that expresses your views, to play—if only tentatively and provisionally—the game called philosophy for yourself. Such engaged participation on your part may be stimulated by the suggestions "For Further Thought" in each chapter.

When you pose your own questions to these thinkers, you will sometimes find an answer that satisfies you. Sometimes you won't. More often you will find there are too many answers, all with some plausibility. And then you must choose.

But this is all to the good. Reflecting on the ideas in this book should help you to choose *more wisely* than you otherwise would. Part of wisdom is being willing to take responsibility for your life. You can fulfill that responsibility better if you make your choices with your eyes more fully open, being more alive to the options available.

Thinking well, moreover, is a kind of craft—just like cabinetmaking, or pottery, or gourmet cooking. As a common practice, people who want to learn these crafts apprentice themselves for a time to a master craftsman, learning the basic skills and getting acquainted with the key moves to make and the cardinal errors to avoid. You might think of the course in which this book is used as an apprenticeship in thinking, with Socrates, Plato, Kant, and the rest as the master thinkers. By thinking for a time as they think, you will improve your own skills and be able to set up shop responsibly on your own.

I will not try to give a comprehensive treatment of each thinker but will focus attention on four major concerns shared by those we call philosophers, together with some characteristic questions that express each one:

Metaphysics:	What is the nature of reality?
	What kinds of things are there?
	Is there a God?
	What, if anything, is the soul?
	Is free will a possibility?
Epistemology:	What is knowledge?
	What—if anything—can we know?
	Are there different kinds of knowledge?
	What is truth?
Ethics:	What is good?
	Are certain actions right or wrong? If so, which? And why?
	How should we live?
Human nature:	What kind of creature is a human being?

One motif, or theme, will appear again and again, most of our philosophers constructing some variation of their own on the theme. We can express the theme in various ways: knowledge versus skepticism, belief versus doubt, objectivism versus relativism. The issue is whether there is available to us a perspective, a point of view, or a method that will get us beyond the prejudices and assumptions peculiar to ourselves as individuals or as members of a culture. Is there a way to understand the world, ourselves, and human good that is universally acceptable, that is more than just the expression of how we happen to have been brought up or of the peculiarities of our own narrow experience?

This problem, which first came into prominence in classical Greece, has persisted to this day. For the most part, as we will see, the Western philosophical tradition has been one of resisting skepticism and relativism—though it is significant that philosophers have felt again and again that they *needed* to combat these views. Apparently they often felt like frontline soldiers fending off the barbarian hordes of chaos, darkness, and disorder. Whether relativism actually yields such chaos is, of course, itself an issue. Not everyone agrees.

Our own age has the distinction, perhaps, of being the first age ever in which the basic assumptions of most people, certainly of most educated people, are relativistic. So the theme we will be tracing has a peculiar poignancy for us. We will want to understand how we came to this point and what it means to be here. We will want to understand the arguments on both sides of the relativism issue.

Starting before Socrates, we will follow the thread of the conversation into our own century.

Exciting things have been happening in all the major areas of philosophy. And the relativism debate
is very much alive.

NOTE: This is Volume II of a connected two-volume work. (It is also available as a single, complete hardback book.) This volume begins with the transition from medieval to modern conceptions of the world and takes us up to important twentieth-century thinkers. The first volume deals with the dawning of philosophical thought in the West and ends with the beginning of the modern period. That transitional chapter and the chapter on Descartes are present in each volume.

   You will find cross-references throughout this book, some of them to thinkers presented in Volume I. I hope these will not be confusing to you, but may stimulate you to look further into the origins of our more recent philosophical conceptions.

For Max and Julian, Xavier and Nicholas

I was aware that the reading of all good books
is indeed like a conversation with the noblest men
of past centuries who were the authors of them,
nay a carefully studied conversation,
in which they reveal to us
none but the best of their thoughts.
—René Descartes

What is education?
I should suppose that education was the curriculum
one had to run through
in order to catch up with oneself,
and he who will not pass through this curriculum
is helped very little by the fact that he was born in
the most enlightened age.
—Søren Kierkegaard

14

Moving from
Medieval to Modern

It is not clear just when the modern era begins. But it cannot be denied that something of immense significance happens in the sixteenth and seventeenth centuries that changes life and thought startlingly. In philosophy the beginnings of modernity are usually attributed to René Descartes (1596–1650). Though there are other plausible candidates for the title of "father of modern philosophy," it is the work of Descartes that sets the agenda for most of what we call "modern" in philosophy. Despite the fact that he shares many medieval concerns and convictions, Descartes sees clearly that a new beginning is required. He dramatically poses fundamental questions. And, although his own answers to these questions will satisfy few of his successors, they all see that an answer is required. Generations of philosophers will worry about solving the problems Descartes uncovers.

We can classify these problems under three heads.

1. Descartes, himself a distinguished mathematician and contributor to physics, sees with blinding clarity the need to assimilate the methods and results of the *new sciences* into our picture of the world. Copernicus, Kepler, and Galileo had reoriented thinking about both earth and the heavens. Their new conceptions clash badly with the old. So some tearing down and rebuilding is called for.

2. Paradoxically, and to some extent accidentally, *skepticism* has arisen once more from its ashes—this phoenix that first Plato and then Au-gustine seek to slay.* Fueled by Reformation quarrels among the churches and lack of agreement among philosophers and scientists, the doubts of Sextus Empiricus spread rapidly among Renaissance intellectuals.† Descartes sees that skepticism cuts at the root of the claims made by science, philosophy, and religion alike. If we are going to rely on any one of them to tell us how things are, skepticism will have to be taken on again—and this time killed for good.

3. Both of the first two problems mean that much closer attention will have to be paid to *knowledge.* Epistemological questions begin to take center stage. Can we know anything at all? And if so, by what means? Do the sciences give us knowledge of reality? If they do, how can we be sure of that? This preoccupation with epistemological questions is the principal heritage of Descartes. In ancient and medieval philosophy, questions about knowledge are just one sort of question among many others. But after Descartes they seem absolutely preeminent. *Unless you can solve these problems, no other problems can be solved.*

Those are Descartes' problems: the problems of modern philosophy. But to feel the force of them *as problems* we need to back up a bit and sketch the context. His age is intellectually, and in other

---

*For Plato's attempt at refutation, see pp. 107–108; for Augustine's, p. 221.

†For a discussion of ancient skepticism, featuring the views of Sextus, see "The Skeptics," in Chapter 10.

ways as well, one of the most tumultous we have ever lived through. Though we are interested primarily in the intellectual ferment, we cannot help but note some of the social, political, and economic factors that make this an age of change. It will be useful to start with a review of the medieval picture of the world.

The World God Made for Man

Though there was by no means unanimity in the late Middle Ages about details, there was broad agreement about a certain picture of the world.[1] The universe, people thought, is a harmonious and coherent whole, created by an infinite and good God as an appropriate home for human beings, for whose sake it was made. It is difficult for us now to put ourselves into the place of medieval men and women and see the world as they saw it. We have been shaped by our education, which has very different presuppositions. But let us try.

It will help if we try to set aside all we have learned in school about the structure of the universe and attempt to recapture a more direct and naive interpretation of our experience. Consider the sky as you see it on a clear day or night. If you look *at* it, rather than *through* it, as those with our picture of the world tend to do, you will almost certainly conclude that it has a certain shape. It is *something* (as our term "the sky" tends to suggest). And the shape it has is roughly that of an upside down bowl. It is the roof of the earth, the "firmament" of Genesis 1 that God created to separate the primeval waters and make a place for dry land and living creatures. This view of the heavens is very common among primitive people and among children, too. We have to *learn* that the sky is not a thing.

This primitive view of the sky undergoes a great deal of rather sophisticated development by the later Middle Ages. But two things remain constant. It is still considered a thing. And its nature is defined in terms of its relation to the earth. The de-

velopment is largely due to the efforts of ancient philosophers (particularly Plato and Aristotle) and astronomers, especially an Egyptian astronomer of the second century C.E. named Ptolemy. How do they modify this primitive view?

For one thing, the earth is recognized to be roughly a sphere. So the heavens can't be completely analogous to the roof of a house or a tent. They, in fact, are spherical, too. The basic picture is of two spheres, the smaller one solid and stationary directly in the center of a much larger sphere, which is hollow and moving. The sphere in the center is, of course, the earth. And the outer sphere, composed of aether, a crystalline, weightless solid, is that of the stars, which revolve around the inner sphere once each day.

Astronomical observations complicate this picture considerably. Neither the sun nor the moon fits neatly into such a scheme, and they are given spheres of their own. Even more recalcitrant to neatness are those "wanderers" in the heavens, the planets. They seem to move in more complicated patterns, both speed and direction varying at irregular times. Much astronomical ingenuity had been devoted to the mathematical description of their paths; postulations of circles revolving around centers that are themselves revolving on circles are used to solve these problems. But the basic pattern is the same: each planet is assigned an aetherial sphere. Saturn occupies the sphere just below that of the fixed stars, and the moon occupies that nearest to the earth, with the sun and the other planets arranged between.

This universe is said to be finite. Aristotle holds that outside the outer sphere there is literally nothing—no matter, no space, not even a void.* For

---

* Aristotle does not accept the atomists' conception of a void, that is, a space in which nothing exists. His reasoning depends on the notion of potentiality. Wherever there is space, there is potentially some substance. But potentiality is just the possibility of having some form; and what is formed into a substance is matter. So wherever there is space there is matter; matter never exists unformed; and the idea of empty space is a contradiction in terms. There could not be other worlds out in space beyond this world; this world is not just the only world there is, but the only world there *could be*.

medieval Christians, however, there is something beyond the sphere of the stars. It is often called simply Heaven, but sometimes also the Empyrean, the place of perfect fire or light; it is the dwelling place of God and the destination of saved souls. (Note that heaven, on this view, has a physical location.)

In this universe everything has its natural place. The earth is the center toward which heavy objects naturally fall. The heavy elements, earth and water, find their natural place as near this center as they can. Between the earth and the sphere of the moon is the natural home for the lighter elements, air and fire. But these four elements are continually being mixed up with one another and suffer constant change.*

This change is explained by the motions of the heavens. Aristotle supplies a mechanism to explain such change. The outermost celestial sphere rotates at great speed, as it must to return to the same position in only twenty-four hours. (Compare the speed at the inside of a merry-go-round with that at its edge.) This motion drags the sphere of Saturn (just inside it) along by friction; and this process is repeated all the way to the spheres of the sun and moon. These then produce changes in the air and on the earth below them: the tides, the winds, and the seasons, for example, and the generation of plants and animals. Why, we may wonder, does the sphere of the stars move, though? Dante, whose *Divine Comedy* is a perfect expression of this view of the world, offers an Aristotelian explanation.

> However, beyond all these [crystalline spheres], the Catholics place the Empyrean Heaven . . . , and they hold it to be immovable, because it has within itself, in every part, that which its matter demands. And this is the reason that the *Primum Mobile* [or ninth sphere] moves with immense velocity; because the fervent longing of all its parts to be united with those of this most quiet heaven, makes it revolve with so much desire that its velocity is almost incomprehensible.[2]

---

* See the pre-Socratic speculations about the vortex, p. 10.

The celestial spheres are quite different from anything on earth. Here on earth all is subject to change, generation, and decay. But the spheres in which the heavenly bodies are located revolve in immutable splendor. Only one conclusion can be drawn: terrestrial and celestial substances are made of different material and governed by different laws. Spiritual beings—angels, for instance, whom Saint Thomas holds to be pure forms without matter—have their natural home in these more perfect regions.

The obvious fact that the heavens, particularly the sun, influence what happens here on earth means that what we today distinguish as astronomy and astrology are considered one science. Signs in the heavens—comets and eclipses, for instance—are considered omens that need interpretation. And the question of what they mean is scarcely distinguishable from the question of what the spiritual beings that dwell in those regions mean to convey by means of them. Virtually every astronomer is also an astrologer; as late as the seventeenth century, Kepler, recognized to possess unusually accurate astronomical data, is consulted for horoscopes. Reference to astrological phenomena is common in the work of Dante and Chaucer. Everything in the heavens is significant, since it all exists for the sake of man.

Here we come to the heart of the medieval world view. The earth is not only physically at the center of the universe; it is also the religious center. For on this stationary globe lives the human race, made in the image of God himself, the summit of his creative work. Around human beings everything revolves, both literally and symbolically. The earth is the stage whereon is enacted the great drama of salvation and damnation. It is on the earth that human beings fall from grace. It is to the earth that God's Son comes to redeem fallen men and women, graciously to save them from their sins and lead them to that heavenly realm in which they can forever enjoy blessedness in the presence of light eternal.

Nothing expresses this drama in its intimate connection with the medieval picture of the world better than Dante's great poem. The journey on which he is led, first by Virgil and later by Beatrice, traverses the known universe. As we follow that journey we learn both physical and religious truths, inextricably linked. Let us trace the outline of that journey.

Dante begins his great poem by telling us that he had lost his way and could not find it again.

> Midway life's journey I was made aware
>   That I had strayed into a dark forest,
>   And the right path appeared not anywhere.
> Ah, tongue cannot describe how it oppressed,
> This wood, so harsh, dismal and wild, that fear
> At thought of it strikes now into my breast.
>
> (INFERNO 1.1–6)[3]

The pagan poet Virgil appears and offers to lead him down through hell and up through purgatory as far as the gates of heaven. There he will be supplanted by another guide, as Virgil is not allowed into paradise. A vision of these moral and religious realities, embedded as they are in the very nature of things, should resolve Dante's crisis and show him the way again. It may also serve as a guide to the blessed life for all of us who read the poem.

The poem is a long and complex allegory, and it is possible to read it with an eye only to the values it expresses. But there is little doubt that Dante means its cosmology to be taken with equal seriousness, at least in its basic outlines. The point we need to see is that the cosmos, as envisaged by late medieval thinkers, is not an indifferent and value-less place; every detail speaks of its creator, and the "right path" is inscribed in the very structure of things.*

We can do no more than briefly indicate that structure. There are three books in the poem, *Inferno, Purgatorio,* and *Paradiso.* In each a portion of the physical and moral/religious universe is explored. The first thing to note is that to get to hell (the inferno), one goes *down*—deep into the earth. Hell is a complex place of many layers; as one descends, the sins of its occupants become more

serious, the punishments more awful, and the conditions more revolting. After an antechamber in which the indifferent reside (offensive both to God and to Satan), Dante and Virgil cross the river Acheron and find hell set up as a series of circles, descending ever deeper into the earth. The first circle is Limbo, in which are found the virtuous pagans, including Homer and Aristotle; this is Virgil's own home. Here there is no overt punishment; only the lack of hope for blessedness.

After this there are the circles containing, in an order of increasing evil:

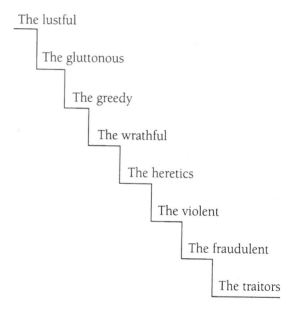

The lustful
The gluttonous
The greedy
The wrathful
The heretics
The violent
The fraudulent
The traitors

These last are frozen up to their necks in ice at the very center of the earth, guarded over by Satan—the arch traitor—in whose three mouths are the mangled bodies of Judas, Brutus, and Cassius.

Virgil and Dante climb down past Satan and climb up again through a passage in the earth until they come out on the opposite side from which they began. There they find themselves on a shore, facing a mountain that rises to the sky. This is the mountain of Purgatory, where those who will ultimately be saved are purified of their remaining faults. Here there are seven levels (corresponding to the "seven deadly sins"), each populated by

---

*Dante's *Divine Comedy* was written in the first decades of the fourteenth century.

persons whose loves are not yet rightly ordered.* These have repented and will be saved, but they still love earthly things too much, or not enough, or in the wrong way. From the lower levels to the higher, the unpurged sins are ranked from more to less serious, those highest on the mountain being furthest from hell and closest to heaven. Let us list them in that "geographical" order, so that we can imagine Virgil and Dante mounting from the bottom of the list to the top:

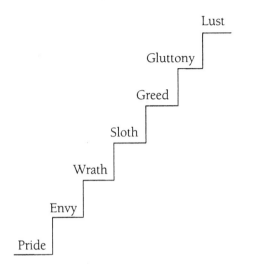

Those who dwell at each level are purging their predominant passion by suffering penances of an appropriate kind. The proud, for example, are bowed down by carrying heavy stones, so that they can neither look arrogantly about nor look down on their fellows. It is worth noting that the "spiritual" sins of pride, envy, and anger are judged to be more serious (farther from heaven) than the "fleshly" sins of gluttony and lust; this ranking roughly corresponds to the evaluations of church fathers such as Augustine, for whom pride is the root of all sin.†

At the top of the purgatorial mountain Virgil disappears, and Beatrice, who represents Christian love, takes his place. She transports Dante through

---

*For the concept of a proper ordering of one's loves, see Augustine, p. 235.
†For Augustine on pride, see pp. 237–238.

the sphere of fire above the earth to the lowest celestial sphere, that of the moon. She answers Dante's question about why the moon seems to have shadows on it and in the process gives a fine description of the celestial realm, which looks roughly like this:

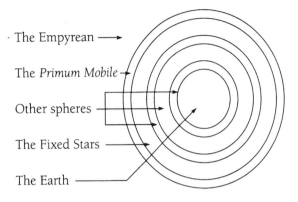

You can see that it conforms nicely to the Aristotelian/Ptolemic astronomical view we sketched earlier. Motion (energy) is imparted from outside toward the center, each of the spheres displaying in its own magnificent way the glory of God. This vision of the heavens as the visible image of the creator is summed up in the first canto of *Paradiso*.

> The glory of Him who moveth all that is
>   Pervades the universe, and glows more bright
>   In the one region, and in another less. . . .
>
> "All things, whatever their abode, [*Beatrice says*]
>   Have order among themselves; this Form it is
>   That makes the universe like unto God.
> Here the high beings see the imprint of His
>   Eternal power, which is the goal divine
>   Whereto the rule, aforesaid testifies.
> In the order I speak of, all natures incline
>   Either more near or less near to their source
>   According as their diverse lots assign.
> To diverse harbors thus they move perforce
>   O'er the great ocean of being, and each one
>   With instinct given it to maintain its course."
>
> (PARADISO 1.1–3, 103–14)

The spheres of paradise which Beatrice leads Dante through correspond to the various virtues, though Dante is careful to say that the appearance of the souls of the virtuous in each sphere is not to be taken literally. One and all, blessed souls inhabit the Empyrean realm with God himself.

The key notions in Dante's vision of the universe are order, harmony, justice, and, finally, love. The poem ends with Dante trying to describe, inadequately he admits, the vision of God. This vision is both intelligible and emotional. Its object both explains the universe and draws Dante's soul towards itself. In the end imagination fails to communicate the glory.

> But like to a wheel whose circling nothing jars
> Already on my desire and will prevailed
> The Love that moves the sun and the other stars.
>
> (PARADISO 33.143–45)

Such is the world for late medieval man: harmonious, ordered, finite, displaying the glories of its creator. Physics, astronomy, and theology are one in a marvelous integration of life and knowledge. Everything in the universe embodies a goal and purpose set within it by the divine love, which governs all. To understand it is to understand this purpose, to gain guidance for life, and to see that absolutely everything depends on and leads to God.

The Humanists

One of the influences on that magnificent flowering of arts and letters we call the Renaissance is the rediscovery of classical poetry, histories, essays, and other writings, which followed by a century or two the recovery of Aristotelian philosophy. These Greek and Roman works breathe a spirit quite different from the extreme otherworldliness expressed in the self-denial of monk's vows, on the one hand, and from the arid disputations of scholastic theologians on the other. They present a model of style, both in language and life, that seems worthy of emulation. And a rather diffuse

movement called "humanism" spreads gradually northward from Italy.

Some of the humanists are churchmen, but many are not. They belong to that aristocratic stratum of society which has leisure to cultivate the arts, paint, compose, or write. They are not, on the whole, antagonistic to the Church; nor do most of them pit the old pagan classical works against Christianity. On the contrary, they tend to see a profound harmony between Christianity and the classics. In this they are, of course, following in the steps of Augustine and Aquinas.* But there is a difference. These earlier theologians hold that pagan philosophy can be a servant to Christian understanding—but never its equal. Many humanists, however, tend to equate faith with virtue and move toward a kind of universalism: the virtuous sage is blessed, whether he knows of (or accepts) Christ as savior or not.

In a dialogue called "The Godly Feast," printed in 1522, Erasmus (the "prince of humanists") has one of the characters say,

> . . . whatever is devout and contributes to good morals should not be called profane. Sacred Scripture is of course the basic authority in everything; yet I sometimes run across ancient sayings or pagan writings—even the poets—so purely and reverently and admirably expressed that I can't help believing their authors' hearts were moved by some divine power. And perhaps the spirit of Christ is more widespread than we understand, and the company of saints includes many not in our calendar.[4]

One of his partners in the conversation, on being reminded of Socrates' attitude at his death, exclaims,†

> An admirable spirit, surely, in one who had not known Christ and the Sacred Scriptures. And so, when I read such things of such men, I can hardly help exclaiming, "Saint Socrates, pray for us!"[5]

---

* To see how Augustine used Platonic philosophy in the service of the faith, see pp. 224–225. Aquinas did much the same for Aristotle.

† Contrast this with Dante's vision 200 years earlier, in which virtuous pagans are consigned—at best—to Limbo. See *Inferno*, canto IV. For the last moments of Socrates' life, see *Phaedo*.

In another dialogue, "The Epicurean," Erasmus argues that those who spend their lives pursuing fine food, sex, wealth, fame, and power in a quest for pleasure actually miss the greatest pleasures: those of righteousness, moderation, an active mind, and a calm conscience. It is Epicurus, of course, who holds that pleasure is the one true good.* It follows that the *successful* Epicurean—the one who gets the most pleasure out of life—will live righteously and moderately, preferring the approval of God to the satisfaction of bodily appetites. But these are precisely the virtues cultivated by the Christian!

> . . . if people who live agreeably are Epicureans, none are more truly Epicurean than the righteous and godly. And if it's names that bother us, no one better deserves the name of Epicurean than the revered founder and head of the Christian philosophy [Christ], for in Greek *epikouros* means "helper." He alone, when the law of Nature was all but blotted out by sins, when the law of Moses incited to lusts rather than cured them, when Satan ruled in the world unchallenged, brought timely aid to perishing humanity. Completely mistaken, therefore, are those who talk in their foolish fashion about Christ's having been sad and gloomy in character and calling upon us to follow a dismal mode of life. On the contrary, he alone shows the most enjoyable life of all and the one most full of true pleasure.[6]

This gives us an insight into why these thinkers are called humanists.† Their concern is the development of a full and rich human life—the best life for a human being to live. Their quest is stimulated by the works of classical antiquity, which they read, edit, translate, and imitate with eagerness. They live, of course, in a culture dominated by Christianity and express that quest in basically Christian terms. But their interests focus on the human. To that end they recommend and propagandize for what they call "humane studies": an education centering on the Greek and Latin classics, on languages, grammar, and rhetoric. They are convinced that "the classics represent the highest level of human development."[7]

The ideal is a person who can embody all the excellences a human being is capable of: music, art, poetry, science, soldiery, courtesy, virtue, and piety. This renewed passion for human excellence is expressed in the art of Bellini, Titian, Tintoretto, Raphael, Holbein, Dürer, and Michelangelo. In these Renaissance painters and sculptors one finds the ideal human form, often in an idealized natural setting—whether the subject is the Christian Madonna and child or Greek gods and heroes. And sometimes classical and Biblical themes are found in the same painting.* The man who embodies this Renaissance ideal most completely is perhaps Leonardo da Vinci. His many accomplishments show what humans are capable of. He represents what humanists admired and worked for: a celebration of the human being as the central fact in all the created world.

In the 1480s, a twenty-four-year-old Italian wrote a preface to nine hundred theses that he submitted for public debate. As it turned out, the debate was never held, but the *Oration on the Dignity of Man* by Giovanni Pico della Mirandola has seldom been equalled as a rhetorical tribute to the glory of being human. We could say it is the apotheosis of humanism. Pico finds the unique dignity of man in the fact that human beings alone have no "archetype" they are predetermined to exemplify. Everything else has a determinate nature, but it is man's privilege to be able to *choose* his own nature. He imagines God creating the world. All is complete, from the Intelligences above the heavens to the lowest reaches of earth.

> But, when the work was finished, the Craftsman kept wishing that there were someone to ponder the plan of so great a work, to love its beauty, and to wonder at its vastness. Therefore, when everything

---

*See p. 190.

†Note that Erasmus here follows the lead of much Greek thought, from Homer to Epicurus. Pursuit of virtue is recommended on ground of *self-interest*. Why be moral? Because you will be happier that way. See the following pages: for Plato, pp. 132–133; for Aristotle, pp. 182–183; for Epicurus, pp. 187–192.

---

*We already find this unification in Dante; but there the classical is still severely subordinated to the Christian.

was done. . . . He finally took thought concerning the creation of man. But there was not among His archetypes that from which He could fashion a new offspring, nor was there in His treasurehouses anything which He might bestow on His new son as an inheritance, nor was there in the seats of all the world a place where the latter might sit to contemplate the universe. All was now complete. . . .

At last the best of artisans ordained that that creature to whom He had been able to give nothing proper to himself should have joint possession of whatever had been peculiar to each of the different kinds of being. He therefore took man as a creature of indeterminate nature and, assigning him a place in the middle of the world, addressed him thus: "Neither a fixed abode nor a form that is thine alone nor any function peculiar to thyself have we given thee, Adam, to the end that according to thy longing and according to thy judgment thou mayest have and possess what abode, what form and what functions thou thyself shalt desire. The nature of all other beings is limited and constrained within the bounds of laws prescribed by Us. Thou, constrained by no limits, in accordance with thine own free will, in whose hand We have placed thee, shalt ordain for thyself the limits of thy nature. We have set thee at the world's center that thou mayest from thence more easily observe whatever is in the world. We have made thee neither of heaven nor of earth, neither mortal nor immortal, so that with freedom of choice and with honor, as though the maker and molder of thyself, thou mayest fashion thyself in whatever shape thou shalt prefer. Thou shalt have the power to degenerate into the lower forms of life, which are brutish. Thou shalt have the power, out of thy soul's judgment, to be reborn into the higher forms, which are divine."

O supreme generosity of God the Father, O highest and most marvelous felicity of man! To him it is granted to have whatever he chooses, to be whatever he wills.[8]

Man as "maker and molder" of himself, able "to have whatever he chooses, to be whatever he wills." What a concept! Pico exclaims, "Who would not admire this our chameleon?"[9] With such possibilities open to them, it is no wonder that human beings should develop in so many different ways. Along with the theme of an essential unity that runs through humanity, the diversity of individuals comes to be valued more and more. Individualism, the idea that there is value to sheer uniqueness, begins to counter the uniformity of Christian schemes of salvation. Portrait painters strive to capture the unique character of each one of their subjects. And variety and invention in music and literature are praised.

Finally, the humanists recapture some of the confidence that had characterized Athenians of the Golden Age. Human failings are more apt to be caricatured as foolishness (as Erasmus satirically did in *Praise of Folly*) than to be condemned as sins. And this reveals a quite different attitude and spirit. Though the humanists do not deny sin and God's grace, they tend to focus on our capability to achieve great things. As often happens in such cases, they thereby help to make great things happen.

Reforming the Church

The world view Dante expresses in his great poem was institutionalized in the Church. The Church was the keeper and protector of Christian truths and the harbor of salvation for those at sea in sin. But the institutional Church had strayed far from the precepts of humility and love enjoined by Jesus. It had become a means of securing worldly prestige, power, and wealth for those who were clever and ruthless enough to bend it to their will.

The Church in the West was dominated by the papacy in Rome, whose occupants had, through the centuries, succeeded in bringing under their control a great variety of incomes, privileges, and powers. Popes were engaged continually in political intrigues to establish and extend their power. More than one pope during this period exceeded in influence, wealth, and power any secular prince, king, or emperor. His court was more splendid, his staff more extensive, and his will more feared than theirs. For a king could, if need be, torture and kill the body; but the pope had the power to cast the soul into Hell. If displeased with a monarch, the pope could put an entire land under the "interdict," which meant that no masses and no sacraments could be celebrated there—a dire threat indeed for those who depended on them for their eternal salvation.

No one doubts—and few doubted even then—that the Church had grown corrupt. Already in the fourteenth century Dante had set several popes, bishops, friars, and priests in the Inferno. There had been numerous attempts at reform. The establishment of new monastic orders by Saint Francis and Saint Dominic had been motivated by a desire to recapture the purity of Christian life by renouncing wealth and power. Unfortunately, their very success ensured the acquisition of wealth and power, with all the inevitable outcomes. Heretical groups, such as the Albigenses in southern France, mixed moral rigor with unacceptable theologies. (The Albigenses were exterminated after a twenty-year "crusade" called for by Pope Innocent III.)

The notorious Inquisition was established in 1231 under Pope Gregory IX, and heresy hunting gained official sanction. Heresy was considered "the greatest of all sins because it was an affront to the greatest of persons, God; worse than treason against a king because it was directed against the heavenly sovereign; worse than counterfeiting money because it counterfeited the truth of salvation; worse than patricide and matricide, which destroy only the body." If a heretic recanted under torture, he "might be granted the mercy of being strangled before being burned at the stake."[10]

From a philosophical point of view, we should note that the institution known as the Inquisition rests on several presuppositions: (1) that truth about God and man not only can be known, but is clearly identifiable and available to all; (2) that it is the Church who is the custodian of this truth; and (3) that whether one affirms these truths or not *matters terribly*. Perhaps even these assumptions do not suffice to justify such extreme measures; but it is clear both that these were actually in the background and that nothing less than these will do. These assumptions are the heritage of that blend of Judeo-Christian prophetism and classical Greek philosophy worked out first by Augustine

using the Platonic tradition and later by Thomas Aquinas using the Aristotelian. A further (but not irrelevant) question is to what extent the Inquisition was simply a technique used by those in power for consolidating their power and suppressing dissent.

Unless they could be assimilated into the structure of the Church, as the monastic orders were, reformers were harshly dealt with. The followers of John Wycliffe in England (the Lollards) were sent to the stake in 1401. Jan (John) Hus of Bohemia was burned in 1415. Savanarola of Florence was hanged and then burned in 1498. Meanwhile the Church, clutching its pomp and privileges, went from corruption to corruption. Here are a few examples. Pope Alexander VI had four illegitimate children (including Cesare and Lucrezia Borgia), though clerical celibacy was the rule. Pope Julius II led his own troops in armor to regain certain papal territories. And Leo X, made a Cardinal through family influence at the age of thirteen, is said to have exclaimed after his election as pope, "The papacy is ours. Let us enjoy it."[11]

Albert of Brandenburg, already bishop of two districts, aspired to be also Archbishop of Mainz, which would make him the top churchman in Germany. The price demanded by the Pope was high—ten thousand ducats. Since his parishes could not supply that fee, he paid it himself, borrowing the money at 20 percent interest from the banking house of Fugger. It was agreed that "indulgences" (we'll hear more about these later) would be sold in his territories; half of the income he could use to repay the loan and half would go to Rome to help build Saint Peter's Cathedral.

Such examples, which could be multiplied indefinitely, called forth a steady stream of critical responses. In the eyes of many, they discredited the claim of the Church to be the repository of truth about God and man. But it was not until the protests of Martin Luther (1483–1546) that the situation was ripe for such moral objections to make a real difference. Luther's appeal for reform coincided with a new assertion of the rights of nations against domination by the church. Princes heard not only the cry for religious reform but also an opportunity to stop wealth and power from flowing interminably to Rome.

It was religious reform that Luther was interested in. But he could address the German nobility in terms that encouraged them to think of papal taxes, fees, and benefits as exploitation of the German people. For example:

> If ninety-nine per cent of the papal court were abolished and only one per cent were left, it would still be large enough to deal with questions of Christian faith. At present there is a crawling mass of reptiles, all claiming to pay allegiance to the pope, but Babylon never saw the like of these miscreants. The pope has more than 3,000 secretaries alone, and no one can count the others he employs, as the posts are so numerous. It is hardly possible to number all those that lie in wait for the institutions and benefices of Germany, like wolves for the sheep. . . . It is not at all astonishing if princes, aristocracy, towns, institutions, country, and people grow poor. We ought to marvel that we still have anything left to eat.[12]

This is strong stuff, and it had its effect. But it is a *consequence* of Luther's views and not the heart of them. We need to understand the religious center from which such protests arose.

Luther was a monk troubled about his sins and in mortal terror of God's justice. His sins did not in fact seem so terrible in the eyes of the world, for he was a monk of a most sincere and strict kind. But he had early seen the point that God looks not to externals, but to motivations; and he could not be sure that his motives were pure.* No matter how much he confessed, he was never confident that he had searched out every tinge of selfishness, greed, lust, and pride. And these sins the righteous God would judge. Luther did penances of a rigorous sort, going so far as to scourge himself. But he could never be sure: had he done enough to make himself worthy of salvation? He suffered agonies of doubt and self-accusation.

> Though I lived as a monk without reproach, I felt that I was a sinner before God with an extremely disturbed conscience. I could not believe that he was placated by my satisfaction. I did not love, yes, I hated the righteous God who punishes sinners, and secretly, if not blasphemously, certainly murmuring greatly, I was angry with God.[13]

He was assigned by his superior to study the Bible and become a professor of theology. As he wrestled with the text of the Psalms and the letters of Saint Paul, it gradually dawned on him that his anxieties about sin were misplaced. He was, to be sure, a sinner. But the righteous God, whom Luther had so much feared, had sent Jesus, his Son, the Christ, precisely to win forgiveness for such sinners. This was an undeserved gift of grace and needed only to be believed to be effective. Even though one was not just in oneself, God "justified" the unjust by means of the cross and resurrection of Christ, who had taken upon on himself the sins of the world. Salvation did not have to be *earned*! It was a *gift*!

> . . . I began to understand that the righteousness of God is that by which the righteous lives by a gift of God, namely by faith. And this is the meaning: the righteousness of God is revealed by the gospel, namely, the passive righteousness with which merciful God justifies us by faith, as it is written, "He who through faith is righteous shall live." Here I felt that I was altogether born again and had entered paradise itself through open gates. . . .
>
> Thus that place in Paul was for me truly the gate to paradise. Later I read Augustine's *The Spirit and the Letter,* where contrary to hope I found that he, too, interpreted God's righteousness in a similar way, as the righteousness with which God clothes us when he justifies us.[14]

With this insight, the Reformation was born. The power of this idea was first demonstrated in relation to the indulgences being sold under the authority of the pope and Archbishop Albert of Mainz. An indulgence was a piece of paper assuring the purchaser of the remission of certain penalties—perhaps in this life, perhaps in pur-

---

* See the discussion of Jesus on pp. 209–211, and the similar point made by Augustine on pp. 231–235 and 242. It is perhaps significant that Luther was a monk of the Augustinian order.

gatory, and perhaps escape from hell itself. The practice of promising such spiritual benefits in return for worldly goods can be traced back to the Crusades. Popes offered heavenly blessings in return for military service in the Holy Land against the Turks. But for those who could not serve or were reluctant to go, a payment in cash to support the effort was accepted instead. This practice had proved so lucrative that, as we have seen, it was extended for other purposes—including the repayment of loans for the purchase of an archbishopric.

The set of indulgences sponsored by Albert were peddled in 1517 by a Dominican monk named Tetzel, who advertised his wares with a jingle:

As soon as the coin in the coffer rings,
The soul from purgatory springs.[15]

Although prohibited in Wittenberg, where Luther was both parish priest and teacher of theology, indulgences were sold near enough that his parishioners traveled to buy them. They came back boasting that they could now do what they liked, for they were guaranteed heaven. Luther was troubled. Was this Christianity—to buy salvation for a few gold coins? Didn't this make a mockery of repentance and the attempt to reform one's life? Indeed, didn't it make a mockery of God's grace, which was sold for worldly gain like any other commodity? On the eve of All Saints' Day, 1517, Luther posted ninety-five theses to the door of the Castle Church. He had drafted them quickly and meant them only to form the substance of a scholarly debate among theologians. But they caused a sensation, escaped his control, and were published and disseminated widely. Among the theses were these:

27. There is no divine authority for preaching that the soul flies out of purgatory immediately the money clinks in the bottom of the chest.
36. Any Christian whatsoever, who is truly repentant enjoys plenary remission from penalty and guilt, and this is given him without letters of indulgence.

43. Christians should be taught that one who gives to the poor, or lends to the needy, does a better action than if he purchases indulgences.
44. Because, by works of love, love grows and a man becomes a better man; whereas, by indulgences, he does not become a better man, but only escapes certain penalties.[16]

Let us think about Thesis 27 for a moment. Here Luther says there is no "divine authority" for Tetzel's rhyme. What does he mean by this? There clearly was ecclesiastical authority for it, at least in the sense that the selling of the indulgences was sponsored by an archbishop and the pope. But for Luther, who had spent five years trying to understand the Bible and who knew well the works of the early church fathers, particularly Augustine, this does not settle the matter at all. It didn't take a great deal of historical knowledge to discover that popes and councils of the Church had disagreed with one another and were often flatly in disagreement with the words of Scripture. So the fact that the practice was backed by the highest Church authority is just that for Luther—a fact. It does not make the practice *right*. Only a *divine* authority can determine that.*

What, then, does Luther mean by "divine authority"? Above all, he means the words and deeds of Christ. But secondarily, he means the testimony of the apostles who had known Jesus or of those (like Paul) to whom Christ had specially revealed himself. So Luther appeals to the Bible, that collection of the earliest records we have of the life and impact of Jesus. This was Luther's authority, against which the words of archbishops and popes alike had to be measured.

It is precisely here that his conflict with the established Church is sharpest. In a certain sense, the Church does not deny that Scripture is the ultimate authority; however, Scripture needs to be interpreted. And the proper interpretation of Scripture, according to the Church, is that given by the Church itself in the *tradition* that reaches

---

*Compare the speech in which Antigone defends her action defying the king's command, p. 44.

back in a long, unbroken historical sequence to the apostles. Ultimately the authority to interpret Scripture resides in the pope, the successor of the apostle Peter, of whom Jesus had said, "You are Peter, and on this rock I will build my church" (Matt. 16:18).

In an interview with Cardinal Cajetan (during the tumult over indulgences) the cardinal reminded Luther of these points. Luther was unmoved. "'His Holiness abuses Scripture', retorted Luther. 'I deny that he is above Scripture.' The cardinal flared up and bellowed that Luther should leave and never come back unless he was ready to say, 'Revoco'—'I recant.'"[17]

In a great debate at Leipzig in 1519, Luther went as far as to say,

> A simple layman armed with Scripture is to be believed above a pope or a council without it.

His opponent in the debate replied,

> When Brother Luther says that this is the true meaning of the text, the pope and councils say, "No, the brother has not understood it correctly." Then I will take the council and let the brother go. Otherwise all the heresies will be renewed. They have all appealed to Scripture and have believed their interpretation to be correct, and have claimed that the popes and the councils were mistaken, as Luther now does.[18]

This exchange gives the tenor of the arguments that continued for about four years while the Church was trying to decide what to do about the rebel. Luther appeals to the Scriptures against the Pope and the ecclesiastical establishment. They in turn point out the damaging consequences—heresy and the destruction of the unity of Christendom—if Luther is allowed to be right.

In 1521 Luther was formally excommunicated from the Church, and the split between "Protestants" and "Roman Catholics" became official. There is much more to this story, but we have enough before us to draw some lessons relevant to our philosophical conversation.

For more than a thousand years there had been a basic agreement in the West about how to settle questions of truth. Some questions could be settled by reason and experience; the great authority on these matters for the past few centuries had been Aristotle, whom Aquinas had called simply "the Philosopher." But above these questions were others—the key questions about God and the soul and the meaning of life—which were answered by *authority,* not reason. And the authority had been that of the Church, as embedded in the decision-making powers of its clergy, focused ultimately in the papacy.

When Luther challenges this authority, he attacks the very root of a whole culture. It is no wonder that there is so much opposition. His appeal to the authority of Scripture sets up a standard for settling those higher questions that is different from the accepted one. And we can now see that the crisis Luther precipitates is a form of the old skeptical *problem of the criterion,* one of the deepest and most radical problems in our intellectual life.* By what criterion or standard are we going to tell when we know the truth? If a criterion is proposed, how do we know that it is the right one? Is there a criterion for choosing the criterion?

In the religious disputes of the following century, each side busies itself in demolishing the claims of the other side. On the one hand, Protestants show that if we accept the Catholic criterion, we can be sure of nothing, because—as Luther points out—popes and councils disagree with one another. If there are contradictions in the criterion itself, how can we choose which of the contradictory propositions to accept? Moreover, popes had certainly sanctioned abuses contrary to the spirit of the Scriptures; so the claim that the interpretations of the Church constitute the criterion seems more and more hollow.

Catholics, on the other hand, argue that reliance on one's individual conscience after reading Scripture could not produce certainty, for the con-

---

* For a discussion of the problem about the criterion, see pp. 199–200.

science of one person may not agree with the conscience of another. Indeed, it is not long before the Protestants are as divided among themselves as they are united in opposing the Catholics. Luther's assumption that Scripture speaks unambiguously enough to serve *of itself* as a criterion begins to look rather naive, and the Roman insistence on the need for an authoritative interpreter of Scripture seems to be supported by the chaotic course of events.

The consequence is that each side appeals to a criterion that is not accepted by the other side; but neither can find a criterion to decide which of these criteria is the correct one!

This quarrel, moreover, is not just an intellectual and religious debate. A long series of savage and bloody quasi-religious wars ensues, in which princes try not only to secure territories, but also to determine the religion of the people residing in them.* Indeed, one outcome of these wars is that southern Germany is to this day overwhelmingly Catholic, whereas northern Germany is largely Protestant.

What the Reformation does, philosophically speaking, is to unsettle the foundations. Though the reformers only intend to call an erring Church back to its true and historical foundations, the consequences are lasting divisiveness, with those on each side certain of their own correctness and of the blindness (or wickedness) of their opponents. This unsettling of the foundations by the reformers is one of the factors that lies behind Descartes' attempt to sink the piles so deep that beliefs built on them could never again be shaken.

But these disputes of the Reformation are not the only source of Descartes' concern. We must consider next the revival of skeptical thought in the sixteenth century.

---

*Here you may be reminded of Socrates' point in *Euthyphro* 7b–d that the gods do not quarrel about length and weight and such matters, but about good and justice. Where there are accepted criteria (rules of measurement, for instance) for settling disputes, wars are unlikely. But where there are apparently irresolvable disagreements, involving appeal to differing standards, might may seem like the only thing that *can* make right.

Skeptical Thoughts Revived

As we have noted, the recovery of ancient scientific and philosophical texts (in particular, the works of Aristotle) was followed by the recovery of Greek and Roman poetry, histories, and essays. Somewhat later still another rediscovery exerted an influence.[19] In 1562 the first Latin edition of a work by Sextus Empiricus was published, and within seven years all his writings were available.* Sextus calls his views "Pyrrhonism," after one of the earliest Greek skeptics, Pyrrho. In this period of divisiveness and strife between Catholics and Protestants, Pyrrhonism strikes a responsive chord in more than one thinker who considers that an impasse has been reached. But we will focus on just one man, Michel de Montaigne.

Montaigne (1533–1592) was a Frenchman of noble birth who, after spending some years in public service as a magistrate, retired at the age of thirty-eight to think and write. His essays are one of the glories of French literature. We are interested not in his style, however, but in his ideas—ideas that a great many people begin to find attractive in the late sixteenth and early seventeenth centuries.

His point of view comes out mostly clearly in a remarkable essay called *Apology for Raymond Sebond*. Sebond had been a theologian of the fifteenth century who had exceeded the claims of Augustine, Anselm, and Aquinas by claiming not only that the existence and nature of God could be proved by reason, but also that rational proofs could be given for *all* the distinctive doctrines of Christianity. This is an astonishing claim; if true, it would mean that clear thinking alone would suffice to convince us all (Jews, Muslims, and pagans alike) that we should be Christians. No one had ever gone so far before. And, as you can imagine, Sebond attracted critics like clover attracts bees.

In his youth, Montaigne had translated Sebond's book into French at his father's request.

---

*For a discussion of the skeptical philosophy of Sextus, see Chapter 10.

Much later, he set out to defend Sebond's thesis. ("Apology" here means "defense," as it does in the title of Plato's account of Socrates' trial.) It is an unusual defense, however; and Sebond, had he been alive, might well have exclaimed that he needed no enemies with friends like this!

Montaigne's strategy is to assert first that Christianity depends entirely on faith and then to demonstrate extensively that Sebond's "proofs" of Christian beliefs are not in the slightest inferior to reasons offered for any other conclusion whatsoever. He claims that Sebond's arguments will

> be found as solid and as firm as any others of the same type that may be opposed to them. . . .
>
> Some say that his arguments are weak and unfit to prove what he proposes, and undertake to shatter them with ease. These must be shaken up a little more roughly. . . .
>
> Let us see then if man has within his power other reasons more powerful than those of Sebond, or indeed if it is in him to arrive at any certainty by argument and reason. (ARS, 327–28)[20]

Montaigne, then, is going to "defend" Sebond's claim to prove the doctrines of the faith by showing that his arguments are as good as those of his critics—because *none* of them are any good at all!

The essay is a long and rambling one, but with a method in its madness. It examines every reason that has been given for trusting our conclusions and undermines each with satire and skeptical arguments. Are we capable of knowing the truth because of our superiority to the animals? In example after example, Montaigne causes us to wonder whether we are superior at all. Have the wise given us insight into the truth? He collects a long list of the different conceptions of God held by the philosophers, and then exclaims:

> Now trust to your philosophy . . . when you consider the clatter of so many philosophical brains! (ARS, 383)

He adds,

> Man is certainly crazy. He could not make a mite, and he makes gods by the dozen. (ARS, 395)

Can we not at least rely on Aristotle, the "master of those who know"? But why pick out Aristotle as our authority? There are numerous alternatives.

> The god of scholastic knowledge is Aristotle. . . . His doctrine serves us as magisterial law, when it is peradventure as false as another. (ARS, 403)

Still, surely we can depend on our senses to reveal the truth about the world.

> That things do not lodge in us in their own form and essence, or make their entry into us by their own power and authority, we see clearly enough. Because, if that were so, we should receive them in the same way: wine would be the same in the mouth of a sick man as in the mouth of a healthy man; he who has chapped or numb fingers would find the same hardness in the wood or iron he handles as does another. . . .
>
> We should remember, whatever we receive into our understanding, that we often receive false things there, and by these same tools that are often contradictory and deceived. (ARS, 422–24)

But can't we at least depend on science? Haven't scientists discovered the truth about things? Montaigne reminds us that in old times most people thought that the sun moved around the earth, though some thought the earth moved.

> And in our day, Copernicus has grounded this doctrine so well that he uses it very systematically for all astronomical deductions. What are we to get out of that, unless we should not bother which of the two is so? And who knows whether a third opinion, a thousand years from now, will not overthrow the preceding two? (ARS, 429)

Well, maybe it is difficult or impossible to know the truth about the universe. But surely reason can demonstrate truth about right and wrong?

> Truth must have one face, the same and universal. If man knew any rectitude and justice that had body and real existence, he would not tie it down to the condition of this country or that. It would not be from the fancy of the Persians or the Indians that virtue would take its form. . . .

But they are funny when, to give some certainty to the laws, they say that there are some which are firm, perpetual and immutable, which they call natural, which are imprinted on the human race by the condition of their very being. And of those one man says the number is three, one man four, one more, one less: a sign that the mark of them is as doubtful as the rest. . . .

It is credible that there are natural laws, as may be seen in other creatures; but in us they are lost; that fine human reason butts in everywhere, domineering and commanding, muddling and confusing the face of things in accordance with its vanity and inconsistency. . . .*

See how reason provides plausibility to different actions. It is a two-handled pot, that can be grasped by the left or the right. (ARS, 436–38)

Finally Montaigne gives us a summary of the chief points of skeptical philosophy. Whenever we try to justify some claim of ours, we are involved either in a *circle,* or in an *infinite regress* of reason-giving. In neither case can we reach a satisfactory conclusion.

To judge the appearances we receive of objects, we would need a judicatory instrument; to verify this instrument, we need a demonstration; to verify the demonstration, an instrument: there we are in a circle!

Since the senses cannot decide our dispute, being themselves full of uncertainty, it must be reason that does so. No reason can be established without another reason; there we go retreating back to infinity.

Our conception is not itself applied to foreign objects, but is conceived through the mediation of the senses; and the senses do not comprehend the foreign object, but only their own impressions. And thus the conception and semblance we form is not of the object, but only of the impression and effect made on the sense; which impression and the object are different things. Wherefore whoever judges by appearance, judges by something other than the object.

And as for saying that the impressions of the senses convey to all the soul the quality of the foreign objects by resemblance, how can the soul and understanding make sure of this resemblance, having of itself no communication with foreign objects? Just as a man who does not know Socrates, seeing his portrait, cannot say that it resembles him.

Now if anyone should want to judge by appearances anyway, to judge by all appearances is impossible, for they clash with one another by their contradictions and discrepancies, as we see by experience. Shall some selected appearances rule the others? We shall have to verify this selection by another selection, the second by a third, and thus it will never be finished.*

Finally, there is no existence that is constant, either of our being or of that of objects. And we, and our judgment, and all mortal things go on flowing and rolling unceasingly. Thus nothing certain can be established about one thing by another, both the judging and the judged being in continual change and motion. (ARS, 454–55)

Let us pause to note one point in this juggernaut of an argument. Montaigne remarks that if the senses do not simply record external realities (as Aristotle assumes, using the image of a seal impressing its form on the wax), then our ideas may not correspond at all to those realities.[†] Even worse, we are never in a position to find out whether they do or not. We may be in the position of having only pictures, without ever being able to compare these pictures to what they are pictures of. Here is that depressing and familiar image of the mind as a prisoner within its own walls, constantly receiving messages but forever unable to determine which of them to trust, and utterly incapable of understanding what is really going on. This image plagues many modern thinkers, not least of all Descartes.

Like all radical skeptics, Montaigne is faced with the question of how to manage the business of living. To live, one must choose, and to choose

---

* Note that Montaigne is making essentially the same point as Pico (p. 276). There are no determinate laws for human nature. But whereas Pico takes this to be the *glory* of man, Montaigne draws from it a *despairing* conclusion: the truth is unavailable to us.

* Here we have a statement of that problem of the criterion that was identified by Sextus. For a more extensive discussion of it, see pp. 199–200.

† For a discussion of Aristotle's view of sense experience, see p. 154.

is to prefer one course as better than another. But this seems to require precisely those beliefs (in both facts and values) that skeptical reflections undermine. Montaigne accepts the solution of Protagoras and Sextus Empiricus before him of simply adapting himself to the prevailing opinions. We see, he says, how reason goes astray—especially when it meddles with divine things. We see how

> when it strays however little from the beaten path and deviates or wanders from the way traced and trodden by the Church, immediately, it is lost, it grows embarrassed and entangled, whirling round and floating in that vast, troubled, and undulating sea of human opinions, unbridled and aimless. As soon as it loses that great common highroad it breaks up and disperses onto a thousand different roads. (ARS, 387)

> . . . since I am not capable of choosing, I accept other people's choice and stay in the position where God put me. Otherwise I could not keep myself from rolling about incessantly. Thus I have, by the grace of God, kept myself intact, without agitation or disturbance of conscience, in the ancient beliefs of our religion, in the midst of so many sects and divisions that our century has produced. (ARS, 428)

You can see that skepticism is here being used as a defense of the status quo. Montaigne was born and brought up a Catholic. No one can bring forward reasons for deserting Catholic Christianity that are any better than Raymond Sebond's reasons for supporting Catholic Christianity. Reason supports the Roman view just as strongly as it supports the Protestant view or, indeed, any other view—which is, of course, *not at all*! So to keep from "rolling about incessantly," the sensible course is to stick with the customs in which one has been brought up.* In one of his sharpest aphorisms, Montaigne exclaims:

> The plague of man is the opinion of knowledge. That is why ignorance is so recommended by our religion as a quality suitable to belief and obedience. (ARS, 360)

It is not knowledge, note well, that Montaigne decries as a plague, but the opinion that one possesses it. If you are reminded of Socrates, it is no coincidence.* He was known to his admirers as "the French Socrates."

Such is Montaigne's "defense" of the rational theology of Raymond Sebond. In an age when everyone's conscience seems to demand that those who disagree are either blind or wicked, the view has a certain attractiveness. While despairing and pessimistic in one way, it seems at least to promote tolerance. Someone who is a Catholic in Montaigne's sense is unlikely to have any incentive to burn someone who differs. This is no doubt one, but only one, of the reasons for the spread of Pyrrhonism among intellectuals and even among some of the clergy.

Copernicus to Kepler to Galileo: The Great Triple Play

Renaissance humanism, the Reformation, and the undermining of accepted certainties by the new Pyrrhonists all contribute to a general sense of chaos and lost unity. But there is also a spirit of expectation. Something new is in the air; the tumults and controversies of the time are a testimony to it. The invention of the printing press together with a growing literacy spreads the new ideas. Imagination is enlarged by the discovery of the New World, and a sense of excitement is generated by the voyages around the globe. New wealth flowing into Europe from America and from the new

---

* Note how different this religiosity is from both that of the Catholic Dante (for whom the "indifferent" are rejected by both God and Satan) and the reformer Luther (for whom commitment and certainty are essential to Christianity). Can it count as being religious at all? What do you think?

* For the claim that Socrates is the wisest of men because he knows that he doesn't know, see Plato's *Apology*, 20e–23b. Socrates, however, is not a Pyrrhonian sceptic; he does not doubt that knowledge is possible; he just confesses that (with some possible few exceptions), he does not possess it.

routes to the East stimulates growth and a powerful merchant class. The isolation of Europe is coming to an end, and the reverberations are felt on every side—not least in the sphere of the intellect. The ancient authorities had been wrong about geography. Perhaps they were wrong about other things as well, and better understanding might lie in the future rather than in the past.

But nothing else can compare, in its long-term impact, with the development of the new science. More than all these other factors combined, this changes people's view of themselves, of the world, and of their place in it. Before we examine the philosophy of Descartes, who was himself a contributor to these new views, we need to look briefly at one tremendously significant shift in perspective—one that decisively overturns the entire Medieval world view and undermines forever the authority of its philosophical bulwark, Aristotle. It is traditionally called the Copernican Revolution. Though there were anticipations of it before Copernicus, and the revolution was carried to completion only in the time of Newton, it is the name of Copernicus we honor. For his work is the turning point. The key feature of that work is the displacement of the earth from the center of the universe.

We saw earlier how the centrality of the earth had been embedded in the accepted astronomical and physical theories. A stationary earth, moreover, had intimate links with the entire medieval Christian view of the significance of man, of his origins and destiny, and of God's relation to his creation. If the earth is displaced and becomes just one more planet whirling about in infinite space, we can expect consequences to be profound. And so they are, though the more radical consequences are not immediately perceived.

The earth-centered, multisphere universe had dominated astronomy and cosmology for eighteen hundred years. As developed by Ptolemy, with a complex system of epicycles to account for the "wanderings" of the planets, it was an impressive mathematical achievement, and its accuracy in prediction was not bad. But it never quite worked. And Copernicus (1473–1543) tells us that this fact

led him to examine the works of previous astronomers to see whether some other system might improve accuracy. He discovered that certain ancient thinkers had held that the earth moved.

> Taking advantage of this I too began to think of the mobility of the Earth; and though the opinion seemed absurd, yet knowing now that others before me had been granted freedom to imagine such circles as they chose to explain the phenomena of the stars, I considered that I also might easily be allowed to try whether, by assuming some motion of the Earth, sounder explanations than theirs for the revolution of the celestial spheres might so be discovered.[21]

It is important to recognize that the heart of Copernicus' achievement is in the mathematics of his system—in the geometry and the calculations that filled most of his 1543 book, *De Revolutionibus*. As he himself puts it, "Mathematics are for mathematicians."[22] He expects fellow astronomers to be the ones to appreciate his results; from nonmathematicians he expects trouble.

We cannot go into the mathematical details. But we should know in general what Copernicus does—and does not do. He does not entirely abolish the Ptolemaic reliance on epicycles centered on circles to account for apparent motion. His computations are scarcely simpler than those of Ptolemy. He retains the notion that all celestial bodies move in circles; indeed, the notion of celestial spheres is no less important for Copernicus than for the tradition. And he accepts the idea that the universe is finite—though considerably larger than had been thought. Even the sun is not set clearly in the center, as most popular accounts of his system state.[23]

But his treatment of the apparently irregular motions of the planets is a breakthrough. The planets appear to move, against the sphere of the fixed stars, slowly eastward. But at times they reverse course and move back westward. This "retrograde" motion remains a real puzzle as long as it is ascribed to the planets themselves. But Copernicus treats it as merely an *apparent* motion, the appearance being caused by the *actual* motion of the observers on an earth that is not itself stationary. And this works; at least, it works as well as the traditional assumptions in accounting for the observed phenomena. Moreover, it is aesthetically pleasing, unlike the inexplicable reversals of earlier theory. Copernicus' view, though not less complex and scarcely more accurate in prediction, allows for a kind of unity and harmony throughout the universe that the renegade planets had previously spoiled. Until the availability of better naked-eye data and the invention of the telescope (about fifty years later) these "harmonies" are what chiefly recommend the Copernican system to his astronomical successors.

At first some of them simply use his mathematics without committing themselves to the truth of this new picture of the universe. Indeed, in a preface to Copernicus' major work, a Lutheran theologian, Osiander, urges this path. Copernicus' calculations are useful, but to give up the traditional picture of the universe would mean an overhaul of basic beliefs and attitudes that most are not ready for. So if one could treat the system merely as a calculating device, without any claims to truth, one could reconcile the best of the new science with the best of ancient traditions.*

Johannes Kepler (1571–1630), however, is not content with this restricted view of the theory. A lifelong Copernican, he supplies the next major advance in the system by taking the sun more and more seriously as the true center. Oddly enough, his predilection for the sun as the center has its roots not so much in observation, or even in mathematics, as in a kind of mystical Neoplatonism, which takes the sun to be "the most excellent" body in the universe.† Its essence, Kepler says

is nothing else than the purest light, than which there is no greater star; which singly and alone is the

producer, conserver, and warmer of all things; it is a fountain of light, rich in fruitful heat, most fair, limpid, and pure to the sight, the source of vision, portrayer of all colours, though himself empty of colour, called king of the planets for his motion, heart of the world for his power, its eye for his beauty, and which alone we should judge worthy of the Most High God, should he be pleased with a material domicile and choose a place in which to dwell with the blessed angels.[24]

It may be somewhat disconcerting to hear this sort of rhetoric from one we honor as a founder of the modern scientific tradition; but it is neither the first nor the last time that religious or philosophical views function as a source of insights later confirmed by more exact and pedestrian methods.

Part of Kepler's quasi-religious conviction is that the universe is fundamentally mathematical in nature. God is a great mathematician, and his creation is governed by mathematically simple laws. This view can be traced back through Plato to the Pythagoreans, who hold (rather obscurely) that all things are numbers. In the work of Kepler and his successors, this conviction is to gain an unprecedented confirmation. Mathematics must be devised to fit the phenomena, and the phenomena are given a mathematical description.

Drawing on more accurate data compiled by the great observer of the heavens, Tycho Brahe, Kepler made trial after trial of circular hypotheses, always within the Copernican framework; but none of them exactly fit the data. He tried various other kinds of ovals without success. For the greater part of ten years he worked on the orbit of Mars. At last, he noticed certain regularities suggesting that the path of a planet might be that of an ellipse, with the sun at one of the two foci that define it. And that worked; the data and the mathematical theory fit precisely.

This became the first of Kepler's famous three laws. The second offers an explanation of the varying speeds that must be postulated in the planets' movement around these ellipses: The areas swept out by a line from the sun to the planet are always equal in equal intervals of time. The third law is more complicated, and we need not bother about

---

*Here is foreshadowed one of the intense debates in current philosophy of science: should we understand terms in explanatory theories in a "realistic" way, or take such terms as mere "instruments" for calculation and prediction.

†In *Republic* 506d–509b, Plato uses the sun as a visible image of the Form of the Good (see p. 120ff). And in his later work, *Laws*, he recommends a kind of sun worship as the heart of a state-sponsored religion.

its details; it concerns the relation of the speeds of planets in different orbits. In fact, Kepler formulated a great many laws; posterity has selected these three as particularly fruitful.

The significance of Kepler's work is that for the first time we are presented with a simple and elegant mathematical account of the heavens that matches the data; and it is sun-centered. For the first time we have a really powerful alternative to the medieval picture of the world. Its ramifications are many, however, and will take time to draw out. Part of this development is the task of Galileo.

Galileo Galilei (1564–1642) was, in 1609, the first to view the heavens through a telescope. The result was a multitude of indirect but persuasive evidences for the Copernican view of the universe. New stars in prodigious numbers were observed. The moon's topography was charted; it resembled the earth remarkably, a fact that cut against the distinction between terrestrial imperfection and celestial perfection. Sun spots were observed; it was not perfect either! And it rotated—it was not immutable! The moons of Jupiter provided an observable model of the solar system itself. The phases of Venus indicated that it moved in a sun-centered orbit.

Encouraged by the successful application of mathematics to celestial bodies, Galileo sets himself to use these same powerful tools for the description and explanation of terrestrial motion. Previous thinkers, influenced by Aristotle, had asked primarily *why* bodies move. Why do objects fall to earth when unsupported? Why does a projectile traverse the course it does? Aristotelian answers were at hand. A body falls because it is seeking its natural place. The significance of this answer can be seen by a thought experiment. Imagine that the earth is where the moon now is and that you let go of a rock some distance above the surface of the earth. What would happen? If Aristotle's answer were correct, the rock would not fall to the earth (where it *now* is) but would travel to the place where the center of the earth *used* to be; it would fly away from the earth.[25]

Place, not space, is primary in an Aristotelian world; place is a qualitative term, each place having its own essential character. The place at the center of the celestial spheres is the place of heavy elements. The concept of space, by contrast, which plays such a crucial role in the new science, is the concept of an infinitely extended neutral container with a purely mathematical description.

Note also that the Aristotelian explanation in terms of *final causes* gives no answer at all as to *how* an object falls; no specification of laws that describe its speed and trajectory is given.* But this is just what Galileo supplies in terms of a mathematical theory of motion. It is a theory that applies to *all* motion, terrestrial and celestial alike. For him, as for his two predecessors, the great book of nature is written in mathematical language. And we, by using that language, can understand it.

Let us set down some of the consequences of the new science. First, our sense of the size of the universe changes. Eventually it will be thought to be infinitely extended in space. This means it has *no center,* since in an infinite universe every point has an equal right to be considered the center. As a result, it becomes more difficult to think of human beings as the main attraction in this extravaganza, where quite likely there are planets similar to the earth circling other suns in other galaxies. The universe no longer seems a cozy home in which everything exists for our sake. Blaise Pascal, himself a great mathematician and contributor to the new science, would exclaim a hundred years after Copernicus, "The eternal silence of those infinite spaces strikes me with terror."[26]

Second, our beliefs about the nature of the things in the universe change. Celestial bodies are thought to be made of the same lowly stuff as we find on the earth, so that the heavens are no longer special—eternal, immutable, and akin to the divine. Furthermore, matter seems to be peculiarly *quantitative.* For Aristotle and medieval science alike, mathematics had been just one of the ways in which substances could be described. Quantity was only one of the ten categories, which together supplied the basic concepts for describing and explaining reality. Substances were fundamentally

---

*For a discussion of final causes, see pp. 157–158.

qualitative in nature, and science had the job of tracing their qualitative development in terms of changes from potentiality to actuality.*

But now mathematics seems to be a privileged set of concepts in terms of which to describe and explain things. Only by the application of geometry and mathematical calculation has the puzzle of the heavens been solved; and it is mathematics that can describe and predict the fall of rocks and the trajectory of a cannonball. Mathematics, it seems, can tell us what *really* is. The result is a strong push toward thinking of the universe in purely quantitative terms, as a set of objects with purely quantitative characteristics (size, shape, motion) that interact with each other according to fixed laws. It is no surprise that the implications of the new science move its inventors in the direction of atomism or, as they call it, "corpuscularism."† We will see this at work in Descartes' philosophy.

In the third place, the new science does away with teleological explanations, or final causes. The question about what *end* or *goal* a planet or a rock realizes in behaving as it does is simply irrelevant. Explanations of its behavior are framed in terms of mathematical laws that account for *how* it behaves. Why does it behave in a certain way? Because it is a thing of just this precise quantity in exactly these conditions, and things of that quantity in those conditions necessarily behave in accordance with a given law. It is no longer good enough to explain change in terms of a desire to imitate the perfection of God.‡

As you can see, this way of viewing the universe puts *values* in a highly questionable position. If we assume that the valuable is somehow a goal, something desirable, what we all want—and this is the common assumption of virtually all philosophers and theologians up to this time—where is there room for such goals in a universe like this? A goal seems precisely to be a final cause, something that operates by drawing us onward and upward towards itself. But if everything simply happens as it must in the giant machine that is the universe, how can there be values, aspirations, goals?

It looks like knowledge and value, science and religion are being pulled apart again after two thousand years of harmony. Plato, and Aristotle after him, opposes the atomism of Democritus to construct a vision of reality in which the ultimate facts are not indifferent to goodness and beauty. Christian thinkers take over these schemes and link them intimately to God, the creator. But all this, expressed so movingly in Dante's *Divine Comedy,* seems to be in the process of coming unstuck again.

One more consequence of the new science will prove to be perhaps the most perplexing of all. Galileo sees that the quantitative, corpuscular universe makes the *qualities of experience* highly questionable. If *reality* is captured by mathematics and geometry, then the real properties of things are just their size, shape, velocity, acceleration, direction, weight: those characteristics treatable by numbers, points, and lines. But what becomes of those fuzzy, intimate, and lovable characteristics, such as warm, yellow-orange, pungent, sweet, and harmonious to the ear? It is in terms of such properties that we make contact with the world beyond us; it is they that delight or terrify us, attract or repel us. But what is their relation to those purely quantitive things revealed by Galilean science as the real stuff of the universe?

Our instinctive habit is to consider the apple to be red, the oatmeal hot, cookies sweet, and roses fragrant. But is this correct? Do apples and other such things really have these properties? Here is Galileo's answer:

> . . . that external bodies, to excite in us these tastes, these odours, and these sounds, demand other than size, figure, number, and slow or rapid motion, I do not believe; and I judge that, if the ears, the tongue, and the nostrils were taken away, the figure, the numbers, and the motions would indeed remain, but not the odours nor the tastes nor the sounds, which, without the living animal, I do not believe are anything else than names, just as tickling is precisely nothing but a name if the armpit and the nasal mem-

---

*See Aristotle's development of these ideas on pp. 156–159. For Aristotle's categories, see pp. 147–149.

†The key notions of ancient atomism are discussed on pp. 29–31.

‡Compare the teleological explanations of Aristotle (pp. 158–160) and Dante (pp. 270–274).

brane be removed; . . . having now seen that many affections which are reputed to be qualities residing in the external object, have truly no other existence than in us, and without us are nothing else than names; I say that I am inclined sufficiently to believe that heat is of this kind, and that the thing that produces heat in us and makes us perceive it, which we call by the general name fire, is a multitude of minute corpuscles thus and thus figured, moved with such and such a velocity; . . . But that besides their figure, number, motion, penetration, and touch, there is in fire another quality, that is heat—that I do not believe otherwise than I have indicated, and I judge that it is so much due to us that if the animate and sensitive body were removed, heat would remain nothing more than a simple word.[27]

Galileo is here sketching a distinction between two different kinds of qualities: those which can be attributed to things themselves and those which cannot. The former are often called **primary qualities** and the latter **secondary qualities.** Primary qualities are those that Galilean mathematical science can handle: size, figure, number, and motion. These qualities are now thought to characterize the world—or what we might better call the *objective* world—exhaustively. All other qualities exist only *subjectively*—in us. They are caused to exist in us by the primary (quantitative) qualities of things.

Heat, for example, experienced in the presence of a fire, no more exists in the fire than a tickle exists in the feather brushing my nose. If we try to use the term "heat" for something out there in the world, it turns into "nothing but a name"—that is, it does not describe any reality, since the reality is just the motion of "a multitude of minute corpuscles." The tickle exists only in us; and if the term "heat" (or for that matter "red" or "sweet" or "pungent") is to be descriptive, then what it describes is also only in us. Take away the eye, the tongue, the nostrils, and all that remains is figure and motion.

Democritus, the ancient atomist, draws the same conclusion. He remarks in a poignant phrase, "By this man is cut off from the real." * The prob-

lem that Galileo's distinction between primary and secondary qualities bequeaths to subsequent philosophers is this: if, in order to understand the world, we must strip it of its experienced qualities, where do those experienced qualities exist? If they exist only *in us,* what then are *we*? If they are mental, or subjective, what is the *mind*? And how is it related to the corpuscular world of the new science? Suppose we agree, for the sake of the mastery of the universe given us by these new conceptions, to kick experienced qualities "inside." Then how is this "inside" related to the "outside"? Who are these men that, in Democritus' phrase, are cut off from reality? Galileo, concerned as he is with the objective world, can simply relegate secondary qualities to some otherwise specified subjective realm. But the question will not go away.

It is a new world, indeed. The impact of all these changes on a sensitive observer is registered in a poem by John Donne in 1611.

> And new philosophy calls all in doubt,
> The element of fire is quite put out;
> The sun is lost, and th' earth, and no man's wit
> Can well direct him where to look for it.
> And freely men confess that this world's spent,
> When in the planets, and the firmament
> They seek so many new; they see that this
> Is crumbled out again to his atomies.
> 'Tis all in pieces, all coherence gone;
> All just supply, and all relation:
> Prince, subject, father, son, are things forgot,
> For every man alone thinks he hath got
> To be a phoenix, and that then can be
> None of that kind, of which he is, but he.
> This is the world's condition now.[28]

Here is a lament founded on the new developments. Point after point recalls the detail we have just surveyed; Pyrrhonism, secondary qualities (why is the sun, source of light, heat, and color "lost"?), the moving earth, the expanding universe, corpuscularism, and in the last few lines, the new individualism, which seems to undermine all traditional authority. The medieval world has vanished: "'tis all in pieces, all coherence gone."

---

* See p. 31.

It did not go quietly, of course. The Roman Catholic Counter-Reformation tried to preserve as much as it could. The argument about Copernicanism, which seemed to be the key, was long and fierce; we all know the story of the Church's condemnation of Galileo's opinions and his recantation and house arrest. In 1633, the Church prohibited teaching or believing that the earth moved around the sun. And many Protestants were no more friendly, citing biblical passages that seemed to support the claim that the earth was stationary.* These conservative forces were not interested in the new science per se, but in the fact that it seemed subversive of the "coherence" Christian society had enjoyed for so long. It questioned everything and seemed to turn it all upside down. When one part of a coherent world view is undermined, all the rest seems suddenly unstable.

But the new science proves irresistible, and in one way or another religion, morality, world view, and the structure of society would have to make peace with it. The question of what to make of this science is perhaps the major preoccupation of philosophers in the modern era.

If we wanted to sum up, we could say that the new science bequeaths to philosophers four deep and perplexing problems:

1. What is the place of mind in this world of matter?
2. What is the place of value in this world of fact?
3. What is the place of freedom in this world of mechanism?
4. Is there any room left for God at all?

Descartes, among others, sees the radical nature of these problems and sets himself to solve them.

Basic Questions

1. Describe the Aristotelian/Ptolemaic picture of the universe.
2. Why, given that picture of the universe, is it appropriate for Virgil and Beatrice to take Dante on a tour of the world in order to show him "the right path"?

_____

* For example, Joshua 10:13, Ecclesiastes 1:4, 5, and Psalm 93:1.

3. What do the levels in hell and purgatory show us about virtue and vice?
4. What rediscoveries stimulate the movement we know as Renaissance humanism?
5. Describe the ideal human life, as pictured by the humanists.
6. In what feature of human beings does Pico della Mirandola find their "dignity"?
7. In what ways had the church grown corrupt?
8. What does Luther find in the New Testament that leads to his objection to indulgences?
9. To what authority does Luther appeal?
10. How did the challenge posed by the Reformation raise again the problem of the criterion?
11. What is Montaigne's strategy in "defending" Raymond Sebond?
12. What does Montaigne have to say about depending on authority? Our senses? Science? Reason?
13. How does Montaigne try to show that we are involved either in a circle or in an infinite regress?
14. How does he recommend we live?
15. How does Copernicus resolve the puzzle about the apparent irregularity in the motions of the planets?
16. What is the impact of a moving earth on Dante's picture of the world?
17. What does Kepler add to the Copernican picture?
18. Contrast Aristotelian explanations of motion with those of Galileo.
19. What impact does giving up final causes have on values?
20. What happens to the qualities we think we experience in objects? Explain the difference between primary and secondary qualities.
21. What questions does the new science pose to the philosophical quest for wisdom?

For Further Thought

Imagine that you are a philosopher living at the beginning of the seventeenth century. You are acquainted with the writings of the humanists, with Luther's reforming views of Christianity, with Montaigne's skeptical arguments, and with the new science. A friend asks you, "What should I live for? What is the point of life?" How do you reply?

Notes

1. I am indebted for much in this chapter to the excellent book by Thomas Kuhn, _The Copernican_

Revolution (Cambridge: Harvard University Press, 1957).

2. Quoted in Kuhn, *Copernican Revolution,* 112.

3. Quotations from Dante, *The Divine Comedy,* in *The Portable Dante,* ed. Paolo Milano (New York: Penguin Books, 1947), are cited in the text by canto and line numbers.

4. Erasmus, "The Godly Feast," in *The Colloquies of Erasmus,* trans. Craig R. Thompson (Chicago and London: University of Chicago Press, 1965), 65.

5. Erasmus, "Godly Feast," 68.

6. Erasmus, "The Epicurean," in *Colloquies,* 549.

7. Ernst Cassirer, Paul Oskar Kristeller, and John Herman Randall, Jr., *The Renaissance Philosophy of Man* (Chicago and London: University of Chicago Press, 1948), 4.

8. Giovanni Pico della Mirandola, *Oration on the Dignity of Man,* in Cassirer, Kristeller, and Randall, *Renaissance Philosophy of Man,* 224–25.

9. Pico, *Oration,* 225.

10. Roland H. Bainton, *Christendom: A Short History of Christianity and Its Impact on Western Civilization* (New York: Harper and Row, 1964), 218.

11. Bainton, *Christendom,* 249.

12. Martin Luther, "An Appeal to the Ruling Class of German Nationality as to the Amelioration of the State of Christendom," in *Martin Luther: Selections from His Writings,* ed. John Dillenberger (New York: Anchor Books, 1981), 418–21.

13. Quoted in Dillenberger, "Preface to the Complete Edition of Luther's Latin Writings," in *Martin Luther,* 11.

14. Quoted in Dillenberger, *Martin Luther,* 11–12.

15. Quoted in Roland H. Bainton, *Here I Stand: A Life of Martin Luther* (London: Hodder and Staughton, 1951), 78.

16. Luther, "The Ninety-Five Theses," in Dillenberger, *Martin Luther,* 493–94.

17. Bainton, *Here I Stand,* 96.

18. Quoted in Bainton, *Here I Stand,* 117.

19. I rely here on Richard H. Popkin's *History of Scepticism from Erasmus to Descartes* (Assen, Netherlands: Van Gorcum & Comp, N.V., 1960).

20. Quotations from Michel de Montaigne, *Apology for Raymond Sebond,* in *The Complete Works of Montaigne,* trans. Donald M. Frame (Palo Alto, Calif.: Stanford University Press, 1958), are cited in the text using the abbreviation *ARS*. References are to page numbers.

21. Quoted from Copernicus, *De Revolutionibus,* in Kuhn, *Copernican Revolution,* 141.

22. Quoted in Kuhn, *Copernican Revolution,* 142.

23. Kuhn, *Copernican Revolution,* 164–70.

24. Quoted in Edwin Arthur Burtt, *The Metaphysical Foundations of Modern Physical Science* (London: Routledge and Kegan Paul Ltd., 1924), 48.

25. Kuhn, *Copernican Revolution,* 86.

26. Blaise Pascal, *The Pensées,* trans. J. M. Cohen (New York: Penguin Books, 1961), sec. 91, p. 57.

27. Quoted in Burtt, *Metaphysical Foundations,* 78.

28. John Donne, "An Anatomy of the World," in *John Donne: The Complete English Poems* (New York: Penguin Books, 1971), 276.

15

René Descartes:
Doubting Our Way to Certainty

When he is just twenty-three years old, René Descartes (1596–1650) experiences a vision in a dream. He writes down:

> 10, November 1619; I discovered the foundations of a marvellous science.[1]

This discovery decisively shapes the intellectual life of the young man. Before we focus on the philosophy of his *Meditations,* we need to understand something about that discovery and its importance for his method of approaching problems.

Descartes had received a good education, as he himself acknowledges. But he is dissatisfied. He had expected to obtain "a clear and certain knowledge . . . of all that is useful in life." Instead, he tells us,

> . . . I found myself beset by so many doubts and errors that I came to think I had gained nothing from my attempts to become educated but increasing recognition of my ignorance. (*DM* 1.4, p. 113)[2]

Mathematics delights him "because of the certainty of its demonstrations and the evidence of its reasoning," though he is surprised that more has not been done with it. As for philosophy, he says,

> Seeing that it has been cultivated for many centuries by the most excellent minds, and yet there is still no point in it which is not disputed and hence doubtful, I was not so presumptuous as to hope to achieve

any more in it than others had done. (*DM* 1.8, pp. 114–15)

What is a serious young man, who has always had "an earnest desire to learn to distinguish the true from the false," to do? (*DM* 1.10, p. 115).

> . . . I entirely abandoned the study of letters. Resolving to seek no knowledge other than that which could be found in myself or else in the great book of the world, I spent the rest of my youth travelling, visiting courts and armies, mixing with people of diverse temperaments and ranks, gathering various experiences, testing myself in the situations which fortune offered me, and at all times reflecting upon whatever came my way so as to derive some profit from it. (*DM* 1.9, p. 115)

A striking move! He does not give up learning, but he does give up "letters"—learning what other men had written. In this, Descartes is both a reflection of the age and an immense influence furthering the individualism we earlier remarked on. Where would he seek truth? Not in the writings of the ancients, but in *himself* and in *the great book of the world.* Since he concludes—echoing Socrates—that hardly anyone knows anything worth learning, he would have to *discover* the truth.* If

---

*Do you find it surprising that two thousand years after Socrates someone should still echo the same complaint? Could we say the same today? If not, why not?

he is going to "learn to distinguish the true from the false," he would have to look to himself.

He joins an army (a traditional way to "see the world") and in his travels meets a Dutchman interested in mathematics and the new physics. Descartes' interest is sparked, and he begins to think about using mathematics to solve problems in physics. While working on these problems, he has his dream.

What is this "marvellous science" that forms the content of his "vision"? Apparently it is analytic geometry, which Descartes invents.* Descartes sees in a flash of insight that there is an isomorphism between algebraic symbols and geometry. He sees, moreover, that this opens the door to a mathematical treatment of everything that can be geometrically represented. But *nature* seems to be something that can be geometrically represented, natural things having size, figure, volume, and geometrical relations to each other. Suppose that the things in the world were just objects having such geometrical properties; suppose that whatever other properties they have can in one way or another be reduced to purely geometrical properties; then the stunning prospect opens up of a science of nature—a physics—that is *wholly mathematical*. Mathematics, the only discipline that impressed him in his college days as clear and certain, would be the key to unlock the secrets of nature. Surely this is a vision fit to motivate a research program! And that is exactly what it does.

For the rest of his life Descartes works on this program, in constant communication with the best minds at work on similar problems. In 1633 he is about to publish a *Treatise on the World,* when he learns of the Catholic Church's condemnation of Galileo and the burning of his books. He holds the treatise back, for in it he has endorsed the Copernican view of the moving earth. Four years later, however, he ventures to publish several works on light, on meteors, and on geometry. These are accompanied by a *Discourse on Method,* which

---

*So-called Cartesian coordinates are, of course, named for Descartes.

we will examine in more detail. But we may first note something of the scope and character of his science.

He writes on a wide variety of topics: on the sun, moon, and the stars; on comets; on metals; on fire; on glass; on the magnet; on the human body, particularly on the heart and the nervous system (for which he gathers observations from animal bodies at a local slaughter house). He formulates several "laws of nature." Here are two influential ones:

> . . . that each thing as far as in it lies, continues always in the same state; and that which is once moved always continues to move.

> . . . that all motion is of itself in a straight line; and thus things which move in a circle always tend to recede from the centre of the circle that they describe. (*PP* 2.37–39, p. 267)[3]

Newton will later adopt both of them, and so they pass into the foundations of classical physics; but they were revolutionary in Descartes' day. Both laws contradict Aristotelian assumptions built into the world view of medieval science. It had been thought that rest (at or near the center of the universe) is the natural state of terrestrial things, while the heavenly spheres revolve naturally in the most perfect of geometrical forms, perfect circles. To say that rest is not more "natural" than motion and that motion is "naturally" in a straight line is radical indeed. It could make sense only in a world of infinite space, where there is no such thing as a natural center. And it fits only with a moving earth.

Descartes applies these principles to a world that he takes to be geometrical in essence. He tries to do without concepts of weight and gravity, for these seem to be "occult" qualities like those in the nonmathematical science of Aristotle. To say that a body falls because it has weight or because it is naturally attracted to another body seems to him no explanation at all; it is just attaching a name to a phenomenon and supposing that we thereby learn something. (These concepts trouble many of the early scientists, including Newton, who does use the concept of gravity but is never happy with it.)

For Descartes, bodies are sheer extended volumes. They interact according to mechanical principles that can be mathematically formulated. Given that a single body in motion would continue in that motion unless interfered with, and given the laws of interaction, the paths and positions of interacting bodies can be plotted and predicted. Since extension is the very essence of body, there can be no vacuum or void. (You can see that if bodies are just extended volumes, the ideal of such a volume containing *no body* is self-contradictory.) So the universe is full, and motion takes place by a continual recirculation of bodies, each displacing another as it is itself displaced. The fall of bodies near the earth is due to the action on them of other bodies in the air, which in turn are being pressed down by others out to the edges of the solar system. This system forms a huge vortex tightly bound in by the vortices of other systems, which force the moving bodies in it to deviate from otherwise straight paths into the roughly circular paths traced by the planets.*

The key idea, as you can see, is that everything in the material world can be treated in a purely geometrical and mathematical fashion. Descartes is one of the most vigorous promoters of that "corpuscularism" noted earlier.† Although he criticizes Democritus and the ancient atomists (for thinking that atoms are indivisible, for positing a void, for believing in gravity, and for not specifying the laws of interaction precisely), it is clear that the general outlines of Descartes' universe bear a striking resemblance to that earlier theory.‡ In particular, the *mechanistic* quality of the picture is identical. He states explicitly that "the laws of mechanics . . . are identical with the laws of Nature" (*DM* 5.54, p. 139).

---

* The notion of a cosmic vortex, a huge, swirling mass of matter, is already found in the speculations of Anaximander; see pp. 10–11. Compare also Parmenides' arguments against the existence of a void, pp. 24–25.

† See p. 288.

‡ For the views of the atomists, see Chapter 4. Descartes' criticisms may be found in Part IV, CCII, of *The Principles of Philosophy.*

The radical nature of this conception can be appreciated by noting a thought experiment Descartes recommends. Imagine, he says, that God creates a space with matter to fill it and shakes it up until there is thorough chaos. All that God then adds is a decree that this matter should behave according to the laws of Nature. What would be the result?

> . . . I showed how, in consequence of these laws, the greater part of the matter of this chaos had to become disposed and arranged in a certain way, which made it resemble our heavens; and how, at the same time, some of its parts had to form an earth, some planets and comets, and others a sun and fixed stars. Here I dwelt upon the subject of light, explaining at some length the nature of the light that had to be present in the sun and the stars. . . . From that I went on to speak of the earth in particular: how, although I had expressly supposed that God had put no gravity into the matter of which it was formed, still all its parts tended exactly towards its centre; . . . how mountains, seas, springs and rivers could be formed naturally there, and how metals could appear in mines, plants grow in fields, and generally how all the bodies we call 'mixed' or 'composite' could come into being there. (*DM* 5.43–44, p. 132)

Of course, Descartes does not actually succeed in demonstrating all that. No one yet has solved all these problems, and they are in fact insoluble with the limited resources that Descartes allows himself. But it is the conception and the daring it expresses that counts. This vision of a universe evolving itself in purely mechanistic ways has been enormously influential; and we haven't yet finished exploring its ramifications.

Descartes is quick to add that he does not infer from this thought experiment that the world was actually formed in that way, only that it could have been. Careful still about charges of heresy, he says it is "much more probable" that God made it just as it now is. But in either case, it is pretty clear that God is excluded from the day to day operations of the universe, which in Descartes' view proceeds as it must according to purely mathematical and mechanistic laws.

The Method

While working on these physical problems, and feeling certain that progress is being made virtually every day, Descartes asks himself why more progress hadn't been made in the past. It is surely not, he thinks, that he is more clever or intelligent than earlier thinkers. No, the problem is that they lacked something. And it gradually becomes clear to him that what they lacked is a *method*. They did not proceed in as careful and principled a way as they might have. Acceptance of obscurity, the drawing of hasty conclusions, avoidable disagreements, and general intellectual chaos are the results.

Descartes sets himself to draw up some rules for the direction of the intellect. It is of some importance to recognize that these rules of method formulate what Descartes takes himself to be doing in his scientific work. In particular, they are indebted to his experience as a mathematician. They are not picked arbitrarily, then, but are an expression of procedures that actually seem to be producing results. If only other thinkers could be persuaded to follow these four rules, he thinks, what progress might be made!

> The first was never to accept anything as true if I did not have evident knowledge of its truth: that is, carefully to avoid precipitate conclusions and preconceptions, and to include nothing more in my judgments than what presented itself to my mind so clearly and distinctly that I had no occasion to doubt it.
>
> The second, to divide each of the difficulties I examined into as many parts as possible and as may be required in order to resolve them better.
>
> The third, to direct my thoughts in an orderly manner, by beginning with the simplest and most easily known objects in order to ascend little by little, step by step, to knowledge of the most complex, and by supposing some order even among objects that have no natural order of precedence.
>
> And the last, throughout to make enumerations so complete, and reviews so comprehensive, that I could be sure of leaving nothing out. (*DM* 2.18–19, p. 120)

"It is much easier to have some vague notion about any subject, no matter what, than to arrive at the real truth about a single question." —RENÉ DESCARTES

He says of these four rules that he thought they would be "sufficient, provided that I made a strong and unswerving resolution never to fail to observe them" (*DM* 2.18, p. 120). They are difficult to follow, as any attempt to do so will convince you immediately. But let us explore their content more carefully.

The first one has to do with a condition for accepting something as true. It is pretty stringent. You want to avoid two things: "precipitate conclusions" (hastiness) and "preconceptions" (categorizing something before you have good warrant to do so). How do you do this? By accepting only those things which are *so clear and distinct that you have no occasion to doubt them.* Descartes clearly has in mind as models such propositions as "$3 + 5 = 8$" and "the interior angles of a triangle are equal to two right angles." Once you understand these, you really cannot bring yourself to doubt that they are true. Can you?

What do the key words "clear" and "distinct" mean? In *The Principles of Philosophy* (*PP* 1.45,

p. 237) he explains them as follows. Something is "clear" when it is "present and apparent to an attentive mind, in the same way as we assert that we see objects clearly when, being present to the regarding eye, they operate upon it with sufficient strength." Seeing an apple in your hand in good light would be an example. We are not to accept any belief unless it is as clear as that. Nothing obscure, fuzzy, dim, indefinite, indistinct, vague, ambiguous—only what is *clear*!

By "distinct" he means "so precise and different from all other objects that it contains within itself nothing but what is clear." An idea not only must be clear in itself but also impossible to confuse with any other idea. Ideas must be as distinct as the idea of a triangle is from the idea of a square.

Ask yourself how many of *your* beliefs are clear and distinct in this way. Descartes is under no illusions about the high standard he sets. "There are even a number of people who throughout all their lives perceive nothing so correctly as to be capable of judging it properly." But the first rule of the method is to *accept nothing as true* that does not meet that high standard. In the first of the *Meditations* we shall see how much that excludes.

The second rule recommends analysis. Problems are typically complex, and an essential step in their solution is to break them into smaller problems. Anyone who has tried to write a computer program to solve a certain problem will have an excellent feel for this rule. Often more than half the battle is to discover smaller problems we already have the resources to solve, so that by combining the solutions to these more elementary problems we can solve the big problem. We move, by analysis, not only from the complex to the simple, but also from the obscure to the clear and distinct, and so we also follow the first rule.

The third rule recognizes that items for consideration may be more or less simple. It recommends beginning with the simpler ones and proceeding to the more complex. Here is a mathematical example. If we compare a straight line to a curve, we can see that there is a clear sense in which the straight line is simple and the curve is not; no straight line is more or less straight than another,

but curves come in all degrees. If we know a line is straight, we know something perfectly definite about it; if we know it is curved, we do not. And it is in fact possible to analyze a curve into a series of straight lines at various angles to each other, thus "constructing" the more complex curve from the simple straights.

For Descartes, this serves as a model of all good intellectual work. There are two basic procedures: a kind of *insight* or *intuition* of simple natures (which must be clear and distinct), and then *deduction* of complex phenomena from perceived relations between the simples. A deduction, too, is in fact just an insight: insight into the connections holding between simples. Geometry, again, provides many examples. Theorems are proved by deduction from the axioms and postulates. The latter are simply "seen" to be true; for example, through two points in a plane one and only one straight line can be drawn. The same kind of "seeing" is required to recognize that each step in a proof is correct.

Deductions, of course, can be very long and complex, even though each of the steps is clear and distinct. That is the reason for the fourth rule: to set out all the steps completely (we all know how easily mistakes creep in when we take something for granted) and to make comprehensive reviews.

Descartes is extremely optimistic about the results we can obtain if we follow this method.

> These long chains composed of very simple and easy reasonings, which geometers customarily use to arrive at their most difficult demonstrations, had given me occasion to suppose that all the things that can fall under human knowledge are interconnected in the same way. And I thought that, provided that we refrain from accepting anything as true which is not, and always keep to the order required for deducing one thing from another, there can be nothing too remote to be reached in the end or too well hidden to be discovered. (*DM* 2.19, p. 120)

We will see this optimism at work when Descartes tackles knotty problems like the existence of God and the relation between soul and body. But first we need to ask: why does Descartes feel a need to address these *philosophical* problems at all? Why doesn't he just stick to mathematical physics?

For one thing, he is confident that his method will allow him to succeed where so many have failed. But a deeper reason is that he needs to show that his physics correctly describes the world, that it is more than just a likely story. In short, he needs to demonstrate that his physics is *true.* He is quite aware of the skeptical doubts of the Pyrrhonists, of the way they undermine the testimony of the senses and cast doubt on our reasoning. In particular, he is aware of the problem of the criterion.* Unless this can be solved, no certainty is possible.

Descartes thinks he has found a way to solve this problem of problems. He will outdo the Pyrrhonists at their own game; when it comes to doubting, he will be the champion doubter of all time. The first rule of his method already gives him the means to wipe the slate clean—unless, perhaps, there remains something that is *so clear and distinct that it cannot possibly be doubted.* If there were something like that, the rest of the method could gain a foothold, deductions could lead us to further truths, and perhaps, from the depths of doubting despair, we could be raised to the bliss of certainty.

This is Descartes' strategy. And it is his attempt to *justify* his physics that makes Descartes not just a great scientist, but a great philosopher as well. We are now ready to turn to this philosophy as expressed in the *Meditations.*

The *Meditations*

The *Meditations on First Philosophy* is Descartes' most famous work. We will focus our attention on the text itself, as we did earlier with certain dialogues of Plato. It is a remarkably rich work; and if you come to understand it, you will have mastered many of the concepts and distinctions that philosophers use to this day. So it will repay careful study. I cannot emphasize too much that in this section it is the *text,* the words of Descartes himself you must wrestle with. It is he who is your partner in this conversation, and you must make him speak to you and—as far as possible—answer your questions. What I will do is offer some commentary on particularly difficult aspects, fill in some background, and ask some questions.

Though it is usually known just as the *Meditations,* the full title of the work is *Meditations on First Philosophy in Which the Existence of God and the Distinction of the Soul from the Body Are Demonstrated.* The title gives you some idea what to expect. But as you will see, his experience as a mathematician and physicist is everywhere present. It was first published in 1641.

Although not represented in our text, the *Meditations* are prefaced by a letter to "the Wisest and Most Distinguished Men, the Dean and Doctors of the Faculty of Theology in Paris." The motivation behind this letter is fairly transparent. It had been just eight years since the condemnation of Galileo's opinions; and, as we have seen, Descartes has allied himself with the basic outlook of Galileo. The Faculty of Theology in Paris had indeed been an illustrious one for some centuries. If he could secure their approval, he could almost certainly escape Galileo's fate. The *Meditations,* as it turns out, was examined carefully by one of the theologians, who expressed his approval; but twenty-two years later it was nonetheless placed by the Roman Catholic Church on the *Index Librorum Prohibitorum* of books dangerous to read.*

Descartes had also asked one of his close friends, the priest and scientist Mersenne, to circulate the text to some distinguished philosophers, who were then invited to write criticisms of it. These criticisms, including some from his English contem-

---

*For a discussion of this problem by the ancient skeptics, see pp. 199–200. For the impact of skepticism nearer to Descartes' time, see pp. 281–284.

*The *Index* was created in 1571 by Pope Pius V, after approval by the Council of Trent; the latter was a general council of the Roman Catholic church, called to deal with problems created by the Protestant Reformation. It set in motion the Catholic Counter-Reformation, and the *Index* was one of its tools.

porary, Thomas Hobbes, were printed along with Descartes' replies at the end of the volume.*

In the letter to the theologians, Descartes refers to "believers like ourselves." He professes to be absolutely convinced that it is sufficient in these matters to rely on Scripture. But there is a problem. On the one hand, God's existence, he says, is to be believed because it is taught in Scripture. Scripture, on the other hand, is to be believed because God is its source. Now it doesn't take a lot of thought to realize that there is a circle here, a pretty tight circle. It comes down to believing that God exists because one believes that God exists. (Recall skeptics like Sextus and Montaigne, who maintain that all our claims to know are either involved in such circular thinking or are strung out in an infinite regress.)

To break into the circle Descartes thinks it necessary to *prove rationally* that God exists and that the soul is distinct from the body. His claim that reason should be able to do this is no innovation; Augustine, Anselm, Aquinas, and others had said as much before. Descartes, however, claims to have proofs superior to any offered by these thinkers.

He refers to some thinkers who hold that it is rational to believe the soul perishes with the body. Aristotle seems in the main to think so (though he waffles).[†] Christian Aristotelians like Thomas Aquinas labor mightily, but inconclusively, to reconcile this view with the tradition of an immortal soul. Descartes thinks he has a proof of the soul that is direct, simple, and conclusive.[‡] He claims, in fact, that his proofs will "surpass in certitude and obviousness the demonstrations of geometry." A strong claim indeed! You will have to decide whether you agree.

These are meditations on *first philosophy*. This is a term derived from Aristotle, who means by it a search for the *first principles of things*. First philosophy is also called **metaphysics.** In a letter to the man who translated his *Principles of Philosophy* from Latin to French, Descartes uses a memorable image.

> Thus the whole of philosophy is like a tree; the roots are metaphysics, the trunk is physics, and the branches that issue from the trunk are all the other sciences.[4]

Note that all the sciences, in 1641, are still counted as parts of philosophy, the love of wisdom.

So Descartes is inquiring into *what kinds of things there ultimately are,* about which physics and the other sciences give us more detailed information. What he wants to find is a set of concepts that will give us an inventory of the *basic kinds of being.* Aristotle calls such fundamental concepts "categories."*

Descartes' inventory of what there is actually looks fairly simple. We can diagram it this way:

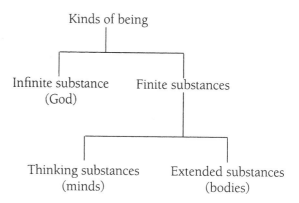

But by itself this chart isn't very informative. It is time to turn to the *Meditations* themselves, to see how Descartes fills in this schema and why it turns out just that way.

The text of *Meditations on First Philosophy* is printed at the end of this chapter, beginning on page 311. You should read through one of the meditations quickly to get a general feel for the argument. After reading it, come back to the com-

---

*We will discuss the views of Hobbes in the next chapter. For his criticisms of the *Meditations,* see the "Third Set of Objections" in Haldane and Ross, *The Philosophical Works of Descartes,* volume 2.
[†]For Aristotle's view of the soul as "the form of a living human body" see pp. 168–171.
[‡]Descartes tends to use the terms "soul," "mind," and "spirit" interchangeably. They are all terms for "the thing that thinks." Some philosophers and theologians make distinctions among them.

---

*See p. 145.

mentary and questions below, using them as a guide to go through the text again, this time paying close attention to Descartes' exact words. He is a careful and clear writer and says exactly what he means. If you proceed in this way, you will not only learn some philosophy but also gain skill in reading a text of some difficulty—a valuable ability. Writing out brief answers to the questions will increase your understanding. Repeat this procedure for each of the six meditations.

Read Meditation I: On What Can Be Called Into Doubt Note the personal, meditative character of the writing. Descartes is inviting us to join him in thinking certain things through, asking us to mull them over and see whether we agree. He is not making authoritative pronouncements. Just as he reserves the right to be the judge of what *he* should believe, so he puts you on the spot. You will have to be continually asking yourself: Do I agree with this or not? if not, why not? This familiar first-person style is quite different from most of medieval philosophy; it harks back to Augustine's *Confessions* in the late fourth century. Descartes is, as it were, having a conversation with himself. So the structure of *Meditation I* is dialectical: proposal, objection, reply, objection, reply. . . . Try to distinguish the various "voices" in this internal dialogue.

Note that there are three stages in the "tearing down" of opinions, and one principle running throughout. The principle is that we ought to withhold assent from anything uncertain, just as much as from what we see clearly to be false. This is simply a restatement of the first rule of his method, but is of the greatest importance.* The three stages concern (1) the senses, (2) dreams, and (3) the evil demon hypothesis.

Q1. Aren't you *strongly* inclined to think, just like Descartes by the fire, that you *can't deny* that

you are now reading this book which is "right there" in your hands? Should you doubt it anyway?

Q2. What do you think of Descartes' rule that we shouldn't completely trust those who have cheated us even once? Does this rule apply to the senses?

Q3. *Could* you be dreaming right now? Explain.

Q4. What is the argument that even in dreams *some* things—for example, the truths of mathematics—are not illusory?

Q5. How does the thought of God, at *this* stage, seem to reinforce skeptical conclusions—*even* about arithmetic? *

Here Descartes avails himself of the techniques of the Pyrrhonists, who set argument against plausible argument until they find themselves no more inclined to judge one way than another. But he acknowledges that this equilibrium or suspension of judgment is difficult to achieve. "Habit" strongly inclines him to believe some of these things as "probable." Like Descartes, you almost certainly take it as *very* probable that you are now looking at a piece of paper, which is located a certain determinate distance before your eyes, that you indeed have eyes, and that 2 plus 3 really does equal 5. And you almost certainly find it very hard *not* to believe these things. You very likely find yourself so committed to them that you almost *can't* doubt them. (Ask yourself whether this is the case.) How can we overcome these habits of believing? We now know, if Descartes is right so far, that we *should* doubt them. As a remedy against these habitual believings, Descartes determines *deliberately* (as an act of will) to suppose that all his prior beliefs are false.

Q6. How does the hypothesis of the evil demon help?

Descartes now thinks that he has canvassed every possible reason for doubting. We cannot rely on our senses; we cannot even rely on our rational

---

*A brief look back at the four rules of the method will be of use at this point. See p. 295. It is the principle expressed in this first rule which the pragmatists in our century reject. (See Peirce's critique on p. 525). Once, when a friend of mine stumbled on an unusually high first step of a staircase, I formulated what came jokingly to be known as Norman's First Law: Watch that first step; it's a big one. Good advice for appraising philosophical systems.

---

*Review the consequences William of Ockham draws from the doctrine of God's omnipotence (pp. 265–267).

faculties for the simplest truths of mathematics, geometry, or logic. All our beliefs, it seems, are dissolved in the acid of skeptical doubt.

Q7. Before going on to *Meditation II,* ask yourself the question: Is there anything at all that I am *so certain* of that I could not *possibly* doubt it? (Meditate on this question a while.)

Read Meditation II: On the Nature of the Human Mind, Which Is Better Known Than the Body
Descartes seems to have gotten nowhere by doubting. What to do? He resolves to press on, suspecting that the terrors of skepticism can be overcome only by enduring them to the end. The monster in the child's closet will only disappear if the child can muster the courage to look at it directly. If we avert our eyes in fear, we will not conquer.

The particular horror, of course, is that all our beliefs might be false—that nowhere would they connect at all with reality. If Descartes has carried us with him to this point, we know that we have lots of ideas and beliefs, but whether any one of them represents something that really *exists* must seem quite uncertain. Perhaps they are just webs of illusion, like those spun by a master magician— or the evil demon.

Descartes here represents a pattern of thought which deserves a name. Let us call it the representational theory of knowledge and perception, or the **representational theory** for short. The basic ideas of this theory are very widely shared in modern philosophy. We can distinguish five points.

1. We have no immediate or direct access to things in the world, only to the world of our ideas.
2. "Ideas" must be understood broadly to include all the contents of the mind, including perceptions, images, memories, concepts, beliefs, intentions, and decisions.
3. These ideas serve as *representations* of things other than themselves.
4. Much of what these ideas represent, they represent as "out there," or "external" to the mind containing them.

5. It is in principle possible for ideas to represent these things correctly; but they may also be false and misleading.

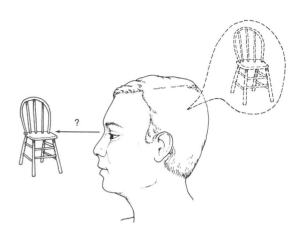

In *Meditation I,* Descartes draws a certain consequence of the representational theory. It seems that mind and world could be disconnected in a perplexing way, that even the most solid ideas might represent things all wrong—or maybe even not represent anything at all! This possibility, foreshadowed by the ancient skeptics and by William of Ockham in his reflections on God's omnipotence, provokes thinkers to try to find a remedy. What we need is a bridge across the chasm between mind and world; and it is clear that it will have to be built by inference and argument. We want *good reasons* to believe our ideas represent the "external" world truly. But the good reasons must be of a peculiar sort. It is as if we have to start this construction project while isolated on one side, restricted in our choice of materials to those available there. It is from the vantage point of the mind that we try to stretch the girders of our argument across the gulf to the world.

We will examine Descartes' effort to build such a rational bridge. Other thinkers after him will struggle with the problem. Hume will despair of a bridge, Kant will redefine the problem so as to make the gulf partially disappear, Hegel will deny that there is a gulf at all, and Kierkegaard will open it up again. In our century, there have been several attempts to show that the notion of a chasm needing to be bridged is itself an illusion.* In those first few pages of the *Meditations,* formulated in an incomparable way, is a dramatic rehearsal of the old skeptical worries about knowledge. They are now seen to hover around the theses of the representational theory of knowledge and perception.

To change the metaphor, we might remember Archimedes, who says, "Give me a lever long enough, and a place on which to rest it, and I can move the earth." Descartes thinks that if he can find just one certainty, he might, like Archimedes, do marvels. He might just build that bridge.

Q8.   To what certainty does Descartes' methodical doubt lead? Is he right about that?†

The principle "I think, therefore I am" is often referred to as the *cogito,* from the Latin "I think" and we will use that shorthand expression from time to time.

Note that Descartes rejects the standard, long-accepted way of answering the question, What am I? (p. 313). According to a tradition that goes back to Socrates (and is codified by Aristotle), the way to answer such a question is to give a *definition.* The traditional way to define something will tell you (a) what *genus* it belongs to and (b) the *difference* between it and other things in that genus. Not surprisingly, this is called *definition by genus and difference.* A human being is said to belong to the genus *animal;* and the difference between a human and other animals is that a human is *rational.* Human beings, Aristotle says, are *rational animals.*

Descartes objects to such a definition because it simply calls for more definitions; you need next a definition of *animal* and a definition for *rational.*

---

* Other thinkers who struggle with this problem are John Locke (1632–1704) and George Berkeley (1685–1753). It is the latter who shows that Galileo's distinction between primary and secondary qualities (see p. 289) cannot resolve the problem; size and shape, as we experience them, are just as much ideas in the mind as are colors and smells. Berkeley's *Three Dialogues between Hylas and Philonus* is an accessible source for this argument. See also the "snapshot" discussions of Locke on p. 341 and of Berkeley on p. 350.

† Descartes' central idea here is anticipated by Augustine in his refutation of the skeptics. See p. 221.

Then, presumably, you will require definitions for the terms used to define *them.* And so on.

This whole process has to come to ground somewhere. There must be some terms, Descartes thinks, that do not need definition of this sort, but whose meaning can just be "seen." These will be the *simple* terms. From them, more complex terms can be built up. We see in Descartes' rejection of the traditional definition-procedure an application of the second and third rules of his method. He is searching for something so simple, clear, and distinct that it just presents itself without any need for definition. He is looking for something *self-evident.* If that can be found, he can use it as a foundation on which to build more complex truths.

Q9.   What, then, does Descartes conclude that he is?

Note that Descartes briefly considers the view that he may after all *be* a body, or some such thing, even though he does not *know* he is (p. 314).* But he does not try to refute it here; that proof comes in *Meditation VI.* Here he is interested in what he knows that he *is*— not in what he can infer that he *is not.*

Q10.   Why does Descartes rule out the use of the imagination in answering the question, What am I?

Q11.   What all is included in "thinking," as Descartes understands the term? (See p. 314.) Note how broad the term is for him.

Q12.   Suppose I feel certain that I see a cat on the mat. Is it certain that there is a cat on the mat? What, in this situation, *can* I be certain of?

How difficult it is to stay within the bounds of what I know for certain! As Descartes says, his "mind enjoys wandering." And so it is with us. I, too, keep slipping back into the error of thinking that I know *sensible* things best—this desk, this computer keyboard, this hand. (Do you find that too?)

It is to cure this inclination to rely on the senses

---

* This is the view that Thomas Hobbes urges against Descartes. See "Minds and Motives" in Chapter 16.

that Descartes considers the bit of wax. Read that passage once more (pp. 314–15). All the sensible qualities by means of which we recognize the wax can change. But we still judge that it is the same wax.

The distinction between *ordinary perception* and *judgment* is crucial for Descartes. It is illustrated by the hats and coats we see through the window. We say that we *see* men passing; but this is inaccurate, for they may be just robots dressed like men. What is actually happening in ordinary perception is that our intellect is drawing an *inference* on the basis of certain *data* (supplied by the senses) and issuing a *judgment*. Judging is an activity of the mind—indeed, as we'll see in *Meditation IV,* of the will.

Perceiving, then, is not a purely passive registration by the senses. Implicit in all perception is judgment, or *giving assent*. In ordinary perception, these judgments are apt to be obscure, confused, and just plain wrong. But fortunately they can be corrected by the application of ideas that are clear and distinct, for example, the mathematical simples. (These points will be crucial in *Meditation IV,* where Descartes explains how it is possible for us to err.)

With respect to the bit of wax, the moral is that it is "grasped, not by the senses or the power of having mental images, but by the understanding alone." When based wholly on sense, our perception is "imperfect and confused." When directed, however, to "the things of which the wax consists" (the mathematically determinable simples of extension, figure, and motion), knowledge of the wax can be *clear and distinct.*

Now we can understand why Descartes introduces the wax example. If even here knowledge cannot be found in sensation, but only in a "purely mental inspection," then we should have less difficulty remembering that knowledge of *what we are* must also be approached in this way. Our tendency to think of ourselves as what we can *sense* of ourselves—these hands, this head, these eyes—is considerably undermined. Indeed, I must know myself "much more truly and certainly" even than the wax.

And there follows a remarkable conclusion: "I

can't grasp anything more easily or plainly than my mind." (What would Freud have said to that?)

Q13. What qualities, then, belong to the wax essentially? (Look again at the basic principles of Descartes' physics on pp. 293–294.)

Q14. Why is our imagination incapable of grasping these qualities of the wax? By what faculty do we grasp it?

Q15. How does the wax example help to cure our habitual inclination to trust the senses?

Q16. How does our language tend to mislead us?

Read Meditation III: On God's Existence   In the first paragraphs Descartes resolves to explore more carefully his own mind. But then what alternative does he have, now that he has resolved to consider everything else "as empty illusions"?

A momentous step is taken: he *solves* (or at least he thinks he solves) the problem of the criterion! Here are the steps.

1. He is certain that he exists as a thinking thing.
2. He asks himself: What is it about this proposition that accounts for my certainty that it is true?
3. He answers: The fact that I grasp it so clearly and distinctly that I perceive it could not possibly be false.
4. He concludes: Let this then be a general principle (a *criterion*): Whatever I grasp with *like* clarity and distinctness must also be true.

He then reviews (yet again) the things he had at one time thought were true, and reminds himself that no matter how sure he feels about them, he can't be absolutely certain.

Q17. Why does he feel a need to inquire about the existence and nature of God?

Descartes now tries to make clear a crucial distinction between *ideas* on the one hand and *volitions, emotions,* and *judgments* on the other (p. 316). This distinction is embedded in an inventory of the varied contents of the mind (which is all that we can so far be certain of). Here is a schematic representation of that inventory.

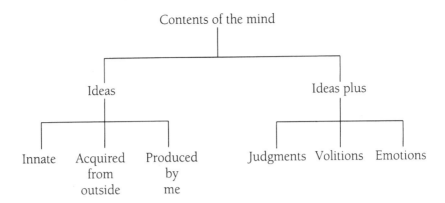

Q18. What is the key difference between ideas and judgments?

Q19. What is the key difference between judgments on the one hand, and volitions and emotions on the other?

Q20. What question arises with respect to the ideas that seem to be acquired from outside myself?

Q21. What (provisional) examples does Descartes give of each class of ideas?

We need to comment on the notion of **innate ideas.** In calling them "innate," Descartes does not mean to imply that they are to be found in babies and mentally defective adults, as some of his critics suppose. He merely means there are some ideas that we would have even if nothing existed but ourselves. These ideas do not require external causes for their existence in us; every developed rational mind will possess them from its own resources. Thus, the idea of a *thing* can originate with the *cogito*, which gives me the certainty that I exist as a thing that thinks—even if nothing else exists. Perhaps my idea of an antelope is caused in me by seeing antelopes in a zoo (though this remains to be proved). But we would have the ideas of thing, thought, and truth in any case.

Q22. Why do you think Descartes believes the ideas of truth and thought are innate?

Q23. Why is he inclined to believe that some ideas do originate from objects outside himself? He gives two reasons (p. 317).

Q24. Are these two reasons conclusive?

Q25. What is the difference between being taught "by nature" and being taught "by the light of nature"? (See p. 317.) What is the **light of nature?** *

We come now to a point of terminology. Descartes distinguishes *subjective* reality on the one hand from *formal* and *eminent* reality on the other. If we are going to understand Descartes' argument, we must be clear about how he uses these terms and keep his use firmly in mind.

It is easier to begin with formal reality. Something has formal reality if it is, in our terms, actual or existing. If there really are giraffes and angels, then giraffes and angels have formal reality. You also, because you exist, have formal reality. And when you form an image of a giraffe in your mind, that image also has formal reality—that is, it actually exists *as an image* in your mind. So any idea actually present in a mind is formally real. This means that (if there are giraffes) both the idea of a giraffe (when being thought) and the giraffe you are thinking of are formally real. They are distinct realities, but related: the one *represents* the other.

What you are thinking about when you entertain an idea has *subjective* reality. Giraffes and angels have subjective reality whenever you think of

---

* It is interesting to compare this with what Augustine says about the Interior Teacher and the light within. (See Chapter 12.) Descartes' view is less explicitly theological and is a step on the road to secularization. It should also be compared to what Heidegger says about "the clearing" (p. 611).

them. But there are ideas whose objects have *only* subjective reality: the tooth fairy, for instance, or unicorns. These, of course, are examples of ideas "produced by us." But if we look carefully, we can see that they have not been invented out of nothing. The idea of a unicorn comes from the ideas of a horse and a single horn. And (though Descartes has not proved it yet) it may be that horses and horns are *formally* real. Already he remarks (p. 318) that although one idea may be derived from others, this cannot go on to infinity: there must eventually be a *cause* for these ideas; and the reality of that cause must be more than "merely subjective." If this were not so, we would have gotten something "from nothing." And the light of nature assures us that this is impossible. There is an old Latin saying: *ex nihilo nihil fit,* or "from nothing, nothing comes."

Descartes does not, of course, make these distinctions for their own sake. There is a problem he is trying to solve: given that I can be certain that *I* exist (together with all my ideas), can I be certain of the *formal* existence of anything else? Although thoroughgoing skepticism may have been refuted (we do know something in the *cogito*), we have not got beyond solipsism. **Solipsism** is the view that each of you (if there is anyone out there!) must state for yourself in this way: "I am the only thing that actually exists."

Another step in solving that problem is to note that there are *degrees of reality:* some things have more reality than others. This is the cardinal principle of the great chain of being.* Descartes gives two examples, framed in terms of subjective reality (pp. 317–318), though the same is true for formal reality as well.

Q26.   Why does the idea of *substance* contain more subjective reality than that of *modification or accident*? (Think of a fender and the dent in it.)†

Q27.   Why does the idea of infinite substance

have more subjective reality than that of finite substance?

On the basis of these distinctions, Descartes formulates a *causal principle:* that there must be at least as much reality in the cause as there is in the effect. A cause is said to be *formally* real when it has the same degree of reality as the effect it produces; it is said to be *eminently* real when it has even more reality than its effect.

Q28.   What examples does Descartes offer to illustrate this causal principle?

Once more Descartes canvasses the various kinds of ideas he finds in himself as a thinking thing. He is looking for some idea of which he himself could not possibly be the cause. Such an idea must have a cause (since nothing comes from nothing). If (1) he is not the cause, and (2) there is a cause, then (3) he knows that he is not alone in the universe. Something else exists!

Descartes thinks his meditations to this point give him the materials with which to prove that God exists. In its bare bones, his argument looks like this:

> I have an idea of an infinitely perfect substance. Therefore, such a substance exists.

Now you no doubt think that, stated in this stark way, this is a terrible argument. And it is. But when properly filled in with other premises, Descartes thinks it is a proof that is as good as the best mathematical proofs.

Q29.   Fill in the premises that complete Descartes' argument that God exists.
Q30.   Why could not Descartes himself be the cause of his idea of God?

Meditation III contains two separate arguments for God's existence. The first one, which we have now examined, begins with the fact that each of us has an *idea* of God. The second one begins (on p. 319) with the fact that it is certainly true that

---

* See pp. 228–230.

† I owe this nice example to Ronald Rubin, the translator of these *Meditations.*

I exist. The argument then addresses whether I could exist if God does not. It is an argument by exclusion; it considers the other plausible candidates for the cause of my existence and shows in each case that it won't do. Note that both of these arguments are *causal* arguments. The first inquires about the cause of my *idea* of God, the second about the cause of my own *existence*. Both make use of the causal principle Descartes has formulated.

Q31. Set down briefly, in numbered sentences, the essential steps of this second argument.
Q32. What does Descartes conclude is the origin of his idea of God? And why?
Q33. Explain why Descartes says we cannot "comprehend" God, but can "reach" him in thought. (Compare touching an elephant and wrapping your arms around it.)

At the end of the third *Meditation*, Descartes feels he has achieved his aim. He now knows that he is not alone. In addition to himself there is at least one other being—a substance infinite in intelligence and power, and perfect in every way. This latter fact will prove to be of very great significance, for Descartes will use it to defeat the hypothesis of the evil demon; a perfect being could not be a deceiver. Thus he thinks he can overcome the deepest ground for skepticism about knowledge of the external world. But that is a line of argument pursued in the remaining meditations.

Read Meditation IV: On Truth and Falsity   Note the transitional character of the first paragraph. Descartes sums up the argument so far, expresses his confidence that God's existence is more certain than anything else (except the *cogito*), and looks forward to further progress.

Q34. Is Descartes' assertion (p. 321) that deception is an evidence of weakness rather than power plausible? Explain your answer.

Before God's existence was proved, it was unclear whether any of our beliefs were true. Now there is a new puzzle: how any of them can be false? (Do you see why this puzzle arises?) So Descartes has to provide an explanation of the obvious fact that we can and do make mistakes.

For the basic framework he depends again upon the idea of the great chain of being. He finds that he is an "intermediate" between God and nothingness, having less reality than God, whose perfection excludes error, but more reality than sheer nonbeing. Error, in any case, is not a positive reality; it is only a defect, as weakness is only the absence of strength and cold the absence of heat. So it should not be too surprising that Descartes, and we, too, should be liable to error.

Two points he makes in passing are worth noting.

1. Why did God create me so that I could make mistakes? I don't know, he says, but if I could see the world as God sees it, it is quite possible that I would judge it to be for the best.*

Q35. How does recognizing that I am only a part of a larger whole help answer this question?

2. Among the many things we do not know are God's purposes. It follows that Aristotelian final causes—the what for—are not appropriate in the explanations given by physics. Thus Descartes buttresses the mechanistic character of his (and the modern world's) scientific work. We can come to know *how* things happen, but not *why*.

A more detailed analysis of error can be given. It depends on another distinction: that between entertaining a belief, or having it in mind (which is the function of the *understanding*), and assenting to that belief, or accepting it (which is the function of the *will*).

---

* Here is one expression of that attitude expressed in Leibniz and other later writers to the effect that "this is the best of all possible worlds." It is this optimism which Voltaire caricatures so savagely in *Candide*. These reflections of Descartes form part of a project known as theodicy—the justification of the ways of God to man. For another attempt at theodicy, see Hegel (pp. 435–439). And you might review the Stoic notion that evil does not exist in the world, but only in our perception of it (p. 194).

Q36. How does this distinction between understanding and will explain the possibility of error?

Q37. In what way is the will more perfect than the understanding?

Q38. Can God be blamed for our errors?

Q39. How can we avoid error?

Read Meditation V: On the Essence of Material Objects and More on God's Existence This brief meditation is a transition to the more important sixth meditation. Though Descartes says at the beginning that he wants to investigate whether anything can be known about material things (so far, only God and the soul are known), he doesn't solve that problem here. But he does take a significant step towards its solution. And, along the way, he discovers a third proof that God exists.

Again we find the typical Cartesian strategy at work. He wants to know whether material things exist independently of himself. How can he proceed? He can't just look to see, since he has put the testimony of the senses in doubt. So he must consider more carefully the *idea* of material things, which is all that is available to him. And again he finds that some of these ideas are confused and obscure, while others are clear and distinct. The latter are those of extension, duration, and movement—the qualities that can be treated geometrically or mathematically. Material things, then, are *essentially* extended volumes.* Once we are clear about their *essence,* it makes sense to inquire about their *existence;* and that is the subject of *Meditation VI.*

Note that these mathematical ideas are not just imaginary inventions. I cannot put them together any way I like, as I can construct fantastic creatures by combining heads, bodies, and hides at will. I may not yet know whether there are any triangular things outside myself, but the idea of a triangle "can't be said to be nothing" (p. 324). It has a *nature* that is "immutable and eternal." This nature does not depend upon me.

The point can be put in this way. Suppose you

imagine a creature with wings covered with scales, a long furry tail, six legs, and an elephantlike nose covered with spikes. Then I ask you, does this creature have a liver? You will have to *invent* the answer. You cannot discover it. But if you imagine a triangle and I ask you whether the interior angles equal two right angles, you do not have to invent an answer. Even if you had never thought about that question before, you could investigate and discover that the answer is yes. With respect to these geometrical properties, there are *truths.** And these, remember, are the very properties that determine the essence of material things.

Since the idea of a material thing is the idea of something extended, and since extended things can be treated geometrically, it follows that the *idea* of a material thing is one which is clear and distinct. Material substances have an essence or nature that would make a *science* of them a possibility—if only we could be assured that they exist. And we know that such a science is a possibility merely from an examination of their ideas. So, provided we can discover a proof that some *formal* reality corresponds to the *subjective* reality of our ideas of material things, we can have a science of material things. In this way, then, he hopes to give a metaphysical foundation to his mechanistic physics.

The discovery that certain ideas have a nature or essence of their own, quite independent of our inventions, also supplies Descartes with material for a third proof of God's existence.† If we simply pay close attention to what is necessarily involved in our idea of *what* God is (his essence or nature), we can discover, Descartes argues, *that* God is (that

---

* Review the discussion of the bit of wax in *Meditation II* and on p. 302.

---

* Socrates thinks that we can never be taught anything other than what we in some sense already know; what we call learning is in fact just remembering. (See pp. 97–98.) Descartes alludes to this doctrine here; in discovering the properties of a triangle I am "noticing for the first time something that had long been in me without my having turned my mind's eye towards it." Descartes is not, however, committed to the Socratic doctrine of the preexistence of the soul as an explanation of this phenomenon, since he thinks God's creation of a soul possessing certain innate ideas will suffice.
† This proof is a version of the ontological argument first worked out by Anselm of Canterbury in the eleventh century. See Chapter 13.

he exists). God's existence is included in his essence. Notice that, unlike the first two arguments, this is not a *causal* proof.

Q40. Set out briefly, in numbered sentences, the essential points of this argument.
Q41. Is the argument, in your opinion, a sound one? Explain.

This last proof of God's existence allows Descartes to lay to rest a final worry that has been tormenting him. You really cannot help believing, he suggests, that your clear and distinct thoughts are true—while you are thinking them. But later you may not be so sure! You may then think you were dreaming what earlier seemed so certain. But now this worry can be dealt with. And *Meditation V* closes on a note of reassurance.

Q42. How are the dream and demon worries finally disposed of?
Q43. Can an atheist do science? (See the last paragraph.)

Read Meditation VI: On the Existence of Material Objects and the Real Distinction of Mind from Body We now know what the essence of material things is: to be such a thing is to be extended in space in three dimensions, to have shape and size, to endure, and to be movable and changeable in these dimensions. This is what a material thing would be—if there were any. At last we face the haunting question: Are there any?

The first thing to note is that they *can* exist.

Q44. What is Descartes' reason for thinking this?

If, moreover, we examine our *images* of material things, it seems that the imagination produces these images by turning "to the body" and looking "at something there" (p. 326). It is as though a representation of a triangle were physically stored in the body (or brain); and imagination is looking, not at a real triangular thing, but at that stored representation. Since we can undoubtedly form mental images, it certainly seems as though some material things exist, namely, our bodies.

But to make this clearer, Descartes draws a sharp distinction between *imagining* something and *conceiving* it.

Q45. How does the example comparing the triangle with the chiliagon help to clarify this distinction? (See p. 326.)

We still have no proof, of course, that there are any bodies. But again, progress has been made; for we now have an account of how one of the faculties of the mind works—on the assumption that there really are bodies. If we can find a proof of this assumption, it will "fit" with what we know about our mental capacities.

Descartes now turns from imagining to sensing. On pages 327–328, he reviews first his reasons for confidence in the senses and then his reasons for doubt.* At the end of this review he concludes again that what he is taught "by nature" does not deserve much credence.

However, the situation is now very different from that of the first *Meditation*. For now he knows that God exists and is not a deceiver. And in short order Descartes offers proofs that the soul is distinct from the body and that material things exist. Both of these depend on clear ideas of the essence of material things, which he arrived at in the fifth *Meditation*.

Q46. Set out briefly, in numbered sentences, the essential steps in the argument that the soul can exist without the body.
Q47. Is there a tension between this conclusion and the assertion (p. 329) that I am not in my body the way a sailor is in his ship?

---

*In the course of this review he paraphrases one of the basic principles of Thomas Aquinas, who derives it from Aristotle; that there is no idea in the intellect which was not previously in the senses. This is, for instance, the foundation for Thomas' rejection of the ontological argument (see p. 257). Descartes allows that this principle is superficially plausible; but in the light of his skeptical doubts he considers it naive. Not only do we know that we have ideas before we know we have senses, we know that some of these ideas must be innate—that is, they could not plausibly be derived from sensible experience. Such are the ideas of thing, thought, truth, and God.

Q48. Set out briefly, in numbered sentences, the essential steps in the proof that material things exist (pp. 328–329).

At this point Descartes has, he thinks, achieved his main objectives. Skepticism and solipsism have been defeated. The basic structure of reality has been delineated. God, souls, and material things. Reality, then, is composed of infinite substance and two kinds of finite substances—thinking and extended. The bridge has been built. Knowledge has been shown to be possible. Physics has been supplied with a foundation. And all this with a certainty that rivals that of geometry!

The rest of *Meditation VI* attends to a few details that are still left.

Q49. Compare what Descartes says on p. 329 to Galileo's view of "secondary qualities" (pp. 288–289).

Q50. If the senses present external things in such an inadequate way, what use are they?

Q51. How are we to account for certain errors the senses seem to lead us to (such as the pain in an amputated limb or the desire of a person with dropsy to drink)?

Q52. What is the final disposition of the problem arising from dreams?

What Has Descartes Done?

It is possible to argue whether Descartes is the last of the Medievals or the first of the Moderns. Like most such arguments about transitional figures, there is truth on both sides. But that both philosophy and our general view of the world have been different ever since is indisputable. Descartes develops a philosophy that reflects the newly developing sciences and, in turn, gives them a legitimacy they otherwise lack. A measure of his lasting influence is the fact that a significant part of phi-losophy since World War I has been devoted to showing that he was crucially wrong about some basic things (which would not be worth doing unless his influence was still powerfully felt).* Descartes is *our* ancestor.

Let us sum up several key features of his thought and then indicate where certain problems crop up.

A New Ideal for Knowledge

One commentator says of the Cartesian revolution that it "stands for the substitution of free inquiry for submission to authority, for the rejection of Faith without reason for faith *in* reason, and the replacement of Faith by Demonstration."[5] Though Descartes is far from trying to reject religious belief (indeed, he thinks he can rationally justify its two most important parts, God and the soul), in the last analysis everything comes down to what the rational mind finds clear and distinct enough to be indubitable. Nothing else will be accepted, regardless of its antiquity or traditional claims to authority. We each contain within ourselves the criterion for truth and knowledge. This radical individualism is qualified only by the conviction that rationality is the same for every individual (just as mathematics is the same for all). No longer can we put the responsibility for deciding what to believe on someone else, whether priest, pope, or king. It lies squarely on each of us.

Moreover, the ideal for such belief is the clarity and certainty of mathematics. Probability or plausibility is not enough. Being vaguely right is not enough. The habits of thought developed in us by nature are not enough. By analysis we can resolve problems into their simple elements; by intuition we can see their truth; and by demonstration we can move to necessary consequences. Knowledge has the structure of an axiomatic system. All this is possible. Anything less is unacceptable. To be

---

* Among the critics are C. S. Peirce, Martin Heidegger, and Ludwig Wittgenstein. See the chapters on their philosophies.

faithful to this ideal is to free oneself from error and to attain truth.

In all this Descartes deserves his reputation as Prince of the Rationalists.* The ultimate court of appeal is Reason—the Light of Nature. We ought to rely on intellect rather than sense, on intuition and deduction rather than imagination; "for true knowledge of external things seems to belong to the mind alone, not the composite of mind and body" (p. 329).

A New Vision of Reality

Descartes' metaphysics makes explicit and complete the world view that was emerging already in the work of Copernicus, Kepler, and Galileo. Our world is a giant mechanism, not unlike a clock (see Descartes' analogy on p. 330). It was, to be sure, created by God. But now it runs on the principles of mechanics, and our science is mechanistic in principle. If we abstract from the fact of creation, the entire material universe, including the human body, is just a complex machine. The world has become a *secular* world. What happens can be explained and predicted without reference to any purposes or intentions of the creator. We are, we might say, worlds away from the intrinsically purposive, inherently value-laden, God-directed world of the Medievals. Dante now begins to look like a fairy tale or, at best, a moral allegory with no literal truth value at all. It is, perhaps, no great surprise that the *Meditations* ends up on the *Index* of forbidden books.

There are, to be sure, human minds or souls, and they are not caught up in the mechanism of the material world. They are, in fact, radically free. Even God does not have more freedom than a soul see *Meditation IV*). But as we'll see, this disparity between soul and body is not as much the solution to a problem as it is a problem in itself.

---

* Though (almost) all philosophers try to reach their conclusions rationally, a rationalist is one who emphasizes the *exclusive* role of reason in the formation of knowledge. For one of Descartes' most distinguished predecessors in this tradition, see the discussion of the pre-Socratic thinker, Parmenides, in Chapter 3.

Problems

Great as Descartes' achievement is, he bequeaths to his successors a legacy of unsolved problems. There are those who refuse to accept his radical beginning point and remain true to a more traditional approach, usually Aristotelian. But his methodological doubt has been powerfully persuasive to many, and the continued progress of physics seems to be evidence that his basic view of the world is correct. For the next hundred and fifty years, Cartesianism, together with its variants, will be the dominating philosophy on the continent. As we'll see, different assumptions are at work in Britain, but even here the Cartesian spirit of independence is pervasive. Still, there are nagging worries. Let us note three of them.

The Place of Humans in the World of Nature

Descartes is intent on legitimizing the new science. And this he does. But what place is there for us in the universe of the new physics? Is it plausible to think that we, too, are just cogs in this universal machine? We assume that we have purposes and act to realize certain values. But where is there room for purposes and values in this mechanistic world? Is our assumption just an illusion? We assume that we can make a difference in the outcome of physical processes. But if the world is a closed mechanism, how can this be? We experience ourselves as conscious beings, aware of ourselves and the world around us. But can a machine be conscious? These are very contemporary questions, the sort cognitive science aims to sort out and solve.

All these questions force themselves on us once we take Descartes' vision of the universe seriously. Descartes is not unaware of them. His basic strategy for dealing with them consists in the radical split that he makes between mind and body. Bodies, he holds, are parts of the mechanical universe; minds are not. Physics can deal with the body, but not with the mind. We know that we are not merely automata because (1) we can use language, (2) we are flexible and adaptable in a way no machine could be; reason, Descartes says, "is a universal instrument which can be used in all kinds of situations." It is quite possible, he says, that we could construct a machine that utters words—even one that utters words corresponding to movements of its body. But it is not possible, he thinks, for a machine to "give an appropriately meaningful answer to whatever is said in its presence, as the dullest of men can do" (*DM* 6.56–57, p. 120.*

But merely dividing mind from body does not completely solve the problem. The question arises: how are they related?

The Mind and the Body   Descartes concludes that the mind is one thing and the body another; each is so independent of the other that either could exist without the other. They are, moreover, of a radically different character. The essence of a mind is thinking; minds are in no sense extended objects. The essence of a material thing is extension; but extended things such as bodies cannot think. Still, he says, mind and body are so intimately related as to form "a single unified thing" (p. 329).

But how can I be two things and yet one single thing? No explanation is given. Clearly he must insist that what happens to the body affects the mind, as when I get hungry, or am hurt, or open my eyes to a blue wall in daylight. And what the mind decides, the body may do, as when I choose to walk or eat an ice cream cone. There seems to be a two-way causal relation between mind and body. This view is called *interactionism*.

Yet it is completely puzzling how this can be. How can something that is not extended reach into the closed system of the mechanical world and work a change there, where all changes are governed by mechanical principles? And how can an alteration in the shape or position of certain material particles cause us to feel sad or think of Cleveland? No explanation is forthcoming. It seems entirely mysterious. To save the integrity of his

physics, Descartes pushes the mental out of the physical world entirely. But then it is inexplicable how physics itself can be done at all, since it seems to depend on interactions between nonphysical minds and physical bodies. Here is the problem that Schopenhauer would later call "the world knot." It is safe to say that a philosophy that does not solve the mind-body problem cannot be considered entirely acceptable.

God and the Problem of Skepticism   As we have seen, Descartes takes the skeptical problem very seriously. He pushes skeptical arguments about as far as they can be pushed. And he thinks that in the *cogito* he has found the key to overcoming skepticism. But even if we grant that each of us knows, by virtue of the *cogito,* that we exist, knowledge of the *world* depends on the fact that God is not a deceiver. And that depends on the proofs for the existence of God.

What if those proofs are faulty? Then we are back again in solipsism, without a guarantee that anything exists beyond ourselves. Are the proofs—or at least one of them—satisfactory? Descartes is quite clear that everything depends on that question; "the certainty and truth of all my knowledge derives from one thing: my thought of the true God" (p. 326). He is sure that the proofs are as secure as the theorems of geometry. But is he right about that?

The Preeminence of Epistemology

In earlier philosophies there are many problems—the one and the many, the nature of reality, explaining change, the soul, the existence of God—and the problem of knowledge is just one among the rest. Descartes' radical skepticism changes that. After Descartes and until very recent times most philosophers think that epistemological problems are absolutely foundational. Among these problems of knowledge, the problem about knowing the external world is the sharpest and most dangerous. Can we know anything at all beyond the contents of our minds? Unless this skeptical question can be satisfactorily answered, nothing else

---

*This, of course, is precisely the aim of research on artificial intelligence. Will it be successful? Descartes bets not.

can be done. Epistemology is, for better or worse, the heart of philosophy for the next several hundred years.

These are problems that Descartes' successors wrestle with, as we'll see. Next, however, we want to look at a figure who is often neglected in the history of modern philosophy, Thomas Hobbes. Hobbes is more interesting to us than to previous generations, perhaps, because he presents an alternative response to the new science. Some recent thought about the mind—that associated with artificial intelligence—can be thought of as a struggle to replace the paradigm of Descartes with that of Hobbes.

Meditation I:
On What Can Be Called Into Doubt

For several years now, I've been aware that I accepted many falsehoods as true in my youth, that what I built on the foundation of those falsehoods was dubious, and accordingly that once in my life I would need to tear down everything and begin anew from the foundations if I wanted to establish any stable and lasting knowledge. But the task seemed enormous, and I waited until I was so old that no better time for undertaking it would be likely to follow. I have thus delayed so long that it would be wrong for me to waste in indecision the time left for action. Today, then, having rid myself of worries and having arranged for some peace and quiet, I withdraw alone, free at last earnestly and wholeheartedly to overthrow all my beliefs.

To do this, I don't need to show each of them to be false; I may never be able to do that. But, since reason now convinces me that I ought to withhold my assent just as carefully from what isn't obviously certain and indubitable as from what's obviously false, I can justify the rejection of all my beliefs if in each I can find some ground for doubt. And, to do this, I need not run through my beliefs one by one, which would be an endless task. Since a building collapses when its foundation is cut out from under it, I will go straight to the principles on which all my former beliefs rested.

Of course, whatever I have so far accepted as supremely true I have learned either from the senses or through the senses. But I have occasionally caught the senses deceiving me, and it's prudent never completely to trust those who have cheated us even once.

But, while my senses may deceive me about what is small or far away, there may still be other things that I take in by the senses but that I cannot possibly doubt—like that I am here, sitting before the fire, wearing a dressing gown, touching this paper. And on what grounds might I deny that my hands and the other parts of my body exist?—unless perhaps I liken myself to madmen whose brains are so rattled by the persistent vapors of melancholy that they are sure that they're kings when in fact they are paupers, or that they wear purple robes when in fact they're naked, or that their heads are clay, or that they are gourds, or made of glass. But these people are insane, and I would seem just as crazy if I were to apply what I say about them to myself.

This would be perfectly obvious—if I weren't a man accustomed to sleeping at night whose experiences while asleep are at least as far-fetched as those that madmen have while awake. How often, at night, I've been convinced that I was here, sitting before the fire, wearing my dressing gown, when in fact I was undressed and between the covers of my bed! But now I am looking at this piece of paper with my eyes wide open; the head that I am shaking has not been lulled to sleep; I put my hand out consciously and deliberately and feel. None of this would be as distinct if I were asleep. As if I can't remember having been tricked by similar thoughts while asleep! When I think very carefully about this, I see so plainly that there are no reliable signs by which I can distinguish sleeping from waking that I am stupefied—and my stupor itself suggests that I am asleep!

Suppose, then that I am dreaming. Suppose, in particular, that my eyes are not open, that my head is not moving, and that I have not put out my hand. Suppose that I do not have hands, or even a body. I must still admit that the things I see in sleep are like painted images which must have been patterned after real things and, hence, that things like eyes, heads, hands, and bodies are real rather than imaginary. For, even when painters try to give bizarre shapes to sirens and satyrs, they are unable to give them completely new natures; they only jumble together the parts of various animals. And, even if they were to come up with something so novel that no one had ever seen anything like it before, something entirely fictitious and unreal, at least there must be real colors from which they composed it. Similarly, while things like eyes, heads, and hands may be imaginary, it must be granted that some simpler and more universal things are real—the "real colors" from which the true and false images in our thoughts are formed.

Things of this sort seem to include general bodily nature and its extension, the shape of extended things, their quantity (that is, their size and number), the place in which they exist, the time through which they endure, and so on.

Perhaps we can correctly infer that, while physics, astronomy, medicine, and other disciplines that require the study of composites are dubious, disciplines like arithmetic and geometry, which deal only with completely simple and universal things without regard to whether they exist in the world, are somehow certain and indubitable. For, whether we are awake or asleep, two plus three is always five, and the square never has more than four sides. It seems impossible even to suspect such obvious truths of falsity.

Nevertheless, the traditional view is fixed in my mind that there is a God who can do anything and by whom I have been made to be as I am. How do I know that He hasn't brought it about that, while there is in fact no earth, no sky, no extended thing, no shape, no magnitude, and no place, all of these things seem to me to exist, just as they do now? I think that other people sometimes err in what they believe themselves to know perfectly well. Mightn't I be deceived when I add two and three, or count the sides of a square, or do even simpler things, if we can even suppose that there is anything simpler? Maybe it will be denied that God deceives me, since He is said to be supremely good. But, if God's being good is incompatible with His having created me so that I am deceived always, it seems just as out of line with His being good that He permits me to be deceived sometimes—as he undeniably does.

Maybe some would rather deny that there is an omnipotent God than believe that everything else is uncertain. Rather than arguing with them, I will grant everything I have said about God to be fiction. But, however these people think I came to be as I now am—whether they say it is by fate, or by accident, or by a continuous series of events, or in some other way—it seems that he who errs and is deceived is somehow imperfect. Hence, the less power that is attributed to my original creator, the more likely it is that I am always deceived. To these arguments, I have no reply. I'm forced to admit that nothing that I used to believe is beyond legitimate doubt—not because I have been careless or playful, but because I have valid and well-considered grounds for doubt. Hence, I must withhold my assent from my former beliefs as carefully as from obvious falsehoods if I want to arrive at something certain.

But it's not enough to have noticed this: I must also take care to bear it in mind. For my habitual views constantly return to my mind and take control of what I believe as if our long-standing, intimate relationship has given them the right to do so, even against my will. I'll never break the habit of trusting and giving in to these views while I see them for what they are—things somewhat dubious (as I have just shown) but nonetheless probable, things that I have much more reason to believe than to deny. That's why I think it will be good deliberately to turn my will around, to allow myself to be deceived, and to suppose that all my previous beliefs are false and illusory. Eventually, when I have counterbalanced the weight of my prejudices, my bad habits will no longer distort my grasp of things. I know that there is no danger of error here and that I won't overindulge in skepticism, since I'm now concerned, not with action, but only with gaining knowledge.

I will suppose, then, not that there is a supremely good God who is the source of all truth, but that there is an evil demon, supremely powerful and cunning, who works as hard as he can to deceive me. I will say that sky, air, earth, color, shape, sound, and other external things are just dreamed illusions that the demon uses to ensnare my judgment. I will regard myself as not having hands, eyes, flesh, blood, and senses—but as having the false belief that I have all these things. I will obstinately concentrate on this meditation and will thus ensure by mental resolution that, if I do not really have the ability to know the truth, I will at least withhold assent from what is false and from what a deceiver may try to put over on me, however powerful and cunning he may be. But this plan requires effort, and laziness brings me back to my ordinary life. I am like a prisoner who happens to enjoy the illusion of freedom in his dreams, begins to suspect that he is asleep, fears being awakened, and deliberately lets the enticing illusions slip by unchallenged. Thus, I slide back into my old views, afraid to awaken and to find that after my peaceful rest I must toil, not in the light, but in the confusing darkness of the problems just raised.

Meditation II:
On the Nature of the Human Mind, Which Is Better Known Than the Body

Yesterday's meditation has hurled me into doubts so great that I can neither ignore them or think my way out of them. I am in turmoil, as if I have accidentally fallen into a whirlpool and can neither touch bottom nor swim to the safety of the surface. I will struggle, however, and try to follow the path that I started on yesterday. I will reject whatever is open to the slightest doubt just as though I have found it to be entirely false, and I will continue until I find something certain—or at least until I know for certain that nothing is certain. Archimedes required only one fixed and immovable point to move the whole earth from its place, and I too can hope for great things if I can find even one small thing that is certain and unshakeable.

I will suppose, then, that everything I see is unreal. I will believe that my memory is unreliable and that none of what it presents to me ever happened. I have no senses. Body, shape, extension, motion, and place are fantasies. What then is true? Perhaps just that nothing is certain.

But how do I know that there isn't something different from the things just listed that I do not have the slightest reason to doubt? Isn't there a God, or something like one, who puts my thoughts into me? But why should I say so when I may be the author of those thoughts? Well, isn't it at least the case that I am something? But I now am denying that I have senses and a body. But I stop here. For what follows from these denials? Am I so bound to my body and to my senses that I cannot exist without them? I have convinced myself that there is nothing in the world—no sky, no earth, no minds, no bodies. Doesn't it follow that I don't exist? No, surely I must exist if it's me who is convinced of something. But there is a deceiver, supremely powerful and cunning whose aim is to see that I am always deceived. But surely I exist, if I am deceived. Let him deceive me all he can, he will never make it the case that I am nothing while I think that I am something. Thus having fully weighed every consideration, I must finally conclude that the statement "I am, I exist" must be true whenever I state it or mentally consider it.

But I do not yet fully understand what this "I" is that must exist. I must guard against inadvertently taking myself to be something other than I am, thereby going wrong even in the knowledge that I put forward as supremely certain and evident. Hence, I will think once again about what I believed myself to be before beginning these meditations. From this conception, I will subtract everything challenged by the reasons for doubt that I produced earlier, until nothing remains except what is certain and indubitable.

What, then, did I formerly take myself to be? A man, of course. But what is a man? Should I say a rational animal? No, because then I would need to ask what an animal is and what it is to be rational. Thus, starting from a single question, I would sink into many that are more difficult, and I do not have the time to waste on such subtleties. Instead, I will look here at the thoughts that occurred to me spontaneously and naturally when I reflected on what I was. This first thought to occur to me was that I have a face, hands, arms, and all the other equipment (also found in corpses) which I call a body. The next thought to occur to me was that I take nourishment, move myself around, sense, and think—that I do things which I trace back to my soul. Either I didn't stop to think about what this soul was, or I imagined it to be a rarified air, or fire, or ether permeating the denser parts of my body. But, about physical objects, I didn't have any doubts whatever: I thought that I distinctly knew their nature. If I had tried to describe my conception of this nature, I might have said this: "When I call something a physical object, I mean that it is capable of being bounded by a shape and limited to a place; that it can fill a space so as to exclude other objects from it; that it can be perceived by touch, sight, hearing, taste, and smell; that it can be moved in various ways, not by itself, but by something else in contact with it." I judged that the powers of self-movement, of sensing, and of thinking did not belong to the nature of physical objects, and, in fact, I marveled that there were some physical objects in which these powers could be found.

But what should I think now, while supposing that a supremely powerful and "evil" deceiver completely devotes himself to deceiving me? Can I say that I have any of the things that I have attributed to the nature of physical objects? I concentrate, think, reconsider—but nothing comes to me; I grow tired of the pointless repetition. But what about the things that I have assigned to soul? Nutrition and self-movement? Since I have no body, these are merely illusions. Sensing? But I cannot sense without a body, and in sleep I've seemed to sense many things that I later realized I had not really sensed. Thinking? It comes down to this: Thought and thought alone cannot be taken away from me. I am, I exist. That much is certain. But for how long? As long as I think— for it may be that, if I completely stopped thinking, I would completely cease to exist. I am not now admitting anything unless it must be true, and I am therefore not admitting that I am anything at all other than a thinking thing—that is, a mind, soul, understanding, or reason (terms whose meaning I did not previously know). I know that I am a real, existing thing, but what kind of thing? As I have said, a thing that thinks.

What else? I will draw up mental images. I'm not the collection of organs called a human body. Nor am I some rarified gas permeating these organs, or air, or fire, or vapor, or breath—for I have supposed that none of these things exist. Still, I am something. But couldn't it be that these things, which I do not yet know about and which I am therefore supposing to be nonexistent, really aren't distinct from the "I" that I know to exist? I don't know, and I'm not going to argue about it now. I can only form judgments on what I do know. I know that I exist, and I ask what the "I" is that I know to exist. It's obvious that this conception of myself doesn't depend on anything that I do not yet know to exist and, therefore, that it does not depend on anything of which I can draw up a mental image. And the words "draw up" point to my mistake. I would truly be creative if I were to have a mental image of what I am, since to have a mental image is just to contemplate the shape or image of a physical object. I now know with certainty that I exist and at the same time that all images—and, more generally, all things associated with the nature of physical objects—may just be dreams. When I keep this in mind, it seems just as absurd to say "I use mental images to help me understand what I am" as it would to say "Now, while awake, I see something true—but, since I don't yet see it clearly enough, I'll go to sleep and let my dreams present it to me more clearly and truly." Thus I know that none of the things that I can comprehend with the aid of mental images bear on my knowledge of myself. And I must carefully draw my mind away from such things if it is to see its own nature distinctly.

But what then am I? A thinking thing. And what is that? Something that doubts, understands, affirms, denies, wills, refuses, and also senses and has mental images.

That's quite a lot, if I really do all of these things. But don't I? Isn't it me who now doubts nearly everything, understands one thing, affirms this thing, refuses to affirm other things, wants to know much more, refuses to be deceived, has mental images (sometimes involuntarily), and is aware of many things "through his senses"? Even if I am always dreaming, and even if my creator does what he can to deceive me, isn't it just as true that I do all these things as that I exist? Are any of these things distinct from my thought? Can any be said to be separate from me? That it's me who doubts, understands, and wills is so obvious that I don't see how it could be more evident. And it's also me who has mental images. While it may be, as I am supposing, that absolutely nothing of which I have a mental image

really exists, the ability to have mental images really does exist and is a part of my thought. Finally, it's me who senses—or who seems to gain awareness of physical objects through the senses. For example, I am now seeing light, hearing a noise, and feeling heat. These things are unreal, since I am dreaming. But it is still certain that I seem to see, to hear, and to feel. This seeming cannot be unreal, and it is what is properly called sensing. Strictly speaking, sensing is just thinking.

From this, I begin to learn a little about what I am. But I still can't stop thinking that I apprehend physical objects, which I picture in mental images and examine with my senses, much more distinctly than I know this unfamiliar "I," of which I cannot form a mental image. I think this, even though it would be astounding if I comprehended things which I've found to be doubtful, unknown, and alien to me more distinctly than the one which I know to be real: my self. But I see what's happening. My mind enjoys wandering, and it won't confine itself to the truth. I will therefore loosen the reigns on my mind for now so that later, when the time is right, I will be able to control it more easily.

Let's consider the things commonly taken to be the most distinctly comprehended: physical objects that we see and touch. Let's not consider physical objects in general, since general conceptions are very often confused. Rather, let's consider one, particular object. Take, for example, this piece of wax. It has just been taken from the honeycomb; it hasn't yet completely lost the taste of honey; it still smells of the flowers from which it was gathered; its color, shape, and size are obvious; it is hard, cold, and easy to touch; it makes a sound when rapped. In short, everything seems to be present in the wax that is required for me to know it as distinctly as possible. But, as I speak, I move the wax toward the fire; it loses what was left of its taste; it gives up its smell; it changes color; it loses its shape; it gets bigger; it melts; it heats up; it becomes difficult to touch; it no longer makes a sound when struck. Is it still the same piece of wax? We must say that it is: not one denies it or thinks otherwise. Then what was there in the wax that I comprehended so distinctly? Certainly nothing that I reached with my senses—for, while everything having to do with taste, smell, sight, touch, and hearing has changed, the same piece of wax remains.

Perhaps what I distinctly knew was neither the sweetness of honey, nor the fragrance of flowers, nor a sound, but a physical object that once appeared to me one way and now appears differently. But what exactly is it of which I now have a mental image? Let's pay careful attention, remove everything that doesn't belong to the wax, and see what's left. Nothing is left except an extended, flexible, and changeable thing. But what is it for this thing to be flexible and changeable? Is it just that the wax can go from round to square and then to triangular, as I have mentally pictured? Of course not. Since I understand that the wax's shape can change in innumerable ways, and since I can't run through all the changes in my imagination, my comprehension of the wax's flexibility and changeability cannot have been produced by my ability to have mental images. And what about the thing that is extended? Are we also ignorant of its extension? Since the extension of the wax increases when the wax melts, increases again when the wax boils, and increases still more when the wax gets hotter, I will be mistaken about what the wax is unless I believe that it can undergo more changes in extension that I can ever encompass with mental images. I must therefore admit that I do not have an image of what the wax is—that I grasp what it is with only my mind. (While I am saying this about a particular piece of wax, it is even more clearly true about wax in general.) What then is this piece of wax that I grasp only with my mind? It is something that I see, feel, and mentally picture— exactly what I believed it to be at the outset. But it must be noted that, despite the appearances, my grasp of the wax is not visual, tactile, or pictorial. Rather, my grasp of the wax is the result of a purely mental inspection, which can be imperfect and confused, as it was once, or clear and distinct, as it is now, depending on how much attention I pay to the things of which the wax consists.

I'm surprised by how prone my mind is to error. Even when I think to myself non-verbally, language stands in my way, and common usage comes close to deceiving me. For, when the wax is present, we say that we see the wax itself, not that we infer its presence from its color and shape. I'm inclined to leap from this fact about language to the conclusion that I learn about the wax by eyesight rather than by purely mental inspection. But, if I happen to look out my window and see men walking in the street, I naturally say that I see the men just as I say that I see the wax. What do I really see, however, but hats and coats that could be covering robots? I *judge* that there are men. Thus I comprehend with my judgment, which is in my mind, objects that I once believed myself to see with my eyes.

One who aspires to wisdom above that of the common man disgraces himself by deriving doubt from common ways of speaking. Let's go on, then, to ask when I most clearly and perfectly grasped what the wax

is. Was it when I first looked at the wax and believed my knowledge of it to come from the external senses— or at any rate from the so-called "common sense," the power of having mental images? Or is it now, after I have carefully studied what the wax is and how I come to know it? Doubt would be silly here. For what was distinct in my original conception of the wax? How did that conception differ from that had by animals? When I distinguish the wax from its external forms—when I "undress" it and view it "naked"—there may still be errors in my judgments about it, but I couldn't possibly grasp the wax in this way without a human mind.

What should I say about this mind—or, in other words, about myself? (I am not now admitting that there is anything to me but a mind.) What is this "I" that seems to grasp the wax so distinctly? Don't I know myself much more truly and certainly, and also much more distinctly and plainly, than I know the wax? For, if I base my judgment that the wax exists on the fact that I see it, my seeing it much more obviously implies that I exist. It's possible that what I see is not really wax, and it's even possible that I don't have eyes with which to see— but it clearly is not possible that, when I see (or, what now amounts to the same thing, when I think I see), the "I" that thinks is not a real thing. Similarly, if I base my judgment that the wax exists on the fact that I feel it, the same fact makes it obvious that I exist. If I base my judgment that the wax exists on the fact that I have a mental image of it or on some other fact of this sort, the same thing can obviously be said. And what I've said about the wax applies to everything else that is outside me. Moreover, if I seem to grasp the wax more distinctly when I detect it with several senses than when I detect it with just sight or touch, I must know myself even more distinctly—for every consideration that contributes to my grasp of the piece of wax or to my grasp of any other physical object serves better to reveal the nature of my mind. Besides, the mind has so much in it by which it can make its conception of itself distinct that what comes to it from physical objects hardly seems to matter.

And now I have brought myself back to where I wanted to be. I now know that physical objects are grasped, not by the senses or the power of having mental images, but by understanding alone. And, since I grasp physical objects in virtue of their being understandable rather than in virtue of their being tangible or visible, I know that I can't grasp anything more easily or plainly than my mind. But, since it takes time to break old habits of thought, I should pause here to allow the length of my contemplation to impress the new thoughts more deeply into my memory.

Meditation III:
On God's Existence

I will now close my eyes, plug my ears, and withdraw all my senses. I will rid my thoughts of the images of physical objects—or, since that's beyond me, I'll write those images off as empty illusions. Talking with myself and looking more deeply into myself, I'll try gradually to come to know myself better. I am a thinking thing— a thing that doubts, affirms, denies, understands a few things, is ignorant of many things, wills, and refuses. I also sense and have mental images. For, as I've noted, even though the things of which I have sensations or mental images may not exist outside me, I'm certain that the modifications of thought called sensations and mental images exist in me insofar as they are just modifications of thought.

That's a summary of all that I really know—or, at any rate, of all that I've so far noticed that I know. I now will examine more carefully whether there are other things in me that I have not yet discovered. I'm certain that I am a thinking thing. Then don't I know what's needed for me to be certain of other things? In this first knowledge, there is nothing but a clear and distinct grasp of what I affirm, and this grasp surely would not suffice to make me certain if it could ever happen that something I grasped so clearly and distinctly was false. Accordingly, I seem to be able to establish the general rule that whatever I clearly and distinctly grasp is true.

But, in the past, I've accepted as completely obvious and certain many thoughts that I later found to be dubious. What were these thoughts about? The earth, the sky, the stars, and other objects of sense. But what did I clearly grasp about these objects? Only that ideas or thoughts of them appeared in my mind. Even now, I don't deny that these ideas occur in me. But there was something else that I used to affirm—something that I used to believe myself to grasp clearly but did not really grasp at all: I affirmed that there were things besides me, that the ideas in me came from these things, and that the ideas perfectly resembled these things. Either I erred here, or I reached a true judgment that wasn't justified by the strength of my understanding.

But what follows? When I considered very simple and easy points of arithmetic or geometry—such as that two and three together make five—didn't I see them

clearly enough to affirm their truth? My only reason for judging that I ought to doubt these things was the thought that my God-given nature might deceive me even about what seems most obvious. Whenever I conceive of an all-powerful God, I'm compelled to admit that, if He wants, He can make it the case that I err even about what I take my mind's eye to see most clearly. But, when I turn to the things that I believe myself to grasp very clearly, I'm so convinced by them that I spontaneously burst forth saying, "Whoever may deceive me, he will never bring it about that I am nothing while I think that I am something, or that I have never been when it is now true that I am, or that two plus three is either more or less than five, or that something else in which I recognize an obvious inconsistency is true." And, since I have no reason for thinking that God is a deceiver— indeed since I don't yet know whether God exists—the grounds for doubt that rest on the supposition that God deceives are very weak and "metaphysical." Still, to rid myself of these grounds, I ought to ask as soon as possible whether there is a God and, if so, whether He can be a deceiver. For it seems that, until I know these two things, I can never be completely certain of anything else.

The structure of my project seems to require, however, that I first categorize my thoughts and ask in which of them truth and falsity really reside. Some of my thoughts are like images of things, and only these can properly be called ideas. I have an idea, for example, when I think of a man, of a chimera, of heaven, of an angel, or of God. But other thoughts have other properties: while I always apprehend something as the object of my thought when I will, fear, affirm, or deny, these thoughts also include a component in addition to the likeness of that thing. Some of these components are called volitions or emotions; others, judgments.

Now, viewed in themselves and without regard to other things, ideas cannot really be false. If I imagine a chimera and a goat, it is just as true that I imagine the chimera as that I imagine the goat. And I needn't worry about falsehoods in volitions or emotions. If I have a perverse desire for something, or if I want something that doesn't exist, it's still true that I want that thing. All that remains, then, are my judgments; it's here that I must be careful not to err. And the first and foremost of the errors that I find in my judgments is that of assuming that the ideas in me have a similarity or conformity to things outside me. For, if I were to regard ideas merely as modifications of thought, they could not really provide me with any opportunity for error.

Of my ideas, some seem to me to be innate, others acquired, and others produced by me. The ideas by which I understand reality, truth, and thought seem to have come from my own nature. Those ideas by which I hear a noise, see the sun, or feel the fire I formerly judged to come from things outside me. And the ideas of sirens, hippogriffs, and so on I have formed in myself. Or maybe I can take all of my ideas to be acquired, all innate, or all created by me: I do not yet clearly see where my ideas come from.

For the moment, the central question is about the ideas that I view as derived from objects existing outside me. What reason is there for thinking that these ideas resemble the objects? I seem to have been taught this by nature. Besides, I find that these ideas are independent of my will and hence of me—for they often appear when I do not want them to do so. For example, I now feel heat whether I want to or not, and I therefore take the idea or sensation of heat to come from something distinct from me: the heat of the fire by which I am now sitting. And the obvious thing to think is that a thing sends me its own likeness, not something else.

I will now see whether these reasons are good enough. When I say that nature teaches me something, I mean just that I have a spontaneous impulse to believe it, not that the light of nature reveals the thing's truth to me. There is an important difference. When the light of nature reveals something to me (such as that my thinking implies my existing) that thing is completely beyond doubt, since there is no faculty as reliable as the light of nature by means of which I could learn that the thing is not true. But, as for my natural impulses, I have often judged them to have led me astray in choices about what's good, and I don't see why I should regard them as any more reliable on matters concerning truth and falsehood.

Next, while my sensory ideas may not depend on my will, it doesn't follow that they come from outside me. While the natural impulses of which I just spoke are in me, they seem to conflict with my will. Similarly, I may have in me an as yet undiscovered ability to produce the ideas that seem to come from outside me—in the way that I used to think that ideas came to me in dreams.

Finally, even if some of my ideas do come from things distinct from me, it doesn't follow that they are likenesses of these things. Indeed, it often seems to me that an idea differs greatly from its cause. For example, I find in myself two different ideas of the sun. One, which I "take in" through the senses and which I ought therefore to view as a typical acquired idea, makes the sun look very small to me. The other, which I derive from astronomical reasoning (that is, which I make, perhaps by composing it from innate ideas), pictures the sun as many times larger than the earth. It clearly cannot be that both of these are accurate likenesses of a sun that exists outside me, and reason convinces me that the one least like the sun is the one that seems to arise most directly from it.

All that I've said shows that, until now, my belief that there are things outside me that send their ideas or images to me (perhaps through my senses) has rested on blind impulse rather than certain judgment.

Still, it seems to me that there may be a way of telling whether my ideas come from things that exist outside me. Insofar as the ideas of things are just modifications of thought, I find no inequality among them; all seem to arise from me in the same way. But, insofar as different ideas present different things to me, there obviously are great differences among them. The ideas of substances are unquestionably greater—or have more "subjective reality"—than those of modifications or accidents. Similarly, the idea by which I understand the supreme God—eternal, infinite, omniscient, omnipotent, and creator of all things other than Himself—has more subjective reality in it than the ideas of finite substances.

Now, the light of nature reveals that there is at least as much in a complete efficient cause as in its effect. For where could an effect get its reality if not from its cause? And how could a cause give something unless it had it? It follows both that something cannot come from nothing and that what is more perfect—that is, has more reality in it—cannot come from what is less perfect or has less reality. This obviously holds, not just for those effects whose reality is actual or formal, but also for ideas, whose reality we regard as merely subjective. For example, it's impossible for a non-existent stone to come into existence unless it's produced by something containing, either formally or eminently, everything in the stone. Similarly, heat can only be induced in something that's not already hot by something having at least the same degree of perfection as heat. Also, it's impossible for the *idea* of heat or of stone to be in me unless it's been put there by a cause having at least as much reality as I conceive of in the heat or the stone. For, although the cause doesn't transmit any of its actual or formal reality to the idea, we shouldn't infer that it can be less real than the idea; all that we can infer is that by its nature the idea doesn't require any formal reality except what it derives from my thought, of which it is a modification. Yet, as the idea contains one particular subjective reality rather than another, it must get this reality from a cause having at least as much formal reality as the idea has subjective reality. For, if we suppose that an idea has something in it that wasn't in its cause, we must suppose that it got this thing from nothing. However imperfect the existence of something that exists subjectively in the understanding through an idea, it obviously is something, and it therefore cannot come from nothing.

And, although the reality that I'm considering in my ideas is just subjective, I ought not to suspect that it can fail to be in an idea's cause formally—that it's enough for it to be there subjectively. For, just as the subjective existence of my ideas belongs to the ideas in virtue of their nature, the formal existence of the ideas' causes belongs to those causes—or, at least, to the first and foremost of them—in virtue of the causes' nature. Although one idea may arise from another, this can't go back to infinity; we must eventually arrive at a primary idea whose cause is an "archetype" containing formally all the reality that the idea contains subjectively. Hence, the light of nature makes it clear to me that the ideas in me are like images that may well fall short of the things from which they derive, but cannot contain anything greater or more perfect.

The more time and care I take in studying this, the more clearly and distinctly I know it to be true. But what follows from it? If I can be sure that the subjective reality of one of my ideas is so great that it isn't in me either formally or eminently and hence that I cannot be the cause of that idea, I can infer that I am not alone in the world—that there exists something else that is the cause of the idea. But, if I can find no such idea in me, I will have no argument at all for the existence of anything other than me—for, having diligently searched for such an argument, I have yet to find one.

Of my ideas—besides my idea of myself, about which there can be no problem here—one presents God, others inanimate physical objects, others angels, others animals, and still others men like me.

As to my idea of other men, of animals, and of angels, it's easy to see that—even if the world contained no men but me, no animals, and no angels—I could have composed these ideas from those that I have of myself, of physical objects, and of God.

And, as to my ideas of physical objects, it seems that nothing in them is so great that it couldn't have come from me. For, if I analyze my ideas of physical objects carefully, taking them one by one as I did yesterday when examining my idea of the piece of wax, I notice that there is very little in them that I grasp clearly and

distinctly. What I do grasp clearly and distinctly in these ideas is size (which is extension in length, breadth, and depth), shape (which arises from extension's limits), position (which the differently shaped things have relative to one another), and motion (which is just change of position). To these I can add substance, duration, and number. But my thoughts of other things in physical objects (such as light and color, sound, odor, taste, heat and cold, and tactile qualities) are so confused and obscure that I can't say whether they are true or false—whether my ideas of these things are of something or of nothing. Although, as I noted earlier, that which is properly called falsehood—namely, *formal* falsehood—can only be found in judgments, we can still find falsehood of another sort—namely, *material* falsehood—in an idea when it presents what is not a thing as though it were a thing. For example, the ideas that I have of coldness and heat are so unclear and indistinct that I can't tell from them whether coldness is just the absence of heat, or heat just the absence of coldness, or both are real qualities, or neither is. And, since every idea is "of something," the idea that presents coldness to me as something real and positive could justifiably be called false if coldness were just the absence of heat. And the same holds true for other ideas of this sort.

For such ideas, I need not posit a creator distinct from me. I know by the light of nature that, if one of these ideas is false—that is, if it doesn't present a real thing—it comes from nothing—that is, the only cause of its being in me is a deficiency of my nature, which clearly is imperfect. If one of these ideas is true, however, I still see no reason why I couldn't have produced it myself—for these ideas present so little reality to me that I can't even distinguish it from nothing.

Of the things that are clear and distinct in my ideas of physical objects, it seems that I may have borrowed some—such as substance, duration, and number—from my idea of myself. I think of the stone as a substance—that is, as something that can exist on its own—just as I think of myself as a substance. Although I conceive of myself as a thinking and unextended thing and of the stone as an extended and unthinking thing so that the two conceptions are quite different, they are the same in that they both seem to be of substances. And, when I grasp that I exist now while remembering that I existed in the past, or when I count my various thoughts, I get the idea of duration or number, which I can then apply to other things. The other components of my ideas of physical objects—extension, shape, place, and motion—can't be in me formally, since I'm just a thinking thing. But, as these things are just modes of substance, and as I am a substance, it seems that they may be in me eminently.

All that's left is my idea of God. Is there something in this idea of God that couldn't have come from me? By "God" I mean a substance that's infinite, independent, supremely intelligent, and supremely powerful—the thing from which I and everything else that may exist derive our existence. The more I consider these attributes, the less it seems that they could have come from me alone. So I must conclude that God necessarily exists.

While I may have the idea of substance in me by virtue of my being a substance, I who am finite would not have the idea of infinite substance in me unless it came from a substance that really was infinite.

And I shouldn't think that, rather than having a true idea of infinity, I grasp it merely as the absence of limits—in the way that I grasp rest as the absence of motion and darkness as the absence of light. On the contrary, it's clear to me that there is more reality in an infinite than in a finite substance and hence that my grasp of the infinite must somehow be prior to my grasp of the finite—my understanding of God prior to my understanding of myself. For how could I understand that I doubt and desire, that I am deficient and imperfect, if I didn't have the idea of something more perfect to use as a standard of comparison?

And, unlike the ideas of hot and cold which I just discussed, the idea of God cannot be said to be materially false and hence to come from nothing. On the contrary, since the idea of God is completely clear and distinct and contains more subjective reality than any other idea, no idea is truer *per se* and none less open to the suspicion of falsity. The idea of a supremely perfect and infinite entity is, I maintain, completely true. For, while I may be able to suppose that there is no such entity, I can't even suppose (as I did about the idea of coldness) that my idea of God fails to show me something real. This idea is maximally clear and distinct, for it contains everything that I grasp clearly and distinctly, everything real and true, everything with any perfection. It doesn't matter that I can't fully comprehend the infinite—that there are innumerable things in God which I can't comprehend fully or even reach with thought. Because of the nature of the infinite, I who am finite cannot comprehend it. It's enough that I think about the infinite and judge that, if I grasp something clearly and distinctly and know it to have some perfection, it's present either formally or eminently—perhaps

along with innumerable other things of which I am ignorant—in God. If I do this, then of all my ideas the idea of God will be most true and most clear and distinct.

But maybe I am greater than I have assumed; maybe all the perfections that I attributed to God are in me potentially, still unreal and unactualized. I have already seen my knowledge gradually increase, and I don't see anything to prevent its becoming greater and greater to infinity. Nor do I see why, by means of such increased knowledge, I couldn't get all the rest of God's perfections. Finally, if the potential for these perfections is in me, I don't see why that potential couldn't account for the production of the ideas of these perfections in me.

None of this is possible. First, while it's true that my knowledge gradually increases and that I have many as yet unactualized potentialities, none of this fits with my idea of God, in whom absolutely nothing is potential; indeed, the gradual increase in my knowledge shows that I am *imperfect*. Besides, I see that, even if my knowledge were continually to become greater and greater, it would never become actually infinite, since it would never become so great as to be unable to increase. But I judge God to be actually infinite so that nothing can be added to his perfection. Finally, I see that an idea's subjective being must be produced, not by mere potentiality (which, strictly speaking, is nothing), but by what is actual or formal.

When I pay attention to these things, the light of nature makes all of them obvious. But, when I attend less carefully and the images of sensible things blind my mind's eye, it's not easy for me to remember why the idea of an entity more perfect than I am must come from an entity that really is more perfect. That's why I'll go on to ask whether I, who have the idea of a perfect entity, could exist if no such entity existed.

From what might I derive my existence if not from God? Either from myself, or from my parents, or from something else less perfect than God—for nothing more perfect than God, or even as perfect as Him, can be thought of or imagined.

But, if I derived my existence from myself, I wouldn't doubt, or want, or lack anything. I would have given myself every perfection of which I have an idea, and thus I myself would be God. And I shouldn't think that it might be harder to give myself what I lack than what I already have. On the contrary, it would obviously be much harder for me, a thinking thing or substance, to emerge from nothing than for me to give myself knowledge of the many things of which I am ignorant, which is just an attribute of substance. But surely, if I had given myself that which is harder to get, I wouldn't have denied myself complete knowledge, which would have been easier to get. Indeed, I wouldn't have denied myself *any* of the perfections that I grasp in the idea of God. None of these perfections seems harder to get than existence. But, if I had given myself everything that I now have, these perfections would have seemed harder to get than existence if they were harder to get—for in creating myself I would have discovered the limits of my power.

I can't avoid the force of this argument by supposing that, since I've always existed as I do now, there's no point in looking for my creator. Since my lifetime can be divided into innumerable parts each of which is independent of the others, the fact that I existed a little while ago does not entail that I exist now, unless a cause "recreates" me—or, in other words, preserves me—at this moment. For, when we attend to the nature of time, it's obvious that exactly the same power and action are required to preserve a thing at each moment through which it endures as would be required to create it anew if it had never existed. Hence, one of the things revealed by the light of nature is that preservation and creation differ only in the way we think of them.

I ought to ask myself, then, whether I have the power to ensure that I, who now am, will exist in a little while. Since I am nothing but a thinking thing—or, at any rate, since I am now focusing on the part of me that thinks—I would surely be aware of this power if it were in me. But I find no such power. And from this I clearly see that there is an entity distinct from me on whom I depend.

But maybe this entity isn't God. Maybe I am the product of my parents or of some other cause less perfect than God. No. As I've said, there must be at least as much in a cause as in its effect. Hence, since I am a thinking thing with the idea of God in me, my cause, whatever it may be, must be a thinking thing having in it the idea of every perfection that I attribute to God. And we can go on to ask whether this thing gets its existence from itself or from something else. If it gets its existence from itself, it's obvious from what I've said that it must be God—for it would have the power to exist on its own and hence the power actually to give itself every perfection of which it has an idea, including every perfection that I conceive of in God. But, if my cause gets its existence from some other thing, we can go on to ask whether this other thing gets its existence from itself or from something else. Eventually, we will come to the ultimate cause, which will be God.

It's clear enough that there can't be an infinite regress here—especially since I am concerned, not so much with the cause that originally produced me, as with the one that preserves me at the present moment.

And I can't suppose that several partial causes combined to make me or that I get the ideas of the various perfections that I attribute to God from different causes so that, while each of these perfections can be found somewhere in the universe, there is no God in whom they all come together. On the contrary, one of the chief perfections that I understand God to have is unity, simplicity, inseparability from everything in Him. Surely the idea of the unity of all God's perfections can only have been put in me by a cause that gives me the ideas of all the other perfections—for nothing could make me aware of the unbreakable connection of God's perfections unless it made me aware of what those perfections are.

Finally, even if everything that I used to believe about my parents is true, it's clear that they don't preserve me. Insofar as I am a thinking thing, they did not even take part in creating me. They simply formed the matter in which I used to think that I (that is, my mind, which is all I am now taking myself to be) resided. There can therefore be no problem about my parents. And I am driven to this conclusion: The fact that I exist and have an idea in me of a perfect entity—that is, God—conclusively entails that God does in fact exist.

All that's left is to explain how I have gotten my idea of God from Him. I have not taken it in through my senses; it has never come to me unexpectedly as the ideas of sensible things do when those things affect (or seem to affect) my external organs of sense. Nor have I made the idea myself; I can't subtract from it or add to it. The only other possibility is that the idea is innate in me, like my idea of myself.

It's not at all surprising that in creating me God put this idea into me, impressing it on His work like a craftsman's mark (which needn't be distinct from the work itself). The very fact that it was God who created me confirms that I have somehow been made in His image or likeness and that I grasp this likeness, which contains the idea of God, in the same way that I grasp myself. Thus, when I turn my mind's eye on myself, I understand, not just that I am an incomplete and dependent thing which constantly strives for bigger and better things, but also that He on whom I depend has all these things in Himself as infinite reality rather than just as vague potentiality and hence that He must be God. The whole argument comes down to this: I know that I could not exist with my present nature — that is, that I could not exist with the idea of God in me—unless there really were a God. This must be the very God whose idea is in me, the thing having all of the perfections that I can't fully comprehend but can somehow reach with thought, who clearly cannot have any defects. From this, it's obvious that He can't deceive—for, as the natural light reveals, fraud and deception arise from defect.

But before examining this more carefully and investigating its consequences, I want to dwell for a moment in the contemplation of God, to ponder His attributes, to see and admire and adore the beauty of His boundless light, insofar as my clouded insight allows. As I have faith that the supreme happiness of the next life consists wholly of the contemplation of divine greatness, I now find that contemplation of the same sort, though less perfect, affords the greatest joy available in this life.

Meditation IV:
On Truth and Falsity

In the last few days, I've gotten used to drawing my mind away from my senses. I've carefully noted that I really grasp very little about physical objects, that I know much more about the human mind, and that I know even more about God. Thus, I no longer find it hard to turn my thoughts away from things of which I can have mental images and toward things completely separate from matter, which I can only understand. Indeed, I have a much more distinct idea of the human mind, insofar as it is just a thinking thing that isn't extended in length, breadth, or depth and doesn't share anything else with physical objects, than I have of physical objects. And, when I note that I doubt or that I am incomplete and dependent, I have a clear and distinct idea of a complete and independent entity: God. From the fact that this idea is in me and that I who have the idea exist, I can clearly infer both that God exists and that I am completely dependent on Him for my existence from moment to moment. This is so obvious that I'm sure that people can't know anything more evidently or certainly. And it now seems to me that, from the contemplation of the true God in whom are hidden all treasures of knowledge and wisdom, there is a way to derive knowledge of other things.

In the first place, I know that it's impossible for Him ever to deceive me. Wherever there is fraud and deception, there is imperfection, and, while the ability to deceive may seem a sign of cunning or power, the desire to deceive reveals malice or weakness and hence is inconsistent with God's nature.

Next, I find in myself an ability to judge which, like everything else in me, I've gotten from God. Since He doesn't want to deceive me, He certainly hasn't given me an ability which will lead me wrong when properly used.

There can be no doubt about this—except that it may seem to imply that I don't err at all. For, if I've gotten everything in me from God and He hasn't given me the ability to err, it doesn't seem possible for me ever to err. Thus, as long as I think only of God and devote all my attention to Him, I can't find any cause for error and falsity. When I turn my attention back to myself, however, I find that I can make innumerable errors. In looking for the cause of these errors, I find before me, not just the real and positive idea of God, but also the negative idea of "nothingness"—the idea of that which is completely devoid of perfection. I find that I am "intermediate" between God and nothingness, between the supreme entity and nonentity. Insofar as I am the creation of the supreme entity, there's nothing in me to account for my being deceived or led into error, but, insofar as I somehow participate in nothingness or the nonentity—that is, insofar as I am distinct from the supreme entity itself and lack many things—it's not surprising that I go wrong. I thus understand that, in itself, error is a lack, rather than a real thing dependent on God. Hence, I understand that I can err without God's having given me a special ability to do so. Rather, I fall into error because my God-given ability to judge the truth is not infinite.

But there's still something to be explained. Error is not just an absence, but a deprivation—the lack of knowledge that somehow ought to be in me. But, when I attend to God's nature, it seems impossible that He's given me an ability that is an imperfect thing of its kind—an ability lacking a perfection that it ought to have. The greater the craftsman's skill, the more perfect his product. Then how can the supreme creator of all things have made something that isn't absolutely perfect? There's no doubt that God could have made me so that I never err and that He always wants what's best. Then is it better for me to err than not to err?

When I pay more careful attention, I realize that I shouldn't be surprised at God's doing things that I can't explain. I shouldn't doubt His existence just because I find that I sometimes can't understand why or how He has made something. I know that my nature is weak and limited and that God's is limitless, incomprehensible, and infinite, and, from this, I can infer that He can do innumerable things whose reasons are unknown to me. On this ground alone, I regard the common practice of explaining things in terms of their purposes to be use-less in physics: it would be foolhardy of me to think that I can discover God's purposes.

It also seems to me that, when asking whether God's works are perfect, I ought to look at all of them together, not at one in isolation. For something that seems imper-fect when viewed alone might seem completely perfect when regarded as having a place in the world. Of course, since calling everything into doubt, I haven't established that anything exists besides me and God. But, when I consider God's immense power, I can't deny that He has made—or, in any case, that He could have made—many other things, and I must therefore view myself as having a place in a universe.

Next, turning to myself and investigating the nature of my errors (which are all that show me to be imper-fect), I notice that these errors depend on two concur-rent causes: my ability to know and my ability to choose freely—that is, my understanding and my will. But, with my understanding, I just grasp the ideas about which I form judgments, and error therefore cannot properly be said to arise from the understanding itself. While there may be innumerable things of which I have no idea, I can't say that I am deprived of these ideas, but only that I happen to lack them—for I don't have any reason to think that God ought to have given me a greater ability to know than He has. And, while I understand God to be a supremely skilled craftsman, I don't go on to think that He ought to endow each of his works with all the perfections that He can put in the others.

Nor can I complain about the scope or perfection of my God-given freedom of will—for I find that my will doesn't seem to me to be restricted in any way. Indeed, it seems well worth noting that nothing in me other than my will is so great and perfect that it couldn't conceiv-ably be bigger or better. If I think about my ability to understand, for example, I realize that it is very small and restricted and I immediately form the idea of some-thing much greater—indeed, of something supremely perfect and infinite. And, from the fact that I can form the idea of this thing, I infer that it is present in God's nature. Similarly, if I consider my other abilities, like the abilities to remember and to imagine, I clearly see that they all are weak and limited in me, but boundless in God. My will or freedom of choice is the only thing I find to be so great in me that I can't conceive of anything greater. In fact, it's largely for this reason that I regard myself as an image or likeness of God. God's will is in-comparably greater than mine, of course, in virtue of the associated knowledge and power that make it stronger and more effective, and also in virtue of all its greater range of objects. Yet, viewed in itself as a will, God's will seems no greater than mine. For having a will just amounts to being able either to do or not to do (affirm or deny, seek or avoid)—or, better, to being inclined to affirm or deny, seek or shun what the understanding offers, without any sense of being driven by external forces. To be free, I don't need to be inclined towards both alternatives. On the contrary, the more I lean to-wards one alternative—either because I understand the truth or goodness in it, or because God has so arranged my deepest thoughts—the more freely I choose it. Nei-ther divine grace nor knowledge of nature ever dimin-ishes my freedom; they increase and strengthen it. But the indifference that I experience when no consideration impels me towards one alternative over another is free-dom of the lowest sort, whose presence reveals a defect or an absence of knowledge rather than a perfection. For, if I always knew what was good or true, I wouldn't ever deliberate about what to do or choose, and thus, though completely free, I would never be indifferent.

From this I see that my God-given ability to will is not itself the cause of my errors—for my will is great, a perfect thing of its kind. Neither is my power of under-standing the cause of my errors; whenever I understand something, I understand it correctly and without the possibility of error, since my understanding comes from God. What then is the source of my errors? It is just that, while my will has a broader scope than my understand-ing, I don't keep it within the same bounds, but extend it to that which I don't understand. Being indifferent to these things, my will is easily led away from truth and goodness, and thus I am led into error and sin.

For example, I've asked for the last few days whether anything exists in the world, and I've noted that, from the fact that I ask this, it follows that I exist. I couldn't fail to judge that which I so clearly understood to be true. This wasn't because a force outside me compelled me to believe, but because an intense light in my under-standing produced a strong inclination of my will. And, to the extent that I wasn't indifferent, I believed sponta-neously and freely. However, while I now know that I exist insofar as I am a thinking thing, I notice in myself an idea of what it is to be a physical object and I come to wonder whether the thinking nature that's in me—or, rather, that is me—differs from this bodily nature or is identical to it. Nothing occurs to my reason (I am sup-posing) to convince me of one alternative rather than the other. Accordingly, I am completely indifferent to affirming either view, to denying either view, and even to suspending judgment.

And indifference of this sort is not limited to things of which the understanding is completely ignorant. It extends to everything about which the will deliberates in the absence of a sufficiently clear understanding. For, however strong the force with which plausible conjectures draw me towards one alternative, the knowledge that they are conjectures rather than assertions backed by certain and indubitable arguments is enough to push my assent the other way. The past few days have provided me with ample experience of this—for I am now supposing each of my former beliefs to be false just because I've found a way to call them into doubt.

If I suspend judgment when I don't clearly and distinctly grasp what's true, I obviously do right and am not deceived. But, if I either affirm or deny in a case of this sort, I misuse my freedom of choice. If I affirm what is false, I clearly err, and, if I stumble onto the truth, I'm still blameworthy since the light of nature reveals that a perception of the understanding should always precede a decision of the will. In these misuses of freedom of choice lies the deprivation that accounts for error. And this deprivation, I maintain, lies in the working of the will insofar as it comes from me—not in my God-given ability to will, or even in the will's operation insofar as it derives from Him.

I have no reason to complain that God hasn't given me a more perfect understanding or a greater natural light than He has. It's in the nature of a finite understanding that there are many things it can't understand, and it's in the nature of created understanding that it's finite. Indeed, I ought to be grateful to Him who owes me absolutely nothing for what He has bestowed, rather than taking myself to be deprived or robbed of what God hasn't given me.

And I have no reason to complain about God's having given me a will whose scope is greater than my understanding's. The will is like a unity made of inseparable parts; its nature apparently will not allow anything to be taken away from it. And, really, the wider the scope of my will, the more grateful I ought to be to Him who gave it to me.

Finally, I ought not to complain that God concurs in bringing about the acts of will and judgment in which I err. Insofar as these acts derive from God, they are completely true and good, and I am more perfect with the ability to perform these acts than I would be without it. And, the deprivation that is the real ground of falsity and error doesn't need God's concurrence, since it's not

a thing. When we regard God as its cause, we should say that it is an absence rather than a deprivation. For it clearly is no imperfection in God that He has given me the freedom to assent or not to assent to things of which He hasn't given me a clear and distinct grasp. Rather, it is undoubtedly an imperfection in me that I misuse this freedom by passing judgment on things that I don't properly understand. I see, of course, that God could easily have brought it about that, while I remain free and limited in knowledge, I never err: He could have implanted in me a clear and distinct understanding of everything about which I was ever going to make a choice, or He could have indelibly impressed on my memory that I must never pass judgment on something that I don't clearly and distinctly understand. And I also understand that, regarded in isolation from everything else, I would have been more perfect if God had made me so that I never err. But I can't deny that, because some things are immune to error while others are not, the universe is more perfect than it would have been if all its parts were alike. And I have no right to complain about God's wanting me to hold a place in the world other than the greatest and most perfect.

Besides, if I can't avoid error by having a clear grasp of every matter on which I make a choice, I can avoid it in the other way, which only requires remembering that I must not pass judgment on matters whose truth isn't apparent. For, although I find myself too weak to fix my attention permanently on this single thought, I can—by careful and frequent meditation—ensure that I call it to mind whenever it's needed and thus that I acquire the habit of avoiding error.

Since the first and foremost perfection of man lies in avoiding error, I've profited from today's meditation, in which I've investigated the cause of error and falsity. Clearly, the only possible cause of error is the one I have described. When I limit my will's range of judgment to the things presented clearly and distinctly to my understanding, I obviously cannot err—for everything that I clearly and distinctly grasp is something and hence must come, not from nothing, but from God—God, I say, who is supremely perfect and who cannot possibly deceive. Therefore, what I clearly and distinctly grasp is unquestionably true. Today, then, I have learned what to avoid in order not to err and also what to do to reach the truth. I surely will reach the truth if I just attend to the things that I understand perfectly and distinguish them from those that I grasp more obscurely and confusedly. And that's what I'll take care to do from now on.

Meditation V:
On the Essence of Material Objects and More on God's Existence

Many questions remain about God's attributes and the nature of my self or mind. I may return to these questions later. But now, having found what to do and what to avoid in order to attain truth, I regard nothing as more pressing than to work my way out of the doubts that I raised the other day and to see whether I can find anything certain about material objects.

But, before asking whether any such objects exist outside me, I ought to consider the ideas of these objects as they exist in my thoughts and see which are clear and which confused.

I have a distinct mental image of the quantity that philosophers commonly call continuous. That is, I have a distinct mental image of the extension of this quantity—or rather of the quantified thing—in length, breadth, and depth. I can distinguish various parts of this thing. I can ascribe various sizes, shapes, places, and motions to these parts and various durations to the motions.

In addition to having a thorough knowledge of extension in general, I grasp innumerable particulars about things like shape, number, and motion, when I pay careful attention. The truth of these particulars is so obvious and so consonant with my nature that, when I first think of one of these things, I seem not so much to be learning something novel as to be remembering something that I already knew—or noticing for the first time something that had long been in me without my having turned my mind's eye toward it.

What's important here, I think, is that I find in myself innumerable ideas of things which, though they may not exist outside me, can't be said to be nothing. While I have some control over my thoughts of these things, I do not make the things up: they have their own real and immutable natures. Suppose, for example, that I have a mental image of a triangle. While it may be that no figure of this sort does exist or ever has existed outside my thought, the figure has a fixed nature (essence or form), immutable and eternal, which hasn't been produced by me and isn't dependent on my mind. The proof is that I can demonstrate various propositions about the triangle, such as that its angles equal two right angles and that its greatest side subtends its greatest angle. Even though I didn't think of these propositions at all when I first imagined the triangle, I now clearly see their truth

whether I want to or not, and it follows that I didn't make them up.

It isn't relevant that, having seen triangular physical objects, I may have gotten the idea of the triangle from external objects through my organs of sense. For I can think of innumerable other figures whose ideas I could not conceivably have gotten through my senses, and I can demonstrate facts about these other figures just as I can about the triangle. Since I know these facts clearly, they must be true, and they therefore must be something rather than nothing. For it's obvious that everything true is something, and, as I have shown, everything that I know clearly and distinctly is true. But, even if I hadn't shown this, the nature of my mind would have made it impossible for me to withhold my assent from these things, at least when I clearly and distinctly grasped them. As I recall, even when I clung most tightly to objects of sense, I regarded truths about shape and number—truths of arithmetic, geometry, and pure mathematics—as more certain than any others.

But, if anything whose idea I can draw from my thought must in fact have everything that I clearly and distinctly grasp it to have, can't I derive from this a proof of God's existence? Surely, I find the idea of God, a supremely perfect being, in me no less clearly than I find the ideas of figures and numbers. And I understand as clearly and distinctly that eternal existence belongs to His nature as that the things which I demonstrate of a figure or number belong to the nature of the figure or number. Accordingly, even if what I have thought up in the past few days hasn't been entirely true, I ought to be at least as certain of God's existence as I used to be of the truths of pure mathematics.

At first, this reasoning may seem unclear and fallacious. Since I'm accustomed to distinguishing existence from essence in other cases, I find it easy to convince myself that I can separate God's existence from His essence and hence that I can think of God as nonexistent. But, when I pay more careful attention, it's clear that I can no more separate God's existence from His essence than a triangle's angles equaling two right angles from the essence of the triangle, or the idea of a valley from the idea of a mountain. It's no less impossible to think that God (the supremely perfect being) lacks existence (a perfection) than to think that a mountain lacks a valley.

Well, suppose that I can't think of God without existence, just as I can't think of a mountain without a valley. From the fact that I can think of a mountain with a valley, it doesn't follow that a mountain exists in the world. Similarly, from the fact that I can think of God as existing, it doesn't seem to follow that He exists. For my thought doesn't impose any necessity on things. It may be that, just as I can imagine a winged horse when no such horse exists, I can ascribe existence to God when no God exists.

No, there is a fallacy here. From the fact that I can't think of a mountain without a valley it follows, not that the mountain and valley exist, but only that whether they exist or not they can't be separated from one another. But, from the fact that I can't think of God without existence, it follows that existence is inseparable from Him and hence that He really exists. It's not that my thoughts make it so or impose a necessity on things. On the contrary, it's the fact that God does exist that necessitates my thinking of Him as I do. For I am not free to think of God without existence—of the supremely perfect being without supreme perfection—as I am free to think of a horse with or without wings.

Now someone might say this: "If I take God to have all perfections, and if I take existence to be a perfection, I must take God to exist, but I needn't accept the premise that God has all perfections. Similarly, if I accept the premise that every quadrilateral can be inscribed in a circle, I'm forced to the patently false view that every rhombus can be inscribed in a circle, but I need not accept the premise." But this should not be said. For, while it's not necessary that the idea of God occurs to me, it is necessary that, whenever I think of the primary and supreme entity and bring the idea of Him out of my mind's "treasury," I attribute all perfections to Him, even if I don't enumerate them or consider them individually. And this necessity ensures that, when I do notice that existence is a perfection, I can rightly conclude that the primary and supreme being exists. Similarly, while it's not necessary that I ever imagine a triangle, it is necessary that, when I do choose to consider a rectilinear figure having exactly three angles, I attribute to it properties from which I can rightly infer that its angles are no more than two right angles, perhaps without noticing that I am doing so. But, when I consider which shapes can be inscribed in the circle, there's absolutely no necessity for my thinking that all quadrilaterals are among them. Indeed, I can't even think that all quadrilaterals are among them, since I've resolved to accept only what I clearly and distinctly understand. Thus my false suppositions differ greatly from the true ideas implanted in me, the first and foremost of which is my idea of God. In many ways, I see that this idea is not a figment of my thought, but the image of a real and immutable nature. For one thing, God is the only thing that I can think of whose existence belongs to its essence. For another thing, I can't conceive of there being two or more such Gods, and, having supposed that one God now exists, I see that He has necessarily existed from all eternity and will continue to exist into eternity. And I also perceive many other things in God that I can't diminish or alter.

But, whatever proof I offer, it always comes back to the fact that I am only convinced of what I grasp clearly and distinctly. Of the things that I grasp in this way, some are obvious to everyone. Some are discovered only by those who examine things more closely and search more carefully, but, once these things have been discovered, they are regarded as no less certain than the others. That the square on the hypotenuse of a right triangle equals the sum of the squares on the other sides is not as readily apparent as that the hypotense subtends the greatest angle, but, once it has been seen, it is believed just as firmly. And, when I'm not overwhelmed by prejudices and my thoughts aren't besieged by images of sensible things, there surely is nothing that I know earlier or more easily than facts about God. For what is more self-evident than there is a supreme entity—that God, the only thing whose existence belongs to His essence, exists?

While I need to pay careful attention in order to grasp this, I'm now as certain of it as of anything that seems most certain. In addition, I now see that the certainty of everything else so depends on it that, if I weren't certain of it, I couldn't know anything perfectly.

Of course, my nature is such that, when I grasp something clearly and distinctly, I can't fail to believe it. But my nature is also such that I can't permanently fix my attention on a single thing so as always to grasp it clearly, and memories of previous judgments often come to me when I am no longer attending to the grounds on which I originally made them. Accordingly, if I were ignorant of God, arguments could be produced that would easily overthrow my opinions, and I therefore would have unstable and changing opinions rather than true and certain knowledge. For example, when I consider the nature of the triangle, it seems plain to me—steeped as I am in the principles of geometry—that its three angles equal two right angles: I can't fail to believe this as long as I pay attention to its demonstration. But, if I were ignorant of God, I might come to doubt its truth as soon as my mind's eye turned away from its demonstration, even if I recalled having once grasped it clearly. For I could convince myself that I've been so constructed by nature that I sometimes err about what I believe myself to grasp most plainly—especially if I remember that, having taken many things to be true and certain, I had later found grounds on which to judge them false.

But now I grasp that God exists, and I understand both that everything else depends on Him and that He's not a deceiver. From this, I infer that everything I clearly and distinctly grasp must be true. Even if I no longer pay attention to the grounds on which I judged God to exist, my recollection that I once clearly and distinctly knew Him to exist ensures that no contrary ground can be produced to push me towards doubt. About God's existence, I have true and certain knowledge. And I have such knowledge, not just about this one thing, but about everything else that I remember having proven, like the theorems of geometry. For what can now be said against my believing these things? That I am so constructed that I always err? But I now know that I can't err about what I clearly understand. That much of what I took to be true and certain I later found to be false? But I didn't grasp any of these things clearly and distinctly; ignorant of the true standard of truth, I based my belief on grounds that I later found to be unsound. Then what can be said? What about the objection (which I recently used against myself) that I may be dreaming and that the things I'm now experiencing may be as unreal as those that occur to me in sleep? No, even this is irrelevant. For, even if I am dreaming, everything that is evident to my understanding must be true.

Thus I plainly see that the certainty and truth of all my knowledge derives from one thing: my thought of the true God. Before I knew Him, I couldn't know anything else perfectly. But now I can plainly and certainly know innumerable things, not only about God and other mental beings, but also about the nature of physical objects, insofar as it is the subject-matter of pure mathematics.

Meditation VI:
On the Existence of Material Objects and the Real Distinction of Mind from Body

It remains for me to examine whether material objects exist. Insofar as they are the subject of pure mathematics, I now know at least that they can exist, because I grasp them clearly and distinctly. For God can undoubtedly make whatever I can grasp in this way, and I never

judge that something is impossible for Him to make unless there would be a contradiction in my grasping the thing distinctly. Also, the fact that I find myself having mental images when I turn my attention to physical objects seems to imply that these objects really do exist. For, when I pay careful attention to what it is to have a mental image, it seems to me that it's just the application of my power of thought to a certain body which is immediately present to it and which must therefore exist.

To clarify this, I'll examine the difference between having a mental image and having a pure understanding. When I have a mental image of a triangle, for example, I don't just understand that it is a figure bounded by three lines; I also "look at" the lines as though they were present to my mind's eye. And this is what I call having a mental image. When I want to think of a chiliagon, I understand that it is a figure with a thousand sides as well as I understand that a triangle is a figure with three, but I can't imagine its sides or "look" at them as though they were present. Being accustomed to using images when I think about physical objects, I may confusedly picture some figure to myself, but this figure obviously is not a chiliagon—for it in no way differs from what I present to myself when thinking about a myriagon or any other many sided figure, and it doesn't help me to discern the properties that distinguish chiliagons from other polygons. If it's a pentagon that is in question, I can understand its shape, as I can that of the chiliagon, without the aid of mental images. But I can also get a mental image of the pentagon by directing my mind's eye to its five lines and to the area that they bound. And it's obvious to me that getting this mental image requires a special mental effort different from that needed for understanding—a special effort which clearly reveals the difference between having a mental image and having a pure understanding.

It also seems to me that my power of having mental images, being distinct from my power of understanding, is not essential to my self or, in other words, to my mind—for, if I were to lose this ability, I would surely remain the same thing that I now am. And it seems to follow that this ability depends on something distinct from me. If we suppose that there is a body so associated with my mind that the mind can "look into" it at will, it's easy to understand how my mind might get mental images of physical objects by means of my body. If there were such a body, the mode of thinking that we call imagination would differ from pure understanding in only one way: when the mind understood something, it would turn "inward" and view an idea that it found in itself, but, when it had mental images, it would turn to the body and look at something there which resembled an idea that it had understood by itself or had grasped by sense. As I've said, then, it's easy to see how I get mental images, if we supposed that my body exists. And, since I don't have in mind any other equally plausible explanation of my ability to have mental images, I conjecture that physical objects probably do exist. But this conjecture is only probable. Despite my careful and thorough investigation, the distinct idea of bodily nature that I get from mental images does not seem to have anything in it from which the conclusion that physical objects exist validly follows.

Besides having a mental image of the bodily nature that is the subject-matter of pure mathematics, I have mental images of things which are not so distinct—things like colors, sounds, flavors, and pains. But I seem to grasp these things better by sense, from which they seem to come (with the aid of memory) to the understanding. Thus, to deal with these things more fully, I must examine the senses and see whether there is anything in the mode of awareness that I call sensation from which I can draw a conclusive argument for the existence of physical objects.

First, I'll remind myself of the things that I believed really to be as I perceived them and of the grounds for my belief. Next, I'll set out the grounds on which I later called this belief into doubt. And, finally, I'll consider what I ought to think now.

To begin with, I sensed that I had a head, hands, feet, and the other members that make up a human body. I viewed this body as part, or maybe even as all, of me. I sensed that it was influenced by other physical objects whose effects could be either beneficial or harmful. I judged these effects to be beneficial to the extent that I felt pleasant sensations and harmful to the extent that I felt pain. And, in addition to sensations of pain and pleasure, I sensed hunger, thirst, and other such desires—and also bodily inclinations towards cheerfulness, sadness, and other emotions. Outside me, I sensed, not just extension, shape, and motion, but also hardness, hotness, and other qualities detected by touch. I also sensed light, color, odor, taste, and sound—qualities by whose variation I distinguished such things as the sky, earth, and sea from one another.

In view of these ideas of qualities (which presented themselves to my thought and were all that I really sensed directly), I had some reason for believing that I sensed objects distinct from my thought—physical objects from which the ideas came. For I found that these

ideas came to me independently of my desires so that, however much I tried, I couldn't sense an object when it wasn't present to an organ of sense or fail to sense one when it was present. And, since the ideas that I grasped by sense were much livelier, more explicit, and (in their own way) more distinct than those I deliberately created or found impressed in my memory, it seemed that these ideas could not have come from me and thus that they came from something else. Having no conception of these things other than that suggested by my sensory ideas, I could only think that the things resembled the ideas. Indeed, since I remembered using my senses before my reason, since I found the ideas that I created in myself to be less explicit than those grasped by sense, and since I found the ideas that I created to be composed largely of those that I had grasped by sense, I easily convinced myself that I didn't understand anything at all unless I had first sensed it.

I also had some reason for supposing that a certain physical object, which I viewed as belonging to me in a special way, was related to me more closely than any other. I couldn't be separated from it as I could from other physical objects; I felt all of my emotions and desires in it and because of it; and I was aware of pains and pleasant feelings in it but in nothing else. I didn't know why sadness goes with the sensation of pain or why joy goes with sensory stimulation. I didn't know why the stomach twitchings that I call hunger warn me that I need to eat or why dryness in my throat warns me that I need to drink. Seeing no connection between stomach twitchings and the desire to eat or between the sensation of a pain-producing thing and the consequent awareness of sadness, I could only say that I had been taught the connection by nature. And nature seems also to have taught me everything else that I knew about the objects of sensation—for I convinced myself that the sensations came to me in a certain way before having found grounds on which to prove that they did.

But, since then, many experiences have shaken my faith in the senses. Towers that seemed round from a distance sometimes looked square from close up, and huge statues on pediments sometimes didn't look big when seen from the ground. In innumerable such cases, I found the judgments of the external senses to be wrong. And the same holds for the internal senses. What is felt more inwardly than pain? Yet I had heard that people with amputated arms and legs sometimes seem to feel pain in the missing limb, and it therefore didn't seem perfectly certain to me that the limb in which I feel a pain is always the one that hurts. And, to these grounds for doubt, I've recently added two that are very general: First, since I didn't believe myself to sense anything while awake that I couldn't also take myself to sense in a dream, and since I didn't believe that what I sense in sleep comes from objects outside me, I didn't see why I should believe what I sense while awake comes from such objects. Second, since I didn't yet know my creator (or, rather, since I supposed that I didn't know Him), I saw nothing to rule out my having been so designed by nature that I'm deceived even in what seems most obviously true to me.

And I could easily refute the reasoning by which I convinced myself of the reality of sensible things. Since my nature seemed to impel me toward many things that my reason rejected, I didn't believe that I ought to have much faith in nature's teachings. And, while my will didn't control my sense perceptions, I didn't believe it to follow that these perceptions came from outside me, since I thought that the ability to produce these ideas might be in me without my being aware of it.

Now that I've begun to know myself and my creator better, I still believe that I oughtn't blindly to accept everything that I seem to get from the senses. Yet I no longer believe that I ought to call it all into doubt.

In the first place, I know that everything that I clearly and distinctly understand can be made by God to be exactly as I understand it. The fact that I can clearly and distinctly understand one thing apart from another is therefore enough to make me certain that it is distinct from the other, since the things could be separated by God if not by something else. (I judge the things to be distinct regardless of the power needed to make them exist separately.) Accordingly, from the fact that I have gained knowledge of my existence without noticing anything about my nature or essence except that I am a thinking thing, I can rightly conclude that my essence consists solely in the fact that I am a thinking thing. It's possible (or, as I will say later, it's certain) that I have a body which is very tightly bound to me. But, on the one hand, I have a clear and distinct idea of myself insofar as I am just a thinking and unextended thing, and, on the other hand, I have a distinct idea of my body insofar as it is just an extended and unthinking thing. It's certain, then, that I am really distinct from my body and can exist without it.

In addition, I find in myself abilities for special modes of awareness, like the abilities to have mental images and to sense. I can clearly and distinctly conceive of my whole self as something that lacks these abilities, but I can't conceive of the abilities' existing without me, or without an understanding substance in which to re-side. Since the conception of these abilities includes the conception of something that understands, I see that these abilities are distinct from me in the way that a thing's properties are distinct from the thing itself.

I recognize other abilities in me, like the ability to move around and to assume various postures. These abilities can't be understood to exist apart from a substance in which they reside any more than the abilities to imagine and sense, and they therefore cannot exist without such a substance. But it's obvious that, if these abilities do exist, the substance in which they reside must be a body or extended substance rather than an understanding one—for the clear and distinct conceptions of these abilities contain extension but not understanding.

There is also in me, however, a passive ability to sense—to receive and recognize ideas of sensible things. But, I wouldn't be able to put this ability to use if there weren't, either in me or in something else, an active power to produce or make sensory ideas. Since this active power doesn't presuppose understanding, and since it often produces ideas in me without my cooperation and even against my will, it cannot exist in me. Therefore, this power must exist in a substance distinct from me. And, for reasons that I've noted, this substance must contain, either formally or eminently, all the reality that is contained subjectively in the ideas that the power produces. Either this substance is a physical object (a thing of bodily nature that contains formally the reality that the idea contains subjectively), or it is God or one of His creations that is higher than a physical object (something that contains this reality eminently). But, since God isn't a deceiver, it's completely obvious that He doesn't send these ideas to me directly or by means of a creation that contains their reality eminently rather than formally. For, since He has not given me any ability to recognize that these ideas are sent by Him or by creations other than physical objects, and since He has given me a strong inclination to believe that the ideas come from physical objects, I see no way to avoid the conclusion that He deceives me if the ideas are sent to me by anything other than physical objects. It follows that physical objects exist. These objects may not exist exactly as I comprehend them by sense; in many ways, sensory comprehension is obscure and confused. But these objects must at least have in them everything that I clearly and distinctly understand them to have—every general property within the scope of pure mathematics.

But what about particular properties, such as the size and shape of the sun? And what about things that I understand less clearly than mathematical properties, like light, sound, and pain? These are open to doubt. But, since God isn't a deceiver, and since I therefore have the God-given ability to correct any falsity that may be in my beliefs, I have high hopes of finding the truth about even these things. There is undoubtedly some truth in everything I have been taught by nature—for, when I use the term "nature" in its general sense, I refer to God Himself or to the order that He has established in the created world, and, when I apply the term specifically to *my* nature, I refer to the collection of everything that God has given *me*.

Nature teaches me nothing more explicitly, however, than that I have a body which is hurt when I feel pain, which needs food or drink when I experience hunger or thirst, and so on. Accordingly, I ought not to doubt that there is some truth to this.

Through sensations like pain, hunger, and thirst, nature also teaches me that I am not present in my body in the way that a sailor is present in his ship. Rather, I am very tightly bound to my body and so "mixed up" with it that we form a single thing. If this weren't so, I—who am just a thinking thing—wouldn't feel pain when my body was injured; I would perceive the injury by pure understanding in the way that a sailor sees the leaks in his ship with his eyes. And, when my body needed food or drink, I would explicitly understand that the need existed without having the confused sensations of hunger and thirst. For the sensations of thirst, hunger, and pain are just confused modifications of thought arising from the union and "mixture" of mind and body.

Also, nature teaches me that there are other physical objects around my body—some that I ought to seek and others that I ought to avoid. From the fact that I sense things like colors, sound, odors, flavors, temperatures, and hardnesses, I correctly infer that sense perceptions come from physical objects that vary as widely (though perhaps not in the same way) as the perceptions do. And, from the fact that some of these perceptions are pleasant while others are unpleasant, I infer with certainty that my body—or, rather, my whole self which consists of a body and a mind—can be benefited and harmed by the physical objects around it.

There are many other things that I seem to have been taught by nature but that I have really accepted out of a habit of thoughtless judgment. These things may well be false. Among them are the judgments that a space is empty if nothing in it happens to affect my senses; that a hot physical object has something in it resembling my idea of heat; that a white or green thing has in it the same whiteness or greenness that I sense; that a bitter or sweet thing has in it the same flavor that I taste; that

stars, towers, and other physical objects have the same size and shape that they present to my senses; and so on.

If I am to avoid accepting what is indistinct in these cases, I must more carefully explain my use of the phrase "taught by nature." In particular, I should say that I am now using the term "nature" in a narrower sense than when I took it to refer to the whole complex of what God has given me. This complex includes much having to do with my mind alone (such as my grasp of the fact that what is done cannot be undone and of the rest of what I know by the light of nature) which does not bear on what I am now saying. And the complex also includes much having to do with my body alone (such as its tendency to go downward) with which I am not dealing now. I'm now using the term "nature" to refer only to what God has given me insofar as I am a composite of mind and body. It is this nature that teaches me to avoid that which occasions painful sensations, to seek that which occasions pleasant sensations, and so on. But this nature seems not to teach me to draw conclusions about external objects from sense perceptions without first having examined the matter with my understanding—for true knowledge of external things seems to belong to the mind alone, not to the composite of mind and body.

Thus, while a star has no more effect on my eye than a flame, this does not really produce a positive inclination to believe that the star is as small as the flame; for my youthful judgment about the size of the flame, I had no real grounds. And, while I feel heat when I approach a fire and pain when I draw nearer, I have absolutely no reason for believing that something in the fire resembles the heat, just as I have no reason for believing that something in the fire resembles the pain; I only have reason for believing that there is something or other in the fire that produces the feelings of heat and pain. And, although there may be nothing in a given region of space that affects my senses, it doesn't follow that there aren't any physical objects in that space. Rather I now see that, on these matters and others, I used to pervert the natural order of things. For, while nature has given sense perceptions to my mind for the sole purpose of indicating what is beneficial and what harmful to the composite of which my mind is a part, and while the perceptions are sufficiently clear and distinct for that purpose, I used these perceptions as standards for identifying the essence of physical objects—an essence which they only reveal obscurely and confusedly.

I've already explained how it can be that, despite God's goodness, my judgments can be false. But a new difficulty arises here—one having to do with the things that nature presents to me as desirable or undesirable and also with the errors that I seem to have found in my internal sensations. One of these errors seems to be committed, for example, when a man is fooled by some food's pleasant taste into eating poison hidden in that food. But surely, in this case, what the man's nature impels him to eat is the good tasting food, not the poison of which he knows nothing. We can draw no conclusion except that his nature isn't omniscient, and this conclusion isn't surprising. Since a man is a limited thing, he can only have limited perfections.

Still, we often err in cases in which nature does impel us. This happens, for example, when sick people want food or drink that would quickly harm them. To say that these people err as a result of the corruption of their nature does not solve the problem—for a sick man is no less a creation of God than a well one, and it seems as absurd to suppose that God has given him a deceptive nature. A clock made of wheels and weights follows the natural laws just as precisely when it is poorly made and inaccurate as when it does everything that its maker wants. Thus, if I regard a human body as a machine made up of bones, nerves, muscles, veins, blood, and skin such that even without a mind it would do just what it does now (except for things that require a mind because they are controlled by the will), it's easy to see that what happens to a sick man is no less "natural" than what happens to a well one. For instance, if a body suffers from dropsy, it has a dry throat of the sort that regularly brings the sensation of thirst to the mind, the dryness disposes the nerves and other organs to drink, and the drinking makes the illness worse. But this is just as natural as when a similar dryness of throat moves a person who is perfectly healthy to take a drink that is beneficial. Bearing in mind my conception of a clock's use, I might say that an inaccurate clock departs from its nature, and, similarly, viewing the machine of the human body as designed for its usual motions, I can say that it drifts away from its nature if it has a dry throat when drinking will not help to maintain it. I should note, however, that the sense in which I am now using the term "nature" differs from that in which I used it before. For, as I have just used the term "nature," the nature of a man (or clock) is something that depends on my thinking of the difference between a sick and a well man (or of the difference between a poorly made and a well-made clock)—something regarded as extrinsic to the things. But, when I used "nature" before, I referred to something which is *in* things and which therefore has some reality.

It may be that we just offer an extrinsic description of a body suffering from dropsy when, noting that it has a dry throat but doesn't need to drink, we say that its nature is corrupted. Still, the description is not purely extrinsic when we say that a composite or union of mind and body has a corrupted nature. There is a real fault in the composite's nature, for it is thirsty when drinking would be harmful. It therefore remains to be asked why God's goodness doesn't prevent *this* nature's being deceptive.

To begin the answer, I'll note that mind differs importantly from body in that body is by its nature divisible while mind is indivisible. When I think about my mind—or, in other words, about myself insofar as I am just a thinking thing—I can't distinguish any parts in me; I understand myself to be a single, unified thing. Although my whole mind seems united to my whole body, I know that cutting off a foot, arm, or other limb would not take anything away from my mind. The abilities to will, sense, understand, and so on can't be called parts, since it's one and the same mind that wills, senses, and understands. On the other hand, whenever I think of a physical or extended thing, I can mentally divide it, and I therefore understand that the object is divisible. This single fact would be enough to teach me that my mind and body are distinct, if I hadn't already learned that in another way.

Next, I notice that the mind isn't directly affected by all parts of the body, but only by the brain—or maybe just by the small part of the brain containing the so-called "common sense." Whenever this part of the brain is in a given state, it presents the same thing to the mind, regardless of what is happening in the rest of the body (as is shown by innumerable experiments that I need not review here).

In addition, I notice that the nature of body is such that, if a first part can be moved by a second that is far away, the first part can be moved in exactly the same way by something between the first and second without the second part's being affected. For example, if A, B, C, and D are points on a cord, and if the first point (A) can be moved in a certain way by a pull on the last point (D), then A can be moved in the same way by a pull on one of the middle points (B or C) without D's being moved. Similarly, science teaches me that, when my foot hurts, the sensation of pain is produced by nerves distributed throughout the foot which extend like cords from there to the brain. When pulled in the foot, these nerves pull the central parts of the brain to which they are attached, moving those parts in ways designated by nature to present the mind with the sensation of a pain "in the foot." But, since these nerves pass through the shins, thighs, hips, back, and neck on their way from foot to brain, it can happen that their being touched in the middle, rather than at the end of the foot, produces the same motion in the brain as when the foot is hurt and, hence, that the mind feels the same pain "in the foot." And the points holds for other sensations as well.

Finally, I notice that, since only one sensation can be produced by a given motion of the part of the brain that directly affects the mind, the best conceivable sensation for it to produce is the one that is most often useful for the maintenance of the healthy man. Experience teaches that all the sensations put in us by nature are of this sort and therefore that everything in our sensations testifies to God's power and goodness. For example, when the nerves in the foot are moved with unusual violence, the motion is communicated through the middle of the spine to the center of the brain, where it signals the mind to sense a pain "in the foot." This urges the mind to view the pain's cause as harmful to the foot and to do what it can to remove that cause. Of course, God could have so designed man's nature that the same motion of the brain presented something else to the mind, like the motion in the brain, or the motion in the foot, or a motion somewhere between the brain and foot. But no alternative to the way things are would be as conducive to the maintenance of the body. Similarly, when we need drink, the throat becomes dry, the dryness moves the nerves of the throat thereby moving the center of the brain, and the brain's movements cause the sensation of thirst in the mind. It's the sensation of thirst that is produced, because no information about our condition is more useful to us than that we need to get something to drink in order to remain healthy. And the same is true in other cases.

This makes it completely obvious that, despite God's immense goodness, the nature of man (whom we now view as a composite of mind and body) cannot fail to be deceptive. For, if something produces the movement usually associated with an injured foot in the nerve running from foot to brain or in the brain itself rather than in the foot, a pain is felt as if "in the foot." Here the senses are deceived by their nature. Since this motion in the brain must always bring the same sensation to mind, and since the motion's cause is something hurting the foot more often than something elsewhere, it's in accordance with reason that the motion always presents the mind a pain in the foot rather than elsewhere. And, if dryness of the throat arises, not (as usual) from drink's

being conducive to the body's health, but (as happens in dropsy) from some other cause, it's much better that we are deceived on this occasion than that we are generally deceived when our bodies are sound. And the same holds for other cases.

In addition to helping me to be aware of the errors to which my nature is subject, these reflections help me readily to correct or avoid these errors. I know that sensory indications of what is good for my body are more often true than false; I can almost always examine a given thing with several senses; and I can also use my memory (which connects the present to the past) and my understanding (which has now examined all the causes of error). Hence, I need no longer fear that what the senses daily show me is unreal. I should reject the exaggerated doubts of the past few days as ridiculous. This is especially true of the chief ground for these doubts—namely, my inability to distinguish dreaming from being awake. For I now notice that dreaming and being awake are importantly different: the events in dreams are not linked by memory to the rest of my life like those that happen while I am awake. If, while I'm awake, someone were suddenly to appear and then immediately to disappear without my seeing where he came from or went to (as happens in dreams), I would justifiably judge that he was not a real man but a ghost—or, better an apparition created in my brain. But, if I distinctly observe something's source, its place, and the time at which I learn about it, and if I grasp an unbroken connection between it and the rest of my life, I'm quite sure that it is something in my waking life rather than in a dream. And I ought not to have the slightest doubt about the reality of such things if I have examined them with all my senses, my memory, and my understanding without finding any conflicting evidence. For, from the fact that God is not a deceiver, it follows that I am not deceived in any case of this sort. Since the need to act does not always allow time for such a careful examination, however, we must admit the likelihood of men's erring about particular things and acknowledge the weakness of our nature.

Basic Questions for this chapter are in the text.

For Further Thought

Descartes argues that there is no way you could tell that your ideas about the external world were correct unless there were a nondeceptive God to guarantee their basic rightness. Can you think of any way you might be able to know there is a world corresponding to your ideas? Try to construct a view that provides this reassurance without depending on God.

Notes

1. Quoted in S. V. Keeling, *Descartes* (London, Oxford, New York: Oxford University Press, 1968).
2. Quotations from René Descartes' *Discourse on the Method of Rightly Conducting One's Reason and Seeking the Truth in the Sciences,* in *The Philosophical Writings of Descartes,* ed. John Cottingham, Robert Stoothoff, and Dugald Murdoch (Cambridge: Cambridge University Press, 1985), are cited in the text using the abbreviation *DM.* References are to part numbers and page numbers in the classic French edition, followed by page numbers in this edition.
3. Quotations from René Descartes, *The Principles of Philosophy,* in *The Philosophical Works of Descartes,* vol. 1, ed. Elisabeth S. Haldane and G. R. T. Ross (n.p.: Dover Publications, 1955), are cited in the text using the abbreviation *PP.* References are to the classic French edition, followed by the page numbers in this edition.
4. Quoted by Martin Heidegger in *The Way Back into the Ground of Metaphysics,* reprinted in *Existentialism from Dostoevsky to Sartre,* ed. Walter Kaufmann (New York: Merchant Books, 1957).
5. Keeling, *Descartes,* 252.

16

Thomas Hobbes: Catching Persons in the Net of the New Science

Descartes is one of the heroes of the new science, but for various reasons he stops short of supposing that geometrical mechanics can account for everything. The most obvious exceptions are mental activities: thinking, imagining, doubting, feeling, and willing. And since Descartes believes it is beyond question that each of us is first and foremost a thinking thing—and as free in our decisions as God himself—there can be no Cartesian physics of human beings. We, as thinkers, escape the net of mechanical causality.*

But do we really? Are Descartes' reasons for thinking we do conclusive? And what would be the result if human beings, too, were wholly and completely included in the physical world of Galilean/Cartesian science? Thomas Hobbes (1588–1679) makes the experiment and draws radical conclusions. It is a new world indeed, with shattering implications for human life.

We will make no comprehensive survey of Hobbes' philosophy. But it will prove useful to bring into our sense of the great conversation what Hobbes has to say about human beings, about our place in the world, and about what this means for our life together. In particular, we will ask what status and justification any moral rules can have in a world such as the one Hobbes describes.

---

*For Descartes' reasons, see his argument for the distinctness of mind and body in *Meditation VI.* There is also his conviction that a rational being is *infinitely adaptable*; this, he thinks, distinguishes human beings from any conceivable automaton, no matter how cleverly designed. See p. 310.

Hobbes accepts without reservation the Galilean/Cartesian physics of the nonhuman world. And he accepts and radicalizes the modern rejection of the medieval/Aristotelian picture of the world. It will be useful to contrast once more the salient features of this new science with the view of the world it was replacing.

- Whereas for Aristotle and his medieval disciples, motion is development toward some fulfilling goal (a change from potentiality to actuality), for the new science, motion is simply a body's change of place in a neutral geometrical space.
- Galileo substitutes the distinction between accelerated motion and constant motion for the Aristotelian distinction between motion and rest. For Galileo, rest is simply a limiting case of motion. In no sense is rest the culmination or fulfillment or goal of a motion.
- Motion is the normal state of things; it does not require explanation, as in the medieval view. Only changes in motion (in direction or rate) need to be explained. And they are explained in terms of other motions.
- Therefore, there is no natural center to the universe where things "rest." Since something in motion continues in a straight line to infinity unless interfered with, the universe is conceived to be infinite rather than finite. And there are no privileged places in it.
- Scientific explanation can no longer mention

the final causes of things—those essences toward which development has been thought to strive. Final causes are derided as explanatorily barren, obscure, and even occult. In the geometrical world of Galileo and Descartes, all explanation is in terms of *contact*, of some prior impetus or push. It is as if the rich Aristotelian world with its four causes is stripped down to only the "efficient cause." Purposiveness is eliminated from the physical world.*

Now Hobbes comes along and insists that there is no reason why human beings should be considered exceptions in this world. In his comments on the *Meditations*, Hobbes claims to be unconvinced by Descartes' arguments concerning the independence of the mind from the body. For all Descartes has said, Hobbes thinks, the thing that thinks may just as well be a physical body! Indeed, Hobbes is convinced that "the subject of all activities can be conceived only after a corporeal fashion."[1] If so, then the mind cannot be thought of as a thing independent of the body. It becomes just one of the ways that bodies of a certain sort function.[†] Can this claim be plausible?

Method

Hobbes is as convinced as Descartes that method is the key to progress. He calls his method—which

he claims to have learned from Galileo and his friend William Harvey (who discovered the circulation of the blood)—the method of *resolution and composition*. The first stage, resolution, consists in the analysis of complex wholes into simple elements. It resembles Descartes' second rule.* In the second stage, the elements are reassembled, or composed again into a whole. This is analogous to Descartes' third rule. When we have both resolved and composed the complex whole we began with, we understand it better than we did before we applied the method. Both Galileo and Harvey offer impressive examples of successes attained by this method.

Galileo explains the path taken by a cannonball by imagining a projectile moving on a frictionless horizontal plane that suddenly comes to an end. At that point, the cannonball will tend both to move in the same direction (since things in motion tend to remain in motion) and to drop (since unsupported objects fall at a specific rate). The path is then *resolved* into these two tendencies, each of which can be mathematically expressed. And when synthesized or *composed* by the laws of motion, it can be seen that the path is that of a semi-parabola. This principle can then be used to make predictions about the actual paths cannonballs take. These predictions (for instance, that the greatest distance is reached when the gun is at 45 degrees) are found to agree with the observations made by gunners in the field.

A somewhat different example is that of Harvey's work on the circulatory system. Here *resolution* is actually taking apart a complex object—dissecting the body of a human or other mammal. The elements figuring in the explanation of the behavior of the blood are the heart together with its chambers and valves, the arteries and veins, and the blood itself. When all these are understood in their complex relations to each other, that is, when they are *composed* again into a whole, we understand what was previously puzzling to us.

We will see Hobbes trying to use these methods

---

*Compare Hobbes in this respect to the Greek atomists ("The World," in Chapter 4). You might also like to remind yourself of Plato's critique of this kind of nonpurposive explanation, pp. 119–121.

[†]Hobbes, like nearly all the moderns, is a great opponent of Aristotle. And yet this conclusion is basically Aristotelian. (See p. 170.) Likewise, his account of how we gain knowledge about the world is Aristotelian in spirit, if not in detail. In more than one way, Hobbes must be counted a "critical Aristotelian." Descartes, by contrast, clearly writes in the Plato-Augustine tradition. The principal difference between Hobbes and Aristotle is the former's repudiation of final causes, of potentiality, and of the essences that make them work. But this difference transforms everything it touches.

---

*See pp. 290–291.

in understanding both mind and society. He aspires to be the Galileo or the Harvey of the human world.

Minds and Motives

Life, says Hobbes,

> is but a motion of limbs, the beginning whereof is in some principle part within; why may we not say, that all *automata* (engines that move themselves by springs and wheels as doth a watch) have an artificial life? For what is the heart, but a spring; and the nerves, but so many strings, and the joints, but so many wheels, giving motion to the whole body, such as was intended by the artificer? (*L,* 129)[2]

The distinction, in other words, between living and nonliving things is not to be found in a soul, or a life-principle, or in anything nonmaterial. Living things are just those things which *move* because they have a source of motion *within* them. They are not in principle different from automata or robots that we ourselves might make. In fact, we say that robots are alive, too; it is just that their life is *artificially created.* That doesn't make it any the less life. The internal motions causing the movements of automata are, in principle, no different from the heart, nerves, and joints of the human body. Living things, whether natural or artificial, are just matter in motion.

In a way, Descartes does not yet disagree. For he thinks that animals are just "machines"; and animals are undoubtedly alive. But what about the life of the mind? What of thought and feeling? What of desire, imagination, and memory? Can these too be plausibly considered just matter in motion? We have seen Descartes' negative answer. Can Hobbes make a positive answer plausible?

Let us begin with thinking. What are thoughts?

> . . . they are everyone a *representation* or *appearance,* of some quality or other accident of a body without us, which is commonly called an *object.* (*L,* 131)

"The light of human minds is perspicuous words . . . ; reason is the pace, *increase of science, the* way, *and the benefit of mankind, the* end." —THOMAS HOBBES

Note that Hobbes expresses no doubt that there are indeed bodies—objects—independent of ourselves. He seems simply not to take the Cartesian reasons for doubting seriously.* Descartes, notoriously, thinks there is a serious problem here—that all our experience might be just as it is while *nothing at all* corresponds to it in the world beyond our minds. That there are bodies, Descartes holds, is something that needs to be *proved.* Hobbes offers no proofs. It is as though he thinks it beyond question. *Of course* our thoughts represent bodies. *Of course* bodies really exist. To be sure, we are sometimes mistaken about them, but these mistakes give us no reason to withhold belief in external

---

*Here again Hobbes stands to Descartes as Aristotle to Plato. See pp. 144–145.

things altogether. In fact, if it were not for those objects, we would not have any thoughts at all!

> The original of them all is that which we call *sense*, for there is no conception in a man's mind which hath not first, totally or by parts, been begotten upon the organs of sense. The rest are derived from that original. (*L*, 131)

The source of all our thoughts is to be found in sensation.* And sensation is an effect in us of the action of those external bodies upon our eyes, ears, nose, skin, and tongue. Motions are communicated to our sense organs from these bodies; these motions set up other motions in the sense organs; and these motions are in turn propagated by the nerves "inwards to the brain and heart." There the pressure of these motions meets a "counterpressure, or endeavor of the heart to deliver itself" (*L*, 131). Because this counterpressure is directed outward, we take the disturbance set up to be a representation or appearance of the object from which the motions originated. Here, then, are the origins of our experiences of colors, sounds, tastes, smells, hardness and softness, and so on. These experiences we call sensations, or, to use Hobbes' seventeenth-century term, "fancy."

But what of these experiences themselves? Can a sensation of red or a smell of rose really be "resolved" into motions? Here is what Hobbes says. In the objects that cause them, these qualities are

> but so many several motions of the matter, by which it presseth our organs diversely. Neither in us that are pressed, are they anything else but divers motions; for motion produceth nothing but motion. But their appearance to us is fancy. (*L*, 131)

It will pay us to consider this passage carefully, for it contains a crucial ambiguity. On the one

hand Hobbes says that sensations are themselves nothing but motion; "for motion produceth nothing but motion." If we take that seriously, then Hobbes is what we call a **materialist.** The entire life of the mind is nothing more than matter in motion. For sensations are motions, and all the rest is built up out of sensations. There are no distinctive *mental qualities* at all. Mind is just matter which is moved in certain distinctive ways.

On the other hand, Hobbes says of these motions that "their appearance to us is fancy." Now if it is not the motions themselves that constitute the sensations, but their *appearance* to us, then the sensations must be distinct from the motions. Under this interpretation Hobbes is not a materialist at all; he is what we call an **epiphenomenalist.** An epiphenomenalist thinks there are unique mental qualities, that they are causally dependent upon physical states, but that they do not in turn affect the physical world. They more or less ride piggyback on the physical, but they have no physical effects.

Is Hobbes a materialist or an epiphenomenalist about the mind? It is probably impossible to decide. He talks both ways, probably because he is simply unaware of the distinction. His intentions, however, are fairly clear. He wants to be a materialist, to resolve everything—including all aspects of mental life—into matter in motion. Let us take his intentions to be more significant than his linguistic lapses from them. We will consider him, therefore, to be a materialist about the mind. In this way, he stands in dramatic opposition to Descartes, for whom mind is a radically different kind of substance from body. Descartes, then, is a metaphysical **dualist,** Hobbes a **monist.** For Hobbes there is only one kind of finite substance.

Sensations, the "original" of thought, are motions. But this poses a problem. Paraphrasing Galileo's laws of inertia, Hobbes admits that "when a body is once in motion, it moveth, unless something else hinder it, eternally" (*L*, 133). Why is it, then, that sensations do not remain with us? The answer is that in a way they do—but in a diminished way only. For new sensations are ever pouring in on us; and by these succeeding motions the

---

* For all Hobbes' tirades against Aristotle, this is a very Aristotelian view. It is the dead opposite of Descartes' belief in innate ideas (see p. 303). It means that he can have no tolerance for Descartes' first proof for the existence of God. In this respect, compare Thomas Aquinas' rejection of the ontological argument of Saint Anselm on essentially similar Aristotelian grounds (see p. 257).

Francis Bacon

Although Francis Bacon (1561–1626) was both a jurist and statesman (rising as high as lord high chancellor in the England of James I) he was most passionately interested in reforming intellectual life and creating a new kind of science. His principal philosophical works are *The Advancement of Learning* (1605) and *Novum Organum* (1620).

Bacon believed that old habits had to change; it was a bad mistake to look to the authorities of the past, since nearly everything about the natural world remained to be discovered. Traditional philosophers, he said, are like spiders, spinning out intricate conceptions from their own insides. Alchemists and other early investigators were like ants, scurrying about collecting facts without any organized method. Rather, we should follow the example of the bees; let scientists cooperate in acquiring data, offering interpretations, conducting experiments, and drawing judicious conclusions.

Bacon identified four "idols" that, he said, have hindered the advance of knowledge: (1) idols of the tribe: tendencies resident in human nature itself, such as imagining that the senses give us a direct picture of their objects or imagining there is more order in experience than we actually find; (2) idols of the den: people's inclination to interpret experiences according to their private dispositions or favorite theories; (3) idols of the marketplace: language that subverts communication through ambiguities in words or in names that are assumed to name something but actually do not; and (4) idols of the theater: the dogmas of traditional philosophy, which portray the universe no more accurately than stage plays portray everyday life.

How can we counter these tendencies to revere the past and idolize the wrong things? Bacon recommended a method of careful experimentation and induction. Supporting a theory by simple enumeration of positive instances, however, is not good enough. We must look particularly, he said, for negative instances—especially if the theory is one we are fond of—and for variations in the degrees of presence and absence of factors so that we can find correlations between then.

Nature, Bacon told us, can be commanded only by obeying her; by submitting to nature's own ways through carefully designed experiments, we can gain knowledge. Knowledge, he said, is power. And the result of a reformed science will be mastery of nature, leading to a higher quality of human life.

---

previous ones are weakened. This *"decaying sense,"* as Hobbes calls it (*L,* 133), is *imagination* and *memory.*

In this way Hobbes can give an account of dreams. The old motions that constitute imagination and memory are reactivated in us during sleep by some condition of the body. He allows, what Descartes makes so much of, that it is a hard matter sometimes to distinguish dreams from waking life. But he finds in this fact quite a different implication. It does not, for Hobbes, constitute a reason to doubt everything. What it does provide is an explanation for belief in satyrs, nymphs, fairies, ghosts, goblins, and witches. Because of the similarity to wakeful experience, the presence of such entities in dreams leads to belief in their reality. Superstitions, false prophecies, and purely private religious certainties have the same source and constitute a threat, Hobbes thinks, to civil peace and well-being.

But let us return to thinking. When an image (the decayed motion left by a sensation) is combined with a sign, he says, we have *understanding*. And this is common to both humans and the higher animals. For instance, a dog who comes when his master whistles gives evidence that he understands what is wanted of him. The whistle is a sign connected in this case to images and tendencies to act. Hobbes, unlike Descartes, is quite content to speak of a dog as thinking this or that. The difference between the dog and ourselves is not absolute (that we have a soul, which the dog completely lacks) but is a matter of degree.

Because sense is the origin of all thinking, it is not possible for us to think of something we have not experienced. We can, of course, combine sense elements in novel ways to produce purely imaginative thoughts, of unicorns or centaurs, for instance. But things that are neither sensed nor invented on the basis of sensations are *inconceivable*. This has an important consequence: we can have, Hobbes says, no positive thought of God. "Whatsoever we imagine," he says, "is *finite*. Therefore there is no idea or conception of anything we call *infinite*" (*L*, 140). We do, of course, have *words* for God; we can call him a "being of infinite perfection"—as Descartes does. But these terms do not really function to describe God; rather, says Hobbes, they are signs of our intention to honor him.

Our thoughts, then, are derived from sense; they too are just motions in the matter of our brains. If we examine them, we find that they can roughly be grouped into two classes: *unregulated* and *regulated* thoughts. The first kind may seem to follow each other in a wholly random way. But it is not so. Upon careful observation, Hobbes tells us, we can see that their order mirrors previous successions of sense experiences. The appearance of randomness comes from the variety of our experiences. If at one time we *see* Mary with John, and then again with Peter, the *thought* of Mary may be accompanied by either that of John or that of Peter. But it will be associated in some way dependent on earlier experiences. In trying to find a pattern to unregulated thoughts, Hobbes is making a suggestion that will be developed into the doctrine of the *association of ideas.**

More interesting, however, are regulated thoughts. These do not even have an appearance of randomness but exhibit a quite definite order. One thing Hobbes has in mind is the kind of thinking that looks for *means* to attain a certain end; a young woman wants to attract a certain man, and she thinks about how that might be done. Another kind of regulated thought consists in inquiry about the *consequences* of taking a certain action; a student considers what her life will be like if she changes her curriculum from history to engineering. In regulated thought about the world, we are always searching for either *causes* or *effects*.

Such a hunt for causes is usually carried out in *words*, which are useful both as aids to memory and as signs representing our thoughts to others. Hobbes is acutely conscious of the benefits we derive from having such objective signs of our inner thoughts. But he also warns us about the errors into which they can easily trap us.

> Seeing then the truth consisteth in the right ordering of names in our affirmations, a man that seeketh precise truth had need to remember what every name he uses stands for, and to place it accordingly, or else he will find himself entangled in words, as a bird in lime twigs, the more he struggles the more belimed. (*L*, 142)

The cure for these evils of confusion is to be found in *definition*, to which Hobbes attributes the success of geometry, "the only science that it hath pleased God hitherto to bestow on mankind" (*L*, 142). Words need to be carefully defined, lest we find ourselves "entangled" in them like the bird in the lime twigs. In an often quoted phrase, Hobbes tells us that

> words are wise men's counters, they do but reckon by them; but they are the money of fools, that value

---

* See the use to which David Hume puts this notion, Chapter 17.

them by the authority of an Aristotle, a Cicero, or a Thomas. (*L*, 143)

Only a "fool" thinks that we can buy truth with the *words* of some authority.* A "wise man" realizes that they are only *signs* that, if properly used to "reckon" or calculate with, may possibly yield us a science.

We use words to *reason*, to think rationally about some matter. What is reasoning? Hobbes has a view of reasoning that some artificial intelligence researchers these days look back to as prophetic. Reasoning, he tells us, is "nothing but *reckoning*, that is adding and subtracting, of the consequences of general names agreed upon for the marking and signifying of our thoughts" (*L*, 133–34). Reasoning, as the cognitive scientist nowadays says, is computation.

Whether we reason about the theoretical consequences of some geometrical axiom, about means to attain a certain end, or about the practical consequences of some course of action, these regulated thoughts are governed by *desire*. We wouldn't bother if we didn't *want* to find out the answer. So the motivation behind all our rational thinking is passion. Hobbes must now ask: can these desires and wants, these likes and dislikes, themselves be accounted for in terms of the metaphysics of motion?†

We have seen that living things are distinguished from nonliving things by having the origins of some of their motions within them. Hobbes must now give a more careful account of this. He distinguishes two sorts of motions peculiar to animals: *vital* and *voluntary* motions. Vital motions are such things as the circulation of the blood, the pumping of the heart, breathing, and digestion. Voluntary motions, by contrast, are those whose

cause is to be found in some *imagination*. John imagines how pleasant it would be to go with Jane to the movies; he walks out of his way in the hope that their paths will cross. It is clear that if imagination itself is nothing but the diminished motions of sense, voluntary motions such as walking in a certain direction have their origin in internal motions.

These small, perhaps infinitesimally small beginnings of motion Hobbes calls *endeavor*. Endeavor can either be toward something (in which case it is called *desire*) or away from something (which is called *aversion*). In desire and aversion we find the sources of all human action.

Desire and aversion allow Hobbes to introduce certain value notions. What we desire, he says, we call good; what we wish to avoid we call evil. And these value distinctions are invariably founded on pleasure and pain, respectively: what gives us pleasure we call good; what causes pain we call evil.* It is important to realize that good and evil are not thought to attach absolutely to things. They are not properties that things have independently of our relation to them. The words "good" and "evil," Hobbes tells us,

> are ever used with relation to the person that useth them; there being nothing simply and absolutely so; nor any common rule of good and evil to be taken from the nature of the objects themselves; but from the person of the man, where there is no commonwealth; or, in a commonwealth, from the person that representeth it; or from an arbitrator or judge, whom men disagreeing shall by consent set up, and make his sentence the rule thereof. (*L*, 150)

The idea that in a "commonwealth," or state, good and evil are not relative to *individuals* is one we will explore shortly. But in what Hobbes calls a "state of nature," where there are no monarchs and judges, good and evil strictly depend on "the person of the man." The *only* judgment possible is that of the individual; if she desires X, she judges X to be good; if he dislikes Y, he considers Y evil. And

---

*Augustine makes a similar point in a quite different context. See p. 225.

†What is at stake here is whether *purpose* and *intention* can be given a mechanistic explanation. We have seen that Plato and, following him, Aristotle, think not. For this reason, Aristotle believes we need to ask about *final* causes in addition to the other three kinds. This question is still hotly debated.

---

*It is clear that Hobbes is a hedonist. See Epicurus, p. 187.

from those judgments there is (in the state of nature) no appeal.*

This analysis is an important step in Hobbes' materialistic program. Goodness is not a Platonic Form or an unanalyzable property that some things have. Everything is just body and motion. But some (living) bodies are related in certain ways to other bodies in such a way that the former bodies utter the words "That is good" about those latter bodies. They do so when the latter produce motions in the former that are pleasurable.

And what is pleasure? Pleasure, Hobbes tells us, is just "a corroboration of vital motion, and a help thereunto," while pains are a "hindering and troubling the motion vital" (L, 150). Feeling good, in other words, is just having all our normal bodily processes working smoothly; the more active and untroubled they are, the better we feel. And what we all want is to feel good.

It seems, then, that regulated thoughts are regulated by desire, that desire is always for the good, and that "good" is our name for whatever produces pleasure. The end point of a train of regulated thoughts is some action on our part—an action we think will gain us some good. These actions, when caused by thoughtful desires in this way, are called "voluntary."

At this point Hobbes meets a natural objection. It is not, someone might claim, *desire* that is the cause of voluntary action; it is *will*. And willpower can override our desires. I desperately *want* another slice of that dark, rich chocolate cake; but I exercise my will and say, "Thank you, but no." Can Hobbes deal with this common experience?

He does so by asking what we mean by "*will*." It cannot be anything else, he thinks, than "*the last appetite in deliberating*" (L, 154). Will, then, is a desire. I do desire that slice of cake. But I also have desires that run counter to that desire: I want not to look piggish; I want not to gain too much weight. On this occasion, these latter desires outweigh the former; they are the ones that dictate my action. And so these are what we *call* my will. Will

is nothing but *effective desire*. It is the desire that *wins*. Since we have already seen that Hobbes believes desire and aversion can be given an analysis in terms of matter in motion, there is no need to bring in nonmaterial mental factors to explain the origin of voluntary actions.*

Our voluntary actions, then, are governed in the last analysis by passion—by our desires and aversions, our loves and hates. And since the good we seek and the evil we try to avoid are rooted in our own pleasures and pains, action is always egoistic. It is my own good that I seek, if Hobbes is right—not yours. As Hobbes puts it, "of the voluntary acts of every man, the object is some *good to himself* (L, 165).

Moreover, we seek such good *continually*. It is not enough to act once for our own pleasure; the next moment demands other acts that have the same end. Happiness—or felicity, as Hobbes calls it—is just a life filled with the satisfaction of our desires.

> *Continual success* in obtaining those things which a man from time to time desireth, that is to say, continual prospering, is that men call *felicity;* I mean the felicity of this life. For there is no such thing as perpetual tranquility of mind, while we live here; because life itself is but motion, and can never be without desire, nor without fear, no more than without sense. (L, 155)

In this life there can be no resting, no "tranquility." No sooner has one desire been fulfilled than another takes its place. And the reason Hobbes gives for this is that life itself is nothing but motion. (We

---

*Compare the doctrine of Protagoras, the Sophist, who said, "Of all things, man is the measure" (p. 41).

*It is clear that Hobbes is a *determinist*—that is, one who thinks that for every event, including all human actions, there is a set of sufficient conditions guaranteeing its occurrence. All actions are caused; and the causes of these causes themselves have causes. This poses a problem, of course: the problem of freedom of the will. We saw that Descartes, who is not a materialist, can hold that our decisions escape this universal determinism that holds for the material world; even God, Descartes says, is not more free than we are. Hobbes cannot think so. He has a solution to this problem, but since the same solution is more elegantly set out by Hume, we will consider it in the next chapter. If you want a preview, see "Rescuing Human Freedom," in Chapter 17.

John Locke

One of the founders of empiricism (see **p. 341**), John Locke (1632–1704) was influential not only in epistemology but also in political philosophy. He held that before setting out a view of reality, it was necessary to determine what the human mind is capable of and what its limitations are. Thus, in 1690, he published the influential *Essay Concerning Human Understanding*. Using what he called the "historical plain method," he inquired about the origin of our ideas, the extent of our knowledge, and the degrees of certainty we might attain.

Opposed entirely to Descartes' theory of innate ideas, Locke held that the mind is "white paper" on which experience writes. Our experience yields ideas of two kinds: ideas of sensation, which are conveyed into the mind from external objects (e.g., blue, warm, and solid), and ideas of reflection, which are acquired when the mind observes its own operations (e.g., thinking, willing, and believing). Knowledge, Locke said, is a matter of the agreement and disagreement among ideas and can reach no farther than our ideas can carry us. Because ideas originate in our obviously limited experience, it is clear that what we can know will be quite limited. So we must be cautious in claiming to know and modest in our claims to know for certain. For most of our beliefs about things independent of the mind, we can say only that they are probable.

Locke advocated tolerance in religious matters. In *A Letter Concerning Toleration* (1689), he argued that religious belief is a matter between an individual and God. Attempts by church or state to compel belief breed only hypocrisy, and, in any case, no one can be so certain of the truth of religious beliefs as to be justified in persecuting others.

In 1690, Locke also published *Two Treatises on Civil Government*. Here he argued against the divine right of kings and set forth a version of the social contract theory. His image of the state of nature was less ruthless than that of Hobbes, so the remedy was less absolute. Locke argued for a representative government in which the legislative and executive powers are separate—thoughts that were influential in the establishment of the United States Constitution.

---

have here a kind of principle of inertia for living things; just as things in motion tend to remain in motion, so the life of desiring tends to perpetuate itself.) So there is a perpetual striving for the satisfaction of desires; when this is successful over some period of time, we say that during that period a person is happy.*

All of us desire this felicity, Hobbes says. But it is easy to see that if we are not to be mere pawns of fortune, we must also control access to it; that is, we must be guaranteed the *power* to satisfy whatever desires we may happen to have.

> . . . I put for a general inclination of all mankind, a perpetual and restless desire of power after power, that ceaseth only in death. And the cause of this, is not always that a man hopes for a more intensive delight, than he has already attained to; or that he cannot be content with a moderate power: but because he cannot assure the power and means to live well, which he hath present, without the acquisition of more. (*L*, 158–59)

This kind of power is, of course, a relative matter. In a world of limited resources, if I gain more

---

* Compare this notion of happiness to that of Epicurus ("The Epicureans," in Chapter 10). Note that there is a fundamental agreement: pleasure is the good. But note also that Hobbes makes no distinction between those desires it is and is not *wise* to try to fulfill. It is hard to see how he could—at least for the state of nature. Desires are just facts—any and all of them; they all, equally, demand satisfaction. And the strongest wins. That, Hobbes might say, is just how it is.

power to guarantee the satisfaction of *my* desires, I naturally diminish *your* power to satisfy your desires. In seeking to assure my own felicity, I threaten yours. So we are naturally competitors. I seek my good. You seek yours. And we each seek to increase our own power to assure that we at least do not lose those goods we now have.*

Although there are natural differences in our power, we are equal enough in natural gifts that each of us has reason to fear the other. As Hobbes says, even "the weakest has strength enough to kill the strongest" (*L,* 159). Because of this equality, the egoistic desire for happiness—plus the need to be assured of it by a continual increase of power—leads human beings to be enemies. So our *natural* condition (i.e., before any artificial arrangements or agreements among us) is one of *war.* Indeed, it is "such a war as is of every man against every man." In such a condition, Hobbes argues,

> there is no place for industry, because the fruit thereof is uncertain; and consequently no culture of the earth; no navigation, nor use of the commodities that may be imported by sea; no commodious building; no instruments of moving and removing, such things as require much force; no knowledge of the face of the earth; no account of time; no arts; no letters; no society; and which is worst of all, continual fear, and danger of violent death; and the life of man, solitary, poor, nasty, brutish, and short. (*L,* 161)

Solitary, poor, nasty, brutish—and short! Such is our life in a state of nature.

Let us remind ourselves of what Hobbes claims to be doing here. He is trying to use the same method on human nature and society that Galileo and Harvey use on the nonhuman world. He resolves human beings into their component elements—the motions characteristic of living things—and finds this competitive and restless striving to be the result.

This analysis is supported, he believes, by ob-

servation. Hobbes lived during extremely troubled times in England. There was a long struggle between king and Parliament over the right to make certain laws and collect taxes. This struggle reflected a broader quarrel between the old nobility and the established Church of England on the one hand and the rising middle classes and religious dissenters of a more radical Protestant sort on the other. Those on each side, in Hobbes' view, were trying to preserve against the other side the means of their own happiness.

The outcome was a protracted and bloody civil war, the execution of King Charles I, a period of government without a king under the Protectorate of Oliver Cromwell, and finally the Restoration of the monarchy under Charles II (to whom Hobbes had been a tutor in mathematics). The "state of nature" into which Hobbes resolves human society was very nearly the actual state of affairs during a good part of the seventeenth century in England. The war of all against all was not just a theoretical construct; it was an observed actuality.

Still, Hobbes does not intend his description of the state of nature to be a description of society at all times and places. Nor is it supposed to be a historical description of the state of society at some time in the distant past. It is intended to picture the results of an analytical decomposition of human society into its elements. Left to their own devices, the theory says, individuals will always act egoistically for their own good. And the inevitable consequence is a state of war—each of us fearing our neighbor and striving to extend our sphere of control at our neighbor's expense. This is the result of the *resolution* phase of Hobbes' method.

We now need to look at the *composition* phase, where the elements are put back together again. And here we are interested primarily in Hobbes' view of the ethical consequences.

The Natural Foundation of Moral Rules

Hobbes has "resolved" human society into its elements. Let us see how he thinks it can be "composed" back again into a whole. If Hobbes suc-

---

*If this seems unrealistic to you as a model of relations among individuals, consider political and economic rivalries among nations. As we will see, Hobbes has an explanation of how we have gotten beyond this competitive situation on the individual level. It is instructive to compare this picture of restless competitiveness to Augustine's two cities, pp. 244–247.

ceeds in this stage, we will have an explanation of the human world, including its ethical and political aspect, in purely mechanistic terms.

In the state of nature, human beings are governed by their egoistic passions, their endeavor to ensure their own happiness. And we have seen how this leads to the "war of everyone against everyone," a deadly competition for the power to guarantee for each person what he considers good. If this is our natural state, how can it be overcome? Partly, Hobbes says, by passion itself, and partly by reason.

One of the strongest passions is the *fear of death*. It is this fear, together with the desire for happiness, that motivates us to find a way to end the state of nature. We must remember that in the state of nature there are no rights and wrongs, no goods and bads, except where an individual thinks there are. We each take as much as we have power to take and keep. An individual's liberty extends as far as his power. But if a person in this state of nature realizes how unsatisfactory this condition is, he will see that

> it is a precept, or general rule of reason, *that every man ought to endeavor peace, as far as he has hope of obtaining it; and when he cannot obtain it, that he may seek and use all helps and advantages of war.* The first branch of which rule containeth the first and fundamental law of nature; which is, to *seek peace and follow it.* The second, the sum of the right of nature; which is, *by all means we can, to defend ourselves.* (L, 163)

Hobbes speaks here of a *right* of nature and of a *law* of nature. What can he mean? In a universe composed merely of matter in motion, how can there be rights and laws *in nature*? Hasn't Hobbes already denied that there is any right or wrong independent of some monarch or judge to declare what is right and wrong?

There has been much debate about how Hobbes means these notions to be understood. If we interpret him sympathetically, however, it seems that a law of nature must simply be an expression of the way things go. Jones, who by nature seeks his own happiness and fears death, is worried about his future. This is just how it is. In reasoning about his situation, Jones sees that if peace were to replace war, then his fear of death would be relieved; and if he didn't have to be so afraid of his neighbors, he could more satisfactorily fill his own life with "felicity." The rule to "seek peace" is a rule that an egoistic but rational creature such as Jones will inevitably—naturally—come upon. He will reason that if he is going to have any chance of a good life, he has to get beyond this state of war. *A law of nature* for Hobbes is simply a rule of prudence that results from the shrewd calculation of a scared human being.

A *right* of nature must have a similar foundation. In the state of nature there are no "rights" in the usual sense. If, in a state of nature, someone injures me, I cannot complain that my "rights" have been infringed. All I can say is that I don't like it and will do whatever I can to see that it doesn't happen again! But precisely because there are no rules, I am *at liberty* to use whatever means I can muster to preserve my life and happiness. Hobbes uses the term "right" to refer to this liberty everyone has in the state of nature. So Jones having the "right" to defend himself is simply the fact that there are no rules that curtail his tendency to preserve his life and happiness. If, however, Jones (and everyone else) exercises this liberty without limit, the results will be, as we have seen, uniformly bad: the war of all against all.

This suggests to the rational person that some of the liberty we have in the state of nature must be given up. To give it up entirely, however, would make no sense at all; if Jones gave up the liberty of defending himself altogether, he would become the prey of everyone—and an egoistic agent could not rationally allow that. So this "right" of self-defense remains something that Jones will always retain.

We have, then, one right and one law, which are used by Hobbes as the foundation for a series of deductions. Once we have these, others "follow" in almost geometrical fashion. For instance, the second law, Hobbes tells us, is

> that a man be willing, when others are so too, as far forth as peace and defense of himself he shall think it necessary, to lay down this right to all things; and be contented

*with so much liberty against other men, as he would al-
low other men against himself.* (L, 163–64)

Each of us, according to this second law, should be
content with as much liberty with respect to others
as we are willing to allow with respect to ourselves.
There should be—in order to end the state of
war—a mutual limiting of rights, as far as this is of
mutual benefit to each. (Note that Hobbes does
not suppose that anyone would do this *altruisti-
cally,* or out of sheer good will. The motivation
throughout is hedonistic and egoistic.)

This agreement to limit one's claims has the flavor of a *contract*. And, indeed, Hobbes' view is one
version of a **social contract** theory.* But you can
see that there is a difficulty at this point. Suppose
Jones and Smith, in a state of nature, each agree to
limit their own liberty to the extent that the other
does as well. Why should they believe each other?
What reason do they have to trust each other to
keep the promise? Is there anything to keep Smith
from violating the contract if she thinks it is in her
interest to do so and calculates that she can get
away with it? It seems not. Hence, in a state of nature contracts and promises are useless. They are
just words! This is a serious problem. It looks like
you cannot get *here* from *there*—that is, to a moral
community from a state of nature. Can Hobbes
solve this problem?

What is necessary to make the contract opera-
tive, Hobbes says, is "a common power set over
them both, with right and force sufficient to compel performance" (L, 167). Only then, when punishment threatens, can Jones trust Smith to keep
her promise. For only then will it clearly be in
Smith's self-interest not to break it. There is, then,
a necessity for

some coercive power, to compel men equally to the
performance of their covenants . . . and such power
there is none before the erection of a commonwealth.
(L, 168)

This is the rationale for that "great *Leviathan*," that
"artificial man," that "mortal god," the state. It is
the state, together with the power of enforcement
that we agree to give it, that gets us beyond the
state of nature. Only in such a community can
moral and legal rules exist and structure our lives.

The details of Hobbes' political philosophy are
of great interest. But we will pass them by. Our
interest lies in the possibility of a world picture
built on the foundations of the new science that
includes human beings, together with their mental
and moral life. And we now have an outline of
what one such attempt looks like. Let us summarize a few of the main points.

- Sensation, thought, motivation, and voluntary
  action are all analyzed in terms of matter in
  motion.
- All events, including human actions, are subject to the same laws of motion that Galileo has
  discovered.
- Only egoistic desires are recognized as motivators; so all actions are performed for the welfare
  of the agent.
- If you peel off the veneer of civilization, what
  you are left with is individuals in conflict.
- This conflict can be resolved on the basis of the
  very passions that produce it, provided people
  reason well about their individual long-term
  interest.
- Morality and law are simply the best means
  available, the *only* means, to stave off imminent
  death and the possible loss of felicity. Being
  moral and law-abiding is no more than a smart
  strategy for self-preservation.
- Unless these rules are enforced by a powerful
  ruler, everything will collapse again into the
  state of nature.

It is a stark vision that Hobbes gives us. He
thinks that acceptance of modern science forces

---

*The idea of a contract or agreement as the basis for society is
taken up by a number of other political thinkers: Spinoza, Rousseau, and—most importantly for the founding of the American
Republic—John Locke. They differ about whether the contract is
with a sovereign (Hobbes) or among individuals (Locke) and
about whether once entered into it could or could not be revoked.
But social contract theories generally stress the rights of individuals and consent as the basis of legitimate government. As such
they are both a reflection of and an influence on the individualism
of the times.

that view upon us. Is that correct? Or are there less forbidding alternatives?

Basic Questions

1. Contrast the world-picture we get from the Galileo-Descartes-Hobbes gang with that of Aristotle and his medieval followers
   - with respect to a description of the universe;
   - with respect to what needs explaining;
   - with respect to kinds of explanation desired; and
   - with respect to the place of values in the world.
2. How does Hobbes try to explain thinking? Compare his views, if you can, with recent work in artificial intelligence.
3. How are good and evil explained by Hobbes? Compare with the view of Augustine (e.g., pp. 223–226).
4. How do Hobbes and Descartes differ on the nature of the will? Relate this to the metaphysics of each.
5. Describe what Hobbes calls "the state of nature," and explain why it has the character it does have.
6. How does Hobbes think we can have gotten, or can get, beyond the state of nature?

7. What makes Hobbes think that a "social contract" will require the "coercive power" of a state?

For Further Thought

Write a dialogue in which Descartes and Hobbes (who were contemporaries and met at least once) debate about the nature of human beings.

Notes

1. Quoted in *Objections III with Replies* in *The Philosophical Works of Descartes,* vol. 2, ed. Elisabeth S. Haldane and G. R. T. Ross (n.p.: Dover Publications, 1955), 62.
2. Quotations from Thomas Hobbes, *Leviathan, or The Matter, Form, and Power of a Commonwealth, Ecclesiastical and Civil,* in *The English Philosophers from Bacon to Mill,* ed. Edwin A. Burtt (New York: Modern Library, 1939), are cited in the text using the abbreviation *L.* References are to page numbers.

17

David Hume:
Unmasking the Pretensions of Reason

The eighteenth century is often called the Age of Enlightenment. Those who lived through this period felt that progress was being made almost daily toward overthrowing superstition and arbitrary authority, replacing ignorance with knowledge and blind obedience with freedom. It is an age of optimism. One of the clearest expressions of this attitude is found in a brief essay by Immanuel Kant (the subject of our next chapter). Writing in 1784, eight years after the death of David Hume, Kant defines what the age understands by "enlightenment."

> *Enlightenment is man's emergence from his self-imposed immaturity. Immaturity* is the inability to use one's understanding without guidance from another. This immaturity is *self-imposed* when its cause lies not in lack of understanding, but in lack of resolve and courage to use it without guidance from another. *Sapere Aude!* "Have courage to use your own understanding!"—that is the motto of enlightenment.[1]

This call to think for oneself, to have the courage to rely on one's own abilities, is quite characteristic of the age. For Kant, the lack of courage is "self-imposed." To overcome it we need only the resolve not to be bound any more by those who set themselves up as our guardians.

> It is so easy to be immature. If I have a book to serve as my understanding, a pastor to serve as my conscience, a physician to determine my diet for me,

and so on, I need not exert myself at all. I need not think, if only I can pay. . . . The guardians who have so benevolently taken over the supervision of men have carefully seen to it that the far greatest part of them (including the entire fair sex) regard taking the step to maturity as very dangerous, not to mention difficult. Having first made their domestic livestock dumb, and having carefully made sure that these docile creatures will not take a single step without the go-cart to which they are harnessed, these guardians then show them the danger that threatens them, should they attempt to walk alone. Now this danger is actually not so great, for after falling a few times they would in the end certainly learn to walk; but an example of this kind makes men timid and usually frightens them out of all further attempts.

> Thus, it is difficult for any individual man to work himself out of the immaturity that has all but become his nature. He has even become fond of this state and for the time being actually incapable of using his own understanding.[2]

Working oneself out of this immaturity is "difficult," but not impossible—as had been clearly shown in the triumphs of the scientific revolution from Copernicus to that most admired of thinkers, Isaac Newton (1642–1727). It was Newton's triumphant integration of his predecessors' work into one unified explanatory scheme for understanding both terrestrial and celestial movements that symbolized what human efforts could achieve—if only they could be freed from the dead hand of the past. And thinkers throughout the eighteenth century busy themselves applying Newton's methods to other subjects: to the mind, to ethics, to religion, and to the state of society.

And yet none of them would think that they have arrived at the goal. Here again is Kant:

> If it is now asked, "Do we presently live in an *enlightened* age?" the answer is, "No, but we do live in an age of *enlightenment*." [3]

The key word is "progress." Newton showed that progress is really possible. And the conviction spreads that this progress can be extended indefinitely if only we can muster the courage to do, in one sphere after another, what Newton had done in physics and astronomy. We were not yet mature; but we were becoming mature.

How Newton Did It

It is almost impossible to exaggerate Newton's impact on the imagination of the eighteenth century. As a towering symbol of scientific achievement, he can be compared only to Einstein in the twentieth century. The astonished admiration his work evoked is expressed in a couplet by Alexander Pope.

> Nature and Nature's laws lay hid in night;
> God said, Let Newton be, and all was light.

Everyone has some idea of Newton's accomplishment, of how his theory of universal gravitation provides a mathematically accurate and powerful tool for understanding not only the motions of heavenly bodies but also such puzzling phenomena as the tides. We won't go into the details of this theory. But every science is developed on the basis of certain methods and presuppositions that may properly be called philosophical. It is these philosophical underpinnings that we must take note of, for they are crucially important to the development of the whole trend of thought in the eighteenth century—not least to the philosophy of David Hume.

How had Newton been able to pull it off? His methods are in fact not greatly different from those of Galileo and Hobbes. There are two stages (like Hobbes' resolution and composition), which he calls *analysis* and *synthesis*. But there is a particular insistence in some of his pronouncements that strike a note somewhat different from those we have heard before. He does not, he says, *frame hypotheses*. What does this mean? By a *hypothesis* he means a principle of explanation not derived from a close examination of the facts. The key to doing science, he believes, is to stay close to the phenomena; the big mistake is to jump prematurely to an explanation. Newton's own long and persistent series of experiments with the prism exemplifies this maxim. The fact that white light is not a simple phenomenon (as it seems to naive sight) is disclosed only by an immensely detailed series of investigations, which reveal its composition out of the many simpler hues of the rainbow. Only an analysis of *facts that disclose themselves to our senses* yields true principles of explanation.

> I frame no hypotheses; for whatever is not deduced from the phenomena is to be called an hypothesis; and hypotheses, whether metaphysical or physical, whether of occult qualities or mechanical, have no place in experimental philosophy. [4]

Principles of explanation are to be "deduced from the phenomena." This emphasis on paying close attention to the facts of experience has a long history in English philosophy even before Newton; it can be traced back through John Locke to Francis Bacon—and, indeed, it is Aristotelian in character. But in Newton its fruitfulness pays off in a way that had never been seen before. In Newton's work we find a suspicion of any principles that have not been derived from a close experimental examination of the sensible facts. We cannot *begin* with what *seems* right to us. Hypotheses, no matter how natural and right they may seem, must be subjected to the test of experience. Hypotheses not arrived at by way of careful analysis of the sensible facts are arbitrary—no matter how intuitively convincing they may seem. And Newton's success is, to the eighteenth-century thinker, proof that his methods are sound.

Note how different this emphasis is from the rationalism of Descartes. Always the mathematician, Descartes seeks to find starting points for science and philosophy that are intuitively certain, axioms that are "so clear and distinct" that they cannot possibly be doubted. He is confident that reason, the "light of nature," will certify some such principles as knowable and known. So the whole structure of wisdom, in Descartes, is the structure of an axiomatic, geometrical system. Intuitive insight and deduction from first principles are the hallmarks of his way of proceeding.

But for eighteenth-century thinkers inspired by the example of Newton, this smells too much of arbitrariness. One man's intuitive certainty, they suspect, is another man's absurdity.* The only cure is to stick closely to the facts. The **rationalism** of Descartes is supplanted by the **empiricism** of thinkers like David Hume.

To Be the Newton of Human Nature

David Hume (1711–1776) aspires to do for human nature what Isaac Newton did for nonhuman nature: to provide principles of explanation both simple and comprehensive.[5] There seem to be two motivations. First, Hume shares with many other Enlightenment intellectuals the project of debunking what they call "popular superstition." By this they usually mean the deliverances of religious enthusiasm together with the conviction of certainty that typically accompanies them.† (The era of religious wars based on such certainties is still fresh in

the memory.) But these thinkers also mean whatever in philosophy cannot be demonstrated on a basis of reason and experience common to human beings. Hume's prose betrays his passion on this score. Remarking on the obscurity, uncertainty, and error in most philosophies, he pinpoints the cause:

> . . . they are not properly a science; but arise either from the fruitless efforts of human vanity, which would penetrate into subjects utterly inaccessible to the understanding, or from the craft of popular superstitions, which, being unable to defend themselves on fair ground, raise these entangling brambles to cover and protect their weakness. Chased from the open country, these robbers fly into the forest, and lie in wait to break in upon every unguarded avenue of the mind, and overwhelm it with religious fears and prejudices. The stoutest antagonist, if he remit his watch a moment, is oppressed. And many, through cowardice and folly, open the gates to the enemies, and willingly receive them with reverence and submission, as their legal sovereigns.
>
> But is this a sufficient reason, why philosophers should desist from such researches, and leave superstition still in possession of her retreat? Is it not proper to draw an opposite conclusion, and perceive the necessity of carrying the war into the most secret recesses of the enemy? (E, 5–6)[6]

The basic strategy in this war is to show what the human understanding is (and is not) capable of. And this is what a science of human nature should give us. If we can show that "superstition" consists in claims to know what no one can possibly know, then we undermine its defenses in the most radical way.

Hume's second motivation is his conviction that a science of human nature is, in a certain way, fundamental. All the other sciences

> have a relation, greater or less, to human nature. . . . Even *Mathematics, Natural Philosophy, and Natural Religion*, are in some measure dependent on the science of Man; since they lie under the cognizance of men, and are judged of by their powers and faculties. 'Tis impossible to tell what changes and improvements we might make in these sciences were we

---

*They feel confirmed in this suspicion by the example of rationalist philosophy after Descartes. First-rate intellects like Malebranche, Spinoza, and Leibniz developed remarkably different philosophical systems on the basis of supposedly "self-evident" truths.

†"Enthusiasm" is the word eighteenth-century thinkers use to describe ecstatic forms of religion involving the claim that one is receiving revelations, visions, or "words" directly from God. This form of religion is far from dead.

thoroughly acquainted with the extent and force of human understanding, and could explain the nature of the ideas we employ, and of the operations we perform in our reasonings. (*T,* xix)

Since all our intellectual endeavors are *products* of human understanding, an examination of that understanding itself should illumine them all. Such an inquiry will reveal how the mind works, what materials it has to operate on, and how knowledge in any area at all can be constructed.

Hume is aware that others before him have formulated theories of the mind (or human understanding). But they have not satisfactorily settled matters.

> There is nothing which is not the subject of debate, and in which men of learning are not of contrary opinions. . . . Disputes are multiplied, as if every thing was uncertain; and these disputes are managed with the greatest warmth, as if every thing was certain. (*T,* xviii)

Consider the wide disagreement between Descartes and Hobbes, for instance. Descartes, as we have seen, believes that the freedom and rationality of our minds exempts them from the kind of causal explanation provided for material bodies. A mind, he concludes, is a thing completely distinct from a body. Hobbes, on the other hand, includes the mind and all its ideas and activities within the scope of a materialistic and deterministic science. "Mind," for Hobbes, is just a name for certain ways a human body operates. Who is right here?

From Hume's point of view, neither one prevails. Hobbes simply *assumes* that our thoughts are representations of objects that exist independently of our minds and that whatever principles explain these objects will also explain the mind. But surely Descartes has shown us that this is something that should not be assumed! Whatever our experience might be, whatever it "tells" us about reality, things could actually be different. That is the lesson of Descartes' doubt. Hobbes' assumption that sensations and thoughts generally represent realities accurately is nothing but a "hypothesis." And, Hume

"As the science of man is the only solid foundation for the other sciences, so the only solid foundation we can give to this science itself must be laid on experience and observation."   —DAVID HUME

says (following Newton), we are to avoid framing hypotheses.

Descartes' positive doctrine of a separate mind-substance, however, is just as "hypothetical" as that of Hobbes. It is derived from principles that may *seem* intuitively obvious, but have not been "deduced from the phenomena." The problem is that neither pays close attention to the data available. Both of them fail because they did not have the example of Newton from which to learn. We do not have, Hume thinks, any insight or intuition into the "essence" of material bodies. Nor do we have such an intuition into the "essence" of minds. We have made progress in the physical realm only by sticking close to the experimental facts; we can

George Berkeley

Believing himself to be a defender of common sense, George Berkeley (1685–1753) quickly established a reputation for paradox. In *The Principles of Human Knowledge* (1710) and *Three Dialogues between Hylas and Philonus* (1713), Berkeley argued against skepticism and atheism by claiming that material substances do not exist.

Locke had held that our ideas of an apple, say, are of two kinds: there are the ideas of its sensible qualities (round, red, sweet, crisp), and the idea of the substance in which these qualities exist. The latter does not originate in sensation; rather, it is an "abstract" idea we form by disregarding the respects in which one apple is different from another. Berkeley noted that if we disregard those qualities of apples, we are left with precisely *nothing*. So, in this sense, there are no abstract ideas. We simply have no idea of material substances.

Berkeley gave an alternative account of "general" ideas in terms of the *use* to which we put terms such as "apple." We use such terms to denote indifferently this apple, that apple, and, indeed, any apple. "Apple" is not a name, so it can't name an abstract idea such as material substance.

But what, then, is an apple? Considerations from optics suggest that what is present to the sense of sight is light and color; taste presents sweetness; touch offers solidity; and so on. All these sensations are contents in the mind: ideas. So an apple is really a collection of ideas present to the mind. Berkeley expressed this in a slogan: *To be is to be perceived.* Is this skepticism? By no means, he said. In knowing the ideas that make up an apple, we know the thing itself; the skeptics are the believers in material things—which we cannot possibly experience!

Berkeley was struck by the remarkable order that exists in such sensible ideas. Where does this regularity in things come from? If there *were* material things, they might account for it; however, this would be an incitement to atheism—it would be as though God were not necessary. Ideas can exist only in a mind or spirit, and *we* clearly are not responsible for this order. Berkeley (a clergyman and bishop) took these facts to be strong proof for the existence of God, in whom all things exist as ideas.

---

hope to progress in constructing a science of human nature only if we do the same in that realm.

> For to me it seems evident, that the essence of the mind being equally unknown to us with that of external bodies, it must be equally impossible to form any notion of its powers and qualities otherwise than from careful and exact experiments, and the observation of those particular effects, which result from its different circumstances and situations. And tho' we must endeavour to render all our principles as universal as possible, by tracing up our experiments to the utmost, and explaining all effects from the simplest and fewest causes, 'tis still certain we cannot go beyond experience; and any hypothesis, that pretends to discover the ultimate original qualities of human nature, ought at first to be rejected as presumptuous and chimerical. (*T*, xxi)

The Newtonian tone is unmistakable. What, then, are the *data* which scientists of human nature must "observe" and from which they may draw principles "as universal as possible"? Hume calls them "perceptions," by which he means all the contents of our minds when we are awake and alert.* Among perceptions are all our ideas, including not only those of the sciences, but also

---

*Here Hume shows that he, like Descartes (and Locke and Berkeley, too), is committed to the representational theory (p. 300). Unlike Descartes, as we will see, Hume believes there are no legitimate inferences from ideas to things.

ideas both arbitrary and superstitious. One of Hume's aims is to draw a line between legitimate ideas and ideas that are confused, unfounded, and nonsensical. To do this, he thinks it necessary to inquire about the *origin* of our ideas.

The Theory of Ideas

A science of human nature must concentrate on what is peculiarly human. A woman's height, weight, and hair color are characteristics of a human being; but these are properties she shares with nonhuman objects, which Newtonian science explains so well. It is human ideas, feelings, and actions that are distinctive and require special treatment. And it is on these that Hume focuses. Ideas are particularly important, since they are involved in nearly all the other activities that are characteristically human. What are ideas? And how do we come to have them?

Hume uses "perceptions" as a general term for all the contents of the mind. Perceptions, he claims, can be divided into two major classes: *impressions* and *ideas*.

> The difference betwixt these consists in the degrees of force and liveliness with which they strike upon the mind, and make their way into our thought or consciousness. Those perceptions, which enter with most force and violence, we may name *impressions*; and under this name I comprehend all our sensations, passions and emotions, as they make their first appearance in the soul. By *ideas* I mean the faint images of these in thinking and reasoning. (*T*, 1)

You can get a vivid illustration of the difference between the two classes if you bring your hand down suddenly on the table (the sound you hear is an impression), and then, a few seconds later, recall that sound (the content of your memory is an idea).

Hume thinks that this difference is one we are all familiar with. There may be borderline cases such as a terrifying dream, in which the ideas are

very nearly as lively as the actual impressions would be. But on the whole, the distinction is not only familiar, but clear. One other important distinction must be observed: that between *simple* and *complex*. The impression you have when you slap the table is simple; the impression you have when you hear a melody is complex. Complex impressions and ideas are built up from simples.

Hume is trying to pay close attention to the data. The next thing he notices is "the great resemblance betwixt our impressions and ideas" (*T*, 2). It seems as though "all the perceptions of the mind are double, and appear both as impressions and ideas" (*T*, 3). No, he adds, this is not quite correct. For you have the idea of a unicorn, but you have never experienced a unicorn impression. (Ah, you say; but I have seen a *picture* of a unicorn! True enough, but your experience on that occasion did not constitute an impression of a unicorn, but of a unicorn picture. Your idea of a unicorn is not the idea of a picture.) So you do have an idea that does not correspond to any impression; so not all our perceptions are "double."

But a closer look, Hume thinks, will convince us that although this principle does not hold for *complex* ideas, it does hold for all *simple* ideas. The idea of a unicorn, after all, is a very complex idea. We need not analyze it very far to notice that it is made up of two simpler ideas: that of a horse and that of a single horn. Impressions do correspond to these simpler ideas, for horses and horns we have all seen. So the revised principle is that to every *simple idea* corresponds a *simple impression* that resembles it.

If impressions and simple ideas come in pairs like this, so that there is a "constant conjunction" between them, the next question is: which comes first? Hume again notes that *in his experience* it is always the impression that appears first; the idea comes later.

> To give a child an idea of scarlet or orange, of sweet or bitter, I present the objects, or in other words, convey to him these impressions; but proceed not so absurdly, as to endeavour to produce the impressions by exciting the ideas. . . . We cannot form to

ourselves a just idea of the taste of a pine-apple, without having actually tasted it. (*T*, 5)

This suggests that there is a relation of *dependence* between them; Hume concludes that every simple idea has some simple impression as a causal antecedent. Every simple idea, in fact, is a *copy* of a preceding impression.* What is the origin of all our ideas? The impressions of experience—no impression, no idea.

This is an apparently simple principle. But Hume warns us that taking it seriously will have far-reaching consequences. It contains, in fact, a rule of procedure that Hume makes devastating use of.

> All ideas, especially abstract ones, are naturally faint and obscure: The mind has but a slender hold of them: They are apt to be confounded with other resembling ideas; and when we have often employed any term, though without a distinct meaning, we are apt to imagine it has a determinate idea, annexed to it. On the contrary, all impressions, that is, all sensations, either outward or inward, are strong and vivid: The limits between them are more exactly determined: Nor is it easy to fall into any error or mistake with regard to them. When we entertain, therefore, any suspicion, that a philosophical term is employed without any meaning or idea (as is but too frequent), we need but enquire, *from what impression is that supposed idea derived*? And if it be impossible to assign any, this will serve to confirm our suspicion. (*E*, 13)

Every meaningful term, Hume tells us, is associated with an idea. Some terms, however, have no clear idea connected with them. We get used to them and think they mean something, but we are deceived. Hume in fact thinks this happens all too frequently! How can we discover whether a term really means something? Try to trace the associ-

ated idea back to an impression. If you can, it is a meaningful term that expresses a real idea. If you try and fail, then all you have are meaningless noises or nonsensical marks on paper.

Hume has here a powerful critical tool. It seems innocent enough, but Hume makes radical use of it. The rule is a corollary to Hume's Newtonian analysis of the phenomena. It is a result of the theory of ideas.

The Association of Ideas

The results so far constitute the stage of analysis. What we find, on paying close attention to the contents of the human mind, are impressions and ideas, the latter in complete dependence upon the former. Hume now needs to proceed to the stage of synthesis; what are the principles that bind these elements together to produce the rich mental life characteristic of humans? Like Newton, he finds that the great variety of phenomena can be explained by a few principles, surprisingly simple in nature. These are principles of *association,* and they correspond in the science of human nature to universal gravitation in the purely physical realm.

> It is evident that there is a principle of connexion between the different thoughts or ideas of the mind, and that, in their appearance to the memory or imagination, they introduce each other with a certain degree of method and regularity. . . . Were the loosest and freest conversation to be transcribed, there would immediately be observed something, which connected it in all its transitions. Or where this is wanting, the person, who broke the thread of discourse, might still inform you, that there had secretly resolved in his mind a succession of thought, which had gradually led him from the subject of conversation. (*E*, 14)

Whether this observation is correct or not you should be able to test by observing your own trains of thought, or noting how one topic follows another in a conversation you are party to.

If Hume is right here, then the obvious next

---

*Compare Hobbes, p. 336. Hume's theory of the origin of ideas is similar, but without the mechanistic neurological explanation, and also without the assumption that external objects are the cause of our impressions. In trying to stick to the phenomena, Hume considers both these claims to be merely "hypotheses." The perceptions of the mind are our data; beyond them we may not safely go.

question is, What are these principles of association?

> To me, there appear to be only three principles of connexion among ideas, namely *Resemblance, Contiguity* in time or place, and *Cause* or *Effect.*
>
> That these principles serve to connect ideas will not, I believe, be much doubted. A picture naturally leads our thoughts to the original [Resemblance]: The mention of one apartment in a building naturally introduces an enquiry or discourse concerning the others [Contiguity]: And if we think of a wound, we can scarcely forbear reflecting on the pain which follows it [Cause and Effect]. (*E,* 14)

There is some question about whether this list of three principles of association is complete; Hume thinks it probably is and invites you to try to find more if you think otherwise. The world of ideas, then, is governed by the "gentle force" of association. He likens it to "a kind of Attraction, which in the mental world will be found to have as extraordinary effects as in the natural, and to shew itself in as many and as various forms" (*T,* 10, 12–13).

It is important to note that this "gentle force" operates entirely without our consent, will, or even consciousness of it. It is not something in our control, any more than we can control the force of gravity. If Hume is right, it just happens that this is how the mind works. He does not think it possible to go on to explain *why* the mind works the way it does; explanation has to stop somewhere, and, like Newton, he does not "frame hypotheses." But these principles can be "deduced from the phenomena."

Causation: The Very Idea

We now have the fundamental principles of the science of human nature Hume is trying to construct: an analysis into the elements of the mind (impressions and ideas), the relation between them (dependence), and the principles that explain how ideas interact (association). We are now

ready for the exciting part: What happens when this science is applied?

One more distinction will set the stage.

> All the objects of human reason or enquiry may naturally be divided into two kinds, to wit, *Relations of Ideas,* and *Matters of Fact.* Of the first kind are the sciences of Geometry, Algebra, and Arithmetic; and in short, every affirmation, which is either intuitively or demonstratively certain. *That the square of the hypothenuse is equal to the square of the two sides,* is a proposition, which expresses a relation between these figures. *That three times five is equal to the half of thirty,* expresses a relation between these numbers. Propositions of this kind are discoverable by the mere operation of thought, without dependence on what is anywhere existent in the universe. Though there never were a circle or triangle in nature, the truths, demonstrated by Euclid, would forever retain their certainty and evidence.
>
> Matters of fact, which are the second objects of human reason, are not ascertained in the same manner; nor is our evidence of their truth, however great, of a like nature with the foregoing. The contrary of every matter of fact is still possible; because it can never imply a contradiction, and is conceived by the mind with the same facility and distinctness, as if ever so conformable to reality. *That the sun will not rise to-morrow* is no less intelligible a proposition, and implies no more contradiction, than the affirmation, *that it will rise.* We should in vain, therefore, attempt to demonstrate its falsehood. Were it demonstratively false, it would imply a contradiction, and could never be distinctly conceived by the mind. (*E,* 15–16)

The contrast drawn in these paragraphs is an important one. Let's be sure we understand it. Suppose we contrast these two statements:

A: Two plus three is not five.
B: The sun will not rise tomorrow.

Assume that the sun does rise tomorrow. Then both statements are false. But what Hume draws our attention to is that they are *false in different ways. A* is false simply because of the way in which the ideas "two," "plus," "three," "five," and "equals" are related to each other. To put them together as

A does is not just to make a false statement; it is to utter a *contradiction,* to say something that cannot even be clearly conceived. As Hume puts it, we can know it is false "by the mere operation of thought." We do not have to make any experiments or look to our experience. The opposite of *A* can in turn be known to be true, no matter what is "anywhere existent in the universe."

However, we can clearly conceive *B* even though it is false. It is not false because the ideas in it are related the way they are; given the way they are related, it might possibly be true. We can clearly conceive what that would be like: we wake up to total and continuing darkness. Whether *B* is true or false depends on the *facts,* on what actually happens in nature. And to determine its truth or falsity we need to do more than just think about it. We need to consult our experience. The falsity of *B,* Hume says, cannot be *demonstrated.* Reason alone will not suffice to convince us of matters of fact; here only experience will do.

And he suggests one further difference between them: about *A* we can be certain; but with respect to propositions stating matters of fact, our evidence is never great enough to amount to certainty.*

At this point we need to remind ourselves once again that Hume is committed to sticking to the phenomena: the perceptions of the mind, its impressions and ideas. These are the data that need explaining in a science of human nature. But now it is obvious that a question forces itself on us. Is that all we can know about?

We don't usually think so. We talk confidently

of things beyond the reach of our senses and memory—of what's going on in the next room or on the moon, of what happened long before we were born, of a whole world of objects that exist (we think) quite independently of our minds; and many of us think it quite sensible to talk of God and the soul. All this is common sense. And yet it all goes far beyond the narrow bounds of Hume's data. What can we make of this? Or rather, what can Hume make of it? He considers some examples:

* A man believes that his friend is in France. Why? Because he has received a letter from his friend.
* You find a watch on a desert island and conclude that some human being had been there before you.
* You hear a voice in the dark and conclude there is another person in the room.

In each of these cases, where someone claims to know something not present in his perceptions, you will find that a connection is being made by the relation of *cause and effect.* In each case a present impression (reading the letter, seeing the watch, hearing the voice) is *associated* with an idea (of the friend's being in France, of a person's dropping the watch, of someone speaking). And in each case, the idea is an idea of something not present. The way we get beliefs about matters of fact beyond the present testimony of our senses and memory is by relying on our sense of causal relations. The letter is an *effect* of our friend's having written and sent it; the watch was *caused* to be there on the beach by another person; and voices are *produced* by human beings. Or so we believe. It is causation that allows us to reach out beyond the limits of present sensation and memories.

> All reasonings concerning matter of fact seem to be founded on the relation of *Cause and Effect.* By means of that relation alone we can go beyond the evidence of our memory and senses. (*E,* 16)

This seems like progress, though it is hardly very new. Descartes, you will recall, escapes the

---

*Hume is here suggesting a revolutionary understanding of the kind of knowledge we have in mathematics. A contrast with Plato will be instructive. For Plato (see pp. 108–110), mathematics is the clearest case of knowledge we have. Not only is it certain and enduring; it is also the best avenue into acquaintance with absolute reality, for its *objects* are independent of the world of sensory experience—eternal and unchanging Forms. What Hume is suggesting is that mathematics is certain not because it introduces us to such a world of realities, but simply because of how it relates *ideas* to one another. Mathematics *has no objects.* This suggestion undermines in a radical way the entire Platonic picture of reality. It is further developed in this century by Ludwig Wittgenstein and the logical positivists. See pp. 560–561 and 569.

solipsism of having his knowledge limited to his own existence by a causal argument for the existence of God.* But Hume now presses these investigations in a novel direction. How, he asks, do we arrive at the knowledge of cause and effect?

The first part of his answer to this question is a purely negative point. We do not, and cannot, arrive at such knowledge independently of experience, or *a priori* (a term which simply means "independent of experience"). To put this in a now familiar way, our knowledge of causality is not a matter of the *relations of ideas.* Consider two events that are related as cause and effect. To use a typical eighteenth-century example, think about two balls on a billiard table, the cue ball striking the eight ball, causing the eight ball to move. Suppose we know all about the cue ball—its weight, its direction, its momentum—but have never had any experience whatsoever of one thing striking another. Could we predict what would happen when the two balls meet? Not at all. For all we would know, the cue ball might simply stop, reverse its direction, pop straight up in the air, go straight through, or turn into a chicken. Our belief that the effect will be a movement of the second ball is *completely* dependent on our having observed that sort of thing on prior similar occasions. Without that experience, we would be at a total loss.

> No object ever discovers, by the qualities which appear to the senses, either the causes which produced it, or the effects which will arise from it; nor can our reason, unassisted by experience, ever draw any inference concerning real existence and matter of fact. . . . *causes and effects are discoverable, not by reason, but by experience.* (E, 17)

My expectation that the second billiard ball will move when struck is based entirely on *past experience* with balls and similar things. I have seen that sort of thing happen before. This seems entirely reasonable: I make a prediction on the basis of past experience. But if that prediction is reasonable, we

ought to be able to set out the reason for it. Reasons can be given in arguments. Let us try to make the argument explicit.

1. I have seen one ball strike another many times.
2. Each time the ball which was struck has moved. Therefore:
3. The struck ball will move this time.

If we look at the matter this way, however, it is easy to see that (3) does not *follow* from (1) and (2). It seems quite possible that this time something else could happen. To be sure, none of us believes that anything else will happen; but it is precisely this belief, the belief that the first one *causes* the second to move, which needs explanation. Hume is searching for what, if anything, makes this a *rational* thing to believe. This time could be very different from all those past times. The ball *could* fail to move. So the argument is invalid and does not give us a good *reason* to believe that the second ball will move. Can we patch the argument up?

Suppose we add a premise to the argument.

1a. The future will (in the relevant respect) be like the past.

Now the argument looks valid. (1a), (1), and (2) do indeed entail (3). If we know that (1a) is true, then, in the light of our experience summed up in (1) and (2), it is rational to believe that the second billiard ball will move when struck by the first one. We could call (1a) the principle of *the uniformity of nature.*

But how do you know that (1a) is true? Think about that a minute. How *do* you know that the future will be like the past? It is surely not *contradictory* to suppose that the way events hang together might suddenly change; putting the kettle on the fire after today *could* produce ice. So (1a) is not true because of the relation of the ideas in it.* Whether (1a) is true or false must surely be a *matter of fact.* So if we know it, we must know it on the

---

*You might review the argument in *Meditation III,* noting especially the role played by the causal principle that nothing comes from nothing.

---

*You should review the discussion of the distinction between relations of ideas and matters of fact, p. 353.

basis of experience. What experience? If we look back, we can see that the futures we were (at various points) looking forward to always resembled the pasts we were (at those points) recalling. This suggests another argument.

4. I have experienced many pairs of events which have been constantly conjoined in the past.
5. Each time I found that similar pairs of events were constantly conjoined in the future. Therefore:
1a. The future will (in these respects) be like the past.

But it is clear that this argument is no better than the first one; we are trying to justify our general principle (1a) in *exactly* the same way as we tried to justify the expectation that the struck billiard ball would move, (3). If it didn't work the first time, it surely won't work now. The fact that past futures resembled past pasts is simply no good reason to think that future futures will resemble their relevant pasts.

Yet we all think that is so. Don't we? Our practical behavior surely testifies to that belief; we simply have no hesitation in walking about on the third floor of a building, believing that it will support us now just as it always has in the past. We all believe in the uniformity of nature. But why? For what *reason*? Here is Hume's response to that question.

> These two propositions are far from being the same,
> *I have found that such an object has always been attended with such an effect, and*
> *I foresee, that other objects, which are, in appearance, similar, will be attended with similar effects.*
> I shall allow, if you please, that the one proposition may justly be inferred from the other: I know in fact, that it always is inferred. But if you insist, that the inference is made by a chain of reasoning, I desire you to produce that reasoning. The connexion between these propositions is not intuitive. There is required a medium, which may enable the mind to draw such an inference, if indeed it be drawn by reasoning and argument. What that medium is, I must

confess, passes my comprehension; and it is incumbent on those to produce it, who assert, that it really exists, and is the origin of all our conclusions concerning matter of fact. (*E*, 22)

Let us review. Hume is inquiring into the foundation of ideas about things that go far beyond the contents of our present consciousness. These ideas all depend on relations of cause and effect: they are effects caused in us by impressions of some kind. But what is the foundation of these causal inferences? It can only be experience. But now we see that *experience cannot supply a good reason* for believing that my friend is in France—not even my impression that I hold in my hand a letter which seems to have a Paris postmark. There is a gap between the premise and the conclusion; it seems always possible that the premise might be true while the conclusion is false; I might have such a letter even though she is not in France but is taking a holiday in Istanbul. The gap is certainly there; and it seems there is no possible *reason* that can fill that gap. Reason does not seem to be the right "medium" to fill the gap.

And so we have the first part of Hume's answer to the question about what justifies us in believing in so many things independent of our present experience: *not any reason!*

We must be careful here. Hume is not advising us, on that ground, to give up such beliefs; he thinks we could not, even if we wanted to. "Nature will always maintain her rights," he says, "and prevail in the end over any abstract reasoning whatsoever" (*E*, 27). The fact that these beliefs do not rest on any rational foundation is an important result in his science of human nature. And, as we'll see, its philosophical consequences are dramatic. But he acknowledges that these are beliefs living creatures such as ourselves really cannot do without. Our survival depends on them.

If we allow that these beliefs about the world are not rationally based, the next obvious question is this: What is their foundation? Hume suggests a thought experiment.

> Suppose a person, though endowed with the strongest faculties of reason and reflection, to be brought

on a sudden into this world; he would, indeed, immediately observe a continual succession of objects, and one event following another; but he would not be able to discover any thing farther. He would not, at first, by any reasoning, be able to reach the idea of cause and effect; since the particular powers, by which all natural operations are performed, never appear to the senses; nor is it reasonable to conclude, merely because one event, in one instance precedes another, that therefore the one is the cause, the other the effect. Their conjunction may be arbitrary and casual. There may be no reason to infer the existence of one from the appearance of the other. And in a word, such a person, without more experience, could never employ his conjecture or reasoning concerning any matter of fact, or be assured of any thing beyond what was immediately present to his memory and senses.

Suppose again, that he has acquired more experience, and has lived so long in the world as to have observed similar objects or events to be constantly conjoined together; what is the consequence of this experience? He immediately infers the existence of one object from the appearance of the other. (E, 27–28)

This seems plausible. But what is the difference between the first and the second supposition? The only difference is that in the first case the man lacks sufficient experience to notice which events are "constantly conjoined" with each other. But what difference does this difference make? What allows him in the second case to make inferences and have expectations, when he cannot do that in the first case? If it is not a matter of reasoning, then there must be

some other principle, which determines him to form such a conclusion. This principle is CUSTOM or HABIT. (E, 28)

Note carefully what Hume is saying. Our belief that events are related by cause and effect is a completely *nonrational* belief. We have no good reason to think this. So we also have no good reason to think what we do in fact think: that all those things we believe are going on beyond the range of our present impressions and memories really exist. We

do believe these things. We cannot help it. But it is simply by virtue of a kind of natural instinct. That is just how human nature works: when we experience the *constant conjunction* of events, we form a habit of expecting the second when we observe the first. (We can think of Hume's thesis here as an ancestor of the contemporary psychological notion of conditioning.)

Custom, then, is the great guide of human life. It is that principle alone, which renders our experience useful to us, and makes us expect, for the future, a similar train of events with those which have appeared in the past. Without the influence of custom, we should be entirely ignorant of every matter of fact, beyond what is immediately present to the memory and senses. (E, 29)

Hume is here turning upside down the major theme of nearly all philosophy before him. Almost everyone in the philosophical tradition has agreed that a person has a right to believe something only if a good reason can be given for it. This goes back at least to Plato.* The major arguments among the philosophers concern what can (and what cannot) be adequately supported by reason. This commitment to the rationality of belief is most prominent, of course, in a rationalist such as Descartes, who determines to doubt everything that cannot be certified by the "light of reason." The skeptics, on precisely these same grounds, argue that virtually nothing can be known, since virtually nothing can be shown to be reasonable. Hume seems to agree that virtually nothing can be shown to be reasonable; is he, then, a skeptic? We will return to this question.

For now, let us note his conclusion that almost none of our most important beliefs (all of which depend on the relation between cause and effect) can be shown to be rational. We hold them simply out of habit. Our tendency to form beliefs about the external world is just a *fact* about us; this is the way human nature works. Experiencing the constant conjunction of pairs of events leads us to ex-

---

*Review Plato's distinction of knowledge from opinion in terms of the former being "backed up by reasons" (pp. 106–108).

pect the one when we experience the other. Hume does not try to explain *why* human nature functions this way—it just does. We should not try to frame hypotheses!

There is a corollary, which Hume is quick to draw. Sometimes a certain event is *always* conjoined with another event. But in other cases two events are more loosely connected in our experience, so that it is only *often*, or *mostly*, the case that when the one occurs the other also occurs. Water always boils when put on a hot fire, but it only sometimes rains when it is cloudy. These facts are the foundation of *probabilistic* expectations. Our degree of belief corresponds to the degree of connection that our experience reveals between the two events. The more constant the conjunction between event *A* and event *B*, the more probable we think it that a new experience of *A* will be followed by *B*. Again, note that for Hume this is not the result of a rational calculation. We do not *decide* to believe with a particular degree of assurance. It just happens. We *find ourselves* believing those things most confidently which are most regular in our experience. That is how we are made.*

One more fact about our causal beliefs needs to be accounted for. We have seen that they are founded on a habit, or custom, of expecting one event whenever we have observed it to be constantly conjoined with another event. But this does not seem to exhaust the notion of causality. When we say that *X* causes *Y*, we don't just mean that whenever *X* occurs *Y* also occurs. We mean that if *X* occurs, *Y* *must* occur, that *X* *produces* *Y*, that *X* has a certain *power* to bring *Y* into being. In short, we think that in some sense the connection between *X* and *Y* is a *necessary connection*. This is part

of what we mean by the idea of a *cause*. Hume owes us an account of this aspect of the idea.

How can he proceed? The idea of cause is one of those metaphysical ideas we are all familiar with, but whose exact meaning is obscure. Hume has already given us a rule to deal with these cases: try to trace the idea back to an impression. What happens if we try to do that?

Think again about the billiard balls on the table. Try to describe with great care your exact experience when seeing the one strike the other. Isn't it your impression that the cue ball moves across the table, it touches the eight ball, and the eight ball moves? Is there anything else you observe? In particular, do you observe the *force* that *makes* the second ball move? Do you observe the *necessary connection* between them? Hume is convinced that you do not.

> . . . we are never able, in a single instance, to discover any power or necessary connexion; any quality which binds the effect to the cause, and renders the one an infallible consequence of the other. We only find, that the one does actually, in fact, follow the other. . . . Consequently, there is not, in any single, particular instance of cause and effect, any thing which can suggest the idea of power or necessary connexion. (*E*, 41)

Mental phenomena are no different. If I will to move my hand, my hand moves. If I try to recall the first line of "The Star Spangled Banner," I can (usually) do it. But no matter how closely I inspect these operations, all I can observe is one thing being followed by another. I never get an impression of the *connection* between them. All relations of cause and effect must be learned from experience; and experience can show us only "the frequent CONJUNCTION of objects, without being ever able to comprehend any thing like CONNEXION between them" (*E*, 46).

Where then do we get this idea of cause? Is it one of those ideas that is simply meaningless? Should we discard it? Try to do without it? That seems hardly possible. Yet a close inspection of all the data seems to confirm Hume's conclusion:

---

*A qualification needs to be made here. While our degree of confidence in our beliefs is usually governed by this principle, there are exceptions. We can be misled by confusions in our terms, thinking that certain ideas have meaning when they do not. Or we can generalize too soon, on the basis of limited information. These mistakes lead to what Hume calls "superstition." A superstition is usually an erroneous belief, held with too high a degree of confidence, about causes and effects. Think about the bad luck supposedly associated with breaking a mirror or walking under a ladder.

. . . upon the whole, there appears not, throughout all nature, any one instance of connexion, which is conceivable by us. All events seem entirely loose and separate. One event follows another; but we can never observe any tie between them. They seem *conjoined*, but never *connected*. And as we can have no idea of any thing, which never appeared to our outward sense or inward sentiment, the necessary conclusion *seems* to be, that we have no idea of connexion or power at all, and that these words are absolutely without any meaning, when employed either in philosophical reasonings, or common life. (*E*, 49)

"All events seem entirely loose and separate." And the conclusion *seems* to be that we have no idea of cause at all—because there is no corresponding impression. But then it is really puzzling why this idea should be so natural, so pervasive, and so useful. It is an idea we all have, and one we can hardly do without.

This puzzle, Hume thinks, can be solved. He can explain why we have this idea. To understand this explanation, we have to go back to the fact that exposure to constant conjunctions of events builds up an associationistic *habit* of expecting one event on the appearance of the other. This habit is the key to understanding the concept of a cause.

> . . . after a repetition of similar instances, the mind is carried by habit, upon the appearance of one event, to expect its usual attendant, and to believe that it will exist. This connexion, therefore, which we *feel* in the mind, this customary transition of the imagination from one object to its usual attendant, is the sentiment or impression, from which we form the idea of power or necessary connexion. . . . When we say, therefore, that one object is connected with another, we mean only, that they have acquired a connexion in our thought, and give rise to this inference, by which they become proofs of each other's existence. (*E*, 50–51)

Hume is able, in this way, to give a certain legitimacy to the concept of cause. In fact he ventures to give a *definition* of a cause. A cause, he says, is

> an object, followed by another, and where all the objects, similar to the first, are followed by objects similar to the second. Or in other words, *where, if the first object had not been, the second never had existed*. (*E*, 51)

And there is a second definition equivalent to that which mentions our experience of the constant conjunction involved:

> an object followed by another, and whose appearance always conveys the thought to that other. (*E*, 51)

In this way Hume explains why causation is a natural, universally shared concept among humans by giving us an account of how it arises: we all *feel* this tendency to expect a second event when we experience a first one, provided they have been uniformly connected in our past experience. And this feeling *in the mind* is the impression that gives rise to the idea of a necessary causal connection.

Although the concept is explained and we can understand how humans naturally come to have it, the concept itself is a *fiction*. We cannot help applying it to observed events, but nothing in our observation of those events *ever* gives us a warrant for so applying it.

Remember that the relation of cause and effect is the foundation of all our beliefs about matters beyond immediate consciousness. It follows that the entire world of common sense (and science, too) is a *construction*—one *without any reason behind it*. If knowledge is belief based on reason, there is precious little we can claim to know! The confidence of Descartes and Hobbes (in their different ways) that we have good reason to think modern science tells us the truth about reality seems very naive. And the major philosophical tradition since Plato and Aristotle, one dedicated to finding what is reasonable to believe, is shown to be built on sand. What do we have *reason* to believe about the nature of reality? Virtually nothing.

Again we should ask, Is this just skepticism all over again—this time on the foundation of an attempt to construct a science of human nature? But again, let us put off the question.

The Disappearing Self

Philosophers since Plato have struggled with the question about the nature of human beings. This metaphysical problem is puzzling and difficult because the phenomena of mind—consciousness, thinking, feeling, willing, deciding to act—seem to be so different from nonmental phenomena—size, motion, weight, inertia. Plato argues that a person is really an entity distinct from the body, a *soul;* residence in a body is a temporary state, and the soul survives the body's death. The tradition in the West generally follows him, though there are dissenters. The atomists and Epicureans think of the soul as material and mortal; Aristotle holds (with qualifications) that the soul is a functional aspect of a living body; the skeptics, of course, suspend judgment on the whole question.

In modern times, Descartes follows the lead of Plato, holding not only that the soul or mind is a distinct substance and immortal, but also that it is better known than any body could be. Hobbes, by contrast, interprets human beings in a thoroughly materialistic way. The issue is certainly not settled before the age of Enlightenment.*

Hume can hardly avoid dealing with the problem, since he claims to be constructing a science of human nature. The first thing we need to do, to the extent possible, is to clarify the meaning of the central term. What Plato called "soul" and Descartes the "mind," Hume names the "self." A self is supposedly a substance or thing, simple (not composed of parts), and invariably the same through time. It is the "home" for all our mental states and activities, the "place" where these characteristics are "located." (The terms in quote marks are, of course, used metaphorically.) My self is what is supposed to account for the fact that I am one and the same person today as I was at the age of four, even though nearly all my characteristics have changed over the years. I am larger, stronger and

---

*Discussions of these various doctrines can be found as follows: Plato, pp. 128–130; Aristotle, pp. 168–170; atomism, pp. 31–32; Descartes in *Meditation VI;* and Hobbes on pp. 335–336.

smarter; I have different hopes and fears, different thoughts and memories; my interests and activities are remarkably different. Yet I am the *same self.* The thing that I most deeply am has not changed. This selfsame, identical thing—this is *I.* Or so the story goes.

It is clear what Hume will ask here. Remember his rule: If there is a term which is in any way obscure, or about which there is much controversy, try to trace it back to an impression.

> . . . from what impression cou'd this idea be derived? This question 'tis impossible to answer without a manifest contradiction and absurdity; and yet 'tis a question, which must necessarily be answer'd, if we wou'd have the idea of self pass for clear and intelligible. It must be some one impression, that gives rise to every real idea. But self or person is not any one impression, but that to which our several impressions and ideas are suppos'd to have a reference. If any impression gives rise to the idea of self, that impression must continue invariably the same, thro' the whole course of our lives; since self is suppos'd to exist after that manner. But there is no impression constant and invariable. (*T,* 251)

Let us be clear about the argument here. The term "self" is supposed to represent an idea of something that continues unchanged throughout a person's life. Since the idea is supposed to be a simple one, there must be a simple impression that is its "double." But there is no such impression, Hume claims, "constant and invariable" through life. It follows, according to Hume's rule, that *we have no such idea!* The term is one of those meaningless noises that we suppose (through inattention or confusion) means something, when it really doesn't.

This is a most radical way of undermining belief in the soul or self. Some philosophers claim to have such an idea and to be able to prove the self really exists. Others claim to be able to prove that it doesn't exist. But Hume undercuts both sides; they are just arguing about words, he holds, because neither side really knows what it is talking about. Literally! There simply is no such idea as the (supposed) idea of the self. So it doesn't make sense either to affirm it *or* to deny it.

This claim, of course, rests on the theory of ideas. It is only as strong as that theory is good. Is that a good theory? This is an important question; we will meet other philosophers who investigate this question.* But for now, let us explore in a bit more depth why Hume thinks there is no impression that corresponds to the (supposed) idea of the self. In a much-quoted passage, Hume says,

> For my part, when I enter most intimately into what I call *myself*, I always stumble on some particular perception or other, of heat or cold, light or shade, love or hatred, pain or pleasure. I never can catch *myself* at any time without a perception, and never can observe any thing but the perception. When my perceptions are remov'd for any time, as by a sound sleep; so long am I insensible of *myself*, and may truly be said not to exist. And were all my perceptions remov'd by death, and cou'd I neither think, nor feel, nor see, nor love, nor hate after the dissolution of my body, I shou'd be entirely annihilated, nor do I conceive what is farther requisite to make me a perfect non-entity. If any one upon serious and unprejudic'd reflexion, thinks he has a different notion of *himself*, I must confess I can reason no longer with him. All I can allow him is, that he may be in the right as well as I, and that we are essentially different in this particular. He may, perhaps, perceive something simple and continu'd, which he calls *himself*; tho' I am certain there is no such principle in me. (*T,* 252)

Again, Hume tries to pay close attention to the phenomena and tries not to frame hypotheses that go beyond them. If we look inside ourselves, do we find an impression of something simple, unchanging and continuing? He confesses that *he* can find no such impression; his suggestion that maybe *you* can, that maybe *you* are "essentially different" in this regard is surely ironic. His claim is

that none of us ever finds more in ourselves than fleeting perceptions—ideas, sensations, feelings, and emotions.

So we have no reason to suppose that we are selves, or minds, or souls, if we understand those terms to refer to some simple substance that underlies all our particular perceptions. But what, then, are we? If we set aside any of us that are, perhaps, "essentially different," here is Hume's answer:

> . . . I may venture to affirm of the rest of mankind, that they are nothing but a bundle or collection of different perceptions, which succeed each other with an inconceivable rapidity, and are in a perpetual flux and movement. . . . The mind is a kind of theatre, where several perceptions successively make their appearance; pass, re-pass, glide away, and mingle in an infinite variety of postures and situations. There is properly no *simplicity* in it at any one time, nor *identity* in different; whatever natural propensity we may have to imagine that simplicity and identity. The comparison of the theatre must not mislead us. They are the successive perceptions only, that constitute the mind; nor have we the most distant notion of the place, where these scenes are represented, or of the materials, of which it is compos'd. (*T,* 252–53)

The idea of self, like the idea of cause, is natural and inevitable. But, like the idea of cause, it too is a fiction. As selves or minds, we are nothing but a "bundle" of perceptions. Anything further is sheer, unsupported hypothesis. We have not only no reason to believe in a world of "external" things independent of our minds, but also no reason to believe in mind as a thing.*

In thinking of ourselves, Hume suggests, the analogy of a theater is appropriate. In this theater, an amazingly intricate and complex play is being performed. The players are just all those varied perceptions that succeed each other, as Hume says, with "inconceivable rapidity." But if we are to understand the analogy correctly, we must think

---

*Kant, for instance, denies a key premise of the theory of ideas: that all our ideas (Kant calls them "concepts") arise from impressions. Some of our concepts, Kant claims, do not *arise out of* experience, though they may *apply to* experience. See pp. 377–378 and 384–385.

---

*This "bundle theory" of the self is remarkably like the Buddha's view of the self.

away the walls of the theater, think away the stage, think away the seats and even the audience. What is left is just the performance of the play. Such a performance each of us *is*.

But what distinguishes one performance from another—the bundle of perceptions that I am from the bundle that you are? We might think that my bundle is distinguished from others by the fact that it is associated with my body. But this can't be the right answer, in Hume's terms. My awareness of my body is through an impression or idea. So the question arises for that impression or idea too: What makes *that* perception one of mine? Hume's answer is that personal identity must be a matter of the *relations between* the perceptions I call mine. But since Hume himself is never satisfied with his answer, we won't discuss it in detail.

However, we do need to see how the bundle theory of the self bears on Descartes' *cogito:* "I think, therefore I am." Descartes takes this as something each of us knows with certainty. And in answer to the question, "What, then, am I?" he says, "I am a thing (a substance) that thinks." Hume is in effect saying that Descartes is going beyond what the phenomena reveal. A twentieth-century Humean, Bertrand Russell, puts it this way: The most that Descartes is entitled to claim is that there is thinking going on. To claim that there is a mind or self—a thing—doing the thinking is to frame a hypothesis, to go beyond the evidence available.[7] If this criticism is correct, it clearly undermines Descartes' dualistic metaphysics; we cannot know that the mind is a substance distinct from the body because we cannot know it is a substance at all! All we have is acquaintance with that bundle of perceptions.

Rescuing Human Freedom

Another topic a science of human nature must address is whether human actions are in some sense *free*. This question takes on a new urgency with the adoption of the mechanistic physical theories of Galileo and Newton. As long as the entire world is conceived in Aristotelian terms, where a key mode of explanation is teleological,* the question of freedom is not pressing. If *everything* acted for the sake of some end, pursuing its good in whatever way its nature allowed, human actions would seem to fit the general pattern of explanation neatly. Humans simply have more alternatives available than do petunias and snails and have to use their reason to make choices between the available goods. But the pattern of explanation is common to all things.

In the mid eighteenth century, however, the situation is quite different. Explanation in terms of ends or goals has been banished; explanation by prior causes is "in." The model of the universe is mechanical; the world is compared to a gigantic clock. Stones do not fall *in order to* reach a goal (their natural place); and oak trees do not grow because of a *striving* to realize the potentiality in them. Everything happens as it *must happen,* according to laws that make no reference to any end, goal, or good. Every movement takes place with the same inexorability as we find in the hands of a clock.

What about human actions in a world like this? Are they as strictly determined by law and circumstance as the fall of the stone? In the context of the new science, this question gains a new poignancy. How are we to think of our lives, now that we think of everything else in this mechanical way? The view that human actions constitute no exception to the universal rule of causal law is known as **determinism.** The successes of modern science give it plausibility. But it seems to clash with a deeply held conviction that sometimes we are *free* to choose, will, and act.

Descartes shows us one way to deal with this problem: Make an exception for human beings! Mechanical principles might govern material bodies, but they can get no leverage on a nonmaterial mind. The will, Descartes says, is completely free;

---

* An explanation is teleological if it makes essential reference to the realization of a goal or end state. Aristotle's discussion of "final causes" provides a good case study (see pp. 159–160).

even the will of God could not conceivably be more free than the human will. And by "free" he means "not governed by causal laws."

But Hume cannot take this way. For he is convinced we have no idea of a substantial self; and so we can have no reason to think such a nonmaterial mind or soul exists. Hume's solution to this puzzle is quite different from Descartes', and it is justly famous. Its basic pattern is defended by numerous philosophers (but not all) even today.

He begins by asserting that "all mankind" is and always has been of the same opinion about this matter. Any controversy is simply due to "ambiguous expressions" used to frame the problem. In other words, if we can get our terms straight, we should be able to settle the matter to everyone's satisfaction. What we need is a set of *definitions* for what Hume calls "necessity" on the one hand and "liberty" on the other.

> I hope, therefore, to make it appear, that all men have ever agreed in the doctrine both of necessity and of liberty, according to any reasonable sense, which can be put on these terms; and that the whole controversy has hitherto turned merely upon words. (*E,* 54)

We already know what Hume says about *necessity.* The idea of necessity is part of our idea of a cause but is a kind of fiction. It arises, not from impressions, but from that habit our minds develop when confronted with regular conjunctions between events. All we ever observe, when we believe that one event causes another, is the constant conjunction of events of the first kind with events of the second.

Are human actions caused? If we understand this as Hume thinks we must, we are simply asking whether there are *regularities* detectable in human behavior. And he thinks we all must admit that there are. He gives some examples (*E,* 55–61):

- Motives are regularly conjoined to actions: greed regularly leads to stealing, ambition to the quest for power.

- My actions are carried out in a context where I count on being able to predict yours; I depend on the regularity of your behavior.
- If a foreigner acts in unexpected ways, there is always a cause—some condition (education, perhaps) that regularly produces this behavior.
- Where we are surprised by someone's action, a careful examination always turns up some unknown condition that allows it to be fit again into a regular pattern.

If all that we can possibly mean by "caused" is that events are regularly connected, we should all agree that human behavior is caused. Why do some of us resist this conclusion? Because, Hume says,

> men still entertain a strong propensity to believe, that they penetrate farther into the powers of nature, and perceive something like a necessary connexion between the cause and the effect. When again they turn their reflections towards the operations of their own minds, and *feel* no such connexion of the motive and the action; they are thence apt to suppose, that there is a difference between the effects, which result from material force, and those which arise from thought and intelligence. (*E,* 61)

But this is just a confusion! In neither case, material or intelligent, is there any *constraint* observed. And Hume's account of causality has made that clear. Causality on the side of the objects observed is just regularity; on the side of the observer, it is the setting up of a habit or custom on the basis of those regularities. Causality and its accompanying fiction, necessity, apply as much to the mind (when considered as an object of reflection) as to the physical world.

What then of freedom or liberty?

> . . . it will not require many words to prove, that all mankind have ever agreed in the doctrine of liberty as well as in that of necessity, and that the whole dispute, in this respect also, has been hitherto merely verbal. For what is meant by liberty, when applied to voluntary actions? We cannot surely mean, that ac-

tions have so little connexion with motives, inclinations, and circumstances, that one does not follow with a certain degree of uniformity from the other, and that one affords no inference by which we can conclude the existence of the other. For these are plain and acknowledged matters of fact. By liberty, then, we can only mean a *power of acting or not acting, according to the determinations of the will;* that is, if we choose to remain at rest, we may; if we choose to move, we also may. Now this hypothetical liberty is universally allowed to belong to everyone, who is not a prisoner and in chains. (*E,* 63)

This requires some comment. Perhaps the most accessible way to understand Hume's point is to think of cases where a person is said to be *unfree.* Hume's example is that of a man in chains. What is it that makes this a case of unfreedom? Isn't it just this: that he cannot do what he *wants* to do? Even if he *yearns* to walk away, *wills* to walk away, *tries* to walk away, he will *be unable* to walk away. He is unfree because his actions are *constrained—* against his will, as we say.

Suppose we remove his chains. Then he is free, at liberty to do what he wants. And isn't this the very essence of freedom: to be able to do whatever it is that you want or choose to do? We could put this more formally in the following way:

A person *P* is *free* when the following condition is satisfied: *If P chooses to do action A, then P does A.*

If this condition were *not* satisfied (if *P* should choose to do *A,* but be *unable* to do it) then *P* would *not be at liberty* with respect to *A.*

Now we can see what Hume is up to. He wants to show us that it is possible to *reconcile* our belief in causality (or necessity) with our belief in human freedom. We do not have to choose between them. We can have both modern science and human freedom. Newtonian science and freedom to act would clash only if freedom entailed exemption from causality. But causes are simply regularities; and freedom is not an absence of regularity, but the "hypothetical" power to do something *if* we choose to do it. It is, in fact, a certain kind of regularity. It is the regularity of having the actions we

choose to do follow regularly upon our choosing to do them.

There is no reason, then, in human liberty, to deny that a science of human nature—a causal science of a Newtonian kind—is possible. And Newtonian, mechanistic science is no reason to deny or doubt human freedom. In particular, human freedom gives us no reason to postulate a Cartesian mind, quite independent in its substance and operations of the basic laws of the universe. Hume's **compatibilism,** as it is sometimes called, is an important part of a kind of **naturalism,** a view that takes the human being to be a natural fact, without remainder.

Is It Reasonable to Believe in God?

After doubting everything doubtable, Descartes finds himself locked into solipsism—unless he can demonstrate that he is not the only thing that exists. The way he does this, you recall, is to try to demonstrate the existence of God. He looks, in other words, for a good reason to believe that something other than his own mind exists. If he can prove that God exists, he knows he is not alone; and, God being what God is, he will have good reason to trust at least what is clear and distinct about other things as well. Thus everything hangs, for Descartes, on whether it is reasonable to believe that there is a God.*

What does Hume say about this quest to show that belief in God is more reasonable than disbelief? We will review briefly two of the arguments Descartes presents, together with a Humean response to each, and then look at a rather different argument that was proving very popular in the atmosphere after Newton.

Descartes' first argument, you will recall, begins

---

* Earlier thinkers, too, from Aristotle on, think they can give good reasons for concluding that some ultimate perfection exists and is in one way or another responsible for all other things. Review the proofs given by Augustine (pp. 222–223), Anselm (pp. 252–256), and Aquinas (pp. 258–263). The arguments of Descartes are in *Meditations III* and *V.*

from the fact that we have an idea of God—an idea of an infinite and perfect being. Descartes argues roughly in the following way:

1. Such an idea requires a cause.
2. The cause must be equal in "formal" reality to the "subjective" reality of the idea.
3. I myself could not possibly be the cause.
4. The only plausible alternative cause is God himself. Therefore:
5. God exists.

Where could Hume attack this argument? Consider premise 3. This premise concerns the *origin* of a certain idea. As we have seen, Hume has a theory about the origin of ideas: Each and every one stems from some impression. Can Hume show that there is an impression which could be the origin of the idea of God?

> Even those ideas, which, at first view, seem the most wide of this origin, are found, upon a nearer scrutiny, to be derived from it. The idea of God, as meaning an infinitely intelligent, wise, and good Being, arises from reflecting on the operations of our own mind, and augmenting, without limit, those qualities of goodness and wisdom. (*E,* 11)

The idea of God, Hume says, also has its origin in impressions. We reflect on ourselves and find impressions of intelligence and a certain degree of goodness. Not perfect intelligence or complete goodness, of course. But we also have, from our impressions, the ideas of more and less. If we combine the idea of more with the ideas of intelligence and goodness, we get the idea of a being more intelligent and good than we are. We can reiterate this operation, over and over again, until we get the idea of a being that is perfectly intelligent and completely good. And this is the idea of God.*

If Hume is correct, you can see that he has undercut one of the premises Descartes uses in his first argument. He *can* be the origin of his idea

---

*Descartes foresees this line of argument and tries to block it. See his discussion in *Meditation III,* p. 319.

of God, contrary to premise 3. Since the argument absolutely depends on the correctness of that premise, it no longer can give us a good reason to believe in God.

Think about Descartes' third argument, which goes something like this:

1. You cannot think of God without thinking that God exists, any more than you can think of a mountain without a valley or a triangle without three sides.
2. You do have the thought of God.
3. You must, therefore, think (believe) that God exists. Therefore:
4. God exists.

The first premise states a set of relations between ideas we have. The idea of a mountain necessarily involves the idea of a valley (or at least of a plain). In the same way, Descartes says, you cannot have the idea of God without also having the idea that he exists. You should remember, however, that Hume has drawn a sharp contrast between *relations of ideas* on the one hand and *matters of fact* on the other. Propositions concerning the relations of ideas, he holds, are independent in their truth value of "what is anywhere existent in the universe." It may be that thinking of God entails thinking that he exists; but that concerns only how those *ideas* are related to each other. It has nothing whatever to do with whether God *in fact* exists. Yet it is the latter that Descartes is vitally concerned with; unless God exists *in fact,* he is stuck in solipsism. Likewise, it is this question that we, believers and nonbelievers alike, are interested in. Does God *in fact* exist? Simply pointing out that one thought involves another does not answer that question—even if one of the thoughts is the thought of God's existence.

If we analyze the argument this way, it may be quite correct through step 3. But the transition from step 3 to step 4 is illegitimate; for a relation among ideas—even a necessary relation—gets no grip on how things actually are in the world. If it did, then the truth of matters of fact could be discovered "by the mere operation of thought." And that cannot be done, Hume is convinced, because "the contrary of every matter of fact is still possible" (*E*, 15–16). In the realm of fact, it is just as possible that God does not exist as that God does exist—no matter how the ideas are logically related in our scheme of ideas. If it is God's existence as a matter of *fact* that we are interested in (and surely it is), then logical proof moving only within the realm of our ideas will not get us there. Belief in God's existence cannot be made reasonable, then, simply by considering the idea of God. Relations of ideas can't be used to prove matters of fact. About matters of fact we must consult *experience*.

The most popular argument for God during the Enlightenment, among common folk and intellectuals alike, does begin from experience. It can be called the *argument from design*. If there had ever been suspicions that the universe was not a perfectly ordered, magnificently integrated piece of work, Newton's work sets such suspicions at rest. The image of a great machine, or clockwork, dominates eighteenth-century thought about the nature of the world. And it suggests a powerful analogy. Just as machines (and clocks in particular) are the effects of intelligent design and workmanship, so the universe is the work of a master craftsman, supremely intelligent and wonderfully skilled. Machines don't just happen. And neither does the world.

In a set of dialogues that Hume did not venture to publish during his lifetime, one of the participants sets out the argument:

Look round the world: Contemplate the whole and every part of it: You will find it to be nothing but one great machine, subdivided into an infinite number of lesser machines, which again admit of subdivisions to a degree beyond what human senses and faculties can trace and explain. All these various machines, and even their most minute parts, are adjusted to each other with an accuracy which ravishes into admiration all men who have ever contemplated them. The curious adapting of means to ends, throughout all nature, resembles exactly, though it much exceeds, the productions of human contrivance; of human design, thought, wisdom, and intelligence. Since therefore the effects resemble each other, we are led to infer, by all the rules of analogy, that the causes also resemble, and that the Author of Nature is somewhat similar to the mind of man, though possessed of much larger faculties, proportioned to the grandeur of the work which he has executed. By this argument *a posteriori*, and by this argument alone, do we prove at once the existence of a Deity and his similarity to human mind and intelligence. (*D*, 15)

Before considering Hume's appraisal of this argument, let us note several points. It is an argument, Hume says, **a posteriori**; that is, it is an argument that depends in an essential way upon experience. Our experience of the world as an ordered and harmonious whole provides one crucial premise; our experience of how machines come into being provides another. Note also that it is an argument *by analogy*. Its structure looks like this (*M* = a machine; *I* = intelligence; *W* = the world):

1. *M* is the effect of *I*.
2. *W* is like *M*. Therefore:
3. *W* is the effect of something like *I*.

Finally, you should recognize that this, like Descartes' first two arguments, is a *causal* argument. Both the first premise and the conclusion deal with causal relations.

Hume says many interesting things about this argument, partly through his spokesmen in the dialogue. Here we'll be brief, simply listing a number of the points he makes.

1. No argument from experience ever can establish a certainty. The most that experience can yield is a certain probability (since experience is always limited and cannot testify to what is beyond its limits). So even if the argument is a good one (of its kind), it does not give us more than a probability that the "Author of Nature" is analogous to the human.

2. There is a sound principle to be observed in all causal arguments: that "the cause must be proportioned to the effect."

A body of ten ounces raised in any scale may serve as a proof, that the counterbalancing weight exceeds ten ounces; but can never afford a reason that it exceeds a hundred. . . . If the cause be known only by the effect, we never ought to ascribe to it any qualities, beyond what are precisely requisite to produce the effect. (*E*, 94)

If we look around at the world, can we say that it is perfectly good? That is hard to believe. If we think of this proof as an attempt to demonstrate the existence of God as he is traditionally conceived—infinite in wisdom and goodness—it surely falls short. For the proportion of goodness we are *justified* in ascribing to the cause (God) cannot far exceed the proportion of goodness (in the world) that needs to be explained.

3.   The analogy is supposed to exist between the productions of intelligent human beings and the world as an effect of a supremely intelligent designer. But a number of consequences follow if we take the analogy seriously.

- Many people cooperate to make a machine; by analogy, the world may have been created through the cooperation of many gods.
- Wicked and mischievous people may create technological marvels; by analogy, the creator(s) of the world may be wicked and mischievous.
- Machines are made by mortals; by analogy, may not the gods be mortal?
- The best clocks are a result of a long history of slow improvements; by analogy,

Many worlds might have been botched and bungled, throughout an eternity, ere this system was struck out; much labor lost; many fruitless trials made; and a slow but continued improvement carried on during infinite ages in the art of world-making. (*D*, 36)

The point here is not that any of these possibilities is likely but that analogies always have resemblances in certain respects and differences in others. How do we know which are the similarities in this case and which are the differences? Unless we have some principle to make this distinction, any one of these conclusions is as justified as the one theists wish to draw.

4.   Finally, we have to ask what we can learn from a single case. Here Hume applies his analysis of the idea of causality to the case of the cause of the world.

It is only when two *species* of objects are found to be constantly conjoined, that we can infer the one from the other; and were an effect presented, which was entirely singular, and could not be comprehended under any known *species*, I do not see, that we could form any conjecture or inference at all concerning its cause. If experience and observation and analogy be, indeed, the only guides which we can reasonably follow in inferences of this nature; both the effect and cause must bear a similarity and resemblance to other effects and causes, which we know, and which we have found, in many instances, to be conjoined with each other. (*E*, 101–2)

There is one respect in which this universe is entirely *unlike* the clocks and automobiles and stereos of our experience: it is, in our experience, "entirely singular." We can infer that the cause of a new stereo is some intelligent human because we have had past experience of the constant conjunction of stereos and intelligent designers. In this case, we have had experience of instances of *both* the effects *and* the causes. To apply this kind of analogical reasoning to the universe, we would need past experience of the making of worlds; and in our experience of each making, there would have to have been a conjoined experience of an intelligent being. On the basis of such a constant conjunction, we could infer justly that this world, too, is the effect of intelligence. But since the universe is, in our experience, "entirely singular," we can make no such inference. These, and more, are the difficulties Hume finds in the design argument.

You can see that according to Hume's principles *any* causal argument for God is subject to this last criticism. But now we are in a position to see that our situation is much worse than we ever imagined. These reflections not only undercut causal arguments for God's existence, but also undermine all causal arguments for the existence of *anything at all* beyond our own impressions! For causal judgments are always founded on experience—and that means on the constant conjunction *within our experience* of pairs of events. To judge that some extra-mental object is the cause of some experience, we would need to be able to observe a constant conjunction of that perception with its extra-mental cause. To do that we would need to jump out of our own skins, to observe the perceptions in our minds from outside, and compare them with the external things correlated with them. And that is something we surely cannot do.

Descartes thinks we need to prove the existence of God in order to ground our belief that the material world (described by his physics) is more than merely a set of ideas. His argument involves the claim that God is the (extra-mental) cause of an idea he has. But if Hume is right about the origin of the concept of causality *within* experience, we could never have the evidence required to validate this claim. All we can do is relate perceptions to perceptions. And if Descartes is right that without *good reason* to believe in God we are caught within the web of our own ideas, then solipsism seems (rationally) inescapable.* A dismal and melancholy conclusion.

After reviewing these attempts to make belief in God reasonable, it seems that this must be our conclusion: We have so far not found good reason to believe in God. Now we must add that neither have we found good reason to believe in the existence of a material world independent of our perceptions. We can think of this as a radical consequence of the representational theory (p. 300). Hume shows us that if we begin from ideas in the mind, there is no way to build that bridge to the world beyond.

This is not, however, Hume's last word on the subject of religion. In a passage that has puzzled many commentators, one of Hume's characters goes on to say:

> A person, seasoned with a just sense of the imperfections of natural reason, will fly to revealed truth with the greatest avidity: While the haughty dogmatist, persuaded that he can erect a complete system of theology by the mere help of philosophy, disdains any further aid and rejects this adventitious instructor. To be a philosophical skeptic is, in a man of letters, the first and most essential step towards being a sound, believing *Christian.* (D, 89)

What can we make of this? Is Hume serious here? Or, more importantly, is this a serious possibility, this combination of religious faith and philosophical skepticism? What would this be like?*

Understanding Morality

You and I find ourselves making judgments like this: "That was a bad thing Jones did," "Smith is a good person," "Telling the truth is the right thing to do," and "Justice is a virtue." You see twenty dollars on a desk in a room down the hall; no one is around, and you could pick it up; you say to yourself, "That would be wrong," and walk away. Such "moral" judgments are very important to us, both as evaluations of the actions of others and as guides to our own behavior. They are no less important to society. A science of human nature ought to have something to say about this feature of human life, so Hume tries to understand our propensity to make judgments of this kind. As we might anticipate by now, he puts his question this way: Are these judgments founded in some way on reason? Or do they have some other origin?

Reason Is Not a Motivator

> Nothing is more usual in philosophy, and even in common life, than to talk of the combat of passion and reason, to give the preference to reason, and to assert that men are only so far virtuous as they conform themselves to its dictates. Every rational creature, 'tis said, is oblig'd to regulate his actions by reason; and if any other motive or principle challenge the direction of his conduct, he ought to oppose it, 'till it be entirely subdu'd, or at least brought to a conformity with that superior principle. . . . In order to shew the fallacy of all this philosophy, I shall endeavour to prove *first,* that reason alone can never be a motive to any action of the will; and *secondly,* that it can never oppose passion in the direction of the will. (T, 413)

---

*Solipsism is explained on p. 304.

*Fideism, as this view is sometimes called, is explored in the work of Søren Kierkegaard. See "The Religious," in Chapter 20.

Hume's claim that "reason alone" can never motivate any action has clear moral implications. For moral considerations can be motivators. We sometimes refrain from taking something that belongs to another person, not because we are afraid of the consequences, but simply because we judge that it would be *wrong* to do so. Morality is a practical matter. It has implications for what we *do*. If reason alone cannot motivate an action, it seems to follow that morality cannot be a matter of reason alone.

But what does this mean, that reason alone can neither motivate an action nor oppose passion (e.g., desire or inclination)? Recall Hume's claim that "all the objects of human reason or enquiry may naturally be divided into two kinds, to wit, *Relations of Ideas* and *Matters of Fact*" (*E*, 15). If reason is going to motivate action, it must do so in one of these two ways. Let us examine each possibility.

Consider adding up a sum, which Hume takes to be a matter of the relations of ideas. Suppose I am totaling up what I owe to my dentist, Dr. Payne. Will this reasoning lead to any action? Not by itself, says Hume. If I *want* to pay Payne what I owe her, this reasoning will contribute to what I do: I will pay her the total and not some other amount. But in the absence of that (or another) want, the reasoning alone will not produce an action. The motivator is the want; and a want is what Hume calls a *passion*.

Consider next these examples of reasoning about matters of fact:

> Ask a man *why he uses exercise;* he will answer *because he desires to keep his health.* If you then enquire *why he desires health,* he will readily reply *because sickness is painful.* If you push your enquiries further and desire a reason *why he hates pain,* it is impossible he can ever give any. This is an ultimate end, and is never referred to any object.
>
> Perhaps to your second question, *why he desires health,* he may also reply that *it is necessary for the exercise of his calling.* If you ask *why he is anxious on that head,* he will answer, *because he desires to get money.* If you demand why? *It is the instrument of pleasure,* says he. And beyond this it is an absurdity

to ask for a reason. It is impossible there can be a progress *in infinitum;* and that one thing can always be a reason why another is desired. Something must be desirable on its own account, and because of its immediate accord or agreement with human sentiment and affection. (*PM*, 268–69)

Here we have reasoning about matters of fact; it is a matter of fact that exercise is conducive to health, that health is required to pursue a profession successfully, and so on. But mere knowledge of these matters of fact will not motivate action unless one cares about the end to which they lead. And this caring is not itself a matter of reason. It is a matter of *sentiment* or *passion*. Hume draws the conclusion:

> It appears evident that the ultimate ends of human actions can never, in any case, be accounted for by *reason*, but recommend themselves entirely to the sentiments and affections of mankind, without any dependence on the intellectual faculties. (*PM*, 268)

So reason alone can never motivate us to action. But Hume goes even further; he claims that reason can never oppose passion. One passion can oppose another. For example, as I contemplate the roller coaster ride, fear fights with the desire for thrills. Likewise, one rational proposition can be opposed to another when they are contradictories. But for reason to oppose passion, it would have to be a motivator in itself; and Hume argues that it is not. Reason, we might say, is *inert*.

> We speak not strictly and philosophically when we talk of the combat of passion and of reason. Reason is, and ought only to be the slave of the passions, and can never pretend to any other office than to serve and obey them. (*T*, 415)

Reason can instruct us how to satisfy our desires, but it cannot tell us what desires to have.* Reason

---

*You might think there is an obvious exception: Can't reason tell me that it would be better for me if I didn't have this desire to smoke cigarettes? And isn't this a case of reason opposing a desire I have? What would Hume say?

can only be the "slave" of the passions. In a few dramatic sentences, Hume drives this point home.

> Where a passion is neither founded on false suppositions, nor chuses means insufficient for the end, the understanding can neither justify nor condemn it. 'Tis not contrary to reason to prefer the destruction of the whole world to the scratching of my finger. (T, 416)

What would Plato have said about this?* Plato's idea that reason can grasp the Good, and therefore should *rule* the passions, simply misses the point if Hume is right here. Reason is motivationally impotent; it cannot rule. Its role is that of a slave! The master says, "I want that," and it is the job of the slave to figure out how it can be got. The slave deals with *means*. Reason has an important place in action, since if we calculate wrong or make a mistake about the facts, we will be likely to miss our ends. But those ends are dictated by the non-rational part of our nature, the wants and desires, the passions and sentiments, that are simply given with that nature. If I truly prefer the destruction of the world to the scratching of my finger, reason cannot oppose me. There is nothing *irrational* about that.

The Origins of Moral Judgment

What, then, of morality, which is supposed to govern human actions? It is clear that if moral judgments are to have any effect on actions, they cannot be purely rational judgments. They must be the expression of passions of some sort. This is just what Hume claims.

Let us again consider the two possible classes of things subject to reason. Could morality be simply a matter of the relations between ideas? It is plausible to think that there is a conceptual relation between the ideas of murder and wrong. All murder is wrong—because what "murder" means is "wrongful killing." So the connection in this case *is*

a matter of relations of ideas. But this can hardly be all that is involved in morality, because morality is supposed to be applied to the facts. Just pointing out that murder involves the idea of wrongful killing is no help at all when we are asking of a certain action: is this murder—that is, is this a wrongful killing? So morality, if it is going to have any practical effects, cannot be merely a matter of the relations between ideas.

Can morality be a matter of fact (the second province of reason)?

> Take any action allow'd to be vicious: Wilful murder, for instance. Examine it in all lights, and see if you can find that matter of fact, or real existence, which you call *vice*. In whichever way you take it, you find only certain passions, motives, volitions and thoughts. There is no other matter of fact in the case. The vice entirely escapes you, as long as you consider the object. You can never find it, till you turn your reflexion into your own breast, and find a sentiment of disapprobation, which arises in you, towards this action. Here is a matter of fact; but 'tis the object of feeling, not of reason. It lies in yourself, not in the object. So that when you pronounce any action or character to be vicious, you mean nothing, but that from the constitution of your nature you have a feeling or sentiment of blame from the contemplation of it. Vice and virtue, therefore, may be compar'd to sounds, colours, heat and cold, which, according to modern philosophy, are not qualities in objects, but perceptions in the mind. (T, 468–69)

This analysis should be compared to Hume's discussion of causation. When we observe carefully any instance of a causal relation, we never observe the causing itself. We claim that one event causes another on the basis of building up a habit (in ourselves) of expecting the one on the appearance of the other; the concept of "necessary connection" we attribute to the relation between the events is founded on a "feeling" in our minds. Moral judgments, Hume is saying, are perfectly parallel to judgments of causality. Here, too, we project onto the facts an idea whose origin is simply a feeling in the mind. In this case, the feelings are those of approval and disapproval, which

---

* See Plato's discussion of the role of reason in the life of the just and happy person, pp. 135–137.

are expressed in terms of the concepts "right/good" and "wrong/bad." No matter how closely you examine the facts of any action, you will never discover in them its goodness or badness. The moral quality of the facts is not read off them; it is a matter of how the author of the moral judgment "feels" about them.

In a famous passage that widely influences subsequent moral philosophy, Hume marks out clearly the distinction between *the facts* on the one hand (expressible in purely descriptive language) and *the value qualities of the facts* on the other (expressible in evaluations).

> In every system of morality, which I have hitherto met with, I have always remark'd, that the author proceeds for some time in the ordinary way of reasoning, and establishes the being of a God, or makes observations about human affairs; when of a sudden I am surpriz'd to find, that instead of the usual copulations of propositions, *is,* and *is not,* I meet with no proposition that is not connected with an *ought,* or *ought not.* This change is imperceptible; but is, however, of the last consequence. For as this *ought* or *ought not,* expresses some new relation or affirmation, 'tis necessary that it shou'd be observ'd and explain'd; and at the same time that a reason should be given, for what seems altogether inconceivable, how this new relation can be a deduction from others, which are entirely different from it. But as authors do not commonly use this precaution, I shall presume to recommend it to the readers; and am persuaded, that this small attention wou'd subvert all the vulgar [i.e., common] systems of morality, and let us see, that the distinction of vice and virtue is not founded merely on the relations of objects, nor is perceiv'd by reason. (*T,* 469–70)

Hume is here pointing to what is often called the fact/value gap, or the is/ought problem.* Reason

---

*Reflection should tell you that this problem, too, is a consequence of the change produced by the development and acceptance of modern science. Dante's world contained no such gap; he could find the "right way" by discovering the facts about the universe. In general, where *final causes* are an intrinsic part of the *way things are* no such gap exists. For the ends of things are part of their very being. When final causes are cast out, however, values lose their rootedness in the way things are.

can tell us what the facts are, but it cannot tell us how to value them.

We do make value judgments; it is hard to imagine human life without them. And Hume is not advising us to refrain from doing so, any more than he advises against making causal judgments. But a science of human nature tries to understand both kinds of judgment; what it discovers, Hume thinks, is that neither of them is founded on reason. Both have their origins in sentiment or feeling; both are projections onto a world in which they cannot be discovered.

The foundation, or "origin," of morality, then, is to be found in sentiment—in feelings of approval and disapproval—not in reason. A scientific examination of morality ought to do more than discover these foundations, however. It ought also to reveal what *kinds of things* we approve and disapprove, and why. Hume has many interesting things to say about this matter; we'll be brief.

Hume claims that we tend to approve of those things which are either *agreeable* or *useful,* either to *ourselves* or to *others.* Some things naturally elicit our immediate approval (e.g., white sand on a warm beach); those are the agreeable things. Others do not but are valued as means, useful in promoting the occurrence of agreeable things (e.g., a visit to Dr. Payne). Hume believes that we often feel a kind of approval for things agreeable to others, as well as to ourselves; for example, we can take pleasure in another person's enjoyment of a good meal. If Hume is right, an egoistic account of human motivation (such as that of Hobbes) is inadequate.* A Hobbesian might claim, of course, that when we approve of another's enjoyment we do so because such approval is a *means* to our own pleasure. But Hume argues that this can't be right. The pleasure or satisfaction we feel on viewing another's enjoyment *is* our approval of it; so, it could not possibly be that for the sake of which we approve.

There is a passion in human beings that makes possible this apparent "disinterestedness" of moral

---

*Compare Hobbesian egoism, pp. 339–342.

judgments. Hume calls it *sympathy* or *humanity* or *fellow feeling.* Sympathy plays a large role in our moral judgments, since it is characteristic of moral judgments not to be purely self-interested. As evidence, Hume notes that we make moral judgments about figures in past history, where there is no possible impact on our present or future interests. So we tend to approve of benevolent or generous acts, even when they are not directed toward ourselves.

We will not follow the development of Hume's ideas about the particular virtues. But we should note one aspect. His insistence that morality is not founded on reason would seem to catapult him directly into moral relativism, since feelings seem so personal. What I approve, we may think, might be quite different from what you approve. But the insistence on sympathy as an original passion in human nature—within every individual—works toward a commonality in the moral sense of us all. It does not make moral disagreements between cultures or individuals impossible, but it is a pressure built into us all that explains the large agreement in moral judgment we in fact find.

Is Hume a Skeptic?

On topic after topic Hume sets himself against the majority tradition in the West. No doubt he feels this is only to be expected. Galilean and Newtonian science had overthrown traditional views about the nonhuman world; it should be no surprise that an attempt to apply the same methods to human nature should have the same result. Aristotle had defined man as a rational animal; ever since the emphasis had been on the "rational" aspect. In deciding what to believe, what to do, how to live, and how to judge, philosophers had looked to reason. The prerogatives of reason had lately been exalted in an extreme way by Descartes, who held that we shouldn't accept *anything* unless it was attested by rational insight or rational deduction. What Hume thinks he has shown is that *if this*

is the right rule, then there is *virtually nothing* we should accept.

Let us review.

- The principles governing the way ideas succeed each other are nonrational principles: those of sheer mechanical association, analogous in their function to the principle of gravitation.
- All knowledge of anything beyond our perceptions depends on the relation of cause and effect; but the origin of our idea of causality is a nonrational custom or habit that builds up in our minds whenever impressions succeed each other in a constant conjunction.
- We have no reason to believe in a substantial self; any such belief is a fiction foisted on us by detectable mistakes.
- We have no reason to believe in God.
- Our actions are governed by nonrational passions.
- Our liberty in action is not a matter of reason freeing us from the causal order, but simply a matter of nothing standing in the way of following those passions.
- Moral judgments, too, whether used as guides to our own action or as evaluations of the actions of others, are founded on nonrational sentiments that are simply a given part of human nature.

In every area Hume discovers the passivity, the limits, the impotence of reason. There is no good reason to believe in an objective causal order, in the existence of a material world independent of our perceptions, in God, in a soul or self, or in objective moral values. These certainly seem to be skeptical themes. Is Hume, then, a skeptic?

He makes distinctions between several kinds of skepticism. Let us examine two. There is Descartes' type, which Hume calls "antecedent" skepticism, since it is supposed to come before any beliefs are deemed acceptable. About this sort he says:

It recommends an universal doubt, not only of all our former opinions and principles, but also of our very faculties; of whose veracity, say they, we must assure ourselves, by a chain of reasoning, deduced from some original principle, which cannot possibly be fallacious or deceitful. But neither is there any such original principle, which has a prerogative above others, that are self-evident and convincing: Or if there were, could we advance a step beyond it, but by the use of those very faculties, of which we are supposed to be already diffident. The CARTESIAN doubt, therefore, were it ever possible to be attained by any human creature (as plainly it is not) would be entirely incurable; and no reasoning could ever bring us to a state of assurance and conviction upon any subject. (*E*, 103)

His criticism of Descartes' project is twofold. First, you cannot *really* bring yourself to doubt everything; belief is not that much under your control. You find yourself believing in, for example, the reality of the world independent of your senses, whether you want to or not. Second, if you could doubt everything, there would be no way back to rational belief; to get back you would have to use your reasoning faculties, the competence of which is one of the things you are doubting.* So Hume dismisses Cartesian "antecedent" skepticism as both unworkable and barren.

There is another kind of skepticism, however, which Hume thinks is quite useful. This is not an attempt to doubt everything in the futile hope of gaining something impossible to doubt, but an attempt to keep in mind "the strange infirmities of human understanding."

> The greater part of mankind are naturally apt to be affirmative and dogmatical in their opinions. . . . But could such dogmatical reasoners become sensible of the strange infirmities of human understanding, even in its most perfect state, and when most accurate and cautious in its determinations; such a reflection would naturally inspire them with more modesty and reserve, and diminish their fond opinion of themselves, and their prejudice against an-

tagonists. . . . In general there is a degree of doubt, and caution, and modesty, which, in all kinds of scrutiny and decision, ought for ever to accompany a just reasoner. (*E*, 111)

This "mitigated" skepticism, Hume says, makes for modesty and caution; it will "abate [the] pride"(*E*, 111) of those who are haughty and obstinate. It will teach us the limitations of our human capacities and encourage us to devote our understanding, not to abstruse problems of metaphysics and theology, but to the problems of common life.

In sponsoring such modesty about our intellectual attainments, Hume reflects Enlightenment worries about the consequences of dogmatic attachments to creeds that have only private backing. And if reason is really as broken-backed as Hume says, then dogmatic attachment to what appears rational is just as worrisome. One of the virtues of his examination of human nature, he feels, is that it makes such dogmatism impossible.

There might be an opposite worry, however. Could the consistently skeptical conclusions of Hume's philosophy undermine our lives to the point of paralysis? Hume himself reports, in an introspective moment, that after pursuing his researches for a while he finds himself

> ready to reject all belief and reasoning, and [to] look upon no opinion even as more probable or likely than another. Where am I, or what? From what causes do I derive my existence, and to what condition shall I return? Whose favor shall I court, and whose anger must I dread? What beings surround me? and on whom have I any influence, or who have any influence on me? I am confounded with all these questions, and begin to fancy myself in the most deplorable condition imaginable, inviron'd with the deepest darkness, and utterly depriv'd of the use of every member and faculty. (*T*, 268–69)

Reason has no answer to these questions. Depressing indeed!

What is the solution?

Most fortunately it happens, that since reason is incapable of dispelling these clouds, nature herself

---

* Hume seems to be saying that we must be content with the things we are, in Cartesian terms, "taught by nature." See *Meditation III.* Is this criticism of Descartes correct? Compare also the critique of Descartes by Charles Peirce, pp. 525–526.

suffices to that purpose, and cures me of this philosophical melancholy and delirium, either by relaxing
this bent of mind, or by some avocation, and lively
impression of my senses, which obliterate all these
chimeras. I dine, I play a game of back-gammon, I
converse, and am merry with my friends; and when
after three or four hours' amusement, I wou'd return
to these speculations, they appear so cold, and
strain'd, and ridiculous, that I cannot find in my
heart to enter into them any farther. (*T*, 269)

We need not worry, he assures us, that the results
of philosophical study will paralyze us by taking
away all our convictions. "Nature," he says, "is
always too strong for principle" (*E*, 110). Custom and habit, those nonrational instincts that are
placed in our natures, will ensure that we don't sit
shivering in terror at our lack of certainty.

But Hume does not mean that we should cease
to pursue philosophy. Indeed, his conviction that
nothing is more useful than the science of human
nature remains untouched. Only such an enquiry
into the nature and limits of human understanding
can free us from the natural tendency toward dogmatism and superstition that plagues human society. All our knowledge falls into one of two camps:
relations of ideas or matters of fact. The former
concern logical and mathematical matters; these,
Hume thinks, are irrelevant to real existence. The
latter are based wholly on experience, can get us
probability at best, and are founded in any case on
mere instinct, which we cannot prove is reliable.
Here are Hume's last words in *An Enquiry Concerning Human Understanding*.

> When we run over libraries, persuaded of these
> principles, what havoc must we make? If we take
> in hand any volume of school metaphysics, for in-
> stance; let us ask, *Does it contain any abstract reason-
> ing concerning quantity or number?* No. *Does it contain
> any experimental reasoning concerning matter of fact
> and existence?* No. Commit it then to the flames: For
> it can contain nothing but sophistry and illusion. (*E*,
> 114)

Hume represents a kind of crisis point in modern
philosophy. Can anyone build anything on the
rubble he leaves behind?

Basic Questions

1. Using the quotations from Immanuel Kant as a cue, explain the notion of *enlightenment*.
2. Contrast rationalism, materialism, and empiricism, and relate each to Newton's rule about not framing hypotheses.
3. How does Hume explain the origin of our ideas? (Distinguish complex from simple ideas.)
4. What principles govern transitions from one idea or impression to another?
5. Contrast relations of ideas with matters of fact. Give some examples of your own.
6. What is Hume's argument for the conclusion that causes and effects are discoverable not by reason but by experience?
7. If our beliefs about causation are dependent on experience, what experiences are of the relevant kind?
8. How does Hume explain our judgments of probability?
9. Granted that the idea of *necessary connection* is an important part of our idea of a cause, how does Hume account for that?
10. What part of our idea of causation is a fiction, according to Hume? What part is not?
11. What does Hume fail to find when—as he says—he enters most intimately into what he calls *himself*?
12. What conclusions does Hume draw about the nature of a "self"?
13. Explain how Hume thinks the necessity of actions (i.e., that they have causes) is compatible with the fact of liberty in actions (i.e., that sometimes we act freely).
14. How, according to Hume, does the idea of God originate? Compare Hume's view to Descartes' view.
15. How does Hume use the notion of relations of ideas to block the ontological arguments of Anselm (pp. 254–255) and Descartes (*Meditation V*)?
16. State clearly the argument from design, and sketch several of Hume's criticisms.
17. Explain what Hume means when he says that reason is the slave of the passions.
18. How does Hume explain our judgment that a certain action is bad or wrong or vicious? In what do we find the viciousness of a vicious action?
19. What sort of skepticism does Hume criticize? What sort does he advocate?

20. What does Hume hope his philosophizing will accomplish? Does it do that for you?

For Further Thought

Both Descartes and Hume can be compared to Robinson Crusoe. Each tries to construct "a world" out of the resources available only to an isolated individual. Sketch the similarities and differences in their projects, noting the materials they have available and the tools with which they work.

Notes

1. Immanuel Kant, "An Answer to the Question: What Is Enlightenment?" in *Perpetual Peace and Other Essays,* trans. Ted Humphrey (Indianapolis: Hackett Publishing Co., 1983), 41.
2. Kant, "What Is Enlightenment?" 41.
3. Ibid., 44.
4. From Newton's *Principia Mathematica,* General Scholium to Book III, reproduced in John Herman Randall, *The Career of Philosophy,* vol. 1 (New York: Columbia University Press, 1962), 579.
5. I have benefited from the excellent study of Hume by Barry Stroud: *Hume* (London: Routledge and Kegan Paul, 1977).
6. References to Hume's works are as follows:
   E: *Enquiry Concerning Human Understanding,* ed. Eric Steinberg (Indianapolis: Hackett Publishing Co., 1977).
   D: *Dialogues Concerning Natural Religion,* ed. Richard H. Popkin (Indianapolis: Hackett Publishing Co., 1980).
   T: *A Treatise of Human Nature,* ed. L. A. Selby-Bigge (Oxford: Oxford University Press, 1888).
   PM: *An Enquiry Concerning the Principles of Morals,* abridged in *Hume's Moral and Political Philosophy,* ed. Henry D. Aiken (New York: Hafner Publishing Co., 1948).
7. Bertrand Russell, *A History of Western Philosophy* (New York: Simon and Schuster, 1945), 567.

18

Immanuel Kant:
Rehabilitating Reason
(Within Strict Limits)

David Hume had published *A Treatise of Human Nature* at the early age of twenty-three. Immanuel Kant (1724–1804) published the first of his major works, *The Critique of Pure Reason,* in 1781, when he was fifty-seven. He enters the great conversation rather late in life because it has taken him some time to understand the devastating critique of Hume, "that acute man."

> I openly confess that my remembering David Hume was the very thing which many years ago first interrupted my dogmatic slumber and gave my investigations in the field of speculative philosophy a quite new direction. (*P,* 5)[1]

> . . . since the origin of metaphysics so far as we know its history, nothing has ever happened which could have been more decisive to its fate than the attack made upon it by David Hume. (*P,* 3)

Kant sets himself to solve what he calls "Hume's problem": whether the concept of cause is indeed objectively vacuous, a fiction whose origin can be traced to a merely subjective and instinctive habit of human nature. We have seen the skeptical consequences Hume draws from his analysis; these, we can imagine, are what wakes Kant from his "dogmatic slumber."

Human thought seems naturally to recognize no limits. It moves easily and without apparent strain from bodies to souls, from life in this world to life after death, from material things to God. One aspect of Enlightenment thought is the acute con-

sciousness of how *varied* thoughts become when they move out beyond the ground of experience—and yet how *certain* people feel about their own views. This is the dogmatism (or superstition) that Hume tries to debunk. Stimulated by Hume, Kant too feels this is a problem. It is true that in mathematics we have clear examples of knowledge independent of experience. But it does not follow (as thinkers like Plato suppose) that we can extend this knowledge indefinitely in a realm beyond experience. Kant uses a lovely image to make this point.*

> The light dove, leaving the air in her free flight, and feeling its resistance, might imagine that its flight would be still easier in empty space. It was thus that Plato left the world of the senses, as setting too narrow limits to the understanding, and ventured out beyond it on the wings of the ideas, in the empty space of the pure understanding. He did not observe that with all his efforts he made no advance—meeting no resistance that might, as it were, serve as a support upon which he could take a stand, to which he could apply his powers, and so set his understanding in motion. (*CPR,* 47)

Could the dove fly even better in empty space? No, it could not fly there at all; it absolutely depends on some "resistance" to fly. In the same way,

---

*Plato believes that the non-sensible, purely intelligible world of Forms is not only knowable but also *more* intelligible than the world of experience, and *more real,* too. See pp. 110–114.

Kant suggests, human thought needs a medium that supplies "resistance," some discipline, to work properly. In a resistance-free environment, everything is equally possible (as long as formal contradiction is avoided), and the conflicts of dogmatic believers (philosophical, religious, or political) are inevitable.

Kant is convinced that Hume is right to pinpoint *experience* as the medium that disciplines reason, as the limit within which alone reason can legitimately do its work. But Kant doubts that Hume has correctly understood experience. Why? Because Hume's analysis has an unacceptable consequence. We did not explicitly draw this consequence when discussing Hume (because he does not draw it). But if Hume is right, Newtonian science itself is basically an irrational and unjustified fiction.* Recall that for Hume *all* our knowledge of matters of fact beyond present perception and memory are founded on the relation of cause and effect. And causes are nothing more than projections onto a supposed objective world from a feeling in the mind.

Kant is convinced that in Newtonian science we do have rationally justified knowledge. And if Hume's examination of reason forces us to deny that we have this knowledge, something must be wrong with Hume's analysis. What we need, Kant says, is a more thorough and accurate *critique of reason*—a critique that will lay out its *structure*, its *relationship to its objects,* and inscribe precisely the line that sets the *limits* within which it can legitimately work. Hume thinks that what we need is a science of human nature. Kant agrees; but he thinks it must be done better than Hume manages to do it. This is the project Kant sets for himself, now that he has awakened from his dogmatic slumber and is no longer, like the dove, trying to fly in empty space.

---

*You can see that Hume ends up exactly where Descartes fears to be; you just can't trust what custom and habit supply—what you are "taught by nature." In order to escape this fate for his own physics, Descartes thinks you need to prove the existence of a nondeceptive God. But by undermining any such proofs, Hume finds himself unable to escape from solipsism—except by joining a game of backgammon and ignoring the problem.

He makes an absolutely revolutionary suggestion.

> Hitherto it has been assumed that all our knowledge must conform to objects. But all attempts to extend our knowledge of objects by establishing something in regard to them *a priori,* by means of concepts, have, on this assumption, ended in failure. We must therefore make trial whether we may not have more success in the tasks of metaphysics, if we suppose that objects must conform to our knowledge. . . . We should then be proceeding precisely on the lines of Copernicus' primary hypothesis. Failing of satisfactory progress in explaining the movements of the heavenly bodies on the supposition that they all revolved round the spectator, he tried whether he might not have better success if he made the spectator to revolve and the stars to remain at rest. A similar experiment can be tried in metaphysics, as regards the *intuition* of objects. (*CPR,* 22)

This requires some explanation. Nearly all previous philosophy (and science and common sense, too) has made a very natural assumption—as natural as the assumption that the heavenly bodies revolve around us. But perhaps it is just as wrong.

What is that assumption? It is that we acquire knowledge and truth when our thoughts "conform to objects." According to this assumption, objects are *there,* quite determinately *being* whatever they are, completely *independent of our apprehension* of them. And when we know them, we have to "get it right" in the sense that our beliefs must be brought to *correspond* to these independently existing things. Aristotle's classical definition of truth expresses this assumption perfectly: to say of what is that it is, and of what *is not* that it is not, is true.* Truth (and knowledge, too) is a matter of getting what we *say* (or believe) lined up to correspond to what there *is.* The assumption is integral to the representational theory of knowledge and perception (p. 300).

But Hume has shown us the impossibility of thinking about representation in this way. To know whether an idea corresponds to some independent

---

*See Aristotle's discussion of this on pp. 149–150.

object, we would have to be able to compare that idea with the idea-less object.* But the object can be known *only* via an idea. We may have ideas (like the idea of a cause) which are supposed to cross this gulf. Descartes thought he could use this idea to get from his idea of God to the reality of God. But the gulf is impassable. On the basis of mere concepts alone, we can know nothing at all about objects existing outside our minds. Ideas that have their origin in experience (e.g., green, warm, solid) can go no further than experience. And ideas that don't (e.g., cause) are mere illusions. By using such concepts we can know nothing at all about objects. All this follows if (1) we are acquainted only with the ideas in our experience, (2) objects are thought to exist independently of our experience, and (3) knowledge requires that we ascertain a correspondence between ideas and objects.

But what if this assumption is wrong? What if, to be an object at all, a thing has to conform to certain concepts? What if objects couldn't exist—simply couldn't *be* in any sense at all—unless they were related to a rational mind, set in a context of rational concepts and principles? Think about the motion of the planets in their zigzag course across the sky. On the assumption that this motion is *real,* accurate understanding proves to be impossible. Copernicus denies this assumption. He suggests that this motion is only *apparent.* It is *contributed by us,* the observers. On this new assumption, we are able to understand and predict the behavior of these objects.

Perhaps, Kant is suggesting, the same is true in the world of the intellect. Perhaps the objects of experience are (at least in part) the result of a construction by the rational mind. If so, they have no reality independent of that construction. Like the motion of the planets, the objects of our experience are merely apparent, not independently real. If this is so, it may well be that concepts like cau-

sation, which cannot be *abstracted* from experience (the lesson of Hume), still *apply* to experience, simply because objects of experience that are *not* structured by that concept are *inconceivable.* The suggestion is that the rational mind has a certain structure, and whatever is knowable by such a mind must necessarily be known in terms of that structure. This structure is not derived from the objects known. It is *imposed* on them—but not arbitrarily, since the very idea of an object not so structured makes no sense.

This is Kant's "Copernican Revolution" in philosophy. To the details of this novel way of thinking we will now turn.

Critique

If we are going to take seriously this possibility that objects are partially constituted—as objects—by the rational mind, we must examine how that constitution takes place. We need to peer reflectively behind the scenes and catch a glimpse of the productive machinery at work. So we are interested in the *processes* involved in knowing anything at all. A prior question, of course, is *whether* we can know anything at all. But Kant thinks that Newton's science has definitely settled that question. Assuming, then, that a rational mind can have some knowledge, we want to ask, How does it manage that? We need to engage in what Kant calls "critique." A "critical" philosophy is not one that criticizes, in the carping, censorious way where "nothing is ever right." Critique is the attempt to get behind knowledge claims and ask, What makes them possible?

The objects of human knowledge seem to fall into four main classes. We can see what Kant is up to if we frame a question with respect to each of these classes.

1. How is *mathematics* possible?
2. How is *natural science* possible?
3. How is *metaphysics* possible?
4. How is *morality* possible?

---

*Montaigne compares the problem to that of a man who does not know Socrates and is presented with a portrait of him. How can he tell whether it resembles Socrates or not? See p. 283. This perplexity is obviously a consequence of the representational theory, once one has become skeptical of inferences from our ideas to external things existing independently of these ideas.

These are, in Kant's sense, "critical" questions. We are not now going to develop mathematics, physics, metaphysics, or morality. But in each case we are going to look at the rational foundations on which these disciplines rest. What is it, for instance, about human reason that makes it possible to develop mathematics? What *structure, capacities,* and *concepts* must reason have for it to be *able* to do mathematics?

These are *reflective* questions, which together constitute a *critique of reason,* a critical examination of the way a rational mind works. Kant also calls this kind of investigation **transcendental.*** A transcendental inquiry reaches back into the activities of the mind and asks how it produces its results. If this kind of investigation succeeds, we'll know what the powers of reason are—and what they are not. We can, Kant thinks, determine the *limits* of rational knowledge. And this is most important. For if we can determine both the capacities and the limitations of human reason, we may be able to escape both of those evils between which philosophy has so often swung: *dogmatism* on the one hand, and *skepticism* on the other. From Kant's point of view, these extremes are well illustrated by Descartes and Hume, respectively.

"Two things fill the mind with ever new and increasing admiration and awe . . . the starry heavens above me and the moral law within me." —IMMANUEL KANT

Judgments

Since all our claims to know are expressed in the form of judgments, the first task is to clarify the different kinds of judgments there are. Hume had divided our knowledge into relations of ideas and matters of fact.† Kant agrees that this is roughly right, but not precise enough. Hume's distinction runs together two quite different kinds of consideration. (1) There is an *epistemological* question involved: Does a bit of knowledge rest on experience, or not? (2) There is also a *semantic* question: How do the meanings of the words we use to express that knowledge relate to each other? Kant

sorts these matters out, and the result is a classification of judgments (which might be known to be true) into *four* groups rather than into Hume's two.

1. Epistemological
   1a. A judgment is *a priori* when it can be known to be true without any reference to experience. "7 + 5 = 12" is an example.
   1b. A judgment is *a posteriori* when we must appeal to experience to determine its truth or falsity. For instance, "John F. Kennedy was assassinated," cannot be known independently of experience.
2. Semantic
   2a. A judgment is **analytic** when its denial

* The term "transcendental" must be carefully distinguished from the similar term "transcendent." See p. 392.
† Hume's discussion of these is found on pp. 353–354.

yields a contradiction. Here is an example Kant gives: "All bodies are extended." This is analytic because the predicate "extended" is already included as part of the subject, "bodies." To say that there is some body that is *not* extended is, in effect, to claim there can be some extended thing that is not extended. And that is contradictory. If an analytic judgment is true, it is *necessarily true*. The opposite of an analytic judgment is *not possible*. Since it is analytic that every father has a child, it is not possible that there should be a father without a child. And every father necessarily has a child.

2b. A judgment is **synthetic** when it does more than simply explicate or analyze a concept. Here are some examples: "Every event has a cause," "Air has weight," and "John F. Kennedy was assassinated." Consider the first example. The concept *having a cause* is not part of the concept *being an event*. This is something Hume teaches us.* We can imagine that an event might simply occur without any cause. Even if we don't believe that ever happens, there is no contradiction in supposing it might. The opposite of synthetic judgments is always *possible*.

These two pairs can be put together to give us four possibilities. In Kant's view, every judgment that is a candidate for being knowledge will belong to one or another of these four classes. Let us give some examples.

• Analytic *a priori*: "All bodies are extended." This is analytic, as we have seen, because "extended" is part of the definition of "body." It is *a priori* because we don't have to examine our experience of bodies to know it is true; all we need is to understand the meanings of the terms "body" and "extended."

• Analytic *a posteriori*: This class seems empty; if the test for analyticity is examining a judgment's denial for contradiction, it seems clear that we do not *also* have to examine experience. Every analytic judgment must be *a priori*.

• Synthetic *a posteriori*: Here belong most of our judgments about experience, judgments of science and common sense alike, from particular judgments (e.g., "The water in the tea kettle is boiling") to general laws (e.g., "Water always boils at 100°C at sea level").

• Synthetic *a priori*: This is a puzzling and controversial class of judgments. If we were to know such a judgment as true, we would have to be able to know it quite independently of experience. This means that if such a judgment is true, it is true no matter what our experience shows us. Even if the events of experience were organized in a completely different way, a true judgment of this kind would remain true. And yet it is true *not* because it is analytic; its denial is not logically contradictory.

We can represent these possibilities in a matrix:

	A priori	*A posteriori*
Analytic	"Every mother has a child."	✕
Synthetic	"?"	"There is a Waterloo in both Iowa and Wisconsin."

There is something very odd about synthetic *a priori* judgments. Consider a judgment that is about experience. Suppose that it is synthetic, but that we can know it *a priori*. Because it is synthetic, its opposite is (from a logical point of view) a real possibility. And yet we can know—without appealing to experience—that this possibility is never realized! How can this be?

---

* Recall Hume's claim that "all events seem entirely loose and separate." Neither experience nor reason, he claims, ever discloses that necessary "connexion" which might link them inseparably together. See p. 359.

Kant believes that the solution to the dilemmas of past philosophy lies precisely in the recognition that we are in possession of synthetic *a priori* judgments. It is his Copernican revolution in philosophy that makes this recognition possible. Think: On the assumption that objects are realities independent of our knowing them, it would be crazy to suppose that we could know them without observing or experiencing them in some way; our thoughts about them would be one thing, the objects something quite different; and they could vary independently.* What could possibly guarantee that things would match our thoughts *a priori*? On the traditional correspondence assumption, then, *a priori* knowledge that is synthetic would be impossible.

But suppose that objects *are* objects only because they are structured in certain ways by the mind in the very act of knowing them. Then it is not at all implausible to think that there might be *principles* of that structuring and that some of these principles might be synthetic. Moreover, a reflective, critical study of rationality might uncover them. And those principles would be known *a priori*—independently of the character of the objects they are structuring. So if Kant's Copernican revolution makes sense, there will be such *a priori* synthetic principles for every domain of objects.

It is time to give some examples of judgments Kant considers to be both *a priori* and synthetic. You may be surprised by some of them.

- All the judgments of mathematics and geometry
- In natural science, such judgments as "Every event has a cause"
- In metaphysics, "There is a God,"and "The soul is a simple substance, distinct from the body"
- In morality, the imperative to treat others as ends, not merely as means to some end of your own

I do not mean to suggest that we *know* all these judgments, or that they are all true. That remains

---

* Compare Ockham's reflections on God's omnipotence, pp. 265–266.

to be seen. But if you examine them, you should be able to see that they are all examples of judgments which would have to be known *a priori* (i.e., not from experience), if at all. And examination should also confirm, Kant thinks, that they are all synthetic. None of them is true simply in virtue of how the terms are related to each other.

Kant wants to understand how mathematics, natural science, metaphysics, and morality are possible. In the light of his Copernican revolution, we can see that he is asking how the rational mind structures its objects into the objects of mathematics, natural science, metaphysics, and morality. It must be that implicit in the foundations of all these disciplines are some judgments that are synthetic and *a priori*, judgments that do not arise out of experience but *prescribe* how the objects of experience *must* be. All four of these areas are *constituted* by synthetic *a priori* judgments. The objects we encounter are—in part—*constructions*. And these judgments are *principles for the construction of objects*.

Kant sometimes calls *a priori* judgments "pure." By this, he means that they are not "contaminated" by experience. We can now restate his questions:

1. How is *pure* mathematics possible?
2. How is *pure* natural science possible?
3. How is *pure* metaphysics possible?
4. How is *pure* morality possible?

Let's examine his answers.

Geometry, Mathematics, Space, and Time

It would be useful to have a criterion by which we could distinguish *a priori* knowledge from *a posteriori* knowledge. Kant suggests that there are two tests we can use: *necessity* and *universality*.

> Experience teaches us that a thing is so and so, but not that it cannot be otherwise. First, then, if we have a proposition which in being thought is thought as *necessary*, it is an *a priori* judgment. . . . Secondly, experience never confers on its judgments true or

strict, but only assumed and comparative *universality,* through induction. . . . Necessity and strict universality are thus sure criteria of *a priori* knowledge, and are inseparable from one another. (*CPR,* 43–44)

As Hume has taught us, necessity cannot be discovered by means of experience; as far as experience tells us, all events are "entirely loose and separate." Further, we all know that experience is limited in extent; so experience cannot demonstrate that a proposition is universally true (i.e., true everywhere and at all times). It follows that if we nonetheless find a judgment that is either necessarily true or universally true, we can be sure that it does not have its justification in experience. Such a judgment must be *a priori.*

Mathematical truths are both necessary and universal. They are, therefore, clear examples of *a priori* judgments. But they also, Kant tells us,

are all synthetic. This fact seems hitherto to have altogether escaped the observation of those who have analyzed human reason; it even seems directly opposed to all their conjectures, though it is incontestably certain and most important in its consequences. . . .

It might at first be thought that the proposition 7 + 5 = 12 is a mere analytic judgment, following from the concept of the sum of seven and five, according to the principle of contradiction. But on closer examination it appears that the concept of the sum of 7 + 5 contains merely their union in a single number, without its being at all thought what the particular number is that unites them. The concept of twelve is by no means thought by merely thinking of the combination of seven and five; and analyze this possible sum as we may, we shall not discover twelve in the concept. We must go beyond these concepts by calling to our aid some intuition corresponding to one of them, i.e., either our five fingers or five points . . . ; and we must add successively the units of the five given in the intuition to the concept of seven. . . .

All principles of geometry are no less analytic. That a straight line is the shortest path between two points is a synthetic proposition. For my concept of straight contains nothing of quantity, but only a quality. The concept of the shortest is therefore altogether additional and cannot be obtained by any analysis of the concept of the straight line. Here, too, intuition must come to aid us. (*P,* 13–14)

What is Kant trying to show through these examples? Hume suggests that the truths of mathematics are simply matters of how ideas are related to each other—that they are analytic and can be known by appeal solely to the principle of contradiction. Kant argues that this is not so. For "7 + 5 = 12" to be analytic, the concept "12" would have to be implicitly included in the concept "7 + 5." But all that concept tells us, if Kant is right, is that two numbers are being added. It does not, of itself, tell us what the sum is.

What can tell us what the sum is? Only some *intuition,* Kant says.* An intuition is not anything mysterious or occult. By "intuition" Kant simply means the presentation of some sensible object to the mind. That is why we need the five fingers (or something similar). We must "add successively" the units presented in the intuition: we count, one finger at a time. Knowing that 7 + 5 = 12 is a *process.* We *construct* mathematics by inscribing it on a background composed of sensible objects or sets of objects.

But we need to understand these objects more clearly. Since geometry and mathematics are *a priori* disciplines, their objects cannot be the ordinary objects of sensible experience (e.g., apples and oranges), for those objects we can only know *a posteriori,* through experience. If mathematics were only about the objects of experience, then it could neither be necessary nor universal. We might know that *these* five oranges and *those* seven oranges happen to make twelve oranges. But we wouldn't know that *all* such groups of oranges (examined or not) make twelve and *must* make twelve. If we know this with necessity and universality (as we surely do), the objects that justify mathematical truths must themselves be known in a purely *a priori* manner. There must be *pure* intuitions, forms of *pure sensibility.* But what could they be?

_____

* Kant is the ancestor of a school in the philosophy of mathematics that still has distinguished adherents. The viewpoint is called "intuitionism" but might more accurately be termed "constructivism."

Now the intuitions which pure mathematics lays at the foundation of all its cognitions and judgments . . . are space and time. . . . Geometry is based upon the pure intuition of space. Arithmetic attains its concepts of numbers by the successive addition of units in time. (*P*, 27)

Think about space a moment. According to our ordinary experience, space is filled with things. But suppose you "think away" all these things—all the household goods, the clothes, the houses, the earth itself, sun, moon, and stars. Have you thought away space? Kant thinks not. (Newton would have agreed.) But you have "subtracted" (in this thought experiment) everything *empirical*—that is, everything that gives particular content to our experience. All that is left is a kind of container, a form or structure, in which empirical things can be put. But, since you have gotten rid of everything empirical, what is left is *pure*. And it can be known *a priori*. Geometry is the science of this pure intuition of space.*

But what is the status of the intuition itself? Could space simply be one more (rather abstract and esoteric) object independent of our perception of it? Kant doesn't think so. And the reason is this: The truths of geometry, like those of mathematics, are not probabilistic, but *necessary*. If you ask, "How *likely* is it that any given straight line is the shortest distance between its end points?" you demonstrate that you haven't *understood* geometry! Moreover, that a straight line in a plane is the shortest distance between two points is something we know to be *universally* true, not only for spaces that we have examined. If space were an object independent of our minds, knowing this would be impossible. We would have to say that this is true *for all the spaces we have examined*, but beyond that, who knows? Geometers do not proceed in this manner. They neither make experiments concerning space nor suppose that unexamined space could have a different structure. Yet geometry is the science of space. How can this be?

The explanation must be this: Space is not

---

* Kant is referring to Euclidean geometry, of course. Various non-Euclidean geometries were discovered—or constructed—in the nineteenth century.

something "out there" to be discovered; space is a form of the mind itself. It is a pure intuition providing a "structure" into which all our more determinate perceptions *must fit*. When you handle an apple, your experience is constituted on the one hand by sensations (color, texture, weight, and so on) and on the other hand by a form or structure into which these sensations fit (the pure intuition of space). About this intuited form, we can know necessary truths: truths that are synthetic but *a priori*. The apple as we experience it is not an object entirely independent of our perception of it. Part of that very experience is constituted by the intuition of space, which we do not *abstract from* the experience, but *bring to* the experience.

This has an important consequence. We cannot experience the apple as it is *in itself*, independent of our perception of it. Why not? Because part of what it is to *be* an apple is to be in space; and space is an aspect of our experience that comes from the side of the subject. So the apple, as we can know it, is the apple *as it appears to us*, not the apple *as it is in itself*. What goes for the apple goes for the entire world. We can only know how things *appear*.

> . . . things as objects of our senses existing outside us are given, but we know nothing of what they may be in themselves, knowing only their appearances, i.e., the representations which they cause in us by affecting our senses. Consequently, I grant by all means that there are bodies without us, that is, things which, though quite unknown to us as to what they are in themselves, we yet know by the representations which their influence on our sensibility procures us, and which we call bodies. This word merely means the appearance of the thing, which is unknown to us but is not therefore less real. (*P*, 33)

Just as space is the pure intuition that makes geometry possible, time is the pure intuition that makes mathematics possible. Geometrical figures are constructed on the pure (spatial) form in which external objects are experienced. Numbers and their relations are constructed on the pure (temporal) form in which any objects whatsoever (including all mental events) are experienced. An elementary example of constructing in time is counting, where we construct one number *after* another.

Kant has now answered his first question. Pure geometry and mathematics are possible because their objects are not independent of the knowing rational mind; space and time are pure forms of sensible intuition. He has shown, moreover, that geometry and mathematics essentially involve judgments that are synthetic (because they are constructive) and *a priori* (because they are necessary and universal).

Because experience is always experience in time (if it is experience of external objects, it is experience in space as well), it is made up of the *appearances* of things; it is a *product* of contributions from two sides: the objective and the subjective. Nowhere can we know things as they are in themselves, independent of our contribution to their natures. It is not that we know things in themselves in a confused and inadequate way that can be continually improved. We do not know them at all! And we can know *a priori* just the part of their natures that we ourselves, as rational minds, necessarily supply in experiencing them.

Common Sense, Science, and the *A Priori* Categories

Pure mathematics does not exhaust our knowledge. We know many things in the course of our ordinary life and through Newtonian science. What is the application of Kant's Copernican revolution in these spheres? One thing we know already. Whatever common sense and science may reveal, they will not be able to penetrate behind the veil of our pure sensible intuitions, which structure all possible objects in space and time. In these fields, too, we will be unable to reach to things in themselves; all our knowledge will concern how these things *appear* to us.

To deal with his second question, how pure natural science is possible, Kant needs to clarify a distinction between two aspects or powers of the mind. He calls them *sensibility* and *understanding*. The former is a passive power, the ability to receive impressions. The latter is an active power, the power to think objects by constructing a representation of them using concepts.

> Our knowledge springs from two fundamental sources of the mind; the first is the capacity of receiving representations (receptivity for impressions), the second is the power of knowing an object through these representations (spontaneity [in the production] of concepts). Through the first an object is *given* to us, through the second the object is *thought*. . . . Intuition and concepts constitute, therefore, the elements of all our knowledge, so that neither concepts without an intuition in some way corresponding to them, nor intuition without concepts, can yield knowledge. Both may be either pure or empirical. When they contain sensation (which presupposes the actual presence of the object), they are empirical. When there is no mingling of sensation with the representation, they are pure. (*CPR*, 92)

Kant's general term for the contents of the mind is "representation." He is here telling us that our representations can be of several different kinds: pure or empirical, intuitive or conceptual. In fact, this gives us a matrix of four possibilities; let us set them out with some examples.

Representations

	Pure	Empirical
Intuitions (from sensibility)	Space and time	Sensations of red, warm, hard, etc.
Concepts (from understanding)	Straight, cause, substance, God, the soul	Cherry pie, otter, water, the sun, unicorn, etc.

We have not determined at this point whether all these representations actually *represent* something. But we do know that any concept which succeeds in representing something will have to do it in tandem with some intuition. For "neither concepts without an intuition in some way corresponding to them, nor intuition without concepts, can yield knowledge." The dove cannot fly in empty space.

Kant has contrasted sensibility with understanding, intuitions with concepts. But he is also convinced that they must work together.

> To neither of these powers may a preference be given over the other. Without sensibility no object would be given to us, without understanding no object would be thought. Thoughts without content are empty, intuitions without concepts are blind. It is, therefore, just as necessary to make our concepts sensible, that is, to add the object to them in intuition, as to make our intuitions intelligible, that is, to bring them under concepts. . . . The understanding can intuit nothing, the senses can think nothing. Only through their union can knowledge arise. (*CPR*, 93)

We have seen that there are pure intuitions that can be known *a priori* (space and time). There are also *nonpure* or *empirical* intuitions; these are Humean impressions or sensations. Kant thinks of sensations as the *matter* of sensible objects. We can illustrate by imagining a square cut out of wood. The spatial properties of the square can be known *a priori*, quite independent of whether the square is red or brown, warm or cold, smooth or rough. But it can only be *some particular square* if it is either red or some other color, either warm or not, either smooth or less than smooth. Our sensations determine which it is. They provide the "filling" or content for the purely formal intuition of a square.

Are *concepts* like this too? Can there be pure concepts as well as empirical concepts? Kant is convinced that we make use of pure, *a priori* concepts all the time. If there were concepts that we *necessarily* use in thinking *any* object whatsoever, these concepts would be *a priori* concepts. They would satisfy the two criteria of necessity and universality. Pure concepts would do for understand-

ing what space and time do for sensibility: provide a structure within which alone objects could be known. Kant's idea here is that our thinking with concepts also has two sides: the empirical, derived from sensation, and the *a priori* (or formal), supplied by the structure of the understanding.* Like sensibility, the understanding brings something of its own to experience. In neither case is the mind just a blank tablet on which experience writes, as some philosophers have thought.

The question then forces itself upon us: What concepts do we have that apply to objects but are not derived from them? We are searching for a set of concepts we use necessarily in thinking of an object. And these will be *a priori* concepts. Kant calls them *categories,* since they will supply the most general characteristics of things: the characteristics it takes to qualify as a thing or object at all.†

But how can we discover these concepts? Critical philosophy, you will remember, is reflective or transcendental in nature. So we need to reflect on our thinking, to see whether there are some features of our thinking about objects that must be present no matter what the object is.

Let's begin by asking, What is it to think of an *object,* anyway? Consider the contrast between these two judgments:

A: "It seems as if there is a heavy book before me."
B: "The book before me is heavy."

What is the difference? In a certain sense, they both have the same *content:* book, heavy, before me.

---

* Check the examples again in the chart on p. 384.

† You can see that Kant is embarked on a project similar to that of Aristotle: to discover the characteristics of being *qua* being. Aristotle also produces a set of categories, displaying the most general ways in which something (anything) can *be*. (See p. 147.) Kant goes about the project in a roughly similar way: he looks at the language in which we talk about objects. But between Kant and Aristotle there stands the Kantian Copernican revolution. And that makes a tremendous difference. Kant's "categories," the universal and necessary features of objects, originate in the structure of *thinking* about those objects. They apply not to being *as such*, but to being *as it is knowable* by rational minds like ours—that is, to appearance.

Yet there is a crucial difference. What is it? Isn't it just that *B* is a judgment about an *object,* whereas *A pulls back* from making a judgment about that object? *A* is a judgment, not about the book, but about *my perception;* it has only what Kant calls "subjective validity." *B,* however, is a judgment about *the book.* It is an "objective" judgment; whether true or false, it makes a claim that an object has a certain characteristic.

But in what does this difference consist? It can't consist in the empirical concepts involved: "book" and "heavy" and "before me" are the same in *A* and *B.* Nor can the difference be anything *derived from my experience* of the book in the two cases, since my experience may be exactly the same in each. So the difference must be an *a priori* one. It seems to be a difference in the *manner* in which the judgments are made, or in the *form* of the judgments. If we can isolate the feature that distinguishes *A* from *B,* we will have put our finger on something necessary for objective judgments—i.e., for thinking about a world of objects. We will have isolated the contribution the *understanding* makes to our experience of an objective world.

In this case, Kant tells us, the distinguishing feature is that in *B* we are thinking in terms of a *substance* together with its *properties.* These concepts are not derived from what is *given* in my sensations (since the sensations are exactly the same in *A*). These concepts are *brought to* the experience of the book by the understanding in the very form of thinking of the book as an object. The book is a substance that has the property of being heavy. But this means that the concepts "substance" and "property" are *a priori* concepts. And that is just what we are looking for.

The point is this. In thinking of an objective world, thinking necessarily takes certain forms of organization. One of these forms consists of a kind of logical function or rule: *Structure experience in terms of substances having properties.* Unless thoughts take this logical form, Kant says, a world of objects simply cannot be thought at all. Without the application of these *a priori* concepts, there can be no objective world for common sense or science

to know. So a world of objects is, like the world of sensible intuitions, a composite. There is an empirical aspect to it (expressed in empirical concepts like "book" and "heavy"). But there is also an *a priori* aspect to it (expressed in nonempirical concepts such as "substance" and "property"). Experience of an objective world requires both.

Kant works out an entire system of such *a priori* concepts or categories. He thinks he can do this by canvassing all the possible forms objective judgments can take. And he thinks he can do that because he assumes that logic (the science of the forms of judgment) is a closed and finished science; no essential changes, he observes, have occurred in it since Aristotle.* For each possible form of judgment (he thinks there are twelve such forms) he finds an *a priori* concept that we bring to bear on sensations. In each case, the application of this concept produces an *a priori* characteristic of the objective world of our experience. So Kant identifies twelve categories—twelve general ways we know that any objective world *must* be. The fact that the world of our experience must be structured in terms of substances-having-properties is just one of these ways. We will examine only one other, passing over much of the detail of Kant's treatment.

The *a priori* concept of substance gets an opportunity, so to speak, to apply to experience because sensations come grouped together in various ways in *space.* Considered just as sensations, my experience of what I call the book hangs together in a certain way; the color, texture, shape, and so on seem to be closely associated—hanging together, for instance, as they move across my field of vision. If this were not so, I could scarcely unify these sensations under one concept and experience one object, the book. In a similar way, sensations also appear *successively in time.* This provides a foothold for another of the categories: *causation.*

We have examined Hume's powerful argument

---

*We now know that Kant's list of the possible forms of judgments is not, as he thinks, complete. Logic has gone through a revolution since Kant's time.

Baruch Spinoza

Expelled with curses from the Amsterdam synagogue in 1656, Baruch Spinoza (1632–1677) has been characterized as both a "God-intoxicated man" and as an atheistic naturalist. Fundamentally, he was one of the most rationalistic of philosophers. His major work, *The Ethics*, published posthumously, was written in geometrical form; that is, its propositions were deduced from definitions and axioms. Spinoza's aim was to attain a secure happiness by approaching as closely as possible an adequate understanding of absolutely everything.

He defined "substance" as what exists "in itself" and requires nothing beyond itself for its being. He argued that substance must be infinite and that there cannot be two such substances (otherwise each would limit the other and defeat the infinity). So there can be but one substance, which can equally well be called God or Nature. This means that the individuals of our experience—from stones to ourselves—are not substances, but modifications of the one infinite substance.

Mind and body are not substances, as Descartes thought, but attributes under which the one substance can be conceived. In fact, for every natural body, there is an idea; the idea corresponding to a human body is what we call the mind. It follows that mind and body are identical and that every bodily change is a mental change, and vice versa.

Since everything that happens is a necessary expression of the immutable divine nature, there is no free will in the ordinary sense. Freedom, Spinoza claimed, is just the power to act from one's own nature, unconstrained by anything outside oneself. God (or Nature), then, is the only completely free being, since God is the only thing for which there is nothing outside itself.

We, for the most part, are in "bondage," since we are controlled by emotions (desire, love, hate) we passively suffer; emotions are *caused* in us. But our freedom expands as we act from "adequate ideas" that are part of our own nature. Since the only truly adequate ideas are those in God's mind, we move toward freedom by the intellectual love of God, coming to see the necessities of the world as God sees them. Such knowledge is the source of power to act (rather than react), of virtue, and of joy. Thus we can approximate the blessed life of God.

---

that our idea of cause is not an empirical idea—that it is not abstracted from our experience.* Hume concludes that the idea is a fiction, a kind of illusion produced in us by custom. So we cannot really know that objects are related to each other by cause and effect.

But what if the concept of causation (like the concept of substance) represents a necessary aspect of any world of objects? What if there simply couldn't *be* objects at all unless they were set in causal relations with each other? This is the possibility that Kant's Copernican revolution explores. Objects are what we know, both in common sense and in science. If knowing them requires that this knowledge be expressed in judgments making use of an *a priori* concept of causality, we could know (*a priori*) that objects are necessarily and universally related to each other by causality—and avoid Hume's skeptical conclusions.

Again Kant shows us that there is a difference between judgments that refer only to our perceptions and judgments that are about objects. It may *seem* to us that one thing follows necessarily upon another. But once we affirm the idea of a world of

---

*Review this argument on pp. 353–359.

objects, we are committed to there being a rule that it *must* be so. Suppose that something unusual happens. What will we do? We will ask why. We will search for its cause. Will we allow the possibility that this event had no cause? Certainly not. But what if we search and search and do not discover its cause (e.g., the cause for a certain kind of cancer)? Will we finally conclude that it has no cause? Of course not. No degree of failure in finding its cause would ever convince us that it has no cause. *Every* event has a cause.

How do we know that? We have seen that it is not analytic. How do we know that this conviction is not a mere prejudice on our part? Our confidence cannot be based on an induction from past successes in finding causes, for that would never justify our certainty that even unexamined events must have causes. We've learned that from Hume. If we know that every event has a cause, we know it because part of the very idea of a world of objects is that events in it are structured by rules of succession. There *could not be* an objective world that was not organized by cause and effect.

Think of it this way: if there were no necessary order in the succession of events, this succession could not be distinguished from sheer fancy, dream, or imagination. Its being subject to a rule determining that when X happens, Y must necessarily happen is just what makes it objective. Again note the difference between judgments which refer only to perception and judgments which refer to something objective. In the latter, we understand the temporal succession of events in terms of a rule that *makes* the succession objective, a rule of causation. Structuring the world in that way is part of what makes it an objective world that can be experienced. Objective worlds (as opposed to subjective fancies) are just those that do have such a causal structure in time.*

---

* Think again about Descartes' final dismissal of the dream-threat (p. 331). Dreams, he says, do not have that "unbroken connection" to the rest of life that real things have. Kant would love this; it is just such unbroken connections of causality that—in contrast to dreams or flights of fancy—*constitute* a world as an objective world.

The concept of causality *does* apply to the world we experience—not because we discover it there, but because we bring it with us to the experience.

> This complete . . . solution of Hume's problem rescues for the pure concepts of the understanding their *a priori* origin and for the universal laws of nature their validity as laws of the understanding, yet in such a way as to limit their use to experience, because their possibility depends solely on the reference of the understanding to experience, but with a completely reversed mode of connection which never occurred to Hume: they are not derived from experience, but experience is derived from them.
>
> This is, therefore, the result of all our foregoing inquiries: "All synthetic principles *a priori* are nothing more than principles of possible experience" and can never be referred to things in themselves, but to appearances as objects of experience. (*P*, 55–56)

Let us sum up. The principle that every event has a cause is, as we have seen, synthetic (the concept of causation is not included in the concept of an event, but is added to it). And Hume is right that the causal principle cannot be known *a posteriori*, from experience. But we do know that the principle applies universally and necessarily to all experience. We know that *a priori* because, as Kant says, "experience is derived from [it]." The principle that every event has a cause is, then, one of the synthetic *a priori* judgments. Such purely rational, nonempirical principles, Kant believes, lie at the root of both commonsense knowledge and Newtonian science.

Now we can see that Kant has answered how science (including pure science) of nature is possible. Pure knowledge of nature is possible because nature itself (the objective world that is there to be known) is partially constituted by the concepts and principles that a rational mind must use in understanding it. We know *a priori* that nature is made up of substances-having-properties, though we can know only through experience which substances have what properties. We know *a priori* that the world is a causally ordered whole, though we can know only through experience which particular events cause what other events. Science, together with its pure or *a priori* part, is possible only because it is the knowledge of an objective world that is not independent of either our sensibility or our understanding. Natural science is possible only on the basis of Kant's Copernican revolution.

Let us just remind ourselves once more of the consequence: We have, and can have, no knowledge whatever about things as they are "in themselves." Do things in themselves—independently of how we know them—occupy space? *We have no idea.* Are they located in time, so that one event really does happen after another? *We have no idea.* Are there things (substances) at all? Does one event really cause another? *We have no idea.* Our knowledge is solely about the way things appear to us.

But, we must add, it does not follow that our knowledge is in any way illusory. It is not like a dream or a fancy of our imagination. The distinction, in fact, between illusion and reality is one drawn by us *within* this objective world of appearance—not *between* it and something else. Dreams and illusions are just sequences that cannot be ordered by the regularity of causal law; that is why they lack objectivity and are taken to be purely subjective phenomena. We are not capable of knowing anything *more real* than the spatiotemporal world of our experience, structured as it is by the categories of the pure understanding. This world may be "transcendentally ideal" (that is, its basic features are not independent of the knowing mind), but it is *empirically real.*

This, perhaps, needs a bit more explanation.

Phenomena and Noumena

"Thoughts without content are empty," Kant says, and "intuitions without concepts are blind" (*CPR*, 93). Thoughts are made up of concepts united in various ways. But unless those concepts are given a content through some intuition, either pure (as in geometry) or empirical (as in physics), they are "empty"—sheer forms that for all we know may apply to nothing. They provide us with no knowledge. However, merely having an intuition of space, or of blue-and-solid, provides no knowledge either. Intuitions without concepts are "blind." To know, or to "see" the truth, we must have concepts that are applied to some matter.

> We demand in every concept, first, the logical form of a concept (of thought) in general, and secondly, the possibility of giving it an object to which it may be applied. In the absence of such object, it has no meaning and is completely lacking in content, though it may still contain the logical function which is required for making a concept out of any data that may be presented. Now the object cannot be given to a concept otherwise than in intuition. . . . Therefore all concepts, and with them all principles, even such as are possible *a priori*, relate to empirical intuitions, that is, to the data for a possible experience. Apart from this relation they have no objective validity, and in respect of their representations are a mere play of imagination or of understanding. (*CPR*, 259)

Kant insists on this point again and again, for we are

> subject to an illusion from which it is difficult to escape. The categories are not, as regards their origin, grounded in sensibility, like the *forms of intuition*, space and time; and they seem, therefore, to allow of an application extending beyond all objects of the senses. (*CPR*, 266)

We have ideas of, for example, "substance" and "cause." And it seems there is no barrier to applying them even beyond the boundaries of **possible experience.*** In fact, *nearly all previous philosophers* think we can do that! Plato, for example, is convinced that reality is composed of *substances* (the Forms) that cannot be sensed but are purely intelligible. Descartes asks about the *cause* of his

---

*See the principle restricting such concepts to possible experience, p. 388.

Gottfried Wilhelm von Leibniz

Mathematician, physicist, historian, theologian, and diplomat, Gottfried Wilhelm von Leibniz (1646–1714) wrote voluminously; among his most philosophically important works are *Discourse on Metaphysics* (1686) and *Monadology* (1714).

As an inventor of calculus, Leibniz was poised to make use of the principles of continuity and infinity in his philosophical work. He objected to the purely quantitative, geometrical account of matter (as extension) given by Descartes and Spinoza. Sheer extension does not account for resistance, solidity, and impenetrability, he argued, so there must be some real qualitative thing to be extended. A new concept of substance was needed, and Leibniz offered one: a substance is a being capable of action. This makes reality intrinsically dynamic; the ultimate substances are points of activity (force), each with an inherent tendency toward motion (on his view, rest is just infinitesimally small movement). He called these simple substances *monads*.

Though each monad is intrinsically simple, each has infinitely many properties—namely, the ways it is related to each of the infinitely many other monads. So each monad, in a way, mirrors or reflects the entire universe; in certain monads, this reflection is perception and the mind. If you knew any monad completely, you would know everything.

Since each monad mirrors all the others, a change in one would necessitate a change in all the others. The sum total of all the substances that are possible along with a given monad—mirrored in it—constitute a *possible world*. There are many possible worlds, many families of possible monads; this actual world is just one of the possibilities. Contrary to Spinoza, then, Leibniz held that the actual universe does not exist of necessity.

Why is it *this* world, out of all the many possible worlds, that is the actual one? We can figuratively imagine God—the one being that is not merely possible, but necessarily existing—contemplating all the possible worlds and choosing one to actualize. He would clearly choose the "best" one, the one most like God himself, who is perfectly actual. This would be the universe that combines the most actuality (the richest variety of content) with the greatest simplicity of laws. In that sense, Leibniz believed, we live in the best of all possible worlds.

---

idea of God. One of the presuppositions of traditional metaphysics is that these concepts can take us beyond the sphere of experience.* But, if Kant is right, these concepts

---

*Notice how Kant has turned completely upside down Plato's claim that knowledge is restricted to the purely intelligible world of Forms. For Kant, this realm beyond any possible sensory experience cannot be known at all; what we can know is the changing world of the senses, about which Plato thinks we can have only opinions. Here we have yet another example of the radical consequences of modern science for traditional epistemology and metaphysics; for Kant's confidence in knowledge of the sensory world rests ultimately on the achievement of Newton.

---

are nothing but *forms of thought,* which contain the merely logical faculty of uniting *a priori* in one consciousness the manifold given in intuition; and apart, therefore, from the only intuition that is possible for us, they have even less meaning than the pure sensible forms [space and time]. (*CPR,* 266)

The categories, Kant claims, cannot be used apart from sensible intuitions to give us knowledge of objects. Why not? Because they are merely "forms of thought." Compare them to mathematical functions, like x^2. Until some number is given as x, we have no object. If a content for x is supplied, say 2 or 3, then an object is specified, in these cases the numbers 4 or 9. The categories of substance, cause, and the rest are similar. They are merely operators whose function is to unite "in one consciousness the manifold given in intuition." If a certain manifold of sensations is given, our possession of the concept "substance" allows us to produce the thought of a book; a different manifold of sensations produces (under the concept "substance") the thought of a printing press; and the category of "causation" allows us to think a causal relation between the two. Objects are the result of the application of the categories as operators to some sensible material.

It may be helpful to contrast Kant's *concepts* with Hume's *ideas.** Their analyses of this central feature of our intellectual life are as different as can be. For Hume, you will recall, an idea is a kind of *copy* of an impression; so an idea must be analogous to an *image*. Every idea, for Hume, has a *content* that is determined by its ancestry in our experience. It is produced in us passively: no impression, no idea. For Kant, by contrast, a concept is understood as a kind of *formal rule* for uniting intuitions (among which Hume's impressions may be found). Concepts may be suggested by impressions, but they are far from mere copies. Nor are we passive with regard to concepts. The pure concepts (categories) are necessarily *brought to* experience by a rational mind; they do not just reflect experience, they *organize* it. Empirical concepts have the same organizing role, but not so universally. Since a concept is just a formal rule for structuring some material, we can have concepts that reach beyond our experience. Kant holds that these concepts cannot give us *knowledge,* for without the sensible intuitions, there are no objects.

But it *seems* as though there are. This is the illusion.

> The categories . . . extend further than sensible intuition, since they think objects in general, without regard to the special mode (the sensibility) in which they may be given. But they do not thereby determine a greater sphere of objects. (*CPR,* 271)

———————
* See pp. 351–353.

The category of substance, for instance, is not inherently limited to the objects of sensory experience, or even, for that matter, to space and time. It seems we can have the idea of a nonmaterial, nonspatial, nontemporal substance. Nothing easier! But this is profoundly illusory, if Kant is right. Why? Because the concept "substance" is not a complete concept in its own right. It is only a kind of *rule* for organizing some content or other. And the content must be given by intuition.

It is perhaps not impossible for there to be other forms of intuition than those available to us. We human beings, however, are limited to space, time, and sensation. To treat the categories as concepts that can give us knowledge beyond these limitations is to suppose that we have types of intuition that we do not have. And that is to fall into the illusion.

One common form of the illusion is the claim that we can know things as they are *in themselves,* apart from the way they appear to us through our powers of intuition. This is the illusion of speculative metaphysics. The illusion is reinforced because we do have the concept of **things-in-themselves.** Kant even gives it a name: something as it is in itself, independently of the way it reveals itself to us, is called a **noumenon.** This contrasts with a **phenomenon,** its appearance to us.

But it is crucial to observe that this concept of a noumenon is not a concept with any positive meaning. Its role in our intellectual life is purely negative; it reminds us that there are things we cannot know—namely what the things affecting our sensibility are *really* like (if by "really" we mean what they are like independently of our intuitions of them). The phenomenal world of appearance is all we can ever know.

Kant once more drives home the moral:

> *Understanding* and *sensibility,* with us, can determine objects *only when they are employed in conjunction.* When we separate them, we have intuitions without concepts, or concepts without intuitions—in both cases, representations which we are not in a position to apply to any determinate object. (*CPR,* 274)

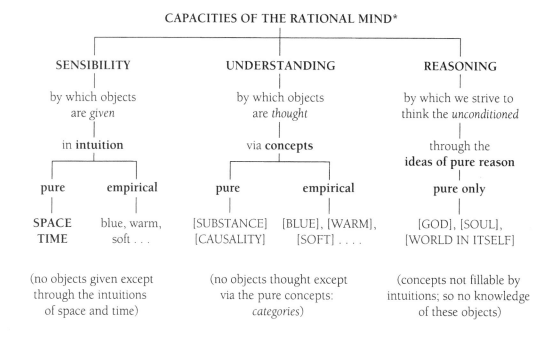

CAPACITIES OF THE RATIONAL MIND*

SENSIBILITY	UNDERSTANDING	REASONING
by which objects are *given*	by which objects are *thought*	by which we strive to think the *unconditioned*
in **intuition**	via **concepts**	through the **ideas of pure reason**

pure	empirical	pure	empirical	pure only
SPACE TIME	blue, warm, soft . . .	[SUBSTANCE] [CAUSALITY]	[BLUE], [WARM], [SOFT]	[GOD], [SOUL], [WORLD IN ITSELF]

(no objects given except through the intuitions of space and time)

(no objects thought except via the pure concepts: *categories*)

(concepts not fillable by intuitions; so no knowledge of these objects)

Reasoning and the Ideas of Metaphysics: God, World, and Soul

Kant's third question concerns metaphysics. The term "metaphysics" has a precise meaning for Kant. Metaphysics contrasts sharply with both common sense and science. We have seen that the entire range of possible experience is governed by the *pure intuitions* of space and time, as well as by the *pure categories* of the understanding. These, together with *sensations,* constitute the way things appear to us, the realm of *phenomena.* Beyond this realm our understanding is without footing. We know there are things that appear to us; but we are completely at sea about what they may be in themselves. "Out there" the dove cannot fly.

It may be useful to set out the basic pattern of Kant's epistemology as a series of steps that together constitute the world of all possible experience.

1. Noumena, or things in themselves,
2. Constitute the phenomenal world of appearance (objects), by
3. Producing in the knower a manifold of sensations (Humean impressions), which are
4. Apprehended through the intuitions of space and time (*a priori* forms of the knower's sensibility), and
5. Structured as substances in causal connections by the *a priori* categories of the understanding.

Experience of the empirical world lies at level 2. This is the domain in which common sense and science can do their work. Critical or transcendental philosophy reveals the levels 3 through 5 by what Kant calls a "critique of pure reason." Mathematics is done at level 4.

Metaphysics looks in two directions. Understood in the traditional way, it is the discipline that tries to gain knowledge about level 1—about things apart from their appearance to us. It is the attempt to go beyond experience in a *transcendent* direction, toward the *noumenal world,* which *tran-*

---

*Concepts are indicated by square brackets.

scends all possible experience. But metaphysics can also look in the opposite direction: to the structures on the side of the subject that condition the being of objects. In this case Kant calls it *transcendental*. It is just that critique of pure reason we have been examining; it tries only to discern the *a priori* conditions of experience. Such a *transcendental* investigation, looking back into the knowing subject, Kant also calls *immanent*.

Not surprisingly, Kant thinks the transcendent kind of metaphysics is impossible. But his discussion of the reasons for the impossibility are full of interesting insights. First, Kant claims to be able to explain why the quest for metaphysical knowledge recurs with such inevitability (despite the critiques of the skeptics) and why it is so difficult to give up. Second, he finds a positive use for the fundamental metaphysical ideas—God, the world, and the soul—even though he denies that these ideas can give us knowledge. Finally, Kant's examination of these ideas propels us into the fourth of his major concerns, the practical use of reason, or morality.

The notion that we can get knowledge of things in themselves is, Kant says, "a *natural* and inevitable *illusion*" (*CPR*, 300). Something in the very structure of rationality gives us that notion; it has to do with *reasoning*. The aim of reasoning is to supply "the reason why" something is true. As we have seen numerous times already, the why-question can always be repeated; we can ask for the reason for the reason. Kant talks of this process as one that seeks the *conditions* which account for a given truth. Grass is green. Why? In answering this question, we refer to some condition in the world that explains that fact. Why is that condition the way it is? Again, we can supply a condition that explains that condition. And we could go on.

As you can see, the quest for reasons will not be satisfied until it finds some condition that doesn't need to be explained by a further condition. Reason is always searching for the *unconditioned*. We can think of this as Kant's version of the search for first principles. This has always been the task of first philosophy, or metaphysics. The search is for

something intelligible in itself, which explains or makes intelligible all the rest.

> Without solving this question, reason will never be satisfied. The empirical use to which reason limits the pure understanding does not fully satisfy reason's own proper destination. Every single experience is only a part of the whole sphere of its domain, but the absolute totality of all possible experience is itself not experience. . . . the concepts of reason aim at the completeness, i.e., the collective unity, of all possible experience, and thereby go beyond every given experience. Thus they become *transcendent*. (*P*, 70)

> . . . when reason, which cannot be fully satisfied with any empirical use of the rules of the understanding, as being always conditioned, requires a completion of this chain of conditions, then the understanding is forced out of its sphere. And then reason partly represents objects of experience in a series so extended that no experience can grasp it, partly even (with a view to complete the series) it seeks entirely beyond experience *noumena*, to which it can attach that chain; and so, having at last escaped from the conditions of experience, reason makes it hold complete. (*P*, 74)

We can understand only what lies within the bounds of possible experience. But reason cannot be content with that. If those bounds are reached, reason still wants to ask why. Why is experience as a whole the way it is? Why is there experience at all? But this question can be answered only by transcending those boundaries. To ask for the condition that explains the "absolute totality of all possible experience" is no longer asking for the explanation of one phenomenon in terms of another—about which we might then ask the same question. It is asking for something absolute, for the unconditioned, which will necessarily involve knowledge of things in themselves.

And so arise, naturally and inevitably, those concepts of God, the world in itself, and the knowing subject or soul. These concepts are very different from all others. They are not empirical concepts abstracted from sensations. Nor are they *a priori* concepts structuring each and every one of our experiences. Kant gives them a special name: *Ideas of Pure Reason.**

> As the understanding stands in need of categories for experience, reason contains in itself the ground of ideas, by which I mean necessary concepts whose object *cannot* be given in any experience. (*P*, 70)

Reason can try to trace out the ultimate conditions in three different directions: back into the *subject* (trying to construct an absolute psychological Idea), out into the *world* (trying to discover the cosmological Ideas), and toward the *absolute condition of anything at all* (searching for the theological Idea). And so we find reason inevitably constructing the ideas of soul, world, and God.

The Soul

The outcome of Descartes' strategy of methodical doubt is that he cannot doubt his own existence. And when he asks himself what he is, the answer seems obvious: a thing that thinks. He "knows" that he is a substance whose essential characteristic is to think. Descartes, as we have seen, further claims that this substance is simple (indivisible), distinct from the body, unchanging through time, and immortal.

It is clear that Descartes is not doing empirical psychology here; there are no experiments, and he gathers no data. Kant calls this kind of thing **rational psychology.** Rational psychology is an attempt to understand the fundamental nature of the self by rational reflection on what the self *must* be if experience is to be possible. It is a quest for the *unconditioned condition* on the side of the subject. Kant is convinced that rational psychology is illusory, that there can be no such knowledge. But he

also thinks that the illusion is a powerful one and difficult to resist. It arises from what Kant calls "the sole text of rational psychology," the judgment "I think" (*CPR*, 330). Reflection on this judgment alone seems to be enough to yield all the conclusions desired by the rational psychologist.

Is the soul a substance? It seems as though I can conclude that I am a substance. Here is the argument. Every thought I have can be preceded (at least implicitly) by the phrase, "I think." I think roses are lovely; I think eggs come from chickens; I think Kant is a great philosopher. All these thoughts belong to me; they are qualities or properties of myself. But what about the "I"? Could this "I" be simply a property or characteristic? Of what? The idea that *I* might be just a property of some other substance doesn't seem to make sense. *I* am the absolute subject of all these determinations. But this is just what we mean by substance; a substance is, by definition, that which cannot be predicated of anything else, but is the subject of properties.* So I, as a thinking thing, must be a substance.

This seems a persuasive argument; but, if Kant is right, it is a mere sophism. Remember that "substance" is one of the *a priori* categories. This means it is a concept that is purely formal in itself, without any content. Its whole function is to serve as a kind of rule for organizing sensible intuitions into experience. But where is the intuition that corresponds to the "I"? Kant agrees with Hume, who claims not to be able to find any perception of the self when he introspects.† When you say "I think," you are not peering at or describing your self. The whole content of what you think is expressed in what comes *after* that phrase.

> The 'I' is indeed in all thoughts, but there is not in this representation the least trace of intuition, distinguishing the 'I' from other objects of intuition.

---

*Kant has Plato explicitly in mind here. In Plato the "Forms" or "Ideas" are purely intelligible entities that can be understood, but not sensed. For Kant, of course, the Ideas are concepts, not realities; and they can give us no knowledge. But they are concepts whose aim seems to be the presentation of realities beyond any possible sensory experience. For Plato on the Forms, see pp. 109–114.

---

* This idea of substance can be traced back to Aristotle's discussion of the categories of being. Substance is basic in the sense that all other modes of being (qualities, relations, and so on) are parasitic on substance. See pp. 148–149 for a brief discussion of this point.
†For Hume on the self, see "The Disappearing Self," in Chapter 17.

We do not have, and cannot have, any knowledge whatsoever of any such subject. (*CPR*, 334)

Reason is always searching for the conditions that make experience possible. In looking back and back into myself, I seem to come upon the idea that there is a substance to which all these activities connected with thinking belong. But this is a kind of grammatical or logical illusion. Just because I need to express my thinking by using subject/predicate forms in which the "I" occurs, I cannot infer that *noumenal reality* is structured that way. I cannot transform a necessity of my mode of representing myself into a metaphysical necessity concerning my nature.

Kant says that the "I" in "I think" is just a kind of formal marker. Concepts like this (others are "now" and "here" and "this") are sometimes called *indexicals;* what is peculiar about them is that they have no determinate content but merely indicate something relative to the circumstances of utterance. About the term "I," Kant says, "we cannot even say that this is a concept, but only that it is a bare consciousness which accompanies all concepts" (*CPR*, 331). All knowledge, however, is through concepts. So the "I" is nothing more than an empty representation of an unknown *X,* "this I or he or it (the thing) which thinks" (*CPR*, 331). What I am in myself is completely unknown to me. For all that rational reflection can tell me, this *X* that I am may be anything at all. I do not know that I am a substance. The self or soul, then, is that unknown *X* to whom the world appears and by which it is structured into objects.

Similar reflections undermine the claims about the soul's simplicity, its unchanging nature, and its immortality. In each case a *merely subjective condition* of thinking is transformed into a concept of a *noumenal object*. The "I," however, is not an object and cannot be known as an object. Objects, remember, can be known in experience only through the application of concepts to intuitions. The "I" is a *subject* and *resists objectification*. As far as rational knowledge goes, the subject of thinking remains merely an *X,* which must express itself *as*

if it were a simple substance, continuously the same through time, and so on. But what it is in itself remains a complete mystery.* The concept of "soul" is an empty idea.

Kant's denial of rational psychology is not equivalent to a denial of the possibility of an *empirical* psychology. Such a psychology, based on experience, is just as legitimate as Newtonian science of nature. Only let psychologists be aware that they are examining appearance, the world of phenomena—in this case, the world of inner phenomena in time. Let them not think that they can discern the ultimate nature of the subject of consciousness!

The World and the Free Will

When we reason about the world, our reasoning seeks completeness, closure. Whatever we experience in the realm of phenomena is conditioned by other things; reason seeks the final condition, a foundation on which it can rest. It is seeking a point where its why-questions can stop. But Kant believes our reason can find no satisfaction in its search for the totality of the world; in fact, it develops internal conflicts. For example, he tries to demonstrate that we cannot decide whether the world had a beginning in time—whether it is temporally finite or infinite. In fact, he has arguments that seem to show that each alternative is false! When reason runs into such a contradiction—he calls it an "antinomy"—this is a sign that reason is overreaching its own powers. In trying to complete the search for the unconditioned, reason frustrates itself. The moral of the story is that the origins of the world *in itself* are unknowable.

A second question, one more pertinent to our concerns here, asks whether we can know that the

---

* Some thinkers have taken this lack of direct insight into the nature of the self to open the door to the Hobbesian possibility that the subject might be a material body after all—perhaps just a human body with a certain type of brain. This is an interesting possibility. There is no evidence that Kant takes this view, though he does point out that the *supposed* simplicity of the soul is the only ground on which it can be distinguished from matter.

world in itself is ordered causally. Phenomena are subject to causal ordering, as we have seen, but only because phenomenal objects are constituted *as objects* by the category of causality. Does this category extend to noumena? No. But then an interesting possibility arises: that our wills might—in themselves—be free.

As we have seen, this problem arises with particular insistence in the modern era. The scientific revolution, which leads to thinking of the world in mechanistic ways (the big clock), raises the question about human actions: Are they, too, just a part of the mechanism?

Descartes takes one possible tack here: mind and all its manifestations are excluded from the universal determinism governing material bodies. For Descartes, will is as free in man as it is in God: absolutely free. It escapes the causal network; when I will to raise my arm, there is no worldly cause in existence sufficient to produce that action. It is my doing—mine alone!

Hobbes and Hume take another tack. Universal determination of events is not denied. Actions, too, have causes: the laws of nature determine what we do just as surely as they determine the fall of a stone. These philosophers try to rescue human freedom, however, by offering a hypothetical analysis of what it is to act freely: *If* you can do what you want to do, *then* you are free. This is a *conditional* account of freedom. In a free action, they say, there are no conditions to constrain us, to keep us from doing what we want. They believe that this view of freedom is quite compatible with the view that (1) our wants themselves have causes and (2) our wants cause our actions. So they hope to reconcile freedom of action with the new physics.*

We should not be surprised if Kant's Copernican revolution in philosophy were to transform the shape of this problem. For, from Kant's point of view, Descartes and Hobbes/Hume share an important presupposition: both sides assume that they are describing things (in this case the will, or

human action) as they are independent of our knowing them. What happens if we recognize that things in themselves are unknown to us and that all we can know is their appearance?

Critical philosophy, Kant thinks, will resolve this puzzle in the nicest possible way.

- We can agree with Descartes that freedom is exemption from causality. Kant calls it "the power of beginning a state *spontaneously*" (*CPR*, 464).
- But we do not have to carve out a part of the world in which causal law does not apply. We can agree with Hobbes and Hume that Newtonian science applies without limits to everything we can possibly experience.

This surely seems like the best of both views! Kant thinks he can give us all this without the questionable moves of Descartes and Hume. Descartes' exemption of the will from causal determination is dubious; it seems like special pleading, a stratagem designed simply to preserve something we are loath to give up. And the definition of "free" that Hobbes and Hume offer is equally questionable; can our actions really be free if they have causes that reach back and back and back in an unbroken chain to some period before we were even born? If Kant can avoid both shortcomings, effectively preserve human freedom, and still allow science unlimited scope, what more could we ask?

What makes this possible, of course, is the distinction between phenomena and noumena, between things as they appear to us and things in themselves.

Is it a truly disjunctive proposition to say that every effect in the world must arise *either* from nature *or* from freedom; or must we not rather say that in one and the same event, in different relations, both can be found? That all events in the sensible world stand in thoroughgoing connection in accordance with unchangeable laws of nature is an established principle . . . and allows of no exception. The question, therefore, can only be whether freedom is completely excluded by this inviolable rule, or whether an effect, notwithstanding its being thus determined in accordance with nature, may not at the same time be

---

*Review the discussion by Descartes in *Meditation IV*, p. 322. For Hume's view, see "Rescuing Human Freedom," in Chapter 17.

grounded in freedom. The common but fallacious presupposition of the *absolute reality* of appearances here manifests its injurious influence. . . . For if appearances are things in themselves, freedom cannot be upheld. Nature will then be the complete and sufficient determining cause of every event. The condition of the event will be such as can be found only in the series of appearances; both it and its effect will be necessary in accordance with the law of nature. If, on the other hand, appearances are not taken for more than they actually are; if they are viewed not as things in themselves, but merely as representations, connected according to empirical laws, they must themselves have grounds which are not appearances. (*CPR*, 466–67)

Every action, even every act of will, has two aspects: (1) it is something that appears in the world of our experience, and (2) it is something in itself. As an appearance, part of the world of nature, it is governed by all the principles that constitute that realm. It appears in time and is related by the category of causality to other events that precede and follow it. In this aspect, every action is causally determined. But as a thing in itself, we cannot even say that it occurs in time! And the category of causality does not extend to what occurs beyond the bounds of experience. So it may well be that in itself an act of will is free in that *absolute* sense of Descartes'; that is, there are no causal conditions sufficient for producing it.

Both Descartes and Hume think you have to choose between a strong noncausal view of freedom and a weaker compatibilist view. If you choose the former, you are committed to events that are exceptions to scientific laws. If you choose the latter, you believe the will is not free (in this absolute sense). Descartes chooses the former, Hume the latter (but adds that acts can be free in another, hypothetical sense). Kant argues that if we keep in mind the distinction between phenomena and things in themselves, we don't have to choose! An act can be both free and determined: free in itself (since the category of causality does not reach so far) and yet causal as it appears to us. The notion that an act couldn't possibly be both is simply due to considering the things we experience as

things in themselves. And that is a mistake that critical philosophy can keep us from making.

> Freedom is therefore no hindrance to natural law in appearances; neither does this law abrogate the freedom of the practical use of reason, which is connected with things in themselves, as determining grounds.
>
> Thus practical freedom, viz., the freedom in which reason possesses causality according to objectively determining grounds, is rescued; and yet natural necessity is not in the least curtailed with regard to the very same effects, as appearances. (*P,* 86–87)

Most of this should now be intelligible to you. "Practical freedom" is freedom in action, freedom to decide what events should occur in the world. This freedom, Kant is convinced, is closely tied to reason and acting for reasons. We can act freely when we act *for a reason* and not just in response to nonrational causes. We'll explain how reason can supply "objectively determining grounds" for action when we discuss Kant's views on morality; for now it will be enough to understand that Kant is thinking of reason itself, in the form of a rational will, as a certain kind of (spontaneous) causality. When you act for good reasons, you bring into being events that *appear* in the causal order of the world, but *in themselves* may have a completely noncausal—but rational—origin.

We need to be very careful, however. Kant does not claim he has proved that there are free actions, or that he has evidence that such free actions exist. Remember, the will in its aspect as free is the will considered noumenally. And about the noumenal world we can know nothing at all. Kant does not even claim to have proved that such freedom is possible. The most he will say is that "causality through freedom is at least *not incompatible with nature*" (*CPR*, 479). There is no contradiction in thinking of an act as free in itself, but determined as appearance.

This means that, from the viewpoint of critical theory, freedom remains merely an Idea of Reason. It is one of those Ideas to which reason is driven when it asks (this time) about the conditions under which it can itself make a difference in the world. But no empirical filling of that concept is available to give us knowledge. More will be said about freedom, however, when we come to the topic of morality.

God

We have seen how our reason, in asking the why-question, inevitably runs through a series of conditions that tends to approach completeness. The end point of each such series must be the concept of some being that is, *in itself,* a foundation for phenomena and a natural stopping place for reason. We have seen how this process generates the Ideas of the soul and of the world in itself. Kant's conclusion in both cases is, of course, that these Ideas are *merely ideas.* Because we have no intuitions providing content for these concepts, knowledge of them is impossible (despite their inevitability). Experience is the only ground our intellect can cultivate. And experience is essentially open-ended; no closure, no completeness will be found there. So the Ideas are sources of illusion. We are drawn to think we can know something about them. But we are mistaken.

There is one more pattern of reasoning we simply cannot avoid. It leads to the concept of God. Let us see how Kant understands this. He agrees with Descartes and the tradition that the idea of God is the idea of an all-perfect being, but he has a very interesting analysis of the way reasoning necessarily leads us to that idea. Like the ideas of soul and world, the idea of God is not an arbitrary invention. Nor is it something we just *might* invent, as Hume claims. Nor is it, as some in the Enlightenment hold, a priestly or political trick foisted on people to keep them in subjection. It is, for any being that reasons, an absolutely unavoidable concept.

Every thing, a philosopher once said, is what it is and not another thing.[2] Very sensible. But what determines what a thing is? In the broadest possible perspective (which is what our reasoning seeks) a thing is only a determinate thing if, given *every possible property* together with its *contradictory opposite,* one out of each pair of such opposites belongs to the thing. This is quite a mouthful; but the idea is really quite simple. Let's take an example.

Think of an egg, an ordinary chicken egg you might have for breakfast. It has certain properties and lacks others. That is what makes it the thing it is. But it isn't fully *determinate* unless every possible question about it has an answer; if there are questions without answers, it isn't any definite thing. Questions can be put in terms of *predicates* that express all the possible properties there are. And we can ask about the egg:

- Is it living, or not living?
- Is it white, or not white?
- Does it weigh thirty pounds, or does it not?
- Is it fragile, or is it not fragile?

And the list goes on and on and on. If the egg is to be a single, determinate thing, then to each such question there must be an answer. And there must be as many questions as there are possible predicates.

For every determinate thing that there is, reason is searching for an answer to the question, What is it? And to get a clear understanding of even one thing, such as our egg, reason would have to encompass in understanding the *complete* system of *all* the properties there could possibly be. Again we have the notion of completeness, finality. And since our egg is a real egg, we are led to think that this sum total of all possibilities cannot itself be merely imaginary. There must actually be, we suppose, *some being* that makes all these possibilities *possible.* There must be a being who is the foundation for the determinate nature of all things, by being the foundation of that enormously long list of possibilities which accounts for things being the things they are.* Such a being, as Thomas Aquinas might say, we call "God."

This is how reason inevitably comes upon the

---

*Even this is not enough. For we can imagine other worlds than this one. And they too would need determinacy. So the being we are led to conceive must be the foundation not only for the actual world but for any other possible world as well. God, if there is a god, must account not only for what the world *is* but for what it *could be.* But this is just to emphasize that such a being could not lack any *possible* perfection.

Idea of God. But the Idea is empty.* The emptiness of the Idea is clear when we realize that finding the sum total of all possible properties is an infinite task we could never complete. No experience, no intuition could ever fulfill the requirements of this Idea. Moreover, it is the Idea of something that cannot just be another phenomenal being; since it is the foundation for the determinate character of all phenomenal things, it must be noumenal—a thing in itself. As we are now abundantly aware, Kant argues that things in themselves are unknowable. So the concept of God is *just* an Idea of Reason. If we keep the principles of critical philosophy firmly in mind, Kant says,

> we can easily expose the dialectical illusion which arises from our making the subjective conditions of our thinking objective conditions of objects themselves, and from making an hypothesis necessary for the satisfaction of our reason into a dogma. (*P*, 89)

These reflections should suffice to inhibit dogmatism, while explaining at the same time how inevitable the temptation to dogmatism is. But Kant adds a critique of the major arguments that purport to show that such a being must actually exist. He divides the arguments into three types: cosmological, design, and ontological. He argues that each of the first two types makes use of the principle of the ontological argument at a crucial stage. So we will focus on that.

The Ontological Argument

We met Descartes' version of this argument in the fifth *Meditation*; the argument is originally presented by Anselm of Canterbury in the eleventh century.† You will remember that this argument is unique because it presupposes nothing but our idea of God as a most perfect being. From that idea

alone, *a priori*, as Kant would say, the existence of God is supposed to follow; it follows just as surely (so Descartes tells us) as a theorem about the interior angles of a triangle follows from the concept of a triangle. Kant's critique of this argument is famous, and we will examine it with some care.

He begins with a general point.

> In all ages men have spoken of an *absolutely necessary* being, and in so doing have endeavoured, not so much to understand whether and how a thing of this kind allows even of being thought, but rather to prove its existence. There is, of course, no difficulty in giving a verbal definition of the concept, namely, that it is something the non-existence of which is impossible. But this yields no insight into the conditions which make it necessary to regard the non-existence of a thing as absolutely unthinkable. It is precisely these conditions that we desire to know, in order that we may determine whether or not, in resorting to this concept, we are thinking anything at all. (*CPR*, 501)

Kant is again insisting on the need for critical philosophy. Previous thinkers have rushed to prove the existence of a supremely perfect being, without examining in a reflective way "how a thing of this kind allows even of being thought." What we need to do, Kant says, is to examine the status of such a concept in our thought. We may find that through this concept we are not "thinking anything at all," that the concept has only a "verbal definition."*

If we give the concept this kind of examination, what do we find? We find that it is supposed to be illuminated by several analogies. Descartes' comments about triangles and mountains without valleys come to mind. God is supposed to have necessary existence in just the same way that a triangle necessarily has three angles. Kant's first criticism shows that these are not in fact analogous.

---

*Remember the slogan, "Thoughts without content are empty, intuitions without concepts are blind." (See p. 389.) The Ideas are thoughts without content.

†For a discussion of the original argument as given by Anselm, see pp. 254–256. Review the argument as presented by Descartes in *Meditation V.*

---

*Kant's doubts here recall the reason that Thomas Aquinas does not accept the ontological argument. Thomas said that the argument assumes we have an adequate grasp of the "essence" of God, but that this is not something we can assume. (See p. 257.) The reason Thomas gives (that all our concepts originate in the senses) is not exactly Kant's reason; but both of them require an examination of our *title* to such a concept, and in that way both are doing "critical" philosophy.

All the alleged examples are, without exception, taken from *judgments,* not from *things* and their existence. But the unconditioned necessity of judgments is not the same as the absolute necessity of things. . . . The above proposition does not declare that three angles are absolutely necessary, but that, under the condition that there is a triangle (that is, that a triangle is given), three angles will necessarily be found in it. . . .

If, in an identical proposition, I reject the predicate while retaining the subject, contradiction results; and I therefore say that the former belongs necessarily to the latter. But if we reject subject and predicate alike, there is no contradiction; for nothing is then left that can be contradicted. To posit a triangle, and yet to reject its three angles, is self-contradictory; but there is no contradiction in rejecting the triangle together with its three angles. The same holds true of the concept of an absolutely necessary being. If its existence is rejected, we reject the thing itself with all its predicates; and no question of contradiction can then arise. (*CPR,* 501–2)

The ontological argument is supposed to show us that the judgment "God does not exist" is self-contradictory because existence is one of the perfections included in the concept of God. (It is supposed to be like saying, "Something that exists does not exist.") The aim of the argument is to show that the atheist is just not thinking coherently. But, Kant says, even if we grant that "God exists" is necessarily true, this is simply a fact about our *concepts.* If the concept of God is given, then the concept of existence is given; and we cannot consistently deny God's existence. But it is quite open to the atheist to simply reject the concept. And if he does, the argument can get no hold on him. As Kant says, "Nothing is then left that can be contradicted."*

You can probably see that defenders of the argument might have a comeback to this point. They might say it is not so clear that the atheist *can* reject the concept. An atheist, in denying God's existence, must understand what it is he is denying, in which case he does have the concept. But Kant has

a second and deeper criticism of the argument, one that will reinforce the first.

The deeper criticism rests on an analysis of what we are doing when we say that something exists.

"Being" is obviously not a real predicate: that is, it is not a concept of something which could be added to the concept of a thing. It is merely the positing of a thing, or of certain determinations, as existing in themselves. (*CPR,* 504)

This is a difficult thought. But we can make it clear by reflecting on definitions. Suppose we have a certain concept *x.* If we want to know what that concept is, we are asking for a definition. And the definition will be given in terms of certain predicates, say *f, g, h.* So we will be told that an *x* is something that is *f, g,* and *h.* A triangle, for example, is a closed plane figure bounded by three straight lines. Could "being" or "existence" be on such a list of predicates? This is what Kant denies. To say that *a triangle is a figure* is one thing. To say that *a triangle exists* is to say something of an altogether different *kind.* If we say that a triangle exists, we are not expressing one of the properties of the triangle; existence is not the kind of thing that should be named in a list of those properties. To say that a triangle exists is to "posit" something that has *all* the properties of a triangle. It is to say that the concept (together with the properties that define it) *applies* to something.

If Kant is right, it follows that *every* judgment of existence is *synthetic.* None of them is simply analytic of the concept expressed by the subject of the judgment—because existence is not a normal predicate and cannot be part of the subject term's definition. And that means that *in no case* is the denial of a judgment asserting existence a contradiction. But this is exactly what the ontological argument claims.*

The fundamental mistake of the argument is the

---

*So far the analysis is similar to that given by Hume. Look again at Hume's discussion on pp. 365–366.

*Modern logic agrees with Kant here. The two propositions "Dogs bark" and "Dogs exist" may *look* very much alike. But their logic is very different. In symbolic notation, the first is $(x)(Dx \supset Bx)$. The second is $(\exists x)(Dx)$.

assumption that existence is a predicate like others and that the concept of a perfect being would have to include it.

> If, now, we take the subject (God) with all its predicates . . . , and say "God is," or "There is a God," we attach no new predicate to the concept of God, but only posit the subject in itself with all its predicates, and indeed posit it as being an *object* that stands in relation to my *concept*. The content of both must be one and the same; nothing can have been added to the concept, which expresses merely what is possible, by my thinking its object . . . as given absolutely. Otherwise stated, the real contains no more than the merely possible. A hundred real thalers do not contain the least coin more than a hundred possible thalers. (*CPR*, 505)

If I say that God does not exist, I am not denying in the predicate part of the sentence what I have implicitly asserted in the subject part. I am simply refusing to "posit" an object of the sort the subject describes. Atheism may be wrong, but it is at least not a logically incoherent view. So the ontological argument fails.

> The attempt to establish the existence of a supreme being by means of the famous ontological argument of Descartes is therefore so much labour and effort lost; we can no more extend our stock of [theoretical] insight by mere ideas, than a merchant can better his position by adding a few noughts to his cash account. (*CPR*, 507)

Is it Kant's purpose to make atheism possible? Not at all. In another famous line, Kant says,

> I have therefore found it necessary to deny *knowledge*, in order to make room for *faith*. (*CPR*, 29)

What sort of faith he has in mind we will discover in examining his moral philosophy.

Let us sum up this section with some reflections on the positive function of these Ideas of Reason: soul, world, and God. We have seen that in no case can we have knowledge of the things-in-themselves these Ideas picture. Taken as sources of knowledge, the Ideas are illusory. But they

do express an *ideal* that reason cannot disregard: the ideal of knowledge as a complete, unified, and systematic whole, with no loose ends and nothing left out. It is this that drives reason forward in asking its why-questions; and it is this goal that, in their various ways, the Ideas of soul, world, and God express. *If* reason could complete its search, it would have to end with such concepts. Since experience, the field in which reason can successfully labor, is essentially open-ended, the search cannot be completed. But these Ideals can serve a regulative purpose, representing the goal toward which rational creatures like ourselves are striving. We want to understand *completely*.

Reason and Morality

We are not only knowers. We are also doers. So far we have seen Kant examining in his critical way our capacities for knowing. The critical investigation into knowledge looks at reason in its *theoretical* aspect; it is concerned with the *a priori* foundations of mathematics and physics, together with the temptations of transcendent metaphysics. As we have seen, it uncovers space and time as pure forms of intuition, the pure concepts (categories) that structure experience, and the Ideas. We are now turning to see what Kant has to say about our actions. The critical inquiry into action concerns reason in its *practical* aspect. It deals with the *a priori* foundations of morality.

Kant takes pains to distinguish his treatment from a common way to look at morality. We might think of morality as just one more empirical phenomenon to be understood. If we take this point of view, we examine what people *in fact* praise and blame, and what motivations (e.g., sympathy) explain these facts. To look at morality this way, Kant says, is to do "practical anthropology" (*G*, 2). This is the way Hume looks at morality.*

There is nothing wrong with studying practical

---

*To make sure you understand the contrast, look back at the way Hume thinks of his moral philosophy, pp. 368–372.

life this way. But Kant is convinced that an empirical study of morality will miss the contribution of *reason* to our practice; and it will be impossible to find *the moral law*. All you will get is a collection of different, probably overlapping, practices or customs. No *universality* can be found this way; nor will the *necessity* that attaches to obligation appear.* (In fact, Kant is right about this; anthropology seems to reveal nothing but customs that vary from culture to culture. Compare the story told by Herodotus on page 42, in the light of which he says that custom—*nomos*—is "king of all." As you read Kant, you should be thinking about whether he succeeds in showing this saying to be a mistake.)

Kant, of course, wants to apply his Copernican revolution to practical life as well as theoretical. We need a transcendental inquiry into the foundations of our practical life to complement his critique of our theoretical life. Morality, he believes, is not just a set of practices in the phenomenal world. It has its foundation in *legislation by pure reason*. Morality, just as much as mathematics and natural science, is constituted in part by *a priori* elements originating in the nature of reason itself. Therefore it is necessary to work out

a pure moral philosophy that is wholly cleared of everything which can only be empirical and can only belong to anthropology. (*G*, 2)

In pursuing such a philosophy, Kant is engaged in nothing less than

seeking out and establishing the supreme principle of morality. (*G*, 5)

This is an ambitious aim. You can see that if Kant succeeds, he will have undercut the moral relativism that seems to be the result of restricting moral philosophy to empirical anthropology. He will have found a *criterion* of moral value that is *nonrelative*.

The Good Will

One way into such a "pure moral philosophy" is to ask whether there is anything at all that could be called *good* without qualification. Now there are many good things in the world.

Intelligence, wit, judgment, and whatever talents of the mind one might want to name are doubtless in many respects good and desirable, as are such qualities of temperament as courage, resolution, perseverance. But they can also become extremely bad and harmful if the will, which is to make use of these gifts of nature and which in its special constitution is called character, is not good. The same holds with gifts of fortune; power, riches, honor, even health, and that complete well-being and contentment with one's condition which is called happiness make for pride and often hereby even arrogance, unless there is a good will to correct their influence on the mind. (*G*, 7)

You can see Kant's line of argument. Money, for example, is surely something good, but it is not good *without qualification;* it is good only if used well. Likewise, intelligence is surely good, but dangerous if put to bad use. Think of a healthy, wealthy, and smart terrorist!

There is no possibility of thinking of anything at all in the world, or even out of it, which can be regarded as good without qualification, except a *good will*. (*G*, 7)

Many earlier philosophers have suggested a connection between being a morally good person and being happy. Plato, for instance, argues that the just man *is* the happy man.* Kant, more realistic perhaps, disagrees. If happiness correlates (as Hobbes claims) with the satisfaction of desires, there is no guarantee that moral goodness will match perfectly with happiness. We can think of the image in Plato's *Republic* of the perfectly just man languishing in prison; it is just too hard, Kant

---

*For *universality* and *necessity* as marks of the *a priori* contributions of reason to experience, see p. 381. What goes for experience, goes for action, too.

*See pp. 134–137. Plato is not the only one to pursue this tack. We find it in Aristotle (pp. 175–177), Epicurus (pp. 191–192), the Stoics (pp. 193–195), and Augustine (pp. 219–223).

seems to suggest, to imagine that he is also perfectly happy! There is a relationship, however.

> The sight of a being who is not graced by any touch of a pure and good will but who yet enjoys an uninterrupted prosperity can never delight a rational and impartial spectator. Thus a good will seems to constitute the indispensable condition of being even worthy of happiness. (*G*, 7)

It may not in fact be the case that happiness correlates perfectly with a good will in this world. But it should be so; any "impartial spectator" will feel uneasy at the sight of some really rotten person who is really happy. Goodness may not guarantee happiness, but it seems to constitute the condition of being worthy of happiness, or of deserving it. And this opinion is reflected in common sayings, such as, "She deserves better." *

We cannot, then, solve the problem about the nature of moral goodness by inquiring (as Aristotle, Epicurus, and Augustine do) into happiness.† If the only thing good without qualification is a *good will*, we must examine that directly. So let us ask, What is a good will? And what makes a good will *good*?

We need first to clarify the notion of will. We will not go far wrong if we think of an *act of will* as a kind of internal command with a content of this kind: "Let me now do *A*!" But not every such imperative qualifies as an act of will. If I decide to do *A* on a whim, or because I want to, or for no reason at all, this will be acting from *inclination,* not from *will.* Only internal commands that come at the end of a process of rational deliberation qualify as acts of will. There is something peculiarly *rational* about will. In fact, it is not too much to say that *will is just reason in its practical employment.* Dogs and cats have inclinations, but only a rational being can have a will.‡ In its theoretical employment, the outcome of a process of reasoning is an indicative, descriptive statement (e.g., "Bodies fall

according to the formula $v = 1/2 \, gt^2$"). When reason deliberates about practical matters, by contrast, the outcome is an imperative, a command, an act of will (e.g., "Let me now help this suffering person").

As this example makes clear, every act of will has a certain content. If we spell out the "*A*" in one of the will's commands, we get what Kant calls a *maxim.* Maxims are rules that express the *subjective intention* of the agent in doing an action. For instance, we might get maxims of the following sort: "Let me now keep the promise I made yesterday," or "Let me now break the promise I made yesterday."

We can think of Kant's moral philosophy as the search for a criterion for sorting maxims into two classes: those which are morally OK, and those which are not. If he can find such a rule (really a metarule, since it is a rule for deciding about maxims, which are themselves rules), he will have found "the supreme principle of morality."

Now we return to the question: what makes an act of will *good*? Kant first makes a negative point. It is *not the consequences* of a good will that make it good. In determining what makes it good, we must altogether set aside what it accomplishes in the world.

> Even if, by some especially unfortunate fate or by the niggardly provision of stepmotherly nature, this will should be wholly lacking in the power to accomplish its purpose; if with the greatest effort it should yet achieve nothing, and only the good will should remain (not, to be sure, as a mere wish but as the summoning of all the means in our power), yet would it, like a jewel, still shine by its own light as something which has its full value in itself. (*G*, 7–8)

If Jane acts out of a truly good will, our estimation of her moral worth is unaffected even if an uncooperative nature frustrates the intended outcome. Her will "sparkles like a jewel," even if the action it produces goes wrong. *

But this just raises the question with more ur-

---

* This connection between moral goodness and happiness is important for what Kant calls "rational religion." See pp. 409–410.
† For another view on this issue, see the utilitarians, Chapter 21.
‡ Contrast this notion of will with that of Hobbes, p. 340.

---

* Compare the Stoic story of the two slaves, p. 196.

gency. What is such a good will? If a good will cannot be defined by anything external to it, something about *the willing itself* must make it good. Now we have seen that every act of will has an intelligible content, expressible as the maxim of that act. Only the maxim, in fact, differentiates one act of will from another. So a good will must be one with a certain kind of maxim. But what kind?

Here we have to distinguish the *form* of a maxim from its *content*. The content of a maxim always refers to some outcome, such as keeping a promise or helping someone in need. But since we must abstract from all outcomes to evaluate its goodness, it is clear that a good will cannot be defined in terms of content. So something about the *form* of a maxim must make it morally OK or not OK. What could it be?

Kant finds a clue in the concept of *duty*. We act out of a good will when we try to do the right thing. In trying to do what is morally right, we do not have our eyes on some advantage to ourselves, but only on the rightness of the action.* We want nothing else but to do our duty. And what is duty?

> Duty is the necessity of an action done out of respect for the law. (*G*, 13)

Duty and law go together. Unless there is a law, there can be no duties. The law tells us what our duties are. The law says, "You *must* do *A*"—the "must" expressing the "necessity" Kant refers to. If an action is done out of a good will, then, it is one that has a peculiar motivation: "respect for law." What law? The moral law, of course. But what does that law say? The answer to this question is the heart of Kant's moral philosophy. But we are not quite ready for it yet.

Let us note that actions can be motivated in two quite distinct ways. We often act out of desires of various kinds. These are the kinds of motivations

that Hobbes and Hume recognize.* Kant groups all these motivations under *inclinations*. But he recognizes one other motivator: *respect for law*. This is a purely rational motivation, quite different from and possibly opposed to even the strongest desire. For Kant, unlike Hume, reason is not just the slave of the passions. Like Plato, Kant thinks that reason can rule, can motivate us to override and control the desires.† And he believes his critical philosophy explains how this can be.

On the assumption that rational respect for law can motivate persons to do their duty, we can classify actions in four ways:

1. *As done from inclination, but contrary to duty:* I do not repay the ten dollars I borrowed because my friend has forgotten about it and I would rather keep it.
2. *As done from calculated self-interest, but according to duty:* Common proverbs, such as "Honesty is the best policy," often express this (partial) overlap of prudence and morality.
3. *As done from a direct inclination, but according to duty:* If I act to preserve my life out of fear, or I am kind simply because I am overwhelmed with pity, I am doing the right thing, but not *because* it is right.
4. *As done from duty, even if it runs contrary to inclinations:* I keep my promise to take my children on a picnic, whether I want to or not.

Only the last is a case of acting from a good will.

We have an answer, then, to the question about what makes a will good. It is not the outcome nor the particular content of the maxim implicit in it. We act from a good will when we act out of a sense of duty, doing what is right solely because it is

---

* In T. S. Eliot's play, *Murder in the Cathedral*, Thomas Becket, the archbishop of Canterbury, is meditating about his possible martyrdom. He says, "The last temptation is the greatest treason:/To do the right deed for the wrong reason." A very Kantian sentiment.

* For Hobbes, you will recall, desire for pleasure and aversion to pain are the sole motivators. Hume adds a nonegoistic source of action in sympathy; but this, too, is simply a passion. See pp. 339 and 371–372.

† See pp. 368–370 for Hume's views of passion and reason. Plato's opposed views are discussed on pp. 130–132.

right, from respect for the moral law. Only such acts have true moral worth.

The Moral Law

We now need to know what the moral law says. We already know that we cannot discover it by empirical investigation; the most we can get that way is anthropology—a description of the rules people *do* live by. We cannot get rules they *ought* to live by.* At best one might be able to cite examples to imitate. But, Kant says,

> worse service cannot be rendered morality than that an attempt be made to derive it from examples. For every example of morality presented to me must itself first be judged according to principles of morality in order to see whether it is fit to serve as an original example, i.e., as a model. But in no way can it authoritatively furnish the concept of morality. Even the Holy One of the gospel must first be compared with our ideal of moral perfection before he is recognized as such. (*G*, 20–21)

If there is going to be a moral law, its origin must be independent of experience. It must be *a priori*; it must be an aspect of practical reason itself.

In order to understand the content of the moral law, as a rule guiding actions, we need one more distinction. Kant distinguishes two kinds of *imperatives:*

1. An imperative is *hypothetical* when it has this form: "If you want *x* in circumstances *C,* do *A.*"

There are several familiar kinds of these hypothetical imperatives.† Kant distinguishes two types:

1a. *Technical* imperatives, such as those of medicine and engineering (e.g., if you want to cure a patient with these symptoms, use this drug); these Kant calls *rules of skill.*

1b. *Pragmatic* imperatives, such as advice about how to be happy; "Dear Abby" is filled with examples; Kant calls these *counsels of prudence.*

2. An imperative is *categorical* when it has this form: "Do *A* (in circumstance *C*)."

Note that there is no reference to your wishes, wants, desires, ends, or goals in a **categorical imperative.** This is what it means to call it "categorical." Given that you are in *C,* it simply says, "Do *A.*" It is not "iffy."

If the moral law expresses our duty and if there is something necessary about our duty, then it seems the moral law must be *categorical.* Hypothetical imperatives are not necessary; they apply to you only if your wants are those specified in the if-clause. If you don't want to build a bridge, then the technical imperatives of engineering get no grip on you. But the moral law applies regardless of your wants.

We can sum up in this way. The moral law must

- Abstract from everything empirical
- Make no reference to consequences of actions
- Be independent of inclinations
- Be capable of inspiring respect

Now if we examine hypothetical imperatives, we find that they one and all

- Make reference to empirical facts
- Concern consequences of actions
- Express our inclinations
- Inspire, at most, approval, not respect

Therefore, the moral law must be a categorical imperative.

We are getting close. The moral law is a rule for choosing among maxims. It is supposed to be a sorting device, separating the morally acceptable

---

* Note that once more Kant is trying to solve a problem that Hume poses. He is trying to answer the question, Where does the "ought" come from? Review Hume's famous challenge on p. 371.

† Hypothetical imperatives, when they function as the conclusions of arguments, are instances of reason being "the slave of the passions." (See Hume, p. 369.) They tell you how to get what you want.

maxims from those not acceptable. Since all empirical content must be left behind, it cannot refer to the *content* of maxims. So it must refer to their *form.* As an imperative, it has the character of law; and the essential feature of a law is that it has a *universal* form.*

> Hence there is only one categorical imperative, and it is this: Act only according to that maxim whereby you can at the same time will that it should become a universal law. (*G*, 30)

Kant has reached his goal: "the supreme principle of morality." This is the first formulation of the famous categorical imperative. Note several features of this rule:

- It is clearly synthetic; no contradiction is produced by denying it.
- It is clearly *a priori*; it has no empirical content.
- It is therefore an example of pure reason at work—this time legislating for actions.

If pure reason in its theoretical employment provides principles according to which things *do in fact happen,* we can now see that in its practical employment pure reason provides a principle according to which things *ought to happen.*

Let us see how it works. You are considering, let us suppose, making a promise; but you have in mind not keeping it if it runs counter to your inclinations. The maxim of your action might be expressed this way: "Let me make this promise, intending not to keep it if I don't want to."

How does the categorical imperative get a grip on this? It tells you that this is a morally acceptable maxim only if you can *universalize* it. To universalize a maxim is to consider the case in which *everyone* acts according to it: "Let us all make promises, intending not to keep them if we don't want to."

And now the question to ask is, Could this be a universal law? It could not; for if everyone acted according to this rule, no one would trust others to keep their promises. And if no one ever trusted others to keep a promise, the very meaning of promising would vanish. Saying "I promise" would become indistinguishable from saying "Maybe." So your original maxim is not one that can be universalized; you cannot will that everyone should act on the principle you are considering for your own action. And it must be rejected as an acceptable moral principle. Whenever you act according to this maxim, you are acting *immorally.*

There is only one categorical imperative, but Kant thinks it can be expressed in a variety of ways. One of the most interesting makes use of the notion of an *end in itself.* All our actions have ends; we always act for the sake of some goal. If our end is one prompted by desire, the end has only *conditional value.* That is, it is worth something *only* because someone desires it. Diamonds have that sort of worth. If no one wanted them, they would be worthless; and how much they are worth depends exactly on how much people want them (taking a certain supply of them for granted). All these ends are relative, not absolute.

> But let us suppose that there were something whose existence has in itself an absolute worth, something which as an end in itself could be a ground of determinate laws. . . .
>
> Now I say that man, and in general every rational being, exists as an end in himself and not merely as a means to be arbitrarily used by this or that will. (*G*, 35)

Rational beings—including extraterrestrial rational beings, if there are any—are different from the ends that have worth only because somebody desires them. How could they fail to be different? They are the *source* of all the relative values there are. How could they just be another case of relative values? They are ends in themselves. In terms of value, then, there are two classes of entities:

1. Things, which have only a *conditional* value, which we can call *price;* their value is *rela-*

---

* Think of laws in science; if a proposition is claimed to be a law, but a counter-instance is found, we conclude that it is not a law after all—because it does not hold universally. Review what Kant says about universality and necessity being the criteria for the *a priori.* (See pp. 381–382.)

tive to the desires for them and correlates to their *use* as *means* to the satisfaction of those desires.

2. Persons, who have *absolute* worth, which we can call *dignity;* their value is *not relative* to what someone desires from them; they have value as *ends* and command *respect.*

In terms of this distinction, the categorical imperative can be stated this way:

> Act in such a way that you treat humanity, whether in your own person or in the person of another, always at the same time as an end and never simply as a means. (*G,* 36)

Don't treat persons like things. Don't *use* people. Don't think of others simply as means to your own ends. These are all admonitions in the spirit of Kant's categorical imperative. You can see that this form of it is merely a variant of the first (universalizing) form: by restricting the maxims of your own actions to those to which *anyone* could subscribe (the first form), you are according to *all* the dignity of personhood (the second form) by respecting them as equal sources of the moral law.

Autonomy

The moral law as categorical imperative arises from pure reason. It imposes itself imperiously upon me, saying: Do this—choose your maxims according to whether they can be universalized. But since it is a principle of reason, and I am a rational being, I am not just subject to it. I am also the *author* of it. It expresses my nature as a rational being. And we are led naturally to

> the idea of the will of every rational being as a will that legislates universal law. . . .
>
> . . . The will is thus not merely subject to the law but is subject to the law in such a way that it must be regarded also as legislating for itself and only on this account as being subject to the law (of which it can regard itself as the author). (*G,* 38)

And this leads Kant to the momentous conclusion that with regard to the moral law each of us is **au-**

tonomous. We each give the law to ourselves. A law to which I cannot give my rational consent according to the universalization principle cannot be a *moral* law.

There are nonmoral (and even immoral) laws; Kant calls them *heteronomous*—having their source outside ourselves. What is characteristic of such laws is that I have no intrinsic reason to obey them. If I find them binding on me, it is only because they appeal to some interest (perhaps by threatening punishment for violations). But with respect to the moral law, no such appeal to the inclinations can work. Not even promises of heaven or threats of hell are relevant. With respect to the moral law, I do not feel bound from without, for the moral law expresses my inmost nature as a rational creature.

As an autonomous legislator of the moral law, I find myself a member of a community of such legislators. This community Kant calls a *realm of ends.*

> For all rational beings stand under the law that each of them should treat himself and all others never merely as means but always at the same time as an end in himself. Hereby arises a systematic union of rational beings through common objective laws, i.e., a kingdom that may be called a kingdom of ends (certainly only an ideal), inasmuch as these laws have in view the very relation of such beings to one another as ends and means.
>
> A rational being belongs to the kingdom of ends as a member when he legislates in it universal laws while also being himself subject to these laws. He belongs to it as sovereign, when as legislator he is himself subject to the will of no other. (*G,* 39–40)

Note that Kant here calls certain laws "objective." These laws contrast with "subjective" rules. A subjective rule or maxim is one that may differ from person to person. The reason is that they are *relative to inclination.* Consider the maxim, "Let me run six miles per day." Is that a good maxim? We would all agree that this depends on what you *want;* it is a good maxim for someone who wants eventually to compete in a marathon. But it is a poor maxim for someone who wants only to maintain basic fitness. Such maxims are neither objective nor universal; they are implicitly hypothetical, relative, and personal. There are many such personal maxims, and Kant has no objection to them.

But, if Kant is right, not all rules are relative and subjective like this. A law legislated by the rational will according to the categorical imperative is "objective." He means it is a law that *any rational being* will agree to. The moral law for me is the moral law for you. Any maxim approved by the universalization test will be the same for all; it is simply not acceptable unless it is fit to be a *universal* law, one that each rational being can legislate for itself. Reason is not, despite Hume, just the "slave of the passions"; reason is the source of a criterion for judging the passions. The inclinations may propose actions, together with their maxims. But reason judges which are acceptable. Reason is legislative. It is autonomous. And its laws are *absolute.**

We can come back at last to the notion of a good will, the only thing good without qualification. We now see that a good will is governed by the categorical imperative; a good will is one that can be universalized. We can even imagine a will so much in harmony with reason that all its maxims are in natural conformity with the moral law. Such a will Kant calls a "holy" will. A holy will would never feel that it *ought* to do something it didn't want to do, because it would always want to do what was right. It would never feel duty to be a constraint. Though we can imagine such a will, we must confess that it is not the will we have. We experience a continual struggle between inclination and duty. So a good will is something we may aspire to, but we can never be completely confident that we have attained it.

> We like to flatter ourselves with the false claim to a more noble motive; but in fact we can never, even by strictest examination, completely plumb the depths of the secret incentives of our actions. For when moral value is being considered, the concern is not with the actions, which are seen, but rather with their inner principles, which are not seen.
>
> . . . if we look more closely at our planning and striving, we everywhere come upon the dear self, which is always turning up, and upon which the intent of our actions is based rather than upon the strict command of duty (which would often require self-denial). (*G,* 19–20)

As Aristotle said, "It is a hard job to be good."*

Freedom

Finally, we need to situate Kant's moral theory in the general critique of reason, to see how the moral law fits with his epistemology and metaphysics. The notion of *autonomy* is the key. An autonomous will must be one that is *free.*

> The will is a kind of causality belonging to living beings insofar as they are rational; freedom would be the property of this causality that makes it effective independent of any determination by alien causes.
>
> . . . freedom is certainly not lawless, even though it is not a property of will in accordance with laws of nature. It must, rather, be a causality in accordance with immutable laws, which, to be sure, is of a special kind. . . . What else, then, can freedom of the will be but autonomy, i.e., the property that the will has of being a law to itself? The proposition that the will is in every action a law to itself expresses, however, nothing but the principle of acting according to no other maxim than that which can at the same time have itself as a universal law for its object. Now this is precisely the formula of the categorical imperative and is the principle of morality. Thus a free will and a will subject to moral laws are one and the same. (*G,* 49)

Freedom, Kant says, is not sheer randomness; nor is it whim or caprice; nor is it arbitrariness. Freedom is giving the law for one's action to oneself. It is not, therefore, lawless. Freedom is in fact a kind of causality—a power of producing actions ac-

---

* Note that in a certain way Kant again agrees with Hume, this time about the fact/value distinction. There are no values just in facts per se. Value comes from the side of the subject. But it does not follow that it is always bestowed by desire or passion; reason has a crucial role that provides a kind of objectivity in morality parallel to the objectivity in science.

---

* See p. 180.

cording to a rule that one legislates for oneself. But this is just autonomy. And autonomy is the principle of a rational will free from the influence of the inclinations. Such a will is bound only by the requirement of lawfulness itself—that is, by universality, by the categorical imperative. So "a free will and a will subject to moral laws are one and the same."

But this presents a problem. If all events in the world can be experienced only under the category of causality (as we saw in Kant's treatment of theoretical understanding), what *room* is there for freedom? Kant's Copernican revolution comes to the rescue. Recall the distinction between phenomena and noumena. What is impossible in the phenomenal world may be quite possible in the noumenal. We seem to have two standpoints from which to consider ourselves.

Phenomenally	Noumenally
I *appear* to myself as an *object* in the world.	I *am* the unknown *subject* to whom the world appears.
All objects are organized by the *a priori* category of causality.	The category of causality does not apply.
I appear to act under causal laws that I do not legislate for myself (heteronomy).	I may act under rational laws I legislate for myself (autonomy).
I do not appear to be free.	I am free, in that I can act on laws that I give to myself.

Since Kant insists that the world of things-in-themselves is strictly unknowable, the propositions on the right cannot be known to be true. (Knowledge is restricted to how things appear, under the pure intuitions of space and time and the categories.) But we can know that they are *possibly* true. We do know that there is a world of things-in-themselves; and we know that our categories do not apply to them, only to how they appear to us.

So from a theoretical point of view, Kant's Copernican revolution creates room for autonomy, freedom, and the moral law.

As agents, Kant says, engaged in practical life, we

> cannot act in any way other than under the idea of freedom. . . . Reason must regard itself as the author of its principles independent of foreign influences. Therefore as practical reason or as the will of a rational being must reason regard itself as free. (*G*, 50)

When we make a decision, we cannot help but think that it is up to us, in our freedom, to decide. And, if Kant is right, nothing in science—empirical psychology, for instance—could show us that we are wrong. For experimental science can only deal with the world as it appears, not with the world as it really is.

This does not constitute a *proof* of freedom, as Kant clearly recognizes. Freedom is a mere Idea, an Idea of Pure Reason. But we ought now to recall Kant's saying that he "found it necessary to deny *knowledge,* in order to make room for *faith*" (*CPR*, 29). Faith in freedom is one thing he has in mind—not an arbitrary faith, but one founded in that practical necessity to think of ourselves "under the idea of freedom." It is not knowledge; but it is a rational faith. And the distinction between things as they are in themselves and things as they appear to us is the metaphysical foundation that allows this freedom to be possible. We *must assume* we are free; and we *may do so.* The assumption of freedom is a *practical necessity* and a *theoretical possibility.*

Morality is the foundation of other articles of a rational faith as well. We can think of morality as giving us the command: "*Do that through which thou becomest worthy to be happy*" (*CPR*, 638). As we have seen, being worthy of happiness does not guarantee that we will be happy, at least not in the world of our experience. Yet goodness and happiness *ought* to go together. It wouldn't make good sense if we were urged by reason to qualify for a condition that would ultimately be denied to us. It seems that reason is telling us that we have *a right to hope* for happiness. The fact that we belong to the noumenal, purely intelligible, world opens up a possibility that it might be more than a mere hope.

For it to be more than a futile hope, however, it seems that a future life must be possible (since we see that goodness and happiness do not coincide in this life). It follows that we must believe in the immortality of the soul (which is, from the point of view of theoretical knowledge, a mere Idea of Reason). And we must also believe that a power exists sufficient to guarantee the eventual happiness of those who strive for moral goodness. This power, of course, is God (also, from the point of view of theory, merely an Idea).

> God and a future life are two postulates which, according to the principles of pure reason, are inseparable from the obligation which that same reason imposes upon us. (*CPR*, 639)

So Kant rounds off his critical philosophy. Wisdom, Kant tells us, requires indeed a certain modesty about our rational powers—as both Socrates and Hume, in their different ways, insist. But our powers are adequate to do mathematics and empirical science, and they provide a sure and certain guide for our practical life. For the rest, faith and hope are at least not irrational. But *knowledge* is limited to the realm of possible experience. After the incisive skeptical probes of Hume, "that acute man," Kant has grounds to claim that he has indeed rehabilitated reason—but only within strict limits.

Kant's critical philosophy has a profound influence on the course of subsequent philosophy. And, as we will see, aspects of its are still alive today.

Basic Questions

1. What is the problem with the *representational theory of knowledge and perception* that Kant thinks can be resolved by imitating in metaphysics what Copernicus did in astronomy. How does a "Copernican turn" help?
2. What does a critique of reason try to uncover? In what sense will the answers be transcendental?
3. Explain the idea of a synthetic *a priori* judgment,

showing clearly both its semantic and its epistemological aspects. Give examples. Why are these judgments puzzling?
4. Explain why Kant thinks that mathematical and geometrical propositions are both *a priori* and synthetic.
5. What is Kant's argument that space and time must be "pure" or *a priori* forms of intuition?
6. How do Kant's reflections on space and time lead to the conclusion that we can know things only as they appear to us, not as they are in themselves?
7. What does it mean that the dove cannot fly in empty space? Relate this aphorism to the notions of concept and intuition.
8. Explain the role Kant assigns to the categories, illustrating it with the examples of substance/properties and cause/effect. How are these *a priori* concepts related to the objects of our common experience?
9. Explain the famous Kantian dictum: "Thoughts without content are empty, intuitions without concepts are blind."
10. Explain the notion that our *a priori* concepts are the source of a powerful illusion—the illusion of speculative metaphysics.
11. What is it about reasoning, in Kant's view, that drives us inevitably to the concepts of God, the soul, and the world in itself?
12. How does Kant attack the Cartesian claim that we are thinking things?
13. Explain how the distinction between noumena and phenomena allows Kant to claim that we can reconcile causality with freedom.
14. Why is it, according to Kant, that the idea of God is an unavoidable idea for any reasoning being?
15. Kant says, "'Being' is obviously not a real predicate." What does this mean? How does Kant use this principle to criticize the ontological argument for the existence of God?
16. If the Ideas of Pure Reason (God, the soul, the world in itself) are such powerful sources of illusion, what good are they?
17. Why can't Kant be satisfied with the kind of view "practical anthropology" gives us of morality? What will be missing in such a view?
18. Kant says that the only thing good without qualification is a good will. What is the relation between will and rationality?
19. What is the connection between a good will and the concept of duty?

20. What is the supreme principle of morality? Why is it categorical (not hypothetical)? And why must it be *a priori*?

21. In what way does the distinction between conditional value and absolute value play a role in the moral law?

22. In what way am I autonomous (rather than heteronomous) in the realm of morality? Why doesn't individual autonomy precipitate social chaos?

23. Kant asks, "What else, then, can freedom of the will be but autonomy, i.e., the property that the will has of being a law to itself? (**p. 397**). Explain the connections between autonomy, rationality, and human freedom.

24. Kant says he has demonstrated the limits of knowledge, but that this makes room for faith. Faith in what? And on what grounds?

For Further Thought

1. Kant does seem to resolve certain puzzles concerning knowledge that are bequeathed to him by Descartes and Hume. But there is a high price to pay for these successes: we have to give up the hope of knowing reality as it really is. Can you think of a way to avoid paying this price?

2. Suppose you are talking things over with Kant and he says, "Lying is wrong, you know." And, in the way undergraduates are apt to these days, you reply, "Who's to say?" What would Kant have to say to you? And would you need to think again about that flippant, but very popular, question?

Notes

1. References to Kant's works will be as follows:

   P: Prolegomena to Any Future Metaphysics, translated by Paul Carus, revised by James W. Ellington (Indianapolis: Hackett Publishing Co., 1977).

   G: Grounding for the Metaphysics of Morals, trans. James W. Ellington (Indianapolis: Hackett Publishing Co., 1981).

   CPR: Immanuel Kant's Critique of Pure Reason, trans. Norman Kemp Smith (New York: St. Martin's Press, 1956).

2. Joseph Butler, *Fifteen Sermons* (London: G. Bell and Sons Ltd., 1949), 23.

19

G. W. F. Hegel:
Taking History Seriously

Since early Greek times, it has been the ambition of those seeking wisdom to give a general account of the universe and our place in it. One after another, philosophers announce to the world that they have succeeded in solving the riddle. But each attempt, though it builds on preceding efforts and tries to correct their shortcomings, seems to raise new occasions for doubt. The persistent jabs of sophists and skeptics always find a target and keep generations of philosophers in business. Some assumptions, however, are taken for granted by most of these thinkers and by Western culture in general. We can set them out in the following way:

- There is a *truth* about the way things are.
- This truth is *eternal* and unchanging.
- This truth can, in principle, be *known* by us.
- It is the job of the *philosopher,* relying on reason and experience, to discover this truth.
- Knowing the truth about ourselves and the universe in which we live is *supremely important,* for only such truth can serve as a secure foundation on which culture can be built: science, religion, ethics, the state, and a good life for all.

As we have seen, both Hume and Kant argue for a severe limitation on these ambitions. Hume drives us toward a skeptical attitude regarding the powers of human reason. And Kant, though he rescues Newtonian science and offers us a rational morality, concedes that we can know things only

as they *appear* to us, structured by our sensibility and rational faculties. What we *really* are, and what reality is *in itself,* is completely and forever hidden from us.

Still, in one important respect, Kant accepts the assumptions common to most of the Western philosophical tradition: that there is a truth about the way things are and that this truth is eternal. He thinks he has found it. Kant's central truths, of course, focus on what it is to be rational. The structures of a rational mind are the same for all rational creatures (and so, of course, for all humans). They are unchanging over time—the same for ancients and moderns, primitives and enlightened philosophers. The receptive structures of Sensibility, the pattern-imposing categories of the Understanding, and the insatiable logical drive of Reason are the given features of mind, identical in every age and every place.

Nineteenth-century thinkers alter this picture and transform it in surprisingly far-reaching ways. Chief among them is Georg Wilhelm Friedrich Hegel (1770–1831), a German philosopher of encyclopedic range who is sensitive to the exciting changes surrounding him in his world. It will be worth spending a little time in setting the scene.

The French Revolution July 14, 1789. A Paris mob storms the fortress-prison known as the Bastille, hated symbol of royal absolutism. Hegel is nineteen. Like youth all over Europe, he is enthralled. The Revolution seems like a new start, an overthrow of the dead weight of centuries. Reason is triumphant over tradition. The people are in control.

It is true that this control turns into the Reign of Terror, that it spawns a series of wars, and that it leads to Napoleon's coup d'etat and his assumption of the title of Emperor. But something deep and remarkable has happened, and Europe will never be the same again. Hegel imbibes the sense of history being made, of real change, of the possibility of progress toward a more rational society. And he never loses it.

> . . . it is not difficult to see that ours is a birth-time and a period of transition to a new era. Spirit has broken with the world it has hitherto inhabited and imagined, and is of a mind to submerge it in the past. Spirit is indeed never at rest but always engaged in moving forward. But just as the first breath drawn by a child after its long, quiet nourishment breaks the gradualness of merely quantitative growth—there is a qualitative leap, and the child is born—so likewise the Spirit in its formation matures slowly and quietly into its new shape, dissolving bit by bit the structure of its previous world, whose tottering state is only hinted at by isolated symptoms. The frivolity and boredom which unsettle the established order, the vague foreboding of something unknown, these are the heralds of approaching change. The gradual crumbling that left unaltered the face of the whole is cut short by a sunburst which, in one flash, illuminates the features of the new world. (*PS*, 6–7)[1]

Hegel's references to the Revolution are obvious here, as is his sense of something new bursting into history. It is not, of course, absolutely new, any more than the new-born child appears from nothing. A long period of preparation marked by the people's increasing dissatisfaction has preceded it. Moreover,

> this new world is no more a complete actuality than is a new-born child; it is essential to keep this in mind. It comes on the scene for the first time in its immediacy or its Notion. Just as little as a building is finished when its foundation has been laid, so little

"What is rational is actual and what is actual is rational."
—G. W. F. Hegel

is the achieved Notion of the whole the whole itself. When we wish to see an oak with its massive trunk and spreading branches and foliage, we are not content to be shown an acorn instead. (*PS*, 7)

Several crucial concepts are introduced in these two quotations, and it is important to get some preliminary understanding of them. The word translated "Spirit" is the German *Geist*. Scholars disagree about whether the best English equivalent is "Spirit," as this translator has it, or "mind." Hegel's use of *Geist* surely includes everything we mean by mind, but it has larger implications that allow Hegel to talk of the Revolution as Spirit breaking with past traditions and maturing as it moves forward in history. The term "Notion" is a translation of *Begriff* and is often rendered "concept." It is the term Kant uses for concepts, including the *a priori* concepts he calls categories. Sometimes I shall use "concept" where it seems appropriate, and sometimes "Notion." In this second quotation we can understand Hegel to be saying that the *concept* of a people united in "Liberty, Equality, and Fraternity" has come on the scene. But to achieve this "Notion" is not yet to achieve the *reality* of a society organized by those principles. That may take a long time, just as it takes a long time for the acorn to develop into the giant oak. Development, movement toward maturity, the sense of history going on—history with direction, purpose, aim—are central characteristics of Hegel's thought.

The Romantics   Hegel lives at what is arguably the high point of German culture. Goethe is just twenty years his senior, Schiller ten. Hegel is a close friend of the poet Hölderlin. Beethoven is almost his exact contemporary. Novalis, Herder, the Schlegel brothers—all react against what they feel is the dry and cold rationality of the Enlightenment. In England it is the time of Wordsworth, Shelley, Keats, Byron, and Blake. They are called the Romantics. What do the Romantics stand for?

They champion imagination and feeling. They are suspicious of science and the picture of the world it provides. They resist "analysis" and the application of logical methods to living things. They agree with Kant that science and reason cannot reveal reality, but they look to other faculties to take us where reason falters: to intuition, to love, to passion.

The Romantics look back to classical Greece—once again! The inexhaustibility of that heritage is remarkable. There they see a somewhat idealized version of what they come to admire. It is the *unity* and *harmony* of Greek life that impresses them. As they see it, there is no conflict in these Greeks between reason and inclination, science and religion, rationality and feeling. Their morality seems to grow naturally out of their sense of being at home in the world and in their society.

This is what they hold against Kant: that he divides human beings, so that their reason is eternally at odds with their passions. For Kant, as we

have seen, morally right actions cannot be motivated by inclination, passion, or feeling—not even the feeling of love. The only acts that are morally good, Kant tells us, are done out of that austere motivation of rational respect for the moral law. And this strikes the Romantics as an almost schizophrenic divisiveness. Are all of our impulses to be dismissed as of no account? Or worse—as evil? Many of them oppose the Christianity they are familiar with, setting its pessimism about sin and evil in humanity against what they perceive as the sunny, optimistic outlook of the Greeks.* Kant's austere morality seems to them merely a remnant of a tradition that has outworn its usefulness. Some, including the young Hegel, explore the possibilities for a new folk religion that would express more adequately the ideals they hold dear.

Hegel cannot be classed as a Romantic; indeed, in some respects he criticizes the movement severely. As we'll see, he is himself a great champion of Reason. But this ideal of harmony within and among human beings he makes thoroughly his own. Nothing will satisfy him that leaves conflicts unresolved, that pits one aspect of a human being against another—or against a neighbor.

Hegel's thought is notoriously difficult, and what you will read here is a considerable simplification. But in an introduction to philosophy, that is quite in order. The main themes and something of Hegel's contribution to the great conversation should be intelligible. As you will surely see, the very idea of the history of philosophy *as* a Great Conversation owes much to Hegel. For him, this conversation *is* philosophy, and to study its history is to immerse oneself in the development of Reason itself.

Epistemology Internalized

Hume calls for the construction of a science of human nature, and Kant attempts a critique of pure reason. In each case, the motivation is to examine

---

* But see Nietzsche, pp. 487–488.

Arthur Schopenhauer

Known for his pessimism, Arthur Schopenhauer (1788–1860) accepted the Kantian distinction between the phenomenal world presented to our understanding and the world as it is in itself. Schopenhauer held that phenomena are organized by a *principle of sufficient reason,* which guarantees that everything we can experience has a cause or ground explaining why it must be as it is. This principle corresponds to the Kantian *a priori* machinery of the mind and entails that the experienced world, including even my body, is "my idea."

In *The World as Will and Idea* (1818), Schopenhauer claimed to go beyond Kant; that is, he claimed to be able to identify the character of the world as it is in itself. We ourselves, he argued, are part of the noumenal world; so we have the most direct and immediate knowledge of its nature. In itself the world is nothing but "will," a blind, ceaseless, striving, the desire for existence. The whole of the phenomenal world, with all its varied individuals, is but a manifestation in time and space of this will. Beneath the surface appearances of things, we see a never-ending struggle for existence, desire succeeding desire, until life finally ends in death.

Unsatisfied desire is painful, but when desire is satisfied, boredom sets in—until we want something else. So life continually swings between pain and ennui. Is there any cure for the disease of life? Schopenhauer held that art, and music in particular, can provide a temporary release from this cycle of frustration. In the peculiarly disinterested character of aesthetic experience, the clamor of the will is quieted. We are freed for a time from the wheel of suffering and lose ourselves in the contemplation of a beautiful object.

A more permanent salvation can be attained only by a denial of the will to live itself. Schopenhauer believed this is the goal of all religions and is found most explicitly in Buddhism. If we realize that individuality (including our own bodily life in the phenomenal world) is *merely* idea—a kind of illusion, and not reality—our striving for individual ends will cease, egoism will be defeated, and we can dwell in a kind of will-less, ascetic, compassionate harmony with all.

---

the "instrument" by which we gain knowledge in order to understand the nature and limits of our cognitive capacities. This seems, on the face of it, a very reasonable thing. But Hegel has an objection.

> In the case of other instruments, we can try and criticize them in other ways than by setting about the special work for which they are destined. But the examination of knowledge can only be carried out by an act of knowledge. To examine this so-called instrument is the same thing as to know it. But to seek to know before we know is as absurd as the wise resolution of Scholasticus, not to venture into the water until he had learned to swim.[2]

If we want to know whether a chisel is an adequate instrument, we can use our sense of touch as a criterion, or we can observe with our eyes how easily it parts the wood. But if we want to know whether our knowledge is an adequate instrument—whether it gets us the truth—we have only our own knowledge to depend on. For coming to know how (and what) we know is an *instance* of knowing, and cannot therefore *precede* it.

To resolve not to enter the water until one has learned to swim is absurd; you learn to swim by swimming. It is, Hegel assures us, just as absurd to think that before we can be sure that we know anything, we have to *know* what our abilities for gaining knowledge *are.*

If this criticism is correct, it completely invalidates the project of epistemology as it has been carried out since Descartes. This tradition holds that to know whether we can know anything, we have to *know* what knowing is. But to know what knowing is *presupposes* that we can know something. And so we are involved in a circle and cannot answer the question. It is obvious that Hegel is posing again the ancient problem of the criterion.* To decide whether a conscious state constitutes knowledge, we must have a criterion or standard to judge by. But by what criterion do we tell whether we have accepted the right criterion? How do we know that our "knowledge" about knowledge really is *knowledge*?

Hegel sees a second difficulty in Kant's project: it concedes too much to skepticism. Our aim in knowledge, at the outset, is to know the way things *really are,* to discover the truth about reality as it exists *in itself.* But if our reason imposes its categories on things, so that objects can exist only *for us,* then this ambition of knowing what is real and true must be given up. Kant bravely draws the consequence: all we can know is how things *appear* to us. The truth about reality is forever hidden from our sight. We can know phenomena, how things are for us. In addition, we know there are things-in-themselves; but *what* they are is forever beyond our powers to discover, since we would have to step outside ourselves and compare whatever ideas we had about them with the things themselves—without using any of the natural equipment of the rational mind! And that is not possible. But this leaves us skeptical about things-in-themselves.

Some of Kant's successors find this unsatisfactory—indeed, self-contradictory. To claim to know that there are things-in-themselves but to deny that we can know anything about them does seem self-undermining. If we don't know anything about them, how do we know there are such things? Hegel agrees with this criticism and works out an alternative view in which the distinction between consciousness and its objects is seen to be a distinction *internal* to consciousness. This is a difficult notion, but a crucial one. Let us see if we can understand it.

Amazingly, Hegel thinks he can solve both problems at once: the problem of the criterion and the problem of how we can gain knowledge of things-in-themselves. The key to his solution is the idea of *development.* As long as we think of a mind as *one* complete and finished entity and that which we intend to comprehend as a *second* complete and finished entity, there can be no solution to these problems. As long as subject and object are thought to be inherently unrelated, there can be no guarantee that they will correspond, and skepticism always looms large. Descartes does not defeat it, Hume resigns himself to it, and Kant cultivates the garden of phenomena in the midst of a vast sea of unknowables. What Hegel proposes to show is that consciousness moves through *stages* (he sometimes calls them "moments"), that it does this with a kind of *necessity,* driven by clear inadequacies at each stage, and that we can "watch" as it develops itself from the simplest and most inadequate consciousness to one that is completely adequate to its object. To "watch" in this way is to do what he calls **phenomenology**—to engage in an attempt to discern the *internal dialectic* through which consciousness moves toward ever more satisfactory relations with its objects.* Phenomenology of mind (Spirit) takes consciousness itself as a phenomenon; it tries to set out the *logos* of this phenomenon—the logic or internal rationale of its development.

Development, for Hegel, is not chaotic or random; though it zigzags towards its goal, it does have a direction. Consciousness, history, forms of life, and reality all develop

- from *implicit* forms to *explicit,*
- from the *potential* to the *actual,*
- from the *abstract* to the *concrete,*
- from *Notion* to *Reality,*
- from *partial truth* to *Absolute Knowledge,* and
- from *less rational* to *more rational.*

Development, in short, is progress.

---

*For earlier discussions of this problem, see Sextus Empiricus, pp. 199–201, Montaigne, p. 283, and Descartes, p. 297.

*For the connection between dialectic and truth in Socrates and Plato, see pp. 61 and 119.

I have several times used the word "internal." This needs to be explained. You can see the significance of what Hegel is doing by comparing it to our "ordinary" way of thinking. For most of us, knowledge (if we think of it at all) is a certain state of mind that *represents* or *corresponds to* some object external to it. I have this idea that my bicycle is in the garage. That is one thing. I also have this bicycle. That is a second thing. These two things, idea and object, seem quite independent of one another and can vary independently.* That is why knowledge is a problem. I can believe my bicycle is in the garage when in fact it has been stolen. I believe something false about the bike; I am in error and do not have the truth. In the possibility of this discrepancy we have the origins of skepticism.†

Notice, though, that every time we are aware of an object, we take it *really to be* (in itself) what it *seems to be* (for us). As long as we are satisfied in our contemplation of this object, no dichotomy between what it really is and how it appears to us arises in our consciousness. You pick up this book, look at it, and are completely satisfied that you have *got it*. The concept or Notion of the book seems to coincide perfectly with the object. But then how does the idea of *appearance* ever arise? How does the idea of how something *is for us* ever get distinguished from the idea of what it *is in itself*? Hegel argues that this *can* happen because consciousness is conscious not only of the object but also of itself (as related to the object); and it *does* happen whenever we become aware of some discrepancy between our "knowledge" of the object and our "experience" of the object.

> For consciousness is, on the one hand, consciousness of the object, and on the other, consciousness of itself; consciousness of what for it is the True, and consciousness of its knowledge of the truth. Since

both are *for* the same consciousness, this consciousness is itself their comparison; it is for this same consciousness to know whether its knowledge of the object corresponds to the object or not. (*PS*, 54)

The crucial phrase here is this: "both are *for* the same consciousness." The *object* and our *awareness of that object are given together*—in the same consciousness! This is why Hegel thinks a critique of knowledge can be *internal* to consciousness and why it can proceed by means of phenomenology. The comparison between concept and object is made by the same consciousness that is aware of both. The object of consciousness is not, never has been, and *could not be* some completely independent thing-in-itself. Every object, indeed, every *conceivable* object, is an object *for a subject*. The slogan "no object without a subject" expresses the key idea in what is called **idealism**. We shall discuss this view further below.

What we discover if we just "watch" consciousness at work is that it reveals—by itself, and with a certain kind of inevitability—the discrepancies between its own awareness and its objects. It corrects itself to make its awareness more adequate to the object; but in changing itself, it finds that the object has not stayed put but has changed correspondingly. And what the object was previously taken to *be* is now seen only to *appear* to be. Its former status as thing-in-itself (a status it had only because the former consciousness *ascribed* that status to it) is now withdrawn, and it is now seen as having been only an object *for us*. Thus arises the distinction *within consciousness* between appearance and reality, that very distinction we naively (together with Kant and almost all previous philosophers) thought had to exist between the realm of consciousness as a whole and something entirely independent of consciousness.

As an example, think of a movie in which you "see" Smith kill Jones. As the plot develops, more facts are assembled, a larger context is elaborated, and new evidence comes to light. Eventually it becomes clear that it was not Smith, but Brown dressed up like Smith, who was the killer. What you had taken to be reality is now seen to be

---

*Again we note the key elements of the representational theory. See p. 300.

†You should review Descartes' first *Meditation* at this point. It is the classic modern source for the way skeptical problems arise. Note that it all depends on the absolute independence of idea and object.

merely appearance. But, of course, you are now taking something else to be real. And it is always possible that a larger picture may upset your convictions yet again.

Phenomenology is the discipline that traces the dialectical succession of these more and more adequate stages of consciousness.

> Consequently, we do not need to import criteria, or to make use of our own bright ideas and thoughts during the course of the inquiry; it is precisely when we leave these aside that we succeed in contemplating the matter in hand [knowledge] as it is *in and for itself.* (*PS,* 54)

There is no need for us philosophers to come up with the criterion for knowledge, Hegel tells us. The problem of the criterion is in the process of solving itself. Nor should we despair because it seems we cannot compare our thoughts with their objects and test definitively for their correctness. In examining its own adequacy, consciousness is continually engaged in such comparison and testing; "all that is left for us to do is simply to look on" (*PS,* 54). Hegel claims that by pursuing philosophy this way, by simply "looking on," we will see the criterion for knowledge develop naturally and necessarily *from within consciousness itself;* consciousness corrects itself.

Hegel's *Phenomenology of Spirit* can be thought of as a kind of biography of consciousness, the story of its development toward maturity. As consciousness develops, it grows ever more adequate to its object (and its object to consciousness), until at the end we discover a stage that deserves to be called **absolute knowledge.** At this point there will be no more discrepancy between reality and the knower; what there is will *be* what it is *known to be;* and what we *know* will correspond perfectly to *what there is*—because there has been a long process of mutual adjustment of each to the other. At that point Reason will be satisfied, because it will see that *what is real is what is rational, and what is rational is the real.*

> The series of configurations which consciousness goes through along this road is, in reality, the de-

tailed *education* of consciousness itself to the standpoint of Science. (*PS,* 50)

There is an ambiguity in the way I have presented Hegel to this point, but it is an ambiguity present in Hegel's thought. Is this development to be thought of as a series of stages within the life of *each human consciousness,* as it matures toward adequacy? Or is it to be regarded as a historical process, through which the *human race* travels from stages of primitive culture to the most advanced science, religion, and philosophy? The answer is that it is both. And in some sense it is a *logical* progression as well. The reason is to be found in the concept of Spirit. Individuals are manifestations of Spirit. But so are civilizations and cultures. And throughout all, Hegel holds, there is present the *World Spirit,* which develops in individuals and cultures toward self-knowledge, rationality, and freedom. But of this, more later.

So far this is all rather abstract. We need to look at several examples. Let us begin where Hegel does in his book, *Phenomenology of Spirit,* with the simplest sort of knowledge—what he calls **sense-certainty.** *

Think of the simple presence of some object to your consciousness, for example, the paper on which this sentence is written. Now, as Hegel says, you have to be very careful here. You may now be *thinking* of this experience. But in the *consciousness* of the piece of paper there is no thinking going on. There is just the presence of the paper to your consciousness. You are just *sensing* the presence of the paper. The fact that there is no thinking involved—no use of concepts to characterize the

---

* Philosophers have often looked to something like this to serve as the *foundation for knowledge.* It may be that you are deceived that there is a dagger before you. But, apparently, you cannot be mistaken that it is *as if* there were a dagger before you. How things *seem* to you, what you *sense* (as opposed to what objects you *perceive*), seems immune from doubt and so is fit to be a foundation. Recall what Descartes claims is certain even if his senses deceive him about external objects. Hume's impressions also play this role (p. 351). There are later examples as well, right into the twentieth century. But if Hegel is right in his critique here, a lot of modern epistemology is simply based on a mistake.

paper—is crucial for the *certainty* of this kind of experience. It is a very basic, extremely elementary kind of experience—an experience of the sheer presence of something to consciousness without any "work" being done on it by the consciousness. This sort of consciousness is wholly *receptive*. It is like one of Hume's *impressions*. There seem to be no Kantian "conceptual filters" at work organizing, relating, and structuring the material. The knowledge is "unmediated" by any interpretive scheme of the mind which has it. That is why this kind of experience seems to exclude the possibility of mistake. Hegel calls this kind of experience *immediate*.

We, of course, are using language and quite sophisticated concepts in doing this phenomenology of sense-certainty. But we want to characterize it "from the inside," so to speak, as it experiences itself. So we must be careful not to import our external descriptions into that consciousness itself. What, then, is it like? All we can say by way of description is that there is a "This" presented to an "I." And perhaps, to make the "This" more clear, we can add that it is presented *Now* and *Here*. Sense-certainty presents what philosophers have called a *particular* (the "This") in its sheer particularity, without attributing any *universal* characteristics to it.* Sense-certainty does not know this page as white, or as dotted with black marks—or, for that matter, as a page. Such characterizations import interpretive concepts into the experience, but it is wholly bare of such notions. There is just that sheer presence in your visual field. (Take a minute to see whether this description does capture an elementary aspect of your current experience.)

But now we notice that this "I" might direct its attention elsewhere, and a new "This" is presented—a can of cola, perhaps. But the cola can be characterized by "This" just as well as the paper. And there is a new "Now" and "Here" as well. The "This," "Now," and "Here," however, have not changed; they just apply to a different object. But what this shows us is that these are themselves *concepts;* they are, in fact, universals. And they are among the *most universal* of all universals, since they can apply to *every* object.

Moreover, another consciousness might become aware of this piece of paper. In that case, there is another "I" involved. It is no less an "I" than the first. And this shows that the "I" is also a universal. Like the others, it is *universally* universal. And so it is essentially empty.* It reveals nothing at all about the *nature* of the "I" in question.

What does all this mean? We can observe, Hegel says, that this most fundamental kind of consciousness turns into its opposite. It seemed to be the most concrete, rich, dense, real kind of knowledge there is. It seemed to be "immediate," by which Hegel means uninterpreted, unconceptualized, and unmodified by any conscious activity. It seemed to be an apprehension of the pure particularity of things. But it turns out that this "knowledge" is the most bare, most abstract, most universal, and most empty of content imaginable.

> Because of its concrete content, sense-certainty immediately appears as the *richest* kind of knowledge. . . . Moreover, sense-certainty appears to be the *truest* knowledge; for it has not as yet omitted anything from the object, but has the object before it in its perfect entirety. But, in the event, this very *certainty* proves itself to be the most abstract and poorest *truth*. (PS, 58)

What does such a consciousness *know*? It *cannot say*. But is knowledge that cannot be expressed really knowledge at all? Imagine a world in which the only consciousnesses that exist are instances of such brute awareness; there would be no classification, no characterization, no comparison, no relating of one thing to another, no narratives, no laws, no explanations, no remembrance of things

---

* The distinction between particulars and universals goes back at least to Plato, who notes that some things have properties in common—squareness, redness, humanity, and so on. These common features, Plato thinks, are (peculiar) things themselves; he calls them "Forms." (See p. 112.) Aristotle and the medieval philosophers call the common properties of things "universals." For Kant, it is *concepts* that supply this universal aspect. Hegel has this part of the great conversation clearly in mind here.

* There are echoes here of Kant's critique of rational psychology. Review pp. 394–395.

past or expectations of things to come—and virtually no language! Consciousness could not even be aware of a tree *as a tree*, for that involves the application of the concept "tree" and a classification of it with like things. Would such a world qualify as one in which *knowledge* exists? Hegel, for one, is sure that it would not.

So sense-certainty, which seemed to be the most secure form of knowledge, immune from the ravages of doubt, turns out not to be knowledge at all. And consciousness is impelled to go beyond it. Note well: It is consciousness *itself* that is forced beyond this minimal stage. Indeed, in necessarily using the universal concepts of "This" and "I," it is already beyond this stage. *We* are not imposing this from the outside. We are not supplying some criterion according to which this stage is unsatisfactory. There is an internal dialectic at work, forcing consciousness to recognize the inadequacy of sense-certainty and to move to a new level of sophistication. We are just "looking on."

Suppose that we "personalize" consciousness for a moment (as Hegel tends to do anyway) and think of it as having intentions and goals. We can then ask, What is it that "motivates" consciousness to develop beyond this primitive stage? Hegel answers this question in a somewhat peculiar, but characteristic, way. Consciousness, in its "attempt to be" simply sense-certainty, *negates itself*. In the stage of sense-certainty, it "intends" to be nothing more than a knowledge of what is immediately present to it. But, as we have seen, it fails. The insufficiency of this attempt is *displayed* to consciousness itself in its very attempt. It *cannot* be what it tries to be, since it necessarily interprets even this minimal experience in terms of universal concepts ("This," "Here," "Now," and "I"), which, moreover, are completely inadequate to capture the experience.

But, Hegel points out, this negation of itself as certain knowledge is not a kind of blank rejection. It is not equivalent to skepticism (which can be thought of as a *general* sort of negation of knowledge). It is a quite determinate and specific negation: the negation of the sufficiency of sense

certainty for knowledge. And this drives consciousness not into skepticism, but into a quite determinate new form.

What consciousness has learned is that it cannot find the certainty of true knowledge by retreating to elementary beginning points.* So it has no other alternative but to plunge ahead, make use of concepts, interpret its experience, and hope that somehow a correspondence of subject and object lies in the direction of conceptual elaboration. If knowledge is to be possible, consciousness cannot be merely receptive, for what it has discovered is that any attempt to merely "register" what is present to it *already* makes use of universal concepts, but these are concepts so poor that *what* is being sensed cannot be expressed. Mind *must* play a more active role.†

We can learn one more thing from this first bit of the dialectic of consciousness. Sense-certainty is negated. Its pretensions to knowledge are *false*. But when consciousness goes on to another stage, it will not leave the contents of sense behind, to start afresh. When consciousness begins to interpret in terms of richer concepts, it will interpret *precisely what has been negated:* the sense experience that does not itself suffice for knowledge. So the earlier stage is not lost; what is *true* in it is preserved and incorporated in the next level.

Hegel finds this dialectical pattern repeated again and again, both in the progress of consciousness toward Absolute Knowledge and in the sequence of stages the human race goes through in history. A "moment" develops until it displays its own inadequacy. It is then negated and supplanted by a second (as the universally universal supplants the purely particular in sense-certainty). Then a stage emerges that incorporates the valuable and

---

* Compare Descartes' project of discovering a foundation in simple certainties and Hume's recommendation to trace ideas back to impressions.
† Here Hegel agrees with Kant's Copernican revolution and supplies an argument to back it up. Knowledge cannot be like the wax tablet that passively receives impressions from objects. The knower cannot help but play an active role in conceptualizing the object.

true in each of these stages. That stage then begins to develop, and the process repeats itself.* It is this *internal* dialectic that he thinks will supply at last the criterion for knowledge and close off the possibility of skepticism.

We cannot here follow the immensely elaborate and complex dialectic Hegel displays for us. Let us instead sketch briefly the progress of the next few stages, then discuss more fully several of the most famous and influential of them.

The inadequacy of sense-certainty leads consciousness on to the stage Hegel calls

* *Perception,* in which objects are characterized using concepts (universals) that describe their properties. Perception's structure is consciousness of *things* that *have* these properties. But what is a thing? Is it a mere collection of the properties? That hardly seems right, since it misses the *unity* of a thing. Is it then something lying behind all the properties? But then it becomes an unknowable *X,* since we know things by perception only in terms of their properties. And that can't be right either. This dilemma forces consciousness on to the next stage of
* *Understanding,* in which things are understood in terms of *laws,* as in Newtonian science. These laws are thought to express the *truth of things*—their inner nature or essence. They *explain* the properties we ascribe to things in perception and give us an account of the unity of things—of why a given thing has just the properties it does have. But in producing such explanations, consciousness is *active,* not merely passive. And in recognizing this contribution by itself, consciousness reaches the stage of explicit
* *Self-consciousness.*

What Hegel says here is justly famous; let's examine it more carefully.

*Hegelians have often called these moments the *Thesis,* the *Antithesis,* and the *Synthesis.* Hegel does not often use these terms, but this triadic structure is common in his analyses.

Self and Others

There is, within the stage of self-consciousness, a dialectic that structurally resembles the one in sense-certainty. In a passage that is the despair of commentators, Hegel seems to suggest that the most basic form of self-consciousness is *Desire.* Why should this be? Any answer, in view of the obscurity of Hegel's text here, is somewhat speculative. But perhaps this is what he has in mind.

Consciousness faces a world of objects that is *other* than itself. Yet, in the stage of Understanding, it recognizes that the inner essence or "truth" of these objects (revealed in science) is its own work. So it really isn't *other* after all. And yet, obviously, it isn't just itself. It both is other and it *isn't.* Consciousness wants to resolve this unsatisfactory situation and it tries to do so by *incorporating the other into itself.* And that is the essence of desire: wanting to make what is other than oneself into one's own. In this way the previous dialectic of consciousness leads inexorably to Desire as the next development.

But Desire is not merely conscious; it is explicitly *self*-conscious. Think about what it is like to desire something. You say, "*I* want a million dollars." In the very expression of your desire, there is consciousness of self, of the "I"—and also of the fact that your self is not all there is. To be conscious of your *self,* you need to have a contrast. Desire provides that contrast in abundance. It is what you do not have, but want to have, that defines for you what *you* are!

Still, there is something incomplete about this stage of self-consciousness. We might put it this way. Desire reveals the poignancy of being *other* than the world revealed to sense, perception, and understanding. And so it is a form of *self*-consciousness. But it does not yet reveal this self as *being self-conscious.* All we have in desire is the disclosure of a difference between two poles, between oneself and the other, together with a project to close up the gap. But the *nature* of oneself is not yet clear.

Think of the way a child develops a consciousness of herself. At first there is a stage where no distinction is made between self and other. What breaks this seamless unity of the child's world is frustration—when something *desired* is not attained. She becomes aware of the difference between herself and Mama, between herself and the bottle, between herself and the teddy bear. But this is not yet full-blown self-conciousness, explicit consciousness *of herself as a self-conscious being*. This comes much later and requires—as Hegel is among the first to recognize—another self-consciousness with which to contrast herself.

Self-consciousness achieves its satisfaction only in another self-consciousness.

Self-consciousness exists in and for itself when, and by the fact that, it so exists for another; that is, it exists only in being acknowledged. (PS, 110–11)

Self-consciousness is achieved, Hegel is telling us, only by being *recognized* as such by another self-consciousness. *Recognition* of a mutual sort between persons *creates* self-conscious beings. My self-consciousness exists "in and for itself" only insofar as it "exists for another." I cannot be *for myself* a self-conscious being unless I am acknowledged as such by another self-consciousness and *recognize* this acknowledgement. Self-consciousness is a *social* fact.*

But if Hegel is right, this mutual recognition is not an easy process. It is filled with conflict of the most desperate sort. It is a dialectical achievement that involves—as does all such dialectical progress—radical negation. How does this work? We can make Hegel's tortuous and abstract discussion more intelligible if we talk of two individuals, Jones and Smith.

Jones recognizes Smith as *like himself*—as a self-consciousness constituted by Desire. But this is not

a happy recognition; for it means that in a certain sense Jones has "lost" himself; he recognizes himself now as an "*other* being"—for Smith. Who is Jones? He is what Smith takes him to be. Jones becomes conscious of himself as an object of Smith's Desire. Remember that Desire is an attempt to make one's own what is felt to be alien to oneself. The ominous aspect of this attempt can be brought out if we think in terms of *control;* to make something one's own is to bring it within the sphere of one's power to control it. So Jones experiences Smith as someone who is trying to control him. Naturally, Jones resists this. From the other side, meanwhile, Smith is having analogous experiences; he feels himself to be the object of a hostile take over attempt by Jones—to be nothing more than what Jones takes him to be. He, too, struggles against this status. Neither Jones nor Smith can allow himself to be simply defined as an object for the other.*

But this does not yet bring out the full complexity of the situation. Each wants to make the other his own. Each recognizes the other as having a similar project. And in this recognition each implicitly acknowledges the other as an "equally independent and self-contained" consciousness. So each implicitly admits that the other cannot simply be controlled like a mere thing, used without consent. In this admission, "They *recognize* themselves as *mutually recognizing* one another" (*PS*, 112). So their consciousness of each other is of a distinctive sort; it is different in kind from their consciousness of things like stones or pencils.

At first, however, this mutual recognition is necessarily inadequate. From each side the situation is this: one is the being doing the *recognizing*,

---

* Contrast this with the view of Descartes, who holds that it is quite possible that *he alone* exists (the specter of solipsism—see p. 304). If Hegel is right, this individualism is simply *impossible*. Humans are *made* into self-conscious individuals, persons in the full sense, by their interactions with other human beings. No one is a self-made man.

* Kant's second formulation of the categorical imperative (p. 407) commands us to treat others as ends, not as means only. What Hegel is identifying here is an unavoidable tendency in self-conscious beings to treat each other *precisely* as means. Relations between the sexes often take this dialectical form, and complaints that someone is perceived only as a "sex object," or is being "used," get a natural interpretation in this Hegelian context. Hegel agrees, of course, with the rationality and rightness of Kant's imperative; but he is pointing out how difficult it is to achieve the state in which it is actualized.

and the other is the being *being recognized.* Look at it from the side of Jones, remembering that the same can be said for Smith's point of view. Jones recognizes Smith as both *like* himself and as *other* than himself. Smith (from Jones' point of view) is the one being recognized. But Jones cannot yet recognize Smith as a *pure* self-consciousness.* He sees him as an embodied, living individual: an *object* in the world, but one who (like himself) wants to control the *other*—that is, to control him. Jones thinks:

* Smith is like me, an independent, self-conscious being.
* Smith is aware of me.
* Smith recognizes that I am aware of him.
* He realizes that *for me,* he is just another object in the world.
* Like me, Smith is constituted by Desire.
* Hence, Smith will not be content to leave me in my independence, since that will mean I may come to control him.
* So I had better not leave Smith in his independence, lest he control me.
* Therefore, I must *kill* Smith, even if this means risking my life to do so.

Smith, of course, has exactly parallel thoughts. Once again, it is the unsatisfactory nature of a stage—the immediate self-certainty of Desire—that drives self-consciousness into the next. Desire produces conflict. Each consciousness is driven to *negate* the other, to control it, to turn it into a mere means for the satisfaction of its own Desire.* And it is this negating that reveals to each consciousness its true nature as a *pure self-consciousness.* Why? Because each is willing to risk everything worldly—even *life*—in the struggle for domination.

> Thus the relation of the two self-conscious individuals is such that they prove themselves and each other through a life-and-death struggle. They must engage in this struggle, for they must raise their certainty of being *for themselves* to truth, both in the case of the other and in their own case. And it is only through staking one's life that freedom is won; only thus is it proved for self-consciousness, its essential being is not [just] being, not the *immediate* form in which it appears, not its submergence in the expanse of life, but rather that there is nothing present in it which could not be regarded as a vanishing moment, that it is only pure *being-for-itself.* The individual who has not risked his life may well be recognized as a *person,* but he has not attained to the truth of this recognition as an independent self-consciousness. (*PS,* 113–14)

Hegel's thought here is an extreme one. Spirit, which comes on the scene explicitly for the first time in self-consciousness, cannot *realize itself* (become an actuality) except in mutual recognition by independent and free self-conscious individuals. But such mutual recognition is hazardous and tricky; it involves the necessity of tearing oneself—and the other—away from everything immediate and merely natural. And the only proof of that is the willingness to confront death in the struggle to demonstrate that one is *not simply an object for another.*

But what happens next is a surprise. Suppose Jones wins the struggle and kills Smith. Has he achieved what he wanted? Not at all. For in eliminating Smith, he deprives himself of precisely that source of recognition that he needs to realize him-

---

*Hegel has a very strong sense of "self-consciousness" in mind here. Think of it like this. You can become conscious of your height and weight, but that is a minimal self-consciousness indeed. You can go farther and become aware of your inclinations, of your character, of your personality, of your thoughts. Indeed, for *any fact* about yourself, you could become conscious of it—make it into an *object* for yourself. So being self-conscious in this strong sense is engaging in an *absolute abstraction* from *all* the facts that make you the existing individual that you are, turning every facet of yourself into an *object* for yourself. To use the title of a recent book by Thomas Nagel, this is *The View From Nowhere* (New York: Oxford University Press, 1986). With this possibility of *pure* self-consciousness, Hegel tells us, Spirit first makes its *explicit* appearance in the dialectic.

---

* There are echoes here of Hobbes' description of the state of nature. See again pp. 341–342. In Jean-Paul Sartre's play *No Exit,* we find three people engaged in just such control games. Eventually we discover they are in hell, from which there is "no exit"; they cannot die. One of the characters says, "Hell is other people."

self as a self-conscious being! He has shattered the mirror in which he might have discovered who he is. In some fashion (either in the course of history or in some dim way within each developing consciousness, or perhaps in both—Hegel does not make this clear), self-conscious individuals become aware of this self-defeating character of the life-and-death struggle. And the result is a compromise.

What happens is this: the stronger makes the weaker into his slave.* Let us imagine that Jones makes himself the master. Then he has, in relation to Smith, a very real independence and freedom; and he experiences Smith as recognizing that independence. Jones, then, exists *for himself* and has apparently achieved what he needs: the recognition of himself as a free and independent self-consciousness. But has he really? Oddly enough, he has not. For consider the consciousness of the slave. It is a *dependent* consciousness—unfree and subject to the will of the master. But such a consciousness is not fit to provide the recognition that the master needs to confirm himself as free and independent. That can only be given by another free and independent individual. From Jones' own point of view, Smith (his slave) is almost indistinguishable from a mere brute. What could "recognition" by such a creature *mean*? So the master does not win what he needs by enslaving the other, any more than he could win it by killing the other.

Consider the consciousness of the slave. It is completely at its master's beck and call. The slave must work at the master's bidding. Smith's work is not done for Smith's sake, but for the sake of Jones, who rules him. It would seem that Smith, too, has failed to achieve that self-consciousness that Spirit is driving toward. But again something odd happens.

Think of Smith's work. He is oriented toward things in the world. Suppose he is a cobbler; he takes leather and nails and *changes* them until they become shoes. He does this not to satisfy his own Desire, of course, but to satisfy the Desire of his master, Jones. But in working on the things of the world, he expresses himself; he *puts himself into the products of his labor.* These products exist independently of him; he recognizes himself in them and so achieves in his *work* a kind of self-realization that is denied the master. He *objectifies* himself and so can recognize himself in what he produces. "I," he can say, "am the one who made this; this object reveals what I can do and who I am; I have put *myself* into this object." Thus he achieves a definite kind of self-consciousness. In the independence of these objects, of the products of his labor, he recognizes his own independence.*

But that is not all. In addition to this "positive moment" in Smith's attainment of self-consciousness, there is a pervasive fear in the slave that constitutes a "negative moment."

> For this consciousness has been fearful, not of this or that particular thing or just at odd moments, but its whole being has been seized with dread. In that experience it has been quite unmanned, has trembled in every fibre of its being, and everything solid and stable has been shaken to its foundations. But this pure universal movement, the absolute melting-away of everything stable, is the simple, essential nature of self-consciousness, absolute negativity, *pure being-for-itself,* which consequently is *implicit* in this consciousness. (*PS*, 117)

The fear of the slave, a kind of universal dread, drives Smith back into himself, distances him from the master and even from the things on which he works. The entire material world is "negated"; the slave in his fear says "no" to it all—and discovers himself as a pure self-consciousness. In this way,

---

* It is worth noting that ancient societies, including Greek, Roman, and Hebrew, were all slave societies. Indeed, as we know, slavery was not abolished even in America until relatively recently. Hegel's discussion here has a historical cast that the earlier, more purely epistemological studies lack.

* Some forty years later, Karl Marx would take up this dialectic of master and slave. For Marx, of course, it is not consciousness that is at stake, but real material life and well-being. He accepts Hegel's point that one objectifies oneself in one's labor, and goes on to emphasize that if the product of one's labor is not one's own, if it belongs to another, then one becomes alienated *from oneself.* From this point arises his critique of capitalism. See "Marx: Beyond Alienation and Exploitation," in Chapter 20.

too, he becomes aware of himself as something *other* than everything else that exists. Moreover, he has objectively before him an example of self-consciousness in the master, although the master fails to experience himself that way (not having an independent consciousness in which to mirror himself). He becomes what the master can never become: a being who exists as an object *for himself*. He, rather than the master, is the bearer of Spirit in its progress toward new heights of development.

And yet all is not well in the self-consciousness of the slave. It recognizes itself in the products of its labor and it has an image of itself in the self-conscious independence of the master. But, as Hegel says, these two "moments" *fall apart*. They are not brought together in one unified self-consciousness. And the dialectical story must go on.

Stoic and Skeptical Consciousness

Hegel thinks that the next stage in the development of Spirit appeared first at a definite point in our historical past. After the death of the Greek city-states came the era of empires, first Alexander's, then, after a period of uncertainty, the empire of Rome. The vastness of the empire, its impersonality and bureaucracy, and the sheer weight of established institutions caused most people to feel helpless to shape their destiny in this world. In this context, Spirit, now acutely conscious of itself, withdraws from everything that it cannot control; in effect, it withdraws *into itself*, finding there an independence and freedom that is denied it in the hostile world.

This is the key idea in Stoic thought, which distinguishes *what is in one's power* from *what is not in one's power*; it identifies as in one's power such conscious states as "opinion, aim, desire, aversion." * These Hegel calls "thinking." Why? Note that with respect to absolutely any experience—pain, pleasure, boredom, and so on—the Stoic

---

* See p. 193.

will ask, "Now, what shall I do about that? How shall I consider that? What opinion shall I have of it?" The *immediacy* of sensory experience is completely transcended, and the self-conscious Stoic must *think* about how to respond.* This reflective self is apparently in complete control of its own happiness, since it can always "negate" or consider *as nothing* anything that threatens it. Consequently, it experiences itself as perfectly free. The Stoic claims that this way of life produces both happiness and freedom.

> This freedom of self-consciousness when it appeared as a conscious manifestation in the history of Spirit has, as we know, been called Stoicism. Its principle is that consciousness is a being that *thinks*, and that consciousness holds something to be essentially important, or true and good only in so far as it *thinks* it to be such. (*PS*, 121)

As you might have guessed by now, Hegel is not content just to describe the Stoic form of consciousness. He proposes to show that it, too, is one-sided and inadequate, that Spirit has not yet found a satisfactory resting place. His critique of Stoicism is that its form of self-consciousness is still too abstract.

> The freedom of self-consciousness is *indifferent* to natural existence and has therefore *let this equally go free*: the *reflection* is a *twofold* one. Freedom in thought has only *pure thought* as its truth, a truth lacking the fullness of life. Hence freedom in thought, too, is only the Notion of freedom, not the living reality of freedom itself. (*PS*, 122)

The thought of the Stoic, Hegel tells us, frees the Stoic from "natural existence"; but by the same token, it lets natural existence "go free," too. Consequently, there is a lack of *reality* in the Stoic's freedom, and his much-prized thinking lacks "the fullness of life." That is why Hegel says the Stoic

---

* Epictetus says, "Men are disturbed not by things, but by the view they take of things." And what view we take is something, he says, that is in our own control. It will be helpful to review the discussion of Stoicism in Chapter 10.

has only the "Notion" (the concept) of freedom, not its "living reality." What is still required is that this concept be embedded in the Stoic's life, so that he does not *need* to abstract himself from it in order to find his happiness. The Stoic mode of life does have a certain "truth" to it; it is possible to withdraw into "pure thought." But this truth is a partial truth, an *abstraction* from what would be the whole truth about conscious existence. This truth—perhaps *the Truth*—lies in the unity of a life where what thinking declares to be valuable is *actually realized in natural existence*. And this integration the Stoic conspicuously lacks.*

Again, the road toward such unity is tortuous and indirect. Things have to get worse before they can get better. Consciousness has to *experience* itself as the negation of all reality. It is not enough, as with Stoicism, to realize that one *could* set the value of everything as nothing. This stage must actually be lived through. Such a life is that of the skeptic.

> *Scepticism* is the realization of that of which Stoicism was only the Notion, and is the actual experience of what the freedom of thought is. This is *in itself* the negative and must exhibit itself as such. (*PS*, 123)

Skeptics actually *live* this negation of the world by thinking; they *suspend judgment* about each and every claim concerning reality. Indeed, they actively use the resources of thought to make this possible by constructing equally plausible arguments on each side of every question.†

But once again, this stratagem on the part of Spirit proves unstable. Notoriously, skeptics need to find a way to *live*. They cannot make judgments about the true, the real, and the good. So how are they to manage it? The standard skeptical line at this point is to "adhere to appearances," as Sextus Empiricus puts it, to "live in accordance with the normal rules of life, undogmatically, seeing that we

cannot remain wholly inactive."* Hegel's analysis of this tactic lays it bare as a sham. Skeptical self-consciousness at one time

> recognizes that its freedom lies in rising above all the confusion and contingency of existence, and at another time equally admits to a relapse into occupying itself with what is unessential. . . . It affirms the nullity of seeing, hearing, etc., yet it is itself seeing, hearing, etc. It affirms the nullity of ethical principles, and lets its conduct be governed by these very principles. Its deeds and its words always belie one another. (*PS*, 124–25)

In short, skeptical self-consciousness is mired deep in self-deception. Priding itself on its freedom, it becomes slave to the customs of the society in which it finds itself, whatever they happen to be. This purely accidental life cannot, Hegel is convinced, be the goal of Reason and Spirit.

Hegel's Analysis of Christianity

The next transition arises naturally—necessarily, Hegel would say—out of this unsatisfactory state.† Again, as Hegel sees it, something very interesting happens.

> In Scepticism, consciousness truly experiences itself as internally contradictory. From this experience

---

* See p. 201. For a modern version of the same principle, recall Montaigne's "defense" of Raymond Sebond and its outcome, p. 284. A somewhat similar pattern is found in David Hume; see pp. 373–374.

† It is perhaps time to pause a moment and reflect. Recall that Hegel's strategy is to discover the criterion for knowledge *from within.* The dialectic we have been tracing can be thought of as a process of sloughing off one proposed but clearly unsatisfactory criterion after another. And by now the goal should be getting clearer, too, though the details still need to be filled in. Nothing will do but a state in which Spirit is not *alienated* from reality, but *identifies* with it, and can see *itself* expressed in whatever it knows to be real. One further aspect of this process needs to be noted. You can see that we have moved from a purely *theoretical* sense of knowledge to one that incorporates *the entire life* of a knower. (This correlates with the increasingly historical cast to the story Hegel is telling.) Hegel, for whom the Truth is always the whole, will be satisfied with nothing less: Reason governs *all*.

---

*It is worth comparing this critique of Stoicism with that of Saint Augustine. See p. 249. Note also that Hegel's internal critique of Stoicism (that it splits a person into two halves) is akin to the Romantics' critique of Kant (p. 414).

† For an example of the techniques of the skeptics, see p. 199.

emerges a *new form* of consciousness which brings together the two thoughts which Scepticism holds apart. Scepticism's lack of thought about itself must vanish, because it is in fact *one* consciousness which contains within itself these two modes. This new form is, therefore, one which *knows* that it is the dual consciousness of itself, as self-liberating, unchangeable, and self-identical, and as self-bewildering and self-perverting, and it is the awareness of this self-contradictory nature of itself. (*PS*, 126)

Spirit recognizes its split nature. And it recognizes the split as a duality *within itself*. It no longer identifies itself only with the thinking, rational side but incorporates into itself both of the opposed aspects. This, too, is a process that takes agonizingly long. Once again, things have to get worse before they can get better. This self-divided consciousness, aware nonetheless that it is *one*, Hegel calls the *Unhappy Consciousness.** On the one side there is the experience of free and rational thinking, of pure universality, which nothing merely contingent or natural can touch. Hegel calls this the *Unchangeable.* On the other side, consciousness experiences itself as a changeable, unessential, "self-bewildering and self-perverting" particular individual, subject to the sheerest happenstance of accident. These two sides are "alien to one another" (*PS*, 127).

Under psychological pressure to resolve this dilemma, consciousnesss identifies itself with the Changeable and experiences the Unchangeable as "an alien Being," as *not itself* (*PS*, 127). The Unhappy Consciousness is essentially a *religious* consciousness; as you can see, Hegel has in mind the two poles around which Augustine's thought revolves: God and the soul.† But there is an obviously radical twist in Hegel's story. The Unchange-

able (experienced as God) is not *actually* a being independent of an individual's consciousness; it only seems so. Actually, it is one *pole* of Spirit's consciousness of itself in this Unhappy stage of its dialectical development. And the desperately unhappy individual, cut off from the Unchangeable (God), does not *actually* exist independently; he only seems to. Still, it does really seem so! It is not an illusion to be brushed aside as trivial.

Christianity appears to Hegel as a subtle and ingenious construction on the part of Spirit to reunite what has been split. What is needed is supplied: a *Mediator.* This mediator must participate in both sides of the duality—that is, he must be both God and man. The (supposed) actuality of this mediator demonstrates that *in principle* the two sides of Spirit—eternal and temporal, infinite and finite, Unchangeable and Changeable—are one. This, Hegel holds, is what the Christian doctrine of the Incarnation really means: Jesus as truly man and truly God manifests the unity of the Spirit. The believer participates in the nature of the Unchangeable through devotion, sacrifice, and thanksgiving and hopes for the completion of this process in the life to come. The Holy Spirit is the sign that the gulf can be bridged, that sinners can become saints, and *individuals* can participate in the life divine.*

So Hegel regards Christianity as expressing a truth, or at least a part of the truth. But it does so in mythological and imaginative forms. It takes philosophy—that is, Reason—to understand its real significance.

---

* Compare Augustine's flirtation with Manicheanism and the essential move in its rejection (pp. 216–217).

† Hegel's characterization of this stage as an *Unhappy Consciousness* brings to mind Saint Paul's despairing cry in Romans 7: ". . . when I want to do the right, only the wrong is within my reach. In my inmost self I delight in the law of God, but I perceive that there is in my bodily members a different law, fighting against the law that my reason approves and making me a prisoner under the law . . . of sin." A quick review of Chapter 11 will be helpful at this point.

* Is Hegel a Christian theologian, explaining "the true meaning of the faith"? Or is he an atheist, proposing a secular interpretation of a religious tradition he does not accept? As is characteristic with Hegel, it is hard to answer this question unambiguously. He is convinced that every stage of consciousness has its truth (as well as its falsity) and that what is true in it will be preserved in successor stages. But there *are* successor stages, which will do more justice to the phenomena than the earlier ones do. Christianity, for Hegel, is one necessary, fruitful stage in the history of Spirit. But it is no more than that. Marx and his followers will emphasize the aspect of surpassing religion and proclaim themselves atheists. Others—"liberal" theologians—will emphasize what is true and must be preserved. Kierkegaard takes offense at the whole notion that *finite individuals* could ever "surpass" the truth in Christianity. See Chapter 20.

Reason and Reality:
The Theory of Idealism

Consciousness, by its own internal development, has now reached the stage of reincorporating its *other* into itself. It recognizes that what it took to be alien—the thing sensed and perceived, the world as understood by science, the object of desire and labor, the self-consciousness of the master and the dependence of the slave, the negatively valued world of Stoic and skeptic, and finally the projection of itself into the heavens as God—is all its own work. Wherever consciousness looks, it sees nothing but *itself!* *

> In grasping the thought that the *single* individual consciousness is *in itself* Absolute Essence, consciousness has returned into itself. (*PS,* 139)

Hegel calls this stage *Reason.* It will help to understand why if we think back to Kant. For Kant, Reason is the faculty that asks and tries to answer why-questions. You will remember that the propensity to ask such questions sets us off in a search for the "condition" that explains the subject we are asking about. Since we can always ask again, we find ourselves driven toward the Idea (a technical term, for Kant, you recall) of a condition that is *unconditioned,* that neither has nor needs any further explanation. (There are in fact three such Ideas: God, the soul, and the world in itself.) But in the realm of phenomena, nothing unconditioned can be found; and noumena are closed to our inspection. So Reason is a drive that must remain forever unsatisfied. This is how Kant limits knowledge to make room for faith.*

But for Hegel there is no need for faith. His elaborate dialectic *from within* has, he thinks, covered all the possibilities that any consciousness could ever be aware of. And everywhere, absolutely everywhere, consciousness discovers *itself;* in every explanation of an *other,* it finds meanings, laws, truths, values it has itself supplied. It is true that there is process involved. But it is a process that consciousness now knows must have a close; for it knows that it—it, *itself*—is the *Unconditioned.* And that is why Hegel calls the stage in which this truth is recognized *Reason.* It is Kantian Reason with this difference: it can achieve its aim!

> Now that self-consciousness is Reason, its hitherto negative relation to otherness turns round into a positive relation. Up till now it has been concerned only with its independence and freedom, concerned to save and maintain itself for itself at the expense of the *world,* or of its own actuality, both of which appeared to it as the negative of its essence. But as Reason, assured of itself, it is at peace with them, and can endure them; for it is certain that it is itself reality, or that everything actual is none other than itself; its thinking is itself directly actuality, and thus its relationship to the latter is that of idealism. . . .
>
> Reason is the certainty of consciousness that it is all reality; thus does idealism express its Notion. (*PS,* 139–40)

To put it in another typically Hegelian way, the *substance* of the world is a *subject* of consciousness!

This conclusion might seem to be outrageous. How could *I,* a "*single* individual consciousness," be *all reality*? Is this some sort of mysticism? Even if we grant Hegel's controversial claim that whatever I can be aware of is something I have constituted myself, *I* am certainly not conscious of *all reality!*

Two things can be said in Hegel's defense. First, his claim is to be understood only as the outcome of the entire dialectical story that has been told up to this point. It is not something that you in your

---

*It may help here to remember the *beginning* of the dialectic. Our natural resistance to this conclusion, our conviction that consciousness cannot be *all* there is, has its basis in "sense-certainty"—in the apparent *brute-fact* character of sensation. It seems absolutely *not up to us* to determine what we sense when we open our eyes. And the sense of something independent of our awareness—something *other,* something *alien*—is very powerful. Hegel does not deny this. But, he asks you to consider that as soon as you try to say *what* it is that you sense, you are in the realm of concepts, interpretation, and reason. *What it is*—even this apparently independent fact—is relative to the consciousness that comprehends it.

* Kant's concept of Reason is discussed on pp. 393–394.

common sense should be expected to immediately assent to. Our feeling of outrageousness may be simply a manifestation of that stage of consciousness in which most of us mostly live; we may occupy a rather lowly rung on the dialectical ladder. Common sense may have its limits, and the question we need to address is this: How sound is the dialectical path that Hegel has sketched for us?

> . . . anyone who has not trodden this path finds this assertion incomprehensible when he hears it in this pure form—although he does as a matter of fact make the assertion himself in a concrete shape [i.e., the assertion is implicit in his behavior]. (PS, 141)

What Hegel means by this last remark is that whenever we act, we implicitly assume that the world is intelligible, rational, and meaningful. We bank on it. But to do that is to "make the assertion" that it is not alien to Reason—that the Reason in it is the same Reason as is in us. We are all, he seems to say, *practical* idealists, whether we admit it or not.

The second reply has to do with the *subject* of consciousness. My outrage is predicated on the assumption that I am merely a single, finite, limited individual. If that were so, of course, the outrage would be justified. But is that so? One thing to consider is our earlier conclusion that mind and forms of consciousness are inherently social.* A completely isolated individual consciousness is not possible. So I, as a conscious subject, represent or manifest a more general consciousness: that of my community, those who share the same language and instruments of interpretation (concepts).

Moreover, Hegel agrees with Kant that Reason is a principle of universality. What is rational cannot differ from mind to mind. If it is rational in *these* circumstances to do just exactly *that,* then it is rational for me, for you, and for anyone else. So when Hegel says that consciousness in its mode of Reason is *all reality,* he does not mean the consciousness that you happen to display today. After

all, the dialectic he has led us through has shown us one after another *inadequate* form of consciousness. And your form of consciousness today is no doubt inadequate in many ways. Hegel means that consciousness, Reason *in itself* or in its *essence,* is identical with all reality. This consciousness is *implicit* in you and me, and we are part of the process in which it is *becoming explicit.* This process is history. In that (implicit) sense, even the single consciousness that *you* are is *all reality.**

In this connection, Hegel often talks in terms of a *World Spirit.* The term has clear religious connotations, but it would be a mistake to identify it with the Christian concept of God. (Recall Hegel's critique of the "alienation" characteristic of traditional religious—unhappy—consciousness.) The World Spirit is consciousness and Reason manifesting itself in the world. Indeed, Hegel thinks history is a process in which "God" is coming to comprehend itself in and through us. In a sense, then, you and I are God—but potentially, implicitly, and in essence, not yet in actuality.

> Consciousness will determine its relationship to otherness or its object in various ways, according to the precise stage it has reached in the development of the World-Spirit into self-consciousness. How it *immediately* finds and determines itself and its object at any time, or the way in which it is *for itself,* depends on what it has already *become,* or what it already is in *itself.* (PS, 141–42)

The endpoint of this process, when subject and object correspond perfectly because each recognizes the other as nothing but itself, the stage of perfect self-consciousness, is the stage Hegel calls *absolute knowledge.*

What is known in absolute knowledge? It is the Kantian *Idea*—the unconditioned explainer of all reality. But it is now known not just as an ever-receding goal serving to regulate our enquiries. It is known as it is *in itself.* For it is the World Spirit's rational consciousness of *itself* as constituting all

---

*See p. 422.

---

*For an enlightening analogy, compare Aristotle's notion of potentiality. The tadpole is not yet *actually* a frog, but it already is a frog *potentially* (see p. 159).

reality—as the Unconditioned. This means that the process of gaining knowledge is not like an infinitely long path we can never hope to traverse. It is more like a loop; it closes and comes back on itself. In absolute knowledge the problem of the criterion will be solved, because all possible grounds for skeptical doubt will have been analyzed and *surpassed* in the dialectical progression that gets us to that point. Spirit will not just know reality; it will know that it knows.

It is not for you and me, but for the World Spirit that objects are (or rather, will be) completely intelligible. For us there remains opacity and darkness and an alien character to the things of the world. They continue to be experienced as *other*. But if Hegel is right, this otherness is merely appearance; even now it is in the process of being surpassed. In themselves, things are illuminated by the light of Reason and are comprehensible without remainder. There are no dark and unintelligible Kantian noumena hiding behind the face of appearance. Apart from being known, things do not even exist—*could not* exist; they have their reality only *for a subject*. That is what idealism means. Hegel's idealism is an *absolute idealism,* because reality is thought to be constituted in the self-consciousness of the Absolute—in God, Reason, the World Spirit. For the World Spirit *is* all of reality.

Spirit Made Objective: The Social Character of Ethics

The recognition on the part of Reason that it encompasses all reality is not yet the end of the dialectic. For this is, as we might say, "mere" recognition and has a formal or abstract character to it. Hegel would say it merely expresses the "Notion" of Reason.* It remains for Reason to *make itself* into what it recognizes that it truly is; Reason must *objectify* itself. It must come out of itself and express itself in its objects, so that these objects are made to display explicitly that rationality

which, so far, is theirs only implicitly. Reason must become Practical Reason and actually shape the life of the community of self-conscious beings. Reason must become ethics.

The realm of **objective spirit,** as Hegel calls it, is the realm of culture—of art, religion, custom, morality, the family, and law. Here Spirit makes itself into an actual object for itself and can comprehend itself in contemplating its products. But this process, too, is tortuous; like all the rest, it is a process involving complication, negativity, and inadequacy. Again we will simplify.

Hegel looks back to ancient Greece before the controversy between Socrates and the Sophists for an example of unity and harmony.* At this time, the judgments of individuals about what should and should not be done, what is valuable, and what the good life consists in reflect the "ethos" of the Greek city-state. Individuals simply absorb the standards of their city; these standards are theirs without question and without reflection. Citizens do not experience a conflict between their individual conscience and what is required of them by the state, since they cannot be said to have an "individual" conscience at all.† Their desires are simply molded by the customs of the community, which they take for granted. We must not think that there is anything sinister about this process. It is the most natural thing in the world, since children grow up *necessarily* internalizing the standards of the society in which they live.

There are consequences: (1) citizens do not experience the welfare of their community as hostile to their own welfare, but naturally identify their own good with the good of the state to which they belong; so there is harmony between individual and community; (2) they experience themselves as free in their actions—so free, indeed, that they

---

* Compare the passage about the French Revolution, p. 413.

---

* Hegel would not want to deny that there have been many such "traditional societies" (as they are often called); but the Greeks, whom Hegel here interprets in line with the Romantic view of them, are unique because it seems to have been they who first move away from the "immediacy" of traditional modes of community to a more rational and reflective mode.

† Hegel says, "An Athenian citizen did what was required of him, as it were from instinct" (*RH,* 53). Compare Heidegger on "the One" ("The 'Who' of Dasein," in Chapter 26).

need not even remark on it, since the experience of unfreedom is not present to them as a contrast. We can call this the stage of *custom*.

But this stage, Hegel notes, is marked by an *immediate* identity between an individual and the community. And, as we should now know, immediacy is a state that needs to be overcome and will be overcome by producing some *negative* to itself. Immediacy is always simplistic, naive, and abstract, for Hegel. In this case, it lacks the character of being *for itself,* which is essential to a developed consciousness; it is not a *self-conscious* harmony and freedom. It does not represent a rational decision, just an unexamined way of life that is taken for granted.

The negative "moment" in Greek history is represented by the Sophists and Socrates. Influenced by the wider knowledge of the non-Greek world brought about through trade and warfare, the Sophists express the view that Greek customs are not "natural," not matters of *physis,* but mere matters of "convention" or *nomos.** This represents a giant step toward becoming self-conscious, for it suggests that customs and traditions have been invented by consciousness and can be changed. Socrates, for his part, engages in his ceaseless questioning in order to discover the *reason why* something is considered just or pious or courageous.† It is self-consciousness as *Reason* that comes on the scene with Socrates. The detachment of consciousness from its immediacy in the traditional society of the Greeks is a fateful step; it detaches the individual from that sense of natural solidarity with his community, and Western civilization is never the same again. Hegel recognizes that our long history since has, in a way, been an exploration of the consequences of this step.

This negative stage of increasing individual self-consciousness reaches a culmination, according to Hegel, in modern times, when the Reformation affirms the criterion of individual conscience, Enlightenment thinkers debunk everything based only on tradition and privilege, and the French Revolution tries overnight to reconstruct society according to the dictates of reason.* Philosophically speaking, Hegel sees this stage reaching a climax in the ethical thinking of Immanuel Kant. He calls this stage *morality*. We need to pay some attention to Hegel's discussion of Kant, since he takes Kant to "typify" this second, self-conscious stage.

Hegel accepts much of Kant's analysis. Morality, he agrees, must be founded on Reason, not Desire. Reason, moreover, gives us universal laws telling us what our duties are. And to do one's duty is to act in a way that is both autonomous and free:†

> I should do my duty for duty's sake, and when I do my duty it is in a true sense my own objectivity which I am bringing to realization. In doing my duty, I am by myself and free. To have emphasized this meaning of duty has constituted the merit of Kant's moral philosophy and its loftiness of outlook. (*PR,* 253)

In all these respects, Kant's thought is the culmination of that tradition of self-reflective rationality begun by Socrates. In fact, Hegel gives the Kantian emphasis on the role of reason additional support.

Think about the claim that you are free when you can do—without hindrance or constraint—what you want to do.‡ It is a view of freedom that has been espoused by many "liberal" thinkers, from Hume and John Stuart Mill to present-day "liberal" economists. What is characteristic of the view is that desires are simply accepted as a *given;* on this view, the question a person faces in seeking happiness is just this: What shall I do to get the most satisfaction for the desires I in fact have? And

---

*See the discussion of the debate about *nomos* and *physis* (Chapter 5).

†Any of the earlier dialogues of Plato will give you the flavor of his questions, *Euthyphro* being a particularly good example.

---

*Take a quick look back at the discussions of conscience in the Reformation (p. 280), Kant on enlightenment (p. 346), and Hume on superstition (p. 348). The French Revolutionaries consciously aimed at a rational society; to this end they introduced a new religion of reason, rationalized the calendar, adopted the metric system, and cut off the king's head.

†For Kant's theory of morality, see "Reason and Morality," in Chapter 18.

‡See Hume's endorsement of this view, pp. 363–364. It is the natural companion of the view that reason is and must be the slave of the passions.

I am free to the degree that no one interferes with my pursuit of that satisfaction.

It is Hegel's view that this is a very shallow kind of freedom. It is no more satisfactory than the abstract view of Stoic and skeptic. Indeed, it is equally abstract, but in a precisely opposite direction.* Just as the Stoic and skeptic abstract themselves from "living reality" and identify themselves with pure thought, reflection, and universality, so the "liberal" theorists about freedom identify themselves solely with their nonreflective, rationally uncriticized, given desires. The former experience themselves as possessing an "infinite will," since their decisions range freely over any alternatives presented to them.† The will of the latter is wholly finite, being simply a set of naturally given (or culturally instilled) inclinations, yearnings, hankerings, wants, and so on. Hegel calls this an "arbitrary will."

> Arbitrariness implies that the content is made mine not by the nature of my will but by chance. Thus I am dependent on this content, and this is the contradiction lying in arbitrariness. The man in the street thinks he is free if it is open to him to act as he pleases but his very arbitrariness implies that he is not free. When I will what is rational, then I am acting not as a particular individual but in accordance with the concepts of ethics in general. (PR, 230)

To be truly free, Hegel claims, we must not be at the mercy of whatever happens to influence and form us, lest we be simply the pawns and dupes of irrational interests and forces. (Think, in this connection, of the ways advertisers or politicians try to mold and persuade us.) To be free we must be rational. And, since rationality is intrinsically universal, to be rational is to be ethical. This is already argued by Kant, and Hegel emphatically agrees. Reason is not, and cannot be, simply the slave of the passions; reason must be a determining factor in action.

Hegel thinks that the Stoic/skeptic view on the one hand and the "liberal" Humean view on the other constitute two abstract moments that need to interact and interpenetrate each other. Abstract reason must become concrete in action, and the arbitrary will needs to be disciplined by reason. In this way Hegel buttresses the Kantian view of reason, freedom, morality, and action.

But, in Hegel's view, Kant does not show us how to make reason actual in the world. Though Kant correctly identifies reason as the key to morality and freedom alike, his discussion remains abstract and, therefore, inadequate as a guide for life. We need to examine Hegel's critique of Kant's ethics.

Recall that Kant's criterion for the moral acceptability of a principle of action is the categorical imperative.* Suppose we are thinking of acting on a certain maxim; the categorical imperative bids us examine it by asking, Can it be universalized? The maxim will be morally acceptable as a basis for acting only if it passes this universalization test. Otherwise, it would be morally wrong to act on that principle. It is important to note that the categorical imperative is a purely formal rule; by itself, it does not bid us do anything in particular. What it does is to test proposed maxims (and hence actions) for moral acceptability.

One of Kant's clearest examples is the proposal to make a promise, intending all the while to break it if it proves inconvenient to keep. Kant argues that this maxim cannot be universalized, because if it were, promising would simply disappear. The universal practice of promising with an intention to break the promise undermines itself and so cannot be an acceptable moral practice. Acting on this maxim will work for individuals only if they can count on nearly everyone else keeping their promises; but that is to make an exception for oneself in order to satisfy some desire of one's own—at the expense of others—the very essence of immorality.

This seems a strong argument. What is Hegel's objection? In effect Hegel asks, And then what? Suppose we grant the entire argument; what are

---

*"The development we are studying is that whereby the abstract forms reveal themselves not as self-subsistent but as false" (PR, 233).

†Compare Descartes' claim in Meditation IV that even God's will is not more free than our own.

---

*The content of the categorical imperative, together with an examination of the "promising" example, is set out on pp. 406–407.

we to do now? We see that the practice of false promising cannot be institutionalized in a society, but that still leaves us with two options:

1. We can make promises, intending sincerely to keep them.
2. We can dispense with the institution of promising altogether.

There seems to be no way the categorical imperative, as a purely formal rule, can decide between these two possibilities; for there seems nothing impossible or contradictory about a society that simply does not have the institution of promising. Kant's formal principle is *too abstract,* since it cannot choose between these two alternatives.*

The criticism can be put in a more politically sensitive way if we consider another example: stealing. Can a maxim that I may steal what is my neighbor's property be universalized? It again seems clear that it cannot, for were it universalized the institution of private property would disappear. Hegel grants that there is a contradiction between the institution of private property and the maxim "Thou mayest steal." You cannot consistently have both. But again, the question is this: Shall we have the institution or not? And again we seem to be left with two consistent possibilities:

3. A society with private property and rules against stealing
4. A society without private property

Kant's purely formal imperative, Hegel argues, is helpless to choose between them.† And the reason is that in itself it has no *content.*

---

*Would a Kantian be able to reply to this argument? Might one say that if faced with the prospect of legislating for society a set of practices which either includes or excludes the practice of promising, the rational choice would be in favor of promising? If so, the same move might be possible for stealing and private property (see below). In either case, however, rationality would probably have to mean more than just absence of contradiction.

†This is obviously another one of the points Karl Marx picks up from Hegel. If a purely formal and individualistic morality like Kant's cannot be a guide in selecting *institutions,* then a guide for life must be given by *society.* And doing that is *politics.*

The absence of property contains in itself just as little contradiction as the non-existence of this or that nation, family, etc., or the death of the whole human race. But if it is already established on other grounds and presupposed that property and human life are to exist and be respected, then indeed it is a contradiction to commit theft or murder; a contradiction must be a contradiction of something, i.e., of some content presupposed from the start as a fixed principle. (*PR,* 90)

The inadequacy of this stage of morality was made dramatically clear, Hegel believes, in the French Revolution. This was an attempt to *impose* on society abstract principles of a universal sort, to *force* recalcitrant reality to be rational and free. But this freedom was a purely *negative* freedom; and the result was the Terror. When negative freedom

turns to actual practice, it takes shape in religion and politics alike as the fanaticism of destruction—the destruction of the whole subsisting social order—as the elimination of individuals who are objects of suspicion to any social order, and the annihilation of any organization which tries to rise anew from the ruins. Only in destroying something does this negative will possess the feeling of itself as existent. Of course it imagines that it is willing some positive state of affairs, such as universal equality or universal religious life, but . . . what negative freedom intends to will can never be anything in itself but an abstract idea, and giving effect to this idea can only be the fury of destruction. (*PR,* 22)

The stage of *morality* is supplanted by what Hegel calls *ethics.* (These terms are often used synonymously, but they are quite distinct for Hegel.) *Ethics* is the next dialectical step in the objectification of Spirit. But let us pause a moment to review. At first there was *custom,* where an unreflective and uncritical harmony existed between the life of the individual and the life of his society. This broke down in the Socratic/Stoic/skeptic realization of oneself as pure reason, distinct from any natural or social realities; the apex of this stage is to be found in the *morality* of Kant.

What is required for Spirit to become what it is, however—fully rational, self-conscious, and free—is for it to be able to recognize itself in its cultural expressions. And so the next step, *ethics,* is the recognition of rationality in institutions—in property, contracts, the family, and the state. Spirit, alienated from its products in a necessary differentiation of itself from them, must reappropriate them, see itself in them, express itself in the social dimension—but now critically, rationally, freely. The abstraction of Kantian morality is to be overcome by the objectification of reason in society.

For Hegel, ethics is virtually indistinguishable from social and political philosophy. Or rather, it is not philosophy at all, but the *realization* of philosophy in an actual community. As he says, "the system of right·is the realm of freedom made actual, the world of mind brought forth out of itself like a second nature" (*PR*, 20). What kind of social system will this incarnation of Spirit be? How will right, duty, rationality, and freedom all manage to coalesce in the society of Spirit objectified?

We won't go into the details of Hegel's social thought; he tends too much to see his own society as approaching or having reached the ideal, and much of his discussion is thus of interest only to historians. But we need to indicate his general idea and to point out one of its consequences.

As we have already noted, an individual must be thought of as socially shaped and constructed; no one is an island. Hobbes' view of the rational origin of a state as a contract made by isolated individuals with a view to their own individual protection is, for Hegel, simply another instance of undue abstraction.* The relation between an individual and the community is more like that between a leg and the body it belongs to. If the leg were to say, "I am an independent entity, and I will go my own way," this would be manifestly absurd. It is no less absurd for individuals to consider themselves distinct from the community that nourishes, educates, shapes and forms them. Indeed, an individual per se is an *abstraction* (there's that word again) from the whole. As separate from the community, a person lacks reality. It is the community, which Hegel calls the *State,* that is the

bearer of the objective reality of Spirit and as such is "higher" than the individual. The State is like an organism, and individuals are like its organs. Hegel goes as far as to say,

> A single person . . . is something subordinate, and as such he must dedicate himself to the ethical whole. Hence if the state claims life, the individual must surrender it.

> The rational end of man is life in the state, and if there is no state there, reason at once demands that one be founded. . . . It is false to maintain that the foundation of the state is something at the option of all its members. It is nearer the truth to say that it is absolutely necessary for every individual to be a citizen. (*PR*, 241–42)

But what kind of state is it that can rightly subordinate persons like this? It must be, Hegel says, a rational state. And that means that it must be one whose laws are universal and impartial, one to which free and rational individuals can give their free and rational consent.* Citizens must be able to live freely and rationally in such a state because the state is the objective correlate of that Reason which is the essence of their very being. Here we see how Hegel thinks to surpass, and yet incorporate, the "moments" of unthinking harmony (*custom*) and rational abstraction from that harmony by individuals (*morality*). There is to be a new harmony, one now founded self-consciously on rational principles. After being merely implicit in traditional societies, and after a long estrangement from a reality that was less than fully rational, Spirit is now to find itself mirrored in the institutions and laws of the organic community. These institutions and laws will not seem restrictive to its citizens, because they express the inner nature of those citizens.

> If men are to act, they must not only intend the good but must know whether this or that particular course

---

* For Hobbes' view of the social contract, see pp. 343–344.

* It does not necessarily mean one in which each citizen has a vote; Hegel's picture of a rational state is a constitutional monarchy where decisions are made by discussion among large scale interests, such as the landed class and corporations.

is good. What special course of action is good or not, right or wrong, is determined, for the ordinary circumstances of private life, by the laws and customs of a state. It is not too difficult to know them. . . . Each individual has his position; he knows, on the whole, what a lawful and honorable course of conduct is. To assert in ordinary private relations that it is difficult to choose the right and good, and to regard it as a mark of an exalted morality to find difficulties and raise scruples on that score indicates an evil and perverse will. It indicates a will that seeks to evade obvious duties or, at least, a petty will that gives its mind too little to do. (*RH*, 37)

The empty form of Kantian morality is thus to be given content by the laws and customs of the state one grows up in. It is true that "each individual is also the child of a people at a definite stage of its development" (*RH*, 37) and that none of us lives in a perfectly rational society. But Hegel seems to say that this is no excuse for trying to go off on our own individualistic tangents. Our ethical life is only realized by actualizing the norms of our society. An individual "*must bring the will demanded by his people to his own consciousness, to articulation*" (*RH*, 38).

The moral of the French Revolution (and of other revolutions since then, we might add) is that Reason cannot (like Descartes in the sphere of ideas) try to sweep the board clean and begin anew. That way leads only to destruction. What is necessary is to recognize what is *already rational* in the present and to nurture and strengthen that. And there is *always* some rationality in current circumstances; Spirit is always already implicit in some stage of realization, though it is usually inadequate, one-sided, and (of course) abstract.

When Spirit becomes fully *concrete,* when its objective expression in culture matches perfectly its rational essence, then individuals—the subjective bearers of self-consciousness—will recognize themselves in the institutions of their society without hesitation. At that point they will be fully free, for the institutions shaping them will not be alien to themselves, but an expression of the rationality and universality that constitute them as persons. They will not be constrained either by their own

nonrationally given desires or by the arbitrariness of irrational laws and institutions. All will be, as in the stage of *custom,* a harmony. But now it will be a rationally founded harmony, approved by the self-conscious, rational citizens of that State.

You can see that there is an uneasy ambiguity in Hegel's treatment of the ideal community. On the one hand, there is some basis for a radical critique of nearly any given society; insofar as its institutions lack rationality—and when will they not?— they are subject to criticism and potential change. On the other hand, Hegel can seem terribly conservative; for whatever there is in the way of social arrangements has *some* rationality to it, is in some way a stage on the way to the Absolute. The State at that stage, moreover, is the shaper of all the individuals who make it up; apart from it, they are mere abstractions, unrealities. Moreover, that stage is in some sense, he tells us, necessary. If it is necessary and is simply working its own way out toward a more adequate embodiment of Reason and Freedom, what sense does it make to interfere? His emphasis that the philosopher must not prescribe, but must simply "look on," seems to indicate that in the social setting, as in epistemology, Spirit takes care of itself.

This ambiguity runs throughout Hegel's thought and explains how after his death there could form two groups of Hegelians, radical and conservative, each claiming to represent the master.* It permeates, moreover, his thought about history, with which we will end our much simplified consideration of this complex system of ideas.

History and Freedom

We have seen that a central concept in Hegel's thought is that of development. Development in the realm of Spirit is complex and dialectical, because Spirit, unlike Nature, is intrinsically in relation to itself; that is why there is always negativity

---

*The most famous of the "left-wing," or radical, Hegelians is of course Karl Marx.

involved: always (1) an object standing in opposition to the subject, (2) typically experienced as *other* (alien), and (3) needing to be recovered so that the subject can recognize itself in its object. As an observer of the development of Spirit, Hegel sees this dialectical process at work everywhere: in the consciousness of the individual, in society, even in concepts themselves. Unlike nearly all previous philosophers, Hegel sees Reason itself developing its own tools, its concepts and Notions, in this dialectical and historical process. That is why it has not been possible previously to solve the problem of the criterion: each philosopher has necessarily been working in a certain stage of the development of Reason and necessarily expresses the way things look at that stage. But each of these stages has been abstract (i.e., not yet the whole, the True) and therefore inadequate. The criterion for knowledge and action, Hegel believes, is in the process of *working itself out in history*. And we "phenomenological" observers need only "look on" to see it happening.

History is meaningful; it has a direction and a purpose; it is going somewhere. And Hegel claims to know where it is going. Its goal is *Freedom*. In a schematic (and surely oversimple) way, Hegel claims we can actually see this process going on. In ancient Oriental societies (e.g., the Persian), he says, only *one* was free (the ruler); in Greek and Roman societies, *some* were free (the citizens, but not the slaves); and in his own time, it has been realized that *all* are free (though the working out of this realization may take a long time yet). But to understand this fully, we need to say a bit more about Freedom and its relation to Reason.

> The sole thought which philosophy brings to the treatment of history is the simple concept of *Reason*: that Reason is the law of the world and that, therefore, in world history, things have come about rationally. (*RH*, 11)

Hegel discusses Reason in exalted terms, saying it is "both *substance and infinite power*," (*RH*, 11) and suggesting that it is what people really mean when they speak of God. Let us see if we can understand this.

Reason is *substance*, Hegel says, because it is "that by which and in which all reality has its being" (*RH*, 11). This should make some sense to us by now, since we have seen that Hegel believes only the universal concepts of rational thought can determine *what something is*. Its very *being* (as that kind of thing) is a function of Reason—and *nothing* can have a nonrational existence.

Reason is *power*, he says,

> for Reason is not so impotent as to bring about only the ideal, the ought, and to remain in an existence outside of reality—who knows where?—as something peculiar in the heads of a few people. . . . [Reason] is its own exclusive presupposition and absolutely final purpose, and itself works out this purpose from potentiality into actuality, from inward source to outward appearance, not only in the natural but also in the spiritual universe, in world history. (*RH*, 11)

Parts of this "working out" we have traced in following the dialectical stages from implicit to explicit self-consciousness, and from a naively traditional to a self-consciously rational and organic society. Reason, then, seems to be simply another term for the Absolute, for the World Spirit.

How is Reason related to Freedom? Well, what is Freedom? Freedom, Hegel tells us, is

> self-contained existence. . . . For when I am dependent, I refer myself to something else which I am not; I cannot exist independently of something external. I am free when I am within myself. This self-contained existence of Spirit is self-consciousness, consciousness of self. (*RH*, 23)

You can see that if there isn't anything in reality *but* Spirit (or Reason)—its objects having existence only relative to it,* so that when Spirit becomes conscious of them it is becoming conscious of itself in them—and if to be free is to be "self-contained," then Spirit is essentially free. But being *essentially* free and being *actually* free are two different things. The former is merely the abstract essence, the lat-

---

* This is the key element in Hegel's absolute idealism.

ter is the concrete reality. History is the dialectical tale by which the former becomes the latter.

> . . . world history is the exhibition of spirit striving to attain knowledge of its own nature.
>
> World history is the progress of the consciousness of freedom. . . .
>
> We have established Spirit's consciousness of its freedom, and thereby the actualization of this Freedom as the final purpose of the world. (RH, 23–24)

But how does this work? It sounds glorious, and perhaps it is. But how does it fit the *facts* of history, where there is so much that seems irrational and evil? Is Hegel just a "cockeyed optimist" about history? On the contrary, Hegel is acutely conscious of the negative side of the story; only, as always, he sees this negativity as an essential aspect of the dialectic leading to freedom. Reason does not conquer easily, but only with agonizing slowness and indirection. He is under no illusions about the motivations behind the acts that make history.

> Passions, private aims, and the satisfaction of selfish desires are . . . tremendous springs of action. Their power lies in the fact that they respect none of the limitations which law and morality would impose on them; and that these natural impulses are closer to the core of human nature than the artificial and troublesome discipline that tends toward order, self-restraint, law, and morality.
>
> When we contemplate this display of passions and the consequences of their violence, the unreason which is associated not only with them, but even—rather we might say *especially*—with *good* designs and righteous aims; when we see arising therefrom the evil, the vice, the ruin that has befallen the most flourishing kingdoms which the mind of man ever created, we can hardly avoid being filled with sorrow at this universal taint of corruption. And since this decay is not the work of mere nature, but of human will, our reflections may well lead us to a moral sadness, a revolt of the good will (spirit)—if indeed it has a place within us. Without rhetorical exaggeration, a simple, truthful account of the miseries that have overwhelmed the noblest of nations and polities and the finest exemplars of private virtue forms a most fearful picture and excites emotions of the profoundest and most hopeless sadness, counter-

balanced by no consoling result. We can endure it and strengthen ourselves against it only by thinking that this is the way it had to be—it is fate; nothing can be done. (RH, 26–27)

Hegel compares history to a "slaughter bench," at which the happiness, wisdom, and virtue of countless individuals and peoples have been sacrificed. When this image takes hold, the question forces itself upon us:

> To what principle, to what final purpose, have these monstrous sacrifices been offered? (RH, 27)

Hegel's answer, of course, is Freedom. But we need to say a bit more about how he thinks Freedom will come out of this protracted and bloody process.

He is under no illusions, as we have noted, about individuals acting from Reason. In fact, he goes as far as to say,

> We assert then that nothing has been accomplished without an interest on the part of those who brought it about. And if "interest" be called "passion" . . . we may then affirm without qualification that *nothing great in the world* has been accomplished without passion. (RH, 29)

But that is only half the story. The other half is equally important: Reason, or what Hegel calls the *Idea*.*

> Two elements therefore enter into our investigations: first the Idea, secondly, the complex of human passions; the one the warp, the other the woof of the vast tapestry of world history. (RH, 29)

Individuals, then, act out of their passions and desires. Like the threads in a tapestry that run in one direction only, they are unaware that they are held in place by a rationality which, fixing their actions into a pattern they can scarcely discern, works out a purposeful progress toward Absolute Knowledge and Freedom.

---

*Remember that "Idea," for Hegel, represents the unconditioned explainer of everything and that the nature of Spirit (self-conscious, universal Reason) is that it functions as the Idea.

The burden of historical development is carried particularly, Hegel thinks, by certain persons, whom he calls "world-historical individuals." Alexander, Caesar, and Napoleon are examples he cites. What is true of them is that

their own particular purposes contain the substantial will of the World Spirit.

Such individuals have no consciousness of the Idea as such. They are practical and political men. But at the same time they are thinkers with insight into what is needed and timely. They see the very truth of their age and their world, the next genus, so to speak, which is already formed in the womb of time. It is theirs to know this new universal, the necessary next stage of their world, to make it their own aim and put all their energy into it. (*RH*, 40)

They do not pursue this "new universal" consciously, of course. They may simply seek to consolidate their own power. And they may do so quite ruthlessly; "so mighty a figure must trample down many an innocent flower, crush to pieces many things in its path" (*RH*, 43). But in pursuing their private aims, they unknowingly serve a larger purpose. There are unintended effects to their actions, and whether they will it or not, they serve the purposes of reason. This Hegel calls the

cunning of Reason—that it sets the passions to work for itself, while that through which it develops itself pays the penalty and suffers the loss. . . . The particular in most cases is too trifling as compared with the universal; the individuals are sacrificed and abandoned. The Idea pays the tribute of existence and transience, not out of its own funds but with the passions of the individuals. (*RH*, 44)

Individuals, then, are the *means* by which the World Spirit actualizes its Reason in the world. And if we see this, we can be reconciled to the agony and the tragedy of world history. It is all worthwhile because it is necessary to realize the goal.

The insight then to which . . . philosophy should lead us is that the actual world is as it ought to be,

that the truly good, the universal divine Reason is the power capable of actualizing itself. This good, this Reason, in its most concrete representation, is God. God governs the world. (*RH*, 47)

What Hegel gives us in his reflections on history, is a **theodicy,** a justification of the ways of God to human beings; it is one solution to the old problem of evil. Hegel's is perhaps the most elaborate theodicy since Augustine wrote *The City of God* in the early fifth century.* But notice the price that is paid: the actual world *is as it ought to be.* Remembering Hegel's own lament over the "slaughter bench" of history, this is a remarkable conclusion. All this is worthwhile because it leads to a supremely valuable end.

And what, in particular, is that end to be? We already know. It is "the union of the subjective with the rational will; it is the moral whole, the *State*" (*RH*, 49). Once again, note that the State does not exist for the sake of satisfying the desires of its citizens.

Rather, law, morality, the State, and they alone, are the positive reality and satisfaction of freedom. The caprice of the individual is not freedom. It is this caprice which is being limited, the license of particular desires.

The subjective will, passion, is the force which actualizes and realizes. The Idea is the interior; the State is the externally existing, genuinely moral life. It is the union of the universal and essential with the subjective will, and as such it is *Morality*. (*RH*, 50)[†]

It is the realization of Freedom, of the absolute,

---

* See the discussion of Augustine's view of history, pp. 244–247. One crucial difference is that for Augustine the justification of history lies *beyond* it in the life to come, whereas for Hegel it lies *within* history itself in an attainable historical condition. A second difference is that Augustine looks for the *peace* of the blessed, whereas Hegel justifies everything in terms of the rational *freedom* to be enjoyed by citizens of a rational state. A third difference is in the conception of God. For Augustine, God is a being quite independent of the world he created, having his being even outside of time; for Hegel, the world *is* God coming to self-actualization in time through self-conscious knowers like ourselves.

[†] Hegel here uses the term "morality" to designate what he elsewhere has called "ethics," perhaps to indicate that only in the actuality of the State does Kantian morality realize its inner nature.

final purpose, and exists for its own sake. All the value man has, all spiritual reality, he has only through the state. For his spiritual reality is the knowing presence to him of his own essence, of rationality, of its objective, immediate actuality present in and for him. Only thus is he truly a consciousness, only thus does he partake in morality, in the legal and moral life of the state. For the True is the unity of universal and particular will. And the universal in the state is in its laws, its universal and rational provisions. The state is the divine Idea as it exists on earth. (*RH*, 52–53)

Here again we feel that ambiguity we noted before. When Hegel says the state is the "divine Idea as it exists on earth," does he mean *any* state? Or does he mean only the ideal, perfectly rational state? On the one hand, as we have seen, the actual world is as it ought to be. This suggests that, if things are not as good as they *might* be, still they are as good as they realistically *can* be (at this stage), and there is no sense complaining. On the other hand, there is the ideal of a rational state in which individuals will actually find themselves at home because it expresses perfectly their inner nature as rational beings. No actually existing state seems to measure up. Again we find the ambivalence between conservative and radical points of view.

But perhaps this ambivalence can be reduced if we note that Hegel is quite self-consciously *not* a "world-historical individual." He is a philosopher. And it is not the job of philosophy, he holds, to change the world; it is the philosopher's job simply to understand it. Remember that we began our consideration of Hegel's philosophy with the problem of the criterion. Hegel suggests that this problem does not need to be solved by the philosopher, because it is in process of solving itself; all the philosopher needs to do is "look on" and describe. Near the end of his life, Hegel comes back to that same point in a memorable image.

One more word about giving instruction as to what the world ought to be. Philosophy in any case always comes on the scene too late to give it. As the thought of the world, it appears only when actuality is already there cut and dried after its process of formation has been completed. . . . When philosophy paints its grey in grey, then has a shape of life grown old. By philosophy's grey in grey it cannot be rejuvenated but only understood. The owl of Minerva spreads its wings only with the falling of the dusk. (*PR*, 12–13)

Basic Questions

1. How does the problem of the "instrument" called knowledge involve us again in the old "problem of the criterion"?
2. In what sense does Hegel think Kant concedes too much to the skeptics?
3. How does the distinction between appearance and reality arise within consciousness, if Hegel is right?
4. What is phenomenology?
5. What would absolute knowledge be—if we could get it?
6. What is sense-certainty? What is it "certain" about? Can it say? Sketch Hegel's critique of sense-certainty.
7. Define the term "immediate," as Hegel uses it. Why is immediacy something that has to be surpassed?
8. How does a dialectic of consciousness develop? Explain how perception and understanding are dialectical developments from sense-certainty.
9. Why does Hegel think desire is the first stage of self-consciousness?
10. Explain the role that recognition plays in the development of self-consciousness.
11. In the dialectic of master and slave, in what sense does the slave win?
12. What is the "truth" in Stoicism? Why is Stoicism, in Hegel's view, nonetheless inadequate?
13. How does Stoicism lead to the pure negativity of skepticism? Why does Hegel think skepticism, too, is inadequate?
14. How does the inadequacy of skepticism lead to the unhappy consciousness? How does Hegel utilize this concept to try to understand Christianity?
15. Explain idealism as the theory of how reason and reality are related.
16. Relate, as Hegel might, the World Spirit, absolute knowledge, and yourself.
17. What does Hegel mean by *objective spirit*?
18. What transition in our history does Hegel believe Socrates represents?

19. What does Hegel praise in Kant's account of morality? What, nonetheless, is his critique of the categorical imperative?
20. What is Hegel's critique of an arbitrary will?
21. How does Hegel understand ethics?
22. How does Hegel think that individuals are related to the state?
23. What is there in Hegel's thought that explains why both conservatives and radicals could claim him as their ancestor?
24. What is the goal of history, according to Hegel? What all does it justify?
25. Explain the notion of the *cunning* of reason. What are world-historical individuals?
26. How does Hegel think of God? How is God related to the world? To us?
27. Explain the image of the owl of Minerva. What does it say about the task of the philosopher?

For Further Thought

If you were to understand yourself in terms of Hegel's philosophy, how would you characterize (a) your real nature, (b) your relation to society, and (c) your place in history? Would you find this satisfactory?

Notes

1. References to Hegel's works will be as follows:
   PS: Phenomenology of Spirit, trans. A. V. Miller (Oxford: Clarendon Press, 1977).
   PR: Hegel's Philosophy of Right, trans. T. M. Knox (Oxford: Oxford University Press, 1952).
   RH: Reason in History, trans. Robert S. Hartman (New York: The Liberal Arts Press, 1953).
2. Quoted from *The Logic of Hegel,* trans. William Wallace (Oxford, 1892), in Richard Norman, *Hegel's Phenomenology: A Philosophical Introduction* (Published for Sussex University Press by Chatto and Windus Ltd., London, 1976), 11.

20

Kierkegaard and Marx:
Two Ways to "Correct" Hegel

The influence of Hegel was enormous. Everywhere he was read and discussed, dissected and analyzed, damned and admired. The synthesis of so much learning and the forging of so many insights could hardly help but shape the next generation of philosophers.

Despite the range and depth of Hegel's thought, some readers had the sense (which perhaps you share) that this magnificent system was extravagant, that it promised more than it could deliver. In a certain way, moreover, and contrary to Hegel's explicit intentions, it seemed too *abstract*; it did not seem to deal concretely enough with the actuality of people's lives as they led them, making specific choices in specific circumstances. This was an ironic complaint indeed, because abstraction is Hegel's great enemy.

In this chapter we will glance at two thinkers who are deeply in Hegel's debt. They can both be considered Hegelians, but they are renegade Hegelians, each in his own way. Both have contributed in lasting ways to our thinking in many spheres of human life, from religion to politics, from art to economics, from the anxieties of individual psychology to the sociology of class struggle. Their intellectual progeny in our time go by the names of **existentialist** and Marxist. So we shall examine some of the central contributions of Søren Kierkegaard and Karl Marx to the great conversation.

Kierkegaard: On Individual Existence

The "authorship" of Søren Kierkegaard (1813–1855) is exceedingly varied and diverse. For one thing, about half of it is pseudonymous (written under other names—and quite a number of them, too). Why? Not for the usual reason, to hide the identity of the author; nearly everyone in little Copenhagen knew Kierkegaard, and they knew he had written these books. There is a deeper reason: the various "authors"—a romantic young man known simply as A; Judge William (a local magistrate), Johannes *de silentio* (John the silent), the Seducer (who writes a famous diary), Victor Eremita (the Hermit), Johannes Climacus (the Climber), to name only a few—represent different views. Through their voices Kierkegaard expresses certain possibilities for managing the problem of having to exist as a human being. This is a problem, he believes, that we all face. Moreover, it is a problem that cannot be solved in the abstract, by thinking about it—though it cannot be solved without thinking about it either!* A solution is worked out in one's life by the choices one actually makes, thereby defining and creating

---

*Kierkegaard, who thinks of himself as the "gadfly of Copenhagen," agrees with Socrates' dictum that "the unexamined life is not worth living." (See Plato's *Apology*, 38a.)

the self one becomes. His pseudonymous authors "present themselves" to the reader as selves in the process of such self-creation. They thereby function as models for possibilities that you or I might also actualize in our own lives; they awaken us to alternatives and stimulate us to self-examination.

Kierkegaard calls this technique "indirect communication." His motive for adopting it is his conviction that most of us live in varying forms and degrees of self-deception. We are not honest with ourselves about the categories that actually structure our lives. He attempts to provoke the shock of self-recognition by offering characters with which the reader may identify and then revealing slowly, but inexorably, what living in that way really means. He is particularly concerned with an "illusion" he discerns in many of his contemporaries in nineteenth-century Denmark: the impression that they are *Christians*. He wants to clarify what it means actually to live as a Christian. And it is his particular concern to distinguish such a life from two things: (1) from the average bourgeois life of a citizen in this state-church country, where everyone is baptized as a matter of course, and (2) from the illusion that intellectual speculation of the Hegelian type is a modern successor to faith.

In the course of this elaborate literary production, Kierkegaard offers us insights that many recent philosophers, psychologists, and theologians have recovered and used in their own work.* For our present purposes, we will sketch several of these life possibilities and then draw some conclusions about how Hegel needs to be modified, if Kierkegaard is right. We will follow Kierkegaard and call them the **esthetic**, the ethical, and the religious.

The Esthetic

In the first part of a two-part work called *Either/ Or*,† we find the somewhat chaotic papers of an unknown young man whom the editor of the volume (himself a pseudonymous character) elects simply to call "A." The fond desire of A's life is simply to *be* something. His ideal is expressed in a line by the twentieth-century poet T. S. Eliot: "You are the music while the music lasts."[1] This kind of complete absorption, which we experience occasionally in pleasurable moments, seems wonderful to him. If only the whole of life could be like that! If only he could evade reflection, self-consciousness, thought, the agony of choice, and this business of always having to *become* something! If he could just enjoy life in its *immediacy*.* A's dream is to live unreflectively a life of pleasure.

But A is a clever and sophisticated young man. He realizes that this is not possible. For one thing, immediacy never exists where it is sought; to take it as one's *aim* or *ideal* entails directly that one has missed the goal. As soon as you think, "What I really want is a life of pleasure," you prove that you are already beyond simply *having* such a life. You are reflecting on how nice that would be. No human, in fact, can attain the placid, self-contained immediacy of the brutes. And it is clear to A that pleasure is not his life, but the chief preoccupation of his life.

This becomes clear to A through his reflections on the figure of Don Juan. As A imagines him, he is pure, undifferentiated, unreflective desire—nothing more than embodied sensuality. Don Juan wants women wholesale, and he gets what he wants. In Mozart's opera, *Don Giovanni*,† the Don's servant keeps a list of his conquests, which he displays in a comic aria, informing us that they number 1003 in Spain alone! Don Juan represents something analogous to a force of nature—an avalanche or hurricane—but for this very reason there is something subhuman about him. A con-

---

*We will later examine one twentieth-century thinker who owes much to Kierkegaard, Martin Heidegger. See Chapter 26.

†Already in the title of this early work, we see an attack on central themes in Hegel, for whom "both/and" might be an appropriate motto. As we have seen, the progress of Hegelian dialectic is a suc-

cessively reiterated synthesis, gathering in the truth contained in earlier stages until we reach in the end a stage of absolute knowledge. Kierkegaard is convinced that such a stage is impossible for existing human beings. We'll see why.

*"Immediacy," of course, is a Hegelian category. Look back to pp. 419–420 for Hegel's phenomenological critique of immediacy as a foundation for knowledge.

†Kierkegaard admired this opera extravagantly, attending many performances of it.

cludes that this "pure type" can exist only in art and that music is the appropriate vehicle for its expression. Sensuality (together with its associated pleasure) is not human reality, but an aspect of human reality. Considered in itself, it is an abstraction.*

What, then, to do? There seems to A one obvious solution: make one's life itself into a work of art. Then one could enjoy it as one enjoys any fine esthetic object. The pleasures of immediacy may be vanishing, but the pleasures of esthetic appreciation are all the more available. The most damning comment on a movie or novel is: boring! So one wants above all to keep life interesting. Toward this end A writes a little "how-to" manual called *Rotation of Crops*.

> People with experience maintain that proceeding from a basic principle is supposed to be very reasonable; I yield to them and proceed from the basic principle that all people are boring. Or is there anyone who would be boring enough to contradict me in this regard? . . . Boredom is the root of all evil.
>
> This can be traced back to the very beginning of the world. The gods were bored; therefore they created human beings. Adam was bored because he was alone; therefore Eve was created. Since that moment, boredom entered the world and grew in quantity in exact proportion to the growth of population. Adam was bored alone; then Adam and Eve were bored together; then Adam and Eve and Cain and Abel were bored *en famille*. After that, the population of the world increased and the nations were bored *en masse*. To amuse themselves, they hit upon the notion of building a tower so high that it would reach the sky. This notion is just as boring as the tower was high and is a terrible demonstration of how boredom had gained the upper hand. (*EO* 1, 285–86)[2]

Here we have an expression of the categories under which A organizes his life. Everything is evaluated in terms of the pair of concepts:

interesting/boring

The rotation method is a set of techniques for keeping things interesting. Let us just note a few of the recommendations.

---

*Here A is echoing, of course, Hegel's own critique of immediacy.

"The biggest danger, that of losing oneself, can pass off in the world as quietly as if it were nothing; every other loss, an arm, a leg, five dollars, a wife, etc. is bound to be noticed."   —SØREN KIERKEGAARD

Variety, of course, is essential, since nothing is as boring as the same old thing. But it is no use trying to achieve variety by varying one's surroundings or circumstances, though this is the "vulgar and inartistic method."

> One is weary of living in the country and moves to the city; one is weary of one's native land and goes abroad; one is europamüde [weary of Europe] and goes to America, etc; one indulges in the fanatical hope of an endless journey from star to star. (*EO* 1, 291)

What one must learn to do is vary *oneself*, a task A compares to the rotation of crops by a farmer. The key idea is a developed facility for remembering and forgetting. To avoid boredom, we need to remember and forget artistically, not randomly as most of us do. Whoever develops this art will have a never-ending source of interesting experiences at hand.

> No part of life ought to have so much meaning for a person that he cannot forget it any moment he wants to; on the other hand, every single part of life ought to have so much meaning for a person that he can remember it at any moment. (*EO* 1, 293)

In addition, one requires absolute freedom to break away at any time from anything, lest one be at the mercy of something or someone boring. Thus, one must beware of entanglements and avoid commitments. The rule is no friendships (but acquaintances aplenty), no marriage (though an occasional affair adds to the interest), and no business (for what is so boring as the demands of business?).

The key notion is to stay in control. As A writes in one of a series of aphoristic paragraphs,

> Real enjoyment consists not in what one enjoys but in the idea. If I had in my service a submissive jinni who, when I asked for a glass of water, would bring me the world's most expensive wines, deliciously blended, in a goblet, I would dismiss him until he learned that the enjoyment consists not in what I enjoy but in getting my own way. (*EO* 1, 31)

This project of living for the interesting is explored in a variety of ways in A's papers, but its apex is surely the lengthy manuscript known as *The Seducer's Diary.* In some prefatory remarks, A claims to have stolen the diary from the desk of an acquaintance, though the "editor" of *Either/Or,* in which it appears, doubts this. He speculates that it was written by A himself, in which case it may represent a kind of dream on the part of A, in which A explores possibilities that he knows he is capable of—and perhaps we are, too.*

The essentials of the plot are simple. Johannes, the diarist, sees a young girl, Cordelia, and is fascinated. He insinuates himself into her family. While paying little attention to her, but much to her fussy old aunt, he sets things up so that he appears interesting to Cordelia. He promotes Edward, a rather conventional and boring young man in love with Cordelia, as a suitable match; but slowly and cleverly he brings her to see Edward—in comparison with himself—as boorish and common. He manipulates an engagement with himself. But then, so subtly that she seems to be making the decisions, he leads her to believe that a marriage is merely an external impediment to true love. *She* breaks the engagement. There is a passionate night together. And then he leaves her.

Everything is arranged by Johannes to intensify the interesting. As a result, the diary is a far cry from those novels of sexual athleticism whose characters are as thin as their bodies are voluptuous. The focus is on the psychological rather than the physical. And it must be so, for the Seducer is the polar opposite of Don Juan (within the sphere of the esthetic).* Whereas the latter is supposed to be wholly nonreflective, an embodiment of pure immediacy, the seducer lives so completely in reflection that he seems to touch down in reality only occasionally. All is planning, arranging, scheming, plotting, and enjoying the results, as one would enjoy a play at the theater. Johannes is at once the playwright, the actor, and the audience in the drama of his life. It is not the actual seduction that matters to him (one moment of physical conquest is much like another), but the drama leading up to that moment. That is where the art lies. That is what is really interesting. And to preserve the esthetic character of his experience, he must keep the necessary esthetic distance, even from himself.

---

*Note how possibilities are piled up here. Kierkegaard presents Victor Eremita (the nonreal, merely possible editor of the volume), who presents A (the literary embodiment of certain possibilities), who (possibly) presents the Seducer. Everything conspires to hold

---

the reader at a distance, as if to say: *this* is not your life; it is merely a reflection of it. By its very intensification of possibility, it accentuates—by contrast—the actual. The medium is itself part of the message.

*Remember that the esthetic is defined as that style of life in which everything is judged in terms of the pair of categories: interesting/boring.

I scarcely know myself. My mind roars like a turbulent sea in the storms of passion. If someone else could see my soul in this state, it would seem to him that it, like a skiff, plunged prow-first down into the ocean, as if in its dreadful momentum it would have to steer down into the depths of the abyss. He does not see that high on the mast a sailor is on the lookout. Roar away, you wild forces, roar away, you powers of passion; even if your waves hurl foam toward the clouds, you still are not able to pile yourselves up over my head—I am sitting as calmly as the king of the mountain. (*EO* 1, 324–25)

Other aspects of this project to treat one's life like an esthetic object reveal themselves subtly in the diary. The project must be carried out in secret; to reveal his intentions to Cordelia would bring the whole enterprise to ruin. And so he must, necessarily, deceive Cordelia. He is, in terms Kant and Hegel would find appropriate, *using* her for ends she not only does not consent to, but of which she has not the slightest hint.

Does Johannes love Cordelia? He asks himself this question.

Do I love Cordelia? Yes! Sincerely? Yes! Faithfully? Yes—in the esthetic sense. (*EO* 1, 385)

He flatters himself that he is benefiting her. In what sense? Why, in the only sense he recognizes: he is making her life more interesting! He found her a naive young girl; he will leave her a sophisticated woman. She was innocent, uninitiated into *possibility;* he has taught her the delights and terrors of the possible. He found her nature; he will leave her spirit. So, at least, he tells himself.

Whether Cordelia agrees is another matter. A includes a letter she sent to Johannes after the break, which Johannes had returned unopened (*EO* 1, 312):

Johannes,
    Never will I call you "my Johannes," for I certainly realize you have never been that, and I am punished harshly enough for having once been gladdened in my soul by this thought, and yet I do call you "mine": my seducer, my deceiver, my enemy, my murderer,

the source of my unhappiness, the tomb of my joy, the abyss of my unhappiness. I call you "mine" and call myself "yours," and as it once flattered your ear, proudly inclined to my adoration, so shall it now sound as a curse upon you, a curse for all eternity. . . . Yours I am, yours, yours, your curse.
Your Cordelia

It appears that even within the sphere of the esthetic there might be no clear answer to whether Johannes has benefited Cordelia. But, as we'll see, that is not the only kind of question that can be asked.

The Ethical

The bulk of the second part of *Either/Or* is composed of several long letters from a magistrate in one of the lower courts, a certain Judge William. They are addressed to A. The main topic is love; but the Judge has his eye on a larger issue: what it means for an existing human being to be a *self*.

To see the relevance of this issue, let us look back to another of A's aphorisms. He says,

My life is utterly meaningless. When I consider its various epochs, my life is like the word *Schnur* in the dictionary, which first of all means a string, and second a daughter-in-law. All that is lacking is that in the third place the word *Schnur* means a camel, in the fourth a whisk broom. (*EO* 1, 36)

A recognizes that there is no continuity in his life. It is as if he were a succession of different people, one interested in this, another in that. The different periods of his life have no more relation to each other than do the meanings of the word *Schnur*. In a sense, A has no self—or rather, he is splintered into a multiplicity of semi-selves, which comes to much the same thing. The Judge has a remedy.

Taking his cue from A's own preoccupations, the Judge gives us an analysis of romantic love. Its "mark" is that it is *immediate*. Its watchword is "To see her was to love her." And indeed, that is how we think about love, too; we talk about "falling in love"—something that can *happen* to one, a condition in which one may, suddenly, just find oneself. Falling in love is not something one *does* deliberately after reflection.

> Romantic love manifests itself as immediate by exclusively resting in natural necessity. It is based on beauty, partly on sensuous beauty. . . . Although this love is based essentially on the sensuous, it nevertheless is noble by virtue of the consciousness of the eternal which it assimilates, for it is this that distinguishes all love from lust: that it bears a stamp of eternity. The lovers are deeply convinced that in itself their relationship is a complete whole that will never be changed. (*EO* 2, 21)

This conviction, however, since it is based merely on something natural, on *what happens to one,* is an illusion. If you can fall into love, you can fall out of it again. For this reason, it is easy to make romantic love look ridiculous; it promises what it cannot deliver: faithfulness, persistence, *eternity.* (Just listen to popular love songs.) The Judge notes that a lot of modern literature expresses cynicism about love. The culmination of this cynicism is either (1) giving in to the transience of nature, resigning the promise of lasting love, and making do with a series of affairs, or (2) the marriage of convenience, which gives up on love altogether.

The Judge deplores both alternatives. He believes A is right in valuing romantic love. But, he says to A, what you want, you can't have on your terms. The promise of eternity in romantic love can be realized, but not if you simply "go with the flow" (as we say). What is required is choice, a determination of the will.

The Judge is a defender of *conjugal* love, a defender of marriage, the mark of which is precisely the engagement of the will. The bride and groom *make promises* to each other. They promise to *love.* The Judge argues that what one hears from the Romantic poets, that marriage is the enemy of romantic love, is simply false. For what romantic love seems to offer, but cannot deliver, is exactly what the engagement of the will can provide: the continuity and permanence of love. Marriage, as an expression of the will, is not the death of romantic love; it comes to its aid and provides what it needs

in order to endure. Without the will, love is simply inconstant and arbitrary nature.*

It is true, the Judge admits, that conjugal love is not a fit subject for art. Love stories usually go like this: The handsome prince falls in love with the beautiful princess, and after much opposition and struggle (ogres and dragons, wicked uncles and unwilling fathers), they are married; the last line of the story is "And they lived happily ever after." But, says the Judge, these stories end just where the really interesting part begins. Nevertheless, the marriage cannot be represented in art, "for the very point is time in its extension." The married person "has not fought with lions and ogres, but with the most dangerous enemy—with time."

> The faithful romantic lover waits, let us say for fifteen years; then comes the moment that rewards him. Here poetry very properly perceives that the fifteen years can easily be concentrated; now it hastens to the moment. A married man is faithful for fifteen years, and yet during these fifteen years he has had possession; therefore in this long succession he has continually acquired the faithfulness he possessed, since marital love has in itself the first love and thereby the faithfulness of the first love. But an ideal married man of this sort cannot be portrayed, for the point is time in extension. . . .
>
> And although this cannot be portrayed artistically, then let your consolation be, as it is mine, that we are not to read about or listen to or look at what is the highest and the most beautiful in life, but are, if you please, to live it.
>
> Therefore, when I readily admit that romantic love lends itself much better to artistic portrayal than marital love, this does not at all mean that it is less esthetic than the other—on the contrary, it is more esthetic. (*EO* 2, 138–39)

The Judge is defending the *esthetic* validity of marriage and, with it, the self. For the Judge sees marriage as an example of a style of life quite other than that which A has been leading. The ethical life requires the development of the *self.*

---

* Compare what Hegel has to say about the "arbitrariness" of a will (by which he means merely natural or conditioned desires) that has not been subjected to reason. See pp. 431–432.

The crucial difference between the esthetic and the ethical is *choice*. In a certain sense, of course, the esthetic life is full of choices. But, with that clear-sighted irony that an intelligent esthete brings to his experience, A sees that none of them are *significant choices*. Any choice might as well have been the opposite—and can be tomorrow. After all, if your aim is "the interesting," you must not get stuck in commitments. None of these esthetic choices really mean anything for the self doing the choosing. Among A's papers, this is expressed in "An ecstatic lecture."

> Marry, and you will regret it. Do not marry, and you will also regret it. . . . Whether you marry or do not marry, you will regret it either way. Laugh at the stupidities of the world, and you will regret it; weep over them, and you will also regret it. . . . Whether you laugh at the stupidities of the world or weep over them, you will regret it either way. Trust a girl, and you will regret it. Do not trust her, and you will also regret it. . . . Whether you trust a girl or do not trust her, you will regret it either way. Hang yourself, and you will regret it. Do not hang yourself, and you will also regret it. . . . Whether you hang yourself or do not hang yourself, you will regret it either way. This, gentlemen, is the quintessence of all the wisdom of life. (*EO* 1, 38–39)

In a certain sense, "either/or" is A's watchword. But *how* one says this makes all the difference. And the Judge urges that A's manner of saying it means the loss of the self.

> Imagine a captain of a ship the moment a shift of direction must be made; then he may be able to say: I can do either this or that. But if he is not a mediocre captain he will also be aware that during all this the ship is ploughing ahead with its ordinary velocity, and thus there is but a single moment when it is inconsequential whether he does this or does that. So also with a person . . . there eventually comes a moment where it is no longer a matter of Either/Or, not because he has chosen, but because he has refrained from it, which also can be expressed by saying: Because others have chosen for him—or because he has lost himself. (*EO* 2, 164)

And so it is with us; if we drift, if we fail to decisively take hold of our lives, if we treat every ei-ther/or as indifferent, we will lose our selves; there will be nobody who we are.*

So the Judge pleads with A to adopt a different either/or, the mark of which is *seriousness of choice*. When one chooses seriously, when one *engages oneself*, one chooses *ethically*.†

> Your choice is an esthetic choice, but an esthetic choice is no choice. On the whole, to choose is an intrinsic and stringent term for the ethical. Wherever in the stricter sense there is a question of an Either/Or, one can always be sure that the ethical has something to do with it. The only absolute Either/Or is the choice between good and evil, but this is also absolutely ethical. (*EO* 2, 166–67)

And yet the Judge is not—at least not directly—urging A to choose the good. He just wants him to *choose*.

> What, then, is it that I separate in my Either/Or? Is it good and evil? No, I only want to bring you to the point where this choice truly has meaning for you. . . .
>
> Rather than designating the choice between good and evil, my Either/Or designates the choice by which one chooses good and evil or rules them out. Here the question is under what qualifications one will view all existence and personally live. That the person who chooses good and evil chooses the good is indeed true, but only later does this become manifest, for the esthetic is not evil but the indifferent. And that is why I said that the ethical constitutes the choice. Therefore, it is not so much a matter of choosing between willing good or willing evil as of choosing to will, but that in turn posits good and evil. (*EO* 2, 168–69)

The Judge's either/or, then, has to do with the categories under which things are evaluated. One

---

* This thought is developed by Martin Heidegger, who holds that without a resolute seizing of oneself, one's life is dominated by what "they" say, or what "One" does or doesn't do. See "The 'Who' of Dasein," in Chapter 26.

† This does not mean that one necessarily chooses the right, but that one's choice, whether right or wrong, lies within the domain of the ethical; it is a choice *subject to ethical evaluation*. From the esthetic point of view, such evaluation is simply not meaningful (since the categories of evaluation are restricted to "interesting/boring").

will lead a radically different life if everything is decided according to

good / evil (ethical choice)

rather than

interesting / boring (esthetic choice).

And the basic either/or, the really significant or deep one, is not either one of these alternatives, but that which poses this question:

esthetic *or* ethical?

If the Judge is right, the mark of making that choice is the *way* one chooses: with the entire seriousness and passion of the will (in which case the categories of good and evil *automatically* arise), or in that ironic, detached, amoral way in which one can say, "Choose either, you will regret both."

We can now see why marriage is for the Judge an example and symbol of the ethical. What one says at the altar is a decisive expression of the will, a choice that one makes for the future, a choice *of oneself*. One chooses to be the sort of self who will continue to nurture and come to the aid of romantic love. It is no longer a matter of what happens to you; it is a matter of what you do with what happens to you. The ethical person gives up the futile project of simply trying to *be* something, and takes up the project of *becoming* something—of becoming a *self*.

It will be helpful before moving on to summarize some of the chief differences between these two ways of life. It is striking how different everything looks from the two perspectives.

- *Immediacy,* which in the esthetic stage has the status of a condition to be aspired to, looks from the ethical point of view like *nature,* that is, material for the will to act upon—to shape and form.
- The possibility of *reflection* in the esthetic (the spectator's view of one's own life) takes on in

the ethical the aspect of *practical freedom* (the ability to take the givens of one's life and make something of them).
- The necessity for *secrecy* in the esthetic life (remember the Seducer) is supplanted by a requirement of *openness* in the ethical.
- The prominence of the *accidental* in the esthetic (what happens to one) finds its ethical contrast in the notion of the *universal* (what duty requires of every human being).
- The *abstraction* of the esthetic, hung as it is between the impossible immediacy of Don Juan and the incredible reflectiveness of the Seducer, is contrasted with the *concreteness* of an individual's self-construction, where the accidental givens are taken over and shaped by the universal demands of duty.
- The attempt to *be* is given up in favor of the striving to *become*.
- The emphasis on *the moment* is superseded by the value of *the historical* (as in an affair versus a marriage).
- The *fragmentariness* of an esthetic life stands in contrast to the *continuity* of the ethical.

These contrasts pave two distinct avenues for human life. The question arises: Are there any other possibilities?

The Religious

If the key characteristic of the esthetic style of life is enduring or enjoying (and perhaps arranging) what happens to one, and that of the ethical stage is taking oneself in hand and creating oneself, it seems apparent that human existence involves a tension between two poles. Kierkegaard characterizes them differently in various works: immediacy and reflection; nature and freedom; necessity and possibility; the temporal and the eternal; the finite and the infinite. On the one hand, we simply *are* something: a collection of accidental facts. "I am American, five feet ten inches tall, and balding." On the other hand, we are an awareness of this, together with some attitude toward these facts and the need to do something about them. This aspect of ourselves seems to elude all limitation, since it is not definitely this nor that. It seems to be a capacity for distancing ourselves from anything finite, temporal, and given.*

From the ethical point of view, this duality defines the task facing an individual: to become oneself. The task is to bring these two poles together so that they interpenetrate and inform each other: the immediate and finite takes a definite shape, and the reflective and infinite loses its abstract indefiniteness. One becomes a definite and unique thing: oneself.†

If you listened only to the Judge, you might think that becoming yourself by melding your immediate and reflective aspects is an achievable, if difficult, task. Further reflection, however, casts doubt on that optimistic assumption. These two sides of a person, the material out of which a self is to be constructed, have a disconcerting tendency to drift apart. We slide into identifying ourselves now with one aspect, now with another. Indeed, this is not something that just happens to us; it is a tendency we acquiesce in, accede to, cooperate with. We refuse the anxiety-filled role of having to hold the two poles together. Our problem is that we are *not willing to be ourselves* and always want to be something more or something less: *either* something approaching God *or* something analogous to an unthinking brute.

As soon as we discover this tendency, we are beyond the ethical. What use is more determination to succeed in the task of being yourself if you continually undermine this determination by your unwillingness to be yourself?* All this huffing and puffing and moral seriousness begin to look like impossible attempts to lift yourself by your own bootstraps. You might as well try to raise yourself off the ground by wrapping your arms around your chest and lifting!

Even the Judge seems to have an inkling of this; the last thing we hear from him concerns a "sermon" that he sends along to A. The Judge tells A that the sermon has caused him to think about himself, and also about A. The sermon was composed by an "older friend" of the Judge's, a pastor out on the heaths of Denmark; it is a meditation on the thought that "as against God, we are always in the wrong." The pastor says that this is an edifying thought, a helpful thought, a thought in which we can find rest. Struggling with the ethical task, we inevitably discover ourselves failing. What then should we do? Perhaps, the pastor says, we try to console ourselves by saying, "I do what I can." But, he asks, doesn't that provoke a new anxiety?

> If a person is sometimes in the right, sometimes in the wrong, to some degree in the right, to some degree in the wrong, who, then, is the one who makes that decision except the person himself, but in the decision may he not again be to some degree in the right and to some degree in the wrong?
>
> Doubt is again set in motion, care again aroused; let us try to calm it by deliberating on:
> THE *UPBUILDING* THAT LIES IN THE THOUGHT THAT IN RELATION TO GOD WE ARE ALWAYS IN THE WRONG. (*EO* 2, 345–46)

These thoughts take us into the domain of religion; it is no coincidence that they are presented in a sermon. Kierkegaard's views on religion are complex and extensive; he expresses some of them under still other pseudonyms and some under his own name. He distinguishes two levels of religion:

---

*See the note on p. 423 where I discuss Hegel's notion of pure self-consciousness. See also Pico della Mirandola on the dignity of human beings, pp. 275–276.

†We need to be careful here. Kierkegaard does not present the ethical self as unique in the sense that it defines itself as *different from other selves*, for that would be to define it in terms external to itself. Becoming oneself involves the embodiment of those rational and universally human aspects which Kant and Hegel focus on in their treatment of morality and ethics. And these are shared by all. But the *way* in which these are embodied will depend on the particular given facts about oneself, and in that respect no one individual will be exactly like any other.

---

*Compare what Augustine has to say about the bondage of the will. See pp. 218 and 239. The "unhappy consciousness" of Hegel, at once self-liberating and self-perverting, is another expression of this stage. See p. 427.

a basic level of religious consciousness in general (as it is shared by pagan figures like Socrates and Old Testament patriarchs, such as Abraham) and a more intense level distinctive, he thinks, of Christianity. One of his "authors" calls the first "religiousness A" and the second "religiousness B." Let us look at each in turn.

In a haunting little book by Johannes *de silentio* (John the silent) called *Fear and Trembling,* he poses this question: Is there anything beyond the ethical? If so, what would it be like? Johannes meditates on Abraham, in particular on a story in Genesis 22. God asks Abraham to take his only son, Isaac, to Mount Moriah and there offer him up as a sacrifice. Abraham does what God asks, and only at the last moment, as Abraham raises the knife, is Isaac spared. If there is a stage of life beyond the ethical, this seems an appropriate story to contemplate. As Johannes makes clear, from a strictly ethical point of view,* Abraham is the moral equivalent of a murderer; he was willing to do the deed. Yet he is remembered as *the father of faith*. What can this mean?

Johannes says that he cannot understand Abraham, cannot explain him. Before Abraham he is "silent." The reason is that Abraham seems to do two contradictory things at once. On the one hand, he apparently gives up Isaac, resigns any claim to him, emotionally lets him go; how else could he travel those three long days to Moriah? But on the other hand, he clearly continues to love Isaac as dearly as ever and even to believe that Isaac will not be required of him! The proof, Johannes says, is that Abraham was not embarrassed before Isaac after having raised the knife, that he received him back with joy. How could anyone do both things, simultaneously make both these "movements" of the spirit? It seems impossible, paradoxical, absurd.

But, Johannes suggests, this absurdity is precisely the secret life of faith. If there is anything

beyond the ethically human, it must be something like this. It must be a state in which one lives in an absolute relationship to God, where even the universally human requirements of the ethical drop away into relative insignificance.* And yet it is not an escape from this world, but a life wholly engaged in the concrete finitude of one's earthly being.

Johannes illustrates these two internal movements by describing two "knights." The Knight of Infinite Resignation withdraws into the interior chambers of the spirit, makes no claims on anyone, asks for nothing worldly. He no longer identifies himself with his possessions, his worldly relationships, or even his body. Like the Stoic philosopher or the monk, this Knight identifies with the infinite, reflective side of himself, with his "eternal consciousness."

> In infinite resignation there is peace and rest; every person who wills it . . . can discipline himself to make this movement, which in its pain reconciles one to existence. Infinite resignation is that shirt mentioned in an old legend. The thread is spun with tears, bleached with tears; the shirt is sewn in tears— but then it also gives protection better than iron or steel. The defect in the legend is that a third person can work up this linen. The secret in life is that each person must sew it himself, and the remarkable thing is that a man can sew it fully as well as a woman. (*FT*, 45)

Johannes stresses how difficult it must be to make this movement. It would seem to require absolutely all one's energy, all one's strength, all one's passion. What could be left over to make still another movement? And yet that is just what the Knight of Faith does. He also resigns everything, sets himself adrift from the world, takes refuge in the eternal side of himself. But as he is making the movements of infinite resignation, the Knight of

---

* The ethical is here understood as the highest human thought can reach with respect to our duties to one another. Johannes, like Kant, takes ethics to be composed of rules that we rationally understand to be binding on us all. From the ethical standpoint, then, taking one's son out to slaughter him is clearly forbidden.

* It is not, of course, that a religious life of faith is an *unethical* life. Just as the Judge argues that an ethical life is *more* esthetic than a life lived specifically for esthetic enjoyments, so does a relation to God preserve and enhance whatever is of value in the ethical life. As Johannes points out, Abraham did not become the father of faith by *hating* his son.

Faith comes back again into the world. How does he do that? Where does he find the strength? Johannes doesn't know. He can't understand it.

He admires the Knight of Resignation extravagantly; he can understand, he says, how someone could resign everything, thinks he might even be capable of it himself, difficult though it is. But faith he can't understand. It seems absurd to him that this should be possible. And yet, if there is to be anything beyond the ethical, it would have to be something like this paradoxical life, simultaneously beyond and totally within this world. Johannes imagines that he meets such a Knight of Faith.

> The instant I first lay eyes on him, I set him apart at once; I jump back, clap my hands, and say half aloud, "Good Lord, is this the man, is this really the one—he looks just like a tax collector!" But this is indeed the one. I move a little closer to him, watch his slightest movement to see if it reveals a bit of heterogeneous optical telegraphy from the infinite, a glance, a facial expression, a gesture, a sadness, a smile that would betray the infinite in its heterogeneity with the finite. No! I examine his figure from top to toe to see if there may not be a crack through which the infinite would peek. No! He is solid all the way through. . . . He belongs entirely to the world; no bourgeois philistine could belong to it more. . . . He finds pleasure in everything, takes part in everything. . . . He attends to his job. . . . He goes to church. . . . In the afternoon, he takes a walk to the woods. He enjoys everything he sees, the swarms of people, the new omnibuses. . . . Toward evening, he goes home, and his gait is as steady as a postman's. On the way, he thinks that his wife surely will have a special hot meal for him when he comes home—for example, roast lamb's head with vegetables. If he meets a kindred soul, he would go on talking all the way to Østerport about this delicacy with a passion befitting a restaurant operator. It so happens that he does not have four shillings to his name, and yet he firmly believes that his wife has this delectable meal waiting for him. If she has, to see him eat would be the envy of the elite and an inspiration to the common man, for his appetite is keener than Esau's. His wife does not have it—curiously enough, he is just the same. . . . And yet, yet—yes, I could be infuriated over it if for no other reason than envy—and yet this

man has made and at every moment is making the movement of infinity. He drains the deep sadness of life in infinite resignation, he knows the blessedness of infinity, he has felt the pain of renouncing everything, the most precious thing in the world, and yet the finite tastes just as good to him as one who never knew anything higher. (*FT*, 38–40)

Several points stand out in this portrait. The first is that faith is not something to be understood, is not a doctrine to be memorized and accepted. Faith is something to be lived. Second, the life of faith is not an otherworldly or particularly ascetic sort of life. There are, of course, many sorts of lives that someone who is every moment making the movement of infinite resignation would simply not be interested in; but it is definitely a life *in* the world. Third, it is not easy to recognize a Knight of Faith. What distinguishes such Knights from other people is not external but a matter of their "inwardness"; it concerns not so much what they do but how and why they do what they do. And fourth, because of its interiority it may seem easy to "have faith"; it may seem to be something everybody and her brother has already got. But that is an illusion. In fact, no other sort of life is as difficult, as demanding, as strenuous as the life of faith. For, Johannes tells us, faith is a *passion*, the highest passion of all.

Johannes is full of scorn for Hegelian philosophers who think they have "understood" faith, and now want to "go further." Here, he says, there is nothing to understand, nothing that can be learned in a formula from someone else. It is not like a theorem that has been proved, which you can use to prove still other theorems. Here we have a way of life. To aspire to get beyond it is to show that you haven't the slightest idea what sort of life is lived by Knights of Faith. In an entire lifetime, he says, Abraham did not get further than faith. If it is possible at all, it is apparent that the life of faith is the greatest and most arduous life one could live.

In a large and difficult book, *Concluding Unscientific Postscript,* the philosopher among the pseudonyms, Johannes Climacus, offers an intriguing image. An existing individual, he says, cannot be in two places at the same time; "when he is nearest to being in two places at the same time he is in passion" (*CUP*, 178). What does he mean?

Suppose you are facing a chemistry exam tomorrow and it is important to you to do well. Here are two possibilities: (1) you have been attending class, doing the homework, and have easily passed the quizzes so far; (2) you have been neglecting the course but are hoping an all-nighter will pull you through. It is as if you were in two places at once, the place you actually are and the place you want to be. And it is clear that the "distance" between these two points is greater in situation (2) than in (1). Correspondingly, passion is heightened in situation (2): fear, anxiety, desperation, and panic make themselves felt. The greater the distance between where you are and where you want to be, the greater the passion.

We can apply this principle to the sorts of lives that Kierkegaard's pseudonymous authors are presenting for our consideration. There is certainly passion in the esthete's life. But there is no *great* passion, because the esthete is wholeheartedly committed to nothing. If we live this way, we fritter life away pursing momentary passions, always ready to move on if interest flags; there is nothing for which we are willing to live or die.

There is much greater passion, much greater intensity in the life the Judge recommends. Why? Because the distance between where the Judge is and where he genuinely wants to be is much greater: His aim is to construct himself as a concrete ethical individual over a lifetime, making his moment-to-moment particularity an exemplary instance of what is universally required of all. Now that's reaching pretty far; that's a task! And that's why the Judge insists that the way to reach it is committed, passionate, whole-hearted choice.

Johannes *de silentio* tells us, as we have seen, that faith is the highest of the passions. Can we understand what he means by this? Let us take Socrates as an example, remembering that the first religious stage is exemplified in paganism as well as in Old Testament patriarchs like Abraham. Socrates wants the truth, the truth about human excellence. He wants to understand courage, piety, justice, and what makes a life worth living. We see him still pursuing the same goal daily at the age of

seventy, still asking questions, not satisfied that he *knows*. Now that's passion!

Is Socrates wise? Does he understand? The oracle at Delphi had said there was no one wiser, and after his long search Socrates concludes that the god was right. Those persons are wisest who know that they don't know, who understand that true wisdom belongs to the god alone. But Socrates never relaxes into a "who's to say?" or "true-for-me" mode. Thinking that something is true doesn't in itself *make* it true, he holds. And so, though he is never satisfied, he keeps faith in truth. For humans, Socrates believes, it is the search for truth that is the very best way of life.*

Johannes Climacus understands Socratic passion in this way: There is a disparity between individuals who exist in time and what is eternally true; it is paradoxical to think that existing individuals like you and me could actually *grasp* that truth. So if that is what we want, we are in two places that are very far from each other—much farther from each other than you are from an "A" in chemistry, even if you haven't been studying. And so the passion is intensified. Like Abraham's faith in God (maintained though he can't understand God's asking for the sacrifice of his son), Socrates' life exemplifies a passionate faith in the existence of a truth about human existence. This faith manifests itself in a lifelong search.

Is it possible that the passion guiding a life should be still more intense than that? Climacus says yes. How might that be? The sermon that caused the Judge to rethink his own life has already given us a hint. (Remember that the theme of the sermon is that before God we are always in the wrong.) Suppose, Climacus says, that the situation is worse than it seems to Socrates. Suppose that we are not just lacking the truth but that we are continually engaged in distorting the truth—hiding it from ourselves, deceiving ourselves, pretending that we are other than in fact we are. If that were our situation, we would be even further from the eternal truth than Socrates thinks. And once again, passion would be intensified.

---

* For a discussion of Socrates' character and philosophical convictions, see Chapters 6 and 7.

This, Climacus tells us, is the possibility Christianity puts before us; this is what distinguishes Christianity from all sorts of paganism, from mysticism, from Socratic and Abrahamic religion, and (he might add today) from New Age optimism. Christianity (religiousness B) tells us that we are sinners. But what is sin? It is a very shallow view of sin to think of it as rule-breaking, as occasional lapses from the straight and narrow. No, sin is a condition of the self. Sin is despair. And what is despair? We already know; despair is not being willing to be oneself.

The many varieties of despair are examined in a little book by Anti-Climacus, *The Sickness Unto Death.** Being able to be in despair is our advantage over the other animals, but actually to be in despair is "the greatest misfortune and misery" (*SUD*, 45). Despair is a sickness in the self; unless cured it leads to death—not the death of the body, but the death of the self. And that is the worst sort of death there is, for if we are not a self, what are we?

We usually think of despair as something that overcomes us, something produced in us by unfavorable events.

> Someone in despair despairs over *something*. So, for a moment, it seems, but only for a moment. That same instant the true despair shows itself, or despair in its true guise. In despairing over *something* he was really despairing over *himself,* and he now wants to be rid of himself. (*SUD*, 49)

My wife leaves me or the stock market crashes, and I am in despair. Am I in despair over my wife leaving or over the market crash? No, Anti-Climacus says; that is a shallow view. I am in despair over myself; my despairing is my not being willing to be this self that I now am—this self whose wife has left him, whose stock portfolio is worthless. I would rather be someone else, perhaps almost anyone else. That is my sickness. That is the essence of despair.

---

*Johannes Climacus tells us that he is not a Christian, but he claims to know what it is to be or become a Christian. Anti-Climacus writes from the point of view of a sort of super-Christian. Together they give us a view from beneath and a view from above of what a Christian life would be like.

But what is a self? In a passage often cited for obscurity, Anti-Climacus says

> The self is a relation which relates to itself, or that in the relation which is its relating to itself. The self is not the relation but the relation's relating to itself. A human being is a synthesis of the infinite and the finite, of the temporal and the eternal, of freedom and necessity. In short a synthesis. (*SUD*, 43)

Here we have our old friends, the duality of (1) what we immediately, factually, are and (2) the possibility of reflecting on that and (freely) doing something about it. But we are not yet selves, Anti-Climacus says, just in virtue of this duality in us, this synthesis of two opposing factors. No, being a self is having to relate these factors to each other, bringing them into balance, creating a harmony between them. Being a self, as the Judge also says, is a task. It is a task we can fail at. And our failure is despair, an imbalance in the factors of the synthesis that manifests our unwillingness to be ourselves.

We cannot reproduce here the subtlety of Anti-Climacus' analysis of the many forms despair can take in our lives. But a few examples will give the flavor. If we reflect on the factors of the synthesis, we can see that there can be a despair of infinitude and a despair of finitude. Infinitude's despair is to lack finitude. This form of despair manifests itself in becoming "fantastic." Emotion becomes fantastic in abstract sentimentality; I melt with sympathy for suffering mankind, but I cannot stand my neighbor. Understanding becomes fantastic in squandering itself in the pursuit of inhuman and useless knowledge, in merely satisfying idle curiosity. Will becomes fantastic when it builds castles in the air. It is full of all the many things it will do, but it does not concentrate on the nearest act at hand that would move one step along the way. All these are forms of despair, of not being willing to be oneself.

Finitude's despair lacks infinitude. The self that lacks infinitude, has no sharp edges, has been ground smooth by its commerce with others, assumes the only possibilities are those well ensconced in "how things are done." This sort of self allows itself to be cheated of itself by "the others." *

> By seeing the multitude of people around it, by being busied with all sorts of worldly affairs, by being wise to the ways of the world, such a person forgets himself, in a divine sense forgets his own name, dares not believe in himself, finds being himself too risky, finds it much easier and safer to be like the others, to become a copy, a number, along with the crowd.
>
> Now this form of despair goes practically unnoticed in the world. Precisely by losing oneself in this way, such a person gains all that is required for a flawless performance in everyday life, yes, for making a great success out of life. Here there is no dragging of the feet, no difficulty with his self and its infinitizing, he is ground smooth as a pebble, as exchangeable as a coin of the realm. Far from anyone thinking him to be in despair, he is just what a human being ought to be. Naturally the world has generally no understanding of what is truly horrifying. . . .
>
> Yes, what we call worldliness simply consists of such people who, if one may so express it, pawn themselves to the world. They use their abilities, amass wealth, carry out worldly enterprises, make prudent calculations, etc., and perhaps are mentioned in history, but they are not themselves. (*SUD*, 63, 64, 65)

So we can despair by identifying ourselves with our infinitude, and we can despair by identifying ourselves with our finitude. In either case, there is a lack of balance in the synthesis.

There are many other variations in Anti-Climacus' rich description of despair. But we will here note only one other possibility, a surprising one, given the general definition of despair. Despair can take this form: being willing (in despair) to be oneself. This is the despair of defiance, in which

> the self wants in despair to rule over himself, or create himself, make this self the self he wants to be, determine what he will have and what he will not

have in his concrete self. . . . That is to say, he wants to begin a little earlier than other people, not at and with the beginning, but 'in the beginning'; he does not want to don his own self, does not want to see his task in his given self, he wants . . . to construct it himself. (*SUD*, 99)

"In the beginning" is obviously a reference to the first words of Genesis; this self wants to be its own god, to create itself completely. That is why Anti-Climacus says such a person "does not want to don his own self" but to construct it—out of nothing, as it were.

Defiance, too, can take several forms. There is an active and a passive form of this despair. Its active form is really a matter of experimenting with itself; in this form there is nothing firm, since

> it can, at any moment, start quite arbitrarily all over again. . . . So, far from the self succeeding increasingly in being itself, it becomes increasingly obvious that it is a hypothetical self. The self is its own master, absolutely (as one says) its own master; and exactly this is the despair, but also what it regards as its pleasure and joy. But it is easy on closer examination to see that this absolute ruler is a king without a country, that really he rules over nothing; his position, his kingdom, his sovereignty, are subject to the dialectic that rebellion is legitimate at any moment. Ultimately it is arbitrarily based upon the self itself.
>
> Consequently, the despairing self is forever building only castles in the air. . . . (*SUD*, 100)

In its passive form, the despair of defiance finds something objectionable about itself. Perhaps it is a flaw, or seems to be a flaw, a deficiency, or a disability. But how does the offended one react? He

> uses it as an excuse to take offense at all existence; he wants to be himself in spite of it. . . . (*SUD*, 102)
>
> The demonic despair . . . wants to be itself in hatred toward existence, to be itself according to its misery. . . . Rebelling against all existence, it thinks it has acquired evidence against existence, against its goodness. The despairer thinks that he himself is this evidence. . . . It is, to describe it figuratively, as if a writer were to make a slip of the pen, and the error became conscious of itself as such—perhaps it wasn't a mistake but from a much higher point

---

* Martin Heidegger's more recent discussion of human existence as "falling-in-with-the-One" is obviously indebted to Kierkegaard's discussion of despair. See Chapter 26.

of view an essential ingredient in the whole presentation—and as if this error wanted now to rebel against the author, out of hatred for him forbid him to correct it, and in manic defiance say to him: 'No, I will not be erased, I will stand as a witness against you, a witness to the fact that you are a second-rate author.' (SUD, 104–5) *

Even this form of willing to be oneself, however, conforms to the general formula for despair; it, too, is a way of being unwilling to be oneself. This becomes apparent when we see what it would be for a self to be without despair.

> This then is the formula which describes the state of the self when despair is completely eradicated: in relating to itself and in wanting to be itself, the self is grounded transparently in the power that established it. (SUD, 43)

In wanting to be its own creator, to begin "a little earlier than other people," the defiant self imagines that it can establish itself from the ground up. But no one can do that. There are no self-made people. And so the defiant self is in fact unwilling to be the self that is: a self grounded in the "power that established it." Anti-Climacus takes this power to be God; so defiance is rebellion, offense, and despair after all.

What does Anti-Climacus mean by saying that when despair is completely eradicated, the self is grounded "transparently" in God? This means, I take it, that it is not that there are *two* things to do: (1) be willing to be oneself, and (2) establish a relation to God. Rather, doing the first *is* doing the second, and vice versa. Is there a name for this state of self without despair? There is. It is not *virtue*, Anti-Climacus tells us, but *faith* that is the opposite of despair. And so we come back again to that passion of inward intensity we met earlier in the Knight of Faith. Only now the passion is ever so much more intense; for now we can see how far, far away from a true way of life we really are.

But how could we come to accept ourselves as we are, knowing what we now know about despair,

about sin? Isn't this just as impossible as the Judge actually living the perfectly ethical life? What we require is forgiveness. And this, too, Christianity has a word about. But it is a word that once more intensifies the passion, for it is the word about Christ, the God-Man who makes our forgiveness possible. Kierkegaard and his pseudonyms all agree that this pushes the truth out beyond all understanding. If, with Socrates, the relation between an existing individual and the eternal truth had an element of paradox about it, Christianity makes it far worse. If there is any truth in Christianity, it is absolutely paradoxical, paradoxical in itself. If we know anything about God, we know God is not human; and if we know anything about humans, we know they are not God. And yet Christianity proclaims our healing through the life and death of the God-Man.

What does this mean? It means, Kierkegaard is certain, that faith should never be confused with knowledge. (Philosophy is just confused, a subject for ridicule, if it thinks that by human reason it can "go further" than faith; faith is not a matter of understanding anything, for the Absolute Paradox rebuffs our understanding.) It means that proofs for the existence of God and evidence for the divinity of Jesus are beside the point; faith is not a matter of accepting certain propositions as true, but of *existing* in a certain manner. (Christianity resists being understood; it invites a certain form of life.) It means that a life trusting in the forgiveness of sins, a life in imitation of Christ, is inherently risky— that there are no guarantees that it will "pay off." Such a life is the ultimate risk, stretched as it is between recognition of one's sinfulness and the paradox of possible forgiveness. But such is the life of faith; for faith is the highest passion.

But does Christianity present us with the truth about ourselves, about our sickness and its healing? Or not? That is not a question Kierkegaard thinks he can answer for us. That is something we all have to answer for ourselves. And answer it we will—one way or another—in our lives.

The Individual

You might think that the pattern we have seen in the relations between esthetic, ethical, and reli-

---

* This passively defiant despair is perfectly captured in the spiteful voice that speaks in Dostoevsky's *Notes From Underground*.

gious forms of life is just the Hegelian pattern all over again. Inadequacies in earlier stages are exposed and remedied by later stages, toward which consciousness moves with a kind of inexorable logic. But this would be a serious mistake. To see why, we must examine the way Kierkegaard understands the position of the individual human being.

One reason he resorts to indirect communication is to combat the Hegelian view of the natural and necessary evolution of consciousness to ever higher levels. Each pseudonymous "author" presents to the reader a "possibility" for life; in that respect, they are all on the same level. Each invites the reader to identify with him.

- *The esthete:* You have only one life to live, so you might as well arrange to make it enjoyable. It is true that the kind of ironic detachment this requires means that life is ultimately meaningless and that there are no serious choices; but that's just how life is.
- *The ethicist:* Life *is* neither this way nor that; it all depends on what you *do* with it. And that is a matter of choice, the sort of serious choice that constitutes a continuing self. You *are* what you *make* of yourself. And far from being meaningless, nothing could possibly matter more.
- *The Christian:* You can't successfully create yourself. We are all failures at this task. What is required is acknowledgement of this fact, together with faith in God's forgiveness through Christ. In this way we can come to accept ourselves in spite of our unacceptability; only thus can we be free simply to *be* ourselves.*

It is Kierkegaard's claim that among these three possibilities (and they may not be the only ones) existing human beings must *choose*. And they must choose without being able to attain a position in

which they could know for certain which choice was the right or best one. For existing human beings, the key concepts are choice, decision, and *risk*. A move from one kind of life to another is less like the result of rational persuasion and more like conversion. If one makes such a move it is by a *leap*.

It is true that *within* each of these frameworks each occupant thinks it can characterize and explain the others. To the Judge, A looks like a man who has lost himself; to A, the Judge's marriage looks overwhelmingly boring. The Christian sees them both as examples of despair—of not willing to be oneself; and no doubt the Christian could be accused, from some other framework, of irrationality and of going beyond the evidence. Where does the truth lie? In order to determine this, it seems one would have to take up a point of view outside them all and consider them all *objectively*. But it is Kierkegaard's conviction that no such point of view is available to an existing human being. There is no such vantage point for us as Hegel imagines absolute knowledge to be—no coincidence of subjectivity and objectivity, no identification of ourselves with Absolute Spirit, no *good reason* to choose one life rather than another, and no *knowledge* here at all. You and I, he thinks, are free to choose among the possibilities. But we are not free to choose *for good reasons*—from an objective point of view. Neither are we free *not to choose*. Simply by living, we are making our choices; we cannot help it.

Hegel and the Hegelians Kierkegaard knew suppose that the process of living well can be organized in an objective and rational way. In particular, they think that philosophy can construct a *system* in which every aspect of life and reality is given its necessary and proper place. To this supposition Johannes Climacus responds in scathing tones.

> I shall be as willing as the next man to fall down in worship before the System, if only I can manage to set eyes on it. Hitherto I have had no success; and though I have young legs, I am almost weary from running back and forth. . . . Once or twice I have been on the verge of bending the knee. But at the

---

*It is worth noting that Kierkegaard's stage of *faith* is worlds away from the sort of "self-acceptance" urged upon us by so much contemporary psychology (and advertising!). The "I'm OK, you're OK" syndrome is one that is basically esthetic, in Kierkegaard's terms. What it lacks is both the seriousness of the ethical and the consciousness of sin. Dietrich Bonhoeffer, a German theologian influenced by Kierkegaard and killed by the Nazis, would have called it "cheap grace."

last moment, when I already had my handkerchief spread on the ground, to avoid soiling my trousers, and I made a trusting appeal to one of the initiated who stood by: "Tell me now sincerely, is it entirely finished; for if so I will kneel down before it, even at the risk of ruining a pair of trousers (for on account of the heavy traffic to and from the system, the road has become quite muddy),"—I always received the same answer: "No, it is not yet quite finished." And so there was another postponement—of the System, and of my homage.

System and finality are pretty much one and the same, so much so that if the system is not finished, there is no system. . . . A system which is not quite finished is an hypothesis; while on the other hand to speak of a half-finished system is nonsense. (*CUP*, 97–98)

Climacus makes a distinction between a *logical system* and what he calls an *existential system*. And he claims that a logical system is possible, but an existential system is not. Geometry is a good example of a logical system; it is founded on axioms, postulates, and definitions, from which we can prove theorems using the rules of logic. Characteristic of a logical system is that all the theorems are already implicit in the premises. That is the respect in which "finality" is an essential characteristic of a system—if a proposition that cannot be deduced from the axioms is introduced, it follows that a mistake has been made. Given a certain set of axioms, the set of derivable theorems is also given; no new truths can be added later, and none of the theorems can be altered. In particular, Climacus says, nothing must be incorporated into such a logical system "that has any relation to existence, that is not indifferent to existence" (*CUP*, 100). Existence, after all, makes headway, like the ship in the Judge's image, and may always falsify any "system" that purports to describe it. So far as its relation to existence goes, a logical system merely presents a possibility, a hypothesis.*

The reason why an existential system is not possible (at least for us) is that "existence is precisely the opposite of finality." (*CUP*, 107)

Respecting the impossibility of an existential system, let us then ask quite simply . . . "Who is to write or complete such a system?" Surely a human being; unless we propose again to begin using the strange mode of speech which assumes that a human being becomes speculative philosophy in the abstract, or becomes the identity of subject and object. So then, a human being—and surely a living human being, i.e., an existing individual. . . . It is from this side . . . that objection must be made to modern philosophy; not that it has a mistaken presupposition, but that it has a comical presupposition, occasioned by its having forgotten in a sort of world-historical absent-mindedness, what it means to be a human being. Not indeed, what it means to be a human being in general; for this is the sort of thing that one might even induce a speculative philosopher to agree to; but what it means that you and I and he are human beings, each one for himself. (*CUP*, 109)

The problem is that in constructing a system that supposedly captures existence, the speculative philosopher supposes that he can be finished with existence before existence is finished with him! As long as he lives, he must choose; his own existence is precisely not something finished. To suppose that at some point in his life he (or we, or the human race in its history) could attain the finality that comes with a system is simply comic.* Such a philosopher, Climacus says, "has gradually come to be so fantastic a being that scarcely the most extravagant fancy has ever invented anything so fabulous" (*CUP*, 107).

We have seen that the problem of the criterion has plagued philosophers since Sextus Empiricus, who first formulates it clearly. By what mark can we tell when we have latched onto truth and goodness? Hegel's answer to this problem is that we will

---

*About this point Climacus seems to be more correct than he could have known. Since the discovery of non-Euclidean geometries in the latter part of the nineteenth century, any system of geometry has to be regarded, as far as its application goes, as a hypothesis about the nature of space. For all these systems themselves can tell us, space may be either Euclidean or non-Euclidean.

* There is some reason to believe Kierkegaard's criticism here may be more apt against some enthusiastic "right-wing" Hegelians than against Hegel himself. You will recall that we noted several times a deep ambivalence running through Hegel's thoughts. For a strain that sounds very Kierkegaardian, see again the famous "Owl of Minerva" passage on p. 439.

know *in the end*—that is, when we see how everything hangs together in a systematic way. What Kierkegaard is denying is that this kind of sight is possible for existing human beings. Perhaps that *would* do as a criterion. But we can't get there from here. And so we have to live without a criterion, without certainty, without good reason. We live by a *leap*.

The essential task for an existing human being, then, is not to speculate philosophically about absolute knowledge, but to become himself. As we have seen, this is a task involving risky choices, choices that must be made without the comfort of objective certainty. Speculative philosophers who try to present a *system* explaining existence imagine they can reach such a degree of objectivity that they revoke the risk in living; but this is sheer illusion. As Climacus plaintively asks, "Why can we not remember to be human beings?" (*CUP*, 104).

The tendency of modern philosophy is entirely toward objectivity. Kierkegaard sets himself absolutely against this tendency. He deplores

> . . . the objective tendency, which proposes to make everyone an observer, and in its maximum to transform him into so objective an observer that he becomes almost a ghost, scarcely to be distinguished from the tremendous spirit of the historical past. (*CUP*, 118)

He endorses a saying by G. E. Lessing (a noted eighteenth-century German dramatist) to this effect: that if God held in his right hand the truth and in his left hand the striving for the truth, and asked the existing individual to choose one, the appropriate choice would be the left hand.

With respect to the individual's relation to the truth, there are two questions: (1) whether it is indeed the truth to which one is related; and (2) whether the mode of the relationship is a true one. Call the former an *objective* question and the latter a *subjective* question. The former concerns *what* is said or believed, the latter *how* it is said or believed.

For an existing individual, there is no way to settle that first question definitively. As a result,

the *how* is accentuated.* For an individual, the quality of life depends on the intensity, the passion, the decisiveness with which this relation is maintained. (Remember the advice of the Judge to A about choice; remember also the way in which the consciousness of sin—of actually being already in error and separated from the truth—intensifies the situation in the Christian framework.) Climacus offers a formula that expresses the appropriate knowledge relation of the individual to the truth.

> *An objective uncertainty held fast in an appropriation-process of the most passionate inwardness is the truth,* the highest truth available for an *existing individual.* (*CUP*, 182)

Objectively speaking, the individual never has more than "uncertainty"; this uncertainty correlates subjectively with the riskiness of the choice made; and the riskier the choice the more intense the "passionate inwardness" with which it is made. For the individual, living in this subjectivity *is* living in the truth.

Kierkegaard is interested in two questions: (1) What is it to be an existing human being? and (2) What is it to be a Christian? He is convinced that unless we get an adequate answer to the first question, we will get the second one wrong. He believes most people do get it wrong. In an age in which everyone considers himself a Christian as a matter of course, Kierkegaard means to unsettle this complacency by drawing our attention back to the first question.

If the problem that faces each individual is this problem of how to manage the duality implicit in being a self, then it becomes evident that being a Christian must be a certain way of solving the problem. It cannot be just a matter of church membership, or of being baptized, or of having the right

---

* Climacus is here thinking of truth about the best life choices. But an analogy from general epistemology might be helpful. Knowledge is commonly defined as *justified true belief.* Unless our belief is true—that is, objectively correct—it cannot constitute knowledge. But the best we can do is believe for good reasons. Nothing we can do will guarantee truth.

(i.e., orthodox) beliefs, or of "understanding" one-self and one's place in the "system" (in the manner of Hegelian philosophy). It is a problem that cannot be solved in any other way than by the construction of the self through the choices, momentous and trivial, that one makes when faced with life's multifarious possibilities.

In a whimsical passage, Johannes Climacus tells us the story of how he became an author. He was smoking his cigar on a Sunday afternoon in a public garden and ruminating on how he might best spend his life to be of benefit to mankind. He was thinking about all those

". . . celebrated names and figures, the precious and much heralded men who are coming into prominence and are much talked about, the many benefactors of the age who know how to benefit mankind by making life easier and easier, some by railways, others by omnibuses and steamboats, others by the telegraph, others by easily apprehended compendiums and short recitals of everything worth knowing, and finally the true benefactors of the age who make spiritual existence in virtue of thought easier and easier, yet more and more significant. And what [he asks himself] are you doing?" Here my soliloquy was interrupted, for my cigar was smoked out and a new one had to be lit. So I smoked again, and then suddenly this thought flashed through my mind: "You must do something, but inasmuch as with your limited capacities it will be impossible to make anything easier than it has become, you must, with the same humanitarian enthusiasm as the others, undertake to make something harder." This notion pleased me immensely, and at the same time it flattered me to think that I, like the rest of them, would be loved and esteemed by the whole community. For when all combine in every way to make everything easier, there remains only one possible danger, namely, that the ease becomes so great that it becomes altogether too great; then there is only one want left, though it is not yet a felt want, when people will want difficulty. Out of love for mankind, and out of despair at my embarrassing situation, seeing that I had accomplished nothing and was unable to make anything easier than it had already been made, . . . I conceived it as my task to create difficulties everywhere. (*CUP*, 165–66)

What sort of difficulties? Those that remind us of what a hazardous and risky business it is, this business of having to be an existing human individual.

Marx: Beyond Alienation and Exploitation

As we have noted, several themes become prominent at the close of the Enlightenment and the beginning of the nineteenth century. They are most systematically developed in Hegel. We can summarize these themes as follows:

- *The significance of history.* The classical quest for eternal truths, knowable at any time and in any circumstances, is replaced by the notion of the development of culture and of reason itself. Moreover, this development is thought of as *progress* toward a more encompassing truth, rationality, and freedom.
- *The role of opposition and antagonism in this progress.* Hegel notices, indeed emphasizes the role of the *negative* in development, that is, that struggle and loss are an essential part of any move forward.* William Blake, the English Romantic poet, puts it this way: "Without contraries is no progression."[3]
- *The attainment of the goal by the race, not the individual.* Since the progress is a historical one and since individuals cannot jump out of their own cultural setting, the goal (self-consciousness, rationality, freedom) must be one toward which the race is moving, rather than one which an individual could completely attain.
- *The justification of the evil that accompanies this progression.* Hegel, as we have seen, acknowledges the suffering that individuals endure on the "slaughter bench" of history but argues that all is worthwhile because of the incomparable

---

*In a way, this is a very old thought. See Heraclitus on the necessity for opposition and strife, p. 18.

value of the end: the realization of Absolute Spirit in the wholly rational state. As Lenin was later to put a similar point: You can't make an omelet without breaking some eggs.

Karl Marx (1818–1883) accepts these views. Indeed, he accepts them in their Hegelian guise; as a young man, Marx was self-consciously one of the left-wing Hegelians. Like Kierkegaard, whom he did not know, he complains that Hegelian philosophy is speculative and abstract. But unlike Kierkegaard, his remedy for this abstraction is not to focus on the plight of the anxious individual, forced to make choices without rational warrant; such a focus on "subjectivity" would seem to him an abstraction of a different, but no less deplorable, kind. Marx develops his critique along other lines.

Hegel believes (1) that reality is Spirit, (2) that the human being is Spirit unknown to itself, alienated from its objects (and so from itself), and (3) that the cure for this **alienation** is the knowledge that there is nothing in the object which is not put there by the subject—by Spirit itself. The human being is God coming to consciousness of himself through history. Marx comes to believe that this is exactly right, but only in a funny kind of way. For what Hegel has done, Marx thinks, is to take reality and "etherealize" it. It is as though the real world has been transposed into another key and played back to us—all there, but with everything looking weirdly distorted. Hegel, Marx believes, has taken philosophy off its feet and turned it upside down on its head. It is Marx's determination to put philosophy back on its feet again. In an early work written with Friedrich Engels, Marx expresses this determination.

In direct contrast to German philosophy which descends from heaven to earth, here we ascend from earth to heaven. That is to say, we do not set out from what men say, imagine, conceive, nor from men as narrated, thought of, imagined, conceived, in order to arrive at men in the flesh. We set out from real, active men, and on the basis of their real life-process we demonstrate the development of the ideological reflexes and echoes of this life-process. The phan-

toms formed in the human brain are also, necessarily, sublimates of their material life-process, which is empirically verifiable and bound to material premises. Morality, religion, metaphysics, all the rest of ideology and their corresponding forms of consciousness, thus no longer retain the semblance of independence. They have no history, no development; but men, developing their material production and their material intercourse, alter, along with this their real existence, their thinking and the products of their thinking. Life is not determined by consciousness, but consciousness by life. (*GI,* 118–19)[4]

Consider the last sentence. Hegel writes as if the forms of consciousness, traced in his phenomenology of Spirit, are independent of the material world. Forms of life, Hegel holds, depend on forms of consciousness, the level to which knowledge has evolved: sense-certainty, perception, understanding, desire, the unhappy consciousness, morality, and so on. But to Marx and Engels, this puts the cart before the horse. Those forms of consciousness do not have the kind of independence Hegel ascribes to them. And so they do not, in themselves, have a history. There is, however, an underlying reality that does have a history. This *material* reality has to do first and foremost with *economic* matters—with putting bread on the table. It is the reality of "men in the flesh," of "real, active men" and their "life processes." Hegel's forms of consciousness are simply "sublimates" or ideological reflections of this more basic reality.

The most essential need of real people is the sustenance of their material life. Marx calls this the

first premise of all human existence, and therefore of all history, the premise, namely, that men must be in a position to live in order to be able to "make history." But life involves before everything else eating and drinking, a habitation, clothing and many other things. The first historical act is thus the production of the means to satisfy these needs, the production of material life itself. (*GI,* 119–20)

This premise is followed by other no less basic points: that producing the means of subsistence requires instruments of production; that this multiplies needs; that people propagate their own kind and so create families; and, most important, that these activities involve people from the start in social relationships.

> It follows from this that a certain mode of production or industrial stage is always combined with a certain mode of co-operation, or social stage, and this mode of co-operation is itself a "productive force." (*GI*, 121)

It is Marx's intention, then, to substitute for Hegelian speculative philosophy a discipline that looks carefully at the actual, empirically ascertainable facts about human beings. Marx is an influential figure in the history of both sociology and economics. He holds that if you want to understand a certain form of consciousness—of religion, perhaps, or of literature—you need to understand the material (economic and social) conditions in which it is produced. It is no good simply looking at texts or practices in isolation; you need to understand the context in which they arise.* He also believes that certain forms of intellectual and spiritual life are merely compensations for an unsatisfactory life here on earth; religion, for instance, an opiate of the people, will simply vanish if we can get society straightened out.

Understanding is not enough, however, even for the intellectual. What is called for is action. Perhaps no one has put the philosopher in such a central role since Plato had proposed that philosophers should become kings and kings philosophers.† In a famous line, Marx writes,‡

> The philosophers have only *interpreted* the world, in various ways; the point, however, is to *change* it. (*TF,* 109)

---

*Vigorous controversies exist among literary critics over precisely this point, the "New Critics" arguing that the text itself must speak, and more or less Marxist opponents replying that the text is not an independent entity that has a voice of its own.

†For the rationale behind this proposal of Plato's, see "The State," in Chapter 8. In a way, Marx proposes a similar role for the intellectual in the struggles of his time.

‡Look once more at the "Owl of Minerva" passage in Hegel (p. 439). This is what Marx is attacking.

"From each according to his ability, to each according to his needs!" —KARL MARX

In what ways is philosophy supposed to change the world? To answer this question, we must consider what Marx sees when he undertakes to describe "real" people in their actual existence.

Alienation, Exploitation, and Private Property

In an early work (1844), unknown until the 1930s, Marx presents an analysis of the condition these "real" people had reached in the middle of the nineteenth century. We need to remind ourselves that this is the heyday of the industrial revolution—of the steam engine, the coal mine, and the knitting mill, of the twelve- or fourteen-hour work day, of child labor, and of a widening gap between those who own the means of production and the masses who give their labor in factories they have no stake in. In understanding these conditions, Marx relies heavily on the major political economists who analyze the new industrial situation, Adam Smith and David Ricardo.

Here is how Marx sees things.

> *Wages* are determined through the antagonistic struggle between capitalist and worker. Victory goes necessarily to the capitalist. The capitalist can live longer without the worker than can the worker without the capitalist. (*EPM*, 65)

The capitalist, of course, owns the means of production, the factories and tools. A separation of ownership from labor is characteristic of the industrial age. In the days when cobblers made shoes, virtually all cobblers had their own shops and tools; perhaps they had an apprentice or two and maybe even a servant. But ownership and labor were typically combined in the same person. In the nineteenth century, however, there is a split between the class of people who own the very large and expensive means of industrial production and the class that provides the labor, a split that takes on the characteristics of a "struggle."

To increase their profits and meet the competition of other industrial entrepreneurs, the capitalists pay the workers no more than is necessary to keep the workers alive, working, and reproducing. This is possible in part because there are typically more workers than jobs. So the worker takes on the characteristic of a *commodity* in the system; like all commodities, the capitalist tries to buy it as cheaply as possible. As a commodity, of course, the worker is not thought of as a human being, but "only as a working animal—as a beast reduced to the strictest bodily needs" (*EPM*, 73). The worker could be (and often is) replaced by a machine.

The worker must face not only the capitalist but also the landlord. Formerly, the landed gentry could live solely by the productivity of the land. But the vigorous activity of the capitalist has forced competition here, too; and landowners are either driven out of this class altogether or become capitalists in their own right, seeking a profit from the land. They, therefore, seek to make rents as high as possible, and tenant farmers join the industrial workers as commodities on the market.

Private property is one fact political economy takes for granted, Marx says. But that should not be taken for granted; it needs an explanation. Marx's explanation leans heavily on his Hegelian background. For example, suppose you take a piece of wood from the floor of the forest, sit down, and painstakingly carve into it the face of Lincoln. We can say that you have "put something of yourself into it." No longer raw nature, it now is an expression of yourself. It is, in fact, your labor *objectified.* In confronting it, you are confronting yourself: you are the person who *did that.* In contemplating this object, you become aware at one and the same time of it and of yourself, for part of what you are stands there in objectified form before you. Before you put your labor into it, you would not have been harmed had someone stolen it; but now, if it is stolen, the thief steals part of *you.**

We humans are active, productive, creative beings. In producing objects we create not only them, but ourselves. The products of our labor show us to ourselves as in a mirror. Do you want to know what humans are? Don't examine just their physiology and individual psychology. Look at their art, their laws, their religion, their societies, their technologies, their industrial products; these things will tell you, because they are humanity itself in objectified form. It is in such *externalization* that we make ourselves fully human, that is, self-consciously human.

But in the industrial age this process has become perverted. For the worker labors and produces a *commodity.* What does that mean?

1. It means that workers do not experience their work as an affirmation of themselves. On the contrary, they feel *alienated* from their work. Their labor is not an expression of their lives but external to their lives. As Marx puts it, the worker

> . . . does not affirm himself but denies himself, does not feel content but unhappy, does not develop freely his physical and mental energy but mortifies his body and ruins his mind. . . . His labor is there-

---

*Compare Hegel on master and slave, pp. 422–425.

fore not voluntary, but coerced; it is *forced labor*. It is therefore not the satisfaction of a need; it is merely a *means* to satisfy needs external to it. Its alien character emerges clearly in the fact that as soon as no physical or other compulsion exists, labor is shunned like the plague. (*EPM*, 110–11)

Rather than being fulfilled in their work, workers experience a loss of themselves. They are *dehumanized;* they feel active and productive only in their animal functions. In what should be their highest human functions (productive, creative labor), they become no more than animals, or worse, machines.*

2. Workers are alienated not only from their labor but also from the products of their labor, which belong not to them but to the capitalist. The workers have just their wages, which are necessarily only enough for bare subsistence. The products they make stand over against them as independent powers; although they have put themselves into these products, they have no control over them. They put their lives into the objects they produce but then find that their lives no longer belong to them.

3. In the early days of the Industrial Revolution, there was no solidarity among workers, no labor union, no force to rival the superior power of the employer. Workers competed against each other for jobs, and there were too many workers. For every worker who faltered or expressed dissatisfaction with working conditions, there were a dozen waiting at the employer's door. As a result, workers were also alienated from each other and, of course, from the capitalist, who was making money from their exploitation.

This is all more intelligible if we note that according to the economists of the day, *value* is defined in terms of labor. The value of something (including money) represents a certain amount of labor. The worker produces value, but value in the hands of another: the one with the means to purchase the labor of the worker, that is, the capitalist.

---

*Those of you who have worked on an assembly line can perhaps verify from your own experience Marx's description of such work.

In plain words, what the worker is producing is capital, and with it the capitalist.

Workers, then, are alienated from their labor and from the products of their labor; in neither can they find themselves. If we return now to the question about the origin of private property, we can see, Marx says, that it has its foundation in *alienated labor*. And since the classical political economists formulate their laws in terms of private property, we can see that they are formulating the laws of estranged labor—the laws of a condition of society in which workers are exploited, dehumanized.

> All these consequences result from the fact that the worker is related to the *product of his labor* as to an *alien* object. For on this premise it is clear that the more the worker spends himself, the more powerful becomes the alien world of objects which he creates over and against himself, the poorer he himself—his inner world—becomes, the less it belongs to him as his own. It is the same in religion. The more man puts into God, the less he retains himself. The worker puts his life into the object; but now his life no longer belongs to him but to the object. . . . The *alienation* of the worker in his product means not only that his labor becomes an object, an *external* existence, but that it exists *outside him*, independently, as something alien to him. It means that the life which he has conferred on the object confronts him as something hostile and alien. . . .
>
> It is true that labor produces for the rich wonderful things—but for the worker it produces privation. It produces palaces—but for the worker, hovels. It produces beauty—but for the worker, deformity. It replaces labor by machines, but it throws a section of the workers back to a barbarous type of labor, and it turns the other workers into machines. It produces intelligence—but for the worker stupidity, cretinism. (*EPM*, 108–10).

In the condition of alienated labor—of private property—the natural human needs of people become perverted. "Man becomes ever poorer as man, his need for *money* becomes ever greater if he wants to overpower hostile being" (*EPM*, 147). The need for money, of course, is insatiable; schemes for multiplying human needs are devised to increase one's money wealth. The process is fueled by *greed*. Greed and the money system, Marx says, are corollaries; devotion to money becomes a kind of secular religion.

Communism

Private property, then, has a history; it is not a natural, given fact. Private property is the result of alienated labor. And this alienation of labor itself has a history. Marx's view of this history is sketched in the first part of the *Manifesto of the Communist Party,* which he wrote with Engels in 1848.

> The history of all hitherto existing society is the history of class struggles.
> Freeman and slave, patrician and plebeian, lord and serf, guild-master and journeyman, in a word, oppressor and oppressed, stood in constant opposition to one another, carried on an uninterrupted, now hidden, now open fight, a fight that each time ended, either in a revolutionary reconstitution of society at large, or in the common ruin of the contending classes. . . .
> Our epoch, the epoch of the bourgeoisie, possesses, however, this distinctive feature: it has simplified the class antagonisms. Society as a whole is more and more splitting up into two great hostile camps, into two great classes directly facing each other: Bourgeoisie and Proletariat. (*MCP,* 35–36)

The bourgeoisie is the class of owners, including both capitalists (in the narrower sense) and landlords. Marx characterizes it in the following way:

> The bourgeoisie, wherever it has got the upper hand, has put an end to all feudal, patriarchal, idyllic relations. It has pitilessly torn asunder the motley feudal ties that bound man to his "natural superiors," and left remaining no other nexus between man and man than naked self-interest, than callous "cash payment." It has drowned the most heavenly ecstasies of religious fervor, of chivalrous enthusiasm, of philistine sentimentalism, in the icy water of egotistical calculation. It has resolved personal worth into exchange value, and in place of the numberless indefeasible chartered freedoms, has set up that single,

unconscionable freedom—Free Trade. In one word, for exploitation, veiled by religious and political illusions, it has substituted naked, shameless, direct, brutal exploitation. (*MCP,* 38)

In pursuit of wealth, the bourgeoisie constantly revolutionizes the instruments of production and thus transforms relations among people in society into competitive relations. It produces a world market and interdependence among nations. It converts all other nations, on pain of extinction, into bourgeoisie as well. It concentrates property in a few hands. And it produces its own opposition: the proletariat.

> In proportion as the bourgeoisie, *i.e.,* capital, is developed, in the same proportion is the proletariat, the modern working class, developed—a class of labourers, who live only so long as they find work, and who find work only so long as their labour increases capital. (*MCP,* 42)

The proletariat is the class of nonowners, of workers who have nothing but their labor to call their own. We have already characterized the life of the worker, as Marx sees it. We can now add that the lower strata of the middle classes—small tradespeople, shopkeepers, craftsmen, peasants—tend to sink gradually into the proletariat. As the proletariat grows in size, it begins to feel its strength and becomes the only really revolutionary class. As Marx sees it,

> The development of Modern Industry . . . cuts from under its feet the very foundation on which the bourgeoisie produces and appropriates products. What the bourgeoisie, therefore, produces, above all, is its own grave diggers. Its fall and the victory of the proletariat are equally inevitable. (*MCP,* 48)

Historical development, as Marx sees it, has led us to the point where society is divided into two great classes whose interests are diametrically opposed.

The interests of the proletariat, Marx believes, are best represented by the communists, "the most advanced and resolute section of the working class parties of every country," who have "the advantage of clearly understanding the line of march, the conditions, and the ultimate general results of the proletarian movement" (*MCP*, 49). (This insight is the result of taking Hegelian dialectical philosophy off its head and setting it back on its feet.) What communism stands for, then, is the abolition of private property. About this claim Marx and Engels make the following remarks:

The distinguishing feature of Communism is not the abolition of property generally, but the abolition of bourgeois property. But modern bourgeois private property is the final and most complete expression of the system of producing and appropriating products, that is based on class antagonisms, on the exploitation of the many by the few. . . .

Hard-won, self-acquired, self-earned property! Do you mean the property of the petty artisan and of the small peasant, a form of property that preceded the bourgeois form? There is no need to abolish that; the development of industry has to a great extent already destroyed it, and is still destroying it daily. . . .

You are horrified at our intending to do away with private property. But in your existing society, private property is already done away with for nine-tenths of the population; its existence for the few is solely due to its non-existence in the hands of those nine-tenths. You reproach us, therefore, with intending to do away with a form of property, the necessary condition for whose existence is, the non-existence of any property for the immense majority of society.

In one word, you reproach us with intending to do away with your property. Precisely so; that is just what we intend. . . .

Communism deprives no man of the power to appropriate the products of society; all that it does is to deprive him of the power to subjugate the labour of others by means of such appropriation. (*MCP*, 50–54)

If the history of the world has, as Marx says, been the history of class struggles, then there seems to be something final and apocalyptic about this division of society into bourgeoisie and proletariat, into the few who have all and the many who have nothing. And if this picture is taken seriously,

it seems as though a final revolution, in which the workers take control of the means of production, might be the goal toward which history is moving. This is, in fact, the "theoretical advantage" that the communists claim—that they can see this line of development.

Marx agrees with Hegel about the character of the end: all this suffering is worthwhile only for *freedom*.* But it is not the freedom of pure self-consciousness—knowing itself to be all there is, both subject and object—that Marx praises. Rather, it is the freedom of real, active, working men and women, who no longer find themselves alienated from their work, the products of their work, and their fellow workers.

When, in the course of development, class distinctions have disappeared, and all production has been concentrated in the hands of a vast association of the whole nation, the public power will lose its political character. Political power, properly so called, is merely the organized power of one class for oppressing another. If the proletariat during its contest with the bourgeoisie is compelled, by the force of circumstances, to organize itself as a class, if, by means of a revolution, it makes itself the ruling class, and, as such, sweeps away by force the old conditions of production, then it will, along with these conditions, have swept away the conditions for the existence of class antagonisms and of classes generally, and will thereby have abolished its own supremacy as a class.

In place of the old bourgeois society, with its classes and class antagonisms, we shall have an association, in which the free development of each is the condition for the free development of all. (*MCP*, 59–60)

It is indeed not enough to understand the world; what is required is to change it. The *Manifesto* ends with a ringing call to action (*MCP*, 74):

The Communists disdain to conceal their views and aims. They openly declare that their ends can be attained only by the forcible overthrow of all ex-

---

* See Hegel's discussion of freedom as the goal of history, pp. 436–438.

isting social conditions. Let the ruling classes tremble at a Communistic revolution. The proletarians have nothing to lose but their chains. They have a world to win.

WORKING MEN OF ALL COUNTRIES, UNITE!

If things have not worked out as Marx and Engels expected, it must nonetheless be allowed that their vision of a world where the "free development of each is the condition for the free development of all," a world without exploitation and without class antagonisms, has done as much actually to change the world (in one way and another) as any system of thought has ever done.

Basic Questions

KIERKEGAARD

1. What is "indirect communication"? Why did Kierkegaard write so much under pseudonyms?
2. Under what categories does an esthete organize his or her life? Describe two ways this might work out, using the examples of Don Juan and the Seducer.
3. Explain Judge William's fundamental Either/Or. How does it relate to choice? And how is this choice different from the many choices made by an esthete?
4. What is the Judge's view of the relation between romantic love and marriage?
5. What two "movements" does a Knight of Faith make? Why does Johannes de silentio think this is "absurd," or beyond human understanding?
6. Characterize in several ways the two aspects of human life that fascinate Kierkegaard and his "authors."
7. How do these two aspects look to the esthete, to the ethical person, and to someone who lives in religious categories?
8. What is despair? What is the condition of a self when despair is completely eradicated? How can this be attained?
9. What, according to Kierkegaard and Johannes Climacus, is distinctive about Christianity? Why is it characterized as "the highest passion"?
10. What is characteristic of a system? What would an existential system be? How does Kierkegaard attack this notion?
11. What, according to Johannes Climacus, is the proper relation of an existing human individual to the truth?

MARX

1. What does Marx mean when he says that "life is not determined by consciousness, but consciousness by life"?
2. Characterize the struggle between capitalist and worker.
3. What is the origin of private property, according to Marx?
4. Describe some forms of worker alienation.
5. Characterize the bourgeoisie and the proletariat as Marx saw them in the mid-nineteenth century. How did he think they were related?
6. What does communism intend? And why?

For Further Thought

1. Does the pattern of your life seem to match (more or less) that of any of Kierkegaard's pseudonymous writers? Write a brief story to illustrate.
2. Argue for one or another of the following theses:
   a. If we could satisfactorily meet people's material needs (whether through communism or in some other way), the sorts of concerns expressed by Kierkegaard would seem merely neurotic symptoms to us and would very likely vanish.
   b. Even if we completely satisfied everyone's material and bodily needs, the spiritual and existential questions that concerned Kierkegaard would be as lively as ever.

Notes

1. T. S. Eliot, *Four Quartets: The Dry Salvages*, V, in *The Complete Poems and Plays 1909–1950* (New York: Harcourt, Brace and Co., 1958), 136.
2. References to the works of Søren Kierkegaard are as follows:
   EO: Either/Or, vols. 1 and 2, trans. Howard V. Hong and Edna H. Hong (Princeton: Princeton University Press, 1987). References in text are to volume numbers and page numbers.
   FT: Fear and Trembling, trans. Howard V. Hong and Edna H. Hong (Princeton: Princeton University Press, 1983).
   SUD: The Sickness Unto Death, trans. Alistair Hannay (London: Penguin Books, 1989).

PF: Philosophical Fragments, trans. Howard V. Hong and Edna H. Hong (Princeton: Princeton University Press, 1985).

CUP: Concluding Unscientific Postscript, trans. David F. Swenson and Walter Lowrie (Princeton: Princeton University Press, 1944).

3. William Blake, "The Marriage of Heaven and Hell," in *William Blake,* ed. J. Bronowski (New York: Penguin Books, 1958), 94.

4. References to the works of Karl Marx are as follows: *GI: The German Ideology,* in *The Marx-Engels Reader,* ed. Robert C. Tucker (New York: W. W. Norton and Co., 1972).

TF: Theses on Feuerbach, in Tucker (ed.), *The Marx-Engels Reader.*

EPM: The Economic and Philosophic Manuscripts of 1844, ed. Dirk J. Struik (New York: International Publishers, 1964).

MCP: Manifesto of the Communist Party (with Friedrich Engels), trans. Samuel Moore (Moscow: Progress Publishers, 1971).

21

The Utilitarians:
Moral Rules and the Happiness of All
(Including Women)

At about the same time that Kant is working out his views on duty and the rational justification of the moral law, a quite different orientation for ethics is being developed in England. The utilitarians, as they come to call themselves, are much more empirical than Kant or Hegel, and in their own way nearly as radical in their critique of society as Marx; however, they advocate reform rather than revolution. They draw on sources in their own English-speaking history, particularly on Hobbes and Hume, but develop these themes in a quite distinctive fashion.

The Classic Utilitarians

Two thinkers stand out in connection with **utilitarianism,** though others contribute to the doctrine. Jeremy Bentham (1748–1832) and John Stuart Mill (1806–1873) together set out its principal tenets, though there are some basic points on which they disagree. We can begin our investigation of this still influential view of morality with a quotation from Mill's little booklet, *Utilitarianism* (1861).

All action is for the sake of some end, and rules of action, it seems natural to suppose, must take their whole character and color from the end to which they are subservient. When we engage in a pursuit, a

clear and precise conception of what we are pursuing would seem to be the first thing we need. (*U, 2*)[1]

Note the *teleological* orientation here.* Suppose I want to know what I ought to do, or what would be the right thing to do. Since everything I do is intended to accomplish something—that is, is "for the sake of some end"—it seems sensible to pay attention to that end. Mill suggests that the end in fact determines whether what I do is the morally right thing. The consequences of my action fix its rightness and wrongness.†

But what consequences do we look to? Every act always has many, many consequences. Which of them are morally relevant? Bentham and Mill answer this question by claiming that in everything we do, no matter what the particular end, we are aiming at a single thing: happiness. But does this help? Aristotle has already noted that people disagree widely over what happiness is.‡ If happiness means one thing to Jones and another to Smith, how will it help to note that all their actions are aiming at happiness?

---

*You may recall that this word comes from the Greek *telos,* meaning "end" or "goal." Something is teleological if it points to an outcome. See the earlier discussion on p. 159. See also pp. 174–175.
†Consequences are precisely what Kant says morality must *not* be concerned with. For Kant, the morally relevant facts concern only a person's intention: does the individual act out of *duty,* out of respect for the moral law. Consequences are completely irrelevant to morality. See p. 403.
‡See pp. 174–176.

Bentham and Mill are convinced, however, that this variability is only superficial; at its core, happiness is everywhere alike. As Bentham puts it,

> Nature has placed mankind under the governance of two sovereign masters, *pain* and *pleasure*. It is for them alone to point out what we ought to do, as well as to determine what we shall do. On the one hand the standard of right and wrong, on the other the chain of causes and effects, are fastened to their throne. They govern us in all we do, in all we say, in all we think: every effort we can make to throw off our subjection, will serve but to demonstrate and confirm it. (*PML*, 1)[2]

Our goal in whatever we do, Bentham says, is to avoid pain and to secure pleasure. And that is what happiness is.* Note that Bentham here makes two distinct claims. The first is a thesis about motivation; this is a psychological thesis, proposing that considerations of pain and pleasure always determine our actions. This psychological or causal thesis has a name: *psychological hedonism*.[†]

The second is an ethical or moral thesis, which holds that right and wrong are tied to pleasure and pain. That is, in judging the moral rightness of an action, we must consider the pleasure and pain that action produces. This claim is called *ethical hedonism*. As you can see, it is distinct from the former; it is a claim, not about what we in fact do, but about what we ought to do. It is in these terms that Bentham and Mill formulate the principle of utility.

> By the principle of utility is meant that principle which approves or disapproves of every action whatsoever, according to the tendency which it appears to have to augment or diminish the happiness of the party whose interest is in question: or what is the same thing in other words, to promote or oppose that happiness. (*PML*, 2)

So far this doesn't have a moral ring to it. If the "party whose interest is in question" is I, then I fol-

"The happiness which forms the utilitarian standard of what is right in conduct is not the agent's own happiness, but that of all concerned." —JOHN STUART MILL

low this principle in doing what will make me happy, that is, what will provide me the greatest proportion of pleasure over pain. That may be prudent, but not, it seems, especially moral. It doesn't seem to have that peculiar moral *bite*; after all, pursuing my own interests may sometimes be held to be wrong. The utilitarians, however, give the principle of utility a moral character by insisting that what is ethically relevant is not my happiness or yours, but happiness itself. In this form it is sometimes also called the greatest happiness principle and is summed up in the slogan "The greatest happiness for the greatest number." So the utilitarian standard, as Mill tells us,

> is not the agent's own greatest happiness, but the greatest amount of happiness altogether. (*U*, 11)

---

* This is what Hobbes calls "felicity." See p. 340.

[†] The term "hedonism" is discussed on p. 187.

Suppose you are facing a choice between actions and wondering what, morally speaking, you ought to do. Here is what the utilitarian advises. Estimate how much total pleasure and pain each alternative action will produce for you and everyone concerned. The action that produces the best pleasure/pain ratio overall is the one you ought to perform. Note that it is not more important that *you* should be happy as a result of your action than other people. But neither is it less important. The utilitarian principle is an *impartial* principle. The happiness of each is to be weighed equally.

It is of great importance to see that the utilitarians were not thinking just of private actions by individual citizens. They were one and all active in politics, in the reform of law, and in trying to produce better legislation. The principle of utility was to function not just as a moral guide, but as a tool of social criticism and reform. In the early nineteenth century many felt that the law in England was a mess—a tangled skein of contradictory precedents originating in forms of society very different from the one in which these thinkers were living. The law seemed designed chiefly to secure a livelihood for the lawyers.* All the utilitarians, Bentham in particular, used the principle of utility to criticize this maze by asking, Does this law, this institution, this way of doing things contribute to happiness or misery? This tool was sufficiently sharp to earn them the appellation "philosophical radicals." In the name of general happiness, they demanded parliamentary reform, prison reform, the extension of the right to vote, full legal rights for women, greater democracy, ways of making government officials accountable, changes in punishments, and so on. The principle of utility is a sharp tool for reformers; it can pinpoint social evils and suggest remedies.

But how is this tool to be used? Bentham believes that one of the great advantages of the principle of utility is the detail and precision of thought it makes possible in these moral and political issues. In fact, he tries to work out something like a calculus of pleasures and pains, so that one can simply *calculate* the right thing to do by taking into account the various amounts of happiness each alternate course of action or law would produce. Though Mill and other utilitarians have doubts about how strictly this method can work, a brief glance will help us get an understanding of the movement.

One part of Bentham's project is to list the various kinds of pleasures and pains that need to be taken into account. There are a great many; among the pleasures are those of sense, wealth, skill, a good name, piety, power, memory, and so on. Among the pains are those of privation, the senses, awkwardness, a bad name, memory, expectation, and so on. Each of these is explained in sufficient degree, Bentham thinks, so that it can be recognized and taken account of by the judge, the legislator, or the private citizen in dealing with other persons.

But in considering any given pleasure, we see that it differs in several ways from another pleasure of the same kind; the same is true of pains. Pleasures and pains differ in:

- *Intensity* (some toothaches hurt worse than others)
- *Duration* (some last longer)
- *Certainty* or *uncertainty* (some are avoidable, others not)
- *Propinquity* or *remoteness* (some are expected tomorrow, others not for several years)
- *Fecundity* (some pleasures or pains bring further pleasures or pains in their wake; others do not)
- *Purity* (if a pleasures does *not* bring pains along with it, it is "pure")
- *Extent* (how many people are affected by it)

You can see how these considerations might be brought to bear on a practical problem. A more intense pleasure is preferable to one less intense. The longer pains last and the more people they affect, the worse they are judged to be. So if a law will produce quite intense pleasure for a few

---

*Charles Dickens details the terrible effects of interminable suits dragging through the courts in his novel *Bleak House*.

people but condemn a great many to pains of long duration, it is sure to be a very bad law. That law should not be passed. Actual cases are usually more complicated, but this gives the basic idea.

The utilitarians believe that legislation and moral judgment alike can approximate a science. Given the principle of utility and these rules, one should not have to *guess* which law or action is best; one can *discover* it. These thinkers assume that pleasure can be quantified; if this assumption is correct, the legislator or moral agent need only add up the sums to arrive at the right answer. Bentham allows that it may be difficult or too time consuming to engage in this deliberation before every decision. But, he says, it should be kept in view; the closer we can come to it, the more exactly correct our choices will be.

But can pleasures and pains be quantified in this exact way? Here is a point on which Mill differs from Bentham.* Though full of admiration for the older man, Mill says that Bentham is like a "one-eyed man," who sees clearly and far, but very narrowly.[3] To Bentham, pleasure is pleasure, and that's the end of it. In a famous line, Bentham declares that "quantity of pleasure being equal, push-pin [a children's game] is as good as poetry."[4] But Mill thinks this is obviously not true. Some pleasures are worth more than others, even if the *amount* of pleasure in each is the same (supposing that one can determine this). Pleasures, he wants to say, differ not only in quantity, but also in quality.

> It is quite compatible with the principle of utility to recognize the fact that some kinds of pleasure are more desirable and more valuable than others. It would be quite absurd that, while in estimating all other things quality is considered as well as quantity, the estimation of pleasure should be supposed to depend on quantity alone. (*U*, 8)

This may well be right, but it raises two problems. First, it seems to undermine Bentham's claim that legislation and morality might be made scientific. For even if you agree that one could compare *amounts* of pleasure and pain to add up the quantities produced, it seems hard to imagine that *qualities* are likewise quantifiable. If they were, they would just be quantities again, and we would be back with Bentham. The second problem is whether there is any way to *tell* which pleasures are more desirable. To this question Mill has an answer.

> Of two pleasures, if there be one to which all or almost all who have experience of both give a decided preference, irrespective of any feeling of moral obligation to prefer it, that is the more desirable pleasure. (*U*, 8)

Consult the person of experience, Mill tells us: someone who has tried both. Setting aside moral considerations, that person's preference is a sign that one exceeds the other in quality and is more desirable.*

But, you might object, is there any reason to think that people will agree about which pleasure is better? Suppose we take a survey of those who have experienced each of two kinds of pleasure—a day in an amusement park, let us say, and a day spent reading poetry. Do you think we will find anything approaching unanimity? And if we don't, how are we going to take the principle of utility as a practical rule to make decisions? We are supposed to maximize happiness; but if happiness varies so much among individuals, how are we going to decide whether to build more amusement parks or more libraries?

> From this verdict of the only competent judges, I apprehend there can be no appeal. On a question which is the best worth having of two pleasures, or which of two modes of existence is the most grateful

---

* To understand why, it helps to know something of Mill's life. You may enjoy Mill's very readable *Autobiography,* in which he recounts his childhood and remarkable education at the hands of his father, his nervous breakdown and the cure of it, and his twenty-year Platonic love of Harriet Taylor, who became his wife only after the death of her husband. Mill's active involvement with the intellectual and political movements of the day are also detailed.

*We have to set moral consideration aside in making this judgment, lest we beg the question. After all, we are trying to discover where the greatest happiness lies precisely in order to determine what our moral obligations are!

to the feelings, . . . the judgment of those who are qualified by knowledge of both, or if they differ, that of the majority among them, must be admitted as final. (*U*, 11)

So, Mill tells us, democratic politics is the way to make this decision. In fact, he thinks there will be a large measure of agreement because of the similarities among people. But where there are differences, the majority must rule. In personal decisions, of course, this complication is often lacking; we may know quite well the pleasures and preferences of all those concerned, and then it is relatively simple to determine the right thing to do. We should (1) try to foresee the consequences of each action open to us, (2) compare the total happiness produced by each, and (3) choose the one that produces the most happiness overall (understood as pleasure in this qualitative sense).

A key concept of utilitarian moral philosophy is its *consequentialism:* that actions are sorted into the morally acceptable and the morally unacceptable by virtue of their consequences. The early utilitarians identify as relevant the consequences bearing on happiness, understanding happiness to be pleasure and the absence of pain. Utilitarians in our century, while preserving the consequentialism, have sometimes looked to other features than pleasure to justify moral judgments.*

Suppose we ask whether the principle of utility is the right one to use in making a choice. Is it, as the utilitarians hold, the criterion for the morally right? It is not the only option available, as we already know. Aristotle would ask whether the action contributes to our excellence (virtue) as an instance of the human species. Jesus, Saint Paul, and Augustine would have us ask whether what we propose to do is in accord with the will of God. Kant would urge us to submit the maxim of our action to the test of universalization. And Hegel

would presumably have us look to the standards present in our current cultural situation.* Is there anything the utilitarian can say that should convince us that the principle of utility is what Kant said he was searching for: the "supreme principle of morality"?†

Both Bentham and Mill address this question. Both insist that since the principle of utility is held to be the *first* principle of morality, it is not subject to ordinary kinds of proof. Nonetheless, each thinks he can provide arguments to convince us. Let us examine them in turn.

Bentham believes we will be converted to utilitarianism if we just consider the alternatives to it. There are only two, he thinks, though these two may appear in various versions and disguises. The clearest opposite to the principle of utility is what he calls the principle of asceticism. An adherent of this principle would judge many actions to be right that involve a denial of pleasure for themselves and, perhaps, for others. An ancient Stoic, who holds virtue to be the only good, may be an example.‡ Others (e.g., certain religious ascetics) may judge an actual increase of pain to be right, at least for oneself. Luther in the monastery beating himself for his sins is a vivid illustration.

Bentham has two arguments against the principle of asceticism. First, it is never applied consistently. A monk does not torture himself because he thinks it is good in itself, but because he judges it necessary to gain the incomparable pleasures of heavenly bliss. Thus, he bears witness against his will to the principle of utility. The Stoics, according to Bentham, see correctly that some pleasures are sources of pain but generalize hastily to the unwarranted claim that pleasures as such are never good. Nonetheless, they praise the virtues, which in Bentham's eyes are nothing more than producers of pleasure without the accompanying pains. So Bentham thinks the Stoics, too, reject utility inconsistently.

---

*G. E. Moore, for instance, holds that a certain quality of *goodness* is what the moralist is to look to; while pleasure is one good thing, he says, there are numerous other goods not reducible to pleasure, such as knowledge. R. M. Hare takes as fundamental what people *prefer;* whether that is always a matter of pleasure is an open question.

---

* See pp. 175–177 (Aristotle); p. 209 (Jesus); pp. 241–242 (Augustine); p. 406 (Kant); and pp. 433–434 (Hegel).
† See p. 402.
‡ See p. 195.

Second, asceticism has never been applied to government. Even if one thought it would be good to minimize one's own pleasures, or perhaps to increase one's pains, no legislator has ever consciously aimed at stocking the body politic with highwaymen, housebreakers, or arsonists. And if through negligence and ignorance the misery of the populace increases, the government that allows it is justifiably criticized.

Basically, Bentham argues that the ascetic principle cannot be consistently pursued.

> The principle of utility is capable of being consistently pursued; and it is but tautology to say, that the more consistently it is pursued, the better it must ever be for humankind. The principle of ascetism never was, nor ever can be, consistently pursued by any living creature. Let but one tenth part of the inhabitants of the earth pursue it consistently, and in a day's time they will have turned it into a hell. (*PML,* 13)

The other alternative to utility Bentham calls the principle of sympathy and antipathy. Most of the other claimants to the title of moral criterion reduce, he thinks, to this.

> . . . I mean that principle which approves or disapproves of certain actions, not on account of their tending to augment the happiness, nor yet on account of their tending to diminish the happiness of the party whose interest is in question, but merely because a man finds himself disposed to approve or disapprove of them. (*PML,* 15–16)

In a way, Bentham remarks, this is not a principle, but the denial that a principle is needed. All that is required is a sentiment of approval or disapproval on the part of the moral agent. Though such judgments may often coincide with judgments of utility, they need not. People, of course, seldom are content simply to say that an action is right because they approve of it. So they cloak their decisions in fine words. They attribute their approvals and disapprovals to common sense, to a special moral sense, to understanding, to the law of nature, to reason, to good order, to the voice of God,

and more. But all such appeals come down in the final analysis to what the individual in question approves or disapproves. And this seems to Bentham excessively arbitrary.

Bentham ends this defense of utility with a rhetorical flourish. Suppose you say, "This is morally right; I know it is, though I do not know whether it will bring happiness or misery; moreover, I don't care." Bentham asks you to assume it will bring misery. Then he urges you to bring that misery clearly before your mind, to feel it, become sensible of it. Can you still, in the face of that fact, persist in your conviction that to do it is the right thing? (To do the experiment right, of course, it is important that we not imagine that the misery is a means to some further happiness. It must be misery as an end. That, Bentham thinks, none of us can persist in calling right.)

Mill adds arguments of his own. Though he agrees that questions of ultimate ends do not admit of proof, he thinks convincing considerations can be brought forward. Among these considerations, unfortunately, are two arguments that nearly all subsequent philosophers have held to be remarkably poor. They are famous (perhaps even infamous) for that reason alone. We'll examine them briefly.

> The only proof capable of being given that an object is visible is that people actually see it. The only proof that a sound is audible is that people hear it; and so of the other sources of our experience. In like manner, I apprehend, the sole evidence it is possible to produce that anything is desirable is that people do actually desire it. (*U,* 34)

What Mill needs to show is that the general happiness is desirable, that it is what we ought to strive for. But his analogies do not work. "Visible" means "can be seen," and "audible" means "can be heard." But "desirable" is not parallel. It does not mean "can be desired," but "should be desired." So the fact that something is desired (even if that something be the greatest happiness of the greatest number) doesn't mean it *ought* to be desired.

Mill's second argument is no better. The conclusion he needs to support is that each of us, you and I, should (morally speaking) take the general happiness as our end; when we act, that is what we ought to be trying to bring about. He argues that

> happiness is a good, that each person's happiness is a good to that person, and the general happiness, therefore, a good to the aggregate of all persons. (*U*, 34)

We can, perhaps, grant the premises of this argument: that happiness is a good and that for each person that person's own happiness is a good to that person. But all that follows from this premise is that each person's happiness is a good to *someone*. It does not follow that *your* happiness is a good to *me*, just because my own is. Each and every bit of the general happiness is a good to some person; but it may not be, for all the premises tell us, that the general happiness is a good to everyone—that it is what *each* of us ought to pursue. Yet that is what the principle of utility claims.*

But how important are these errors? Both Bentham and Mill, after all, admit that their first principle cannot be proved. Perhaps, then, it is a mistake to try to prove it. We may feel that their consequentialist morality is pointing to something important, even if it cannot be proved correct. The lack of proof does leave open the possibility that there is more to morality than utility. But it may be hard to deny that utility plays an important role.

Let us set aside this attempt at a positive proof and look at another kind of defense of the utilitarian creed. Mill considers various sorts of objections to it and tries to show that they all rest on misunderstandings. It is worth reviewing some of those objections; we will gain a clearer view of the utility principle by seeing what it does *not* mean.

1. Some accuse utilitarians, especially utilitarians who set pleasure as the good, of aiming too low. It is the old objection aimed already at the Epicureans. Since pleasure and pain are something we share with the animals, to make these the standard of right and wrong is to espouse a philosophy for pigs.* To this Mill replies that human beings, having higher faculties than pigs, require more to make them happy; but their happiness is still just pleasure and their unhappiness pain. In this connection Mill pens a famous line.

> It is better to be a human being dissatisfied than a pig satisfied; better to be a Socrates dissatisfied than a fool satisfied. And if the fool, or the pig, are of a different opinion, it is because they only know their own side of the question. (*U*, 10)

2. Some hold that the utilitarian standard is unrealizable. Is it possible that everyone should be happy? First, Mill replies, even if that were impossible, the principle of utility would still be valid. We can do much to minimize unhappiness, even if we cannot attain its opposite. Second, it is an exaggeration to say that happiness—even the general happiness—is impossible. The happiness that utilitarians favor is not, after all, a life of constant rapture, but

> moments of such, in an existence made up of few and transitory pains, many and various pleasures, with a decided predominance of the active over the passive, and having as the foundation of the whole not to expect more from life than it is capable of bestowing. (*U*, 13)

He believes that even now a great many people live this way. If it were not for the "wretched education and wretched social arrangements" prevailing in his society, he thinks, such a life would be attainable by almost all. And he adds,

> When people who are tolerably fortunate in their outward lot do not find in life sufficient enjoyment to make it valuable to them, the cause generally is caring for nobody but themselves. (*U*, 13)

This point is actually so important to Mill that it is a little surprising he doesn't make more of it in

---

*Logicians have a name for this kind of mistake. They call it a *fallacy of composition*, since what applies to every part is erroneously applied to the whole.

*See the discussion of Epicurus on pp. 190–191. You might also look at Aristotle's remark about pleasure on p. 175.

Utilitarianism. In his *Autobiography,* Mill tells us about a period of severe depression that he suffered in his early twenties. He came out of it, he says, with a new certainty.

> I never, indeed, wavered in the conviction that happiness is the test of all rules of conduct, and the end of life. But I now thought that this end was only to be attained by not making it the direct end. Those only are happy (I thought) who have their minds fixed on some object other than their own happiness; on the happiness of others, on the improvement of mankind, even on some pursuit, followed not as a means, but as itself an ideal end. Aiming thus at something else, they find happiness by the way. The enjoyments of life (such was now my theory) are sufficient to make it a pleasant thing, when they are taken *en passant,* without being made a principal object. Once make them so, and they are immediately felt to be insufficient. They will not bear a scrutinizing examination. Ask yourself whether you are happy, and you cease to be so. The only chance is to treat, not happiness, but some end external to it, as the purpose of life. . . . This theory now became the basis of my philosophy of life.[5]

If this is Mill's considered view, it must make quite a difference when we try to estimate the happiness that our actions produce. For if we cannot ensure our own happiness by aiming directly at it, we cannot produce the happiness of others in any direct way, either. At least when thinking about other people's lives as a whole, the most we may be able to do is to produce conditions in which people can work toward their own "ideal ends."*

3. Some critics object that in making happiness the end, utilitarians undercut the most noble motives and the most admirable character. Do we not, they ask, admire the individual who is willing to sacrifice personal happiness? Wouldn't this human virtue be destroyed if we all became happiness seekers?

Mill admits that we admire those who give up their personal happiness for the sake of something they prize even more. But what do they renounce their happiness *for?*

> . . . after all, this self-sacrifice must be for some end; it is not its own end; and if we are told that its end is not happiness but virtue, which is better than happiness, I ask, would the sacrifice be made if the hero or martyr did not believe that it would earn for others immunity from similar sacrifices? . . . All honor to those who can abnegate for themselves the personal enjoyment of life when by such renunciation they contribute worthily to increase the amount of happiness in the world; but he who does it or professes to do it for any other purpose is no more deserving of admiration than the ascetic mounted on his pillar. (*U,* 15–16)

Utilitarians, Mill says, can admire such self-sacrifice as much as any. They only refuse to recognize that it is good in itself. It is admirable only if it tends to increase the total amount of happiness in the world. And that is exactly what the principle of utility urges.

4. Other critics object that it is asking too much of people to aim at general happiness in all their actions. You can think of this as the opposite of the first objection; instead of holding that the standard is too low, some claim it is impossibly high.

To this Mill replies that it is the business of ethics to tell us what our duties are, what is right and what is wrong. But ethics does not go as far as to require that everything we do should be done from a certain *motive.** From a utilitarian point of view, the rightness of an action is judged by what it brings about; why the agent acted in that way is irrelevant. Mill gives an example.

> He who saves a fellow creature from drowning does what is morally right, whether his motive be duty or the hope of being paid for his trouble. (*U,* 18)

---

* Mill's point that happiness is a by-product of other aims, strivings, and successes is one that utilitarians often neglect. If taken seriously, this point would to some extent reconcile the differences between utilitarians and those who (like Kant, Aristotle, and the Stoics) stress virtue as the key to ethics.

* This is exactly what Kant thinks morality does require; that every morally right action be one that is done out of duty, from respect for the moral law. Actions done out of mere inclination are not worth anything, morally speaking. See pp. 403–405.

Does this make ethics seem altogether *too external*? Are people's motives really that irrelevant to what is right and wrong? In a footnote added in response to criticism of that sort, Mill allows that our estimate of the *agent* may vary, depending on whether he saved the drowning person out of duty or greed. In the latter case, we will think less of the man and be less likely to trust him in similar circumstances. But, Mill insists, we must allow that, for whatever motive, the right thing was done.

5.   The above objection easily turns into another. It would seem that utilitarianism

> renders men cold and unsympathizing; that it chills their moral feelings toward individuals; that it makes them regard only the dry and hard consideration of the consequences of actions, not taking into their moral estimate the qualities from which those actions emanate. (*U,* 19)

Here Mill reiterates that we have to distinguish *actions* as good or bad from *persons* as good or bad. It is possible, of course, that a good person occasionally performs a morally bad action, just as a really bad person may do a good thing. And though some utilitarians may stress the moral estimation of action almost to the exclusion of "the other beauties of character which go toward making a human being lovable or admirable" (*U,* 20)—Mill is surely thinking of Bentham here—utilitarianism itself does not forbid valuing character. Moreover, although goodness of character and the rightness of action do not always coincide, "in the long run the best proof of a good character is good actions" (*U,* 20). So utilitarianism need have no chilling effect on us.

6.   To the objection that utilitarianism, which counts only worldly happiness as the mark of moral rightness, is a "godless" doctrine, Mill replies that it all depends on how you think of God.

> If it be a true belief that God desires, above all things, the happiness of his creatures, and that this was his purpose in their creation, utility is not only not a godless doctrine, but more profoundly religious than any other. (*U,* 21)

7.   The last objection we will consider is that the principle of utility is impractical. It requires something there is usually no time to do. Very often we are called upon to act quickly in making a choice; there is no time to do the exhaustive calculations required to determine the consequences of all the alternatives available. To this Mill has a very interesting reply.

> This is exactly as if anyone were to say that it is impossible to guide our conduct by Christianity because there is not time, on every occasion on which anything has to be done, to read through the Old and New Testaments. The answer to the objection is that there has been ample time, namely the whole past duration of the human species. During all that time mankind have been learning by experience the tendencies of actions. (*U,* 23)

The fact that utility functions as a first principle does not in any way rule out secondary principles. These intermediate generalizations, Mill holds, are readily available to us in the common wisdom of our culture and in the law. We do not need to calculate each time whether *this* murder would be all right, or whether *that* lie would be justified, or whether making *this* contribution to the relief of the homeless fits with the first principle. We learn the basic moral rules as children. Such secondary rules may be subject to gradual improvement. They may be more and more perfectly adapted to produce happiness. There may be occasional exceptions to them, too; but a *moral* justification for an exception must be decided by appeal to utility.

> Nobody argues that the art of navigation is not founded on astronomy because sailors cannot wait to calculate the Nautical Almanac. Being rational creatures, they go to sea with it ready calculated; and all rational creatures go out upon the sea of life with their minds made up on the common questions of right and wrong. (*U,* 24)

It is indeed not possible to calculate the utility of each of our actions on the occasion of their performance. But we don't need to. We cannot do without secondary rules in society, which can be learned and relied upon. But these can be improved only by bringing them more closely in line with the first principle: utility. For Mill, Bentham's great value lies in his attempt to improve these subordinate principles, particularly in social institutions and the law.

Let us round out our discussion of utilitarianism by considering a problem Mill addresses that seems unresolved to this day. Can the principle of utility function as the *sole* principle of an acceptable morality? The problem concerns justice. Can the demands of justice be incorporated into the utilitarian framework? Or is justice something different, something that resists the calculation of consequences?

It is easy to dream up cases where there is at least the appearance of conflict between justice and utility. Executing an innocent person may, in certain circumstances, quell a riot and prevent the death of hundreds. It is clear that to execute the innocent is *unjust*. Yet a utility calculation seems to tell us that in this circumstance executing the person is the morally right thing to do, since it would produce more pleasure and less pain overall.* So it seems there is a clash between the claims of justice and the claims of utility. In circumstances like this, justice tells us one thing, utility another. Mill tries to argue that this clash is merely apparent and that justice rightly understood can be seen to be a special case of utility. If his argument is successful, justice and utility are reconciled.

Mill allows that the subjective feeling attached to judgments about justice is different from, and stronger than, the feeling about utility. We think it is a more serious business to violate justice than simply to fail to bring about as much happiness as we can. Why? Because, Mill believes, justice is associated with *rights*. It is unjust, for instance, to violate someone's *legal* right. Or at least it is usually

unjust to do so; there may be bad laws that provide persons with legal rights they *ought* not to have. Perhaps it is not unjust to violate a legal right of that sort, but cases like that are exceptional.

This leads to the notion of *moral* rights—rights that laws ought to protect but sometimes may not. A person may have a moral right even in the absence of any legal protection. Injustice, then, is taking or withholding from someone something to which that person has a moral right. When injustice is done, we have a natural reaction: resentment. And we very much want the perpetrator of injustice to be punished. To be sure, we may punish other acts; but we feel that punishment is particularly appropriate when someone's moral rights have been violated.

> When we call anything a person's right, we mean that he has a valid claim on society to protect him in the possession of it. (*U*, 52)

If I have a right to something, I have a "valid claim" on society to protect me by threatening to punish anyone who violates this right. That is what it is to have a right. But this leaves Mill with further problems. What is the origin of such rights? Are such rights compatible with the principle of utility? And on what grounds can I claim that society owes me such protection?

Mill argues that no reason other than general utility can be given, and none is needed. One part of utility is so basic, so fundamental to our happiness, that without it everything else is in jeopardy: security.

> All other earthly benefits are needed by one person, not needed by another; and many of them can, if necessary, be cheerfully foregone or replaced by something else; but security no human being can possibly do without; on it we depend for all our immunity from evil and for the whole value of all and every good, beyond the passing moment, since nothing but the gratification of the instant could be of any worth to us if we could be deprived of everything the next instant by whoever was momentarily stronger than ourselves. (*U*, 53)

---

*Discussion of such cases has made it clear that from a utilitarian standpoint, it is not so easy to be sure that the circumstances justifying an innocent person's execution ever exist. For instance, we would have to be virtually certain that the fact of the person's innocence would never be known, lest even worse events ensue. And could we ever be certain enough of that?

Security, being safe in our persons and possessions, is the "most indispensable of all necessaries," Mill says (*U*, 53).* And because it is so basic to our happiness, the feelings that attach to its protection are particularly strong. That is why it may *seem* that justice is different from utility. But far from being different from utility, let alone opposed to it, justice is its deepest and most fundamental form.

> I account the justice which is grounded on utility to be the chief part, and incomparably the most sacred and binding part, of all morality. Justice is a name for certain classes of moral rules which concern the essentials of human well-being more nearly, and are therefore of more absolute obligation, than any other rules for the guidance of life; and the notion which we have found to be of the essence of the idea of justice—that of a right residing in an individual—implies and testifies to this more binding obligation. . . . a person may possibly not need the benefits of others, but he always needs that they should not do him hurt. (*U*, 58)

In this way Mill argues there is no conflict between justice and utility. If we return to our example of executing an innocent man for the sake of avoiding a riot, we can see what Mill would say. It is unjust to take his life, so it ought not to be done. To acquiesce in the violation of that man's security imperils the security of us all. And that none of us will tolerate.† The appearance of conflict can be overcome if we reflect that justice is the name we give to the deepest condition for securing our happiness.

_____

*You would be right to hear echoes of Hobbes here. See Hobbes on the deplorable "state of nature" in which no one can feel safe (pp. 340–342).

†Critics of utilitarianism will push the point, however, that it is *possible*—however unlikely—that such an execution will actually increase the general happiness. And if one *could* be sure that the circumstances were right, then utility *would* prescribe the execution. Since this could in no case be a just act, there is in principle an unresolved conflict between justice and utility, and Mill's attempt at reconciliation fails. The principle of justice must have other, independent grounds—perhaps in something like the Kantian imperative that one is never to use a person as a means to an end. See again Kant's discussion of this on p. 407.

Bentham and Mill, together with utilitarians to the present day, urge that there is only one way to decide the morally right thing to do. Think about the consequences of all the actions open to you, estimate (if you can't literally calculate) the effect each action would have on the happiness of all the persons affected (or on the goodness of their lives, or on what they would prefer), and the right thing will become apparent. What remains is simply to do it.

_____

The Rights of Women

By the time Mill wrote *The Subjection of Women* in 1869, slavery had been abolished in the United States and, indeed, in most of the world. But one form of bondage, Mill said, remained: that in which half the world's population, the female half, was still held. Our situation today is so much changed from the circumstances in which Mill wrote (though it may still be far from ideal), that we need to exert our imaginations to grasp the "Woman Question," as it was then known. Together with Mill's little book, we will consider an earlier work by Mary Wollstonecraft, *A Vindication of the Rights of Women* (1792). Wollstonecraft is not clearly a utilitarian, though much of what she writes is in the same spirit.* Mill and Wollstonecraft take a similar view of the "Woman Question," and they recommend similar remedies.[6]

Writing in 1869, Mill reminds us of the state of English law concerning women. (It was scarcely better anywhere else.) Society assumed that women generally would marry, and most did. For this reason, the laws concerning marriage were the crucial ones. Here is what those laws held (*SW*, 246–49):

_____

*Bentham had published *Introduction to the Principles of Morals and Legislation* just three years earlier, in 1789. Wollstonecraft's arguments vary. There are consequentialist arguments of a utilitarian cast, appeals to reason as the arbiter of morality, claims about what is suitable for an individual destined for immortality, and arguments from justice and the will of God. Even though it is a bit hard to find any theoretical unity in the essay, there is no denying its power.

- A married woman can have no property except in her husband; anything she inherits immediately becomes his.
- There is a way for a woman to secure "her" property from her husband, but even so she is not allowed the use of it; if he by violence takes it from her, he can not be punished or compelled to return it to her.
- Husband and wife are called "one person in law," but that means only that whatever is hers is his (not vice versa).
- Her children are by law *his* children. She can do nothing with them except by his delegation. On his death she does not become their legal guardian, unless he by will makes her so.
- If she leaves her husband, she can take nothing with her, not even her children. He can—by force, if it comes to that—compel her to return.

And, of course, women were excluded from voting, from running for Parliament, and (at least by custom) from nearly all nondomestic professions. Mill considers the question of why this should be so. Is it, he asks, because society has experimented with alternative social arrangements and discovered that, all in all, this is best? Of course not. The adoption of this system

> *"Let there be then no coercion established in society, and the common law of gravity prevailing, the sexes will fall into their proper places."* —MARY WOLLSTONECRAFT

> never was the result of deliberation, or forethought, or any social ideal, or any notion whatever of what conduced to the benefit or humanity or the good order of society. It arose simply from the fact that from the very earliest twilight of human society, every woman (owing to the value attached to her by men, combined with her inferiority in muscular strength) was found in a state of bondage to some man. (*SW,* 223)

Mill stresses that the situation which is now sanctioned by law was simply the situation which was actually in place when laws were first written. This amounts to an adoption of *the law of the strongest*, a law that led to kingship and slavery as well as to the subjection of women. So the fact that the subjection of women has been a custom nearly everywhere for ages is no more an argument in its favor than is a similar argument in support of absolute monarchy or slavery—both of which have been done away with in the modern world.

Moreover, it is not hard to explain why this custom has outlasted monarchy and slavery. Each of these had the attractions of power; the same is true of the relation between women and men. But there is an important difference.

> Whatever gratification of pride there is in the possession of this power, and whatever personal interest in its exercise, is in this case not confined to a limited class, but common to the whole male sex. . . . It comes home to the person and hearth of every male head of a family, and of everyone who looks forward to being so. The clodhopper exercises, or is to exercise, his share of the power equally with the highest nobleman. And the case is that in which the desire of power is the strongest: for everyone who desires

power, desires it most over those who are nearest him, with whom his life is passed, with whom he has most concerns in common, and in whom any independence of his authority is oftenest likely to interfere with his individual preferences. . . . We must consider, too, that the possessors of the power have facilities in this case, greater than in any other, to prevent any uprising against it. Every one of the subjects lives under the very eye, and almost, it may be said, in the hands, of one of the masters—in closer intimacy with him than with any of her fellow-subjects; with no means of combining against him, and, on the other hand, with the strongest motives for seeking his favour and avoiding to give him offence. (*SW*, 228)

The fact that women don't complain about this inequality might constitute an argument in its favor; women consent to it, it is said, and even contribute to its continuance. But Mill notes several things: (1) Some women do complain. (2) The common pattern is that those subjected to power of an ancient origin begin by complaining not about the power itself, but only about its abuse; and there is plenty of complaint by women about their husbands' ill use of them. But most importantly, (3)

Men do not want solely the obedience of women, they want their sentiments. All men, except the most brutish, desire to have, in the woman most nearly connected with them, not a forced slave but a willing one, not a slave merely, but a favourite. They have therefore put everything in practice to enslave their minds. The masters of all other slaves rely, for maintaining obedience, on fear, either fear of themselves, or religious fears. The masters of women wanted more than simple obedience, and they turned the whole force of education to effect their purpose. (*SW*, 232)

To us, this may sound exaggerated. But Wollstonecraft cites passages from popular books about how to bring up young women that suggest this is no exaggeration. Let's look at some of her evidence.

The theme running through the popular literature is that a woman exists for the sake of a man.

The female ideal is sketched with that in mind; a woman's virtues are different from a man's because of that, and a woman's daily life is oriented to that end. One of Wollstonecraft's sources is *Émile,* an influential book on education by Jean-Jacques Rousseau, a philosopher of note in his own right. Here is Rousseau on the education of women. (I cite Wollstonecraft's quotations from Rousseau at some length to stimulate the imagination we need to recreate the situation of the time.)

"It being once demonstrated that man and woman are not, nor ought to be, constituted alike in temperament and character, it follows, of course, that they should not be educated in the same manner. . . .

"Woman and man were made for each other, but their mutual dependence is not the same. The men depend on the women only on account of their desires; the women on the men both on account of their desires and their necessities. We could subsist better without them than they without us. . . .

"For this reason the education of women should be always relative to the men. To please, to be useful to us, to make us love and esteem them, to educate us when young, and take care of us when grown up, to advise, to console us, to render our lives easy and agreeable—these are the duties of women at all times, and what they should be taught in their infancy. . . .

"Boys love sports of noise and activity; to beat the drum, to whip the top, and to drag about their little carts; girls, on the other hand, are fonder of things of show and ornament; such as mirrors, trinkets, and dolls: the doll is the peculiar amusement of the females; from whence we see their taste plainly adapted to their destination. . . . And, in fact, almost all of them learn with reluctance to read and write; but very readily apply themselves to the use of their needles. They imagine themselves already grown up, and think with pleasure that such qualifications will enable them to decorate themselves. . . .

"Girls . . . should also be early subjected to restraint. This misfortune, if it really be one, is inseparable from their sex; nor do they ever throw it off but to suffer more cruel evils. They must be subject, all their lives, to the most constant and severe restraint, which is that of decorum; it is, therefore, necessary to accustom them early to such confinement, that it may not afterwards cost them too dear; and to the suppression of their caprices, that they may the more readily submit to the will of others. . . .

"There results from this habitual restraint a tractableness which women have occasion for during their whole lives, as they constantly remain either under subjection to the men, or to the opinions of mankind; and are never permitted to set themselves above those opinions. The first and most important qualification in a woman is good nature or sweetness of temper: formed to obey a being so imperfect as man, often full of vices, and always full of faults, she ought to learn betimes even to suffer injustice, and to bear the insults of a husband without complaint; it is not for his sake, but her own, that she should be of a mild disposition. . . .

"Woman has everything against her, as well our faults as her own timidity and weakness; she has nothing in her favour, but her subtility and her beauty. Is it not very reasonable, therefore, she should cultivate both? . . .

"A man speaks of what he knows, a woman of what pleases her; the one requires knowledge, the other taste; the principal object of a man's discourse should be what is useful, that of a woman's what is agreeable. There ought to be nothing in common between their different conversation but truth.

"We ought not, therefore, to restrain the prattle of girls, in the same manner as we should that of boys, with that severe question, *To what purpose are you talking?* but by another, which is no less difficult to answer, *How will your discourse be received?* In infancy, while they are as yet incapable to discern good from evil, they ought to observe it, as a law never to say anything disagreeable to those whom they are speaking to." (Quoted in *VRW,* 88–95)

There is more to the same effect in Wollstonecraft, quoted from other popular authors of the time. Mill and Wollstonecraft not only agree that this subjection of women to men is unjust, but also argue that it has many bad consequences. Let us examine what they say.

The idea that there are special virtues for a woman, and that these are all oriented around pleasing men, results in morality being very insidiously undermined, in the female world, by the attention being turned to the show instead of the substance. A simple thing is thus made strangely complicated; nay, sometimes virtue and its shadow are set at variance. (*VRW,* 148)

A woman is persuaded to value trivial things: attractiveness, dress, decorum, the short-term pleasures of sex. Thus are women turned toward sensuality and away from understanding.

They who live to please—must find their enjoyments, their happiness, in pleasure! (*VRW,* 129–30)

To satisfy this genus of men, women are made systematically voluptuous, and though they may not all carry their libertinism to the same height, yet this heartless intercourse with the sex, which they allow themselves, depraves both sexes, because the taste of men is vitiated; and women, of all classes, naturally square their behaviour to gratify the taste by which they obtain pleasure and power. (*VRW,* 152)

It is this emphasis on pleasing—and pleasing men particularly—that accounts for the fact that the term "a virtuous woman" has such a narrow connotation. Why should that term direct the mind immediately to sexual behavior, when the term "a virtuous man" does not? Because a woman is regarded as first and foremost a pleaser!

How then can the great art of pleasing be such a necessary study? it is only useful to a mistress. The chaste wife and serious mother should only consider her power to please as the polish of her virtues, and the affection of her husband as one of the comforts that render her task less difficult, and her life happier. But whether she be loved or neglected, her first wish should be to make herself respectable, and not to rely for all her happiness on a being subject to like infirmities with herself. (*VRW,* 32)

Everything is focused on the opinions of others, on how a woman is *regarded.* This constant attention to keep the "varnish" of character fresh often supersedes actual moral obligations. With respect to reputation, Wollstonecraft says,

the attention is confined to a single virtue—chastity. If the honour of a woman, as it is absurdly called, be safe, she may neglect every social duty; nay, ruin her family by gaming and extravagance; yet still present a shameless front—for truly she is an honourable woman! (*VRW,* 150)

Thus the social order makes women worse than they ought to be; this narrow view of their nature gives them the status of secondary beings whose very existence is justifiable only in terms of a relation to another.

> Pleasure is the business of woman's life, according to the present modification of society; and while it continues to be so, little can be expected from such weak beings. Inheriting in a lineal descent from the first fair defect in nature—the sovereignty of beauty—they have, to maintain their power, resigned the natural rights which the exercise of reason might have procured them, and chosen rather to be short-lived queens than labour to obtain the sober pleasures that arise from equality. (*VRW,* 61)

Not much can be expected from such weak beings, Wollstonecraft says. But, of course, they have been deliberately created weak. Mill puts the argument this way:

> All women are brought up from the very earliest years in the belief that their ideal of character is the very opposite to that of men; not self-will, and government by self-control, but submission, and yielding to the control of others. All the moralities tell them that it is the duty of women, and all the current sentimentalities that it is their nature, to live for others; to make complete abnegation of themselves, and to have no life but in their affections. And by their affections are meant the only ones they are allowed to have—those to the men with whom they are connected, or to the children who constitute an additional and indefeasible tie between them and a man. When we put together three things—first, the natural attraction between the sexes; secondly, the wife's entire dependence on the husband, every privilege or pleasure she has being either his gift, or depending entirely on his will; and lastly, that the principal object of human pursuit, consideration, and all objects of social ambition, can in general be sought or obtained by her only through him, it would be a

miracle if the object of being attractive to men had not become the polar star of feminine education and formation of character. And, this great means of influence over the minds of women having been acquired, an instinct of selfishness made men avail themselves of it to the utmost as a means of holding women in subjection, by representing to them meekness, submissiveness, and resignation of all individual will into the hands of a man, as an essential part of sexual attractiveness. (*SW,* 232–33)

Wollstonecraft speaks of women having to resign reason and their natural rights "to maintain their power" (*VRW,* 61). And this leads to further bad consequences. Women become, of necessity, *cunning.*

> Only employed about the little incidents of the day, they necessarily grow up cunning. My very soul has often sickened at observing the sly tricks practised by women to gain some foolish thing on which their silly hearts were set. Not allowed to dispose of money, or call anything their own, they learn to turn the market penny; or, should a husband offend, by staying from home, or give rise to some emotions of jealousy—a new gown, or any pretty bauble, smooths Juno's angry brow.
>
> But these *littlenesses* would not degrade their character, if women were led to respect themselves, if political and moral subjects were opened to them; and, I will venture to affirm that this is the only way to make them properly attentive to their domestic duties. An active mind embraces the whole circle of its duties, and finds time enough for all. (*VRW,* 187)

Thus understanding, strictly speaking, has been denied to woman; and instinct, sublimated into wit and cunning, for the purposes of life, has been substituted in its stead. . . .

I shall not go back to the remote annals of antiquity to trace the history of woman; it is sufficient to allow that she has always been either a slave or a despot, and to remark that each of these situations equally retards the progress of reason. The grand source of female folly and vice has ever appeared to me to arise from narrowness of mind; and the very constitution of civil governments has put almost insuperable obstacles in the way to prevent the cultivation of the female understanding; yet virtue can be built on no other foundation. (*VRW,* 59–60)

On this same narrowness of education another female fault is built: meddlesomeness. Wollstonecraft argues that

> women cannot by force be confined to domestic concerns: for they will, however ignorant, inter-meddle with more weighty affairs, neglecting private duties only to disturb, by cunning tricks, the orderly plans of reason which rise above their comprehension. (VRW, 12)

And Mill adds that men who are considerate of their wives' opinions are often made worse, not better, by the wife's influence.

> She is taught that she has no business with things out of that [domestic] sphere; and accordingly she seldom has any honest and conscientious opinion on them; and therefore hardly ever meddles with them for any legitimate purpose, but generally for an interested one. She neither knows nor cares which is the right side in politics, but she knows what will bring in money or invitations, give her husband a title, her son a place, or her daughter a good marriage. (SW, 255)

Many women do manage to "govern" their husbands, of course. Their weakness and lack of straightforward rationality, however, cause them to do this indirectly, sneakily, with what Rousseau calls "subtility." In fact, Wollstonecraft argues, it is this very weakness that entices women to become tyrants in their families.

> Women are, in fact, so much degraded by mistaken notions of female excellence, that I do not mean to add a paradox when I assert that this artificial weakness produces a propensity to tyrannize, and gives birth to cunning, the natural opponent of strength, which leads them to play off those contemptible infantine airs that undermine esteem even whilst they excite desire. (VRW, 7)

Either women use their beauty, their desirability, to tyrannize men, or they become shrewish. But what is the alternative?

> "Educate women like men," says Rousseau, "and the more they resemble our sex the less power will they have over us." This is the very point I aim at. I do not wish them to have power over men; but over themselves. (VRW, 69)

In this last remark we come near to the heart of the matter. Such, then, are the consequences of restricting the education and dulling the reason of women, of teaching them that their only concern must be to please a man.

What do Wollstonecraft and Mill want for women? Equality with men before the law, independence, freedom to make their own decisions, strength of body, a real education that broadens understanding and doesn't just heighten sensitivity, and the capacity for friendship with men rather than submissive fawning. Wollstonecraft sums it up by declaring that there should be no sexually based virtues. Virtue—moral goodness—is a *human* matter; only evil comes from assuming that there is one virtue for a man and another for a woman, with its corollary that the woman's virtue exists only relative to the man's. True, men and women may to some extent have different duties, but they are one and all, she says, human duties.

> . . . I here throw down my gauntlet, and deny the existence of sexual virtues, not excepting modesty. For man and woman, truth, if I understand the meaning of the word, must be the same. (VRW, 57)

As things are, a woman is denied the independent use of reason and must see everything through her husband's eyes. But the question is, does she have as much capacity for reason and understanding as a man?

> If she have, which, for a moment, I will take for granted, she was not created merely to be the solace of man, and the sexual should not destroy the human character. (VRW, 59)

Very well. But should we take that for granted? How could we tell whether her reason would be as strong as a man's if it were given a chance? Both Mill and Wollstonecraft argue that you can't tell by looking at contemporary society or history, since both are tainted by the corrupting influence of the education and upbringing women have received. The only way to tell is to make the experiment. Wollstonecraft says,

> I have not attempted to extenuate their faults; but to prove them to be the natural consequence of their education and station in society. If so, it is reasonable to suppose that they will change their character, and correct their vices and follies, when they are allowed to be free in a physical, moral, and civil sense.
>
> Let woman share the rights, and she will emulate the virtues of man; for she must grow more perfect when emancipated, or justify the authority that chains such a weak being to her duty. (*VRW*, 214–15)

Mill adds,

> I consider it presumption in anyone to pretend to decide what women are or are not, can or cannot be, by natural constitution. They have always hitherto been kept, as far as regards spontaneous development, in so unnatural a state, that their nature cannot but have been greatly distorted and disguised; and no one can safely pronounce that if women's nature were left to choose its direction as freely as men's, and if no artificial bent were attempted to be given to it except that required by the conditions of human society, and given to both sexes alike, there would be any material difference, or perhaps any difference at all, in the character and capacities which would unfold themselves. (*SW*, 273)

> There are no means of finding what either one person or many can do, but by trying. . . . (*SW*, 243)

Suppose the trial is made and we find that women are not by nature the inferior beings they have been made to be. Suppose that the reforms in law and custom Mill and Wollstonecraft urge come to pass. What good can we expect to come of them? First of all, Mill says, we will have justice rather than injustice, and that is no insignificant gain (*SW*, 296). Second, we would virtually double "the mass of mental faculties available for the higher service of humanity" (*SW*, 198). Third,

women would have a more beneficial influence, though not necessarily a greater influence, on general belief and sentiment (*SW*, 300).* And fourth, there will surely be a great gain in happiness for women (*SW*, 311).

We can close this brief consideration of the "Woman Question" in the last century with an appeal by Wollstonecraft:

> I then would fain convince reasonable men of the importance of some of my remarks; and prevail on them to weigh dispassionately the whole tenor of my observations. I appeal to their understandings; and as a fellow-creature, claim, in the name of my sex, some interest in their hearts. I entreat them to assist to emancipate their companion, to make her a *help-meet* for them.
>
> Would men but generously snap our chains, and be content with rational fellowship instead of slavish obedience, they would find us more observant daughters, more affectionate sisters, more faithful wives, more reasonable mothers—in a word, better citizens. We should then love them with true affection, because we should learn to respect ourselves. (*VRW*, 164)

If our situation is very different from the situation in which these two philosophers wrote, one reason is the impact their thoughts have had on successive generations down to the present day.

Basic Questions

1. What makes utilitarianism a teleological theory?
2. What general features of an action determine whether it is morally right or wrong? Contrast this utilitarian view with Kant's account of what makes actions right or wrong.
3. What makes classic utilitarianism a form of hedo-

---

* As an example of bad consequences caused by narrowness of vision and domination by sentiment, Mill cites the charity given by "ladies" of the upper classes; this does more harm than good, he believes, by making the recipients dependent rather than independent. Opening the minds of women to a broader perspective will forestall such shortsighted response to emotion (*SW*, 303–4).

nism? Distinguish the two hedonic theses that form the core of Bentham's version of utilitarianism.

4. What is happiness, according to the utilitarians, and what does it have to do with morality? (Pieces of their view of happiness are scattered through the chapter; gather them together to form your answer.)

5. Explain the principle of utility. What makes this a moral principle, rather than just prudence or self-interest?

6. How does a person apply the principle of utility to determine whether a particular action is morally right or wrong?

7. How do Bentham and Mill differ in their methods of calculating happiness? How does Mill propose to determine the quality of pleasures?

8. Mill presents two arguments in favor of utilitarianism. Explain each argument. Identify the fallacy in each.

9. How does Mill defend utilitarianism against the charges that (a) pleasure is too low a standard to be appealed to in morality, and (b) the general happiness is too high a standard?

10. Contrast Mill and Kant on the question of whether an agent's motivation is relevant to an appraisal of the morality of an action.

11. What problem is justice thought to raise for the utilitarians? How does Mill argue that, at bottom, there is no conflict between justice and utility?

12. What principles for the education of women does Rousseau advocate?

13. What bad consequences do Wollstonecraft and Mill see flowing from the differential treatment of women?

14. What ideals do they recommend in place of the current beliefs about the position of women in society?

15. What benefits will result from such a change, according to Wollstonecraft and Mill?

For Further Thought

1. Bentham argues that the only alternatives to utilitarianism are asceticism and the "principle of sympathy and antipathy." Look again at Kant's ethics, and try to determine whether it escapes this critique.

2. To a considerable degree, we have made the experiment that Wollstonecraft and Mill recommend. Look at what they anticipate the outcome to be, and estimate to what degree we have achieved their ends.

Notes

1. References to John Stuart Mill's *Utilitarianism*, ed. George Sher (Indianapolis: Hackett Publishing Co., 1979), are cited in the text by the abbreviation *U*. References are to page numbers.

2. References to Jeremy Bentham, *An Introduction to the Principles of Morals and Legislation* (Oxford: Clarendon Press, 1907), are cited in the text by the abbreviation *PML*. References are to page numbers.

3. John Stuart Mill, "Bentham," in *Utilitarianism and Other Essays*, ed. Alan Ryan (New York: Penguin Books, 1987), 151.

4. Quoted in *The Encyclopedia of Philosophy*, vol. 1, ed. Paul Edwards (New York: Macmillan Co., Free Press, 1967), 283.

5. John Stuart Mill, *Autobiography*, in *Essential Works of John Stuart Mill*, ed. Max Lerner (New York: Bantam Books, 1961), 88.

6. Mary Wollstonecraft, *A Vindication of the Rights of Women*, and John Stuart Mill, *The Subjection of Women*, edited by Mary Warnock (London: J. M. Dent Ltd., Everyman's Library, 1986). Subsequent references to these works are cited in the text as follows: *VRW: Vindication of the Rights of Women; SW: The Subjection of Women*. References are to page numbers.

22

Friedrich Nietzsche:
The Value of Existence

Born to a German Lutheran minister's family, Friedrich Nietzsche (1844–1900) lost his father at the age of five. He was strictly brought up in a household of five women (his mother, grand-mother, two aunts, and a sister), where religion was, according to reports, less practiced than preached. He went to excellent schools and stud-ied classical philology at the universities of Bonn and Leipzig. At the unheard-of age of twenty-four, on an extravagant recommendation by a great scholar, Nietzsche became a full professor in phi-lology at the University of Basel, Switzerland.

He served as a medical orderly in the Franco-Prussian War and returned in poor health. But he continued working and published his first book in 1872. In 1879, he resigned his professorship on grounds of ill health and spent the next nine years in lonely apartments or flats in Switzerland and Italy. He was severely ill for a long time, racked with pain and weakness that would have put most men in the hospital. But throughout his illness he kept working, producing book after book. He was deeply disappointed in the reception of his work; very few copies of his books were purchased, the few reviews were based mostly on misunderstand-ings, and he was generally ignored. In the late win-ter of 1888, he broke down and spent the next eleven years insane, cared for by his sister.*

Nietzsche is famous, or infamous, as an influ-ence on the Nazi movement. There is no doubt that he wrote things that rather easily lent them-selves to the distortions of Nazi propagandists, and he is certainly no friend of Christianity, democ-racy, or equal rights for all. But there is also no doubt that he would have been sickened by the whole Nazi business. He was no friend of nation-alism, thinking of himself always as a "good Euro-pean." Scarcely any other writings contain such malicious attacks on "the Germans." And anti-Semitism was diagnosed by Nietzsche as a particu-larly reprehensible form of resentment (about as bad a thing as he could say about anything). But the Nazis made him over in their own image and used perverted versions of his concepts of the *over-man* and *will to power* to their advantage.

Like Kierkegaard (whom he did not know), Nietzsche is concerned primarily with the indi-vidual, not with politics. His basic question is this: In a fundamentally meaningless world, what sort of life could justify itself, could show itself to be worth living? Around that issue all his work circles.*

---

* Walter Kaufmann, famous as Nietzsche's best translator, writes: "His madness was in all probability an atypical general paresis. If so, he must have had syphilis; and since he is known to have lived a highly ascetic life, it is supposed that, as a student, he had visited

a brothel once or twice. This has never been substantiated, and any detailed accounts of such experiences are either poetry or pornog-raphy—not biography. Nor has the suggestion ever been dis-proved that he may have been infected while nursing wounded soldiers in 1870" (*The Portable Nietzsche* [New York: Viking Press, 1954], 13–14).

* Interest in Nietzsche is intense these days, and controversy rages over the proper interpretation of his thought. Perhaps no single

Pessimism and Tragedy

Appropriately enough for a classically trained philologist, Nietzsche's first book, *The Birth of Tragedy*,* is about the Greeks. But its style and content were shocking to his scholarly colleagues. It is not a dry historical treatise filled with footnotes and Greek quotations; it is a passionately argued account of how tragedy allowed an ancient people to solve the problem of "the value of existence" (*BT,* 17), together with a plea for the relevance of that solution today.[1] Nietzsche challenges the received view of the Greeks: that everything they did expressed a noble simplicity and grandeur, a calm and measured naiveté, a spirit in which everything was harmonious and beautiful. Greek statues and temples do reflect such a spirit, and many people had taken this to be the classical ideal. But Nietzsche argues that this spirit doesn't fit tragedy—in particular, it doesn't fit what we know of the origins of tragedy.†

rendering can claim to be *the authentic* Nietzsche. One source of dispute concerns what weight to give to the mass of notes that were published posthumously under the title *Will to Power;* to put my cards on the table, I believe it best to stick to what Nietzsche himself approved for publication, using the rest only to illuminate that. Just as "in the end we must all have to some extent our own Socrates" (p. 47), so we may all have to have our own Nietzsche. Let me encourage you to read widely in Nietzsche, but with the warning that it is easy to get him wrong if you just dip in here and there.

*Published in 1872, its title was originally *The Birth of Tragedy from the Spirit of Music.* In the second half of the book, Nietzsche looked at Richard Wagner's music dramas as an indication that the spirit of tragedy might be reborn. But by 1886, when a later edition came out, Nietzsche had despaired of Wagner as a "romantic" and a "decadent." He changed the title to *The Birth of Tragedy: Hellenism and Pessimism.* This edition also contains Nietzsche's severe appraisal of the book in a preface called "An Attempt at Self-Criticism."

†By tragedy Nietzsche means above all the dramas of Aeschylus and Sophocles. Representative examples are the *Oresteia* trilogy by Aeschylus (which tells the tale of Agamemnon's return from Troy and his murder by his wife, Clytemnestra; the vengeance of their son Orestes; and how the law of blood-guilt was replaced by the establishment of courts of justice in Athens) and the well-known plays of Sophocles, *Oedipus Rex* and *Antigone.* The third great Athenian tragedian, Euripides, is thought by Nietzsche to preside over the death of tragedy.

"We want to be the poets of our life."
—FRIEDRICH WILHELM NIETZSCHE

What is the problem that tragedy is supposed to solve? Nietzsche finds it expressed by Sophocles in the play *Oedipus at Colonus.*

"There is an ancient story that King Midas hunted in the forest a long time for the wise Silenus, the companion of Dionysus, without capturing him. When Silenus at last fell into his hands, the king asked what was the best and most desirable of all things for man. Fixed and immovable, the demigod said not a word, till at last, urged by the king, he gave a shrill laugh and broke out into these words: 'Oh, wretched and ephemeral race, children of chance and misery, why do you compel me to tell you what it would be most expedient for you not to hear? What is best of all is utterly beyond your reach: not to be born, not to *be,* to be *nothing.* But the second best for you is—to die soon.'" (*BT,* 42)

The problem is pessimism. Contrary to the accepted view of Greek cheerfulness, Nietzsche believes that the Greeks looked into the abyss of human suffering without blinking, that they *experienced* the terrors and misery of life—and *they did not look away.* All things considered, said Greek folk wisdom, Silenus is right; the best of all is not to be. And yet the Greeks found a way to live, to affirm life, even to rejoice in life. How did they do that? Nietzsche finds the key to this puzzle in their art, especially in their tragedies.

The first thing to note is that the tragedies were performed at religious festivals. Such a festival was not a pleasant night out for the average Greek family seeking an enjoyable escape from the drudgery of the everyday. Attending these performances was serious business, more like going to a papal mass than taking in the latest hit movie. The second thing to note is that writing plays was a competition. Prizes were given for the best plays at each festival, so playwrights were continually challenged to excel.* But the most important feature of the tragedies is the way they unite two opposing powers in human life. Nietzsche designates these powers with the names of two Greek gods, Apollo and Dionysus; each is the patron of a certain kind of art.

Apollo is the god of order and measure, the god of restraint and calm composure. He is the god who says, "Nothing too much," and "Know thyself." It is the spirit of Apollo that reigns supreme in the harmonious sculptures on the Parthenon, where each individual being reaches a divine perfection without denying the perfection of any other. This spirit also pervades the Homeric epic: Homer's portrayal of Olympus, with its radiant gods, glows with those powers in human nature Apollo represents. Zeus, Hera, Athena, Poseidon, and the rest are a magnificent dream of the human spirit. Nietzsche thinks that these are the right sorts of dreams to dream, the right sorts of gods to have. For these gods live the life of human beings, but in a splendid, dazzling, imposing way.*

> For there is nothing here that suggests asceticism, spirituality, or duty. We hear nothing but the accents of an exuberant, triumphant life in which all things, whether good or evil, are deified. And so the spectator may stand quite bewildered before this fantastic excess of life, asking himself by virtue of what magic potion these high-spirited men would have found life so enjoyable that, wherever they turned, their eyes beheld the smile of Helen, the ideal picture of their own existence, "floating in sweet sensuality." (*BT,* 41)

In the Homeric epic, then, the wisdom of Silenus was

> overcome by the Greeks with the aid of the Olympian *middle world* of art; or at any rate it was veiled and withdrawn from sight. It was in order to be able to live that the Greeks had to create these gods from a most profound need. Perhaps we may picture the process to ourselves somewhat as follows: out of the original Titanic divine order of terror, the Olympian divine order of joy gradually evolved through the Apollinian impulse toward beauty, just as roses burst from thorny bushes. How else could this people, so sensitive, so vehement in its desires, so singularly capable of *suffering,* have endured existence, if it had not been revealed to them in their gods, surrounded with a higher glory? . . . Thus do the gods justify the life of man: they themselves live it—the only satisfactory theodicy!† (*BT,* 42–43)

In this way Nietzsche accounts for the epic, for the glories of Homer's *Iliad* and *Odyssey.* But tragedy is

---

*Nietzsche says that for the Greeks, everything was a contest. Characteristically, he sees envy, ambition, and the struggle to prevail flaring out in every sphere of Greek life, from athletics to poetry. What distinguishes the Greek ethos from our own, he thinks, is that this competitive spirit is *affirmed* and not condemned; "Every talent must unfold itself in fighting" ("Homer's Contest" in *PN,* 37).

---

*See Chapter 1 on the Homeric gods as portrayed in the *Iliad.*
†In his later thought, after all gods have disappeared, Nietzsche reaffirms this principle. The only satisfactory justification for human life lies in *living* it. The question then becomes: What sort of life could constitute such a justification? The answer turns out to be: A life rather like the one the Greek gods themselves lived.

something else. In tragedy, the suffering in human life is not "veiled and withdrawn from sight"; it is presented, explored, and given weight. Tragedy shows us the terror. A different account is required for tragedy.

To account for tragedy, Nietzsche believes we need to bring in another kind of god. Dionysus (also called Bacchus) is the god of wine, of intoxication, of excess and loss of control. Where Dionysus lives, all order, form, and measure break down. Women are caught up in long lines, dancing beyond the civilized towns to orgies in the countryside.* Individual consciousness is drowned in a sea of feelings; conventions are left behind as primal nature rules. The Greeks know this god, too; they also take this power to be divine. Nietzsche hears these Dionysian tones in the art of lyric poetry and folk song, where the passions—desire, anguish, hate, contempt, frenzy, joy—are expressed without reserve. But lyric and folk song are not tragedy. For the birth of tragedy, Dionysus must meet Apollo.

To understand how Nietzsche thinks tragedy solves the problem of the value of existence, we need to grasp one more thing: the metaphysics of Schopenhauer.† In *The Birth of Tragedy* Nietzsche accepts Schopenhauer's view of reality, though not Schopenhauer's evaluation of it.‡ For Schopenhauer, the world of our experience is merely appearance (as it is for Kant); but Schopenhauer thinks he can identify *what appears* in appearance. This world we are so familiar with is just *will* made manifest. In itself—apart from all our representations of it—the world is endless striving, wanting, desiring—without differentiation or individuation. The principles that distinguish you from me, one stone from another—the principles that *individuate* things—are space, time, and causality. And (as Kant taught) these principles apply only in the realm of phenomena; they do not apply to things in themselves. So for Schopenhauer (and Nietz-

sche, too, in this early book) these principles do not apply to will.

There is a fairly neat match between Schopenhauer's realm of individuated phenomena and Apollo (the god of order and measure, of knowledge and morality) on the one hand, and between Schopenhauer's raging depths of urgent reality and Dionysus (whose intoxications break down all distinctions and overwhelm all rules) on the other hand. Apollo is the deity who governs the world of appearance. Dionysus expresses the will.

We are now ready to understand how Nietzsche thinks tragedy can solve the problem of existence and overcome pessimism at one stroke. The key, he believes, lies in grasping the significance of the chorus in Greek tragedy. If you are familiar with these plays, you know that in them a chorus often speaks (or chants) in unison. What does this mean? Various interpretations have been offered: political interpretations, in which the choristers represent the citizens commenting on the actions of royalty; and purely aesthetic interpretations, in which the chorus represents an ideal spectator of the drama with whom the audience can identify. But none of these interpretations, Nietzsche believes, come to grips with two facts. First, early Greek dramas had no roles for individual actors; there was *only* the chorus. Second, the chorus was composed of *satyrs*, half-human and half-goat creatures who were the companions of Dionysus. Nor has any interpretation done justice to the *religious* origins of tragedy. In some way that we need to understand, tragedy *redeems*. Through tragedy we can be *saved*.

Why was the chorus originally made up of satyrs?

> The satyr . . . is the offspring of a longing for the primitive and natural. . . . Nature, as yet unchanged by knowledge, with the bolts of culture still unbroken—that is what the Greek saw in his satyr who nevertheless was not a mere ape. On the contrary, the satyr was the archetype of man, the embodiment of his highest and most intense emotions, the ecstatic reveler enraptured by the proximity of his god, the sympathetic companion in whom the suffering of the god is repeated, one who proclaims wisdom from

---

* Such festivals are chronicled in Euripides' late play, *The Bacchae.*
† See the snapshot of Schopenhauer on p. 415.
‡ Later, as we shall see, Nietzsche rejects this metaphysical view, together with metaphysical theories in general.

the very heart of nature, a symbol of the sexual omnipotence of nature which the Greeks used to contemplate with reverent wonder.

The satyr was something sublime and divine. . . .
(*BT*, 61)

In the songs, the chants, the dances of the satyrs,
Greek spectators recognized something deep and
natural in themselves; they identified with the satyr chorus. Their spirits sang, too, in the surging
rhythms and harmonies of the chorus.* Its Dionysian music originated in that primordial reality,
the *will*, from which derives all the apparent
world—including the spectators themselves.

The Dionysian Greek wants truth and nature in their
most forceful form—and sees himself changed, as by
magic, into a satyr. (*BT*, 62)

But tragedy as we have it is not just music and
dance. There is drama, a story; there are individual
characters who act and suffer. So far we have not
yet accounted for that. But the explanation is not
far away: The drama, Nietzsche tells us, is *the
dream of the chorus*. The Dionysian chorus dreams
an Apollinian dream. And the spectators, identifying with the chorus, dream it too.

. . . the Dionysian reveler sees himself as a satyr, *and
as a satyr, in turn, he sees the god*, which means that in
his metamorphosis he beholds another vision outside himself, as the Apollinian complement of his
own state. With this new vision the drama is
complete.

In the light of this insight we must understand
Greek tragedy as the Dionysian chorus which ever
anew discharges itself in an Apollinian world of images. Thus the choral parts with which tragedy is in-
terlaced are, as it were, the womb that gave birth to
the whole of the so-called dialogue, that is, the entire
world of the stage, the real drama. In several successive discharges this primal ground of tragedy radi-
ates this vision of the drama which is by all means a

dream apparition and to that extent epic in nature;
but on the other hand, being the objectification of a
Dionysian state, it represents not Apollinian redemption through mere appearance but, on the contrary,
the shattering of the individual and his fusion with
primal being. (*BT*, 64, 65)

A play is not, after all, anything real; it is merely
appearance, phenomenon, something imagined.
These *individuals* on the stage who are so distinct
from one another—these kings and queens who
make proclamations, search out riddles, punish,
anguish over their fates, commit murder—all have
a dreamlike quality. No one rushes on stage to prevent Agamemnon's death. Experiencing a tragic
drama is like dreaming, Nietzsche says; it is like a
dream in which one says to oneself, "It is a dream!
I will dream on!" (*BT*, 35).

And now we are ready to understand how
Nietzsche thinks tragedy solves the problem of existence, how it overcomes the pessimistic wisdom
of Silenus. Tragedy does not deny the pessimism.
Oh no; look at what happens in the tragedies.
Oedipus' wife, Jocasta, hangs herself. Oedipus
blinds himself with her brooches and goes into
exile. Agamemnon is murdered by his wife, Clytemnestra, and her lover. Clytemnestra dies at the
hand of her son. Prometheus is chained to a mountain peak where every day an eagle eats at his liver.
What happens in the tragedies is the *destruction of
individuals*.

But now we can see that tragedy is a window
into reality. Just as the drama is the Apollinian
dream of the Dionysian chorus, so—given Schopenhauer's metaphysics—our individual lives are
merely appearance and not reality. We ourselves
are a dream of the will. Reality is found in the
Dionysian depths, where no individuation by
space, time, or causality is possible. And just as
the chorus affirms the dream, *including* the suffering and destruction, so the spectators come to affirm life. They affirm it passionately and joyously,
including the suffering and destruction. For they
know themselves to be other than, more than—
infinitely more than—the petty individualities of

---

*For a modern counterpart, you might think of the audience at a
rock concert. In Oliver Stone's movie, *The Doors*, one of the musi-
cians says to Jim Morrison, "I played with Dionysus, man."

the apparent world. They experience themselves in "fusion with primal being" as the eternal, nonindividualized, primordial root of the world. They experience themselves as willing the creation of the drama—and the creation of their lives.

Tragedy is terror and ecstasy in one. Everything that pessimism can say is true—and yet those truths concern only the dream world of appearance. There is also another truth:

> and this is the most immediate effect of the Dionysian tragedy, that the state and society and, quite generally, the gulfs between man and man give way to an overwhelming feeling of unity leading back to the very heart of nature. The metaphysical comfort—with which, I am suggesting even now, every true tragedy leaves us—that life is at the bottom of things, despite all the changes of appearances, indestructibly powerful and pleasurable— this comfort appears in incarnate clarity in the chorus of satyrs, a chorus of natural beings who live ineradicably, as it were, behind all civilization and remain eternally the same, despite the changes of generations and of the history of nations.
>
> With this chorus the profound Hellene, uniquely susceptible to the tenderest and deepest suffering, comforts himself, having looked boldly right into the terrible destructiveness of so-called world history as well as the cruelty of nature, and being in danger of longing for a Buddhistic negation of the will. Art saves him, and through art—life. (*BT*, 59)

> The metaphysical joy in the tragic is a translation of the instinctive unconscious Dionysian wisdom into the language of images: the hero, the highest manifestations of the will, is negated for our pleasure, because he is only phenomenon, and because the eternal life of the will is not affected by his annihilation. "We believe in eternal life," exclaims tragedy; . . . In Dionysian art and its tragic symbolism . . . nature cries to us with its true, undissembled voice: "Be as I am! Amid the ceaseless flux of phenomena I am the eternally creative primordial mother, eternally impelling to existence, eternally finding satisfaction in this change of phenomena!" (*BT*, 104)

We often think of tragedy as an expression of pessimism about life. But Nietzsche thinks there are two kinds of pessimism: a pessimism of weakness and a pessimism of strength. The former he finds exemplified in Schopenhauer, who wants nothing more than Buddhist relief from willing— rest, escape from life. But in their tragedies the Greeks show us another way, the way of *joyous affirmation in the face of the terror*. Like a primordial artist, the will ceaselessly creates the dreamscape of the phenomenal world. And we, identifying with this Dionysian power, can experience our lives, too, in aesthetically satisfying ways. Our lives may, of course, turn out as tragic as the lives of Oedipus and Agamemnon; there is no guarantee that they won't. But there is nothing else that can give life meaning; there is nothing else that can solve the problem of the value of existence.

> The entire comedy of art is neither performed for our betterment or education nor are we the true authors of this art world. On the contrary, we may assume that we are merely images and artistic projections for the true author, and that we have our highest dignity in our significance as works of art—for it is only as an *aesthetic phenomenon* that existence and the world are eternally *justified*—while of course our consciousness of our own significance hardly differs from that which the soldiers painted on canvas have of the battle represented on it. (*BT*, 52)

In what do we find our dignity and value? What is it that makes life worth living? Not anything moral, Nietzsche says; not *another* life (the "life of the world to come"); not our relation to God. Only its *aesthetic* value justifies our life and makes it worth living. There is something intrinsic to, say, *Oedipus Rex* that leads us to value it, to continue to perform and experience it even after 2,500 years. If *our lives* had that same sort of aesthetic value, that would be enough to justify the living of them. If we come to experience ourselves as "images and artistic projections for the true author" of our lives—for the primordial unity, the will, that Dionysian power projecting the dream of the world drama—pessimism can be overcome. We can accept our lives even if our eyes are wide open to the wisdom of Silenus. We are works of art! Nothing else, Nietzsche tells us, could suffice. That is the way to solve the problem of "the value of existence." That is the only way it *could* be solved.* And that is what tragedy shows us.

Goodbye True World

In *The Birth of Tragedy,* Nietzsche solves the problem of existence with the help of a metaphysical theory. Spectators at a tragedy, he thinks, experience the "metaphysical comfort" of realizing that they are other than, more than—*infinitely* more than—the limited and suffering individuals they normally appear to be. Behind the appearance they discover *reality* in the Dionysian exuberance of the one true will's self-affirmation. They identify with their "true" self and rejoice. This solution is *metaphysical* in its appeal to "another world," a "true world" beyond, behind, or beneath the familiar world of everyday experience. Philosophers have long assured us that things are not really as they seem; from Heraclitus and Parmenides, through Plato and Augustine, to Descartes, Kant, and Hegel, we hear that reality is not what we think—that *we* are not what we think! And Nietzsche's reliance on Schopenhauer's metaphysics of the will is just another example of the same pattern.

But in the period after *The Birth of Tragedy,* Nietzsche comes to believe that no such metaphysics is possible for us. So another solution has to be found for the problem of the value of existence. All of Nietzsche's later work is oriented around this problem. Before we can grasp that solution, however, we need to understand why he thinks we must abandon the traditional philosophers' dream: to tell us what there *really* is.

> Gradually it has become clear to me what every great philosophy so far has been: namely, the personal confession of its author and a kind of involuntary and unconscious memoir; also that the moral

(or immoral) intentions in every philosophy constituted the real germ of life from which the whole plant had grown.

> Indeed, if one would explain how the abstrusest metaphysical claims of a philosopher really came about, it is always well (and wise) to ask first: at what morality does all this (does *he*) aim? (*BGE* 6)

What we need is a psychology of the great philosophers, a psychology that uncovers the real drives and interests that motivate their work. Nietzsche prides himself on his psychological acuity and thinks he has discovered that it is not *reality* that philosophical theories display, but *the philosophers themselves:* what sorts of people they are, how weak or strong they are, how sick or how healthy. Philosophy is "confession." Philosophers, Nietzsche says, want us to believe that they want the truth, that their sole interest is knowledge. They want us to believe—perhaps they themselves believe—that their theories tell us about ultimate reality. But

> they are not honest enough in their work, although they all make a lot of virtuous noise when the problem of truthfulness is touched even remotely. They all pose as if they had discovered and reached their real opinions through the self-development of a cold, pure, divinely unconcerned dialectic . . . ; while at bottom it is an assumption, a hunch, indeed a kind of "inspiration"—most often a desire of the heart that has been filtered and made abstract—that they defend with reasons they have sought after the fact. They are all advocates who resent that name, and for the most part even wily spokesmen for their prejudices which they baptize "truths"—and *very* far from having the courage of the conscience that admits this, precisely this, to itself. . . . (*BGE* 5)

Nietzsche means to apply this critique to all the central conceptions of traditional philosophy: to "soul," "free will," "the 'true' world," "God," "immortality," and "morality" itself—to say nothing of "cause," "substance," "unity," and "sameness of things." Nietzsche is suspicious of such notions; in them he senses dishonesty, the lack of an intellec-

---

* Compare Kierkegaard's aesthetic mode of life, pp. 442–445.

tual conscience, even lying.* What philosophers create is a world that satisfies the "desire of the heart"; their "reasons" come later. A good example of Nietzsche's procedure is his analysis of the Stoics. The great desire of Stoics is to live according to nature.† But what is their conception of nature? Nietzsche addresses the Stoic this way:

> Imagine a being like nature, wasteful beyond measure, indifferent beyond measure, without purposes and consideration, without mercy and justice, fertile and desolate and uncertain at the same time; imagine indifference itself as a power—how *could* you live according to this indifference? . . .
>
> In truth, the matter is altogether different: while you pretend rapturously to read the canon of your law in nature, you want something opposite, you strange actors and self-deceivers! Your pride wants to impose your morality, your ideal, on nature—even on nature—and incorporate them in her; you demand that she should be nature "according to the Stoa," and you would like existence to exist only after your own image—as an immense eternal glorification and generalization of Stoicism. . . .
>
> But this is an ancient, eternal story: what formerly happened with the Stoics still happens today, too, as soon as any philosophy begins to believe in itself. It always creates the world in its own image; it cannot do otherwise. Philosophy is this tyrannical drive itself, the most spiritual will to power, to the "creation of the world," to the *causa prima*.‡ (*BGE* 9)

Nietzsche's notion of "will to power," that "tyrannical drive" displayed in philosophizing, is a central idea for him; we will explore it more fully later. Here we only need to note that this will to power expresses itself in philosophers through their attempts to create the world in their own image. And

that means: according to what they value. And that means: according to what they *need*. The Stoics needed order, law, control; they needed to be safe from disorder, chaos, and helplessness. So they created the world as they needed it: a world of providential orderliness, perfectly organized by the *logos*, the divine reason present in it. To cohere with such a world was virtue, happiness, and perfect freedom. But is nature really like that? Nietzsche doesn't think so, as a glance back to the first quoted paragraph will show. So the Stoics read into nature what they *need* it to be. And *all* the philosophers have done the same.

In addition to such *personal* needs, Nietzsche thinks there are *common* factors that influence metaphysical views. These factors may be grounded in the language we speak or simply in our human nature.

> Over immense periods of time the intellect produced nothing but errors. A few of these proved to be useful and helped to preserve the species: those who hit upon or inherited these had better luck in their struggle for themselves and their progeny. Such erroneous articles of faith, which were continually inherited, until they became almost part of the basic endowment of the species, include the following: that there are enduring things; that there are equal things; that there are things, substances, bodies; that a thing is what it appears to be; that our will is free; that what is good for me is good in itself. It was only very late that truth emerged—as the weakest form of knowledge. (*GS* 110)

Even today, these "articles of faith" seem to be just common sense. But Nietzsche tells us they are *errors*. Kant's famous *categories*, Nietzsche holds, are also errors.* The concept of substance, for instance,

> is indispensable for logic, although in the strictest sense nothing real corresponds to it. . . . The beings that did not see so precisely had an advantage over those that saw everything "in flux." At bottom, every

---

*This suspicion toward traditional philosophizing, which Nietzsche in the nineteenth century shares with Kierkegaard, finds numerous echoes in the twentieth century. Compare the variously motivated rejections by Peirce (pp. 523, 533), Dewey (pp. 536–541), Wittgenstein (pp. 568, 575, 578, 588–593), and Heidegger (pp. 631–639).

†For the Stoic ideal of keeping one's will in harmony with nature, see pp. 194–196.

‡"First cause."

---

*See pp. 384–388.

high degree of caution in making inferences and every skeptical tendency constitute a great danger for life. No living beings would have survived if the opposite tendency—to affirm rather than suspend judgment, to err and *make up* things rather than wait, to assent rather than negate, to pass judgment rather than be just—had not been bred to the point where it became extraordinarily strong. (*GS* 111)

The same is true of the *a priori* concept of causality.

> Cause and effect: such a duality probably never exists; in truth we are confronted by a continuum out of which we isolate a couple of pieces, just as we perceive motion only as isolated points and then infer it without ever actually seeing it. The suddenness with which many effects stand out misleads us; actually it is sudden only for us. In this moment of suddenness there is an infinite number of processes that elude us. An intellect that could see cause and effect as a continuum and a flux and not, as we do, in terms of an arbitrary division and dismemberment, would repudiate the concept of cause and effect and deny all conditionality. (*GS* 112)

You can see that in a sense Nietzsche accepts the Kantian point. It *is* necessary for us to judge the world in terms of very general concepts like this. But Nietzsche's view is radically different from Kant's on two scores: (1) these concepts do *not* apply correctly to the phenomenal world, and (2) there is no noumenal world of things-in-themselves that these concepts fall short of. Their necessity for us is a purely practical necessity; without such "errors" we couldn't survive in the world as it is.* So these errors are not arbitrary or capricious inventions; they serve *life*. But the fact that they are useful doesn't mean that they are *true*.

> *Life no argument.*—We have arranged for ourselves a world in which we can live—by positing bodies,

lines, planes, causes and effects, motion and rest, form and content; without these articles of faith nobody now could endure life. But that does not prove them. Life is no argument. The conditions of life might include error. (*GS* 121)

Human beings as they now are have been formed by their errors; we depend on them. Expanding on the general character of these errors, Nietzsche writes:

> *The four errors.*—Man has been educated by his errors. First, he always saw himself only incompletely; second, he endowed himself with fictitious attributes; third, he placed himself in a false order of rank in relation to animals and nature; fourth, he invented ever new tables of goods and always accepted them for a time as eternal and unconditional. . . . (*GS* 115)

Note that all four concern our knowledge of ourselves.* Though they have taken "Know thyself" as their motto, philosophers go wrong most often just here. They see themselves "incompletely," they endow themselves with "fictitious attributes," they conclude that they are higher in "rank" than the other animals. They endow themselves with souls—immortal souls, no less. And they call this wisdom. But we, Nietzsche says,

> have learned differently. We have become more modest in every way. We no longer derive man from "the spirit" or "the deity"; we have placed him back among the animals. We consider him the strongest animal because he is the most cunning: his spirituality is a consequence of this. On the other hand, we oppose the vanity that would raise its head again here too—as if man had been the great hidden purpose of the evolution of the animals. Man is by no means the crown of creation: every living being stands beside him on the same level of perfection. And even this is saying too much: relatively speaking, man is the most bungled of all the animals, the sickliest, and not one has strayed more dangerously

---

* Nietzsche here anticipates a movement in late twentieth-century philosophy called "evolutionary epistemology." The key idea is that we are natural parts of the natural world and our capacities for knowing this world have been developed by natural selection pressures over vast periods of time. Donald Campbell and Willard Quine are two recent exponents of this line of thought.

---

* Nietzsche's book *On the Genealogy of Morals* begins this way: "We are unknown to ourselves, we men of knowledge—and with good reason. We have never sought ourselves—how could it happen that we should ever *find* ourselves" (*GM*, preface, section 1).

from its instincts. But for all that, of course, he is the most *interesting*.

As regards the animals, Descartes was the first to have dared, with admirable boldness, to understand the animal as *machina*: the whole of our psychology endeavors to prove this claim. And we are consistent enough not to except man, as Descartes still did: our knowledge of man today goes just as far as we understand him mechanistically. Formerly man was given a "free will" as his dowry from a higher order: today we have taken his will away altogether, in the sense that we no longer admit the will as a faculty. The old word "will" now serves only to denote a resultant, a kind of individual reaction, which follows necessarily upon a number of partly contradictory, partly harmonious stimuli: the will no longer "acts" or "moves."

Formerly, the proof of man's higher origin, of his divinity, was found in his consciousness, in his "spirit." To become *perfect,* he was advised to draw in his senses, turtle fashion, to cease all intercourse with earthly things, to shed his mortal shroud: then his essence would remain, the "pure spirit." * Here too we have reconsidered: the development of consciousness, the "spirit," is for us nothing less than the symptom of a relative imperfection of the organism; it means trying, groping, blundering—an exertion which uses up an unnecessary amount of nervous energy. We deny that anything can be done perfectly as long as it is still done consciously. The "pure spirit" is a pure stupidity; if we subtract the nervous system and the senses—the "mortal shroud"—*then we miscalculate*—that is all! (*A* 14)

It is clear that Nietzsche accepts a naturalistic, scientific picture of the world and of our place in it—with the reservation that science, too, must use those falsifying concepts: thing, equal, cause, line, plane, and so on. Science cannot avoid this degree of error, since it must be expressed in language, and language necessarily simplifies and falsifies. The universe of which we are a part, then, is indifferent to good and evil, wasteful beyond measure, without mercy and justice, fertile and desolate, without purpose or reason, composed of mere processes in continuous flux. And we are just

animals of a sickly sort, mechanisms governed by instincts that we are scarcely conscious of. Consciousness itself is scarcely our "essence"; it is "the last and latest development of the organic and hence also what is most unfinished and unstrong" (*GS* 11).* To focus on consciousness is bound to mislead.

This view of things, Nietzsche thinks, is the result of centuries of training in truthfulness; *honesty* has brought us to this point. Philosophers have thought otherwise, but

the total character of the world . . . is in all eternity chaos—in the sense not of a lack of necessity but of a lack of order, arrangement, form, beauty, wisdom, and whatever other names there are for our aesthetic anthropomorphisms. . . . But how could we reproach or praise the universe? Let us beware of attributing to it heartlessness and unreason or their opposites: it is neither perfect nor beautiful, nor noble, nor does it wish to become any of these things; it does not by any means strive to imitate man. None of our aesthetic and moral judgments apply to it. . . . When will all these shadows of God cease to darken our minds? When will we complete our de-deification of nature? When may we begin to "*naturalize*" humanity in terms of a pure, newly discovered, newly redeemed nature? (*GS* 109)

The last words in this quotation are extremely important to Nietzsche, but we are not yet ready to understand them. For the moment let us focus on the situation Nietzsche thinks we have come to: the view of the universe that—unless we continue to deceive ourselves—we *must* come to. Nature is completely "de-deified," vacant of all purposiveness and value; "nature is always value-less, but has been *given* value at some time as a present—and it was *we* who gave and bestowed it" (*GS* 301).† In such a world we live; of such a world are we a part.

In *Twilight of the Idols* Nietzsche gives us a cap-

* Compare Plato on philosophy as a training for dying, p. 130.

* Nietzsche has many interesting things to say about consciousness; he sounds very contemporary. See, for instance, *GS*, sections 11, 179, 333, 354, and 360; and *BGE*, sections 3, 16, 32.
† Compare the early Wittgenstein, p. 563. The difference is that for Wittgenstein we are *not* a part of the world.

sule history of philosophical conceptions of reality. He calls it "HOW THE 'TRUE WORLD' FINALLY BECAME A FABLE: *The History of an Error*":

1. The true world—attainable for the sage, the pious, the virtuous man; he lives in it, *he is it*.

    (The oldest form of the idea, relatively sensible, simple, and persuasive. A circumlocution for the sentence, "I, Plato, *am* the truth.")*

2. The true world—unattainable for now, but promised for the sage, the pious, the virtuous man ("for the sinner who repents").

    (Progress of the idea: it becomes more subtle, insidious, incomprehensible—*it becomes female, it becomes Christian.*)†

3. The true world—unattainable, indemonstrable, unpromisable; but the very thought of it—a consolation, an obligation, an imperative.

    (At bottom, the old sun, but seen through mist and skepticism. The idea has become elusive, pale, Nordic, Königsbergian.)‡

4. The true world—unattainable? At any rate, unattained. And being unattained, also *unknown*. Consequently, not consoling, redeeming, or obligating: how could something unknown obligate us?

    (Gray morning. The first yawn of reason. The cock-crow of positivism.)

5. The "true" world—an idea which is no longer good for anything, not even obligating—an idea which has become useless and superfluous—*consequently,* a refuted idea: let us abolish it!

    (Bright day; breakfast; return of *bon sens* and cheerfulness; Plato's embarrassed blush; pandemonium of all free spirits.)

6. The true world—we have abolished. What world has remained? The apparent one, perhaps? But no! *With the true world we have also abolished the apparent one.*

    (Noon: moment of the briefest shadow; end of the longest error; high point of humanity; INCIPIT ZARATHUSTRA.) (*TI,* 485–86)

Little by little, the "true world" vanishes: Parmenides' One, Plato's Forms, Aristotle's God and Augustine's soul, the Christian heaven, Descartes' free and immortal mind, Kant's world of things-in-themselves, Hegel's Absolute, Schopenhauer's will. All gone. Vapors. Evaporated by a heightened honesty about ourselves and our place in the scheme of things. But what is left? Only the "apparent" world? Proposition 6 tells us that when the contrast between true and apparent vanishes, so does all reason to disparage this world—the one and only world—by calling it "apparent" (or, as many philosophers have said, "*merely* apparent"). There is just the world, and we a part of it.

> The "true world" and the "apparent world"—that means: the mendaciously invented world and reality. (*EH,* 218)

Nietzsche's estimate of his own importance can be gathered from the phrase which characterizes stage 6, the stage of his own philosophy; he calls it the "high point of humanity." He truly believes that he has seen through the shams and pretenses of all our previous philosophical history. Zarathustra, as we shall see soon, is the fictional "prophet" in whose mouth Nietzsche puts his own deepest philosophical thoughts. "INCIPIT ZARATHUSTRA" means "Zarathustra begins." And the time of Zarathustra is noon—when the shadows are shortest, when everything is in light and can be seen for what it is.*

So now we see why Nietzsche has to rethink the problem of the meaning of life. In *The Birth of Tragedy,* he had relied on one version of "the true world" to solve the problem of pessimism. But now the true world has disappeared. And the ques-

---

* In *The Antichrist,* Nietzsche interprets Jesus according to the same formula. The kingdom of God, Jesus says, is "within you." And it is, of course, *Jesus* who says, "I am the way, the truth, and the life" (John 14:6).
† Christianity, Nietzsche thinks, has *betrayed* the spirit of Jesus.
‡ Kant lived in Königsberg. Nietzsche obviously is thinking of the unknowable noumenal world and the categorical imperative.

---

* "Among my writings my *Zarathustra* stands to my mind by itself. With that I have given mankind the greatest present that has ever been made to it so far. This book, with a voice bridging centuries, is not only the highest book there is, the book that is truly characterized by the air of the heights—the whole fact of man lies *beneath* it at a tremendous distance—it is also the *deepest,* born out of the innermost wealth of truth, an inexhaustible well to which no pail descends without coming up again filled with gold and goodness" (*EH,* 219).

tion about the value of existence is posed anew, in an even more stark and dramatic way. How *can* life have any meaning in a world such as we now believe in? But before we can get ourselves out of this hole, we have to dig it still deeper. We must *look into the chasm* if we are to be saved.

The Death of God

The disappearance of the "true world"—our inability to take it seriously any longer—is not an obscure and remote event that is of interest only to a few philosophers. We all need a sense for the meaning of life, and to whatever extent that such meaning is provided by something beyond life itself, a "true world" is involved. For centuries, most people have provided meaning for their lives through religion*—in the West, primarily through Christianity. We in the West have solved the problem of meaninglessness by setting our lives in the larger context of creation and salvation, God's plan, immortality, heaven and hell. So the whole culture—and certainly every Christian, Jew, and Muslim—has been committed to a metaphysics involving a "true world." If "true worlds" vanish like smoke in a clear sky, what will happen?

In one of his best known parables, Nietzsche gives us his answer.

The madman.—Have you not heard of that madman who lit a lantern in the bright morning hours, ran to the market place, and cried incessantly: "I seek God! I seek God!" —As many of those who did not believe in God were standing around just then, he provoked much laughter. Has he got lost? asked one. Did he lose his way like a child? asked another. Or is he hiding? Is he afraid of us? Has he gone on a voyage? emigrated? —Thus they yelled and laughed.

The madman jumped into their midst and pierced them with his eyes. "Whither is God?" he cried; "I will tell you. *We have killed him*—you and I. All of us are his murderers. But how did we do this? How could we drink up the sea? Who gave us the sponge to wipe away the entire horizon? What were we doing when we unchained this earth from its sun? Whither is it moving now? Whither are we moving? Away from all suns? Are we not plunging continually? Backward, sideward, forward, in all directions? Is there still any up or down? Are we not straying as through an infinite nothing? Do we not feel the breath of empty space? Has it not become colder? Is not night continually closing in on us? Do we not need to light lanterns in the morning? Do we hear nothing as yet of the noise of the gravediggers who are burying God? Do we smell nothing as yet of the divine decomposition? Gods, too, decompose. God is dead. God remains dead. And we have killed him.

"How shall we comfort ourselves, the murderers of all murderers? What was holiest and mightiest of all that the world has yet owned has bled to death under our knives: who will wipe this blood off us? What water is there for us to clean ourselves? What festivals of atonement, what sacred games shall we have to invent? Is not the greatness of this deed too great for us? Must we ourselves not become gods simply to appear worthy of it? There has never been a greater deed; and whoever is born after us—for the sake of this deed he will belong to a higher history than all history hitherto."

Here the madman fell silent and looked again at his listeners; and they, too, were silent and stared at him in astonishment. At last he threw his lantern on the ground, and it broke into pieces and went out. "I have come too early," he said then; "my time is not yet. This tremendous event is still on its way, still wandering; it has not yet reached the ears of men. Lightening and thunder require time; the light of the stars requires time; deeds, though done, still require time to be seen and heard. This deed is still more distant from them than the most distant stars—*and yet they have done it themselves.*"

It has been related further that on the same day the madman forced his way into several churches and there struck up his *requiem aeternam deo.* Led out and called to account, he is said always to have replied nothing but: "What after all are these churches now if they are not the tombs and sepulchers of God?" (*GS* 125)

---

*Remember that the Greek tragedies had precisely this function—to answer the question (in the face of pessimism) about the value of existence. Remember, too, that they were performed at *religious* festivals. Note also the religious language Nietzsche uses when he talks about this problem. Art "saves" us, he says; our lives are "redeemed" when we see them in an aesthetic perspective.

Perhaps what Nietzsche means to say in these dramatic paragraphs is clear enough. But some questions and answers might be in order.

- Why is the message concerning the death of God put into the mouth of a madman? Because anyone who brings this message to a culture as dominated by Christianity as ours is bound to seem mad.
- Why does the madman announce the "death" of God rather than merely his nonexistence? Because a death is something that *happens*. It can be dated; it happens at one time and not another. Nonexistence is just not ever having been. God's death, Nietzsche thinks, is something that happened recently.
- What does it mean that God died? It means that people no longer believe—though they may not have noticed this fact. (God "lives" in the prayers of the people.) "The greatest recent event—that 'God is dead,' that the belief in the Christian god has become unbelievable—is already beginning to cast its first shadows over Europe" (*GS* 343).
- Who are the clowns standing around that make fun of the madman? Those who don't take these things seriously; they think God can disappear and everything can go along as it always has.
- Who are the murderers of God? We all are.
- What are the consequences of God's death? We have lost our moorings. We don't know any more where we are, where we are going—or where we should be going. We are without a goal. The one who for centuries supplied the rules for living, the goal to strive for, has died. We are adrift.
- Why does the madman say, "I have come too early?" Because though the deed is done, people are not ready to recognize what they have done. And they certainly are not aware of the consequences. "God is dead; but given the way of men, there may still be caves for thousands of years in which his shadow will be shown" (*GS* 108).

Can we say anything more precise about how God died? Zarathustra says, "When gods die,

they always die several kinds of death" (*Z* 4, 373). Nietzsche offers a number of explanations. For example, in the account we canvassed in the last section, Nietzsche claims that the whole idea of a metaphysical "true world" simply became incredible to us. Christianity, which Nietzsche calls "Platonism for 'the people'" (*BGE* preface, p. 2), disappears with the rest of the "true worlds" killed by "the decline of the faith in the Christian god, the triumph of scientific atheism" (*GS* 357).

But there are other explanations. In the fourth book of *Thus Spoke Zarathustra*, the prophet meets "the last pope," who says that though he is now "retired," he served the old god "until his last hour." Zarathustra asks him how God died: "Is it true what they say, that pity strangled him, that he saw how *man* hung on the cross and that he could not bear it, that love of man became his hell, and in the end his death?" (*Z* 4, 372). The old pope replies:

> "When he was young, this god out of the Orient, he was harsh and vengeful and he built himself a hell to amuse his favorites. Eventually, however, he became old and soft and mellow and pitying, more like a grandfather than a father, but most like a shaky old grandmother. Then he sat in his nook by the hearth, wilted, grieving over his weak legs, weary of the world, weary of willing, and one day he choked on his all-too-great pity." (*Z* 4, 373)

As Zarathustra understands pity, it is the opposite of a life-affirming emotion. In pity one *deplores* the condition of someone's existence.* Since the Christian God is one who pities mankind, it is possible that his "all-too-great" pity might in the end undermine even his own will to live, and he might simply wither away. Pity, Zarathustra thinks, is a very bad thing.

Zarathustra tells the old pope that "it might have happened that way—that way, and also

---

* The thing Nietzsche holds most adamantly against Christianity is that it is (as he sees it) a religion of pity. If pity is the appropriate reaction to human life as a whole—is even the reaction of *God!*—then one is virtually saying it would be better if life did not exist at all. And then one is back with Silenus. Nietzsche condemns Christianity, for giving in to pessimism instead of overcoming it.

in some other way." And he offers another explanation:

> "I love all that looks bright and speaks honestly. But he—you know it, you old priest, there was something of your manner about him, of the priest's manner: he was equivocal. He was also indistinct. How angry he got with us, this wrath-snorter, because we understood him badly! But why did he not speak more cleanly? And if it was the fault of our ears, why did he give us ears that heard him badly? If there was mud in our ears—well, who put it there? He bungled too much, this potter who had never finished his apprenticeship. But that he wreaked revenge on his pots and creations for having bungled them himself, that was a sin against *good taste*. There is good taste in piety, too; and it was this that said in the end, 'Away with *such* a god! Rather no god, rather make destiny on one's own, rather be a fool, rather be a god oneself!'" (*Z* 4, 373–74)

Zarathustra's claim here is that integrity, intellectual conscience, cleanliness of spirit, honesty—and finally just good taste—eventually rejects the comforts of such a god. And where did we learn such honesty? From Christianity itself. Nietzsche calls this atheism

> a triumph achieved finally and with great difficulty by the European conscience, being the most fateful act of two thousand years of discipline for truth that in the end forbids itself the *lie* in faith in God.
>
> You see what it was that really triumphed over the Christian god: Christian morality itself, the concept of truthfulness that was understood ever more rigorously, the father confessor's refinement of the Christian conscience, translated and sublimated into a scientific conscience, into intellectual cleanliness at any price. (*GS*, 357)

Paradoxically, God, the source of Christian morality, is finally done in by that morality itself!

There are also less praiseworthy explanations for the death of God. Nietzsche puts one of them into the mouth of "the ugliest man," whom Zarathustra meets and recognizes as *the murderer of God* who "took revenge on this witness" (*Z* 4, 376). The ugliest man confesses:

> "But he *had* to die: he saw with eyes that saw everything; he saw man's depths and ultimate grounds, all his concealed disgrace and ugliness. His pity knew no shame: he crawled into my dirtiest nooks. This most curious, overobtrusive, overpitying one had to die. He always saw me: on such a witness I wanted to have revenge or not live myself. The god who saw everything, *even man*—this god had to die! Man cannot bear it that such a witness should live." (*Z* 4, 378–79)

Nietzsche does not admire such motives for killing off the Christian god; it is, after all, the "ugliest man" who says these words. Nietzsche wants a life that, unlike the ugliest man's life, can bear examination—especially one's own examination. Moreover, he considers revenge a particularly bad motive (although one that is hard to get beyond). Motives such as these, Nietzsche tells us, have also played a role in the death of God.

Reactions to this great event will, of course, differ. Some people will deny that it has happened; others will despair. But, Nietzsche says, the consequences for himself and others like him

> are quite the opposite of what one might perhaps expect: They are not at all sad and gloomy but rather like a new and scarcely describable kind of light, happiness, relief, exhilaration, encouragement, dawn.
>
> Indeed, we philosophers and "free spirits" feel, when we hear the news that "the old god is dead," as if a new dawn shone on us; our heart overflows with gratitude, amazement, premonitions, expectation. At long last the horizon appears free to us again, even if it should not be bright; at long last our ships may venture out again, venture out to face any danger; all the daring of the lover of knowledge is permitted again; the sea, *our* sea, lies open again; perhaps there has never yet been such an "open sea."—(*GS* 343)

Despite such cheerful thoughts, Nietzsche sees that the death of God poses a serious problem. If our culture has for two thousand years been nourished by these religious roots, what happens when the roots no longer sustain its life? When the source of our values dries up, what happens to them? When the lawgiver disappears, what happens to our law? As the madman says, "Is there still any up or down? Are we not straying as through an infinite nothing?" The threat is **nihilism**. Zarathustra meets a soothsayer who expresses the danger of nihilism this way:

> "—And I saw a great sadness descend upon mankind. The best grew weary of their works. A doctrine appeared, accompanied by a faith: 'All is empty, all is the same, all has been!' And from all the hills it echoed: 'All is empty, all is the same, all has been!' Indeed we have harvested: but why did all our fruit turn rotten and brown? What fell down from the evil moon last night? In vain was all our work; our wine has turned to poison; an evil eye has seared our fields and hearts. We have all become dry; and if fire should descend on us, we should turn to ashes; indeed, we have wearied the fire itself. All our wells have dried up; even the sea has withdrawn. All the soil would crack, but the depth refuses to devour. 'Alas, where is there still a sea in which one might drown?' thus are we wailing across shallow swamps. Verily, we have become too weary even to die. We are still waking and living on—in tombs." (*Z* 2, 245)

When Zarathustra hears the soothsayer, he himself becomes "sad and weary"; he becomes "like those of whom the soothsayer had spoken" (*Z* 2, 246). Weariness of life—finding everything empty, the same, dry, shallow, meaningless—that is the mood of nihilism. Into such a state we might be cast by the death of God. It is against nihilism that Zarathustra and Nietzsche struggle. A new meaning must be forged for life. But the fight for meaning, as we shall see, will take a surprising turn: Christianity itself—the factor that until now had saved us from nihilism—is accused of the greatest nihilism of all.

Revaluation of Values

As we have seen, Nietzsche believes that nature is "value-less." Whatever values we might think are present have been "bestowed" on nature by us. He also puts this claim in the following way:

> *there are altogether no moral facts.* Moral judgments agree with religious ones in believing in realities

which are no realities. Morality is merely an interpretation of certain phenomena—more precisely, a misinterpretation. . . . Moral judgments are therefore never to be taken literally. (*TI,* 501)

Our current values and moral judgments are interpretations that were formed in a context that takes God and a "true world" for granted. But if God is dead for us and we no longer believe in any world but the one revealed by our senses and interpreted by the sciences, we surely need to look again at the received values. Nietzsche asks himself, "*In what do you believe?*" and answers, "In this, that the weights of all things must be determined anew" (*GS* 269).

But how do we do this? Nietzsche thinks that philosophers have not been much help; they have typically busied themselves with the task of providing rational foundations for morality.* But in doing so they have simply taken a certain morality for granted. This prevented them from even laying eyes on

> the real problems of morality; for these emerge only when we compare *many* moralities. In all "science of morals" so far one thing was *lacking,* strange as it may sound: the problem of morality itself; what was lacking was any suspicion that there was something problematic here. (*BGE* 186)

If we are going to determine the "weights" of things anew, we obviously cannot just take the present "weights" for granted. We can avoid doing that if we recognize that there is not just one morality, but many moralities.

> If one would like to see our European morality for once as it looks from a distance, and if one would like to measure it against other moralities, past and future, then one has to proceed like a wanderer who

---

*Think of Plato (pp. 132–137) and Aristotle (pp. 173–180), who try to show that living virtuously is the way to live happily; of the Stoics (pp. 192–197), who try to demonstrate that the good life is integration into the order of the universe; of Kant (pp. 401–407), who claims that morality is a requirement of pure reason alone; of Hegel (pp. 430–435), for whom morality is realized in a perfectly rational state; and of the arguments for utilitarianism (pp. 472–474).

wants to know how high the towers in a town are: he *leaves* the town. "Thoughts about moral prejudices," if they are not meant to be prejudices about prejudices, presuppose a position *outside* morality, some point beyond good and evil to which one has to rise, climb, or fly—and in the present case at least a point beyond *our* good and evil, a freedom from everything "European," by which I mean the sum of the imperious value judgments that have become part of our flesh and blood. (*GS* 380)

So Nietzsche calls for "a *typology* of morals" (*BGE* 186) and makes a contribution to this project in his book *On the Genealogy of Morals*. A genealogy, of course, traces the ancestry of a person; a genealogy for a certain type of morality will shed light on its ancestry by revealing the historical and psychological conditions out of which it grew. Nietzsche thinks that our present morality is actually the result of a "revaluation of values" that took place a long time ago. It evolved from a quite different type of morality. And he believes he can tell us the story of how that happened.

Master Morality/Slave Morality

It is a mistake, Nietzsche says, simply to identify the good with the useful or beneficial, as the utilitarians do; for originally the word "good" was used without any reference to utility. It "did *not* originate with those to whom 'goodness' was shown!" (*GM* 1:2). It is also a mistake to identify the good with intention or the good will, as the Kantians do; for will and intention, like conscious phenomena generally, are much too superficial to be regarded as the causes of behavior (see *BGE* 32). Besides, neither utilitarians nor Kantians ask the *radical* questions about morality that Nietzsche wants to press: Why have morality at all? What good is it? Would we be better off without it?

Nietzsche uses historical and linguistic evidence to make a case that originally the word "good" was used by

"the good" themselves, that is to say, the noble, powerful, high-stationed and high-minded, who felt and established themselves and their actions as good, that is, of the first rank, in contradistinction to all the

low, low-minded, common and plebeian. It was out of this *pathos of distance* that they first seized the right to create values and to coin names for values: what had they to do with utility! (*GM* 1:2)

Here is a morality—the morality of the aristocrats, the well-born, the powerful, the masters. These people of the "first rank" call themselves "noble," "commanders," "the rich," the "happy," the "truthful"—what *need* do they have to lie? They affirm their lives; they say yes to their being. They *feel* themselves to be good. To them, "good" means "what *we* are."

The knightly-aristocratic value judgments presupposed a powerful physicality, a flourishing, abundant, even overflowing health, together with that which serves to preserve it: war, adventure, hunting, dances, war games, and in general all that involves vigorous, free, joyful activity. (*GM* 1:7)

The noble type of man experiences *itself* as determining values; it does not need approval; it judges, "what is harmful to me is harmful in itself"; it knows itself to be that which first accords honor to things; it is *value-creating*. Everything it knows as part of itself it honors: such a morality is self-glorification. In the foreground there is the feeling of fullness, of power that seeks to overflow, the happiness of high tension, the consciousness of wealth that would give and bestow: the noble human being, too, helps the unfortunate, but not, or almost not from pity, but prompted more by an urge begotten by excess of power. (*BGE* 260)

This is the morality of conquerors. Among themselves, they are held in check "by custom, respect, usage, gratitude, and even more by mutual suspicion and jealousy"; in their relations with one another, they show themselves "resourceful in consideration, self-control, delicacy, loyalty, pride, and friendship" (*GM* 1:11). But once they go outside, where the stranger is found,

they are not much better than uncaged beasts of prey. There they savor a freedom from all social constraints, they compensate themselves in the wilderness for the tension engendered by protracted confinement and enclosure within the peace of society, they *go back* to the innocent conscience of the beast of prey, as triumphant monsters who perhaps emerge from a disgusting procession of murder, arson, rape, and torture, exhilarated and undisturbed of soul, as it were no more than a students' prank, convinced they have provided the poets with a lot more material for song and praise. (*GM* 1:11)

Nietzsche obviously has the heroes of Homer's great poems in mind.* These magnificent and terrible human beings claim the right to *define* goodness. *They* are good, they say. There is, of course, a contrast. Those who are not good are *below* them—the common, plebeian, pitiable, unhappy, lying ones. The nobles call these weak, shifty, untrustworthy people "bad." They are despicable, contemptible, almost beneath notice. They are slaves or fit to be slaves. Toward them the nobles have no *duties*. The "bad" have no dignity, no worth—no *goodness*.

So we have the first type of morality, that of the masters. It is characterized by a certain sort of value discrimination. Its categories are

good/bad

and moral judgments are made in those terms. Notice that all the weight lies in the first term; the concept "good" wears the pants in the family. "Bad" is just a contrast term; it designates only a shadow of the good. The masters affirm themselves and find themselves good; others hardly matter. The noble mode of valuation

> acts and grows spontaneously, it seeks its opposite only so as to affirm itself more gratefully and triumphantly—its negative concept, "low," "common," "bad," is only a subsequently-invented pale, contrasting image in relation to its positive basic concept—filled with life and passion through and through—"we noble ones, we good, beautiful, happy ones!" (*GM* 1:10)

It is clear that this sort of moral evaluation is made *from the point of view* of the masters.

Nietzsche also identifies a second type of mo-

rality: that of the slaves. Here there is a value contrast too—not "good/bad," but

good/evil,

and its psychological dynamics are very different. Here "evil" is the primary concept and is driven not by affirmation, but by negation—not by a yes to life, but by a no. So "evil" and "bad" are very different from each other. Correspondingly, the "goods" in the two moralities are also different. But this requires explanation.

Slaves are by definition the powerless. They find themselves at the mercy of those noble "beasts of prey" who call themselves "the good." They suffer from them—and they *resent* it.

> The slave revolt in morality begins when *ressentiment** itself becomes creative and gives birth to values: the *ressentiment* of natures that are denied the true reaction, that of deeds, and compensate themselves with an imaginary revenge. While every noble morality develops from a triumphant affirmation of itself, slave morality from the outset says No to what is "outside," what is "different," what is "not itself"; and *this* No is its creative deed. This inversion of the value-positing eye—this *need* to direct one's view outward instead of back to oneself—is of the essence of *ressentiment*: in order to exist, slave morality always first needs a hostile external world; it needs, physiologically speaking, external stimuli in order to act at all—its action is fundamentally reaction. (*GM* 1:10)

So the slave basically says, "No!" And to whom does the slave say no? Why, to the masters, of course—to those who say of themselves that they are the *good*. What is called "good" from the point of view of the nobles is just what the slaves call "evil." There is no way a slave will agree with the master's self-evaluation; such rapacious monsters are experienced as *evil*.

> —how different these words "bad" and "evil" are, although they are both apparently the opposite of the

---

* See Chapter 1.

* Nietzsche consistently uses the French term because there is no German word with just that nuance. I will use the corresponding English term, "resentment."

same concept "good." But it is *not* the same concept "good": one should ask rather precisely *who* is "evil" in the sense of the morality of *ressentiment*. The answer, in all strictness, is: *precisely* the "good man" of the other morality, precisely the noble, powerful man, the ruler, but dyed in another color, interpreted in another fashion, seen in another way by the venomous eye of *ressentiment*. (*GM* 1:11)

This negation of what is other than themselves, Nietzsche says, is the "creative deed" in slave morality. Picture, Nietzsche says,

> "the enemy" as the man of *ressentiment* conceives him—and here precisely is his deed, his creation: he has conceived "the evil enemy," "*the Evil One,*" and this in fact is his basic concept, from which he then evolves, as an afterthought and pendant, a "good one"—himself! (*GM* 1:10)

What, then, from the slaves' point of view, are the *good* like? Can there be any doubt? The good would have to be such as they themselves are: poor, weak, humble, serving. But this evaluation, just like "bad" for the masters, is not the basic evaluation; in this case "good" is the shadow of the primary word "evil," which expresses a negative reaction: *resistance* to the domineering arrogance of the nobles.

Being weak and powerless, however, slaves cannot immediately express their outrage over the actions of the strong. So their resentment simmers in them. It becomes a longing for revenge and colors their lives with rancor. What sort of revenge, Nietzsche asks, would be most appropriate for those who can not simply overpower their enemies? What sort would be *possible*? The most subtle, shrewd, and insidious revenge of all would be this: to persuade the strong they should adopt the values of the weak, to give them a bad conscience about their "goodness," to get *them* to say of their natural impulses, "These are evil; they must be suppressed. We are sinful. We must become 'good' (as the slaves define good)." What a triumph that would be! How delicious the revenge! How satisfying! And, Nietzsche tells us, that is just what happened.

Nietzsche identifies the Jews as the source of this slave revaluation of values. Having actually been slaves in Egypt and thereafter continually dominated by the powerful nations around them (Egypt, Assyria, Babylon, Greece, Rome), the Jews are the world-historical origin of the most powerful revision in moral values the Western world has seen.

> All that has been done on earth against "the noble," "the powerful," "the masters," "the rulers," fades into nothing compared with what the *Jews* have done against them; the Jews, that priestly people, who in opposing their enemies and conquerors were ultimately satisfied with nothing less than a radical revaluation of their enemies' values, that is to say, an act of the *most spiritual revenge*. For this alone was appropriate to a priestly people, the people embodying the most deeply repressed priestly vengefulness. It was the Jews who, with awe-inspiring consistency, dared to invert the aristocratic value-equation (good = noble = powerful = beautiful = happy = beloved of God) and to hang on to this inversion with their teeth, the teeth of the most abysmal hatred (the hatred of impotence), saying, "the wretched alone are the good; the poor, impotent, lowly alone are the good; the suffering, deprived, sick, ugly alone are pious, alone are blessed by God, blessedness is for them alone—and you, the powerful and noble, are on the contrary the evil, the cruel, the lustful, the insatiable, the godless to all eternity; and you shall be in all eternity the unblessed, accursed, and damned!" . . . With the Jews there begins *the slave revolt in morality*: that revolt which has a history of two thousand years behind it and which we no longer see because it—has been victorious. (*GM* 1:7)

Nietzsche remarks along the way, "One knows *who* inherited this Jewish revaluation" (*GM* 1:7). He means, of course, the Christians.

> . . . from the trunk of that tree of vengefulness and hatred, Jewish hatred—the profoundest and sublimest kind of hatred, capable of creating ideals and reversing values, the like of which has never existed on earth before—there grew something equally incomparable, a *new love,* the profoundest and sublimest kind of love—and from what other trunk could it have grown?
>
> One should not imagine it grew up as the denial of that thirst for revenge, as the opposite of Jewish

hatred! No, the reverse is true! That love grew out of it as its crown, as its triumphant crown spreading itself farther and farther into the purest brightness and sunlight, driven as it were into the domain of light and the heights in pursuit of the goals of that hatred—victory, spoil, and seduction—by the same impulse that drove the roots of that hatred deeper and deeper and more and more covetously into all that was profound and evil. This Jesus of Nazareth, the incarnate gospel of love, this "Redeemer" who brought blessedness and victory to the poor, the sick, and the sinners—was he not this seduction in its most uncanny and irresistible form, a seduction and bypath to precisely those *Jewish* values and new ideals? *

. . . And could spiritual subtlety imagine any *more dangerous* bait than this? Anything to equal the enticing, intoxicating, overwhelming, and undermining power of that symbol of the "holy cross," that ghastly paradox of a "God on the cross," that mystery of an unimaginable ultimate cruelty and self-crucifixion of God *for the salvation of man*?

What is certain at least is that *sub hoc signo*[†] Israel, with its vengefulness and revaluation of all values, has hitherto triumphed again and again over all other ideals, over all *nobler* ideals.— (*GM* 1:8)

So slave morality has triumphed—triumphed in Christianity's domination of our culture for two thousand years. Our values, Nietzsche believes, are Judeo-Christian values. And now we are ready for the big question, the question Nietzsche thinks he is the first to ask: What *value* do these values have?

Our Morality

Think again about Kant and the utilitarians, the sponsors of the two most powerful moral theories of modern times. Although they have many differences, they have something in common: Both assert the equal dignity and value of each individual human being. For Kant, this equality is grounded in the fact that every one of us is equally rational

and that the *same* moral law is legislated categorically for each of us. Utilitarianism specifies that when we calculate the greatest happiness, *each one is to count for one*. In either case, no basic inequality of value is allowed to exist between humans; there is no "order of rank" that would allow moral privileges to certain persons and not others. This emphasis on basic equality in our values, Nietzsche believes, can be traced back to the slave revolt in morality; after all, it is the slaves, not the masters, who have an interest in leveling things out. This insistence on equality is a (more or less secular) consequence of the Christian theme that we are equally children of God, equally precious in his sight.

But is this egalitarianism something we should prize? Or is it a symptom of decadence, weakness, illness, resentment—of a basic dissatisfaction with life? Our morality, Nietzsche thinks, is the morality of *the herd*.

> We have found that in all major moral judgments Europe is now of one mind, including even the countries dominated by the influence of Europe; plainly, one now *knows* in Europe what Socrates thought he did not know and what that famous old serpent once promised to teach—today one "knows" what is good and evil.
>
> Now it must sound harsh and cannot be heard easily when we keep insisting: that which here believes it knows, that which here glorifies itself with its praises and reproaches, calling itself good, that is the instinct of the herd animal, man, which has scored a breakthrough and attained prevalence and predominance over other instincts. . . . *Morality in Europe today is herd animal morality*—in other words, as we understand it, merely *one* type of human morality beside which, before which, and after which many other types, above all *higher* moralities, are, or ought to be, possible. But this morality resists such a "possibility," such an "ought" with all its power: it says stubbornly and inexorably, "I am morality itself, and nothing besides is morality." (*BGE* 202)

In this context, Nietzsche calls himself an "immoralist" (*BGE* 31, 226; *EH,* 327, 328, 331) and a "**free spirit**" (*HA,* 6–8; *GS* 343, 347; *TI,* 554; *EH,* 280, 283). Nietzsche assails "modern ideas"

---

* For Nietzsche's interpretation of Jesus as someone *incapable* of resisting evil, see *The Antichrist*, sections 27–35. The sections following 35 give Nietzsche's view of how Christianity betrayed the spirit of Jesus.

[†] "Under this sign."

and "modern men," with their claims to equality and equal rights and their advocacy of democracy and socialism. Zarathustra says,

> I do not wish to be mixed up and confused with these preachers of equality. For, to *me* justice speaks thus: "Men are not equal." Nor shall they become equal! (*Z* 2, 213)

Why should men not *become* equal? Because the only way that could happen is by leveling down to the average or below the average: to the level of the herd. And to do that is to give in to the morality of resentment, of revenge—the morality of slaves.

Zarathustra's story begins with the prophet high on a mountain, outside his cave, where he has lived alone for ten years. He believes he has some wisdom to share and descends from the heights to impart it to men. He speaks to a crowd in a village market place about a superior kind of human being he calls "the overman" (see the next section), but they don't want to hear it. Then he tries to motivate their interest with a description of "what is most contemptible." Zarathustra calls this "the *last man*":

> "Alas, the time is coming when man will no longer give birth to a star. Alas, the time of the most despicable man is coming, he that is no longer able to despise himself. Behold, I show you the *last man*.
>
> "'What is love? What is creation? What is longing? What is a star?' thus asks the last man, and he blinks.
>
> "The earth has become small, and on it hops the last man, who makes everything small. His race is as ineradicable as the flea-beetle; the last man lives longest.
>
> "'We have invented happiness,' say the last men, and they blink. They have left the regions where it was hard to live, for one needs warmth. One still loves one's neighbor and rubs against him, for one needs warmth.
>
> "Becoming sick and harboring suspicion are sinful to them: one proceeds carefully. A fool, whoever still stumbles over stones or human beings! A little poison now and then: that makes for agreeable dreams. And much poison in the end, for an agreeable death.

> "One still works, for work is a form of entertainment. But one is careful lest the entertainment be too harrowing. One no longer becomes poor or rich: both require too much exertion. Who still wants to rule? Who obey? Both require too much exertion.
>
> "No shepherd and one herd! Everybody wants the same, everybody is the same: whoever feels differently goes voluntarily into a madhouse.
>
> "'Formerly, all the world was mad,' say the most refined, and they blink.
>
> "One is clever and knows everything that has ever happened: so there is no end of derision. One still quarrels, but one is soon reconciled—else it might spoil the digestion.
>
> "One has one's little pleasure for the day and one's little pleasure for the night: but one has a regard for health.
>
> "'We have invented happiness,' say the last men, and they blink." (*Z* 1, 129–30)

Zarathustra is obviously full of contempt for such a safe, cautious, careful, timid, excessively prudent form of life. He sneers at the idea that *here* one finds happiness. But what happens? The crowd interrupts him with "clamor and delight":

> "Give us this last man, O Zarathustra," they shouted. Turn us into these last men! Then we shall make you a gift of the overman!" (*Z* 1, 130)

Our morality, Nietzsche believes, has turned us into such "last men." Or, if we are not yet quite "last men," that is what we long to be: comfortable, easily satisfied, without pain and suffering—"happy." Everyone has an equal right to this, we think. Nietzsche's Zarathustra means to teach us (or those of us with ears to hear) to *despise* such a life.

Zarathustra compares the preachers of equality to tarantulas. He says of them:

> Revenge sits in your soul: wherever you bite, black scabs grow; your poison makes the soul whirl with revenge.
>
> Thus I speak to you in a parable—you who make souls whirl, you preachers of *equality*. To me you are tarantulas, and secretly vengeful. But I shall bring your secrets to light; therefore I laugh in your faces

with my laughter of the heights. Therefore I tear at your webs, that your rage may lure you out of your lie-holes and your revenge may leap out from behind your word justice. For *that man be delivered from revenge,* that is for me the bridge to the highest hope, and a rainbow after long storms. (*Z* 2, 211)

Nietzsche hopes to bring to light the dark and dirty secrets hidden in our highest values—to show us that behind such words as "equality" and "justice for all" stand hatred, revenge, resentment, weakness, and spite. And why does he want to expose those secrets? So that we might at last "be delivered from revenge," from negation and saying, "No!" Our "highest values," those we most pay homage to, have been inherited from that first revaluation of values. But we can see that they are based on lies.

> When the oppressed, downtrodden, outraged exhort one another with the vengeful cunning of impotence: "let us be different from the evil, namely good! And he is good who does not outrage, who harms nobody, who does not attack, who does not requite, who leaves revenge to God, who keeps himself hidden as we do, who avoids evil and desires little from life, like us, the patient, humble, and just"
> —this, listened to calmly and without previous bias, really amounts to no more than: "we weak ones, are, after all, weak; it would be good if we did nothing *for which we are not strong enough*"; but this dry matter of fact, this prudence of the lowest order which even insects possess (posing as dead, when in great danger, so as not to do "too much"), has, thanks to the counterfeit and self-deception of impotence, clad itself in the ostentatious garb of the virtue of quiet, calm resignation, just as if the weakness of the weak—that is to say, their *essence,* their effects, their sole ineluctable, irremovable reality—were a voluntary, achievement, willed, chosen, a *deed, a meritorious act.* (*GM* 1:13)

The "virtues" of slave morality are really just what the weak *cannot help but do.* The weak, however, interpret these virtues as something they choose—something for which they deserve credit. But, Nietzsche says, this is "counterfeit" and "self-deception." He invites us to peer into the work-

shop where ideals are made. Here is the voice of someone who looks carefully.

> "It seems to me one is lying; a saccharine sweetness clings to every sound. Weakness is being lied into something *meritorious,* no doubt of it—so it is just as you said"—
> —Go on!
> —"and impotence which does not requite into 'goodness of heart'; anxious lowliness into 'humility'; subjection to those one hates into 'obedience' (that is, to one of whom they say he commands this subjection—they call him God). The inoffensiveness of the weak man, even the cowardice of which he has so much, his lingering at the door, his being ineluctably compelled to wait, here acquire flattering names, such as 'patience,' and are even called virtue itself; his inability for revenge is called unwillingness to revenge, perhaps even forgiveness. . . . They also speak of 'loving one's enemies'—and sweat as they do so." . . .
> —Go on!
> —"Now they give me to understand that they are not merely better than the mighty, the lords of the earth whose spittle they have to lick (*not* from fear, not at all from fear! but because God has commanded them to obey the authorities)—that they are not merely better but are also 'better off,' or at least will be better off someday. But enough! enough! I can't take any more. Bad air! Bad air! This workshop where *ideals are manufactured*—it seems to me it stinks of so many lies." (*GM* 1:14)

This morality, Nietzsche claims, is *our* morality. Jerusalem has decisively overcome Rome; "consider to whom one bows down in Rome itself today . . ." (*GM* 1:16).

There is one additional, absolutely crucial, lie that Nietzsche believes the weak and impotent tell. They tell it to themselves—and to their enemies. It is the lie about *free will.* In truth, Nietzsche holds, there is no such thing as a free will. Human beings are body entirely; they are animals. As we have seen, he even calls us mechanisms. But unless there were a free will, how could the weak take credit for their "virtues"? And, even more important, how could they blame the strong for their "crimes"? Nietzsche holds that the concept of "free will" is the foulest of all theologians' artifices, aimed at making mankind "responsible" in their sense, that is, *dependent upon them.* . . .

Wherever responsibilities are sought, it is usually the instinct of wanting to judge and punish which is at work. Becoming has been deprived of its innocence when any being-such-and-such is traced back to will, to purposes, to acts of responsibility: the doctrine of the will has been invented essentially for the purpose of punishment, that is, because one wanted to impute guilt. The entire old psychology, the psychology of will, was conditioned by the fact that its originators, the priests at the head of ancient communities, wanted to create for themselves the right to punish—or wanted to create this right for God. Men were considered "free" so that they might be judged and punished—so that they might become *guilty:* consequently, every act had to be considered as willed, and the origin of every act had to be considered as lying within the consciousness. . . . (*TI,* 499–500)

But consciousness, as we have seen, is not where the action is. Consciousness is altogether too superficial to contain the causes for actions, which actually lie in the physiological conditions of the body. So actions could not be due to "free will" for the very good reason that they are not due to will at all. The idea of "free will" is an invention, an interpretation of the facts by those who wanted very much to be able to hold people accountable, to persuade people they were guilty, sinful, and evil in the sight of God—because *they could have done otherwise*!

The truth is quite to the contrary, Nietzsche believes.

One is necessary, one is a piece of fatefulness, one belongs to the whole, one is in the whole; there is nothing which could judge, measure, compare, or sentence our being, for that would mean judging, measuring, comparing, or sentencing the whole. But there is nothing besides the whole. That nobody is held responsible any longer, that the mode of being may not be traced back to a *causa prima,** that the world does not form a unity either as a sensorium or as "spirit"—that alone is the great liberation; with

this alone is the innocence of becoming restored. The concept of "God" was until now the greatest objection to existence. We deny God, we deny the responsibility in God: only thereby do we redeem the world. (*TI,* 500–501)

One of Nietzsche's aims is to restore a sense of the "innocence" of life, freed from the slanders of sin and guilt. "Atheism and a kind of *second innocence* belong together" (*GM* 2:20). Christians believe the world is "redeemed" by the sacrifice of Christ on the cross for human sin. Nietzsche thinks to "redeem" the world by denying sin, Christ, and God altogether. As he sees it, the concepts of free will, sin, guilt, and responsibility are part and parcel of the revolution in values he calls "slave morality." And Nietzsche calls for a new "revaluation of values" in which none of these concepts that "taint" existence has a place.

We would get Nietzsche wrong, however, if we thought that he wants to get back again to the master morality of Homer's epic heroes. Despite their love of life, their self-affirmation and yes-saying, there is something simple-minded, naive, and slightly stupid about these "nobles." The long history of resentment and self-deception has also been a history of self-examination, self-discipline, training, obedience, and hardness toward oneself and others. Through it we have become subtler, deeper, more—human. Through this long process, Nietzsche says, everything became more dangerous,

not only cures and remedies, but also arrogance, revenge, acuteness, profligacy, love, lust to rule, virtue, disease—but it is only fair to add that it was on the soil of this *essentially dangerous* form of human existence, the priestly form, that man first became *an interesting animal,* that only here did the human soul in a higher sense acquire *depth* and become *evil*—and these are the two basic respects in which man has hitherto been superior to other beasts! (*GM* 1:6)

There is no going back. We need to go forward—"beyond good and evil." And with that thought we are ready to consider Nietzsche's concept of the overman.

---

* "First cause"

The Overman

"*Dead are all gods,*" Zarathustra says; "*now we want the overman to live*" (Z 1, 191). When Zarathustra arrives at the village, fresh from his ten-year retreat on the mountain, his first words to the crowd in the market place concern the overman.*

> "*I teach you the overman.* Man is something that shall be overcome. What have you done to overcome him?
>
> "All beings so far have created something beyond themselves; and do you want to be the ebb of this great flood and even go back to the beasts rather than overcome man? What is the ape to man? A laughing-stock or a painful embarrassment. And man shall be just that for the overman: a laughing stock or a painful embarrassment. You have made your way from worm to man, and much in you is still worm. Once you were apes, and even now, too, man is more ape than any ape. . . .
>
> "Behold, I teach you the overman. The overman is the meaning of the earth. Let your will say: the overman *shall be* the meaning of the earth! I beseech you, my brothers, *remain faithful to the earth,* and do not believe those who speak to you of otherworldly hopes!" (Z 1, 124–25)

In *The Birth of Tragedy,* Nietzsche addresses himself to the problem of the meaning of life and the value of existence. He thinks he can solve the problem by accepting a certain metaphysical theory: the view of Schopenhauer that reality *in itself* is will. In the Dionysian affirmation of the primordial will, triggered by tragedy, individuals can be saved from pessimism about life by realizing that they *are* life; they are identical with the surging, nonindividualized, eternal reality of the will. But then we see that Nietzsche comes to

believe that philosophy cannot guarantee a metaphysical theory. "True worlds" of all sorts—Platonic, Christian, Kantian—vanish, Schopenhauer's along with them.

But although God is dead, Nietzsche says, otherworldly values continue to hold sway. The morality of "good and evil" is still our morality. It is a morality of resentment against any natural "order of rank" in life. It is a morality that says no to life as it expresses itself in the strong and healthy, levels down to the mediocre herd, and appeals to the commandments of God for validation. In so doing, this morality sets itself *against life itself.* Because of our morality's negative orientation to the basic conditions of life and its longing for *another* life, Nietzsche thinks pessimism still reigns among us. Nihilism is undefeated, and the problem of the meaning of life is unsolved.

Zarathustra proposes to solve it. And the overman is the key. The overman, he says, "is the meaning of the earth." Nietzsche is obviously drawing on evolutionary theory here. Human beings as they now are—*you and I*—cannot be what all these eons of evolution have been for. That would be too petty, too small, too absurd. It could not be that all the while *life* has been driving at *us*! No, "man is something that shall be overcome."

> "Man is a rope, tied between beast and overman—a rope over an abyss. A dangerous across, a dangerous on-the-way, a dangerous looking-back, a dangerous shuddering and stopping.
>
> "What is great in man is that he is a bridge and not an end: what can be loved in man is that he is an *overture* and a *going under.*" (Z 1, 126–27)

Nietzsche clearly has in mind some mode of life that is not "human, all-too-human" (as our lives typically are) but human, *more than human.* Zarathustra is the prophet of the overman. In the life of the overman, the earth itself will find its meaning, and the problem of "the value of existence" will find its solution.

We need to try to understand what sort of life Nietzsche imagines this to be. What is an overman like? Nietzsche returns to this question again and again, though not always under the rubric of

---

*This is the point at which it must be acknowledged that "overmen" do not seem to include women. Only males, for instance, are among the "higher men" in Zarathustra's cave at the end of his quest for wisdom. Nietzsche writes quite a lot about women, of which this is a representative sample: "Woman wants to become self-reliant—and for that reason she is beginning to enlighten men about 'woman as such': *this* is one of the worst developments of the general *uglification* of Europe" (*BGE* 232).

"overman"; for instance, the last section in *Beyond Good and Evil,* "What is Noble," addresses this same issue. What he says is exceptionally rich and complex, often expressed in poetic form that a brief treatment can hardly do justice to. (There really is no substitute for reading lots of Nietzsche.) But here we will try to set out a number of the principal themes.

1. An overman will "remain faithful to the earth." There will be no hankerings for a "true world"—for the soul, God, immortality, heaven. None of these fictions can solve the problem of the value of existence.

> It was suffering and incapacity that created all afterworlds—this and that brief madness of bliss which is experienced only by those who suffer most deeply.
>
> Weariness that wants to reach the ultimate with one leap, with one fatal leap, a poor ignorant weariness that does not want to want any more: this created all gods and afterworlds. . . .
>
> Many sick people have always been among the poetizers and God-cravers; furiously they hate the lover of knowledge and that youngest among the virtues, which is called "honesty." . . .
>
> Listen rather, my brothers, to the voice of the healthy body: that is a more honest and purer voice. More honestly and purely speaks the healthy body that is perfect and perpendicular: * and it speaks of the meaning of the earth. (*Z* 1, 143–45)

Belief in "afterworlds" is a symptom of suffering and sickness and weariness with life. The overman will have none of it.

2. There is a "physiological presupposition" for the overman (*EH,* 298). The overman will be possessed of "*the great health,* . . . a new health, stronger, more seasoned, tougher, more audacious, and gayer than any previous health" (*GS* 382). The healthy body, Zarathustra says, speaks true, and what it says reveals the meaning of the earth. But how can that be? How can a *body* say anything at all?

> "Body am I, and soul"—thus speaks the child. And why should one not speak like children?

---

* "Perpendicular," no doubt, because it is not on its knees praying.

> But the awakened and knowing say: body am I entirely, and nothing else; and soul is only a word for something about the body.
>
> The body is a great reason, a plurality with one sense, a war and a peace, a herd and a shepherd. An instrument of your body is also your little reason, my brother, which you call "spirit"—a little instrument and toy of your great reason. . . .
>
> Behind your thoughts and feelings, my brother, there stands a mighty ruler, an unknown sage—whose name is self. In your body he dwells; he is your body.
>
> There is more reason in your body than in your best wisdom. (*Z* 1, 146–47)

If we are "body entirely," then in all our thinking and reasoning, the *body* thinks and reasons. Beneath the surface of our conscious life, there are tendencies opposing one another ("war"), quarrels resolved ("peace"), some forces dominant ("shepherd"), others submissive ("herd"). What we experience as our reasoning, our deliberation, our oh-so-highly-prized rationality (our "little reason," Nietzsche says) is nothing more than the body at work—our "great reason."

Why would a *body* invent stories about a soul and an afterlife? Because it is at war with itself; it is ill, "angry with life and the earth" (*Z* 1, p. 147). Sick bodies create "true worlds" as compensation. A body possessing "the great health," by contrast, would need no compensation. An overman would trust the body, and in so doing would trust himself—but then the body of someone who could be called an overman would be a body that *could* be trusted.

Someone possessed of this "great health" would be able to experience in his own body all the drives and pretenses to wisdom that *any* body could experience—the tendencies to lie and deceive oneself born of weakness, as well as the exuberance of great health and strength. Such a person could *diagnose* illness, expose the *actors,* distinguish the true from the false. Nietzsche says of such a person:

> whoever wants to know from the adventures of his own most authentic experience how a discoverer and conqueror of the ideal feels, and also an artist, a saint,

a legislator, a sage, a scholar, a pious man, a sooth-sayer, and one who stands divinely apart in the old style—needs one thing above everything else: the *great health.* . . .

And now, after we have long been on our way in this manner, we argonauts of the ideal, with more daring perhaps than is prudent, and have suffered shipwreck and damage often enough, but are, to repeat it, healthier than one likes to permit us, danger-ously healthy, ever again healthy—it will seem to us as if, as a reward, we now confronted an as yet un-discovered country whose boundaries nobody has surveyed yet, something beyond all the lands and nooks of the ideal so far, a world so overrich in what is beautiful, strange, questionable, terrible, and di-vine that our curiosity as well as our craving to pos-sess it has got beside itself—alas, now nothing will sate us any more.

After such vistas and with such a burning hunger in our conscience and science, how could we still be satisfied with *present-day man?* (*GS* 382)

This "undiscovered country . . . beyond all the lands and nooks of the ideal so far" is where the overman lives. A prerequisite for living there—in-deed, even for discovering its existence—is the great health. Nietzsche clearly thinks of himself as one of those "argonauts of the ideal" who has sailed many a sea to find this place.* He describes it this way:

Another ideal runs ahead of us, a strange, tempt-ing, dangerous ideal to which we should not wish to

---

*The first section of Nietzsche's quasi-autobiographical book *Ecce Homo* (which means, "Behold, the man"—the phrase taken from Pilate's words as he presents the scourged Jesus to the crowd) is titled, "Why I Am So Wise." Here Nietzsche tells us of his long illness, of his weakness, of the incredible pains he suffered. But never to complain. No, he is *grateful* for it. "I took myself in hand, I made myself healthy again: the condition for this—every physi-ologist would admit that—is *that one be healthy at bottom.* A typi-cally morbid being cannot become healthy, much less make itself healthy. For a typically healthy person, conversely, being sick can even become an energetic *stimulus* for life, for living *more.* This, in fact, is how that long period of sickness appears to me *now:* as it were, I discovered life anew, including myself; I tasted all good and even little things, as others cannot easily taste them—I turned my will to health, to *life*, into a philosophy. For it should be noted: it was during the years of my lowest vitality that I *ceased* to be a pessimist; the instinct of self-restoration *forbade* me a philosophy of poverty and discouragement" (*EH,* 224).

persuade anybody because we do not readily con-cede *the right to it* to anyone: the ideal of a spirit who plays naively—that is, not deliberately but from overflowing power and abundance—with all that was hitherto called holy, good, untouchable, divine; for whom those supreme things that the people naturally accept as their value standards, signify danger, decay, debasement, or at least recrea-tion, blindness, and temporary self-oblivion; the ideal of a human, superhuman well-being and be-nevolence that will often appear *inhuman*—for ex-ample, when it confronts all earthly seriousness so far. . . . (*GS* 382)

Note that Nietzsche is not eager to persuade you and me to adopt this ideal. We *probably* do not have the *right* to it. The chances are near to over-whelming that you and I are not overmen, and if we tried to put on this ideal, if *we* thought we could easily go "beyond good and evil," we would almost certainly become mere "actors" of that ideal. And for such "actors" Nietzsche has the greatest contempt.

3.   The notion that the overman "plays naively" with what has hitherto been called good and di-vine, parallels what Zarathustra says about the nec-essary "metamorphoses of the spirit." He tells us "how the spirit becomes a camel; and the camel, a lion; and the lion, finally, a child" (*Z* 1, 137).

What is difficult? asks the spirit that would bear much, and kneels down like a camel wanting to be well loaded. What is most difficult, O heroes, asks the spirit that would bear much, that I may take it upon myself and exult in my strength? (*Z* 1, 138)

The easy path, the soft life of pleasure and indul-gence, is not for an overman. An overman seeks out what is "most difficult" and loads it on his back. Discipline, obedience, and bearing heavy burdens is part of an overman's training. An over-man is someone who is hard on himself and oth-ers. A spirit that would attain great heights cannot *begin* there, any more than an apprentice cabinet-maker can begin as a master craftsman.*

---

*Nietzsche began his career by learning the demanding craft of philology. Students sometimes think they should be able to skip the camel phase—not have to bear the burden of tracing out the

In the loneliest desert, however, the second metamorphosis occurs: here the spirit becomes a lion who would conquer his freedom and be master in his own desert. Here he seeks out his last master: he wants to fight him and his last god; for ultimate victory he wants to fight with the great dragon.

Who is the great dragon whom the spirit will no longer call lord and god? "Thou shalt" is the name of the great dragon. But the spirit of the lion says, "I will." "Thou shalt" lies in his way, sparkling like gold, an animal covered with scales; and on every scale shines a golden "thou shalt."

Values, thousands of years old, shine on these scales; and thus speaks the mightiest of all dragons: "All value of all things shines on me. All value has long been created, and I am all created value. Verily, there shall be no more 'I will.'" (Z 1, 138–39)

The spirit that would attain to overman status cannot be content with bearing the burdens of the camel. In the guise of a lion, the spirit says "No!" to all "Thou shalts" and thus opens up a space for freedom—a space in which new values can be created.

> But say, my brothers, what can the child do that even the lion could not do? Why must the preying lion still become a child? The child is innocence and forgetting, a new beginning, a game, a self-propelled wheel, a first movement, a sacred "Yes." For the game of creation, my brothers, a sacred "Yes" is needed: the spirit now wills his own will, and he who had been lost to the world now conquers his own world. (Z 1, 139)

The "naive play" of the overman is the play of a child—a yes to his own life that grows out of great health. It is the "innocence" of the child "willing his own will."* The child plays "the game of creation." And what does the child create? Values.

4. So the overman is a creator of values. And creation cannot take place without a corresponding destruction—the "No!" of the lion. "Whoever must be a creator always annihilates" (Z 1, 171). But the overman does not create heedlessly or arbitrarily. The child does not play dice with values. The principal thing the overman creates is *himself*. And his values are simply expressions of who he is.*

> We, however, *want to become those we are*—human beings who are new, unique, incomparable, who give themselves laws, who create themselves. (GS 335)

In *Ecce Homo,* Nietzsche says a surprising thing.

> To become what one is, one must not have the faintest notion *what* one is. . . .
>
> The whole surface of consciousness—consciousness *is* a surface—must be kept clear of all great imperatives. Beware even of every great word, every great pose! So many dangers that the instinct comes too soon to "understand itself"—. Meanwhile the organizing "idea" that is destined to rule keeps growing deep down—it begins to command; slowly it leads us *back* from side roads and wrong roads; it prepares *single* qualities and fitnesses that will one day prove to be indispensable as a means toward a whole—one by one, it trains all *subservient* capacities before giving any hint of the dominant task, "goal," "aim," or "meaning." (EH, 254)

The danger is that one gets an idea of *what one is* and then tries to conform to that idea. But in that case one has almost certainly got it *wrong*, and one will become merely the ape of an ideal that is *not* one's own—again, merely an actor. One must not decide too soon what one is or take the idea of what one is from others; this is good advice for everyone, Nietzsche thinks. And it is absolutely essential advice for those few who are possessed of the great health and are capable of becoming overmen. For it is *themselves* they want to create, not some cracked and misshapen image of themselves.

It is not the case, however, that an overman can just lie back and wait for what he is to unfold itself. That way one will get nothing worthwhile. All

---

arguments of Plato, Aristotle, and Kant—and become philosophers immediately, without effort. But one way or another, in everything worth while, one must first be a camel. Great pianists have practiced many scales.

* Compare Augustine on the "innocence" of children, p. 234.

---

* Compare Kierkegaard on being willing to be oneself, pp. 453–455.

creators, Nietzsche tells us, are *hard*—most of all, hard on themselves.

> "Among the conditions for a *Dionysian* task are, in a decisive way, the hardness of the hammer, the *joy even in destroying.* The imperative, "become hard!" the most fundamental certainty *that all creators are hard,* is the distinctive mark of a Dionysian nature." *
> (EH, 309)

An overman demands much, has a right to demand much. He demands most of all from himself. Zarathustra warns:

> But the worst enemy you can encounter will always be you, yourself; you lie in wait for yourself in caves and woods.
> Lonely one, you are going the way to yourself. . . . You must wish to consume yourself in your own flame: how could you wish to become new unless you had first become ashes! . . .
> Lonely one, you are going the way of the lover: yourself you love, and therefore you despise yourself, as only lovers despise. The lover would create because he despises. What does he know of love who did not have to despise precisely what he loved? (Z 1, 176–77)

Not for the overman a sweet contentment with his present state. No easy self-esteem. He climbs over himself on his way to himself. Love of himself is inseparable from contempt—contempt of whatever in himself has not yet become perfect. The overman overcomes himself, "giving style" to his character.

> . . . a great and rare art! It is practiced by those who survey all the strengths and weaknesses of their nature and then fit them into an artistic plan until every one of them appears as art and reason and even weaknesses delight the eye. Here a large mass of second nature has been added; there a piece of original nature has been removed—both times through long

practice and daily work at it. Here the ugly that could not be removed is concealed; there it has been reinterpreted and made sublime. Much that is vague and resisted shaping has been saved and exploited for distant views; it is meant to beckon toward the far and immeasurable. In the end, when the work is finished, it becomes evident how the constraint of a single taste governed and formed everything large and small. (GS 290)

So the overman is the poet of his life, the artist who both creates the work and lives it. In *The Birth of Tragedy,* Nietzsche says that existence and the world can be justified only as an aesthetic phenomenon. On this point Nietzsche has not changed his mind. If the overman is going to become the meaning of the earth, he will do it by creating himself as a work of art. Zarathustra considers those who are "sublime." By "the sublime," he means those who have struggled hard for the heights and attained them, but who still have "tense souls" filled with the exertion of control. He admires them but considers that they have not yet reached the pinnacle.

> To stand with relaxed muscles and unharnessed will: that is most difficult for all of you who are sublime.
> When power becomes gracious and descends into the visible—such descent I call beauty.
> And there is nobody from whom I want beauty as much as from you who are powerful: let your kindness be your final self-conquest.
> Of all evil I deem you capable: therefore I want the good from you.
> Verily, I have often laughed at the weaklings who thought themselves good because they had no claws. (Z 2, 230)

It is the *beauty* of the overman that makes life worthwhile.

5. The overman loves himself. In deliberate opposition to the morality of "good and evil," Nietzsche praises selfishness. Zarathustra, for the first time,

> pronounced *selfishness* blessed, the wholesome, healthy selfishness that wells from a powerful soul— from a powerful soul to which belongs the high

---

*Here we see that Dionysus does not disappear when the "true worlds" of The Birth of Tragedy are left behind. But the conception of the god deepens and changes substantially, as we shall see. An overman is clearly a "Dionysian nature." In his last book, *Ecce Homo,* Nietzsche identifies *himself* with Dionysus.

body, beautiful, triumphant, refreshing, around which everything becomes a mirror—the supple, persuasive body, the dancer whose parable and epitome is the self-enjoying soul. The self enjoyment of such bodies and souls calls itself "virtue." (Z 3, 302)

It is worth noting that it is the selfishness of "a powerful soul" in a "high body" that is praised—not every kind of selfishness. Only an overman has a *right* to such selfishness.

> Self-interest is worth as much as the person who has it: it can be worth a great deal, and it can be unworthy and contemptible. (*TI*, 533)

> There is also another selfishness, an all-too-poor and hungry one that always wants to steal—the selfishness of the sick: sick selfishness. With the eyes of a thief it looks at everything splendid; with the greed of hunger it sizes up those who have much to eat; and always it sneaks around the table of those who give. Sickness speaks out of such craving and invisible degeneration; the thievish greed of this selfishness speaks of a diseased body. (Z 1, 187)

Since we know what Nietzsche thinks of sickness and diseased bodies, there is no question about his attitude toward this kind of selfishness. But what can we say of the higher selfishness, the kind appropriate to the higher man?

Perhaps above all, the higher selfishness is the overman's determination not to be drawn *away from himself*. If *the task* is to become who we are, then all sorts of enticements to betray that task must be resisted—for the sake of the self! In the same passage where Zarathustra praises selfishness, he contrasts it with

- "whatever is cowardly,"
- "anyone who always worries, sighs, is miserable,"
- "anyone who picks up even the smallest advantages,"
- "all wisdom that wallows in grief,"
- "the subservient, the doglike, who immediately lie on their backs, the humble,"
- "those who never offer resistance, who swallow poisonous spittle and evil glances, the all-too-

patient, all-suffering, always satisfied; for that is servile,"
- "especially the whole wicked, nitwitted, witless foolishness of priests," and the
- "'selfless.'" (Z 3, 302–3)

There is one mode of being drawn away from oneself that Zarathustra particularly pillories: what Christians call love of the neighbor.*

> You crowd around your neighbor and have fine words for it. But I say unto you: your love of the neighbor is your bad love of yourselves. You flee to your neighbor from yourselves and would like to make a virtue out of that: but I see through your "selfishness.". . .
> Do I recommend love of the neighbor to you? Sooner I should even recommend flight from the neighbor and love of the farthest. . . . But you are afraid and run to your neighbor. . . . (Z 1, 172–73)

As Zarathustra interprets it, neighbor love is another one of those virtues "lied" into existence by the weak; they are dissatisfied with themselves, and they "flee" to the neighbor. Being occupied with the sufferings of others, Zarathustra thinks, is a way of avoiding the hard task of creating oneself. Selflessness is praised by those who have no self worth prizing. Neighbor love is part of the "morality of timidity," that the herd praises to thwart "everything that elevates an individual above the herd and intimidates the neighbor" (*BGE* 201). But once again, as with selfishness generally, there can be a bad and a good form of loving one's neighbor.

> "Do love your neighbor as yourself, but first be such as *love themselves*—loving with a great love, loving with a great contempt." Thus speaks Zarathustra the godless. (Z 3, 284)

As we have seen, loving oneself is being *hard* on oneself, loving oneself "with a great contempt" for all in one's life that has not yet been "given style."†
Loving one's neighbor "as yourself" would involve the same hardness and contempt.

---

* Compare Jesus' parable of the Good Samaritan, p. 209.
† See p. 512.

6. Zarathustra praises not the accidental and anonymous "neighbor," but the friend.

> I teach you not the neighbor, but the friend. The friend should be the festival of the earth to you and an anticipation of the overman. I teach you the friend and his overflowing heart. . . .
> Let the future and the farthest be for you the cause of your today: in your friend you shall love the overman as your cause. (Z 1, 173–74)

A friend is not *someone who needs you,* and you should not "flee" to your friend out of need. A true friend is one with an "overflowing heart," which, of course, requires the "great health." A friend shares what is highest—the passion for self-overcoming. Friends are not just good-time buddies, occasions for enjoyment. Friends stimulate each other to excel; each demands more and ever more from the other—more, that is, of the other's nobility and self-mastery.

> In a friend one should have one's best enemy. You should be closest to him with your heart when you resist him. (Z 1, 168)

> . . . let us be enemies too, my friends! Let us strive against one another like gods. (Z 2, 214)

7. As the prophet of the overman, Zarathustra is also the prophet of *the will to power.*

> Where I found the living, there I found will to power; and even in the will of those who serve I found the will to be master. . . .
> And life itself confided this secret to me: "Behold," it said, "I am *that which must always overcome itself.* Indeed, you call it a will to procreate or a drive to an end, to something higher, farther, more manifold: but all this is one, and one secret. . . .
> "Whatever I create and however much I love it— soon I must oppose it and my love; thus my will wills it. And you too, lover of knowledge, are only a path and footprint of my will; verily, my will to power walks also on the heels of your will to truth. (Z 2, 226–27)

In every kind of overcoming, every will to a higher state, in every valuation and esteeming, Zarathu-

stra detects the will to power.* It is will to power that seeks truth.† It is will to power that creates tablets of values—as a means to self-control and mastery, to more power!

> A tablet of the good hangs over every people. Behold, it is the tablet of their overcomings; behold, it is the voice of their will to power. (Z 1, 170)

Will to power drives the revenge of the weak and motivates the slave rebellion in morality. And will to power points us toward the overman as the one in whom power is at its peak. That is why the overman can be the meaning of the earth. Overman is what life—all life—is driving towards.

The power of the overman is primarily *self-mastery, self*-overcoming; it is the enjoyment of an overfull, overflowing, abundant life in which one is no longer dominated by need, aching, longing, or wishing that things might be otherwise. The life of an overman is a life *beyond revenge* and *without resentment.*

> But if you have an enemy, do not requite him evil with good, for that would put him to shame. Rather prove that he did you some good. (Z 1, 180)

> One needs only to do me some wrong, I "repay" it—you may be sure of that: soon I find an opportu-

---

*You may be wondering how Nietzsche can identify will to power as the key drive in all existence, when he has attacked the will as superficial and hardly the sort of thing that can serve as a cause. The answer is that will to power is not the *conscious* will; it is not the intention to which we normally ascribe action. Will to power is simply *life itself* climbing over itself, overcoming every plateau, always seeking mastery and control—whether consciously or not. Needless to say, this is not Schopenhauer's *metaphysical* will, either; will to power is meant to be a characterization of life in *this* world.
†In an important speech called "On Immaculate Perception," Zarathustra attacks the idea that there can be any disinterested, purely contemplative, spectator-like knowledge. *All* of our knowing and pursuit of truth is driven by desire, interest, will. The trick is not to pare these passions away, but to multiply them (as "great health" makes possible), to add perspectives so as to gain the *height* from which an overman can survey the truth. "How much truth does a spirit *endure,* how much truth does it *dare*? More and more that became for me the real measure of value. Error (faith in the ideal) is not blindness, error is *cowardice*" (EH, 218).

nity for expressing my gratitude to the "evil-doer" (at times even for his evil deed). . . . (*EH*, 229)

No blaming, no accusations, no complaining. No victim-think. No self-pity. *No pity at all.* The life of an overman will not be without suffering, pain, and struggle; but an overman is strong enough for that, too. More to the point, an overman is *grateful* for it. That, too, can be overcome.

All this may sound attractive; we might like to be overmen, too. But we should not be naive about the power of an overman. It is a life, after all, *beyond good and evil.* And Nietzsche on numerous occasions takes pains to tell us how dangerous overmen can be. In the chapter on "What is Noble," Nietzsche says:

> Refraining mutually from injury, violence, and exploitation and placing one's will on a par with that of someone else—this may become, in a certain rough sense, good manners among individuals if the appropriate conditions are present (namely, if these men are actually similar in strength and value standards and belong together in *one* body). But as soon as this principle is extended, and possibly even accepted as the *fundamental principle of society,* it immediately proves to be what it really is—a will to the *denial* of life, a principle of disintegration and decay.
>
> Here we must beware of superficiality and get to the bottom of the matter, resisting all sentimental weakness: life itself is *essentially* appropriation, injury, overpowering of what is alien and weaker; suppression, hardness, imposition of one's own forms, incorporation and at least, at its mildest, exploitation—but why should one always use those words in which a slanderous intent has been imprinted for ages?
>
> Even the body within which individuals treat each other as equals, as suggested before—and this happens in every healthy aristocracy—if it is a living and not a dying body, has to do to other bodies what the individuals within it refrain from doing to each other: it will have to be an incarnate will to power, it will strive to grow, spread, seize, become predominant—not from any morality or immorality but because it is *living* and because life simply *is* will to power. . . . "Exploitation" does not belong to a corrupt or imperfect and primitive society; it belongs to

the *essence* of what lives, as a basic organic function; it is a consequence of the will to power, which is after all the will of life.* (*BGE* 259)

An aristocracy of overmen will *of course* exploit those beneath them. Again Nietzsche displays his hostility to "modern ideas" of equality and equal rights for all. All this is "superficiality" and "sentimental weakness." Worse, it is "a will to the *denial* of life, a principle of disintegration and decay." Men are *not* equal. And a clear view of the very "*essence* of what lives" should convince us of that.

8.   An overman will know what he is worth. Under no illusions about equality, the noble soul of an overman will sense the immense distance between himself and others. He will be conscious of the "*order of rank,* and of how power and right and spaciousness of perspective grow into the heights together" (*HA,* preface, p. 9) Very much like Plato,[†] Nietzsche thinks there are roughly three classes of human beings.

> The highest caste—I call them *the fewest*—being perfect, also has the privileges of the fewest: among them, to represent happiness, beauty, and graciousness on earth. Only to the most spiritual human beings is beauty permitted: among them alone is graciousness not weakness. . . .
>
> The *second:* they are the guardians of the law, those who see to order and security, the noble warriors, and above all the king as the highest formula of warrior, judge, and upholder of the law. The second are the executive arm of the most spiritual, that which is closest to them and belongs to them, that which does everything gross in the work of ruling for them. . . .
>
> A high culture is a pyramid: it can stand only on a broad base; its first presupposition is a strong and soundly consolidated mediocrity. Handicraft, trade, agriculture, *science,* the greatest part of art, the whole quintessence of *professional* activity, to sum it up, is compatible only with a mediocre amount of ability and ambition. . . . (*A* 57)

---

*Remember Nietzsche's description of the "uncaged beasts of prey" who created master morality (pp. 501–502).
[†] For Plato's ideal ordering of a state, see pp. 137–139.

Nietzsche emphasizes that in this pyramid, with the few at the top, there is nothing unnatural.

> In all this, to repeat, there is nothing arbitrary, nothing contrived; whatever is *different* is contrived—contrived for the ruin of nature. The order of castes, the *order of rank,* merely formulates the highest law of life; the separation of the three types is necessary for the preservation of society, to make possible the higher and the highest types. The *inequality* of rights is the first condition for the existence of any rights at all. (*A* 57)

The overman, then, will look *down*. The *many* will be below him—perhaps far below. But what attitude will these highest few have toward those who are lower in the order of rank? The overman will be filled with contempt, loathing, and nausea wherever he sees resentment and revenge in those lower ranks, deception and self-deception, the rancor of the ill-constituted, the demand for equality (where there *is* none)—in short, the morality of good and evil. But for those mediocre ones who are content, who find their happiness in mediocrity, the situation is different.

> It would be completely unworthy of a more profound spirit to consider mediocrity as such an objection. In fact, it is the very *first* necessity if there are to be exceptions: a high culture depends on it. When the exceptional human being treats the mediocre more tenderly than himself and his peers, this is not mere politeness of the heart—it is simply his *duty*. (*A* 57)

There is certainly more to be said about the life of an overman. But in a word, the overman is one who says "Yes!" to his life, to life itself—who is strong enough for such a yes, healthy enough for such a yes. In such self-affirmation and in continual self-overcoming, the overman finds his joy. And in individuals like that the earth finds its meaning.

There is one problem still facing the overman, a problem Zarathustra faces, too. Can one who has reached these heights really say "Yes!" to *everything*? With that we come to the crucial test for those who aspire to greatness.

Affirming Eternal Recurrence

Thus Spoke Zarathustra tells us not only of Zarathustra's speeches but also of his visions, dreams, and adventures. Most importantly, it chronicles Zarathustra's own growth toward overman status. By the end of the book, if Zarathustra is not yet an overman, he is close. As we have seen, an overman says "Yes!" to his life; an overman turns his back on spite and revenge and all no-saying; an overman remains faithful to the earth. But how could one tell whether one has done that? Self-deception is such a common human characteristic; perhaps one is kidding oneself.

In *The Gay Science*, Nietzsche devises a test.

> *The greatest weight.*— What, if some day or night a demon were to steal after you into your loneliest loneliness and say to you: "This life as you now live it and have lived it, you will have to live once more and innumerable times more; and there will be nothing new in it, but every pain and every joy and every thought and sigh and everything unutterably small or great in your life will have to return to you, all in the same moonlight between the trees, and even this moment and I myself. The eternal hourglass of existence is turned upside down again and again, and you with it, speck of dust!"
>
> Would you not throw yourself down and gnash your teeth and curse the demon who spoke thus? Or, have you once experienced a tremendous moment when you would have answered him: "You are a god and never have I heard anything more divine." If this thought gained possession of you, it would change you as you are or perhaps crush you. The question in each and every thing, "Do you desire this once more and innumerable times more?" would lie upon your actions as the greatest weight. Or how well disposed would you have to become to yourself and to life *to crave nothing more fervently* than this ultimate eternal confirmation and seal? (*GS* 341)

The eternal recurrence of all things.* At one point Zarathustra faces that prospect (*Z* 3, 269–72), but

---

* Scholars are divided about whether Nietzsche actually believed in recurrence as a fact. There is some evidence that he did, but many think it inconclusive. My view is that he probably did not. But whether he did or did not, it is clear that its principal impor-

he sets it aside. He speaks of an "abysmal thought" which, apparently, he cannot bear to face. Some time later he calls it forth.

> Up, abysmal thought, out of my depth! I am your cock and dawn, sleepy worm. Up! Up! My voice shall crow you awake! . . .
>
> I, Zarathustra, the advocate of life, the advocate of suffering, the advocate of the circle; I summon you, my most abysmal thought!
>
> Hail to me! You are coming, I hear you. My abyss speaks. I have turned my ultimate depth inside out into the light. Hail to me! Come here! Give me your hand! Huh! Let go! Huhhuh! Nausea, nausea, nausea—woe unto me! (Z 3, 327–28)

What could this thought be that so terrifies Zarathustra, that fills him with such nausea? Remember the prospect that the demon puts before us: that *all* things should recur—eternally—exactly as they are. Zarathustra's abysmal thought is that this means the small man, the herd man, the "last" man, the man of resentment and revenge, the weak, the priest, the slaves with their nihilistic morality, Christianity—all this would recur again and again and again. . . .

> "The great disgust with man—*this* choked me and had crawled into my throat; and what the soothsayer said: 'All is the same, nothing is worth while, knowledge chokes.' A long twilight limped before me, a sadness, weary to death, drunken with death, speaking with a yawning mouth. 'Eternally recurs the man of whom you are weary, the small man'—thus yawned my sadness and dragged its feet and could not go to sleep. . . . 'Alas, man recurs eternally! The small man recurs eternally!'
>
> "Naked I had once seen both, the greatest man and the smallest man: all-too-similar to each other, even the greatest all-too-human. All-too-small, the greatest!—that was my disgust with man. And the eternal recurrence even of the smallest—that was my disgust with all existence. Alas! Nausea! Nausea! Nausea! (Z 3, 331)

The prospect of eternal recurrence brings the soothsayer's nihilism back with a vengeance. What

is life for, if it isn't going anywhere? If there is no hope for ultimate improvement, for progress, for getting beyond the small and the great—for *overcoming man* once and for all—what would be the point? Man would be a bridge leading nowhere! If it all repeats itself, how could one bear it? But that is just the question the demon asks, isn't it? Suppose this prospect of the eternal recurrence of everything were offered to you. Would you "throw yourself down and gnash your teeth," or would you say, "Never have I heard anything more divine"? The way you answer this question shows "how well disposed" you are "to yourself and to life." It is a test of your yes-saying. Would you say "Yes!" even to this? Would you affirm the eternal recurrence of all things? *

What the thought of eternal recurrence teaches Zarathustra is that the meaning of life cannot be sought in anything beyond it. Eternal recurrence is the ultimate denial of all "true worlds"; there is just *this world*—over and over and over again. With "true worlds" gone, life must justify itself *as it is*, or it cannot be justified at all. Not every life, Nietzsche thinks, can stand this thought. Only the strongest can bear this "greatest weight"—only an overman who says "Yes!" to everything, who affirms life and remains faithful to the earth, who overcomes himself, who gives style to his life, who creates his own values in the very living of his life. The overman says "Yes!" to eternal recurrence. And it is in the life of the overman that the problem of the meaning of life is solved. In *that* life, it doesn't seem a problem!

In *Ecce Homo,* a late work, Nietzsche says, "I am a disciple of the philosopher Dionysus" (*EH,* 217). The *philosopher* Dionysus? When we meet Dionysus in *The Birth of Tragedy,* he is a god; in fact, he is just *one* of the gods, symbolizing a certain feature of human life, but certainly not the whole of it. He is contrasted with Apollo, you will remember, and represents passion unconstrained by reason, measure, and order (these being Apollo's domain). But something interesting has happened in the course of Nietzsche's development. With the disappearance of "true worlds," any contrast be-

---

tance for him is not as a *truth,* but as a thought experiment to test the level of yes-saying in a person's life.

---

* Of the Holocaust too, you ask? Yes, even of that.

tween "opposite values"—by which Nietzsche means values grounded in different realities (see *BGE*, 2, 3)—also vanishes. Every aspect of human life, therefore—virtues, vices, values, science—has to be accounted for in terms of the same fundamental reality. And what is that? Will to power.

We have seen that Nietzsche interprets intelligence and "spirit" as no more than an aspect of body. And each body (slave and master alike) expresses the will to power, the will to overcome, the will to achieve a higher, stronger, more masterful condition. So what Nietzsche thinks of as Apollo in *The Birth of Tragedy*—the powers of reason, order, measure (and surely philosophy, too)—is now seen to be just a manifestation of a body's will to power: its "little reason." (The will to truth, remember is just will to power—one form the will to mastery can take.) So all these Apollinian powers are *not* opposed to Dionysus; they are an aspect of Dionysus, a manifestation of the power of Dionysus—of the will to power. Will to power sublimated into reason—that is how Dionysus can be a *philosopher* and not just the god of irrational intoxication. And that is why at the end only Dionysus remains. A philosophy that remains *faithful to the earth* must be a philosophy of the will to power that says yes to everything earthly—and so is willing to affirm the eternal recurrence of everything. But to affirm life, to rejoice in life, *is* Dionysian.

The affirmation of eternal recurrence is identical with a formula that Nietzsche calls "my formula for greatness in a human being: *amor fati*" (*EH*, 258), that is, love of fate. He explains it in this way:

> that one wants nothing to be different, not forward, not backward, not in all eternity. Not merely bear what is necessary, still less conceal it . . . but *love* it. (*EH*, 258)

Since everything that happens in this world is, Nietzsche believes, necessary and a manifestation of the will to power, to love it is to affirm it. And to affirm it is to say yes even to its eternal recurrence. Whoever can truly do that is an overman—and a disciple of the god and philosopher Dionysus.

Not even death can subvert the gratitude and joy with which an overman experiences life. At one point Zarathustra romances life, declaring his love. But life says softly to him,

> "O Zarathustra, you are not faithful enough to me. You do not love me nearly as much as you say; I know you are thinking of leaving me soon. . . ."
> "Yes," I answered hesitantly, "but you also know—" and I whispered something into her ear, right through her tangled yellow foolish tresses.
> "You *know* that, O Zarathustra? Nobody knows that."
> And we looked at each other and gazed on the green meadow over which the cool evening was running just then, and we wept together. But then life was dearer to me than all my wisdom ever was. (*Z* 3, 339–40)

What does Zarathustra whisper in life's ear? Presumably that you cannot have life without death and to say yes to one is to affirm the other. That thought may be an occasion for sadness, but it does not dim in the slightest Zarathustra's love of life.

Zarathustra meets a number of "higher men" who have risen above the herd in one way or another but have not yet reached Zarathustra's level of development. Among them are the soothsayer, the retired pope, and the ugliest man. Zarathustra invites them to his cave where they have a feast (a sacrilegious parody of Jesus' "last supper") and are merry. The dreaded "spirit of gravity" retreats and they laugh together. Zarathustra notes:

> "Nausea is retreating from these higher men. Well then! That is my triumph. In my realm they feel safe, all stupid shame runs away, they unburden themselves. They unburden their hearts, good hours come back to them, they celebrate and chew the cud: they become grateful. *This* I take to be the best sign: they become grateful. (*Z* 4, 423)

Gratitude is the "best sign" of a "redeemed" life. Gratitude for *everything*—just as Nietzsche himself was grateful for his illness and pain, and for those who did him wrong. That gratitude covers everything is a sign of affirming life—even to the point of willing it all again.

At the banquet, the ugliest man (the murderer of God) says:

> "My friends, all of you, . . . what do you think? For the sake of this day, *I* am for the first time satisfied that I have lived my whole life. And that I attest so much is still not enough for me. Living on earth is worth while: one day, one festival with Zarathustra, taught me to love the earth.
>
> "'Was *that* life?' I want to say to death. 'Well then! Once more!'" (*Z* 4, 429–30)

Meanwhile, Zarathustra overcomes his "last temptation"—pity for the higher men, pity that they had not come—perhaps *could not* come—still higher. Pity is the last, subtlest, most seductive form of no-saying. To pity is to say: *would it were not so*. "Pity is the *practice* of nihilism" (*A* 7). To pity is to give in to suffering, to hallow suffering, to suffer oneself. But Zarathustra believes that suffering and pain are no objection to life! They are, rather, stimulants to self-overcoming, and for them, too, one must be grateful. Zarathustra is like a convalescent recovering from a long illness—from his wandering in search of wisdom, from his nausea, his pity, his lack of ability to affirm life. Zarathustra is approaching the life of an overman.

Nietzsche tells us, out of his own experience, what such a convalescence is like.

> . . . the free spirit again draws near to life—slowly, to be sure, almost reluctantly, almost mistrustfully. It again grows warmer about him, yellower, as it were; feeling and feeling for others acquire depth, warm breezes of all kind blow across him. It seems to him as if his eyes are only now open to what is *close at hand*. He is astonished and sits silent: where *had* he been? These close and closest things: how changed they seem! what bloom and magic they have acquired! He looks back gratefully—grateful to his wandering, to his hardness and self-alienation, to his viewing of far distances and bird-like flights in cold heights. What a good thing he had not always stayed 'at home', stayed 'under his own roof' like a delicate apathetic loafer! He had been *beside himself*: no doubt of that. Only now does he see himself—and what surprises he experiences as he does so! What unprecedented shudders! What happiness even in the weariness, the old sickness, the relapses of the convalescent! How he loves to sit sadly still, to spin out patience, to lie in the sun! Who understands as he does the happiness that comes in winter, the spots of sunlight on the wall! They are the most grateful animals in the world, also the most modest, these convalescents and lizards again half turned towards life: —there are some among them who allow no day to pass without hanging a little song of praise on the hem of its departing robe. And to speak seriously: to become sick in the manner of these free spirits, to remain sick for a long time and then, slowly, slowly, to become healthy, by which I mean 'healthier', is a fundamental *cure* for all pessimism. . . . (*HA*, 8–9)

Such a convalescent could wish for it all again.

Basic Questions

1. What is the "wisdom" of Silenus?
2. Distinguish the human powers symbolized by the gods Apollo and Dionysus.
3. How does Nietzsche use the metaphysics of Schopenhauer in his analysis of tragedy?
4. What is the role of the chorus in a Greek tragedy, according to Nietzsche?
5. What "metaphysical comfort" does tragedy provide?
6. Philosophers claim to tell us about reality, but what do they really reveal, if Nietzsche is right?
7. In what ways can errors be useful? What are some of the errors Nietzsche identifies?
8. What is Nietzsche's "nonmetaphysical" view of the world and human nature?
9. Sketch the stages by which Nietzsche thinks the "true world" became a fable.
10. What does Nietzsche mean when he says "God is dead"?
11. In what ways might God have died?
12. What does Nietzsche understand by a "genealogy" of morals?
13. What is master morality like? Who devised it? What do the central terms "good" and "bad" mean?
14. What is slave morality like? Who devised it? What do the central terms "good" and "evil" mean?
15. What is *our* morality like?

16. In what ways does Nietzsche criticize our morality?
17. Who is the "last man"?
18. How did the idea of free will arise?
19. What does it mean that man is "a bridge and not an end?"
20. What does it mean to "remain faithful to the earth"?
21. Explain the parable of the camel, the lion, and the child.
22. How does one "become what one is"?
23. In what sense is selfishness a virtue? In what sense not?
24. What is the contrast Nietzsche draws between the neighbor and the friend?
25. Explain the notion of an "order of rank."
26. What does it mean to affirm eternal recurrence? What does one's reaction to the prospect of eternal recurrence reveal about oneself?
27. How has the conception of Dionysus changed from the early work to the late?
28. Explain *amor fati* and indicate how this could be Nietzsche's "formula for greatness in a human being."

For Further Thought

1. Suppose that you want to resist Nietzsche's attacks on equality and equal rights. How much else in Nietzsche would you have to reject?
2. Nietzsche believes the interpretation of human beings as sinful is based on a lie, whereas Kierkegaard takes it to be the very truth. Nietzsche pins his hopes for "redemption" on *amor fati* and affirming eternal recurrence; Kierkegaard, on faith. Compare these analyses of the problem of human life and its solution.

Notes

1. References to Nietzsche's works are as follows:
PN: The Portable Nietzsche, trans. Walter Kaufmann (New York: Viking Press, 1954). References are to page numbers.
BT: The Birth of Tragedy, in *The Birth of Tragedy and The Case of Wagner*, trans. Walter Kaufmann (New York: Vintage Books, 1967). References are to page numbers.
HA: Human, All Too Human, trans. R. J. Hollingdale (Cambridge: Cambridge University Press, 1986). References are to page numbers.
GS: The Gay Science, trans. Walter Kaufmann (New York: Vintage Books, 1974). References are to sections.
Z: Thus Spoke Zarathustra, in *The Portable Nietzsche*. References are to part and page number.
BGE: Beyond Good and Evil: Prelude to a Philosophy of the Future, trans. Walter Kaufmann (New York: Vintage Books, 1989). References are to sections.
GM: On the Genealogy of Morals, in *On the Genealogy of Morals and Ecce Homo*, trans. Walter Kaufmann (New York: Vintage Books, 1967). References are to part and section.
A: The Antichrist, in *The Portable Nietzsche*. References are to sections.
TI: Twilight of the Idols, in *The Portable Nietzsche*. References are to page numbers.
EH: Ecce Homo, in *On the Genealogy of Morals and Ecce Homo*. References are to page numbers.

23

The Pragmatists:
Thought and Action

The nineteenth century is a tumultuous century, socially, politically, and intellectually. It is the century of the railroad, the newspaper, and the factory. It is the century of the British Empire, colonialism, and the conquest of the American continent. And it is the century of the principle of the conservation of energy, of non-Euclidean geometries, of non-Aristotelian logic, and of evolution. A topsy-turvy century, indeed, but one convinced on the whole that progress is being made every day.

Nothing bolsters this conviction more substantially than the progress of science; and among the accomplishments of science, none stands out more prominently than that of Darwin. A cause for controversy down to our own day, Darwin's theory of evolution claims to give a scientific account of *life,* in much the same way that Newton masters space, time, and gravitational forces. A basically mechanistic explanation is given for the forms of living things, for their variety, and for their tendency to alter over long spans of time. The basic outlines of Darwin's theory of evolution are well known: genetic changes produce small variations in offspring; some of these changes are beneficial to individuals who possess them; under the pressures of population and scarce resources, these individuals are more likely to reproduce, passing their advantage to their offspring, thus leading eventually to differentiation of species in different ecological niches. The core ideas are those of *random variation* and *natural selection.* Darwinian thought is a

momentous and influential shift, affecting intellectuals of all kinds—not least those philosophers who come to call themselves pragmatists.

Charles Sanders Peirce

Charles Sanders Peirce (1839–1914), the son of a Harvard mathematician, was trained in the techniques of science from an early age. He used to claim that he had been brought up in a laboratory. For a good part of his adult life, he worked as a scientist for the United States Coast and Geodetic Survey. He made some contributions to the theory of the pendulum and was much concerned with problems of accurate measurement. But he was early attracted to problems in logic and probability theory and made a close study of the philosophies of Kant and Hegel. His research in logic is extremely original, contributing to the expansion of logic beyond the Aristotelian syllogism.* In addition to extending the theory of *deductive* inferences, Peirce does much to clarify *inductive* inferences; he also explores that sort of inference which starts from certain facts and leaps to a hypothesis that explains them. He

---

* For a brief account of Aristotle's conception of logic, which dominates Western thought for 2,400 years, see pp. 146–153; the syllogism is discussed on pp. 150–152.

calls this last sort *abductive* inference, a term that has not caught on; it is nowadays usually called *inference to the best explanation.*

Peirce is also a metaphysician of some power, combining in his later thought a version of evolutionary theory with absolute idealism.* But it is not his metaphysics that has been influential, so we shall concentrate on what he calls his **pragmatism**. The word comes from a Greek root meaning "deed" or "act" and is chosen to accentuate the close ties that Peirce sees between our intellectual life (concepts, beliefs, theories) on the one hand and our practical life of actions and enjoyments on the other. Peirce also occasionally calls it *practicalism,* and sometimes *critical common-sensism.* We'll see that John Dewey thinks of **instrumentalism** as a term nearly equivalent in force, this term bringing out the tool-like character of the intellectual conceptions we use.

Others, including most prominently the psychologist and philosopher William James, adopt the term "pragmatism"; it comes to mean a number of subtly different things to different people. In 1908, an American philosopher, Arthur Lovejoy, wrote an article entitled "The Thirteen Pragmatisms." It seemed there were almost as many versions of the doctrine as there were philosophers who adopted the name. Since many of them diverged significantly from what Peirce meant by the term, he invented the term *pragmaticism* for his own views—a word, he said, ugly enough to be safe from kidnappers. He was correct; and in fact history knows his views by the more common term "pragmatism." It is under that heading that we will examine what he has to say.

Fixing Belief

In the late 1870s, Peirce published a series of articles in *Popular Science Monthly,* in which the influence of scientific practice on this lifelong researcher is evident. He distinguishes four ways of coming to a fixed belief about some subject matter, four methods of settling opinion. These are techniques that can be used (indeed, are used) to arrive at what we think, at least, is true. They are ways of resolving doubt.

First there is the *method of tenacity.* If the aim is settlement of opinion, one might ask oneself,

> why should we not attain the desired end, by taking any answer to a question which we may fancy, and constantly reiterating it to ourselves, dwelling on all which may conduce to that belief, and learning to turn with contempt and hatred from anything which might disturb it? (*FB,* 248–49)[1]

Those who adopt this technique enjoy certain benefits. For one, they avoid the uncomfortable state of indecision and doubt. It cannot be denied, Peirce says, "that a steady and immovable faith yields great peace of mind" (*FB,* 249). Moreover, there seems to be nothing that can *rationally* be said in objection; for such persons are content to set rationality aside, and reasons against their beliefs will be (from their point of view) beside the point.

Nonetheless, Peirce believes that this is not a satisfactory method of settling opinion. His reason is an interesting one and sheds light on his pragmatism. One might think that the proper objection to the method of tenacity is that it is bound to leave one with too many false beliefs. But that is not Peirce's objection. The trouble with this method is that it

> will be unable to hold its ground in practice. The social impulse is against it. The man who adopts it will find that other men think differently from him, and it will be apt to occur to him, in some saner moment, that their opinions are quite as good as his own, and this will shake his confidence in his belief. (*FB,* 250)

The right objection is that tenacity *doesn't work!* * This thought, that others may well be as right as

---

*For an account of absolute idealism in its Hegelian guise, see pp. 428–430. The key feature in Peirce's version is that the entire universe has the distinguishing features of mind and that it is moving toward a *rational end* out of love. But such a brief account hardly does it justice.

*Experience with certain sorts of "fanatics" may make one doubt whether Peirce is altogether correct here.

oneself, arises from the "social impulse," Peirce says, "an impulse too strong in man to be suppressed" (*FB*, 250). We are in fact influenced by the opinions of others. So some method must be found that will fix belief not only in the individual, but in the community.

This thought leads us to the second method, *authority*.

Let an institution be created which shall have for its object to keep correct doctrines before the attention of the people, to reiterate them perpetually, and to teach them to the young; having at the same time power to prevent contrary doctrines from being taught, advocated, or expressed. Let all possible causes of a change of mind be removed from men's apprehensions. Let them be kept ignorant, lest they should learn of some reason to think otherwise than they do. Let their passions be enlisted, so that they may regard private and unusual opinions with hatred and horror. Then, let all men who reject the established belief be terrified into silence. Let the people turn out and tar-and-feather such men, or let inquisitions be made into the manner of thinking of suspected persons, and, when they are found guilty of forbidden beliefs, let them be subjected to some signal punishment. When complete agreement could not otherwise be reached, a general massacre of all who have not thought in a certain way has proved to be a very effective means of settling opinion in a country. (*FB*, 250)

This method, Peirce judges, is much superior to the first; it can produce majestic results in terms of culture and art. He even allows that for the mass of humankind, there may be no better method than that of authority. But this method is also unstable: there will always be some people who see that in other ages or countries, different doctrines have been held on the basis of different authorities. And they will ask themselves whether there is any reason to rate their beliefs higher than the beliefs of those who have been brought up differently. These reflections "give rise to doubts in their minds" (*FB*, 252). In the long run, authority does not *work* any better than tenacity in settling opinion.

The unsatisfactory character of the first two methods gives rise to the third, which Peirce calls

"The whole function of thought is to produce habits of action." —CHARLES SANDERS PEIRCE

both *the method of natural preferences* and the *a priori method*. Here we accept what seems "obvious," or "agreeable to reason," or "self-evident," or "clear and distinct." Our opinions are neither those we just happen to have at the beginning nor those imposed by an authority; they are those we arrive at after reflection, conversation with others, and taking thought.

The best examples of such a method, Peirce thinks, are the great metaphysical systems from Plato through Hegel. But history seems to show that one person's self-evidence is another's absurdity, and the method

makes of inquiry something similar to the development of taste; but taste, unfortunately, is always more or less a matter of fashion, and accordingly metaphysicians have never come to any fixed agreement, but the pendulum has swung backward and forward between a more material and a more spiritual philosophy, from the earliest times to the latest. (*FB,* 253)

Again we have an unstable and hence unsatisfactory method for settling our opinions.*

What we need is some method

> by which our beliefs may be caused by nothing human, but by some external permanency—by something upon which our thinking has no effect. . . . It must be something which affects, or might affect, every man. And, though these affections are necessarily as various as are individual conditions, yet the method must be such that the ultimate conclusion of every man shall be the same. Such is the method of science. Its fundamental hypothesis, restated in more familiar language, is this: There are real things, whose characters are entirely independent of our opinions about them; those realities affect our senses according to regular laws, and, though our sensations are as different as our relations to the objects, yet, by taking advantage of the laws of perception, we can ascertain by reasoning how things really are, and any man, if he have sufficient experience and reason enough about it, will be led to the one true conclusion. (*FB*, 253–54)

Several features of the fourth method, the *method of science,* are distinctive. First, there is the attempt to make our beliefs responsive to something *independent* of what any of us thinks—or would like to think; in various ways, the first three methods lack precisely this feature. Second, we see that the method of science is decidedly a *public* method: there is to be no reliance on what is peculiar to you or to me; our beliefs are to be determined by what can affect you *and* me *and* anyone else who inquires. Again, this public character is lacking in the first three methods. Third, because of this essentially public character, the *social impulse* (which wrecks the first three methods) will not undermine opinion that is settled in this scientific way.

According to Peirce's conception of science, however, it rests on an assumption, or "hypothesis" that there *actually is* some reality independent of our thinking about it. Suppose we ask, Why

should we grant this assumption?* For one thing, the practice of science does not itself lead us to doubt the assumption; indeed, Peirce holds, the method "has had the most wonderful triumphs in the way of settling opinion" (*FB*, 254). In this regard, too, it is strikingly different from the other methods: it works! But the fundamental reason to grant this assumption has to do with the very nature of belief and doubt. Peirce's thoughts on this score are original and deep. We need to look at them.

Belief and Doubt

We have been examining methods of "fixing" belief or settling our opinions. But what is it to have a belief? And what is it like to doubt? Doubting and believing are clearly different, but how? Peirce finds three differences. (1) The sensation of believing is different from that of doubting; they just feel different. (2) We are strongly disposed to escape doubt but are content when we have a belief—at least until we are led to doubt it again by some surprise the world has in store for us. (3) The most profound difference, however, gets us to the very nature of belief and doubt. For a belief is a *habit*, and doubt is the lack of such a habit. This needs explaining.

Do you believe the world is (roughly) round? Let's assume you do. What is it to have this belief? It is not a matter of having a thought in your mind; presumably, you have believed this for a long time, although you have not been constantly thinking that thought. And it would be wrong to say that you believed it only when you had this thought actively in mind. Belief, Peirce says, "is not a momentary mode of consciousness" (*WPI*, 279). Nor does it "make us act at once, but puts us into such a condition that we shall behave in a certain way, when the occasion arises" (*FB*, 247). So if you believe the world is round, you are in a "condition" that leads you to behave in the following ways: if

---

*Compare Hume's impatience with intuition as a foundation for knowledge, p. 349.

---

*After all, this seems to be the central issue in modern epistemology; it is what Descartes' methodical doubt undermines and what Hegel's idealism denies. How can Peirce be so naive?

someone asks you whether the world is flat, you say, "No, it is round"; if you win a trip "around the world," you accept it gladly; if you see a picture of the world taken from a satellite, you say, "Yes, that is what I expected it would look like." If you are on the interstate highway in Kansas, you drive confidently and do not worry about running your car off the edge. Being *disposed to behave* in these various ways—and more—is what it is to have the belief that the world is round. To have a belief is to have a habit that allows you to act confidently in the world, expecting that your actions in given circumstances will fulfill their purposes.

Doubting, on the other hand, is being in an uncertain state; it is the lack of a settled habit and so involves not knowing what to do in a given situation. That is why we struggle to escape doubt; it is essentially an anxious and irritating state. Peirce calls the struggle to escape doubt and attain the condition of belief *inquiry,* though he admits that sometimes it is not a very apt term. Inquiry, then, is an attempt to recover the calm satisfactoriness of knowing *what to do when,* which is characteristic of belief. And Peirce is convinced, as we have seen, that only the public, intersubjective methods of scientific inquiry will work in the long run to carry us from doubt to fixed belief.

Three things are essential to inquiry: a stimulus, an end or goal, and a method. Here is how Peirce thinks about these things:

* Stimulus: Doubt
* End: Settlement of opinion
* Method: Science

We need to explore further each of the first two factors. Let us begin with some reflections on doubt.

According to all the pragmatists, inquiry (indeed, thinking in general) always begins with a felt problem. But, they say, not everything that has been thought by philosophers to be problematic really is so.

Some philosophers have imagined that to start an inquiry it was only necessary to utter a question whether orally or by setting it down upon paper, and have even recommended us to begin our studies with questioning everything! But the mere putting of a proposition into the interrogative form does not stimulate the mind to any struggle after belief. There must be a real and living doubt, and without this all discussion is idle. (*FB,* 248)

Peirce obviously has Descartes in mind.* Perplexed by the contradictory things he had been taught, Descartes decides to "doubt everything" until he should come upon something "so clear and distinct" that he could not possibly doubt it. Descartes is embarked on what Dewey is to call "the quest for certainty."

But Peirce simply cannot take this project of methodical doubt seriously. This is not, he thinks, "a real and living doubt"; it is only a "make-believe" (*WPI,* 278). To propose that one begin by doubting everything, Peirce remarks, is to suppose that doubting is "as easy as lying."

We cannot begin with complete doubt. We must begin with all the prejudices which we actually have when we enter upon the study of philosophy. These prejudices are not to be dispelled by a maxim, for they are things which it does not occur to us *can* be questioned. Hence this initial skepticism will be a mere self-deception, and not real doubt; and no one who follows the Cartesian method will ever be satisfied until he has formally recovered all those beliefs which in form he has given up. It is, therefore, as useless a preliminary as going to the North Pole would be in order to get to Constantinople by coming down regularly upon a meridian. A person may, it is true, in the course of his studies, find reason to doubt what he began by believing; but in that case he doubts because he has a positive reason for it, and not on account of the Cartesian maxim. Let us not pretend to doubt in philosophy what we do not doubt in our hearts. (*CII,* 156–57)

Do you call it *doubting* to write down on a piece of paper that you doubt? If so, doubt has nothing to do with any serious business. But do not make believe; if pedantry has not eaten all the reality out of you,

---

*Review Descartes' first *Meditation.*

recognize, as you must, that there is much that you do not doubt, in the least. (*WPI,* 278)

What is the basis of Peirce's condemnation of "make-believe" doubt? It rests on his analysis of what it is to believe something. To believe, as we have seen, is to be possessed of a habit, to have a disposition to behave in certain ways in certain situations; to doubt is to be without such a habit—not to know what to do when. But if that is so, to say "I doubt everything" while going about eating bread rather than stones, opening doors rather than walking into them, and carrying on all the normal business of living is "a mere self-deception." There is *much* we do not doubt at all, and we should not "pretend" to doubt in philosophy what we do not doubt in our hearts.*

It is quite possible, of course, that our experiences will lead us to doubt things that we had not doubted before; the world often surprises us. But then these are *real doubts,* doubts that pose real problems and urge us on to inquiry because we no longer know how to act. This is very different from a philosopher who sits in his dressing gown before the fire and says, "I doubt everything."

Peirce's critique of Descartes' starting point, then, comes to this: (1) it is impossible, since we *cannot* suspend judgment about everything while continuing to live; and (2) it is futile.† What we need is not an absolutely certain starting point, but a method of improving the beliefs that, to begin with, we do not imagine *can* be doubted. We must start where we are, with all the beliefs we actually have; only *real* doubts are to count in nudging us away from them. As long as our beliefs work for us, we will have no motivation to question them. You can perhaps appreciate why Peirce occasion-

ally thinks "practicalism" would be a suitable term for his thought.

We might also wonder whether Peirce has correctly identified the end of inquiry. Can the settlement of opinion really suffice as the end or goal of our inquiries? Isn't that being satisfied with too little? Surely, we are inclined to think, what we are after in science and philosophy is the *truth.* Couldn't we settle our opinions and still be *wrong*?

Truth and Reality

Peirce points out first that we invariably think each of our beliefs to be true as long as we have no cause to doubt it.* It is only in that uneasy state of doubt that we wonder about the truth of our beliefs. Second, when doubt ceases, so does inquiry. If we are satisfied with the belief we come to, what sense does it make to wonder, abstractly, whether it might still be false?† If our belief is fixed, we wouldn't know what else to do to determine whether it is true or false.

Finally, Peirce asks us to consider what we mean by "true."

> If your terms "truth" and "falsity" are taken in such senses as to be definable in terms of doubt and belief and the course of experience (as for example they would be if you were to define the "truth" as that to a belief in which belief would tend if it were to tend indefinitely toward absolute fixity), well and good: in that case, you are only talking about doubt and belief. But if by truth and falsity you mean something not definable in terms of doubt and belief in any way, then you are talking of entities of whose existence you can know nothing, and which Ockham's razor would clean shave off. (*WPI,* 279)

What motivates those "doubts" that we raise occasionally even when we are, for all practical purposes, satisfied with our beliefs? It is the suspicion that our beliefs may not, for all their practical usefulness, *correspond* with reality—that reality

---

*Peirce's sarcastic comment about the detour to the North Pole refers to the fact that Descartes, shortly after "doubting everything," had once again proved—now on a certain foundation!—the existence of God and the distinctness and immortality of the soul, the existence and nature of the external world, and much more that he claimed he had "suspended judgment" about.

†Compare Hume's critique of "antecedent skepticism," pp. 372–373. The similarities are striking, but Peirce's criticism is based on a deeper conception of belief.

---

*Compare Hegel for a similar point: pp. 417–418.

†Compare Descartes' reflections in *Meditation I* about dreams. Are these, as Peirce claims, just "make believe"?

may, for all our care and investigation, still be quite different. And this might be the case, we suspect, even if we could in no way discover the discrepancy. But if that is what we mean, Peirce says, then we "are talking of entities of whose existence [we] can know nothing." **Ockham's razor,** that principle of parsimony in theorizing, would shave them clean off.*

We do not and cannot stabilize our beliefs, Peirce argues, by noticing they are true—by seeing that they correspond with a fact. We never do see this. Peirce's argument for this is complicated, but we can get the gist of it quite simply by using an example he gives. Consider a triangle with one side horizontal at the top and its apex pointing down. And now think of it being dipped into still water.

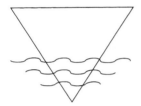

Let the water represent some fact, and let the waterline across the triangle represent some cognition of that fact. Dipping the triangle deeper into the water represents a more and more adequate understanding of the fact, and the horizontal base of the triangle may represent a highly developed understanding of that fact (as we might have in some science). The waterline will be such that, no matter how little the triangle is dipped into the water, other horizontal lines can be drawn between it and the apex. If the distance from the apex up to the waterline is a, then other lines could be drawn at $\frac{1}{2}a$, $\frac{1}{4}a$, and so on—no matter how small a is.

The question is this: Can we get a *pure* conception of the fact, untainted by any previous theoriz-

ing? Can we see the fact *bare,* or *uncontaminated* by any previous cognitions? This is what would be necessary if it were practicable to settle our beliefs by seeing whether they correspond to reality. We would have to be able to apprehend the fact quite independently of any beliefs we already have and then compare that fact with our beliefs. But we can no more do this, Peirce argues, than we can find a waterline on the triangle below which no other line can be drawn. *All* our cognitions, beliefs, hypotheses, theories, and understandings are dependent on other items of that same kind; none of them provides a *test* of correspondence with a fact independent of the beliefs we already have when we have an experience of that fact.*

It would be easy to draw the wrong conclusion from this claim, however. It would be easy to suppose that this makes impossible the understanding of those "external permanencies" which it is supposed to be the genius of science to discern—of those things "upon which our thinking has no effect" (*FB,* 253–54). But Peirce remarks that although

> everything which is present to us is a phenomenal manifestation of ourselves, this does not prevent its being a phenomenon of something without us, just as a rainbow is at once a manifestation both of the sun and the rain. (*CII,* 169)

What Peirce's argument does do, however, is to undercut any claim to be *certain* about a belief on the ground that it represents a "pure intuition," uncontaminated by prior cognitions. But this is an implication Peirce is happy to welcome, since we have seen that he has given up the project of basing our knowledge on a foundation of certain truths in any case. What counts, again, is whether we have

---

*William of Ockham, the fourteenth-century theologian and philosopher, formulates this principle: Do not multiply entities beyond necessity. It is a rule that bids us to make do with the simplest hypothesis in explaining the facts. For a brief look at some of Ockham's views, see pp. 265–267.

---

*Here Peirce agrees with Hegel's attack on immediacy. To try to say what an experience is *of* without relying on the concepts and theories we *bring to* that experience is quite impossible. There is no *unmediated* knowledge, no "theory-free" apprehension of "the facts." Wilfrid Sellars has called the opinion to the contrary "the myth of the given." For the Hegelian view of this matter, see pp. 418–420.

a method to improve our beliefs, not whether we can be certain of them.*

But now we must ask, How does Peirce think of truth? If we cannot understand fixation of belief in terms of the attainment of truth, he suggests we try to define truth in terms of belief and doubt. He offers several attempts at such a definition:

> The opinion which is fated to be ultimately agreed to by all who investigate, is what we mean by the truth. (*HMIC*, 273)

> . . . that to a belief in which belief would tend if it were to tend indefinitely toward absolute fixity. (*WPI*, 279)

> . . . a state of belief unassailable by doubt. (*WPI*, 279)

Note that each of these definitions makes truth dependent on the states of belief and doubt, not the other way around. A true belief, according to them, is a fixed belief—not fixed just for the moment, but *absolutely* fixed, not just undoubted, but *unassailable* by doubt. The truth about some subject matter is what investigators using scientific methods, if they were persistent, would eventually come to agree upon. That is what truth *means*.

Let's draw out some consequences. The truth is a kind of *ideal,* one for which we strive in our inquiries. Since it is what investigators *will* agree upon, no present agreements (no matter how broad and deep) can suffice to give us absolute confidence that what we *now* believe is true. It is always possible that further investigation will upset present beliefs. Nonetheless, it is quite possible that many of our present beliefs are true. What does this mean? It means that many of our beliefs

are ones that future investigators will continue to reaffirm in the light of their inquiries; these beliefs are in fact "unassailable by doubt" because the world holds no surprises that will upset them, though again we cannot ever be certain that this is so for any given belief.

Note, moreover, the truth is something *public.* It is not the case that truth is relative to individuals or cultures. *Evidence* may be relative in such a way, and what one individual has good reason to believe may differ from what another has good reason to believe—because the one may have access to evidence that the other lacks. But we do not have reason to claim for certain that our beliefs are true just because we believe them. It is the *community of inquirers* that defines what is true, not any individual.

We can see how this understanding of truth fits in with Peirce's practicalism by noting a further implication.

> For truth is neither more nor less than that character of a proposition which consists in this, that belief in the proposition would, with sufficient experience and reflection, lead us to such conduct as would tend to satisfy the desires we should then have. To say that truth means more than this is to say that it has no meaning at all.[2]

Beliefs, being habits, invariably lead to conduct in conjunction with desires that move us to act. For example, we believe there is a hamburger before us and, being hungry, pick it up and take a bite. The belief is a true one if, when we act on it, our desire can be satisfied and not frustrated. If I experience the mouth-watering flavor of a Big Mac, then the belief that it was indeed a hamburger is a true one. If my teeth meet a rubber imitation, my belief is a false one; the falsity is testified to by the fact that my action does not satisfy my desire to eat.* True

---

*You may be reminded here of the saying of Xenophanes, the pre-Socratic. "The gods have not revealed all things from the beginning to mortals; but, by seeking, men find out, in time, what is better. No man knows the truth, nor will there be a man who has knowledge about the gods and what I say about everything. For even if he were to hit by chance upon the whole truth, he himself would not be aware of having done so, but each forms his own opinion." For a discussion of this saying, see p. 14. Peirce would add two caveats: (1) Xenophanes is right about no one's knowing the truth only if knowing the truth entails having certainty about it; (2) the "seeking" must be by scientific methods if we are to find out "what is better"; that is how each is to form "his own opinion."

*This notion of satisfaction is an important one for the pragmatists. In the thought of William James, it is subject to certain ambiguities and provoked the outcry of critics: "What? Do you mean to say that any belief that *satisfies you* is to be counted a true one?" But you can see that in Peirce's hands the public nature of truth, together with the requirement of agreement by a community of scientific inquirers, makes this rebuke inapplicable to him.

beliefs, then, are those that can be relied on in our practical activity in the world (including the world of the scientific laboratory). William James puts it this way: they are the beliefs that *pay*. But Peirce would be quick to add that they must pay *for* the community of inquirers and *in the long run*.

It is in terms of truth, so understood, that Peirce thinks we must also understand the concept of reality. What do we mean by "the real"? Peirce says that we may define it as

> that whose characters are independent of what anybody may think them to be. (*HMIC*, 271)

But though that is a perfectly correct definition, it is not, he thinks, a very helpful one. It does not tell us how to recognize reality or give us any instructions about how to find it.

A more satisfactory explanation can be given in terms of truth (which, remember, is itself defined in terms of belief fixed by the methods of scientific investigation). Peirce remarks that scientists are convinced that different lines of inquiry into the same subject matter will come eventually to the same result.

> One man may investigate the velocity of light by studying the transits of Venus and the aberration of the stars; another by the oppositions of Mars and the eclipses of Jupiter's satellites; a third by the method of Fizeau; a fourth by that of Foucault; a fifth by the motions of the curves of Lissajous; a sixth, a seventh, an eighth, and a ninth, may follow the different methods of comparing the measures of statical and dynamical electricity. They may at first obtain different results, but, as each perfects his method and his processes, the results will move steadily together toward a destined centre. So with all scientific research. Different minds may set out with the most antagonistic views, but the progress of investigation carries them by a force outside of themselves to one and the same conclusion. This activity of thought by which we are carried, not where we wish, but to a foreordained goal, is like the operation of destiny. No modification of the point of view taken, no selection of other facts for study, no natural bend of mind even, can enable a man to escape the predestinate opinion. This great law is embodied in the concep-

tion of truth and reality. The opinion which is fated to be ultimately agreed to by all who investigate, is what we mean by the truth, and the object represented in this opinion is the real. That is the way I would explain reality. (*HMIC*, 273)

According to this view, reality is *what true opinion says it is*. And true opinion is that opinion which further scientific inquiry will never upset. But here is a problem. Doesn't this understanding of reality make it *dependent on us* in a way that the former definition (in terms of what is *independent* of what anyone may think) does not? Hasn't Peirce contradicted himself here? He considers this objection and says that

> reality is independent, not necessarily of thought in general, but only of what you or I or any finite number of men may think about it,* . . . though the object of the final opinion depends on what that opinion is, yet what that opinion is does not depend on what you or I or any man thinks. Our perversity and that of others may indefinitely postpone the settlement of opinion; it might even conceivably cause an arbitrary proposition to be universally accepted as long as the human race should last. Yet even that would not change the nature of the belief, which alone could be the result of investigation carried sufficiently far; and if, after the extinction of our race, another should arise with faculties and disposition for investigation, that true opinion must be the one which they would ultimately come to. "Truth crushed to earth shall rise again," and the opinion which would finally result from investigation does not depend on how anybody may actually think. But the reality of that which is real does depend on the real fact that investigation is destined to lead, at last, if continued long enough, to a belief in it. (*HMIC*, 274)

Reality, then, can be independent of the inquiries of any finite number of individuals and yet be what would be revealed in inquiry, provided that inquiry is designed to be sensitive to what is independent of the investigators—that is, provided that inquiry is scientific. For Peirce, then, *science*

---

*Compare Parmenides saying that "thought and being are the same," p. 23.

is the criterion of the real; not science as it exists at any given stage, of course, but that ideal science toward which scientific activity is even now moving.*

> The real, then, is that which, sooner or later, information and reasoning would finally result in, and which is therefore independent of the vagaries of me and you. Thus the very origin of the conception of reality shows that this conception essentially involves the notion of a COMMUNITY, without definite limits, and capable of a definite increase of knowledge. And so those two series of cognition—the real and the unreal—consist of those which, at a time sufficiently future, the community will always continue to reaffirm; and of those which, under the same conditions, will ever after be denied. Now, a proposition whose falsity can never be discovered, and the error of which therefore is absolutely incognizable, contains, upon our principle, absolutely no error. Consequently, that which is thought in these cognitions is the real, as it really is. There is nothing, then, to prevent our knowing outward things as they really are, and it is most likely that we do thus know them in numberless cases, although we can never be absolutely certain of doing so in any special case. (*CII,* 186–87)

Two comments: (1) Peirce is here denying the Kantian doctrine that we *cannot* know things as they really are, but only as they appear to us.† There is no essentially hidden thing-in-itself; things are as they reveal themselves to inquiry. (2) His ground for affirming that we can know things "as they really are" is the "principle" that there is no error possible where it is impossible to discover it. Why does he believe this? To understand his reasoning here, we must turn to what Peirce has to say about *meaning.*

First let us summarize a main theme in all we have examined so far. It goes by the name of **fallibilism:** a readiness to acknowledge that one's knowledge is not yet completely satisfactory, together with an intense desire to find things out.* Peirce would wholeheartedly agree with an aphorism formulated in the early twentieth century by Otto Neurath, one of a group of thinkers known as logical positivists.

> We are like sailors who must rebuild their ship on the open sea, never able to dismantle it in dry-dock and to reconstruct it there out of the best materials.[3]

There is, perhaps, no belief of ours immune from possible revision. But, like the sailors on the open sea, we cannot replace all our beliefs at once. If we revise certain convictions, we do it only by standing on some others, which, for the time being, we must regard as stable.

Meaning

Peirce says that

> pragmatism is, in itself, no doctrine of metaphysics, no attempt to determine any truth of things. It is merely a method of ascertaining the meanings of hard words and of abstract concepts. (*SP,* 317)

We have already, as a matter of fact, seen this method at work on the concepts of belief and doubt, truth and reality. But now we must examine it directly.

Peirce restricts his doctrine of meaning to what he calls *intellectual concepts,* which he contrasts

---

*Here we have a decisively different conception of the problem of the criterion; it is not a criterion *from which to start*—as though we had to solve that problem *first,* before we could do any intellectual work. Peirce would agree that if we think of the problem of the criterion in that way, it is unsolvable; it requires that we know something before we can know something, and skepticism will be the result. According to Peirce's view, however, we know enough about the nature of the criterion to know that we do not now have it in hand; yet we also know how to make definite and regular progress toward it. Peirce's view has certain similarities to Hegel's idea that "absolute knowledge" lies at the end of a process of historical development and that nothing prior to that point can be certain; it differs in recommending empirical science as the method by which to arrive at "fixed beliefs." (See the discussion of Hegel, pp. 414–418.)

†Review Kant's distinction between noumena and phenomena, pp. 389–391.

---

*Once more you should look over that fragment of Xenophanes discussed on pp. 14–15.

with *mere subjective feelings*. An intellectual concept is any concept "upon the structure of which, arguments concerning objective fact may hinge" (*SP*, 318). Examples are concepts like "hard," "ten centimeters," "lithium," and "believes." We may get a better feel for what is distinctive about them by looking at how Peirce characterizes subjective feelings.

> Had the light which, as things are, excites in us the sensation of blue, always excited the sensation of red, and *vice versa*, however great a difference that might have made in our feelings, it could have made none in the force of any argument. In this respect, the qualities of hard and soft strikingly contrast with those of red and blue; because while red and blue name mere subjective feelings only, hard and soft express the factual behaviour of the thing under the pressure of a knife-edge. . . . My pragmatism, having nothing to do with qualities of feeling, permits me to hold that the predication of such a quality is just what it seems, and has nothing to do with anything else. Hence, could two qualities of feeling everywhere be interchanged, nothing but feelings could be affected. Those qualities have no intrinsic significations beyond themselves. (*SP*, 318)

Peirce is here expressing a version of a thought experiment called *the inverted spectrum*. It is often given in a two-person setting. Suppose the sensation I have when I see a ripe tomato is qualitatively identical to the sensation you have when you look at the sky on a clear day, and vice versa. Could we discover this? Apparently we could not, since you cannot directly access my sensations, nor I yours—and everything else would be the same. I would have learned to call ripe tomatoes "red" (doesn't everybody?) despite the fact that the sensation they produce in me is the sensation you call blue. If someone asked me to bring them something red, I might bring a tomato. And I would call the sky "blue," even though the sensation I have when I look at it is the same as the sensation you have when looking at a ripe tomato. Such an inversion of qualities would make absolutely no difference to our behavior, our language, our reasoning, or our science. They are "mere subjective feelings

only." In a fairly clear sense, such sensations have no *meaning*. Nothing else depends on them.

Contrast such a sensation with the quality of hardness (to use Peirce's example). Whether something is hard makes a difference to all those things sensations do not affect: our behavior (we will not be able to crush it in our hand like a sponge), our language (if we call something hard, we communicate something quite definite to our hearers), our reasoning (from the premise that an item is hard, we can conclude that a knife edge will not easily divide it), and our science. "Hard" is a good example of an intellectual concept. It has *implications* that must be understood if we are to understand the concept. If you do not understand that a knife edge will not easily divide a hard object, you do not understand what "hard" means.

These implications have to do with the *behavior* of the objects that are correctly called "hard." They will behave in certain ways under certain circumstances. Indeed, even if a knife edge is never actually drawn across an object, to call it "hard" is to imply that *if* a knife edge *were* put to it, it *would not* divide easily. So the implications of an intellectual concept include what Peirce calls the "would-be's" and the "would-do's" of objects to which the concepts are applicable. These would-be's and would-do's, are of course, nothing else than *habits* or *dispositions*. The rock has a disposition to resist a knife edge; and by virtue of this disposition it is rightly called "hard."

We have looked at one example of an intellectual concept and have noted the ways in which it contrasts with pure subjective sensations. Only the former have meaning. But now we should ask, How can we decide what an intellectual concept means? And this is the same as to ask, How can we make our ideas clear?

> The very first lesson that we have a right to demand that logic shall teach us is, how to make our ideas clear; and a most important one it is, depreciated only by minds who stand in need of it. To know what we think, to be masters of our own meaning, will make a solid foundation for great and weighty thought. . . . It is terrible to see how a single unclear

idea, a single formula without meaning, lurking in a young man's head, will sometimes act like an obstruction of inert matter in an artery, hindering the nutrition of the brain, and condemning its victim to pine away in the fullness of his intellectual vigor and in the midst of intellectual plenty. (*HMIC*, 260–61).

Peirce distinguishes three grades of clearness in ideas. We may first "have such an acquaintance with the idea as to have become familiar with it, and to have lost all hesitancy in recognizing it in ordinary cases" (*HMIC*, 258). If we can identify samples of quartz, for example, from among a variety of stones presented to us, then "quartz" is clear to us to this first degree. A second grade of clearness is provided by a verbal definition, such as one finds in a dictionary and could memorize (or write down in an exam, perhaps). But to attain the third grade of clearness we must follow this rule:

Consider what effects, which might conceivably have practical bearings, we conceive the object of our conception to have. Then, our conception of these effects is the whole of our conception of the object. (*HMIC*, 266)

Let us examine this rule carefully. The first thing to note is that the meaning of an intellectual concept is always something that itself has meaning. Meanings are not things; they are not brute facts; they are not sensations or actions. If you ask what "hard" means, it is not a proper answer for me to clunk you on the head with a rock. Or, if I do, then the meaning of "hard" is still not the rock; nor is it the sensation you felt when you were struck. The word "hard" is a *sign*, and its meaning must be another sign. (We will examine the nature of signs in a moment.)

Next, consider the idea of "effects, which might conceivably have practical bearings." If we ask what "hard" means, we are asking for a conception that can apply to objects that are hard; we are asking what effects these objects have that we can notice, that is, have some impact upon us—for instance, that they will not be scratched by many other substances.

And finally, note that Peirce holds that the whole of our conception of these effects is the whole of the conception we are trying to clarify. There is nothing in our conception of "hard" beyond our conception of these effects. Peirce offers a procedure for identifying these effects.

Proceed according to such and such a general rule. Then, if such and such a concept is applicable to such and such an object, the operation will have such and such a general result; and conversely. (*SP*, 331)

This is a formula for what is sometimes called *operational definition*. Note that applications of this procedure will always have two parts: there will be an operation performed and a result observed. Let us see how it might work in the case of "hard." We can define "*x* is hard" in this way:

- If you apply a knife edge to *x*, you will not cut it.
- If you throw *x* forcefully at a window, the window will (probably) break.
- If you press your hand on *x*, *x* will resist the pressure of your hand.

Note that in each case the structure is the same; an operation is specified, and a result is observed. Some action is performed and in consequence we have an experience of some kind. Note also that an indefinite number of such tests can be made, and all of them together make up the meaning of the concept "hard."

By employing such operational definitions, we can attain the third grade of clearness in ideas. With such clarity we can not only apply the concept to familiar examples or give a verbal definition, but also clear away the fogginess that so often seems to surround our ideas. We sometimes hear that we know how gravity *works*—that is, we know its laws—but we don't know what it *is*. The same is sometimes said of force—that we understand its effects, but not what it *is*. But if Peirce is right about the structure of clear ideas, this is just confusion. Once you know the laws of gravity and the equations of force, once you can predict the results of certain operations correctly so that your experience confirms your predictions, you *do know* what gravity and force are; for there is nothing more in your ideas of them than these effects, which you admit, you are clear about. What else could you possibly mean?

> The idea which the word force excites in our minds has no other function than to affect our actions, and these actions can have no reference to force otherwise than through its effects. Consequently, if we know what the effects of force are, we are acquainted with every fact which is implied in saying that a force exists, and there is nothing more to know. (*HMIC*, 270)

We have already seen this procedure at work, clarifying our ideas of belief and doubt, truth and reality. Let's review. In what does your *belief* that the earth is round consist? The answer is given in terms of operation and result: if you are offered a trip around the world, you will not say, "What? Are you crazy?" What does it mean to *doubt* whether a certain food is spoiled? If it is offered to you, you will be uncertain whether to eat it. What is it for a belief to be *true*? If the community were to inquire sufficiently long about it, there would come a point where the belief would stabilize. What do we mean when we claim that something is *real*? That inquiry concerning it would survive all possible tests. In each case, Peirce has been striving all along for that third grade of clearness, and in each case he applies that hypothetical structure of operation and result. In each case, the operations are such as any member of the community might (in principle) perform, and the results are public in the sense that anyone might observe them. There might, of course, be private associations or feelings associated with these terms—especially with "truth" and "reality"—but these are not part of the meaning of the terms. Language, after all, is a social convention we learn as children and teach others. Were its meanings not founded in something public and common, neither the learning nor the teaching of language would be explicable.

We should note one other consequence of Peirce's discussion of meaning. Consider two beliefs that seem to be different; perhaps they just have a different feel to them or are expressed in different words. Are they really different? If the practical consequences of the two are not different, "then no mere differences in the manner of consciousness of them can make them different beliefs, any more than playing a tune in different keys is playing different tunes" (*HMIC*, 264). William James was later to put this point in terms of a slogan:

> Every difference must make a difference.

If there is no difference in practical effects, then there is no difference in meaning. Peirce draws out the radical consequence of this principle.

> It will serve to show that almost every proposition of ontological metaphysics is either meaningless gibberish—one word being defined by other words, and they by still others, without any real conception ever being reached—or else is downright absurd; so that all such rubbish being swept away, what will remain of philosophy will be a series of problems capable of investigation by the observational methods of the true sciences. (*WPI*, 282)

This seems to be an announcement of the end of philosophy, its true work being taken over by the empirical sciences. Indeed, some twentieth-century thinkers draw just that conclusion from similar premises about meaning.* Peirce himself, however, goes on to argue for a metaphysics of absolute idealism in which mind is the fundamental fact in reality. Because he thinks this conclusion can be warranted on the basis of methods continuous with those of the sciences, he believes that his metaphysics conforms to this radical principle.

To understand the essentials of Peirce's view better, let us contrast it with that of David Hume.†

---

*Compare the logical positivists, pp. 568–572. See also Martin Heidegger for a differently motivated but similar conclusion on p. 636.
† See "The Theory of Ideas," in Chapter 17.

There are some clear similarities to be noted first. Both are interested in getting rid of what they see as fakery and quackery in metaphysics. And both are convinced that clarity about meaning will be helpful in dismissing much of it as sophistry and illusion.

But the differences are more striking than the similarities.

- Hume's method of certifying the meaning of a term is essentially *contemplative*. The philosopher sits in his study and muses over his experiences; if he finds some sensation in his memory from which the idea in question has arisen, it is accepted—otherwise not. For Peirce, on the other hand, the method of clarifying our ideas is *active*. To find out what a term means, we have to *do* something and then experience the consequences.
- Hume's criterion tends to be *individualistic* and *private*; the sensations I have had are not likely to be exactly the sensations you have had. Peirce's criterion is emphatically *public*; he will admit as a practical consequence nothing that could not be experienced by *anyone*.*
- Whereas Hume's investigation of the meaning of our ideas is oriented toward the *past*, toward their origin, Peirce's is *future-looking*, toward use.
- These differences have a consequence. Whereas for Hume the meanings of words are pretty much *fixed* in the light of our past experience, Peirce is able to think of us as much more flexible and *creative* with respect to language. What we do (together with the effects of those actions) determines the meanings of words. And what we do is under our control (though the

result is not). This consequence is quite in line with Peirce's acceptance of evolution and the possibility of progress. Language, too, evolves.

In fact, therefore, men and words reciprocally educate each other; each increase of a man's information involves, and is involved by, a corresponding increase of a word's information. (*CII*, 189)

The meanings of our words are not cut from stone once and for all; they change as relevant information about their objects changes—because for them to have meaning at all is for them to be part of a network of implications. As information changes, so do these implications. The meaning of "heat," for example, is no longer what it was in the days before modern thermodynamics.

Signs

A consideration of some elements of Peirce's doctrine of signs will bring us full circle. The entities that have meaning Peirce calls "signs." Here again Peirce is extremely original; he calls himself a "pioneer," a "backwoodsman," and "first-comer" in this area. His discussion is very complex and never thoroughly or systematically worked out. We will concentrate only on several central features.

Peirce gives the term "sign" (as he does "habit") a very wide sense. He means to include the simplest cases of communication in the animal world as well as the most sophisticated language of science. He believes there is one property which is common to all signs and which differentiates them from anything not a sign. All signs have a certain *triadic structure*: a *sign* stands for an *object* to an *interpretant*.* Being a sign, then, requires all three

---

* In addition, remember that Peirce does not count subjective sensations as part of meaning in any case; when he refers to what anyone can experience, he is talking about something that is already interpreted, already a sign. It is not the pure *sensation* of blue that counts as the relevant experience, but the *judgment* "That is blue" elicited from us in the presence of certain objects, together with all the implications concerning its relations to other colors, to light, to what we know of the surfaces of objects, to our sensory apparatus, and so on.

* We would normally speak here of an "interpreter," thinking primarily, no doubt, of a human who understands the sign. Peirce uses this odd term "interpretant" because he wants to be able to say that there are a variety of ways in which the meaning of a sign can be apprehended, interpretation by a human mind being only one. The behavior of bees in response to a bee dance indicating the direction of nectar (they fly in a certain direction) is, in his terms, an interpretant of the dance. But it would be strange to think of the flight of bees as an "interpreter" of the dance.

of these elements. We do, of course, sometimes just say that "*a* means *b*," but Peirce holds this is an incomplete formulation; if it is spelled out in full, we must say that "*a* means *b* to *c*." For *a* couldn't *mean b* except to some interpreter of *a*.

It is from this triadic structure that modern linguistics and philosophy of language has grown. We may consider language simply as a set of markers or tokens and investigate the permissible relations among them; such an investigation of rules relating signs to each other is called *syntax*. Second, we may pay attention to the relation between words and what they are about, that is, what they stand for: the "word-world" relation. When we do this we are considering the *semantics* of language. Finally, we may think about the way signs affect their users and hearers, and this is known as *pragmatics*.

Let us think for a moment of the semantic aspect of signs. Peirce notes three different ways that a sign can be related to its object. (1) The significance of the sign may depend on an actually existing *causal relation* between it and what it signifies. For example, dark clouds are a sign of rain, and smoke a sign of fire. Thus does Robinson Crusoe infer that he is not alone on his island, for footprints in the sand *mean* another person. Signs that work in this way Peirce calls *indexes*. For example, a weather vane is an index of the direction of the wind. (2). Some signs work because they *resemble* their object. Peirce calls these *icons*. The face in the rock at the Delaware Water Gap is an icon of an Indian. Photographs, as you should be able to see, are both indexes and icons. (3) Some signs are related to their objects in purely *conventional* or *arbitrary* ways. Peirce calls such signs *symbols*. Most of the words in human languages are like this. There is no natural relation between the color red and the word "red"—or, for that matter, "rot" or "rouge." These words stand for red things, rather than for square or heavy things, because a custom or convention of using them in that way has grown up.

But they stand for red things only *to* some interpretant. Without an interpretant, a sign is just a brute fact; nothing, in short, is a sign unless it is used as a sign. What kinds of interpretants can there be? Peirce distinguishes three important kinds. (1) There are *emotional* interpretants for signs. Some words, for instance, produce a lot of feeling when heard or uttered ("freedom," for example), others very little. But the feeling itself is not just a brute fact; it has itself the nature of a sign; it is itself significant. A feeling of pride on observing the flag refers to one's nation just as surely as does the flag itself. (2) There are also *energetic* interpretants. Peirce gives the example of a drill sergeant's order, "Ground arms!" One interpretant of this command is the actual movement by the troops as they lower their muskets to the ground. But by far the most important kind of interpretant is (3) the *logical*. And we need to examine this in more detail.

The first thing to be noted about a logical interpretant is that it is itself a sign. In fact, it is a sign that has the same meaning as the sign it interprets. A dictionary definition might be a good example: "vixen" is defined as "female fox." The latter is the interpretant, and you can see it is about the same class of objects as the former. But, Peirce says, such an interpretant cannot be the *final* or *ultimate* interpretant; because it is itself a sign, it calls for further interpretants of the same kind. And those interpretants require still others, and so on. Can this potential regress be brought to a halt? *

There is an ultimate interpretant, Peirce says. It is a *habit*. Though Peirce's discussion of these matters is somewhat obscure, we can understand his point in this way. One understands a word best when one goes beyond the first and second grades of clearness to the third.† That third grade of clearness, you recall, is given by a set of "if-then" sentences that specify a series of operations together with the results experienced in consequence of performing them. "*x* is hard" means "if you try to cut *x* with a knife, you will fail," and so on. A habit

---

*You should be reminded here of Descartes' second rule, which prescribes analysis into simples, which are clear and distinct ideas requiring no further analysis (p. 295). And Hume, worried about the same problem, traces ideas back to their origin in sensations. Both are ways to halt the regress of meaning-giving. Peirce's way to halt this regress is distinctively different.

†See p. 532.

or disposition is itself precisely such a set of "if-thens." So *having the third grade of clearness* with respect to a concept is *having a habit with respect to the word* that expresses the concept. For example, if I really do understand "hard," then my behavior is such that *if* I want something I can cut with my knife, *then* I will select a stick rather than a stone to practice my whittling.

> Consequently, the most perfect account of a concept that words can convey will consist in a description of the habit which that concept is calculated to produce. But how otherwise can a habit be described than by a description of the kind of action to which it gives rise, with the specification of the conditions and of the motive? (*SP*, 342)

We saw earlier that belief has the nature of a habit; we now see that coming to master the meaning of a word is itself a matter of attaining a habit. So the meaning of an intellectual concept is given by a logical interpretant, and each logical interpretant is subject to further interpretations until anchored finally in a habit of behavior. Two things follow: (1) A linguistic or conceptual sign can function *as a sign* only in the context of an entire working system of signs; nothing can be a sign in isolation; all by itself, a word has *no meaning*. This view is often called "holism." (2) Our entire intellectual life is tied to matters of behavior and experience, to action, and to the quest to establish habits (concepts and beliefs) that will serve us well. To this end, we modify the concepts and beliefs we begin with (and cannot help having), hoping to attain intellectual concepts that will prove ever more adequate to living in our community and in the world. As we have seen, Peirce recommends the methods of science as the way to attain more adequate habits—to "fix" our beliefs. And with this thought we have come full circle.

John Dewey

Intellectually speaking, John Dewey was born in the year that Darwin published *On the Origin of*

Species by Means of Natural Selection. He took seriously Darwin's incorporation of human life into nature and tried to work out its consequences for epistemology, metaphysics, and ethics. He lived a long life, from 1859 to 1952, and wrote voluminously on social, educational, and political matters as well as on these more traditional philosophical topics. He was born in Vermont on the eve of the Civil War and lived through the time of tremendous industrial growth in America, the expansion westward, and both world wars. He lived through the revolution in physics that we associate with Einstein and contributed to theories that made scientific methods applicable also in sociology and psychology. He said of himself that the forces that influenced him and stimulated him to think came not from books, but "from persons and from situations" (*FAE,* 13).[4] He is one of the classic sources of pragmatic ideas in philosophy.

The Impact of Darwin

We will scarcely be able to canvass everything Dewey contributed, even to pragmatic philosophy. But an examination of his *naturalism* in epistemology and metaphysics, together with his *theory of value,* will supplement our discussion of Peirce and give a good overview of the leading pragmatic themes. A 1909 lecture, "The Influence of Darwinism on Philosophy," sets the stage.

> That the publication of the "Origin of Species" marked an epoch in the development of the natural sciences is well known to the layman. That the combination of the very words origin and species embodied an intellectual revolt and introduced a new intellectual temper is easily overlooked by the expert. The conceptions that had reigned in the philosophy of nature and knowledge for two thousand years, the conceptions that had become the familiar furniture of the mind, rested on the assumption of the superiority of the fixed and final; they rested upon treating change and origin as signs of defect and unreality. In laying hands upon the sacred ark of absolute permanency, in treating the forms that had been regarded as types of fixity and perfection as originating and passing away, the "Origin of Species" introduced

a mode of thinking that in the end was bound to transform the logic of knowledge, and hence the treatment of morals, politics, and religion. (*IDP,* 3).

The ancient Greeks assume that to really know something, one has to grasp its essence, its form (*eidos*).* Scholastic philosophy in the Middle Ages, sharing this assumption, translates *eidos* as "species." The cardinal principle is that species (forms) are *fixed,* an assumption that would shape philosophy, science, ethics, and theology for two thousand years.

> The conception of *eidos,* species, a fixed form and final cause, was the central principle of knowledge as well as of nature. Upon it rested the logic of science. Change as change is mere flux and lapse; it insults intelligence. Genuinely to know is to grasp a permanent end that realizes itself through changes. . . . Completely to know is to relate all special forms to their one single end and good: pure contemplative intelligence. . . . The influence of Darwin upon philosophy resides in his having conquered the phenomena of life for the principle of transition, and thereby freed the new logic for application to mind and morals and life. When he said of species what Galileo had said of the earth, *e pur se muove,* he emancipated, once for all, genetic and experimental ideas as an organon of asking questions and looking for explanations. (*IDP,* 6–8)

Obviously Dewey sees a much broader significance to the achievement of Darwin than the merely biological. Dewey thinks there are just two fundamentally different ways to look at knowledge and our place in nature; either we must find "the appropriate objects and organs of knowledge in the mutual interactions of changing things," or we must "seek them in some transcendent and

"At the best, all our endeavors look to the future and never attain certainty." —JOHN DEWEY

supernal region" (*IDP,* 6). It is Darwin's great merit, Dewey believes, that he has shown us the former path.

In the wake of Darwin's work, a great shift of attention and emphasis opens up. Intelligence becomes more concrete, more down-to-earth, more practical. And the new philosophy

> forswears inquiry after absolute origins and absolute finalities in order to explore specific values and the specific conditions that generate them. . . . Interest shifts from the wholesale essence back of special changes to the question of how special changes serve and defeat concrete purposes. . . . To idealize and rationalize the universe at large is after all a confession of inability to master the courses of things that specifically concern us. As long as mankind suffered from this impotency, it naturally shifted a burden of responsibility that it could not carry over to the more competent shoulders of the transcendent cause. But

---

*This is most clear in the work of Plato (see "Knowledge and Opinion," in Chapter 8); for him, knowledge has to be certain and its objects eternal and unchanging: the Forms. For Aristotle, form is always embedded in concrete substances, but he is no less insistent than his teacher Plato that the object of knowledge is always the form of a thing; and, as we have noted before, the dominant form is the one toward which a substance develops: its *final cause.* The final cause of all things, for Aristotle, is that pure actuality he calls the *unmoved mover,* or God.

if insight into specific conditions of value and into specific consequences of ideas is possible, philosophy must in time become a method of locating and interpreting the more serious of the conflicts that occur in life, and a method of projecting ways for dealing with them: a method of moral and political diagnosis and prognosis. (*IDP*, 10–13)

Dewey sees the result of Darwin's evolutionary theory as the prospect of applying scientific, experimental methods to all the pressing, practical human problems. This can't happen overnight, he acknowledges; but he does see it happening and devotes himself to helping the process along.

> Old ideas give way slowly; for they are more than abstract logical forms and categories. They are habits, predispositions, deeply engrained attitudes of aversion and preference. Moreover, the conviction persists—though history shows it to be a hallucination—that all the questions that the human mind has asked are questions that can be answered in terms of the alternatives that the questions themselves present. But in fact intellectual progress usually occurs through sheer abandonment of questions together with both of the alternatives they assume—an abandonment that results from their decreasing vitality and a change of urgent interest. We do not solve them: we get over them. Old questions are solved by disappearing; evaporating, while new questions corresponding to the changed attitude of endeavor and preference take their place. Doubtless the greatest dissolvent in contemporary thought of old questions, the greatest precipitant of new methods, new intentions, new problems, is the one effected by the scientific revolution that found its climax in the *Origin of Species*. (*IDP*, 14)

We have not solved all the old problems of philosophy, but that's all right. Those are problems, Dewey says, that we should just "get over." When we see how the "new methods" of the latest scientific revolution can be applied to the practical problems we already face, the old problems will simply "disappear" or "evaporate."

Dewey thus sets himself against any philosophy that would pose an impassable gulf between knowers and what is known, between subject and object, self and nonself, experience and nature, action and the good.* Human beings are to be understood as embedded without residue in the flux of natural processes—indeed, as a product of such processes. The vaunted cognitive abilities of the human species, including its capacity for sophisticated science, are to be understood as abilities developed through the evolutionary process. This view is often called *naturalism,* and John Dewey is one of the most vigorous exponents.

An epistemological corollary of this naturalistic vision in metaphysics is *giving up the quest for certainty.* All our knowledge is understood to be hypothetical and revisable in the light of future experience. What we know depends as much on our interests and capacities as it does on the objects of knowledge; if our interests shift, so will our concepts, and with them the "world" of our experience.

The same is true of our *values,* Dewey believes. Here, too, no certainty is possible, but it does not follow that all values are equally valuable, or that they are all on a par, or that whatever an individual happens to like is a value. Dewey believes that some views about value are superior to others and that we can improve our opinions about morals and values, though without ever attaining certainty. The situation here is parallel to that in the sciences. Let us explore these matters in more detail.

Naturalized Epistemology

Dewey thinks of intelligence or inquiry as a matter of problem solving. Like Peirce, he understands problem solving as the endeavor to remove doubt and establish habits we can use to advantage.

> The function of reflective thought is to transform a situation in which there is experienced obscurity, doubt, conflict, disturbance of some sort, into a situation that is clear, coherent, settled, harmonious. (*HWT*, 100–101)

---

* This theme Dewey adapts from Hegel; see p. 414.

This is the process: We face a difficulty or perplexity; we take stock of the situation (the facts of the case); we imagine possible courses of action. This leads in turn to further reflection on the facts and thought about outcomes; this may lead to considering other possibilities for action, and then to further investigation of the situation. This interaction between the discovered facts and suggested solutions goes on until we find what moves us toward a more satisfactory state.

Suppose you are walking where there is no regular path. As long as everything goes smoothly, you do not have to think about your walking; your already formed habit takes care of it. Suddenly you find a ditch in your way. You think you will jump it (supposition, plan); but to make sure, you survey it with your eyes (observation), and you find that it is pretty wide and that the bank on the other side is slippery (facts, data). You then wonder if the ditch may not be narrower somewhere else (idea), and you look up and down the stream (observation) to see how matters stand (test of idea by observation). You do not find any good place and so are thrown back upon forming a new plan. As you are casting about, you discover a log (fact again). You ask yourself whether you could not haul that to the ditch and get it across the ditch to use as a bridge (idea again). You judge that idea is worth trying, and so you get the log and manage to put it in place and walk across (test and confirmation by overt action). . . .

The two limits of every unit of thinking are a perplexed, troubled, or confused situation at the beginning and a cleared up, unified, resolved situation at the close. . . .

In between, as states of thinking, are (1) *suggestions,* in which the mind leaps forward to a possible solution; (2) an intellectualization of the difficulty or perplexity that has been *felt* (directly experienced) into a *problem* to be solved, a question for which the answer must be sought; (3) the use of one suggestion after another as a leading idea, or *hypothesis,* to initiate and guide observation and other operations in collection of factual material; (4) the mental elaboration of the idea or supposition as an idea or supposition (*reasoning,* in the sense in which reasoning is a part, not the whole of inference); and (5) testing

the hypothesis by overt or imaginative action. (*HWT,* 105–7)

We must not misunderstand this example. Dewey means it to represent the pattern of *all* our intellectual endeavors. Several points are particularly important. First, human knowers are not passive spectators of the world they come to know. They are involved participants, part of the world. It is one of Dewey's complaints that traditional theories of knowledge make the knower an entity separate from the known, thus erecting barriers between subject and object, knower and known, that could not in any case be bridged again. Dewey rejects the key idea in the representational theory of knowledge (p. 300): that we have direct access only to the world of our own mental states. His own theory, by setting human beings firmly within the natural world, claims to avoid many of the traditional problems of epistemology.* Second, there is a conscious rejection of the rule that we should "not frame hypotheses."† The mind "leaps forward" to possible solutions. Such leaps should not be condemned, but encouraged. We cannot do without framing hypotheses. And third, what is crucial is not whether a proposition represents a leap beyond present evidence, but whether it stands up to future tests by experience and action. A good hypothesis is one that *works.*

You can see that there is an intimate connection between this way of conceiving human knowledge and the futility of a quest for certainty. If the correctness of our beliefs lies open to future tests, to possible correction by future experience (mediated by actions we have not yet taken), then any claim to certainty *now* must be unjustified. Even the most firmly grounded beliefs of science and com-

---

* The solipsism and skepticism that haunts Descartes and Hume, for instance, simply cannot arise on this view; they *begin* with the possibility that *my* experience might be all there is and face the problem of justifying belief in anything else. For Dewey, this is not a real possibility, since we are in *constant interaction* with the world around us.
† For the role of this thought in the views of Newton and David Hume, see pp. 347, 349, 357, and 361.

William James

Often called America's greatest psychologist, William James (1842–1910) was also a distinguished contributor to pragmatist philosophy. In addition to the classic *Principles of Psychology* (1890), James is noted for *The Will to Believe* (1896), *The Varieties of Religious Experience* (1902), *Pragmatism* (1907), and *The Meaning of Truth* (1909).

Like the other pragmatists, James stressed the connection between our beliefs and our practical life. But more than the others, he emphasized the practical consequences of actually believing one thing or another. Since our beliefs are shaped as much by our needs and interests as by the world, we are justified in taking those needs and interests into account when deciding what to believe. With respect to our conception of reality as a whole, James held that the crucial question is this: Does our conception give us cause to hope or cause to despair?

The great philosophical systems, James believed, are in part a reflection of the temperaments of those who devised them, and in this light he sorted philosophies into the tender-minded (rationalistic, idealistic, optimistic, religious, and free-willist) and the tough-minded (empiricist, materialist, pessimistic, irreligious, and fatalistic). James viewed pragmatism as a middle way between these extremes. The key to pragmatism is a revised notion of truth.

Truth, James said, is a human thing; to an unascertainable degree, our truths are a product of our interests. A belief is true, then, when it works for us, when it satisfies our needs; the true is just the useful in the way of ideas. In cases where the evidence does not clearly decide the issue (and he thought nearly all the large questions of philosophy are like that), we are within our rights to believe what will make for a more satisfying life. The question of fatalism is such a case. We are justified in believing that the universe is open to new possibilities of improvement, not a closed system where each future event is already determined by the ancient past, because this belief will have better consequences in our lives than the other.

Nor is there any reason, according to James, why religious faith should be rationally forbidden. If belief in God works to make life more satisfying—offering hope rather than despair—then it is true. And James thought it does work that way.

mon sense may need to be modified as human experience grows more extensive and complex.*

Dewey carries on a constant dialectical debate with traditional philosophy and especially with empiricism. Like William James, he believes that pragmatism is a middle way between the extremes of empiricism and rationalism, incorporating what is best in both. The main problem with these traditional rivals, he believes, is that each operates with an impoverished notion of what experience is. In an essay of 1917, Dewey contrasts the traditional concept of experience with one he thinks more adequate.

(i) In the orthodox view, experience is regarded primarily as a knowledge-affair. But to eyes not looking through ancient spectacles, it assuredly appears as an affair of the intercourse of a living being with its physical and social environment. (ii) According to tradition experience is (at least primarily) a psychical

---

* You can see that Dewey, like Hegel, takes time seriously. Not only our beliefs but also our methods, concepts, and logical tools are part of history. But unlike Hegel, he does not envision a stage in which the progression comes to completion; there is no such thing as *absolute knowledge* for Dewey. In this regard, he resembles Kierkegaard more than Hegel (though he would not have liked Kierkegaard's supernatural religion nor the emphasis on nonrational choice). Compare pp. 456–458.

thing, infected throughout by "subjectivity." What experience suggests about itself is a genuinely objective world which enters into the actions and sufferings of men and undergoes modifications through their responses. (iii) So far as anything beyond a bare present is recognized by the established doctrine, the past exclusively counts. Registration of what has taken place, reference to precedent, is believed to be the essence of experience. Empiricism is conceived of as tied up to what has been, or is, "given." But experience in its vital form is experimental, an effort to change the given; it is characterized by projection, by reaching forward into the unknown; connection with a future as its salient trait. (iv) The empirical tradition is committed to particularism. Connections and continuities are supposed to be foreign to experience, to be by-products of dubious validity. An experience that is an undergoing of an environment and a striving for its control in new directions is pregnant with connections. (v) In the traditional notion experience and thought are antithetical terms. Inference, so far as it is other than a revival of what has been given in the past, goes beyond experience; hence it is either invalid, of else a measure of desperation by which, using experience as a springboard, we jump out to a world of stable things and other selves. But experience, taken free of the restrictions imposed by the older concept, is full of inference. There is, apparently, no conscious experience without inference; reflection is native and constant. (*NRP*, 23)

Important points are made here. Let us review them in order.

- Point (i) is the denial that the knower is a disinterested spectator.
- Point (ii) rejects any notion of experience that would locate it exclusively in a subject, leaving the question of an objective world up in the air.
- Point (iii) captures the inherent purposiveness of experience, the fact that it is always oriented toward the future and concerned about the implications of the present on that future.*

---

*Contrast Hume's rule about ideas: to discover whether a purported idea is a genuine one, trace it *back* to an impression. Here experience is assumed to be *given* whole and complete at any moment, and "the past exclusively counts." Compare Peirce, p. 534.

- Point (iv) attacks the Humean notion that experience presents all events as "loose and separate." *
- Point (v) notes that if reason were a faculty for making inferences that is quite distinct from experience, the result would be the restriction of experience to a purely subjective realm. Then, as long as we wanted to base our knowledge on experience, we would be unable to escape the skepticism plaguing traditional empiricism. But if experience is adequately characterized, it shows itself to be a matter of interactions between an organism and its environment; it is "full of inference" and presents itself in intimate contact with the objective world. There is no such thing as experience that is not already involved in the world.

And once we see that, many of the traditional problems of philosophy (such as the problem of the "reality" of the "external" world) simply "evaporate"; we "get over" them.

Nature and Natural Science

Experience, then, is an affair of nature, since human beings are wholly natural creatures. But what is nature? Dewey resists the imperialism, so to speak, of certain sciences that claim a unique title to reveal the essence of nature. Galileo and Descartes agree that (material) reality is what mathematical physics can tell us about, and Hobbes tries to extend that claim to human nature. The result seems to Dewey an unpalatable dichotomy: either human experience is not a part of the world of nature at all (as in Descartes' dualism), or Hobbesian materialism reigns. But neither seems able to do justice to all we value and hold dear. We saw that "secondary qualities"—the felt, sensory, reds and blues, warms and colds, feelings of hope, love, or despair—are "kicked inside" by the early scientific revolutionaries as being merely effects *in us* of the geometrical, extended things that make up the realm of nature; many philoso-

---

*See p. 359.

phers, acknowledging that physics gives us knowledge of what really is, feel compelled to join them.* This seems wholly inadequate to Dewey. If we identify science with the physical sciences (as traditionally understood), we will cut ourselves off from the uses of intelligence in the more human spheres. The problem, as he sees it, is once again a *spectator theory of knowledge*. It springs from

> the assumption that the true and valid object of knowledge is that which has been prior to and independent of the operations of knowing, . . . [from] the doctrine that knowledge is a grasp or beholding of reality without anything being done to modify its antecedent state—the doctrine which is the source of the separation of knowledge from practical activity. (*QC*, 196)

But as we have seen, experience and knowledge are a matter of interactions (transactions) between the knower and the known; neither is left at the end exactly as it was at the beginning of the affair. What counts as intelligent intervention, Dewey holds, is a matter of *method*. And a method is legitimate if it succeeds in transforming confused situations into clear ones.

> The result of one operation will be as good and true an object of knowledge as any other, provided it is good at all: provided, that is, it satisfies the conditions which induced the inquiry. . . . One might even go as far as to say that there are as many kinds of valid knowledge as there are conclusions wherein distinctive operations have been employed to solve the problems set by antecedently experienced situations. . . .
>
> There is no kind of inquiry which has a monopoly of the honorable title of knowledge. (*QC*, 197, 220)

---

*The loss is poignantly expressed in the poem by John Donne. (See p. 289.) The pattern is an ancient one. Democritus, the contemporary of Socrates, is convinced that reality is made up of atoms and the void, but he recognizes that our access to the world is through the sensory qualities of our experience and laments that "man is cut off from the real." (See p. 32.) Dewey struggles against this conclusion.

Along these lines, Dewey attacks what some call "scientism."

> Thus, "science," meaning physical knowledge, became a kind of sanctuary. A religious atmosphere, not to say an idolatrous one, was created. "Science" was set apart; its findings were supposed to have a privileged relation to the real. In fact the painter may know colors as well as the meteorologist; the statesman, educator and dramatist may know human nature as truly as the professional psychologist; the farmer may know soils and plants as truly as the botanist and mineralogist. For the criterion of knowledge lies in the method used to secure consequences and not in metaphysical conceptions of the nature of the real. . . .
>
> That "knowledge" has many meanings follows from the operational definition of conceptions. There are as many conceptions of knowledge as there are distinctive operations by which problematic situations are resolved. (*QC*, 221)

If we add one more ingredient, we will be ready to see why Dewey thinks that intelligence can be as effective in the realms of value and morality as it is in science. That ingredient is his *instrumentalism*. Because the basic cognitive situation is the problem-situation, and because hypotheses are created to resolve such situations satisfactorily, the concepts involved in hypotheses are necessarily relative to our concerns and interests. Without interests and concerns there would be no problems! Ideas, concepts, and terms, then, are intellectual *tools* we use as long as they serve our purposes and discard when they no longer do. They are *instruments* for solving problems.

Physicists and chemists create concepts that serve the purposes of these sciences: explanation, prediction, and control. But these concepts no more reveal what the world *really* is than any other sort of concept does. They too are merely instruments serving certain purposes; there is nothing prior or more basic about them that should cast a disparaging shadow on concepts serving other purposes. Dewey believes that many philosophers have been misled in thinking that modern physics actually reveals the true nature of reality. Making that assumption seems to shunt the qualities manifest in experience (all those "secondary qualities," whose loss was mourned by John Donne) off the main line onto a siding. But, Dewey says, that is to mistake the purport of scientific knowledge.

> Only when the older theory of knowledge and metaphysics is retained, is science thought to inform us that nature in its true reality is but an interplay of masses in motion, without sound, color, or any quality of enjoyment and use. What science actually does is to show that any natural object we please may be treated in terms of relations upon which its occurrence depends, or as an event, and that by so treating it we are enabled to get behind, as it were, the immediate qualities the object of direct experience presents, and to regulate their happening, instead of having to wait for conditions beyond our control to bring it about. Reduction of experienced objects to the form of relations, which are neutral as respects qualitative traits, is a prerequisite of ability to regulate the course of change, so that it may terminate in the occurrence of an object having desired qualities. (QC, 104–5)

From the point of view of physical science, then, the world appears to be just a sequence of events in certain relations to each other. But we needn't conclude that the world *really* is just such a sequence of events, bare of every quality we prize and delight in. Scientific concepts, like all concepts, are merely tools we use to satisfy certain interests. But the interests served by physical science are not all the interests we have, nor are they our primary interests. In fact, treating nature as physics does (in terms of events and relations between events) serves larger purposes: our interest in controlling change, "so that it may terminate in the occurrence of an object having desired qualities." The concepts of science owe their very being to *values* we have.

"Event" is a concept about as bare and stripped of all that is precious to us as we can find. Yet it applies to everything that happens. Even the things of common sense, such as tables and chairs, can be considered extended, slowly unfolding events. But as we experience them, they are not "bare" events,

but *events with meanings*. And the meanings are multiple. Consider, Dewey suggests, a piece of paper. We call it "a piece of paper," when we are interested in it in a certain way—as something to write on, perhaps, or something to wrap the fish in. But if we consider it in terms of an event (a kind of extended happening), it is clear that it

> . . . has as many other explicit meanings as it has important consequences recognized in the various connective interactions into which it enters. Since the possibilities of conjunction are endless, and since the consequences of any of them may at some time be significant, its potential meanings are endless. It signifies something to start a fire with; something like snow; made of wood-pulp; manufactured for profit; property in the legal sense; a definite combination illustrative of certain principles of chemical science; an article the invention of which has made a tremendous difference in human history, and so on indefinitely. There is no conceivable universe of disclosure in which the thing may not figure, having in each its own characteristic meaning. And if we say that after all it is "paper" which has all these different meanings, we are at bottom but asserting that . . . paper is its ordinary meaning for human intercourse. (EN, 7)

Suppose we insist on asking, But what is it *really*? Is it *really* wood pulp? Or a white surface for writing on? Or atoms and the void? What would Dewey say? He would tell us that we were asking a question to which there is no answer. It is all of these things—and more—since the applicability of any of these concepts merely reflects certain purposes and interests. No one of them can be singled out as the *essence* of the event.

We can see that for Dewey there is no sharp line demarcating science from common sense, any more than there is a gap between knower and the known. Both are ways of dealing with recalcitrant situations and making us better able to cope; science and common sense are different because they serve different purposes, but they are alike in using concepts as *tools* for the realization of those purposes. The same is true of philosophy. Dewey proposes a first-rate test of the value of any philosophy which is offered us: Does it end in conclusions which, when they are referred back to ordinary life-experiences and their predicaments, render them more significant, more luminous to us, and make our dealings with them more fruitful? Or does it terminate in rendering the things of ordinary experience more opaque than they were before, and in depriving them of having in "reality" even the significance they had previously seemed to have? (*EN*, 319–20)

Value Naturalized

Let us apply this criterion to Dewey's own philosophy by looking finally at what he has to say about values.

He notes that the modern problem about values arises with the expulsion of ends and final causes from nature that takes place with the rise of modern science.

For centuries, until, say, the sixteenth and seventeenth centuries, nature was supposed to be what it was because of the presence within it of *ends*. . . . All natural changes were believed to be striving to actualize these ends as the goals toward which they moved by their own nature. Classical philosophy identified *ens* [being], *verum* [truth], and *bonum* [goodness], and the identification was taken to be an expression of the constitution of nature as the object of natural science. In such a context there was no call and no place for any *separate* problem of valuation and values, since what are now termed values were taken to be integrally incorporated in the very structure of the world. But when teleological considerations were eliminated from one natural science after another, and finally from the sciences of physiology and biology, the problem of value arose as a separate problem. (*TV*, 2–3)

Our earlier discussions of Dante and the consequences of Galilean science fit this analysis. The problem of how to understand values in a world of sheer fact is acute. As Dewey sees it, there are two tendencies in modern thought that accept the value-neutral character of nature. On the one hand, value is thought to originate in something above or beyond nature: in God, perhaps, or in pure reason, as Kant claims. At the other extreme, value is identified with purely subjective satisfactions, such as pleasure.

There is either a basic distrust of the capacity of experience to develop its own regulative standards, and an appeal to what philosophers call eternal values, in order to ensure regulation of belief and action; or there is acceptance of enjoyments actually experienced irrespective of the method or operation by which they are brought into existence. Complete bifurcation between rationalistic method and an empirical method has its final and most deeply human significance in the ways in which good and bad are thought of and acted for and upon. (*QC*, 256)

Neither of these alternatives is attractive to Dewey, who wants to account for values in a wholly *naturalistic* way, but without identifying goodness with the arbitrary preference of an individual. What he wants is a way of treating values parallel to the way a scientist treats hypotheses—a way that will make *progress* in valuations possible but without claiming *certainty* at any point.

The problem of restoring integration and cooperation between man's beliefs about the world in which he lives and his beliefs about the values and purposes that should direct his conduct is the deepest problem of modern life. (*QC*, 255)

It is this "integration and cooperation" between facts and values that is disturbed by the rise of modern science in the sixteenth and seventeenth centuries.* Once science is no longer teleological, once it no longer gives us reason to think there are purposes embedded in things, the status of ends and goods in the world becomes problematic. Dewey thinks a pragmatic approach can best restore such integration and solve this "deepest problem." The key idea is this:

that escape from the defects of transcendental absolutism is not to be had by setting up as values enjoy-

---

*See, for instance, Hume on the gap between fact and value, p. 371.

ments that happen anyhow, but in defining value by enjoyments which are the consequences of intelligent action. Without the intervention of thought, enjoyments are not values but problematic goods, becoming values when they re-issue in a changed form from intelligent behavior. (*QC*, 259)

Let us explore this idea. Like Peirce, who holds that we must begin reflection with the beliefs we already have, Dewey thinks we all begin with certain values and cannot help doing so. We do so simply by virtue of the fact that there are things we *like* or *prize*. Some of these likings may be biologically determined, some culturally produced. But there can be no doubt that at any stage of our lives, we do have such likings, desirings, and prizings. How are these to be understood? In accord with his general theory of experience, Dewey denies that these are purely subjective states. To *like* something is to have a certain disposition to behavior; if I like chocolate ice cream, I have tendencies to choose it when buying ice cream, to eat it when it is served to me, and so on. Liking is a matter of interactions between an organism and its environment; it is a transactional matter. To like *X* is to be disposed to try to get it; or, if we already have *X*, liking it is a matter of attempts to preserve, keep, or protect it.

Now, given that we all have such likings, do they constitute values? In one sense they do, Dewey says, but in another sense not. They do represent what we antecedently or *immediately* value (to use a word of Hegel's); but it would be a big mistake to identify these values with values per se. And the reason is that there is a big difference between what we find *satisfying* and that which is *satisfactory*, between what we *desire* and what is *desirable*, between those things we *think good* and the things that *are good*. Dewey is here trying to do justice to the fairly common experience of wanting a certain thing, getting it, and discovering (once we have it) that it does not live up to its advance notices.

What makes the difference between the satisfying and the satisfactory is the intervention of intelligence.

The fact that something is desired only raises the *question* of its desirability; it does not settle it. Only a child in the degree of his immaturity thinks to settle the question of desirability by reiterated proclamation: "I want it, I want it, I want it." . . . To say that something satisfies is to report something as an isolated finality. To assert that it is satis*factory* is to define it in its connections and interactions. The fact that it pleases or is immediately congenial poses a problem to judgment. How shall the satisfaction be rated? Is it a value or is it not? Is it something to be prized and cherished, *to be* enjoyed? Not stern moralists alone but everyday experience informs us that finding satisfaction in a thing may be a warning, a summons to be on the lookout for consequences. To declare something satis*factory* is to assert that it meets specifiable conditions. It is, in effect, a judgment that the thing "will do." It involves a prediction; it contemplates a future in which the thing will continue to serve; it *will* do. It asserts a consequence the thing will actively institute; it will *do*. (*QC*, 260–61)

The ultimate sources of value, then, are our likings, prizings, esteemings, desirings. If we never liked anything, value would not even be on our horizon. But the things we like are always involved in a network of relations to other things. It might be that if we could just have *Y*, we would be satisfied. But *Y* never comes isolated and alone. It requires *X* as a precondition and brings along *Z* as a consequence. And *X* might require such effort and sacrifice that the luster of *Y* is considerably diminished. And *Z* might be so awful that it disqualifies *Y* as a value altogether. (The use of cocaine might be a good example.) Discovering these relations is the work of inquiry, intelligence, and scientific methods, for causal conditions and consequences are matters of fact. So science and values are not two realms forever separated from each other. Finding what is valuable involves the use of methods of intelligence similar to those used in the sciences.

It follows, then, that value judgments can be true and false, for they involve a prediction. To say that something is *good* or to urge that an action *ought* to be done is to say that it *will do*. And that means that we will continue to like it in the light of the entire context in which it is embedded. To call something satisfactory is to say that it will satisfy, given its causal conditions and consequences. And whether that is so is a matter of fact. What is desirable, then, is what is desired after intelligent inquiry and experience have had their say. So not only can value judgments be true and false, they can be supported by methods of intelligent inquiry analogous to scientific methods.

Let us consider a typical objection to this way of looking at things. Suppose we allow that intelligence and the methods of science might have bearing on *means* and on *consequences;* we might nonetheless hold that this does not show how these methods can get any grip at all on what is *good in itself,* what is *intrinsically valuable.** Or we might say that science (sociology or anthropology) can indeed tell us what people do in fact value, but it cannot tell us what is valuable.

What is Dewey's reply? To suppose that there are such things as *ends in themselves* or things that are good no matter what is to make an illegitimate abstraction from the real context in which things are liked and enjoyed. Every end is itself a means to some further end, simply because it is located in time and has consequences. Ends, then, are never absolute; they are what Dewey calls *ends-in-view.* We may take a certain state of affairs to be an end, but that is always provisional and subject to revision in the light of further experience—of the conditions and consequences of that state of affairs. In fact, there is a continuum of ends and means, each means being a means in the light of some end, and

each end a means to some further end. Furthermore, there is a reciprocity between ends and means; any actual end is what it is only as the culmination of those specific means that lead to it, and the means are means only as they lead to that particular end.

Dewey uses the story by Charles Lamb about the origin of roast pork to illustrate these points.

> The story, it will be remembered, is that roast pork was first enjoyed when a house in which pigs were confined was accidentally burned down. While searching in the ruins, the owners touched the pigs that had been roasted in the fire and scorched their fingers. Impulsively bringing their fingers to their mouths to cool them, they experienced a new taste. Enjoying the taste, they henceforth set themselves to building houses, enclosing pigs in them, and then burning the houses down. Now, if ends-in-view are what they are entirely apart from means, and have their value independently of valuation of means, there is nothing absurd, nothing ridiculous in this procedure, for the end attained, the *de facto* termination, *was* eating and enjoying roast pork, and that was just the end desired. Only when the end attained is estimated in terms of the means employed—the building and burning-down of houses in comparison with the other available means by which the desired result in view might be attained—is there anything absurd or unreasonable about the method employed. (*TV,* 40–41)

You simply cannot have ends apart from means, and every means qualifies the end you actually get.* This fact has implications, Dewey believes, for the maxim "the end justifies the means" and also for the popular objection to it. The maxim clearly involves the notion of something which is an end-in-itself, apart from the conditions and consequences of its actual existence. That end is supposed to justify the use of whatever means are necessary to its attainment—no matter how awful they may be. The maxim is plausible, however,

---

* This objection is a version of Hume's principle that reason is and can only be the slave of the passions. (See p. 369.) According to this principle, reason can tell you how to get what you want (means), but it cannot tell you what to want (ends). We have already seen, however, that Dewey challenges just this exclusivity of reason and experience; if he is right, there is no experience that is not already interpreted in terms of certain concepts, and no reason apart from experience. In a way, this echoes Kant's famous motto about concepts and intuitions (see p. 385), but with this difference: that there are no absolutely *a priori* concepts; all concepts are instruments invented to serve certain purposes— which themselves are not absolute but develop reciprocally as a result of the application of the methods of intelligence. Again the closest historical parallel is Hegel (see "Epistemology Internalized," in Chapter 19).

* This is a fact that nations are apt to forget in wartime, to their own detriment. And individuals who take it as their end to be, let us say, rich sometimes discover that in the process they have created themselves as persons they are not happy to be. Means enter into, that is, help determine, the character of the ends you actually get.

only because we assume that only *that* end will be brought into existence. And that assumption is a mistake. You always get more than you intend—for better or worse. A recognition that the relation of ends and means is reciprocal and ongoing clarifies the sense in which the maxim is true (nothing *could* justify a means except a certain end) and the sense in which it is false (no end in isolation from its context could ever justify terrible means to it, simply because there are no such ends). Dewey says that

> nothing happens which is *final* in the sense that it is not part of an ongoing stream of events. . . . Every condition that has to be brought into existence in order to serve as means is, *in that connection,* an object of desire and an end-in-view, while the end actually reached is a means to future ends as well as a test of valuations previously made. Since the end attained is a condition of further existential occurrences, it must be appraised as a potential obstacle and potential resource. If the notion of some objects as ends-in-themselves were abandoned, human beings would for the first time in history be in a position to frame ends-in-view and form desires on the basis of empirically grounded propositions of the temporal relations of events to one another. (*TV,* 43)

It is clear that Dewey has no use for the idea of something good in itself—at least not prior to intelligent reflection. If any pragmatic sense can be made of that notion at all, it will have to be along Peircean lines: that which the intelligent community ultimately comes to agree upon as desirable or good.* We have no hot line to either truth or goodness, and certainty has to be given up with respect to values as well as knowledge. But by inquiring into the conditions and consequences of ends-in-view, we bring our values more and more into line with what we ultimately *would* be satisfied with, if we knew everything there is to know about the facts. If we were to treat our values the same way we treat our scientific beliefs, then

> standards, principles, rules . . . and all tenets and creeds about good and goods, would be recognized

to be hypotheses. Instead of being rigidly fixed, they would be treated as intellectual instruments to be tested and confirmed—and altered—through consequences affected by acting upon them. They would lose all pretense of finality—the ulterior source of dogmatism. It is both astonishing and depressing that so much of the energy of mankind has gone into fighting for (with weapons of the flesh as well as of the spirit) the truth of creeds, religious, moral and political, as distinct from what has gone into effort to try creeds by putting them to the test of acting upon them. The change would do away with the intolerance and fanaticism that attend the notion that beliefs and judgments are capable of inherent truth and authority; inherent in the sense of being independent of what they lead to when used as directive principles. . . . Any belief as such is tentative, hypothetical; it is not just to be acted upon, but is to be *framed* with reference to its office as a guide to action. Consequently, it should be the last thing in the world to be picked up casually and then clung to rigidly. When it is apprehended as a tool and only a tool, an instrument of direction, the same scrupulous attention will go to its formation as now goes into the making of instruments of precision in technical fields. Men, instead of being proud of accepting and asserting beliefs and "principles" on the ground of loyalty, will be as ashamed of that procedure as they would now be to confess their assent to a scientific theory out of reverence for Newton. (*QC,* 277–78)

This theme, that thought and action are reciprocally dependent on each other, that no knowledge worth the name is without implications for practice, and that no action is irrelevant to the utility of our intellectual tools, may be considered the distinctive and essential theme of pragmatism.

Basic Questions

PEIRCE

1. Why, according to Peirce, is the method of science superior to the methods of tenacity, authority, and natural preferences for arriving at fixed beliefs?
2. What is it, actually, to believe something? To doubt something? And what is the function of intellectual inquiry?
3. What is Peirce's critique of Descartes' project of arriving at certainty through doubting?
4. How does Peirce understand truth? How is this dif-

---

*Review what Peirce says about truth, p. 528.

ferent from the way, say, Aristotle (and most of the tradition) understands it? (See pp. 149–150.)

5. How does Peirce understand reality? If you asked him, "Do we now know reality?" what would he say?

6. What is fallibilism? How is it related to the quest for certainty?

7. Contrast intellectual concepts with what Peirce calls mere subjective feelings. Could you be experiencing something different from what I am experiencing when we both look at lush grass? Would that matter? Could we find out?

8. What is Peirce's rule for attaining the "third grade of clearness" about our ideas?

9. What does the slogan "Every difference must make a difference" mean?

10. Contrast Peirce's theory of meaning with that of Hume.

11. Distinguish syntax, semantics, and pragmatics.

12. Distinguish various kinds of signs. Of what sort is most of language composed?

DEWEY

1. What, according to Dewey, is the significance of Darwin for philosophy?

2. What is naturalism? Should we be naturalists? Are you one?

3. What are the stages in problem solving?

4. Why must we give up the quest for certainty?

5. What are Dewey's criticisms of empiricism? Of spectator theories of knowledge?

6. What is Dewey's critique of scientism?

7. What is instrumentalism?

8. In what way are tables and chairs events with meanings? Is there one meaning, or are there more?

9. What is the origin of value? How does Dewey argue that despite this origin, the valuable is not identical to what I happen to like?

10. What is the difference between ends-in-view and absolute ends? How does Dewey think that means and ends should be related?

11. If modern science gives rise to the peculiarly modern problem about values, how does pragmatism claim to resolve that problem? And what role does science itself have in the resolution?

For Further Thought

1. Peirce and Dewey both urge fallibilism, giving up the quest for certainty. Imagine that our culture took

that advice. What would be the result? Do you think that would be mostly good or mostly bad?

2. Naturalism holds that we human beings are, without remainder, parts of the natural world explored by the sciences—not thinking souls (Plato, Descartes), bundles of perceptions (Hume), noumenal selves (Kant), or the World Spirit on its way to self-realization (Hegel). Why should we think so, in the light of all this philosophical history?

Notes

1. References to the works of Charles Sanders Peirce are as follows:
FB, "The Fixation of Belief," and *HMIC,* "How to Make Our Ideas Clear," in *Writings of Charles S. Peirce,* vol. 3 (Bloomington: Indiana University Press, 1986).
WPI, "What Pragmatism Is," CII: "Cognition, Intuition, and Introspection," and SP, "Survey of Pragmatism," in *Collected Papers of Charles Sanders Peirce,* ed. Charles Hartshorne and Paul Weiss, vol. 5 (Cambridge, Mass.: Harvard College, 1934).

2. Note added by Peirce in 1903 to "The Fixation of Belief," in Hartshorne and Weiss, *Collected Papers,* 232.

3. Epigraph (translated from the German) to W. V. O. Quine's *Word and Object* (New York: John Wiley and Sons, 1960).

4. References to the works of John Dewey are as follows:
FAE, "From Absolutism to Experimentalism," and *NRP,* "The Need for a Recovery of Philosophy," in *Dewey: On Experience, Nature, and Freedom,* ed. Richard Bernstein (Indianapolis: Bobbs-Merrill, 1960).
IDP, "The Influence of Darwinism on Philosophy," in *John Dewey: The Middle Works (1899–1924),* vol. 4, ed. Jo Ann Boydston (Carbondale, Ill.: Southern Illinois University Press, 1977).
QC, The Quest for Certainty: A Study of the Relation of Knowledge and Action (1929; New York: G. P. Putnam's Sons, Capricorn Books, 1960).
HWT, How We Think (Boston: D. C. Heath and Co., 1933).
EN, Experience and Nature (New York: W. W. Norton and Co., 1929).
TV, Theory of Valuation (Chicago: University of Chicago Press, 1939).

24

Ludwig Wittgenstein
and the Logical Positivists:
The Limits of Language

One of the major interests in twentieth-century philosophy is language. At first glance, this may seem puzzling. But a second look suggests that it is not so surprising. Our scientific theories, our religious and philosophical views, and our commonsense understandings are all expressed in language. Whenever we try to communicate with someone about a matter of any importance, it is language that carries the freight. What if there were something *misleading* about the language in which we think? What if it set traps for us, catapulted us into errors without our even realizing it? Perhaps we ought not to trust it at all.

This thought is a sort of subtext running through modern philosophy. Descartes notes that we naturally *say* that we see men passing by, but actually we just see colors and shapes and *judge* these are men. So our language misleads us. Hobbes tells us that words are the money of fools who think they can buy truth with them, but that the wise are not deceived. Hume thinks we are misled by language into identifying as ideas what are merely illusions. Kant holds that we do not understand how words like "I" actually work, nor do we grasp the logic of "exists." And so on. But it is only in our century that attention to language becomes a major preoccupation of philosophers, both on the continent and in the Anglo-American world. The interest in language has been so dominant that some speak of "the linguistic turn" in philosophy.

In this chapter and the next we examine two phases of this interest in language as it was expressed primarily in England and America. These two phases are often called *analytic philosophy* and *ordinary language philosophy*. We could do this in a number of ways, but we will focus on one remarkable thinker, Ludwig Wittgenstein, who had an immense impact on each of these ways of doing philosophy.

Language and Its Logic

To understand analytic philosophy, we need to know at least a bit about modern logic. It is a tool of very great power, incredibly magnified in our day by the speed and storage capacities of the digital computer. Every college and university now teaches this "formal," or "symbolic," logic, which was developed in the period near the turn of the century by Gottlob Frege, Bertrand Russell, Alfred North Whitehead, and others.

The power of the new logic derives from abstracting completely from the meaning or semantic content of assertions. It is a *formal* logic in just this sense: that the rules governing transformations from one symbolic formula to another make reference only to the syntactical structures of the formulas in question and not at all to their meaning. Aristotle's logic of the syllogism, of course, is formal in this same sense.* But it is oversimple. The new logic provides a symbolism for the internal structure of sentences that is enormously more powerful than Aristotle's. It can also deal with a more complex set of relations among sentences. For the first time, it really seems plausible that whatever you might want to say can be represented in this formalism. Because this logic abstracts entirely from content, it can be used with equal profit in any field, from operations research to theology. It will tell us what follows from certain premises, which assertions are inconsistent with each other, and so on. Being formal in this sense, it sets out a kind of logical skeleton that can be fleshed out in any number of ways, while preserving the logical relations precisely.

The prospect opened up by the new logic is that of a language more precise and clear than the language we normally speak—a purified, *ideal language,* in which there is no ambiguity, no vagueness, no dependence on emphasis, intonation, or the many other features of our language that may mislead us and are inessential for representing the truth. Bertrand Russell expresses the appeal of such a language in this way:

> In a logically perfect language the words in a proposition would correspond one by one with the components of the corresponding fact, with the exception of such words as 'or,' 'not,' 'if,' 'then,' which have a different function. In a logically perfect language, there will be one word and no more for every simple object, and everything that is not simple will be expressed by a combination of words, by a combination derived, of course, from the words for the simple things that enter in, one word for each simple component. A language of that sort will be completely analytic, and will show at a glance the logical structure of the facts asserted or denied. The language which is set forth in *Principia Mathematica* is intended to be a language of that sort.† It is a

language which has only syntax and no vocabulary whatever. Barring the omission of a vocabulary, I maintain that it is quite a nice language. It aims at being that sort of a language that, if you add a vocabulary, would be a logically perfect language. Actual languages are not logically perfect in this sense, and they cannot possibly be, if they are to serve the purposes of daily life.[1]

Two complementary ideas make the new logic of particular interest to philosophers. The first is the conviction that natural language, such as ordinary English, does not in fact possess this sort of perfection. The language we normally speak is full of vagueness, ambiguity, and confusion. It is by no means what Russell calls "a logically perfect language." The second idea is the suspicion that these tawdry features of our natural languages tend to lead us astray, particularly when we think about philosophical matters, which are always at some conceptual distance from everyday talk "of shoes and ships and sealing wax, of cabbages and kings."

So the dazzling idea of applying the new logic to traditional philosophical problems takes root in the imagination of many philosophers. Perhaps, if we could formulate these problems in terms of the crystalline purity of these formal logical structures, they could finally—after all these centuries—be definitively solved. The excitement is great. And indeed some very impressive analyses of puzzling uses of language are produced. One of the most influential of these is the "theory of definite descriptions" authored by Bertrand Russell. A definite description is a phrase of the form, "the so and so." Sentences containing phrases of this form have a certain paradoxical character. Consider, for example, this sentence: "The golden mountain does not exist." We think this is a true sentence. But ask yourself: "How can it be *true* that the golden mountain does not exist unless the phrase "the golden mountain" is meaningful? And how can it be meaningful unless there is something that it means? And if there *is* something that it means—why, then, the original sentence seems to be *false.* Doesn't it? So the golden mountain must exist after all! This is a puzzle.

---

* See pp. 150–153. For the distinction between syntax and semantics, see p. 535.
† *Principia Mathematica,* written by Bertrand Russell and Alfred North Whitehead between 1910 and 1913, is a classic of modern logic.

Bertrand Russell

Over a long lifetime (1872–1970), Bertrand Russell wrote on nearly every conceivable topic. His books range from *The Principles of Mathematics* (1903) and *Human Knowledge, Its Scope and Limits* (1948) to *The Conquest of Happiness* (1930) and *Common Sense and Nuclear Warfare* (1959). In 1950 he was awarded a Nobel Prize for literature. A pacifist during World War I, Russell was active in social causes all his life. Three passions, he said, governed his life: a longing for love, the search for knowledge, and unbearable pity for the suffering of mankind.

Though his views changed and developed on some topics, he was consistent in wishing philosophy to become more scientific. As one of the major contributors to the new logic, he held that traditional philosophical problems either are not properly the business of philosophy at all (and should be farmed out to the sciences) or are problems of logic. As a maxim for scientific philosophizing, Russell recommended that logical constructions replace inferences whenever possible.

Consider, for example, our knowledge of the external world; suppose I think I am now seeing a table. What I have directly in my acquaintance is a "sense datum"—some brownish, trapezoidal, visual figure or a tactual feeling of resistance. Common sense (and philosophy, too) characteristically *infers* from such data the existence of a table quite independent of my evidence for it. But such inferences are notoriously unreliable and lead easily to skeptical conclusions.

Russell suggested that my knowledge of the table should rather be *constructed* in terms of logical relations between all the sense data (actual and possible) that, in ordinary speech, we would say are "of" the table. Thus the inference to the table external to my evidence is replaced by a set of relations among the data which constitute that evidence. About those items skeptical problems do not arise.

In matters of ethics, Russell took a utilitarian line, holding that right actions are those that produce the greatest overall satisfaction. With respect to religion, he was an agnostic. He was once asked what he would say if after his death he found himself confronted with his Maker. He replied that he would say, "God, why did you make the evidence for your existence so insufficient?"

Russell applies the new logic to this puzzle and shows how it can be made to disappear. The solution goes like this. We go wrong in thinking of the phrase "the golden mountain" as a *name*—like "Socrates" or "New York." Definite descriptions are really disguised *predications,* not names. If we get clear about the *logic* of such phrases, we will see that saying, "The golden mountain does not exist," is equivalent to saying, "There exists no thing which is both golden and a mountain." (In the language of formal logic: "$\sim(\exists x)(Gx \ \& \ Mx)$".) And this is both true and unpuzzling. By getting clear about the logic of the language in which the puzzle is stated, we can see that it is a confusion to suppose that meaningfulness requires that a golden mountain must exist. This analysis has a great impact on many philosophers. It seems to show that the application of this logic to traditional problems of metaphysics and epistemology can produce clarity where before there was confusion. The logical analysis of language, then, seems to promise a definite increase in clarity of thought.*

---

*For example, Plato's semantic argument for the Forms (pp. 111–112) now looks like a mistake of this kind. Lacking an adequate logic, Plato mistakes terms such as "square" and "equal" for names, rather than predicates.

Ludwig Wittgenstein

In 1889 a son was born into the wealthy and talented Wittgenstein family of Vienna. He grew up in an atmosphere of high culture; the most prominent composers, writers, architects, and artists of that great city were regular visitors to his home. His father was an engineer and industrialist, his mother was very musical, and Ludwig was talented both mechanically and musically. It was also, however, a troubled family; there were several suicides among his siblings. He himself seems to have struggled against mental illness most of his life.

Having decided to study engineering, he went first to Berlin and then to Manchester, England, where he did some experiments with kites and worked on the design of an airplane propeller. This work drew his interests toward pure mathematics and eventually to the foundations of mathematics. The early years of the century, as we have seen, were a time of exciting developments in logic and the foundations of mathematics.

It was apparently Frege who advised Wittgenstein to go to Cambridge to study with Russell, which he did in the fall of 1911. Russell tells a story about Wittgenstein's first year there.

> At the end of his first term at Cambridge he came to me and said: "Will you please tell me whether I am a complete idiot or not?" I replied, "My dear fellow, I don't know. Why are you asking me?" He said, "Because, if I am a complete idiot, I shall become an aeronaut; but if not, I shall become a philosopher." I told him to write me something during the vacation on some philosophical subject and I would then tell him whether he was a complete idiot or not. At the beginning of the following term he brought me the fulfillment of this suggestion. After reading only one sentence, I said to him: "No, you must not become an aeronaut."[2]

When the war broke out in 1914, Wittgenstein was working on a manuscript which was to become the *Tractatus Logico-Philosophicus*. He served in the Austrian army and spent the better part of a year in an Italian prisoner-of-war camp, where he finished writing this dense, aphoristic little work that deals with everything from logic to happiness. After the war, he gave away the fortune he had inherited from his father, designating part of it for the support of artists and poets. He considered that he had set out in the *Tractatus* the final solution of the problems addressed there and left philosophy to teach school in remote Austrian villages. He lived, at that time and afterwards, in severe simplicity and austerity.

His days as a schoolmaster did not last long, however, and for a time he worked as a gardener in a monastery. Then he took the lead in designing and building a mansion in Vienna for one of his sisters. Eventually, through conversations with friends, he came to recognize what he thought were grave mistakes in the *Tractatus* and to think he might be able to do good work in philosophy again. He was invited back to Cambridge in 1929, where he submitted the *Tractatus*—by then published and widely read—as his dissertation.

He lectured there (except for a time during the Second World War) until shortly before his death in 1951. He published nothing else in his lifetime, though several manuscripts circulated informally. A second major book, *Philosophical Investigations*, was published posthumously in 1953. Since then many other works have been published from notes and writings he left. This later work is the subject of our next chapter.

Subsequent developments leave no doubt that Wittgenstein is one of the century's deepest thinkers. He is also one of the most complex and fascinating human beings to have contributed to philosophy since Socrates.[3] Wittgenstein's concerns early in life are fundamentally moral and spiritual; the most important question of all, he believes, is *how to live*. As we'll see, however, he also believes there is very little one can *say* about that problem. Like a number of other Viennese in the early decades of this century, he is repelled by the degree to which the hypocritical, the artificial, the ornate and merely decorative, the false and pretentious, and the striving for *effect* characterizes politics, daily life, and art at this time. He is a kindred spirit of the revolt that includes Arnold Schönberg in music and Adolf Loos in architecture. An austere lucidity and ruthless honesty are the values Wittgenstein sets against the confusion of the age. It is not, perhaps, accidental that he masters the new logic of Frege and Russell and becomes an important contributor to it. He sees in it the key by which certain fundamental problems of life and culture can be definitively solved. He also shares the feeling that the new logic might make *all* the difference for philosophy. In the preface to the *Tractatus*, he writes:

> The book deals with the problems of philosophy, and shows, I believe, that the reason why these problems are posed is that the logic of our language is misunderstood. The whole sense of the book might be summed up in the following words: what can be said at all can be said clearly, and what we cannot talk about we must pass over in silence. (*Tractatus* preface, p. 3)⁴

Wittgenstein's thought here is a radical one indeed: the posing of the problems of philosophy is itself the problem. If we can just get clear about "the logic of our language," these problems will *disappear*. They will be part of "what we cannot talk about." About them we must be *silent*.

And how will getting clear about the logic of our language produce such a startling result? If we get clear about the logic of our language, Wittgenstein thinks, we will see what the *limits* of language are. And we will also see that thinkers violate those limits whenever they pose and try to answer the sorts of problems we call philosophical.

> Thus the aim of the book is to set a limit to thought, or rather—not to thought, but to the expression of thoughts: for in order to be able to set a limit to thought, we should have to find both sides of the limit thinkable (i.e., we should have to be able to think what cannot be thought).
>
> It will therefore only be in language that the limit can be set, and what lies on the other side of the limit will simply be nonsense. (*Tractatus* preface, p. 3)

This has a somewhat Kantian ring to it, and it is worth taking a moment to compare it to Kant's view of the limits of knowledge. You will recall that Kant sets himself to uncover the limits of rational knowledge and thinks to accomplish that by a critique of reason. Knowledge, Kant holds, is a product of *a priori* concepts and principles supplied by reason on the one hand and of intuitive material supplied by sensibility on the other. Its domain is phenomena, the realm of possible experience. Beyond this are things-in-themselves (noumena), thinkable, perhaps, but unknowable by us. Knowledge, Kant believes, has definite limits; and we can know what these are.*

Wittgenstein's strategy in the *Tractatus* bears a family resemblance to this Kantian project. But it is more radical on two counts. It aims to set a limit not just to knowledge, but to thought itself. And what lies on the other side of that limit is *not in any way thinkable*. Wittgenstein calls it "nonsense."

He refers, rather opaquely, to a problem standing in the way of such a strategy. In drawing boundaries, we draw a line and say, for example: Here, on this side, is Gary's land; there, on that side, is Genevieve's. But as this example shows, drawing ordinary boundaries or setting ordinary limits presupposes that both sides are thinkable, perhaps even experienceable or knowable. How, then, is it possible to set a limit to *thought*? To do so, it would seem we would have to "think what cannot be thought," survey what is on the *other* side of the boundary line, if only to know what it is we intend to exclude. Wittgenstein's ingenious notion, which we will explore in the next section, is that this limit setting must be done in language—and *from inside* language. He thinks he has found a way to draw the line that doesn't require having to *say* in language what is excluded, what lies outside the limit. One can set the limit, he thinks, by working outward from the center through what *can* be said. The center is defined by what a language *is*, by the *essence* of language. What lies out beyond the boundary *shows itself* to be linguistic nonsense.

---

*A quick review of Kant's Copernican revolution and the idea of critique will bring this back to mind. See pp. 377–379.

The *Tractatus*

Here are the first two sentences in Wittgenstein's youthful work, the *Tractatus Logico-Philosophicus:*

1.   The world is all that is the case.
1.1   The world is the totality of facts, not of things.*

These sayings, announced so bluntly, may seem dark. But the key to unlock these mysteries is at hand: the new logic. Wittgenstein believes that he can use this logic to reveal the *essence of language.* And the essence of language *shows us* what the world must be. But this needs explanation.

Picturing

What is language? We are told that Wittgenstein's thinking about this question takes a decisive turn when he sees a diagram in a magazine story about an auto accident. Let us suppose it looked like this:

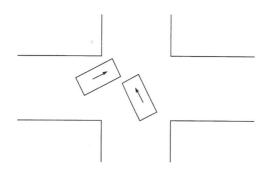

This diagram, we can say, *pictures a state of affairs.* It may not, of course, accurately represent what really happened. Let us call the actual state of affairs *the facts.* We can then say that this is a picture of a **possible state of affairs**—a picture of what

might have been the facts. (We can imagine the lawyers on each side presenting contrasting pictures of the accident.)

2.1   We picture facts to ourselves.
2.12   A picture is a model of reality.
2.131   In a picture the elements of the picture are the representatives of objects.
2.14   What constitutes a picture is that its elements are related to one another in a determinate way.
2.141   A picture is a fact.

The diagram above is itself a fact: it is made up of actual elements (lines on the page) that are related to each other in certain ways. Moreover, each element in the diagram *represents* some object in the world (the edges of the streets, cars). So this fact pictures, or models, another (possible) fact: the way the objects here represented were actually (or possibly) related to each other at a certain time and place.

Every picture has a certain *structure*. By "structure" Wittgenstein means the way its elements are related to each other. Two pictures that are different in many ways might still have a similar structure. Imagine, for instance, a color photograph taken from a helicopter hovering over the corner just after the accident. The elements of this picture (blobs of color) are quite different from the elements of our drawing (black lines on a white background). But if our drawing is accurate, the two pictures have a similar structure: their elements are related to each other in similar ways.

Furthermore, the two pictures not only have a similar structure but also have something in common: what Wittgenstein calls **pictorial form.** It is important to note that pictorial form is not another element in addition to the lines in our drawing or the colors in the photograph, nor is it the actual structure of these two pictures. Rather, pictorial form is the *possibility* that a picture might actually have just this structure, that elements of some sort might actually be arranged in just this way. There needn't ever have been a picture, or a fact, with elements related to each other like this. But even if there never had been, there *could* have been. This possibility is actualized in our diagram; it might be

---

* The *Tractatus* is arranged in short, aphoristic sentences, or small groups of sentences that express a complete thought. These sentences are numbered according to the following scheme. There are seven main aphorisms, 1, 2, 3, and so on. 1.1 is supposed to be a comment on or an explanation of 1; 1.11 is to play the same role with respect to 1.1. It must be admitted that this elegant scheme is sometimes difficult to interpret.

actualized as well in the helicopter photo and in indefinitely many more pictures of the same state of affairs. All these pictures would have the *same* pictorial form.

But it is not just similar pictures that share the same form.

2.16　　If a fact is to be a picture, it must have something in common with what it depicts.

2.161　There must be something identical in a picture and what it depicts, to enable the one to be a picture of the other at all.

2.17　　What a picture must have in common with reality, in order to be able to depict it—correctly or incorrectly—in the way it does, is its pictorial form.

Pictures and what is pictured by them (e.g., the accident itself) must also share the same form. So far we have been thinking of spatial pictures of objects in space. But there are other kinds of pictures, too. We can, for instance, think of an orchestra score as a picture; this is a spatial picture (the notes are laid out next to each other on a page), but what it primarily pictures is not spatial, but temporal: the succession of sounds the orchestra plays in a performance. Yet a score is also a picture, in Wittgenstein's sense, of the grooves in a recording of the work and of the magnetic tracings on a tape or compact disc. And we could think of the grooves in a recording as in turn a picture of the sound produced when it is played (see 4.0141). So while we tend to use the word "picture" rather narrowly, the concept applies very widely. Wherever there are objects in relation representing other objects, there is a Wittgensteinian picture.

Every picture, Wittgenstein claims, is a *logical* picture. And logical pictures can depict the world (2.19). As we have seen, a picture may represent reality correctly or incorrectly. That is why Wittgenstein says that logical pictures *can* depict the world: they depict ways the world might be— possible states of affairs.

If we think of a certain two-dimensional space, such as a desk top, we can see that there are a variety of possible ways the books on it can be arranged. Analogously, we can think of *logical space*.

Logical space consists of all the *possibilities* there are for all the *objects* there are to be *related* to each other in all the possibly different ways there are. Logical space, then, comprises the form not only of all the actual states of affairs but also of all possible states of affairs. Given this notion of logical space, we can say,

2.202　A picture represents a possible situation in logical space.

Some pictures represent reality correctly, and others don't. How can we tell whether what a picture tells us is true?

2.22　　What a picture represents it represents independently of its truth or falsity, by means of its pictorial form.

2.223　In order to tell whether a picture is true or false we must compare it with reality.

2.224　It is impossible to tell from the picture alone whether it is true or false.

2.225　There are no pictures that are true *a priori*.

You can't tell just by looking at our accident diagram, no matter how microscopically you inspect it, whether it represents the accident correctly. And this is the case with *all* pictures, Wittgenstein says. A *true* picture is one that represents a possible state of affairs that is also actual. And actual states of affairs are *facts*. So a true picture depicts the facts. If there were a picture true *a priori* (independent of experience), you wouldn't have to "compare it with reality" to tell whether it is true; you could discover the facts just by examining the picture. But that, Wittgenstein says, is precisely what is not possible. To tell whether a picture is true (represents the facts correctly), you have to check its fit with the facts. In no case can we tell *a priori* whether a picture is true. This is an extremely important feature of pictures.*

---

* If Wittgenstein is right, rationalist attempts to say what the world must be like based on reason alone must be mistaken. No matter how "clear and distinct" one of Descartes' ideas is, for instance, one can't deduce from this that it is true. By stressing that there are no pictures that are true *a priori*, Wittgenstein expresses one version of empiricism. Compare Hume, pp. 353–354.

Thought and Language

Among the logical pictures, there is one sort that is of particular significance.

3.	A logical picture of facts is a thought.
3.001	'A state of affairs is thinkable': what this means is that we can picture it to ourselves.
3.01	The totality of true thoughts is a picture of the world.
3.02	A thought contains the possibility of the situation of which it is the thought. What is thinkable is possible too.

Our thoughts, then, are pictures, too. And, being pictures, they have all the characteristics of pictures we noted earlier: they are composed of elements in a certain arrangement, so they are facts with a certain structure; in virtue of that, they possess pictorial form; they represent possible states of affairs; and they share their pictorial and logical form with what they represent.

And now comes a crucial point.

3.1	In a proposition a thought finds an expression that can be perceived by the senses.
3.11	We use the perceptible sign of a proposition (spoken or written, etc.) as a projection of a possible situation.

So thought finds its expression in perceptible signs, or sentences, that is, in *language*. Now we can understand why Wittgenstein thinks he can set a limit to thought by finding the limits of language. It is in language that thought is expressed. If there are limits to what language can express, these will be the limits of thought as well.

But what is a propositional sign, a sentence? Like all pictures, it is a fact, an arrangement of objects.

3.1431	The essence of a propositional sign is very clearly seen if we imagine one composed of spatial objects (such as tables, chairs, and books) instead of written signs. Then the spatial arrangement of these things will express the sense of the proposition.

Suppose you want to picture the fact that Sarah is standing to the east of Ralph. You might use a table to represent Sarah and a chair to represent Ralph. By putting the table to the east of the chair, you can picture the fact in question. This shows us, Wittgenstein says, "the essence of a propositional sign." What he means is that written or spoken sentences are like this, too; they are made up of elements standing in certain relations.

But it is not obvious that they are like this.

4.002	Everyday language is a part of the human organism and is no less complicated than it. It is not humanly possible to gather immediately from it what the logic of language is. Language disguises thought.

The *essence* of language is hidden, "disguised." Yet it is something that can be disclosed, or shown. What reveals the hidden essence of language? *Logic.* Wittgenstein agrees with Russell that the superficial grammar of what we say may not be a good indication of the logic of what we say. And he holds that the new logic displays for us the internal structure, the essence of language. Still, he is not tempted to discard our natural languages (German or English, for example) in favor of some artificially created "ideal" language. Nor does he have any inclination to reform our language in the direction of some postulated ideal. Since the languages we speak are *languages,* they too must exemplify the essence of language. So logic must reside even there, in the heart of our confusing, vague, and ambiguous languages. What we need is not to junk them in favor of some ideal, but to understand them.

5.5563	In fact, all the propositions of our everyday language, just as they stand, are in perfect logical order.

If they weren't, they wouldn't constitute a language!

But because "language disguises thought," the logical structure of our language is not apparent. To bring it to light we need *analysis.* What sort of analysis, then, can we give of a sentence? We already have the elements of an answer in hand. A sentence is a picture, and we know that a picture, like all facts, is composed of elements set in a certain structure. So there must be elements and a structure in every sentence. It only remains to determine what they are.

Let's consider again the sentence "Sarah is to the East of Ralph." We saw that this could be represented by one object in relation to another, a table and a chair, for instance. The table would in effect be a kind of name for Sarah, and the chair a name for Ralph. Wittgenstein concludes that the *only* elements needed in a language are names. Everything else—all the adjectives and prepositions, for instance—are inessential. If sentences were completely analyzed into their basic elements, all this would disappear. What would be left would be names in a structure.*

> 3.202   The simple signs employed in propositions are called names.
> 3.203   A name means an object. The object is its meaning. . . .
> 3.26   A name cannot be dissected any further by means of a definition: it is a primitive sign.

As you can see, there would be a very great difference between the "look" of a completely analyzed propositional sign and our ordinary sentences. One might have a hard time even recognizing the complete analysis of a familiar sentence, particularly because the names in question have to be *simple* signs. What we take to be names in ordinary language are invariably complex; they can be "dissected . . . by means of a definition." "Santa Claus" is short for "the jolly fat man who brings toys to good children." "George Washington" is a shorthand expression for "the first president of the United States" (and many other descriptions). These descriptions themselves need to be analyzed

if we are to get to the roots of things to understand how language pictures the world.

If we could get to that level of clarity, Wittgenstein thinks, we would see that sentences are composed of names in a logical structure. And names are *simple*. They cannot be further analyzed or "dissected." The meaning of a name cannot be given in a definition using other linguistic elements; the meaning of a name is the object it stands for.*

Now we are ready to go back to the beginning and understand those first mysterious propositions of the *Tractatus*. Just as sentences represent possible states of affairs, true sentences represent facts. True sentences, moreover, are made up of names, and names stand for objects. But a sentence isn't just a list of names; it has an internal structure. And a fact isn't just a jumble of things; it has the same structure as the true sentence that pictures it. Why? Because the pictorial form of sentences mirrors the logical form of facts. The *world* is what is pictured in the totality of true sentences. The world, then, is not just a random collection of objects; it is "the totality of facts, not of things" because it shares the same logical form as the true sentences.

> 1.13   The facts in logical space are the world.

But we do not yet see how to solve the main problem Wittgenstein poses: to set a limit to thought. To do this, we have to look more closely at the logic of propositions.† As Russell shows, ordinary language often disguises the logical form of our sentences, but analysis can reveal it. A complete analysis would leave us with sentences that

---

*Here is a rough analogy. Certain notations in mathematics are merely a convenience and could be eliminated without diminishing the science. x^3, for instance, is just $x \cdot x \cdot x$. And $4y$ can be defined as $y + y + y + y$. So Wittgenstein thinks names standing in certain relations will express whatever we want to express, though we usually use more economical means.

*It is worth noting that Wittgenstein does not offer any examples of these simple names in the *Tractatus*. He argues that such names must be implicit in our language and ultimately reachable by analysis; but just what they are—and what they name—is something of a mystery.

†For our purposes, I will not distinguish sentences from propositions, though some philosophers do; a proposition is often thought of as an abstract feature several sentences can share when they mean the same thing. For example, "Mary hit Sally" and "Sally was hit by Mary" are different sentences but can be said to express the same proposition. Another example is "Snow is white" and "Schnee ist weiss."

could not be further analyzed—simple sentences sometimes called *atomic propositions*. They would have constituents (names in a structure of possibility), but they could not be further broken down into other sentences.

4.221   It is obvious that the analysis of propositions must bring us to elementary propositions which consist of names in immediate combination.

But how are these simple sentences related to each other? Wittgenstein holds that

5.134   One elementary proposition cannot be deduced from another.

What this means is that the truth-value of each is independent of the truth-value of any other. An elementary proposition can remain true while the truth-values of any others (or even all the others) change. This has consequences for our view of the world as well.

2.061   States of affairs are independent of one another.

2.062   From the existence or non-existence of one state of affairs, it is impossible to infer the existence or non-existence of another.

Recall once more the beginning of the *Tractatus:*

1.2   The world divides into facts.

1.21   Each item can be the case or not the case while everything else remains the same.

This view, called **logical atomism,** is reminiscent of Hume's remark that "all events seem entirely loose and separate."* It means that relations existing between atomic facts cannot be *logical* relations. Given one true elementary proposition, it is never *necessary* that another one be true—or false.

There are, of course, logical relations between complex propositions. If we are given the truth-value of *p* and of *q,* we can infer something about

_____
*See p. 359.

the truth of the conjunction, *p and q.* To display these logical relations, Wittgenstein devises *truth tables.* A truth table for a complex proposition sets forth all the logically possible combinations of truth-values for its components and then displays the corresponding truth-values for the whole. Here, for example, are truth tables for conjunctive, disjunctive, and negative propositions.

p	*q*	*p and q*	*p or q*	*not p*
T	T	T	T	F
T	F	F	T	F
F	T	F	T	T
F	F	F	F	T

The two columns on the left set out the possibilities; they show us that two propositions may both be true, one or the other may be true, or neither one may be true. The truth table for the conjunction shows us that the conjunction is true only when both of the components are true, and false otherwise. The truth table for the disjunction (an "or" statement) shows us that the disjunction is true unless both of the components are false. And the truth table for negation shows that negating a proposition changes its truth value.

Propositions may be of any degree of complexity. There may be a very large number of elementary propositions in its makeup, and the logic of their relations may be extremely complicated. The truth table for a proposition such as

if[if(p and q) then not (r or s)]
    then (t if and only if not u)

is very large, but it is calculable. The truth-value of a complex proposition is a function of the truth-values of the component parts; this feature is called *truth functionality.* The logic of the *Tractatus* is a truth-functional logic.

Logical Truth

We noted before that no pictures are true *a priori.* To determine whether a proposition is true or false, then, we must compare it to the world. From the point of view of logic, any elementary proposition might be true, or it might be false. Such propositions are called *contingent:* their truth depends on the facts. The contingency of elementary propositions has another implication: however the world is, whatever the facts are, they *might have been different.* There is never any necessity in the facts. The negation of any true elementary proposition always pictures a possibility. Suppose it is true that it is now raining where I am; then it is false that it is not raining here and now (see the truth table above), but it is not necessarily false. It is a coherent possibility that it should not be raining here and now, even if it is. Given the configuration of the objects in the world, it is raining. But the objects of the world *could have been* otherwise configured.

We might like to ask, Just how far do these unrealized possibilities extend? How many possibilities are there? The answer is that this is what logic shows us. Our experience of the world can tell us what the actual facts are. Logic shows us what they *might be.* Logic is the science of the possible. And everything that it shows us is *necessary* (i.e., not contingent).* Consider, for example, the truth table for a proposition like this:

Either it is raining, or it is not raining.

p	not p	p or not p
T	F	T
F	T	T

The first column gives us the possibilities for the truth of *p.* The next column shows us what is the case when *p* is negated. And the third displays the results of disjoining the first two. The crucial thing to notice is that whatever the truth of *p* (and there are just these two possibilities), *p or not p* is true. In other words, there is no possibility that this

proposition could be false. It is *necessarily* true; it is a **logical truth.** Such a proposition Wittgenstein calls a **tautology.***

There are three important points to notice here.

1.   The sentence represented by *p or not p* is a complex, not an elementary, proposition; *p* may or may not be elementary, but in this complex proposition, it is set in a structure defined by the logical operators, "not" and "or." Only propositions that are logically complex in this way can be necessarily true or false. (That is just another way to say that the truth of an elementary proposition is always contingent.)

2.   Logical words such as "not," "and," "or," and "if-then" are not *names.* These terms do not stand for objects; they have an entirely different function. They are part of the *structure* of sentences, not part of the content.†

4.0312   My fundamental idea is that the 'logical constants' are not representatives; that there can be no representatives of the *logic* of facts.

Wittgenstein illustrates this "fundamental idea" by considering double negation. There is a law of logic stating that negating the negation of a proposition is equivalent to asserting the proposition:

not not p if and only if p.

If it is not true that it is not raining, that it is raining. If the logical operator "not" were a name of something, the left side of this equivalence would picture something quite different from what the right side pictures; the law would then be false. But it doesn't. And the proof of this is that a truth table

---

*If something is possible, it cannot be merely contingent that it is possible, since whatever actually exists must *already* be possible; so what is possible couldn't *depend* on what the facts are.

---

*There are two limiting cases of propositions. Tautologies are one case; contradictions are the other. While tautologies are necessarily true, contradictions are necessarily false. Tautologies do not rule out any possibilities, contradictions rule them all out. In a sense, it is not strictly correct to call tautologies and contradictions "propositions," since propositions are pictures of reality; tautologies and contradictions do not picture states of affairs. They have a different, and very important, role to play.
† Compare Russell's description of a logically perfect language on p. 550.

for this principle is a tautology. So, the logical operators are not names.

3. Suppose we interpret *p* as "It is raining"; then the tautology *p or not p* says, "Either it is raining, or it is not raining." But while "It is raining" gives us some information, the tautology tells us nothing. It says nothing; it is not a *picture*. Why is it that the proposition *p* can tell us something? It can be informative because it picks out one of several possibilities and says that that is how things are. In picking out that possibility, it excludes another. It tells us something about the world by shutting out one possibility and allowing another; *p or not p,* by contrast, excludes nothing. It does not rule out any possibilities, so it does not *say* anything.

> 4.461   Propositions show what they say: tautologies and contradictions show that they say nothing. A tautology has no truth conditions, since it is unconditionally true: and a contradiction is true on no condition.
>
> 4.462   Tautologies and contradictions are not pictures of reality. They do not represent any possible situations. For the former admit *all* possible situations, and the latter *none*.

Saying and Showing

We come now to a distinction that is very important to Wittgenstein: the distinction between *saying* and **showing**. Propositions do two things; they show something and they say something.

> 4.022   A proposition *shows* its sense.
> A proposition *shows* how things stand *if* it is true, and it *says that* they do so stand.

The proposition "All crows are black" shows or presents its sense. We can see what this means if we ask what would be required to *understand* it. To understand this proposition is to grasp its sense; to grasp its sense is to understand what *would be the case* if it were *true*. When we understand the sentence, we know that *if* it is true, any crow we come across will be black. Notice that understanding the sentence is not yet knowing that all crows are black. Given that we understand it, we might won-

der whether it is true or doubt that it is true. It is, after all, possible that some crows aren't black; the proposition might present a possible state of affairs only, not a fact. But we grasp its sense in *knowing what would make it either true or false.* That—its sense—is what a proposition *shows.*

But a proposition like this plays another role. It not only shows its sense but also *says* things are this way, that crows actually are black. It makes an assertion and so is true or false depending on the facts of the world. According to Wittgenstein, this is the most general propositional form, that is, what all propositions have in common:

> 4.5   This is how things stand.

Propositions *show* their sense; they *say* how things are.

But tautologies and contradictions *show* that they *say nothing.* If these limiting cases of propositions say nothing, however, we might wonder whether they have any importance. Couldn't we just ignore or neglect them? No. They are of the very greatest importance. They show us what is possible and what is impossible. They display for us the structure of logical space.

But they have another importance as well.

> 6.1   The propositions of logic are tautologies.

What Wittgenstein here calls the "propositions" of logic are sometimes called the laws of logic. Consider as an example the very basic law called the principle of noncontradiction: that no proposition can be both true and false. We can represent this as

not both p and not p.

If we write a truth table for this formula, we can see that it is a tautology—that is, necessarily true no matter what the truth-values of *p* are.

p	*not p*	*p and not p*	*not (p and not p)*
T	F	F	T
F	T	F	T

So the device of truth tables provides a justification for the laws of logic. Showing they are tautologies is equivalent to demonstrating their necessary truth. The truth table shows that there is no alternative to the laws of logic—no possibility that they might be false.* The *Tractatus* doctrine is that every principle of logical inference can be reduced to a tautology.†

Moreover,

6.113   It is the peculiar mark of logical propositions that one can recognize that they are true from the symbol alone, and this fact contains in itself the whole philosophy of logic.

What this means is that the propositions of logic can be known *a priori*. As we saw above, we can know about the actual world only by comparing a proposition with reality. It is the mark of logical propositions that this is not only unnecessary, but impossible; since they say nothing, they cannot say anything we could check out by examining the facts.

So the propositions of logic are one and all tautologies. And every valid form of inference can be expressed in a proposition of logic. This means that all possible logical relations between propositions can be known *a priori*. And in knowing them, we know the logical structure of the world—logical space, what Wittgenstein calls "the scaffolding of the world" (6.124).

6.1251   Hence there can *never* be surprises in logic.
6.127   All the propositions of logic are of equal status: it is not the case that some of them are essentially primitive proposi-

tions and others essentially derived propositions.
Every tautology itself shows that it is a tautology.

Setting the Limit to Thought

Finally, we are ready to understand how Wittgenstein thinks he can show us the limits of language. An operation discovered by Wittgenstein can be performed on a set of elementary propositions and can produce all the possible complex propositions (truth functions) that can be expressed by that set. Suppose we have just two elementary propositions, p and q. Using this operator, we can calculate that there are just sixteen possible truth functions combining them: *not p, not q, p or q, p and q, if p then q,* and so on. Now imagine that we were in possession of *all* the elementary propositions there are; using this operation on that set, one could simply calculate all the possible truth functions there are and so *generate each and every possible proposition.*

Remembering the picture theory of meaning, we can see that this set of propositions pictures all the possible states of affairs there are, and in all their possible combinations. So, it represents the entirety of logical space; it pictures everything that there could possibly be in reality. Notice that there would be no proposition saying that these are all the possible facts; in fact, there couldn't be such a proposition. But there also doesn't need to be. That these are all the facts there are *shows itself* in these propositions being all there are, in there simply being no more that are possible, calculable, formulable. And we can see there are no more possible propositions, because all the possible ones are part of this set produced by this operator.

This very large set of propositions contains everything it is possible to say, plus the tautologies and contradictions (which say nothing). Beyond this set of possible propositions lies only *nonsense.* So the limit of thought is indeed set from inside. Thought is expressed in language. The essence of language is picturing. And, given this, we can work out from the center to the periphery of language by means of logic. We do not need to take up a

---

* Of course this also shows that the laws of logic *say* nothing, that is, are *about* nothing. The laws of logic are purely formal and empty of content. And that is exactly why they can be noncontingently true.

† In fact this claim is not correct. Truth tables constitute a decision procedure for validity only in *propositional logic*, where the analysis of structure does not go deeper than whole propositions. In *quantificational* (or *predicate*) *logic*, where the analysis reveals the internal structure of propositions, Alonzo Church later proves there is no such decision procedure.

position outside the thinkable in order to draw a line circumscribing it. The limit *shows itself* by the lack of sense that pseudopropositions display when we try to say something unsayable. It is indeed, then, only "in language that the limit can be set, and what lies on the other side of the limit will simply be nonsense" (*Tractatus* preface, p. 3).

> 5.61   Logic pervades the world: the limits of the world are also its limits.
> So we cannot say in logic, 'The world has this in it, and this, but not that.'
> For that would appear to presuppose that we were excluding certain possiblities, and this cannot be the case, since it would require that logic should go beyond the limits of the world; for only in that way could it view those limits from the other side as well. We cannot think what we cannot think; so what we cannot think we cannot *say* either.

Value and the Self

We noted earlier that the young Wittgenstein's concerns were mainly spiritual and moral. But we have just seen that the bulk of the *Tractatus* deals with quite technical issues in logic and the philosophy of language. How are we to understand this apparent discrepancy? In a letter to a potential publisher for the *Tractatus*, Wittgenstein writes,

> The book's point is an ethical one. I once meant to include in the preface a sentence which is not in fact there now but which I will write out for you here, because it will perhaps be a key to the work for you. What I meant to write, then, was this: My work consists of two parts: the one presented here plus all that I have *not* written, and it is precisely this second part that is the important one. My book draws limits to the sphere of the ethical from the inside as it were, and I am convinced that this is the ONLY *rigorous* way of drawing those limits. In short, I believe that where many others today are just *gassing,* I have managed in my book to put everything firmly in place by being silent about it.[5]

What could this mean—that the really important part of the book is the part he did not write? Why

didn't he write it? Was he too lazy? Did he run out of time? Of course not. He didn't write the important part because he was convinced it *couldn't be written.* What is most important—the ethical point of the book—is something that *cannot be said.*

Nonetheless, and again paradoxically, he does have some things to "say" about this sphere, which he also calls "the mystical." * Before we examine his remarks—brief and dark sayings, as many have noted—it will be helpful to set out a consequence of what we have already learned.

> 4.1   Propositions represent the existence and non-existence of states of affairs.
> 4.11   The totality of true propositions is the whole of natural science (or the whole corpus of the natural sciences).

The essence of language is picturing; and to picture is to say, "This is how things stand." The job of natural science is to tell us how things are, to give us a description of the world. And if natural science could finish its job, we would then have a *complete* picture of reality.[†] Nothing—no object, no fact—would be left out. It would include the *totality* of true propositions.

But natural science does not contain any propositions like these: one ought to do *X*; it is wrong to *Y*; the meaning of life is *Z*. It follows that these are not really propositions at all; they look a lot like propositions, but, if Wittgenstein is right, they lie *beyond the limits of language.* Strictly speaking, they are unsayable. Those who utter them may be "just *gassing.*" Or they may be trying to say the most important things of all but failing, because they "run against the boundaries of language." In a "Lecture on Ethics" Wittgenstein gave in 1929 or 1930 (not published until 1965), he says,

> This running against the walls of our cage is perfectly, absolutely hopeless. Ethics so far as it springs from the desire to say something about the ultimate

---

*It is obviously a problem how we are to understand what he "says" about the unsayable. He makes a suggestion we will consider later.
†Compare Peirce's similar conviction, pp. 529–530.

meaning of life, the absolute good, the absolute valuable, can be no science. What it says does not add to our knowledge in any sense. But it is a document of a tendency in the human mind which I personally cannot help respecting deeply and I would not for my life ridicule it.[6]

Ethics "can be no science" because science consists of propositions, and

6.4	All propositions are of equal value.
6.41	The sense of the world must lie outside the world. In the world everything is as it is, and everythig happens as it does happen: *in* it no value exists—and if it did exist, it would have no value.
	If there is any value that does have value, it must lie outside the whole sphere of what happens and is the case.
6.42	And so it is impossible for there to be propositions of ethics.
	Propositions can express nothing that is higher.
6.421	It is clear that ethics cannot be put into words.
	Ethics is transcendental.

We can think of the *Tractatus* as the absolute end point of that road that begins with Copernicus and leads to the expulsion of value from the framework of the world.* The vision of the *Tractatus* is one where everything in the world is flattened out, where nothing is of any more significance than anything else, because nothing is of any significance at all. In the world is no value at all, nothing of importance. There are just the facts. And even if there were such a thing in the world as a value, that thing would itself just be another fact. It would *have* no value.

In Samuel Beckett's play *Endgame*, a character named Hamm, blind and unable to move from his chair, commands his servant, Clov, to "Look at the earth." Clov gets his telescope, climbs a ladder, and looks out of the high window.

---

*Look back again to the discussion of how *final causes,* purposes and goals, are excluded from explanations in the new science. See pp. 287–289.

CLOV:
   Let's see.
   (*He looks, moving the telescope.*)
   Zero . . .
   (*he looks*)
   . . . zero . . .
   (*he looks*)
   . . . and zero.

HAMM:
   Nothing stirs. All is—

C:
   Zer—

H: (*violently*):
   Wait till you're spoken to!
   (*Normal voice.*)
   All is . . . all is . . . all is what?
(*Violently.*)
   All is what?

C:
   What all is? In a word? Is that what you want to know? Just a moment.
   (*He turns the telescope on the without, looks, lowers the telescope, turns toward Hamm.*)
   Corpsed.[7]

Beckett's vision could not be more like Wittgenstein's. And, at the same time, it could not be more unlike. Turn the telescope to the earth (the world) and the verdict is "Zero, zero, zero." "Corpsed." In it no value exists. For Beckett, that is all there is; and that accounts for the sense of desolation and despair you find in his work. But Wittgenstein also knows another "reality." *

Ethics, Wittgenstein says, "cannot be put into words." But what does it mean that ethics is something "higher," that it is "transcendental"? To understand this saying, we need to consider Wittgenstein's views of the subject, the self, the "I." He suggests that if you wrote a book called *The World*

---

*In a phrase as opposed as possible to Beckett's conclusion that the earth is "corpsed," Wittgenstein says, "The world and life are one" (5.621). But in the light of his claim that the world consists wholly of valueless facts, this is a dark saying. It does seem, though, to be related to the idea that the self is the "limit" of the world and to the complementarity of solipsism and realism. We shall examine these ideas below.

As I found It, there is one thing that would not be mentioned in it: *you.* It would include all the facts you found, including all the facts about your body. And it would include psychological facts about yourself as well: your character, personality, dispositions, and so on. But you—the subject, the one to whom all this appears, the one who *finds* all these facts—would not be found.*

5.632	The subject does not belong to the world; rather, it is a limit of the world.
5.641	The philosophical self is not the human being, not the human body, or the human soul, with which psychology deals, but rather the metaphysical subject, the limit of the world—not a part of it.

It seems, then, that there are two "realities" in correlation: the world and the self; however, in the strict sense, the self or subject cannot be *said* to be a reality. Wittgenstein compares the situation to the relation between an eye and its visual field. The eye is not itself part of the visual field; it is not seen. In the same way, all content, all the facts, are "out there" in the world, which is the "totality of facts" (1.1).

5.64	Here it can be seen that solipsism, when its implications are followed out strictly, coincides with pure realism. The self of solip-

sism shrinks to a point without extension, and there remains the reality co-ordinated with it.

5.62	For what the solipsist *means* is quite correct; only it cannot be *said,* but makes itself manifest.*

What the solipsist wants to say is that only he exists, and the world only in relation to himself. But this cannot be *said.* Why? Because to say it would be to use language—propositions—to picture facts. And in picturing facts we are picturing the world, *not* the transcendental self to whom the world appears. So this self "shrinks to a point without extension." And if we ask *what there is,* the answer is the world—"all that is the case" (*Tractatus,* proposition 1). And this is just the thesis of radical **realism,** the antithesis of solipsism.

The concern of ethics is good and evil. But, as we have seen, there is no room for good and evil in the world, where everything just is whatever it is. What application, then, do these concepts have? Ethics must concern itself with the transcendental: the self, the subject. But how? Here is a clue.

6.373	The world is independent of my will.
6.374	Even if all that we wish for were to happen, still this would only be a favour granted by fate, so to speak.

I may will or intend to do something, such as write a check to pay a telephone bill. And usually I can do it. But it is clear that paying a bill by check depends on the cooperation of the world: the neurons have to fire just right, the nerves must transmit the neural signals reliably, the muscles must contract in just the right way, the bank must not suddenly crash, and so forth. And none of that is entirely in my control. That is what Wittgenstein means when he says the world is independent of

---

* Among thinkers we have studied, this should remind you most of Kant, for whom the ego is also transcendental. It is not identical with Kant's view, however. Kant believes that, though we can't come to know the nature of "this I or he or it (the thing) which thinks," we could come to know a lot about it—that it is the source of the pure intuitions, the categories, the *a priori* synthetic propositions, all of which explain the structure of the empirical world. And all this can be stated in meaningful propositions. For Wittgenstein, none of this is possible. The structure of the world is not dictated by the structure of rational minds, because the structure of reality is just logic; and logic, consisting as it does of empty tautologies, neither has nor needs a source. Kant's world needs a structure-giver because its fundamental principles are thought to be synthetic. For Wittgenstein, logic is *analytic.* It requires no source beyond itself because it has no content requiring explanation. This "scaffolding of the world" is not itself a fact in the world, nor is it a fact about the world or about rational minds. It is not a fact at all! It shows *itself.* Look again at the relevant discussions of Kant on pp. 394–395.

* Compare Descartes' struggles to overcome solipsism by proving the existence of God in *Meditation III;* see also pp. 304 and 310. Wittgenstein acknowledges there is a truth in solipsism; but such truth as there is already involves the reality of the world—of which the self is aware. So there is no need to *prove* the world's existence—or that of God, about whom in any case nothing can be said.

my will. If I intend to pay my telephone bill, getting it done is, in a way, a "favour granted by fate."*

Good and Evil, Happiness and Unhappiness

Wittgenstein seems to have proved that good and evil cannot lie in the world. Everything just happens as it does happen. So good and evil must pertain to the will. What I will is in my control, even if the outcome of my willing in the world is not. In a strict sense, my willing *is* my action: the rest is just the result of my action. But now we have to ask what good and evil could be, if they pertain to the will only.

6.422   When an ethical law of the form, 'Thou shalt . . .', is laid down, one's first thought is, "And what if I do not do it?" It is clear, however, that ethics has nothing to do with punishment and reward in the usual sense of the terms. So our question about the *consequences* of an action must be unimportant. At least those consequences should not be events. For there must be something right about the question we posed. There must indeed be some kind of ethical reward and punishment, but they must reside in the action itself. (And it is also clear that the reward must be something pleasant and the punishment something unpleasant.)

Good action (good willing) is rewarded with something pleasant, and evil action is punished with the unpleasant. But these are not rewards and punishments "in the usual sense"; they cannot be external to the action itself. They cannot, in other words, be something added by the world. How could a "favour granted by fate" have anything to do with *ethical* rewards? Such rewards and punishments must be intrinsic to the actions themselves. But what could they be?

6.43   If the good or bad exercise of the will does alter the world, it can alter only the limits of the world, not the facts—not what can be expressed by means of language.
In short the effect must be that it becomes an altogether different world. It must, so to speak, wax and wane as a whole.
The world of the happy man is a different one from that of the unhappy man.

These are difficult sayings, indeed. And I do not claim to understand fully what Wittgenstein means by them. It does seem clear that the reward for good willing is happiness and the punishment for bad is unhappiness. The good person, as Plato also thinks, is the happy person.* But this obviously does not mean that Jones, who lives righteously and well, will get whatever she wants in life. That kind of connection between willing and the world doesn't exist. (This fact is also recognized by Kant.) Goodness does not produce *that kind* of happiness.† What kind does it produce, then?

Strictly speaking, this question cannot be answered. In the *Notebooks, 1914–1916*, Wittgenstein asks:

"What is the objective mark of the happy, harmonious life? Here it is again clear that there cannot be any such mark, that can be *described*. This mark cannot be a physical one but only a metaphysical one, a transcendental one." (*N, 78*)[8]

---

*If these reflections are going to make any sense to you at all, you will have to pause a bit and try to sink into this way of viewing things. It will not be any good to just try to learn the words, or even memorize the sentences. Wittgenstein would insist that if you are able only to parrot the words, you will have understood *nothing*. Here is an exercise that might help. Pick out some fact about your present experience. Focus on it. Try to regard it as merely a fact in the world, one fact among others. Now try to focus on some psychological state in the same way. Practice in this should make even your own psychological states have the same status as any other fact in the world; they will not be "privileged," as it were, but just facts that are *there*. And then ask yourself: for whom are they there? For ideas that are in some ways similar, see the discussion of the Stoics on p. 193.

* See Plato's discussion of the happiness of the just soul, pp. 134–137.
† It might help to remember here that Wittgenstein gave away the considerable fortune he inherited when his father died and lived the rest of his life simply and austerely. What the world can supply cannot *make* you happy!

And we know that nothing can be *said* about the transcendental. Still, there are clues and hints. What could it mean, for instance, that the *world* of the happy person is a different world from that of the unhappy one? That the world waxes and wanes as a whole? Here is a possibility.

Most of us, most of the time, do not occupy the position of the transcendental subject, even though that is what we essentially are—the limit of the world, not some entity within the world. We identify ourselves with a body, with certain desires, with a set of psychological facts. This is, we think, what we are. And in so identifying ourselves, our world narrows, *wanes*. We are concerned with *this* body, with satisfying *these* desires. And *our* world is just the world relevant to these concerns. It is as though the rest didn't exist. If we could, however, identify with the transcendental self, our world would wax larger. Indeed, we would see it just as it is—a limited whole and the totality of facts, none of which are of such importance that they crowd out any other. *Our* world would become *the* world. Only the world of the happy person is identical with the world as it is. The happy see the world with that disinterested enjoyment we experience when we appreciate a fine work of art. In Wittgenstein's words:

6.421   (Ethics and aesthetics are one and the same.)

and

> The work of art is the object seen *sub specie aeternitatis*; and the good life is the world seen *sub specie aeternitatis*. This is the connection between art and ethics.
> The usual way of looking at things sees objects as if it were from the midst of them, the view *sub specie aeternitatis* from outside. (*N*, 84e)

and

> Aesthetically, the miracle is that the world exists. That what exists does exist.
> Is it the essence of the artistic way of looking at

things, that it looks at the world with a happy eye? (*N*, 86e)

To live one's life "from the viewpoint of eternity" is to live in the present.* And here we have another clue:

> Whoever lives in the present lives without fear and hope. (*N*, 76e)

What could this mean? The thought seems to be that fear and hope essentially refer to time; one fears what *may happen,* and one hopes *for the future.* But if one lives entirely in the present, there is no past and future about which to fear and hope. If there is nothing one fears—absolutely nothing— and if there is nothing one hopes (presumably because one lacks nothing), how could one fail to be happy? In his "Lecture on Ethics," Wittgenstein tells us that when he tries to think of something with absolute value, two "experiences" come to mind.

> I will describe this [first] experience in order, if possible, to make you recall the same or similar experiences, so that we may have a common ground for our investigation. I believe the best way of describing it is to say that when I have it *I wonder at the existence of the world.* And I am then inclined to use such phrases as "how extraordinary that anything should exist" or "how extraordinary that the world should exist." I will mention another experience straight away which I also know and which others of you might be acquainted with: it is, what one might call, the experience of feeling *absolutely* safe. I mean the state of mind in which one is inclined to say "I am safe, nothing can injure me what ever happens."[9†]

Wittgenstein adds that the expression of these "experiences" in language is, strictly speaking, nonsense. One can wonder that the world contains kangaroos, perhaps; but there is no proposition

---

* Compare Augustine on the atemporal nature of God, p. 230.
† Such a powerful echo of Socrates! In his defense at his trial, Socrates says, "a good man cannot be harmed either in life or in death" (*Apology* 41d).

that can express the "fact" that the world exists. Why not? Because this "fact" is obviously not one of the facts that make up that totality which *is* the world, and beyond that totality there is nothing. And it is equally nonsense to say that one feels *absolutely* safe; one can be safe from tigers, or protected from polio. But to say, "Nothing whatever can injure me," is just a misuse of language. Yet, that is the only satisfactory expression. Wittgenstein thinks, for what is of absolute value. Here we have an example of running against the boundaries of language.

To "wonder at the existence of the world" is to experience it as a limited whole. And that Wittgenstein calls "the mystical."

> 6.44   It is not *how* things are in the world that is mystical, but *that* it exists.
>
> 6.45   To view the world *sub specie aeterni* is to view it as a whole—a limited whole. Feeling the world as a limited whole—it is this that is mystical.

To live the life of the philosophical self, that metaphysical self which is not a part of the world but its limit, is to have a sense for "the mystical." This life is also the good life, the beautiful life, and the happy life. It is a life of absolute safety.

Remember, though, that all of this is not something that can properly be said. It cannot even really be asked about. It is tempting to think that we can ask, Why does the world exist? or Why is there anything at all rather than nothing? But

> 6.5   When the answer cannot be put into words, neither can the question be put into words.
> *The riddle* does not exist.
> If a question can be framed at all, it is also *possible* to answer it.
>
> 6.52   We feel that even when *all possible* scientific questions have been answered, the problems of life remain completely untouched. Of course there are then no questions left, and this itself is the answer.
>
> 6.521   The solution of the problem of life is seen in the vanishing of the problem. (Is not this the reason why those who have

found after a long period of doubt that the sense of life became clear to them have then been unable to say what constituted that sense?)

> 6.522   There are, indeed, things that cannot be put into words. They *make themselves manifest*. They are what is mystical.

The Unsayable

If you have been following carefully, you have no doubt been wondering how Wittgenstein can manage to say all this stuff that he so explicitly "says" cannot be said. This is indeed a puzzle we must address. What he has been writing is clearly philosophy. But if, as he (philosophically) says, the totality of true propositions is science, what room is there for philosophy?

> 4.111   Philosophy is not one of the natural sciences.
> (The word 'philosophy' must mean something whose place is above or below the natural sciences, not beside them.)
> Philosophy aims at the logical clarification of thoughts.
> Philosophy is not a body of doctrine but an activity.
> A philosophical work consists essentially of elucidations.
> Philosophy does not result in 'philosophical propositions,' but rather in the clarification of propositions.
> Without philosophy thoughts are, as it were, cloudy and indistinct: its task is to make them clear and to give them sharp boundaries.

The key thought here is that philosophy is an activity; its business is clarification. It follows that we should not look to philosophy for *results,* for truths, or for "a body of doctrine." To do so is to mistake the nature of philosophizing altogether. It has been one of the major failings of the philosophical tradition, Wittgenstein believes, that it has tried to produce "philosophical propositions"—that it has thought of itself as something "beside" the sciences, in the same line of work as science. But it is *altogether different* from science. It lies, one might say, at right angles to science. Wittgenstein's view of his predecessors is severe:

4.003   Most of the propositions and questions to be found in philosophical works are not false but nonsensical.
Consequently we cannot give any answer to questions of this kind, but can only establish that they are nonsensical.
Most of the propositions and questions of philosophers arise from our failure to understand the logic of our language.
(They belong to the same class as the question whether the good is more or less identical than the beautiful.)
And it is not surprising that the deepest problems are in fact *not* problems at all.

6.53   The correct method in philosophy would really be the following: to say nothing except what can be said, i.e., propositions of natural science—i.e., something that has nothing to do with philosophy—and then, whenever someone else wanted to say something metaphysical, to demonstrate to him that he had failed to give a meaning to certain signs in his propositions. Although it would not be satisfying to the other person—he would not have the feeling that we were teaching him philosophy—*this* method would be the only strictly correct one.

Plato and Aristotle, Hume and Kant all think they are revealing or discovering truth. But, if Wittgenstein is right, all of their most important claims are nonsensical. They aren't even *candidates* for being true! Their theories—to the extent that they are not absorbable by empirical science—are pseudo-answers to pseudoquestions. Just *gassing*. Such theories arise because these philosophers don't understand the logic of our language; Wittgenstein thinks he has, for the first time, clearly set this forth.

But there is still a worry. Wittgenstein is himself not utilizing "the correct method" in writing the *Tractatus*. How, then, are we to take his own "propositions" here?

6.54   My propositions serve as elucidations in the following way: anyone who understands me eventually recognizes them as nonsensical, when he has used them—as steps—to climb up beyond them. (He must, so to speak, throw away the ladder after he has climbed up it.)
He must transcend these propositions, and then he will see the world aright.

To "see the world aright" is to see it from the viewpoint of eternity, from the point of view of the philosophical self. It is not too farfetched to be reminded of that ladder the mystics talk about as leading to oneness with God. Having climbed Wittgenstein's ladder, we too can wonder at the existence of the world, feel absolutely safe, experience happiness and beauty—and do our science. But we would always have to keep in mind the last "proposition" of the *Tractatus*:

7.   What we cannot speak about we must pass over in silence.

Yet, the things we must "pass over in silence" are the most important of all.

Logical Positivism

In the preface to the *Tractatus*, Wittgenstein writes,

Perhaps this book will be understood only by someone who has himself already had the thoughts that are expressed in it—or at least similar thoughts (*Tractatus* preface, p. 3).

This was to prove prophetic. Russell supplied an introduction that Wittgenstein thought so misunderstood his intentions that he refused to have it printed in the German edition. And his book was studied painstakingly by a group of scientifically oriented philosophers in Vienna (a group that came to be known as the Vienna Circle) who admired its logic and philosophy of language but had no sympathy with what Wittgenstein himself thought most important. Because this latter group proved extremely influential, at least for a time, we will briefly note their major theses. The movement they began had a significant impact on scientists (both natural and social), on philosophy of science, and on the general public. These philosophers are called *logical positivists*.

Logical positivism can be identified with three claims, all of which have recognizable roots in the *Tractatus*. The first is that logic and mathematics are *analytic*. The positivists accept Wittgenstein's analysis of the basic truths of logic: that they are tautological in nature. Both mathematics and logic are empirically or factually empty, providing no knowledge of nature at all.* They are, however, extremely important: they provide a framework in which we can move from one true factual statement to another; that is, they license inferences, just as Wittgenstein says they do.†

The second principle is a criterion for judging the meaningfulness of all nontautological assertions. It is called the **verifiability principle.** The positivists believe they can use it to sweep away not only the confusions of past philosophy, but also everything Wittgenstein holds most dear. Here is Moritz Schlick's explanation of verifiability.

> When, in general, are we sure that the meaning of a question is clear to us? Evidently when and only when we are able to state exactly the conditions under which it is to be answered in the affirmative, or as the case may be, the conditions under which it is to be answered in the negative. By stating these conditions, and by this alone, is the meaning of a question defined.
>
> The meaning of a proposition consists, obviously, in this alone, that is expresses a definite state of affairs. One can, of course, say that the proposition it-

self already gives this state of affairs.* This is true, but the proposition indicates the state of affairs only to the person who understands it. But when do I understand a proposition? When I understand the meanings of the words which occur in it? These can be explained by definition. But in the definitions new words appear whose meanings cannot again be described in propositions, they must be indicated directly: the meaning of a word must in the end be *shown,* it must be *given.* This is done by an act of indication, of pointing; and what is pointed at must be given, otherwise I cannot be referred to it.[10]

The definitions Schlick refers to are Wittgenstein's analyses of complex propositions into elementary or atomic propositions and ultimately into words that are not further definable. For Wittgenstein, as we have seen, elementary propositions are composed of names in a logical syntax. The names stand for objects. He never specifies exactly what objects the names name. He once said, much later, that when he wrote the *Tractatus* he thought of himself as a logician and believed that it wasn't his business to identify the objects that he on logical grounds deduced would have to be there.

But for the Positivists, the truth conditions for elementary sentences are given in *perception.* The simple objects designated by the indefinable words must be the kind of thing you can point to. Schlick uses the Wittgensteinian word "shown" and paraphrases it by "given." The meaning of a word must be something you can *point to* or *indicate* in some way. You have to be able to *show* me what you mean. What Schlick means by "given" is "given in sense experience." This, then, is the bite of the verifiability principle. Unless you can explain what perceptual difference the truth or falsity of your assertion would make, the proposition you are asserting is *meaningless.* Clearly, logical positivism is a kind of empiricism.†

The positivists have no sympathy for a "good" kind of nonsense, no tolerance for "running

---

*Thus they correspond roughly to what Hume calls relations of ideas (see p. 353) and Kant's notion of the analytic *a priori* (see p. 380). Note how different a philosophy of mathematics this is from that of Kant, who believes arithmetic, while *a priori,* is not analytic.
†Review the discussion of the principles of logic on pp. 560–561.

---

*Wittgenstein says, "A proposition *shows* its sense" (4.022).
†Like David Hume, prince of empiricists, the positivists want to base all nonanalytic knowledge on the data our senses provide. See again the discussion of "the theory of ideas" and Hume's rule, "No impression, no idea" (p. 352).

against the boundaries of language." All this they want to *exterminate*. They talk about the *elimination* of metaphysics. (One gets the image of lining metaphysical ideas up against the wall and gunning them down.) What is to be left as meaningful is science—*science alone*! Out with Plato's Forms, Aristotle's entelechy, Augustine's God, Descartes' Mind, Kant's noumena, Hegel's Absolute Spirit—and Wittgenstein's mystical! Out with metaphysics altogether—that attempt to know something beyond what our senses can verify. It is to be purged from human memory.* And the instrument of this purging is the principle of meaningfulness. Since none of these notions are verifiable by sense experience, they are all meaningless.

Note that the positivists are not committed, for example, to the atheist's claim that there is no God. Such a claim they consider to be as much a metaphysical statement as the claim that there is a God. Both claims are shut out from the realm of meaning altogether; if the verifiability criterion is correct, both the believer and the atheist are uttering meaningless noises. Since their claims are without sense, one cannot sensibly ask which is true: neither one is even a possible candidate for truth. So arguments for (or against) the existence of God are completely worthless!

The Positivists work at refining the verifiability principle to avoid obvious counterexamples. For instance, verifiability needn't be *direct,* as when I see something with my own eyes; it can be *indirect,* as when I rely on instrumentation, or (more important) when I test the observable consequences of a hypothesis that is not itself directly testable. And it is enough, they say, for propositions to be verifiable *in principle.* They obviously want to allow for the meaningfulness of propositions that are not now verifiable only because of technological limitations; moreover, something doesn't have to be conclusively verifiable for it to be meaningful. They draw a contrast between *strong* (conclusive) verification and *weak* verification (verification by evidence indicating that something is likely to be

true or probably true). The positivists hold that weak verifiability is enough to qualify a statement as meaningful. But unless a proposition is at least indirectly verifiable, verifiable in principle, and weakly verifiable, it is declared to have no sense.

The third plank of the positivist platform concerns the nature of philosophy. Like Wittgenstein, they hold that philosophy is not in the business of providing knowledge about the supersensible; its task is the clarification of statements. So it is an activity, as Wittgenstein says. But they are convinced that philosophy doesn't have to be classified as nonsense. If the activity of philosophy is clarification, it has certain statable results: it issues in definitions. Much of the writing of the logical positivists is devoted to clarifying what they call "the logic of science." And so they are interested in the concepts of *law* and *theory,* of *hypothesis* and *evidence,* of *confirmation* and *probability.* Much good work is produced in understanding these concepts and how they relate to each other. Under their influence the *philosophy of science* becomes a recognized and important part of philosophy; without their work in this area, it is unlikely that most academic departments would now be teaching courses in this field.*

The fate of ethical statements on positivist principles is particularly interesting. Moral judgments do not seem to be verifiable—even weakly, indirectly, and in principle. So they don't seem to meet the criterion for factual meaningfulness. That raises the question: What kind of statement is a judgment that stealing is wrong?† In an explosive

---

*For a similar sentiment, see David Hume's trenchant remarks at the end of his *Enquiry* (p. 374). It has been said with some justice that logical positivism is just Hume plus modern logic.

*Like most of the distinctive theses of logical positivism, the positivists' understanding of the logic of science is now largely surpassed. It now seems too abstract, too prescriptive, and not mindful enough to how science is actually done. The complaint is, ironically, that positivists are not empirical enough about science itself. Historical studies in the past several decades have significantly modified our understanding of that important cultural institution we call science. One of the milestones in this development is Thomas Kuhn's 1962 work, *The Structure of Scientific Revolutions.*

†Recall Wittgenstein's claim that in the world there is no value—and if there were a value in the world, it would *have* no value. The realm of facts excludes the realm of values. You should also look back to Hume's famous discussion of the distinction between *is* and *ought* (p. 371).

book called *Language, Truth, and Logic,* published in 1936, the English philosopher A. J. Ayer sets out the positivist view of ethics. Ethical concepts, he says, are "mere pseudoconcepts."

Thus if I say to someone, "You acted wrongly in stealing that money," I am not stating anything more than if I had simply said, "You stole that money." In adding that this action is wrong I am not making any further statement about it. I am simply evincing my moral disapproval of it. It is as if I had said, "You stole that money," in a peculiar tone of horror, or written it with the addition of some special exclamation marks. The tone, or the exclamation marks, adds nothing to the literal meaning of the sentence. It merely serves to show that the expression of it is attended by certain feelings in the speaker.

If now I generalize my previous statement and say, "Stealing money is wrong," I produce a sentence which has no factual meaning—that is, expresses no proposition which can be either true or false. It is as if I had written "Stealing money!!"—where the shape and thickness of the exclamation marks show, by a suitable convention, that a special sort of moral disapproval is the feeling which is being expressed. It is clear that there is nothing said here which can be true or false. Another man may disagree with me about the wrongness of stealing, in the sense that he may not have the same feelings about stealing as I have, and he may quarrel with me on account of my moral sentiments. But he cannot, strictly speaking, contradict me. For in saying that a certain type of action is right or wrong, I am not making any factual statement, not even a statement about my own state of mind. I am merely expressing certain moral sentiments. And the man who is ostensibly contradicting me is merely expressing his moral sentiments. So that there is plainly no sense in asking which of us is in the right. For neither of us is asserting a genuine proposition. . . .

We can now see why it is impossible to find a criterion for determining the validity of ethical judgments. It is not because they have an "absolute" validity which is mysteriously independent of ordinary sense-experience, but because they have no objective validity whatsoever. If a sentence makes no statement at all, there is obviously no sense in asking whether what it says is true or false. And we have seen that sentences which simply express moral judgments do not say anything. They are pure expressions of feeling and as such do not come under the category of truth and falsehood. They are unverifiable for the same reason as a cry of pain or a word of command is unverifiable—because they do not express a genuine proposition.[11]

This is pretty radical stuff, at least as judged by the philosophical tradition. Its ancestry lies in the views of the Sophists, that things (at least in the moral sphere) just are as they seem to the individual human being.* If Ayer is right, there are no objective truths about the good life or about right and wrong, so reason (obviously) cannot help us find them. It follows that Socrates' search for the nature of piety, courage, and justice is misguided. And all the philosophers who build on that assumption are mistaken in what they are doing. Plato's Form of the Good, Aristotle's virtues as human excellences, Epicurus' pleasure, the Stoics' keeping of the will in harmony with nature, Augustine's ordered loves, Hobbes' social contract, Kant's categorical imperative, Mill's greatest good for the greatest number—all these are not, if Ayer is right, contributions to a theory of the right and the good for humans, but merely expressions of how these individuals feels about things.†

If we use a different measure, however, Ayer's view isn't so radical. In fact, it is the underpinning of what seems to many these days the sheerest common sense. Nearly every college freshman, in my experience, arrives with the opinion that this view of moral judgments is so obvious that it is

---

* See the motto of Protagoras on p. 41, and the relevance of rhetoric to justice as developed by Gorgias, Antiphon, and Callicles, discussed on pp. 43–46. A major portion of rhetoric might be thought of as techniques for "expressing moral sentiments" in persuasive ways.

† It is important to note that the Wittgenstein of the *Tractatus* would think this turn of events about as awful as could be imagined. While he would agree that value is not a matter of fact, he wants to locate ethics—what really matters—in the life of the transcendental or philosophical self. Positivist ethics construes value as no more than the way some empirical self happens to feel about things. What greater difference could there be? Wittgenstein says, "God does not reveal himself *in* the world" (*Tractatus* 6.432). The positivists make each of us a little god. From Wittgenstein's point of view, if Ayer is right, all we ever get in morality is "just *gassing*." See again Wittgenstein's views on ethics, pp. 562–564.

very near absurd to question it.* (That, of course, is not a very strong argument in its favor.)

Ayer's view, sometimes called *the emotivist theory of ethics,* is stated in a brash and bold fashion. Other thinkers in the same tradition qualify and complicate it to meet obvious objections; but it is good to see it stated in its bare essentials, especially since it has been so widely adopted by the public. It is important to note that the emotivist theory of ethics depends on a stark contrast between the realm of facts and all the rest. And this contrast, at least as the positivists develop it, is based on the verifiability principle's adequacy as a theory of meaning. If that theory of meaning is flawed, we may not be able to get by with such a radically subjectivist theory of morality. We will reexamine the question about meaning when we turn to Wittgenstein's later philosophy.

To their credit, it should be noted that certain difficulties in the verifiability principle are noted and examined by the positivists themselves. For instance, by dividing the analytic statements of logic and definition so sharply from verifiable statements of fact, they provoke the question, What sort of statement is the verifiability principle itself? There seem to be three possibilities:

1. The verifiability principle might be a factual statement. But—by its own terms—the principle, to be factual, must itself be verifiable by sense experience. But what sense experiences could constitute the truth conditions for this principle? The possibility of seeing red roses might constitute the meaning of "Some roses are red." And experiences in a laboratory might (in a complicated and indirect way) verify "Copper conducts electricity." But what experience could show that the only meaningful statements are those verifiable by experience? As Wittgenstein would later remark, the standard meter bar in Paris cannot be said either to be or not to be one meter long. A criterion cannot guarantee itself. So it seems clear that it is not factual.

2. It might be analytic, a definition of "meaningful." But it doesn't seem to capture the *ordinary* sense of meaningfulness. There are lots of unverifiable propositions we think we understand perfectly well. Consider this example: "The last word in Caesar's mind, unuttered, before he died, was 'tu.'" This seems obviously sensible and it is either true or false. But the possibility of verifying it, even weakly, indirectly, and in principle, seems zero. The fact that we cannot in any way *find out* whether it is true, does not subtract from its meaningfulness in the slightest.

3. There seems only one possibility left, given the positivist framework. If it doesn't fit either of the two main favored categories, perhaps the principle functions as a kind of recommendation that this is how we *should* use the word "meaningful," or a proposal that it would be *good* to use the word "meaningful" in this way. This understanding of the verifiability principle would associate it with the positivist view of ethical propositions. Its enunciation would express feelings of approval about this way of understanding meaning and perhaps urge others to feel the same way. But if this is what the verifiability principle amounts to, then there is no *reason* why we all should adopt it, and nonpositivists can (on positivist grounds) simply say, "Well, I feel different about it." And that is not very satisfactory.

Basic Questions

LUDWIG WITTGENSTEIN (THE EARLY YEARS)

1. What is Wittgenstein's aim in the *Tractatus*? And what motivates that aim—that is, why does he want to do that? If he had succeeded, would that have been significant?
2. Explain how a picture is a "model of reality." In what sense is a picture itself a fact?
3. Explain the concepts of pictorial form, possible state of affairs, and logical space.
4. Why are there no pictures that are true *a priori*?
5. In what way does language "disguise" thought? What is the essential nature of a proposition?
6. What is the meaning of a simple name? What are atomic propositions composed of? And why is this view correctly called "logical atomism"?

---

*This fact is one of the centerpieces of Alan Bloom's complaint about today's university education, addressed in his best-seller, *The Closing of the American Mind.*

7. What, then, is the world? And how is it related to logic? To language? To the truth?

8. How do truth-tables work? What is truth functionality?

9. What domain does logic reveal to us? In what way does logic "show itself"?

10. Contrast contingent truth with necessary truth. How do necessary truths reveal themselves in a truth table?

11. Why do tautologies and contradictions "say nothing"? What do they "show"?

12. Explain: "A proposition *shows* its sense . . . and it *says* that 'this is how things stand.'" Give an example.

13. How is the limit to thought set?

14. Why couldn't the "important" part of the *Tractatus* be written?

15. Why must the sense of the world lie outside the world? Why cannot there be "propositions of ethics"?

16. Suppose you wrote a book entitled *The World As I Found It*. Would you appear in the book?

17. How does solipsism coincide with pure realism?

18. In what way is the world of the happy person different from the world of the unhappy person? What does it mean to see the world *sub specie aeternitatis*?

19. Could a person be absolutely safe? (Compare Socrates in his defense to the jury in *Apology* 41c–d, p. 94.)

20. What is the "mystical"? Why does it have absolutely nothing to do with the "occult"?

21. Why won't science solve the problems of life? Why does "the riddle" not exist?

22. What is philosophy? What is its "correct method"? What is the ladder analogy?

THE LOGICAL POSITIVISTS

1. Explain the verifiability principle of factual meaningfulness.

2. In what ways can verification be indirect? Weak? In principle?

3. What is the positivist's analysis of ethical judgments? Compare to Hume; to Kant; to the utilitarians.

4. What difficulties do the positivists identify in the verifiability criterion?

For Further Thought

The young Wittgenstein thought he had found a unique solution to the problem of the meaning of life. The solution is found in the disappearing of the problem—but not through thoughtlessness or inattention. Try to explain this "solution" in terms that could be meaningful to your own life—and then decide whether you accept it or not.

Notes

1. Bertrand Russell, "Logical Atomism," in *Logic and Knowledge* (London: George Allen and Unwin, Publishers, 1956), 197–98.

2. Bertrand Russell, "Philosophers and Idiots," *The Listener* 52, no. 1354 (February 10, 1955): 247. Reprinted in Russell's *Portraits from Memory* (London: George Allen and Unwin, Publishers, 1956), 26–27.

3. A brief and very readable account of Wittgenstein's life can be found in Norman Malcolm's *Ludwig Wittgenstein: A Memoir* (Oxford: Oxford University Press, 1958).

4. Ludwig Wittgenstein, *Tractatus Logico-Philosophicus*, trans. D. F. Pears and B. F. McGuinness (London: Routledge and Kegan Paul, 1961). Quotations from the main text of the *Tractatus* will be identified by the paragraph numbers found in that work.

5. Paul Englemann, *Letters from Ludwig Wittgenstein, with a Memoir* (Oxford: Basil Blackwell, 1967), 143–44.

6. Ludwig Wittgenstein, "Lecture on Ethics," *Philosophical Review* 74 (1965): 12.

7. Samuel Beckett, *Endgame* (New York: Grove Press, 1958), 29–30.

8. Quotations from Ludwig Wittgenstein's *Notebooks, 1914–1916* (Oxford: Basil Blackwell, 1961) are cited in the text using the abbreviation *N*. References are to page numbers.

9. Wittgenstein, "Lecture on Ethics," 8.

10. Moritz Schlick, "Positivism and Realism," in *Logical Positivism*, ed. A. J. Ayer (New York: Macmillan Co., 1959), 86–87.

11. A. J. Ayer, *Language, Truth, and Logic* (New York: Dover Publications, n.d.), 107–8.

25

Ludwig Wittgenstein
and Ordinary Language:
"This Is Simply What I Do"

In the preface to the *Tractatus*, Wittgenstein writes,

> . . . the *truth* of the thoughts that are here set forth seems to me unassailable and definitive. I therefore believe myself to have found, on all essential points, the final solution of the problems.[1]

And he, with great consistency and in perfect conformity with his inexpressible ethics, leaves philosophy to teach elementary school in a remote Austrian village. As the years pass, though, he engages in conversations with other philosophers and scientists, including members of the Vienna Circle. Eventually he comes to believe that he has not after all found "the final solution" of all the problems he had addressed. The vision expressed in the *Tractatus* is powerful and elegant, but Wittgenstein gradually becomes convinced that it is not *true*. And in the first fifty pages of *Philosophical Investigations* he subjects his earlier views to devastating criticism.*

There are certainly difficulties in the *Tractatus*. For one thing, his view that logic consists solely of tautologies is proved by Alonzo Church to be too simple.* Furthermore, there is that strange consequence of the picture theory—that all his own philosophical propositions are nonsensical, despite the fact that many of us seem to understand at least some of them rather well. But it is neither of these things that moves Wittgenstein to criticize the doctrines of the *Tractatus*. Indeed, he is already quite dissatisfied before the publication of Church's Theorem. Wittgenstein begins to feel difficulties in connection with the central thesis of the *Tractatus*—that a proposition is a picture, together with the correlated doctrine of names and simple objects. Norman Malcolm tells a story about a conversation between Wittgenstein and P. Sraffa, a lecturer in economics at Cambridge.

> One day (they were riding, I think, on a train) when Wittgenstein was insisting that a proposition and that which it describes must have the same 'logical form,' the same 'logical multiplicity,' Sraffa made a

---

*Published posthumously in 1953, two years after his death, the *Philosophical Investigations* is written in two parts, the first of which is organized in numbered sections, most of which are a paragraph or two long. Like the *Tractatus*, it is a difficult book, but in quite a different way. Whereas you can read a sentence in the *Tractatus* half a dozen times and still be puzzled about what it means, the *Investigations*, for the most part, reads with some ease. But then you find yourself asking, What does this all amount to?

*Wittgenstein had held that sentences containing quantifiers were capable of analysis into elementary propositions, and so were truth functions of elementary propositions. This meant that truth tables could function as a decision procedure for determining the truth of all logically true propositions. For instance, $(\exists x)Fx$ (there exists something that has the property F) was to be analyzed as (Fa or Fb or Fc . . .) (i.e., object a is F, or object b is F, or object c is F, or . . .). And $(x)Fx$ became (Fa and Fb and Fc . . .). This meant that in principle there could be a truth table written for any generalized sentence, and we would have a *decision procedure* for determining the truth of these sentences. But in 1930, Alonzo Church proved that no such decision procedure is possible for domains that are possibly infinite. (This is called Church's Theorem.)

gesture, familiar to Neapolitans as meaning something like disgust or contempt, of brushing the underneath of his chin with an outward sweep of the fingertips of one hand. And he asked: 'What is the logical form of *that*?' Sraffa's example produced in Wittgenstein the feeling that there was an absurdity in the insistence that a proposition and what it describes must have the same 'form.' This broke the hold on him of the conception that a proposition must literally be a 'picture' of the reality it describes.[2]

A meaningful gesture, surely! It communicates something very effectively. Or think of "Phooey!" or "Nuts!" Bits of language? Of course. But what is their logical form? And of what simple names are they composed? And what possible states of affairs do they picture? Just to ask such questions shows up a deficiency in the *Tractatus* doctrine—if it is to be taken as a description of the very *essence* of language. Even if you were to grant that the picture theory correctly analyzes an important part of language (e.g., the propositions of natural science), it would be at best only partial; it would not reach the essence of language.*

Philosophical Illusion

Wittgenstein allows that the *Tractatus* does express a possible way of seeing things. We can climb the ladder of his "nonsensical" propositions and get a certain vision of things. He had said in the *Tractatus* that we would then "see the world aright" (*Tractatus* 6.54). But he now thinks this way of seeing things is a mistake. Yet, "mistake" is not quite the right word; it is more like an illusion, he suggests, or even a superstition that held him in thrall (*PI* 97, 110).[3] But how could he have been so deceived? What is the source of this illusion that the *Tractatus* presents with such clarity and power?

Philosophers in general, he thinks, are especially subject to this illusion. But all of us can easily be seduced into this kind of error; what trips us up is *the nature of language itself.* Here is one way that the seduction can work.

We sometimes find that others misunderstand what we mean when we talk to them. And we find that these misunderstandings can often be removed by paraphrasing what we mean, by substituting one form of expression for another. It is often helpful to use simpler terms to explain what we mean:

> this may be called an "analysis" of our forms of expression, for the process is sometimes like one of taking a thing apart. (*PI* 90)
> But now it may come to look as if there were something like a final analysis of our forms of language, and so a *single* completely resolved form of every expression. That is, as if our usual forms of expression were, essentially, unanalyzed; as if there were something hidden in them that had to be brought to light. When this is done the expression is completely clarified and our problem is solved.
> It can also be put like this: we eliminate misunderstandings by making our expressions more exact; but now it may look as if we were moving towards a particular state, a state of complete exactness; and as if this were the real goal of our investigation. (*PI* 91)

The Wittgenstein of the *Tractatus* was committed to all these notions: to the idea that there is "something hidden" in our ordinary language that can be "completely clarified" by a "final analysis" into "a *single* completely resolved form of every expression," which would gain us our "real goal"—"a state of complete exactness." The slide to these conclusions is so subtle we scarcely notice it. But it is a slide into illusion.

> This finds expression in questions as to the essence of language, of propositions, of thought. . . . For they see in the essence, not something that already lies open to view and that becomes surveyable by a rearrangement, but something that lies *beneath* the surface. Something that lies within, which we see when we look *into* the thing, and which an analysis digs out.

---

* The positivists recognize this deficiency, too; Ayer's emotivist theory of moral language (that it does nothing more than express and influence feelings) is an attempt to accommodate other uses of language than the literal and descriptive. Wittgenstein's critique, however, is far deeper and more radical.

'*The essence is hidden from us*': this is the form our problem now assumes. We ask: "*What is* language?", "*What is* a proposition?" And the answer to these questions is to be given once for all; and independently of any future experience. (*PI* 92)

Language, propositions—these seem mysterious, strange. And we ask with a baffled kind of emphasis, *What is* language? *What is* thought? *What is* a name? It seems to us that these are *deep* questions, about *deeply hidden* things. (Compare this question: *What are* numbers? Or Augustine's question, *What is* time?)*

We are encouraged to suppose that there *must* be an essence of language—one essence—because it is all called by one name, "language"; further, we assume that because it is all language, every instance of it must have something in common with all the rest. This is a supposition that goes way back; Socrates, in asking about piety, is not content with answers that give him examples of pious behavior. What he wants is the essence of piety, that is, something common to all examples that *makes* them instances of piety.†

About this seductive idea, Wittgenstein now says,

> A *picture* held us captive. And we could not get outside it, for it lay in our language and language seemed to repeat it to us inexorably. (*PI* 115)

This picture is not a *Tractatus* picture. It is a picture in an ordinary, though metaphorical, sense, as when we say, "I can't help but picture her as happy." It is a picture of language as a *calculus*, as something possessing "the crystalline purity of logic" (*PI* 107). This picture, Wittgenstein says, "held us captive."

It is like a pair of glasses on our nose through which we see whatever we look at. It never occurs to us to take them off. (*PI* 103)

We predicate of the thing what lies in the method of representing it. (*PI* 104)

(*Tractatus Logico-Philosophicus*, 4.5): "The general form of a proposition is: This is how things are."—That is the kind of proposition that one repeats to oneself countless times. One thinks that one is tracing the outline of the thing's nature over and over again, and one is merely tracing round the frame through which we look at it. (*PI* 114)

Captive to a picture, we cannot shake off the conviction that language *must* have an essence, that hidden in the depths of our ordinary sentences must be an exact logical structure in which simple names stand for simple objects. Logic, which sets out the structure of possibilities and is the "scaffolding of the world" (*Tractatus* 6.124), *requires* that. Propositions *really* have pictorial form and an isomorphism with what they picture. Never mind that language doesn't actually look like that! That is the way (we think) it *must* be.

But that is just what is wrong with the *Tractatus* vision. It is not just a description of how our language (or some part of it) seems to work and how it seems to be related to the world. Rather, the *Tractatus prescribes* to language. But now we can see the way out of the illusion. We can get out of the grip of superstition about language by confining ourselves solely to *description*.

> It was true to say [in the *Tractatus*] that our considerations could not be scientific ones. . . . And we may not advance any kind of theory. There must not be anything hypothetical in our considerations. We must do away with all *explanation,* and description alone must take its place. And this description gets its light, that is to say its purpose, from the philosophical problems. These are, of course, not empirical problems; they are solved, rather, by looking into the workings of our language, and that in such a way as to make us recognize those workings: *in despite of* an urge to misunderstand them. The problems are solved, not by giving new information, but by arranging what we have always known. Philosophy is a battle against the bewitchment of our intelligence by means of language. (*PI* 109)

---

* For a discussion of Augustine's famous reflections on time, see pp. 230–233. Recall Augustine's remark about knowing what time is as long as no one asks him to explain it but being unable to say when he is asked. Wittgenstein takes this to indicate that the nature of time is something we need to be *reminded* of, just as we need to be reminded of how our language works by "arranging what we have always known" (*PI* 109).

† See Plato's *Euthyphro* 5d–6e and p. 77.

There are clear echoes of the *Tractatus* here. Note that philosophy is still something quite different from the sciences: its problems are "not empirical." And philosophy's job is not to produce theories or explanations. Philosophy is still an activity of clarification rather than a set of results. But Wittgenstein no longer thinks that all philosophical problems can be solved at once, by analyzing "the essence of language." We must proceed in a piecemeal fashion, working patiently at one problem after another by "looking into the workings of our language," by "arranging what we have always known." It is not "new information" that we need to resolve philosophical problems. We need the ability to find our way through the many temptations to misunderstand.

> When philosophers use a word—"knowledge", "being", "object", "I", "proposition", "name"—and try to grasp the *essence* of the thing, one must always ask oneself: is the word ever actually used in this way in the language-game which is its original home?—
>
> What *we* do is to bring words back from their metaphysical to their everyday use. (*PI* 116)

The notion of a **language-game** is one we will have to examine closely. It is clear that philosophical *theories* of knowledge, reality, the self, and the external world are regarded with great suspicion by Wittgenstein, just as they were in the *Tractatus*. Such theories, we may imagine, he still regards as "just gassing." But the reason for suspicion is now different. The words that are being used in these theories—"know," "object," "I," "name"—all are words with common uses. Wittgenstein now suspects that as they are used in these philosophical theories, the words lose their anchors in the uses and activities that make them meaningful. They float free, without discipline, and lose their meaning; yet, it is just *because* they have no anchors in concrete life that they seem to indicate deep problems. This appearance of depth, however, is just part of the illusion. And what is needed is to "bring words back from their metaphysical to their everyday use."

Here is another point of similarity with Wittgenstein's view in the *Tractatus*. There he held that

"At some point one has to pass from explanation to mere description."   —LUDWIG WITTGENSTEIN

the "correct method" in philosophy was to show someone who thinks he is saying something philosophical and deep that "he had failed to give a meaning to certain signs" (*Tractatus* 6.53) and so was not saying anything at all. Here, the alternative to saying something metaphysical is not limited to the propositions of natural science, as the *Tractatus* recommends. The alternative is to come back to home ground in our ordinary ways of talking.

Philosophical problems are *baffling*:

> A philosophical problem has the form: "I don't know my way about". (*PI* 123)

But the solution is not to construct a philosophical theory about the baffling topic. What we need is to clarify the language in which the problem is posed.

> Philosophy may in no way interfere with the actual use of language; it can in the end only describe it. For it cannot give it any foundation either.

It leaves everything as it is. (*PI* 124)

Philosophy simply puts everything before us, and neither explains nor deduces anything.   —Since everything lies open to view there is nothing to explain. For what is hidden, for example, is of no interest to us.

One might also give the name "philosophy" to what is possible *before* all new discoveries and inventions.

The work of the philosopher consists in assembling reminders for a particular purpose.

If one tried to advance *theses* in philosophy, it would never be possible to question them, because everyone would agree to them. (*PI* 126–28)

This is surely a radical view of philosophy, as radical in its way as that of the *Tractatus*. According to this view, the aim of the philosopher is not to solve the big problems about knowledge, reality, God, the soul, and the good. These are not real problems at all; they arise only out of misunderstanding our language. The task of the philosopher is to unmask the ways in which these problems are generated, and by putting "everything before us" and "assembling reminders" bring us back to home ground.* What is the purpose of the reminders? To show us how the language in which these "deep" questions are framed is actually used in those human activities in which they get their meaning. If we understand that, we will be freed from the temptation to suppose these are real questions. Wittgenstein offers the following rule:

don't think, but look! (*PI* 66)

Here are two more striking remarks on this theme.

The philosopher's treatment of a question is like the treatment of an illness. (*PI* 255)

---

* The notion of assembling "reminders" is reminiscent of Socrates' view of the philosopher's task. As a "midwife," he can only help others recollect the truth within them. (See p. 98.) There are two differences: (1) Socrates thinks we recollect truths we were acquainted with before birth, and (2) though what we are reminded of in a Wittgensteinian way are certainties for us, it may not be possible to claim they are *true*, or that we *know* them. We will discuss this further below.

What is your aim in philosophy? To shew the fly the way out of the fly-bottle. (*PI* 309)

The first remark suggests that philosophy is itself the illness for which it must be the cure. There is an old saying by Bishop Berkeley about raising a dust and then complaining that we cannot see. The posing of philosophical problems, Wittgenstein is saying, is like that. Being possessed by a philosophical problem is like being sick; only it is we ourselves who make ourselves sick—confused, trapped, perplexed by paradoxes. We foist these illusions on ourselves by misunderstanding our own language. It is so very *easy* to do that, because language itself suggests these illusions to us. Philosophy, then, is a kind of therapy for relieving mental cramps.

With the second remark we get the unforgettable image of a fly having gotten itself trapped in a narrow-necked bottle, buzzing wildly about and slamming itself frantically against the sides of the bottle, unable to find the way out that lies there open and clear if only the fly could recognize it. We get into philosophical problems so easily but then can't find our way out again.

"But *this* isn't how it is!"   —we say, "Yet *this* is how it has to *be*!" (*PI* 112)

Just like the fly in the bottle! It is Wittgenstein's aim to show us how to put philosophical problems behind us, to help us find the way out of the bottle, rather than to devise theories that will constitute solutions to them. This view is reasonable if we suspect that philosophy as practiced since Socrates and Plato is likely to be based on illusion, like a superstition from which we need to be awakened. And that is Wittgenstein's view.

Language-Games

Let us look in more detail at the way Wittgenstein uses the prescription "Don't think, but look!" in criticizing the characteristic theses of the *Tractatus*. We'll begin with one of the most basic notions in that work, the notion of a *name*.

Wittgenstein now makes use of a device he calls "language-games." A language-game is an activity that involves spoken (or written) words. These words have a natural place in the activity; it is this place, the role they play in the activity, that makes them mean what they do mean. It is sometimes helpful, Wittgenstein suggests, to imagine a language-game more primitive than the ones we engage in.

> It disperses the fog to study the phenomena of language in primitive kinds of applications in which one can command a clear view of the aim and functioning of the words. (*PI* 5)

Here is such a primitive language-game.

> The language is meant to serve for communication between a builder A and an assistant B. A is building with building-stones: there are blocks, pillars, slabs and beams. B has to pass the stones, and that in the order in which A needs them. For this purpose they use a language consisting of the words "block", "pillar", "slab", "beam". A calls them out;　—B brings the stone which he has learnt to bring at such-and-such a call.　—Conceive this as a complete primitive language. (*PI* 2)

The words in this language-game can very naturally be thought of as names. To each word there corresponds an object. Here we have an example of a language that the theory of the *Tractatus* fits. This theory

> does describe a system of communication; only not everything that we call language is this system. And one has to say this in many cases where the question arises "Is this an appropriate description or not?" The answer is: "Yes, it is appropriate, but only for this narrowly circumscribed region, not for the whole of what you were claiming to describe."
> It is as if someone were to say, "A game consists in moving objects about on a surface according to certain rules . . ." —and we replied: You seem to be thinking of board games, but there are others. You can make your definition correct by expressly restricting it to those games. (*PI* 3)

There are language-games in which all the words are names, in which the function of each name is to stand for an object. But not all language is like that. In the following language-game, the *Tractatus* view that names exhaust the meaningful symbols shows itself to be inadequate—if we only *look*.

> I send someone shopping. I give him a slip marked "five red apples". He takes the slip to the shopkeeper, who opens the drawer marked "apples"; then he looks up the word "red" in a table and finds a colour sample opposite it; then he says the series of cardinal numbers—I assume that he knows them by heart—up to the word "five" and for each number he takes an apple of the same colour as the sample out of the drawer.　—It is in this and similar ways that one operates with words. (*PI* 1)

What is interesting in this little example is the very different way in which the shopkeeper operates with each of the three words. "Apple" seems to be a name, like "slab." But what of "red"? And, even more significantly, what of "five"? Both of them are used in ways completely different from "apple" and completely different from each other. Can they all be *names*?* Suppose we ask:

> But what is the meaning of the word "five"?　—No such thing was in question here, only how the word "five" is used. (*PI* 1)

The suggestion that "five" is a name, and that it names a number, is resisted. The point of this language-game, this little "reminder," is to cure us of the hankering to ask about the *meaning* of this word, especially since we are inclined to think its meaning must be an object analogous to apples— only a very mysterious one. We are brought back to the way in which we actually use the word. We say the numbers and take an apple for each number. And there is nothing deep or mysterious here to puzzle us. Note that this example shows us Wittgenstein doing just what he says the job of the philosopher is: dispelling puzzlement by bringing words "back from their metaphysical to their

---

*Consider again Plato's theory of Forms (pp. 109–113). Is Plato someone who falls into the trap of thinking that meaningful words—"eagle," "square," "equal"—are names and that there must be something each one names?

everyday use" (*PI* 116). There is no explanation given, just description. Wittgenstein is merely "arranging what we have always known" (*PI* 109).

Still, the idea that all words *signify* something is hard to resist. We do feel (strongly!) the temptation to ask, But what does the word "five" *mean*? And we can just feel the slide toward asking, "What *really* is a number, anyway? (Don't you feel it?) If we like, Wittgenstein says, we can agree that every word signifies something. But what is gained thereby? Once we know how the words are used, what do we add by saying, "This word signifies *that*"? Assimilating

> the descriptions of the uses of words in this way cannot make the uses themselves any more like one another. For, as we see, they are absolutely unlike.
>
> Think of the tools in a tool-box: there is a hammer, pliers, a saw, a screw-driver, a rule, a glue-pot, glue, nails and screws.   —The functions of words are as diverse as the functions of these objects. (And in both cases there are similarities.)
>
> Of course, what confuses us is the uniform appearance of words when we hear them spoken or meet them in script and print. For their *application* is not presented to us so clearly. Especially not, when we are doing philosophy!
>
> It is like looking into the cabin of a locomotive. We see handles all looking more or less alike. (Naturally, since they are all supposed to be handled.) But one is the handle of a crank which can be moved continuously (it regulates the opening of a valve); another is the handle of a switch, which has only two effective positions, it is either off or on; a third is the handle of a brake-lever, the harder one pulls on it, the harder it brakes; a fourth, the handle of a pump: it has an effect only so long as it is moved to and fro.
>
> When we say: "Every word in language signifies something" we have so far said *nothing whatever;* unless we have explained exactly *what* distinction we wish to make.
>
> Imagine someone's saying: "*All* tools serve to modify something. Thus the hammer modifies the position of the nail, the saw the shape of the board, and so on."   —And what is modified by the rule, the glue-pot, the nails?   —"Our knowledge of a thing's length, the temperature of the glue, and the solidity of the box."   —Would anything be gained by this assimilation of expressions? (*PI* 10–14)

What Wittgenstein is trying to drive home is that the quest for generality and for general explanations of meaning is fruitless. You can engage in this project, but what does it get you? Do you really further your understanding of tools when you say they *all* serve to modify something? Like the handles in the cabin of the locomotive, what counts is how they work; and they work in very different ways. So it is with words. "Five" works in an altogether different way from "red." The quest for general explanations is likely to make us forget that and to lead us into illusions about meaning and language—illusions into which the author of the *Tractatus* was led. The cure is to stick to the details, to "assemble reminders," to "bring words back from their metaphysical to their everyday use."

In the *Tractatus,* Wittgenstein had claimed to give us the *essence* of language. This claim had two implications that he now believes are baseless. The first is that language is *everywhere all-alike;* we have just been examining some reasons to give up this claim. The second is that the account of language he gave was *complete.* We might be inclined to say that these primitive language-games Wittgenstein describes are, by contrast, incomplete. But Wittgenstein now says,

> ask yourself whether our language is complete;   — whether it was so before the symbolism of chemistry and the notation of the infinitesimal calculus were incorporated in it; for these are, so to speak, suburbs of our language. (And how many houses or streets does it take before a town begins to be a town?) Our language can be seen as an ancient city: a maze of little streets and squares, of old and new houses, and of houses with additions from various periods; and this surrounded by a multitude of new boroughs with straight regular streets and uniform houses. (*PI* 18)

Language is something living and growing; creative language users are always adding to it. And there is no rule that new additions have to be like the old. The calculus, for instance (and the new logic, for that matter) are like "new boroughs with straight regular streets." But we must not assume that all language is like that; it is an "ancient city," with all the twists and turns of narrow streets and houses from different eras—like London or Vienna.

In the *Tractatus,* Wittgenstein had held that the proposition was the basic unit and that each proposition pictured a possible state of affairs. Now he asks,

> But how many kinds of sentence are there? Say assertion, question, and command?   —There are *countless* kinds: countless different kinds of use of what we call "symbols," "words", "sentences". And this multiplicity is not something fixed, given once for all: but new types of language, new language-games, as we may say, come into existence, and others become obsolete and get forgotten. (We can get a *rough picture* of this from the changes in mathematics.)

> Here the term "language-*game*" is meant to bring into prominence the fact that the *speaking* of language is part of an activity, or of a form of life.

> Review the multiplicity of language-games in the following examples, and in others:

> Giving orders, and obeying them—

> Describing the appearance of an object, or giving its measurements—

> Constructing an object from a description (a drawing)—

> Reporting an event—

> Speculating about an event—

> Forming and testing a hypothesis—

> Presenting the results of an experiment in tables and diagrams—

> Making up a story; and reading it—

> Play-acting—

> Singing catches [i.e., rounds]—

> Guessing riddles—

> Making a joke; telling it—

> Solving a problem in practical arithmetic—

> Translating from one language into another—

> Asking, thanking, cursing, greeting, praying. (*PI* 23)

In all these ways—and more—we use language. It is absolutely unhelpful—and worse, dangerous!— to suppose that language is everywhere all-alike. It leads into pseudoproblems and illusions, the sorts of dead-ends where we are likely to say, This isn't how it is, but this is how it *must* be.

Ostensive Definitions

Let's think again about names. We are tempted to think that the process of naming is fundamental and that the rest of language can be built on that foundation. We teach the child "ball," "blue," "water." But how do we do this? And when has the child mastered the meaning of these words? We present a ball to a child and get the child to pay attention to it, while we repeat, "ball, ball." This might lead us to generalize again and claim that language gets attached to the world by means of *ostensive definitions* like this. And so we might formulate a *theory* of naming.

But if we look carefully, we see that this assumption cannot be right.

> Now one can ostensively define a proper name, the name of a colour, the name of a material, a numeral, the name of a point of the compass and so on. The definition of the number two, "That is called 'two'"—pointing to two nuts—is perfectly exact.   —But how can two be defined like that? The person one gives the definition to doesn't know what one wants to call "two"; he will suppose that "two" is the name given to *this* group of nuts! . . . an ostensive definition can be variously interpreted in *every* case. (*PI* 28)

Note that Wittgenstein is not denying that ostensive definitions are often useful. What he is attacking is the notion that they are a key to the essence of language, to what is basic in language use. He denies that ostensive definitions can be the simple foundation stone on which all else is built. If I try to show you what a watch is (supposing you don't know) by pointing to the device on my wrist, you may take it that "watch" means a color, a material, a device for keeping time, or a direction. My intention can be "variously interpreted." And what is true for this case is true for every case.

How do ostensive definitions work, then? Well,

I could help you out by saying, "This device on my wrist is a watch." But that presumes, as you can clearly see, that you already are in possession of large portions of the language. You have to understand "device" and "on" and "wrist" if what I say is going to be helpful. So it seems clear that language cannot *begin* with ostensive definitions. And names cannot themselves be absolutely primitive: to understand a name, you have to understand what role it is supposed to play in the language-game.

> So one might say: the ostensive definition explains the use—the meaning—of the word when the overall role of the word in the language is clear. . . .
> One has already to know (or be able to do) something in order to be capable of asking a thing's name. But what does one have to know?
> When one shews someone the king in chess and says: "This is the king", this does not tell him the use of this piece—unless he already knows the rules of the game up to this last point: the shape of the king. . . .
> We may say: only someone who already knows how to do something with it can significantly ask a name. (*PI* 30–31)

An ostensive definition is of use only *within* a language-game. It is of no help in getting into the game in the first place.

But that leaves us with a problem. How do we ever get started with language, if acquiring the use of even names like "ball" and "milk" presupposes an understanding of language in general? Here Wittgenstein again advises us to *look.*

> A child uses such primitive forms of language when it learns to talk. Here the teaching of language is not explanation, but training.
> (I do not want to call this "ostensive definition", because the child cannot as yet *ask* what the name is. I will call it "ostensive teaching of words". . . . This ostensive teaching of words can be said to establish an association between the word and the thing. (*PI* 5–6)

Suppose that such an "association" is established between "apple" and apples by "training" little Jill in that way. Does she now *understand* the word

"apple"? Well, does your dog understand "Come!" when it comes at that command? The process is similar, Wittgenstein suggests, and so are the results. The difference between Jill and Rover is that Jill can eventually go on to learn a lot more about apples by internalizing an ever more complex language in which to talk about them. Understanding comes in degrees; Jill is capable of understanding more than Rover, but they start in the same way. It is not by definitions (ostensive or not) that we enter the gate of language, but by training.

Objects

We are tempted to think, as the *Tractatus* suggests, that "a name means an object. The object is its meaning." But if that were so, Wittgenstein "reminds" us, a word would have no meaning if nothing corresponded to it.

> It is important to note that the word "meaning" is being used illicitly if it is used to signify the thing that 'corresponds' to the word. That is to confound the meaning of a name with the *bearer* of the name. When Mr. N. N. dies one says that the bearer of the name dies, not that the meaning dies. And it would be nonsensical to say that, for if the name ceased to have meaning it would make no sense to say, "Mr. N. N. is dead." (*PI* 40)

It does, of course, make sense to say that John F. Kennedy is dead. So the name is not meaningless, even though its bearer is no longer in existence. It follows that the meaning of a name cannot be the object it names. What, then, is the meaning of a name? It is having a place in a particular language-game, a certain role in a form of life.

> For a *large* class of cases—though not for all—in which we employ the word "meaning" it can be defined thus: the meaning of a word is its use in the language. (*PI* 43)

And that is why it is important not to think, but to look and see how a word is being used.

Names in the *Tractatus* stand for objects, and

these objects are said to be *simple*. In fact, Wittgenstein held at the time he wrote the *Tractatus* that there *must* be simple objects; otherwise, the definition of names could go on forever, and nothing would have any determinate sense. Definitions must come to an end! And they can only end in the absolutely simple.*

> But what are the simple constituent parts of which reality is composed? —What are the simple constituent parts of a chair? —The bits of wood of which it is made? Or the molecules, or the atoms? —"Simple" means: not composite. And here the point is: in what sense 'composite'? It makes no sense at all to speak absolutely of the 'simple parts of a chair'. (*PI* 47)

When talking of simple and composite, we must pay attention to the game we are playing with these words. To suppose that they have meaning quite independently of some concrete activity in which they are being used is to let language "go on holiday" (*PI* 38), a sure way to generate unsolvable philosophical problems.

> If I tell someone without any further explanation: "What I see before me now is composite," he will have the right to ask: "What do you mean by 'composite'? For there are all sorts of things that can mean!" . . .
> But isn't a chessboard, for instance, obviously, and absolutely, composite? —You are probably thinking of the composition out of thirty-two white and thirty-two black squares. But could we not also say, for instance, that it was composed of the colours black and white and the schema of squares? (*PI* 47)

There are circumstances in which we analyze composite things in one way and circumstances in which we analyze them in another way. This is what we find, if we *look*. Why should we insist that there must be one way in which composite things can be analyzed into elements that are absolutely

simple, quite independent of context or language-game? This insistence looks like a prime case of thinking and not looking—a case of prescribing to language and the world. Once again, Wittgenstein invites us to resist the temptation.*

Family Resemblances

Here we come up against the great question that lies behind all these considerations. —For someone might object against me: "You take the easy way out! You talk about all sorts of language-games, but have nowhere said what the essence of a language-game, and hence of language, is: what is common to all these activities, and what makes them into language or parts of language. So you let yourself off the very part of the investigation that once gave you yourself most headache, the part about the *general form of propositions* and of language."

And this is true. —Instead of producing something common to all that we call language, I am saying that these phenomena have no one thing in common, which makes us use the same word for all—but that they are *related* to one another in many different ways. And it is because of this relationship, or these relationships, that we call them all "language". I will try to explain this.

Consider for example the proceedings that we call "games". I mean board-games, card-games, ball-games, Olympic games, and so on. What is common to them all? —Don't say: "There *must* be something common, or they would not be called 'games'"—but *look and see* whether there is anything common to all. —For if you look at them you will not see something that is common to *all*, but similarities, relationships, and a whole series of them at that. To repeat: don't think, but look! —Look for example at board-games; here you find many correspondences with the first group, but many common features drop out, and others appear. When we pass next to ball-games, much that is common is retained, but much is lost. —Are they all 'amusing'? Compare chess with noughts and crosses [tic-tac-toe]. Or is there always winning and losing, or competition between players? Think of patience [solitaire]. In

---

* The commitment to simples has a long history. We find it already in Plato, and versions of it are found in many other thinkers—including Hume and Russell, who hold that although not every idea has to be traceable to a corresponding impression, the simple ones do. (See p. 351.)

* Compare Dewey on the analysis of a concept like "a piece of paper," p. 543.

ball-games there is winning and losing; but when a child throws his ball at the wall and catches it again, this feature has disappeared. Look at the parts played by skill and luck; and at the difference between skill in chess and skill in tennis. Think now of ring-a-ring-a-roses; here is the element of amusement, but how many other characteristic features have disappeared! And we can go through the many, many other groups of games in the same way; can see how similarities crop up and disappear.

And the result of this examination is: we see a complicated network of similarities overlapping and criss-crossing: sometimes overall similarities, sometimes similarities of detail.

I can think of no better expression to characterize these similarities than "family resemblances"; for the various resemblances between members of a family: build, features, colour of eyes, gait, temperament, etc. etc. overlap and criss-cross in the same way.   —And I shall say: 'games' form a family. (*PI* 65–67)

I have quoted this well-known passage at length because it is extremely important. The notion of **family resemblances** has been a *freeing* notion of great significance for thought. Recall that at the beginning of the Western philosophical tradition, dominating it with the kind of power that only unexamined assumptions can have, stands Socrates with his questions: What is piety? Courage? Justice? And what Socrates wants is a definition, the *essence* of the thing. What he wants to discover are those features which (1) any act of justice has, (2) any nonjust act lacks, and (3) *make* the just act just. Are Acts *A* and *B* both just? Then it seems natural to suppose that there must be something they have *in common*, something they *share,* some feature *by virtue of which* they are just. And unless we understand what that is, we will not understand justice.*

-----

* *Euthyphro* on piety is a good example. For other examples, see Plato on knowledge (pp. 105–107) and Descartes on clear and distinct ideas (p. 296). The assumption pervades nearly all of our tradition. I recall some years ago being on a committee to rethink the requirements for a bachelor of arts degree. We expended a lot of energy in trying to discern the *essence* of a bachelor of arts, just what it is that makes a certain degree a bachelor of arts degree—as though this were somehow laid up in the Platonic heaven of Forms. That this discussion was fruitless would not have surprised Wittgenstein.

It is difficult to exaggerate the impact this assumption has had. It certainly lies beneath the *Tractatus* quest for the essence of language; it accounts for the author's certainty that there must be such a thing. But now that we are looking rather than thinking, we discover that, in very many cases, there is no such thing. There is no essence of games, nor of language. And almost surely there is no essence of justice or piety. All are matters of instances, examples, and cases loosely related to each other by crisscrossing and overlapping similarities. What we find when we look are family resemblances. What we find is exactly the kind of thing that Socrates so curtly dismisses when it is offered by Euthyphro!

It follows from this new picture that there may be no sharp boundaries for many of our concepts.

How should we explain to someone what a game is? I imagine that we should describe *games* to him, and we might add: "This *and similar things* are called 'games'". And do we know any more about it ourselves? Is it only other people whom we cannot tell exactly what a game is? But this is not ignorance. We do not know the boundaries because none have been drawn. To repeat, we can draw a boundary—for a special purpose. Does it take that to make the concept usable? Not at all! (Except for that special purpose.) no matter than it took the definition: 1 pace = 75 cm. to make the measure of length 'one pace' usable. And if you want to say, "But still, before that it wasn't an exact measure", then I reply: very well, it was an inexact one.   —Though you still owe me a definition of exactness. (*PI* 69)

One might say that the concept 'game' is a concept with blurred edges.   —"But is a blurred concept a concept at all?"   —Is an indistinct photograph a picture of a person at all? Is it even always an advantage to replace an indistinct picture by a sharp one? Isn't the indistinct one often exactly what we need?

Frege compares a concept to an area and says that an area with vague boundaries cannot be called an area at all. This presumably means that we cannot do anything with it.   —But is it senseless to say: "Stand roughly there"? (*PI* 71)

We may understand Wittgenstein's point more clearly by examining another example. What, people sometimes ask, is a religion? Is belief in a supreme being essential to religion? Then early Buddhism is not a religion. How about belief in life after death? But early Judaism seems to lack that feature. Some people suggest that Communism is essentially religious in character. But how can that be, if it lacks so many of the features of Presbyterianism? If we search for the conditions that are both necessary and sufficient to define "religion," we will probably search in vain. But suppose we proceed this way: Do you want to know what a religion is? Consider Roman Catholicism; this and similar things are called "religions." To treat the question this way is to think of "religion" as a family resemblance concept.

Someone might ask, "How 'similar' to Roman Catholicism does something have to be if it is to qualify as a religion?" We would be right to reply that there is no exact answer to that question.

Suppose someone objects, "But then you haven't drawn a sharp boundary!" We can reply, "That is true. If you want, you can draw a boundary for a special purpose; but don't suppose that in doing so you are answering the original question. It is not our ignorance that makes this way of replying to the question about religion an appropriate one. We don't know more about it ourselves; no one does." The concept "religion" functions in our language in this family resemblance kind of way. And the absence of a set of necessary and sufficient conditions to mark off religions from other things does not mean that the concept is not useful and serviceable, any more than "Stand roughly there" is a useless instruction just because it isn't perfectly precise.*

When he was writing the *Tractatus*, Wittgenstein thought that every proposition had to have a determinate sense and that therefore a completely analyzed proposition would be free of all vagueness and ambiguity. (Remember the ideal presented by Russell's notion of a logically perfect language; see p. 550.) How could it be otherwise, when it was composed of simple names, each standing for a simple object? But if we look, without seeking to prescribe how it *must* be, we see that language is not everywhere exact, like a logical calculus. Like "game," many of our concepts are governed by relationships of family resemblance rather than essences.* And they are none the worse for that. So Wittgenstein assembles his reminders of how our language actually functions, bringing us back to the activities (forms of life) in which

it does its varied jobs. And in so doing, he shows us the way out of various fly bottles we get ourselves into by misunderstanding the logic of our language.

The Continuity of Wittgenstein's Thought

As you can see, virtually every one of the principal theses of the *Tractatus* is undermined and rejected by the later Wittgenstein.

- There is an essence of language.
- The essence of language is picturing facts.
- There is a complete and exact analysis of every sentence.
- The basic elements of language are names.
- The meaning of a name is its bearer.
- Names are simple.
- Names name simple objects.
- The world is pictured as the totality of facts in logical space.

Other thinkers have changed their ways of thinking—Augustine after his conversion to Christianity, Kant after reading Hume—but Wittgenstein's turnabout is as deep and dramatic as any. Is there

---

* Notice how this sort of thing undercuts Descartes' requirement (*Meditation IV*) that we should assent only to ideas that are clear and distinct. Most of our ideas, Wittgenstein holds, are not clear and distinct. And that is not something we should try to fix. On the contrary, our concepts are "in order" as they are.

* But not all. We do have concepts that are governed by strict rules. Many scientific concepts—"triangle," for example, or "force"—are like that. We should not think of the family resemblance claim as a *theory* about the essence of meaning! It is worth noting that recent studies by cognitive psychologists about how people categorize objects have strongly supported Wittgenstein's views about the family resemblance character of many of our concepts.

any line of continuity that one can trace through this shift? Let me suggest that three interrelated themes persist.

The first is an opposition, which seems to amount to a personal revulsion, to what Wittgenstein calls "just *gassing*." A more contemporary term for this phenomenon might be "bullshitting."[4] The second is the idea that one might "set a limit to thought" (*Tractatus* preface, p. 3). And the third is the notion that some things cannot be said, but only shown.

The whole point of the *Tractatus*, you will recall, was to "set a limit to thought" by delineating what can and cannot be said. Whatever can be said can be said clearly. The rest is "nonsense," which we must "pass over in silence" (*Tractatus* preface, p. 3). Wittgenstein felt that most talk about the meaning of life, about value and God and the soul, was "just *gassing*"—an attempt to put into words questions and answers that cannot be put into words. But it is crucial to remember that he also thought that these matters were far and away the most important. The revulsion he felt was grounded in his conviction that prattle about them demeans them, takes them out of the realm in which they properly exist. A good man, for instance, is not someone who talks about goodness, but someone who "shows" it, displays it in his life. "It is clear that ethics cannot be put into words" (*Tractatus* 6.421). But it *can* be put into a life!

That project—to set a limit to thought by identifying nonsense, gassing, and bullshit—is still the driving force of Wittgenstein's later thought. The aim has not changed, but the method by which he thinks it can be done has changed. In the *Tractatus* he tried to do it all at once—with one stroke, as it were—by constructing a theory of language and meaning that would expose nonsense for what it is. But having come to see that he had been prescribing to language, that he had been held captive by the picture of language as a logical calculus, he now gives up the attempt to create a theory. Instead, he "assembles reminders" (*PI* 127) that bring us back from nonsense to the actual uses of language in those varied activities (forms of life) in which words get their meaning. This is something that cannot be done all at once; it requires the care-

ful examination of case after case where language "goes on holiday" (*PI* 38) and misleads us. And so we get the little stories, the language-games, the questions and answers, and the multitudinous examples of the *Philosophical Investigations*.

The *Tractatus* tells us there are some things that cannot be said: these things show themselves. Among them are these:

- The logical structure of language (which displays itself in every proposition)
- The nature of logical truth (manifest in tautologies)
- The relation of the philosophical subject to the world (the coincidence of solipsism and realism)
- The happiness of the good person (who has a different world from that of the unhappy person)
- "The mystical" (that the world is)*

In the *Investigations*, are there still things that can only be shown, not said? There are, but it is not so easy to list them. Rather, the showing has become identical with the *style* of the book. Even the samples we have examined show us a very unusual style full of questions (often unanswered), conversations between the author and an interlocutor, instructions ("Compare," "Imagine"), stories, suggestions, and so on. Surely no other book in the history of philosophy contains so many questions! The aim is still, as in the *Tractatus*, to get us to "see the world aright" (*Tractatus* 6.54). But now that means to see it, and language especially, in all its incredible variety and differentiation. Still, the aim is to *see* it, or, we might almost say, to let it *show itself* to us. It is not, perhaps, by accident that in the preface, Wittgenstein compares his book to an album of sketches.†

---

*I have again just used language to talk about all these things. And, as we have seen, that is paradoxical. But we must remember that according to *Tractatus* doctrine, what I have just said is, strictly speaking, nonsense—part of that ladder that needs to be thrown away.

†Nor is it incidental that the earlier book is called a *treatise* and the later book *investigations*. The former suggests completeness and a theoretical character that is altogether lacking in the latter.

The philosophical remarks in this book are, as it were, a number of sketches of landscapes which were made in the course of . . . long and involved journeyings.

. . . Thus this book is really only an album. (*PI* p. ix)

It would not be going too far to compare Wittgenstein here with an artist, trying in various ways to get us to see the "landscapes" of our language from a variety of points of view, so that we no longer get *lost* in them. There are few if any doctrines to be learned in this book. What it teaches is a way of investigating puzzles and problems—a way, Wittgenstein thinks, that will lead to clarity.

It is not our aim to refine or complete the system of rules for the use of our words in unheard-of ways.

For the clarity that we are aiming at is indeed *complete* clarity. But this simply means that the philosophical problems should *completely* disappear.

The real discovery is the one that makes me capable of stopping doing philosophy when I want to. —The one that gives philosophy peace, so that it is no longer tormented by questions which bring *itself* in question.   —Instead, we now demonstrate a method, by examples; and the series of examples can be broken off.   —Problems are solved (difficulties eliminated), not a *single* problem.

There is not a philosophical method, though there are indeed methods, like different therapies. (*PI* 133)

What would be left if the philosophical problems should completely disappear? Would we be any the worse off? And just what problems is Wittgenstein thinking about here? One can hardly escape the conclusion that Wittgenstein still thinks that most of philosophy is "just *gassing*"—that it is still transgressing the limits of thought. But now the diagnosis cannot be given once and for all by drawing a single limit; now what is required is careful attention to the multifarious language-games we actually play in our forms of life and detailed showing of how philosophical thinking tends to drift away from them into illusion.

In Wittgenstein's later work, we find a number of attempts to show us how traditional problems disappear if we look carefully at the language in which they are framed. There are discussions relevant to problems about understanding, meaning, the status of sensations, and other supposedly private mental states. We find sections dealing with the idea of seeing something, with interpretation, with rule following. These investigations are hard to summarize without doing them an injustice. A brief description of a van Gogh painting stands to the painting itself in much the same way that any summary of Wittgenstein's "conclusions" stands to his "album" of detailed investigations. Just as you really need to immerse yourself in the painting if you are going to appreciate it, so you need to follow the text of the *Investigations* really to understand it.

We can say, however, that these investigations tend to be profoundly subversive, in the sense that they undermine the foundations of many traditional views, for example, Descartes' dualism, Hume's theory of ideas, Kant's transcendental ego. Yet none of them is presented as an *argument*. We find the characteristic examples, questions, stories, and jokes, all designed to get us to *see* things in a different light. The whole point, we might say, is for us to give up the temptation to formulate philosophical theories about mind, reality, perception, or understanding. They are designed to get the fly out of the bottle.

There is one theme in Wittgenstein's later work, closely connected to the idea of a language-game, that we can perhaps pull out. It is a theme directly relevant to a matter that has come up repeatedly in our account of the great conversation: the question about relativism. You will recall that this issue originates in the dispute between Socrates and the Sophists (see those earlier chapters) and is expanded on by most of our philosophers. Can Wittgenstein throw any new light on that old perplexity?

Our Groundless Certainty

Think about the ubiquitous arrow, indicating to us which way to go—to the exit, on the one-way street, to Philadelphia. The arrow is a kind of rule.

Let us ask a question you may never have asked before: How do I know which way I am being directed to go? I do know. I am to go in the direction of the arrow's point. But how do I know this? Why, for instance, don't I go toward the tail of the arrow? Or why don't I go in different directions on different days of the week?

Here are some possible answers: (1) I *decide* in each case to go toward the arrow's head; (2) I *intuit* which way it is directing me to go; (3) I follow the *rule:* Go toward the arrow's head. But (1) is crazy; (2) seems just to put a label on what I do without giving any account of it; and (3) promises an infinite regress—for exactly the same question arises in regard to this rule! Is there a "metarule" that explains to me how *this* rule is to be obeyed?

Wittgenstein suggests a fourth possibility:

> what has the expression of a rule—say a sign-post— got to do with my actions? What sort of connexion is there here?   —Well, perhaps this one: I have been trained to react to this sign in a particular way, and now I do so react to it. (*PI* 198)

Training. Rather like we train a dog to heel, perhaps. But can that be right? An objection is raised by Wittgenstein's "interlocutor," the voice that so often presents our own hesitations to suggestions he makes.

> But that is only to give a causal connexion; to tell how it has come about that we now go by the sign-post; not what this going-by-the-sign really consists in. (*PI* 198)

The objection is that this does not tell us what rule following *is,* but only how we come by it. To explain how we acquire a practice, it seems, is not to explain the practice itself. But Wittgenstein replies,

> On the contrary; I have further indicated that a person goes by a sign-post only in so far as there exists a regular use of sign-posts, a custom. (*PI* 198)

Without such a custom, such a "regular use," there would be no such thing as obeying the sign. If that is right, some interesting consequences follow.

> Is what we call "obeying a rule" something that it would be possible for only *one* man to do, and to do only *once* in his life: —This is of course a note on the grammar of the expression "to obey a rule".
>
> It is not possible that there should have been only one occasion on which someone obeyed a rule. It is not possible that there should have been only one occasion on which a report was made, an order given or understood; and so on.   —To obey a rule, to make a report, to give an order, to play a game of chess, are *customs* (uses, institutions). (*PI* 199)

Wittgenstein's reference to the *grammar* of obeying a rule is a comment about its "logic," in a broad sense. It is part of the concept, he means, that a rule is embedded in institutions, customs, and ways of doing things. There are no rules apart from that kind of setting. We are not to understand this as an empirical remark, as something that we conclude on the basis of observing rules. Rather, he means to say that it is not *possible* that there should be a purely private rule.* And since obeying a rule is part of a custom, it presupposes a community in which such practices exist.

Suppose, then, that you were asked, "But why do you go in the direction of the arrow's point?" What would you say? How *do* you know that is the way to go?

> Well, how do I know?   —If that means "Have I reasons?" the answer is: my reasons will soon give out. And then I shall act, without reasons. (*PI* 211)
>
> "How am I able to obey a rule?"   —If this is not a question about causes, then it is about the justification for my following the rule in the way I do.
>
> If I have exhausted the justifications I have reached bedrock, and my spade is turned. Then I am inclined to say: "This is simply what I do." (*PI* 217)

---

* In a section of the *Investigations* we will not discuss, Wittgenstein uses this principle of the essentially public character of rules to show that there could not be a language in which I give ostensive (private) definitions for my sensations. The supposition that such a language is possible is remarkably pervasive, both in common life and in philosophy. Accordingly, if Wittgenstein is correct, a great deal of confusion is dismissed, and numerous philosophical theories of the mind are shown to be untenable. The sections in which this view is set out (roughly 243–351) are as famous as they are difficult.

In this striking metaphor, Wittgenstein brings us back to the communal practices in which our language-games have their home. It is as if the Platonic and Kantian why-questions have made us dig deeper and deeper. But there comes a point when we can dig no more, find no more justifications for our beliefs, our knowledge claims, or our scientific methods. At that point we reach bedrock, and our "spade is turned." And what is bedrock? Is it some Cartesian clear and distinct idea I cannot possibly doubt? Is it some Humean private impression in my mind? Is it a Kantian synthetic *a priori* truth that reason legislates for itself? Or is it the Hegelian culmination of Reason's inexorable development into Absolute Spirit made explicit for itself? No. None of these things. Bedrock is "simply what I do." And what I do is part of what *we* do, we who live this form of life, engage in these activities, play these language-games, grow up in these customs. There comes a point where explanations and justifications for behaving in a certain way come to an end. Then one just acts. We do as our linguistic community has trained us to do. In the end, it comes down to this:

> When I obey a rule, I do not choose.
> I obey the rule *blindly.* (PI 219)

Custom, practice, the activities that make up a form of life—these have an almost sophistic ring to them, reminding us of Protagoras who says, "Of all things, the measure is man."* Aren't we tempted to object at this point? Does Wittgenstein mean that agreeing among ourselves *makes* things true?

> "So you are saying that human agreement decides what is true and what is false?" —It is what human beings *say* that is true and false; and they agree in the *language* they use. That is not agreement in opinions but in form of life. (*PI* 241)

Think of measuring the length of a table. I do it and report my results: 30. You do it and report 76.

---

*For a comparison with the Sophists' version of relativism, see "Relativism," in Chapter 5.

Is one of us right and the other wrong? It turns out that my rule is graduated in inches and yours in centimeters. So what we both say can be true; the difference is that we were using different measures. If you use my measure, agree in my "language for measuring," we will (usually) agree in "opinion" too. Still, it is not our agreement on 30 that *makes* that opinion true; the length of the table does that. But there is an agreement in language-game that *makes it possible* for us to agree and disagree about opinions. So the measure both is and is not ourselves. It *is not* ourselves in the sense that whatever we agree upon is true. But it *is* ourselves in the sense that all our measures are conventional; they all depend on customs, uses of language, forms of life.

The contrast Wittgenstein draws between what we *say* and the agreement in *language* is another point of similarity and contrast between the later philosophy and the *Tractatus.* There we found the distinction between what can be said and what can only be shown. Here we find that when we get to bedrock, there is no more to say. At that point I can only *display* my form of life, the language-game I play. Here, where the spade is turned, I just *show* you what I do: This is what I do—how I live, the way I understand, mean things, and follow rules; this is my (our) form of life. In the *Tractatus,* it was the logical hardness of tautologies that turned the spade, that could only be shown. Here it is the practice of a certain set of language-games.

But this bedrock cannot, as we have seen, be a purely private form of life, governed by private rules. And Wittgenstein now pushes this point by asking, "What does it mean to "agree in language"?

> If language is to be a means of communication there must be agreement not only in definitions but also (queer as this may sound) in judgments. (*PI* 242)

Imagine that when we measure the table, our results are inconsistent, even if we use the same rule each time. At first we report 30, then 17, then 54, then 1003, and so on. Whatever it was we were doing, could we call that *measuring*? No. *That,* whatever it is, is not measuring. A measure (the yardstick) is analogous to a language. It allows us to say certain things. And just as there has to be some agreement in "results" if we are to have a measure, so also there has to be some agreement in "opinions" or "judgments" if we are to have a language. We have to hold many of the same things true and false.

But which things? Are there any judgments in particular that we need to agree about in order to communicate with one another in a language? Is there a *foundation* of agreement? And if there is, can we identify it?

In an essay called "A Defense of Common Sense," the English philosopher G. E. Moore claims to "know with certainty" a large number of propositions.[5] And he thinks we all know them, too. For instance, he claims each of us knows that

- There exists a living human body which is *my* body.
- My body was born at a certain time in the past.
- My body has existed continuously ever since.
- My body has changed in many ways.
- My body has been since birth close to the surface of the earth.
- My body has been at various distances from other things which also exist.

And we know with certainty that

- The earth existed many years before I was born.
- There have been many other human bodies like my own.
- I have had many different experiences.
- So have other human beings.

This is not Moore's complete list, but you get the idea. It is a list of what seem to be *truisms*.

Wittgenstein says many interesting things about the claim that we *know with certainty* that these propositions are true. (He tends to think the word "know" is inappropriately used here.) But our interest is directed to his idea that these "judgments" might form the basis for an agreement defining a language or a form of life.

How is it that we are so *certain* of these "facts"? Have we carefully investigated each of them and found that the evidence is in their favor? No. They do not have that kind of status. Taken together they are more like a *picture* we accept.*

> But I did not get my picture of the world by satisfying myself of its correctness; nor do I have it because I am satisfied of its correctness. No: it is the inherited background against which I distinguish between true and false. (*OC* 94)[6]

Wittgenstein compares this "inherited background" to a kind of mythology, by which he means that though the truisms of the picture are empirical, they are not acquired by empirical investigation.† He also compares our world picture to the banks of a river within which the water of true and false propositions can flow. The mythology can change; the banks of the river are not unalterable. And in some ways, at least, different pictures are possible for us even at a given time.

> . . . Very intelligent and well-educated people believe in the story of creation in the Bible, while others hold it as proven false, and the grounds of the latter are well known to the former. (*OC* 336)

How are we to account for this? Suppose the doubter talks to the believer. If the reasons for doubt are already well known to someone who believes the biblical story, what could the doubter say to convince the believer? All the doubter's reasons are already on the table—and they don't convince! Moore believes the earth has existed for many, many years. But

---

*Not a *Tractatus* picture, of course; this kind of picture is holistic rather than atomistic, imprecise rather than exact, a system of mutually supporting judgments. It doesn't occur to us, moreover, that this picture *can* be doubted. These matters are explored in another posthumously published book, *On Certainty*.

†Throughout this discussion of the "background" for our beliefs, you should keep in mind the Kantian *a priori* synthetic principles. Wittgensteinian "world pictures" play a similar role. They define a world for us. They are as anchored *for us* as the categories. But they are neither universal nor necessary—nor are they unchangeable.

. . . why should not a king be brought up in the belief that the world began with him? And if Moore and this king were to meet and discuss, could Moore really prove his belief to be the right one? I do not say that Moore could not convert the king to his view, but it would be a conversion of a special kind; the king would be brought to look at the world in a different way. (*OC* 92)

Different language-games (different forms of life) are possible. And arguments in favor of one of them *presuppose* the standards of argument and evidence characteristic of that very form of life. So reasons do not get a grip on a different form of life with different standards and rules of reasoning.

But again we are tempted to think there *must* be something that would constitute a definitive justification, if not for our present view, then for some future one.* Is "conversion" really the final word? What about *science*? Can that be just a matter of "what we do"? Suppose I justify my actions by the propositions of physics; for example, I do not perform rain dances because science tells me dancing is ineffective in bringing rain.

Supposing we met people who did not regard that as a telling reason. Now, how do we imagine this? Instead of the physicist, they consult an oracle. (And for that we consider them primitive.) Is it wrong for them to consult an oracle and be guided by it?   —If we call this "wrong" aren't we using our language-game as a base from which to *combat* theirs?

And are we right or wrong to combat it? Of course there are all sorts of slogans which will be used to support our proceedings.

Where two principles really do meet which cannot be reconciled with one another, then each man declares the other a fool and heretic.

I said I would 'combat' the other man,   —but wouldn't I give him *reasons*? Certainly; but how far do they go? At the end of reasons comes *persuasion*.

(Think what happens when missionaries convert natives.) (*OC* 609–12) *

Combat does not seem to be a form of justification. And conversion is not being convinced by good reasons. Reasons, Wittgenstein reminds us, come to an end.

World pictures, then, may differ; but there is *always* a framework within which we come to believe and think certain things.

I have a telephone conversation with New York. My friend tells me that his young trees have buds of such and such a kind. I am now convinced that his tree is. . . . Am I also convinced that the earth exists?

The existence of the earth is rather part of the whole *picture* which forms the starting-point of belief for me.

Does my telephone call to New York strengthen my conviction that the earth exists? (*OC* 208–10)

Wittgenstein wants us to answer no; it does not strengthen that conviction. That conviction is already as strong as it could possibly be! Is there anything of which I am *more* certain?† Moore's truisms, to which we all consent, are not *known* by us to be true; a claim to know is in order only where doubt is in order, and where one is ready to trot out one's evidence to resolve the doubt.

If you tried to doubt everything you would not get as far as doubting anything. The game of doubting itself presupposes certainty. (*OC* 115)

Why do I not satisfy myself that I have two feet when I want to get up from a chair? There is no why. I simply don't. That is how I act. (*OC* 148)

How does someone judge which is his right and which his left hand? How do I know that my judg-

---

*Compare Peirce's definition of truth as the opinion investigators will eventually agree upon, if they continue to investigate according to scientific methods (p. 528).

---

*Compare these views with the contrast Plato draws between *knowledge* and *opinion* (pp. 105–107). Do Wittgensteinian certainties fall neatly into *either* category?

†Compare Descartes' doubt in *Meditations I* and *II*. He thinks we can be more certain that we are thinking, understanding, doubting. But is that so? Remember Wittgenstein's "reminders" about understanding: that understanding is not a *private state*.

ment will agree with someone else's? How do I know that this colour is blue? If I don't trust *myself* here, why should I trust anyone else's judgment? That is to say: somewhere I must begin with not-doubting; and that is not, so to speak, hasty but excusable; it is part of judging. (*OC* 150)

I should like to say: Moore does not *know* what he asserts he knows, but it stands fast for him, as also for me; regarding it as absolutely solid is part of our *method* of doubt and enquiry. (*OC* 151)

The world picture we have is not something we have checked out; nor is it something we *could* check out. What would I do to assure myself that *this* is my right hand? Ask somebody? But if I have a doubt here, why would I credit a second person's reassurance? (This is not to deny that in certain special circumstances I might have such a doubt and be reassured; perhaps I have put on distorting spectacles.) Can I doubt—Descartes notwithstanding—that I have a body? That I have parents? That I have never been to the moon? These things "stand fast" for us. It is hard to imagine anything *more certain* than these judgments which could cast doubt on them. Is it, for example, *more certain* that my senses have sometimes deceived me than that the sky I'm looking at is blue?*

Might I not believe that once, without knowing it, perhaps in a state of unconsciousness, I was taken far away from the earth—that other people even know this, but do not mention it to me? But this would not fit into the rest of my convictions at all. Not that I could describe the system of these convictions. Yet my convictions do form a system, a structure. (*OC* 102)

And now if I were to say "It is my unshakeable conviction that etc.", this means in the present case too that I have not consciously arrived at the conviction by following a particular line of thought, but that it is anchored in all my *questions and answers*, so anchored that I cannot touch it. (*OC* 103)

All testing, all confirmation and disconfirmation of a hypothesis takes place already within a system.

And this system is not a more or less arbitrary and doubtful point of departure for all our arguments: no, it belongs to the essence of what we call an argument. The system is not so much the point of departure, as the element in which arguments have their life. (*OC* 105)

. . . Much seems to be fixed, and it is removed from the traffic. It is so to speak shunted onto an unused siding. (*OC* 210)

Now it gives our way of looking at things, and our researches, their form. Perhaps it was once disputed. But perhaps, for unthinkable ages, it has belonged to the *scaffolding* of our thoughts. (Every human being has parents.) (*OC* 211)

The use of the *Tractatus* word "scaffolding" in this connection cannot be an accident. In his earlier view, logic (that transparent and absolutely rigid medium) was the scaffolding of the world. Now, in dramatic contrast, what grounds our system of beliefs are such apparently empirical and logically accidental facts as that I have parents, or even that motor cars don't grow out of the earth (279). If certain people believed that, we would suppose they are so different from us as to have entirely different standards of reasonableness; it is not clear we could even understand those who seriously persisted in this belief; they would seem mad. The person who claims—in the face of all our certainties about Chrysler and Honda and engineering and production lines—that cars grow out of the earth is not making a *mistake*. This person would seem *demented*.

In order to make a mistake, a man must already judge in conformity with mankind. (*OC* 156)

The complex system of certainties that make up a world picture does not function like an ordinary foundation. The foundation of a house is that on which everything else rests, but the foundation could stand alone. Our certainties form a system of interrelated judgments.

When we first begin to *believe* anything, what we believe is not a single proposition, it is a whole sys-

---

*Wittgenstein's critique here should remind you of Peirce on doubt and belief. (See again pp. 524–526.)

tem of propositions. (Light dawns gradually over the whole.) (*OC* 141)

> I have arrived at the rock bottom of my convictions. And one might almost say that these foundation-walls are carried by the whole house. (*OC* 248)

Here the atomism of the *Tractatus* is most thoroughly repudiated. We do not first believe a single isolated proposition, then a second, a third, and so on. "Light dawns gradually over the whole" system. In a striking metaphor, Wittgenstein suggests that the foundation walls are themselves borne up by their connection with the rest of the house.

We may still want to ask: What makes us so certain of this picture? What guarantees for us that these judgments are fixed, that they do stand fast? Wittgenstein's answer is that *nothing* guarantees this. There is no guarantee. We are, indeed, certain of these things; but our certainty cannot be anchored in anything objective, in anything more certain than they.

> To be sure there is justification; but justification comes to an end. (*OC* 192)

And in what does it come to an end?

> At the foundation of well-founded beliefs lies belief that is not well-founded. (*OC* 253)

> The difficulty is to realize the groundlessness of our believing. (*OC* 166)

> Giving grounds . . . , justifying the evidence, comes to an end;   —but the end is not certain propositions' striking us immediately as true, i.e., it is not a kind of *seeing* on our part; it is our *acting*, which lies at the bottom of the language game. (*OC* 204)*

> My *life* consists in my being content to accept many things. (*OC* 344)

If the Western philosophical tradition has been a quest for certainty, we can say that Wittgenstein satisfies that quest. For he acknowledges that there are many, many things of which we are certain (many more things than most philosophers ever imagined!). But if philosophy is a quest for objective certainty, for a foundation which guarantees the *truth* of the edifice of knowledge, then, in a certain sense, if Wittgenstein is right, philosophy is *over*. Epistemology is *over*. For there comes a point where the spade is turned, where one cannot dig any deeper. And bedrock comes sooner than most philosophers have wanted it to come. We find it in our form of life. Our life *consists* in "being content to accept many things." This is, Wittgenstein holds, a difficult realization; we keep wanting to ask that good old why-question. Can't we, we yearn to ask, *somehow justify our form of life*? No, says Wittgenstein. It is *groundless*. It is "simply what we do." And what *we* do may not be what *they* do. Philosophy cannot dig deeper than the practices and customs that define our form of life. We do have our certainties. But they are groundless.

> Philosophy may in no way interfere with the actual use of language; it can in the end only describe it.
> For it cannot give it any foundation either.
> It leaves everything as it is. (*PI* 124)

Basic Questions

1. How is philosophy now conceived? What are "philosophical problems" like? What is to happen to them?
2. What is a language-game? What does Wittgenstein think the notion can do for us, and why does he think this is important?
3. How does the example of shopping for five red apples undermine some basic theses of the *Tractatus*? And what is the moral of the tool and locomotive examples?
4. What now happens to the notion of an essence of language? How many kinds of sentence are there, anyway?
5. Why cannot ostensive definitions be basic in language use? And if they are not, how do language-games get started? (How do children learn a language?)

---

*Compare Kierkegaard on the unavoidability of a *leap* (p. 456).

6. What argument purports to show that the meaning of a word cannot be the object to which it refers? Explain, in contrast, the motto: "The meaning of a word is its use in the language."

7. Why does it make no sense to speak absolutely of "the simple parts of a chair"?

8. Must usable concepts have sharp boundaries? What are family resemblances? What are we supposed to learn from the example of games?

9. How has the project of setting a limit to thought changed in Wittgenstein's later philosophy?

10. When we see the sign "EXIT," how do we know which way to go to find the exit?

11. Could there be just one occasion on which someone obeyed a certain rule? Explain.

12. When reasons give out, what do we do then? In what sense do we obey rules blindly?

13. What is bedrock? And what does Wittgenstein mean by "agreement in language"? Why is that important?

14. What kind of status does my "world-picture" have? Am I certain about it? What guarantees its correctness?

15. How is persuasion related to the giving of reasons? And what does it mean to say that our believing is groundless?

For Further Thought

If Wittgenstein is right, philosophy as a quest for foundations, for the absolute truth of things, has suffered shipwreck. Do you think he is right? And if so, what should we do now?

Notes

1. Ludwig Wittgenstein, *Tractatus Logico-Philosophicus* (London: Routledge and Kegan Paul, 1961), preface, 5.

2. Norman Malcolm, *Ludwig Wittgenstein: A Memoir* (Oxford: Oxford University Press, 1958), 69.

3. Quotations from Ludwig Wittgenstein's *Philosophical Investigations* (New York: Macmillan Co., 1953) are cited in the text using the abbreviation *PI*. References are to section numbers.

4. Wittgenstein is mentioned in Harry D. Frankfurt's very interesting piece, "On Bullshit," in his *The Importance of What We Care About* (Cambridge: Cambridge University Press, 1988). Frankfurt identifies the essence of bullshit as the lack of any concern for truth.

5. G. E. Moore, "A Defense of Common Sense," in *Contemporary British Philosophy,* 2d ser., ed. G. Muirhead (London: George Allen and Unwin, Publishers, 1925).

6. Quotations from Ludwig Wittgenstein's *On Certainty* (Oxford: Basil Blackwell, 1969) are cited in the text using the abbreviation *OC*. References are to paragraph numbers.

26

Martin Heidegger: The Meaning of Being

Martin Heidegger was born in the southern German village of Messkirch, near the Swiss border, in 1889. He seldom went far from that area. He felt close to the earth and treasured the fields and woods among which he lived. One can almost hear in his writing the weary tread of peasant shoes. As a youth, he considered studying for the priesthood but turned instead toward philosophy, which he took to be devoted to more fundamental matters. In his adult life he was a professor, mainly at Freiburg, not far from where he was born.

Heidegger lived through both world wars and for a time in the 1930s supported the Nazi party. This disreputable episode has been the occasion for much debate: Was it, or was it not, essentially connected to his philosophy? Opinion is divided. Although Heidegger was not in all respects an admirable person, he is nevertheless a philosopher of great power. He died in 1976.

The difficulty of his writing is legendary. Heidegger's aim is to try to say things that our tradition—the great conversation since Plato—has made it hard to say. Our language has been formed by this tradition; since Heidegger thinks the tradition has "hidden" precisely what he is most interested in, he finds it inadequate. So he devises new terms to express what he wants to say.*

Often these inventions have Greek etymological roots. Sometimes they are ordinary words put together in extraordinary ways or given extraordinary meanings.

The difficulty is compounded because translators do not always agree on the best English rendering of a German term. So the same term may be translated several ways.*

In 1927, Heidegger published a book called *Being and Time*. Actually, the work Heidegger projected was in two parts, and *Being and Time* constituted just two-thirds of the first part. The rest was never published. Why? Apparently he came to believe that the edifice for which *Being and Time* was to provide a foundation could not be built on that foundation. Consequently, there was a "turn" in his thinking, so that (as with Wittgenstein) we can speak of the early and the late philosophy. He never gave up the pursuit of the issue he announced as his concern in *Being and Time*, however; in 1962, he gave a lecture titled *Time and Being*. We will explore this "turn," but we will begin with—and give most of our attention to—the analysis of human existence as it is worked out in that partially completed 1927 book.

---

*Early in our story we see thinkers struggling to find (or invent) language adequate to what they want to say. Compare Anaximander (p. 10), Heraclitus (p. 17), and Democritus (p. 29). Though

we usually assume our language is satisfactory, we see that the struggle to find the right words continues.

* I have had to make some terminological decisions; where a translation is at variance with my decision, I have put the translation I am using in brackets.

What Is the Question?

Tortuous though it is, Heidegger's thought has from the beginning a remarkable single-mindedness. There is one question, and only one, to which all his intellectual effort is directed. Heidegger calls it the question of the meaning of **Being**.* How to understand this question is itself a question. The concern it expresses will become richer and clearer as we explore his philosophy, but we should now address it in a preliminary way.

You have before you a piece of paper on which some words are written. The paper can be described in a variety of ways.† When we describe it, we are saying *what* it is—what kind of thing it is, what its characteristics and functions and uses are. But there is also this curious fact: *that* it is. I call it a curious fact because it tends to remain in the background, taken for granted—even, perhaps, hidden. But it is just this fact Heidegger wishes to ask about. What does it mean for the piece of paper to *be*? Kant, you will recall, urges that "being" is no ordinary predicate, and we have noted that this insight is incorporated into the quantifier of modern logic.‡ To say that the piece of paper *exists*, Kant claims, is not further to describe it, nor to elaborate its concept, but to assert that something corresponds to the description we have given.

So far, so good. But what does this "corresponding" come to? What is it for the piece of paper to *be*? It is hard, perhaps, to get that question clearly in mind, to focus it, to pay attention to it. Heidegger is convinced that Kant doesn't satisfactorily answer this question, nor has anyone else in Western philosophy answered it. But that is precisely the question Heidegger is addressing. What does that *mean*—that the paper *is*?

Heidegger begins *Being and Time* with a quotation from Plato's dialogue *The Sophist,* in which a stranger remarks:

> For manifestly you have long been aware of what you mean when you use the expression 'being.' We, however, who used to think we understood it, have now become perplexed. (*BT,* 1)[1]

That, Heidegger thinks, precisely describes *our* situation. You might think that this is odd. Even if Plato is perplexed, how can it be that all the intervening centuries of thought haven't cleared the matter up? Heidegger's answer is that philosophical reflection about Being has *hidden* as much as revealed the phenomenon—and for deep and interesting reasons, as we will see.

We tend to have conflicting intuitions about the nature of Being. On the one hand, it seems the most obvious thing in the world: it applies to everything! We ourselves and every entity we meet *are*. How could we not know what Being is? On the other hand, if you are asked to define it, your response will probably be like that of Augustine when asked about the nature of time.* One thing is clear, Heidegger says: Being is not itself an entity; it is not one more thing along with all the other things in the world. Imagine that you write down on a long, long list all the things that there are. Would you write down "apples, planets, babies, dirt, . . . , and Being"? No, you would not. Each of the entities on that list, in a strange way, has carried its Being along with it.† But what is this Being

---

*I will follow the usual convention and capitalize the word when it is *Being* that is in question. The word "being" of course has other uses in English. Occasionally I may speak of *a being* or of *beings;* when uncapitalized, the term is the equivalent of "entity" or "item" or "thing" in a very broad sense (not just physical thing)—that is, whatever can *be,* or have *Being.*

†You might look again at all the ways that John Dewey finds for describing such an item (p. 543).

‡See again Kant's discussion of the ontological argument (pp. 400–401).

*See p. 231.

†The early Wittgenstein's contrast between (a) the totality of facts that make up the world and (b) *that* the world exists is essentially the same as Heidegger's contrast between entities (beings) and Being. (See p. 567). Wittgenstein, of course, believes nothing can be said about this "*that* it is"; this is the "unsayable" about which we must be silent—the *mystical.* But it is just this that Heidegger commits all his intellectual energy to trying to say. A caution: what Heidegger means by "world" is *very* different from what the *Tractatus* means by it, and our relationship to it is correspondingly different.

that puts humans and hammers and rocks and stars on the list but unicorns and square circles off? That is the question.

In saying that Being—the object of his inquiry—is not itself *a* being (not a thing, an entity, one of the items that exist), Heidegger means to make clear that he is not engaging in that traditional quest for *the* being who is responsible for all the rest. Heidegger is not searching for or trying to prove the existence of God—at least as God has traditionally been conceived. Heidegger is not asking about the *highest* being, but about what it is that accounts for the fact that there is *anything at all* (rather than nothing). What does it mean that entities *are*?

This sounds like an obscure question. If Heidegger is at all right, it is obscure because the tradition in which we have been raised—indeed, the very language we use—conspires to obscure it. The question seems on the one hand to be so abstract and distant from us as to be of purely academic interest, if that. Yet since we ourselves exist, it seems so intimate and near to us as to be almost too close to examine.* How could we make any progress in answering this question about the meaning of Being?

"What is strange in the thinking of Being is its simplicity. Precisely this keeps us from it."

—MARTIN HEIDEGGER

The Clue

> Any inquiry, as an inquiry about something, has *that which is asked about*. But all inquiry about something is somehow a questioning of something. So in addition to what is asked about, an inquiry has *that which is interrogated*. . . . Furthermore, in what is asked about there lies also *that which is to be found out by the asking*. (*BT*, 24)

The inquiry about the meaning of Being is *asking about* Being; that is the focus of our question. And

what we want to find out by our asking is the meaning of Being. But what will we examine? Where will we look? If our investigation is to be a real, concrete one, it can't just hang in the air; it must tie down to something. There must be something that we *interrogate*.

> "Being is always the Being of an entity." (*BT*, 29)

Being, in other words, is not like the smile of the Cheshire cat, which can remain mysteriously after the cat has vanished. As we have seen, Being comes along with the entities that *are*. What Heidegger is now saying is that apart from entities, there "is" no Being. If we wanted to put this in a slangy slogan, we might say: No *be-ing* without a *be-er*. So if we

---

*Again Wittgenstein comes to mind: recall the analogy of the visual field that does not include the eye that sees it (see p. 564). *Being* is so "close" to us as to be invisible to us. It is one of Heidegger's aims to get us some "distance" from it so that it can appear to us as it is.

want to investigate Being, we must do it in connection with some entity. But which entity do we choose? In principle, any might do, from quarks to gophers to black holes. But is there some entity that would be *best* to interrogate with respect to its Being?

At this point Heidegger notes that an inquiry like this is itself something that has Being. (Asking questions is not just *nothing,* after all.) And we would not have answered our question about the meaning of Being unless we also got clear about the Being of items like inquiries—and of the entities that inquire! This suggests that *we ourselves* might be the entity we interrogate in our inquiry, the focus of our investigation.

Heidegger recognizes, of course, that many sorts of investigation concern themselves with human beings. Many sciences have something to say about us: physics, chemistry, biology, history, psychology, anthropology. But none of these sciences takes the perspective on humans that is relevant to our question. To focus attention on the relevant aspect, he refers to the entity we will interrogate by a term that is usually left untranslated: **Dasein.** This term can be used in German to refer to almost any kind of entity, though it is usually used for human beings. Literally the term means "being there." ("Da" means "there" or sometimes "here"; "sein" is "being.") And Heidegger chooses this term to highlight the aspect of humans he is interested in: not the chemistry of the body nor the history of human society, but their Being.*

The suggestion that Dasein should be the focus of our investigation—the entity to be interrogated—is further supported by noting that we are distinctive among entities in an interesting way.

> Dasein is an entity which does not just occur among other entities. Rather it is ontically distinguished by the fact that, in its very Being, that Being is an *issue* for it. But in that case, this is a constitutive state of Dasein's Being, and this implies that Dasein, in its Being, has a relationship towards that Being—

a relationship which itself is one of Being. And this means further that there is some way in which Dasein understands itself in its Being, and that to some degree it does so explicitly. It is peculiar to this entity that with and through its Being, this Being is disclosed to it. *Understanding of Being is itself a definite characteristic of Dasein's Being.* Dasein is ontically distinctive in that it *is* ontological. (*BT,* 32)

This important paragraph no doubt needs some explanation. Heidegger employs a distinction between two levels at which an entity can be described; he calls them **ontic** and **ontological.** We can think of the ontic level as that of ordinary facts. Each Dasein has a certain physical size, grows up in a certain culture, experiences moods, uses language and tools, remembers and intends, often fears death, and usually thinks its way of life is the right way: these are all ontic facts.

But there is also a deeper level at which Dasein can be described: in its *way of Being*—in the way it is "there," present to things, in the world, together with others. We can think of this level as a matter of structural features of Dasein that make possible all the ontic facts we are ordinarily aware of.* This is the ontological level.

Heidegger holds that, ontically considered, Dasein is unique among entities. And what makes it distinctive is that its own Being "is an issue for it." What he means is that Dasein is the being that is concerned about its own Being; it *matters* to Dasein how things are going with it, how it is doing, what the state of its Being is and will become. So Dasein already has, by virtue of being the sort of entity that it is, a certain understanding of Being.

---

*Like the term "person" in Kant, this term doesn't specify whether human beings are the only beings with the particular *way of Being* we have. Perhaps in other galaxies . . .

*It might be helpful to recall Kant's four questions, for example, "What makes natural science possible?" Kant is asking about the "transcendental" conditions on the side of the subject that must be assumed, given that science (or mathematics, or morality, or metaphysics) actually exists. In a similar way, Heidegger is inquiring about Dasein's basic mode of Being: what must Dasein be for the ontic facts to be what they are? As we will see, Heidegger's project differs from Kant's in two distinct ways: (1) He is not asking about a *subject,* as opposed to an object; (2) he thinks he has a way to reveal to us the very Being of Dasein. So there is no unknowable noumenal entity that has the character of a transcendental ego. Compare Kant on the soul, pp. 394–395.

Its own Being is always, at any given point, "disclosed to it." Because this feature of Dasein is so fundamental, Heidegger asserts that Dasein "is ontological." What does this mean? Ontology is the discipline concerned with Being. So to say that Dasein *is* ontological is to say that Dasein's way of Being involves having an *understanding* of its own Being. This openness to itself is what makes Dasein Dasein!

This feature of Dasein is so central that Heidegger points to it as the *essence* of Dasein. In each case—yours, mine—Dasein "has its Being to be" (*BT*, 33). It is as though Dasein can't just *be* (the way spiders are, for example); Dasein has to *decide* about its Being. How it will *be* is an *issue;* its Being this way or that is not just a given fact. Being, for Dasein, is a *problem* to be solved; but it cannot be solved in a disinterested and theoretical way; it is solved only by living—by existing.*

Heidegger searches for a term to designate the way of Being that is characteristic of Dasein. He settles on "existence." Dasein *exists.* As he uses this term, dogs and cats *are,* but they do not *exist.* Stones and stars are, but they do not exist. They have a different *kind* of Being. "Existence," then, is a technical term for Dasein's way of being. The term "exist" has etymological roots that suggest a kind of projection out from or away from the given situation. Heidegger sometimes writes it as "ek-sist" to emphasize this transcending of the given.† As we will see, Dasein ek-sists: it is always projecting itself beyond the present circumstance to future possibilities. We are aware of the *present* in the light of what we have been (the past) and could become (the future); we are not simply confined in it. It is this feature that makes it possible for Dasein to be concerned about its own Being. (Already we hear intimations of the importance of *time* to the question about the meaning of Being.)

Heidegger can say, then, that the essence of Dasein—what Dasein most essentially is—is its existence. And his first task is an "analytic" of Dasein. If we can get clear about Dasein's way of Being, this should be a step toward the larger question of the meaning of Being in general. Dasein is the best entity to interrogate because Dasein, in existing, already has an understanding of Being. To some degree, Being is "in the open" in Dasein, available in a way it would not be in a chemical compound. Dasein's self-understanding does not yet amount to the clear and comprehensive ontological understanding Heidegger is seeking; it is only an average, everyday kind of understanding, which (as we will see) may hide as much as it discloses. But Heidegger has found the clue as to where to begin.*

Heidegger calls an analysis of Dasein's existence a *fundamental* ontology. The ontological analysis of Dasein (the description of Dasein's basic structures) provides "the condition for the possibility of any ontologies" (*BT*, 34). Since the essence of Dasein is its existence, this will be an *existential* analysis. And what Heidegger will be looking for is something analogous to the traditional *categories,* that is, concepts setting out the most basic sorts of ways that things can be.† The concepts in the analysis of existence that correspond to the traditional categories Heidegger calls *existentials.* We will see what these are.

Let us summarize:

- What we are after is the meaning of Being. The name for such an inquiry is "ontology."
- The place to begin is where Being is "in the open."

---

* Compare Kierkegaard, p. 456.
† "Ek" is a Greek particle that suggests a standing out away from some origin, as in "ecstasy"—standing outside one's normal self.

* Heidegger's reason for turning to Dasein in his attempt to discern the meaning of Being is responsive to the puzzle Plato discusses about searching for the truth: If we don't know the truth, how will we know where to look? And how will we know when we have found it? If we do know the truth, what sense does it make to search for it? See p. 97. Plato thinks learning the truth is "recollecting" what the soul had known in some preexistence. Heidegger thinks Dasein has a "preontological" understanding of Being as part of its essence. This understanding can be deepened into a genuine ontology.
† Compare Aristotle on the categories, p. 147, and Kant, p. 385. Heidegger agrees that "Being can be said in many ways." But he thinks neither of them has discovered the appropriate "categories" for Dasein, the language adequate to our existence.

- Dasein, because it is constituted by an understanding of its own Being, is such a "place."
- So, Dasein is the entity to be interrogated.
- Dasein's way of Being is existence.
- So we want an existential analysis of Dasein.
- This analysis will be formulated in terms of concepts called "existentials," which play the role for Dasein that the traditional categories play for what Heidegger will call "present-at-hand" entities—that is, they give the most general characterizations of its way of Being.
- And this analysis will provide a fundamental ontology, from which the meaning of Being in general can be approached.

This focus on Dasein and its existence has led many to classify Heidegger as an *existentialist*. And perhaps there is no harm in that. But it must be clearly kept in mind that the analysis of existence is not what he is mainly interested in. Heidegger is, from first to last, intent on deciphering the meaning of Being.

Phenomenology

We now know what the aim is. But we do not yet have a very clear idea of how to pursue that goal. Even though Dasein is the kind of being that has an understanding of its own Being, we must not think that philosophy can just take over that understanding—far from it. For one thing, there are many ways in which Dasein has been interpreted in the great conversation, and any of these are available for Dasein to use: as a soul temporarily imprisoned in a body (Plato), as a rational animal (Aristotle), as a creature of God (Augustine), as the *ego cogito* (Descartes), as a material mechanism (Hobbes), as a transcendental ego (Kant), as the absolute subject (Hegel). *None* of these interpretations, Heidegger thinks, is adequate. In one way or another, they all miss the *existence* of Dasein. And even the average, everyday, unsophisticated way in which Dasein understands itself may hide as much

as it reveals about Dasein's true existential nature. Dasein always understands itself in one way or another. But that understanding is as likely to be a misunderstanding as to be an adequate one.

You can see, however, that we have a serious problem. How are we going to approach Dasein? With what method? Heidegger suggests that the analysis should proceed in two stages. In the first stage, we should set aside all the sophisticated theories of the tradition and try just to look at Dasein's "average everydayness."* We want to grasp Dasein as it exists most obviously and naturally. Still, the results of this analysis of everyday Dasein will be merely provisional, because we suspect that Dasein understands itself to some degree *inauthentically,* self-deceptively, hiding its way of Being from itself.

For this reason, the second stage is necessary; we must ask what it would be for Dasein to grasp itself, to own up to what it really is, to exist and understand itself *authentically.* In such an adequate self-understanding of its Being, Dasein will reveal the existentials that define it, and we will have an authentic fundamental ontology. This second stage will reveal *temporality* as the meaning of the Being of Dasein; thus we'll see that *time* is of central importance for the main question. In fact, Heidegger suggests time as the "horizon" within which the meaning of Being must be understood. If that is correct, Being itself is fundamentally temporal in nature.

But this is getting far ahead of our story. We are still faced with the problem of how to go about investigating everyday existence. This must be done, Heidegger tells us, *phenomenologically.* Hegel's use of the term "phenomenology" can serve as a clue to its meaning here.† There, the key idea is that we can "watch" consciousness as it develops through its stages toward more adequate forms. This idea of observing is central for Heidegger,

---

* Compare the later Wittgenstein's motto: "Don't think, but look!" (p. 578). Heidegger goes as far as to talk of "destroying" the ontological tradition that extends from the Greeks to ourselves—so fundamentally misguided does he believe its "thinking" has been!
† See p. 416.

Jean-Paul Sartre

Perhaps the best known of the existentialist philosophers, Jean-Paul Sartre (1905–1980) was a novelist, playwright, biographer, and short-story writer as well as a philosopher. His major philosophical work is *Being and Nothingness* (1943). His literary works include the novel *Nausea* (1938) and the plays *The Flies* (1943) and *No Exit* (1944).

Influenced by the phenomenology of Husserl and Heidegger, Sartre investigated the structures of consciousness. He noted that in ordinary unreflective awareness, the ego or self does not appear; what is present is just an object. We can reflect, of course, and then the ego appears—but then it is an object, too! Consciousness itself is apparently *not any thing*. It is, Sartre said, a pure function, an emptiness, a wind blowing toward being: nothingness. All being is located in the object of consciousness, which is full, opaque, dense: the *in-itself*.

Yet even unreflective consciousness has a kind of diaphanous self-awareness. It is always *for-itself*. As such, no consciousness is ever completely coincident with itself; there is nothing that it definitively *is*. Human reality is the place where in-itself and for-itself meet. You and I are undeniably objects; we do have being. But we are also awareness of ourselves and not just a collection of facts. So we *are not* what we are, and we *are* what we are not.

One of Sartre's most famous claims was that "existence precedes essence," by which he meant that there is no given essential nature to a human being; we first exist, and then by our free choices and actions make ourselves into something. But we are tempted to evade the anxiety and responsibility of having to create ourselves, so we identify with our in-itself or with our for-itself, and thus we slide into various forms of self-deception.

In various ways we try to justify or make meaningful our lives. Ultimately we want simultaneously to *be* something and for that something to be the result of our conscious choice: to be an in-itself/for-itself. But this concept of a self-caused being is just the traditional notion of God. The ultimate project of human beings is to be God. Unfortunately, Sartre believed, the concept of God is self-contradictory. So man, he concluded, is a futile passion.

---

too.* It has nothing to do with bodily eyes, of course; this "watching" is more a matter of attitude, of not imposing preconceived notions on the subject in question. Phenomenology is the disclosing, or uncovering, of a phenomenon by means of discourse about it. We can think of it as the attempt to *let* entities manifest themselves as they truly are.

Phenomena are understood to be "the totality of what lies in the light of day or can be brought to light" (*BT,* 51). A phenomenon, Heidegger says, is "*that which shows itself in itself,* the manifest" (*BT,* 51). Phenomena are not "mere appearances," then. They are not just illusions. Nor are they signs for something else. They are "the things themselves" as they show themselves—and not by means of something else, but "in themselves." And that is

---

*Heidegger's phenomenological method actually owes most to his teacher, Edmund Husserl, who develops phenomenological methods of inquiry. For Husserl, phenomenology is (1) a science which is (2) purely descriptive, rather than deductive or explanatory, (3) which sets aside in a systematic way all prior assumptions and presuppositions, (4) whose subject matter is consciousness—its structure, its contents, and its "intended" objects—and (5) whose outcome is a description of essences—for example, an account of *what it is to be* an act of perception or the object of a remembering. Husserl's motto is "to the things themselves!" Heidegger takes this over, but he understands it in quite a different way.

why phenomenology is relevant to our question about Being—why phenomenology can be ontology. For what we want to do is to let Being itself appear, as it is.

Notice that Heidegger makes a subtle distinction: some matters, he says, "lie in the light of day," and others "can be brought to light." Roughly speaking, entities are what lie in the light of day—the tableware we use at lunch, the daily newspaper, the family dog, your brother. But (and this should be no surprise by now) their Being is not so clearly apparent to us. Their Being must be brought to light, uncovered, disclosed. And this is just what phenomenology is designed to do.

Heidegger suggests three ways in which the phenomenon of Being might be hard to discern: (1) Being might be "hidden," in the sense that it is just too close to us for us to focus on it easily; (2) it might be "covered up," an idea that suggests Being was once known but has been made inaccessible by the tradition; and (3) Being might be "disguised," in the sense that Dasein, unable to face the awful truth about its existence, might draw a veil of camouflage over it (*BT*, 59–60). So the data we are after might not simply be there "in the light of day," manifesting themselves for us to see. We will have to engage in some *interpretation* to bring the phenomena to light. This interpretation Heidegger calls "hermeneutics," drawing this term from the tradition of interpreting texts, particularly Scripture. The meaning of a text is often obscure; to understand it requires an interpretation. Similarly, the meaning of Being is obscure. Even the character of our own existence requires interpretation if we are to penetrate its "disguises." To get to the meaning of Dasein, then, will require a method that is phenomenological and hermeneutical at the same time. Our aim is to let the phenomenon of Being shine forth, as it is in itself.

Being-in-the-World

We are now ready to begin the analysis of Dasein's existential structure. Remember, what we are aiming at is an explicit understanding of Dasein's way of Being, that way which Heidegger calls "existence." The *basic state* of Dasein, he tells us, is this; Dasein essentially, necessarily, *is-in-the-world*. The hyphens in this odd phrase are not accidental; they tell us that we are dealing here with a *unitary* phenomenon. It is not possible to understand Dasein apart from its world; indeed, Dasein without the world would not be "da"—that is, *there*. To be in a world—to "have" a world—is constitutive for Dasein.

We need to unpack this very rich notion. But before we do, it might be useful to contrast it with some others. We can already see that Heidegger's phenomenological analysis of Dasein's Being is completely at variance with the view expressed most clearly by Descartes: that it is a real possibility (one that needs to be ruled out by argument) that I might be the only thing that exists.* As we have seen, this ego (or mind), which Descartes thinks could exist independently of the world, gets trapped inside itself and has a hard time finding the world again. In supposing that such an independent existence is possible for the soul, Heidegger claims, Descartes misses precisely the *Being* of Dasein—namely, its **Being-in-the-world.** Heidegger thinks that Descartes' notion of the *ego*, of "the *thing* which thinks," in fact attributes to Dasein a kind of Being that belongs rather to a different sort of entity, which he will call the **present-at-hand.**† This is just one dramatic example of how the Western philosophical tradition has gone wrong—one example, Heidegger thinks, of how our forgetfulness of Being has warped our perception of things. One finds this pattern, he believes, in the whole history of the conversation since Descartes—in Hume, Kant, and Hegel particularly.‡

---

*Review *Meditation I* with its skeptical arguments from sense deceptions, dreams, and the evil demon. Descartes thinks he can defeat solipsism only by *proving* the existence of God.

†We will explicitly discuss this notion of the present-at-hand below.

‡Heidegger would think that Hume's bundle theory of the self, Kant's transcendental ego, and Hegel's infinite subject (Spirit) as the substance of the world all miss the phenomenon of the Being of Dasein. All are dominated by the heritage of Descartes, for whom the subject is a peculiar kind of *thing* (though they differ about the kind of thing it is).

But its roots can be traced back to Plato's interpretation of the true Being of entities in terms of the Forms.

Our tradition, Heidegger holds, has succumbed to a tendency toward *objectification*. As a result, we have taken the world to be made up of substances, things, objects; and the self or soul or mind has been understood as just another substance or thing. No wonder the crucial question seemed to be the epistemological one: whether the subject (a thinking thing, the mind) can *know* the object (a different kind of thing). Can a subject *transcend* its subjectivity and know the truth about objects existing independently of it? We have seen how Kant's Copernican revolution "solves" this problem by making the knowable objects dependent on the knowing subject, but at the price of leaving things-in-themselves unknowable. All this, Heidegger believes, is a result of our having "covered over" the phenomenon of Being. And, most crucially, it has distorted our understanding of *our own* Being. This covering over is what Heidegger means to combat. And the first shot in this battle is the notion that the basic state of Dasein (which, you will recall, is in each case *mine*) is Being-in-the-world.

What does this mean? For one thing, it means that the fundamental relation between Dasein and the world is not epistemological, but ontological. Knowing is not basic; Being is. We *are* in-the-world, and we are so in a way that is deeper and richer than any propositional knowledge could completely express. What is it to be *in* the world? We can't fully answer this question until we understand more clearly what a "world" is. But in a preliminary way, we can say this: it is not the same as the coffee being *in* the cup, or the pencil being *in* the box. In these cases, we have one "present-at-hand" thing spatially contained in another. Heidegger does not want to deny that for certain purposes the entity that is Dasein can be regarded like this: right now, for instance, I am *in* my study, which is *in* my house in exactly this sense.

But this is not the basic fact about the way I am in the world. (It is not the basic fact, for that matter, about the way I am in my study.) Dasein is *in*-the-world more in the sense in which my brother was *in* the navy, or my son is *in* love. Dasein's way of Being-in-the-world is a matter of being engaged in projects, involved with others, using tools. Dasein *dwells* in the world; it is not just *located* there. Dasein's

> Being-in-the-world has always dispersed itself or even split itself up into definite ways of Being-in. The multiplicity of these is indicated by the following examples: having to do with something, producing something, attending to something and looking after it, making use of something, giving something up and letting it go, undertaking, accomplishing, evincing, interrogating, considering, discussing, determining. . . . All these ways of Being-in have *concern* as their kind of Being—a kind of Being we have yet to characterize in detail. (*BT*, 83)

Concernfully—that is the way Dasein is *in*-the-world. In all these ways and more, Dasein is concernfully engaged in the world. What this means is that there is a more basic mode of relating to the things in the world than knowing them. Knowledge we might have or lack. But Being-in is something we cannot *be* without.

> From what we have been saying, it follows that Being-in is not a 'property' which Dasein sometimes has and sometimes does not have, and *without* which it could be just as well as it could with it. It is not the case that man 'is' and then has, by way of an extra, a relationship-of-Being towards the 'world'—a world with which he provides himself occasionally. Dasein is never 'proximally' an entity which is, so to speak, free from Being-in, but which sometimes has the inclination to take up a 'relationship' towards the world. Taking up relationships towards the world is possible only *because* Dasein, as Being-in-the-world, is as it is. (*BT*, 84)

Being-in-the-world, in other words, is one of the *existentials* that characterizes the fundamental ontology of Dasein. It is one aspect of the essence of Dasein. The world is *given with* Dasein. But what a *world* is we are not yet clear about.

Remember that we are trying to disclose the Being of Dasein by an investigation of "average everydayness." So we now have to ask, How does this phenomenon of Being-in-the-world show itself in Dasein's average everydayness? What form does our Being-in normally take? We can get an answer, Heidegger suggests, via an interpretation of the *entities in the world* "closest" to us.

> We shall call those entities which we encounter in concern "*equipment*". In our dealings we come across equipment for writing, sewing, working, transportation, measurement. The kind of Being which equipment possesses must be exhibited. (*BT*, 97)

If we try to give a phenomenological description of our everyday mode of Being, what we find is that we dwell in a world of gear, of equipment for use. We do not first understand a pen as a "mere thing," and thereafter apprehend its use as a writing instrument. That is not the right description of our way with the pen. We grasp it *to write with*, usually without a thought. It is "on hand," or, as Heidegger puts it, **ready-to-hand.** We simply turn the knob to open the door, often with our mind entirely on other matters—don't we? We deal with the things around us in an engaged, not a detached, manner. We cope with them in a variety of ways. They are elements in our ongoing projects. The things that are phenomenologically "closest" to us are not, then, neutral "objects" which we first stare at in a disinterested way and to which we must subsequently assign some "value."

It is in this engaged manner that we are most primordially in-the-world. Descartes worries about the problem of a transcendent reality: Is there anything "out there" beyond my mind's ideas? But if Heidegger is right, that is not a problem at all. Dasein *is* a kind of transcendence—in its very Being! Dasein is essentially *in-the-world*, engaged with the entities of the world in a concernful fashion. Kant says that the scandal of philosophy is that philosophers have not solved this problem of transcendence. Heidegger thinks the scandal is that philosophy has thought there is a problem here! That there seems to be a problem about "the reality of the external world" is just a sign of how

distant we are from an understanding of our own mode of Being.*

But we still need to clarify the mode of Being of these entities "closest" to us in-the-world. Let us ask, What is it to *be* a hammer? In what does its *being-a-hammer* consist? There is a certain characteristic shape for a hammer, and a hammer is usually made out of certain definite materials, though both shape and materials can vary. But it is neither shape nor composition that *makes* a hammer a hammer. What it is for something to be a hammer is for it to have a certain definite use—a function, a purpose. A hammer is (to oversimplify slightly) *to-drive-nails-with*. That is what a hammer *is*. A hammer *hammers*.

It is important to note that the Being of the hammer involves a reference to something else— to nails. What is it to be a nail? To be a nail is to be something that can be driven into boards to fasten them together. Another reference!

> Taken strictly, there 'is' no such thing as *an* equipment. To the Being of any equipment there always belongs a totality of equipment, in which it can be this equipment that it is. Equipment is essentially 'something in-order-to . . .' A totality of equipment is constituted by various ways of the 'in-order-to', such as serviceability, conduciveness, usability, manipulability.
>
> In the 'in-order-to' as a structure there lies an *assignment* or *reference* of something to something. (*BT*, 97)

It is not possible, in other words, that there should exist just one item of equipment. Being a hammer involves a context of other equipment and, ultimately, the world.†

Let us ask a related question. When do we *understand* something to be a hammer? In what does

---

*Heidegger's analysis of Being-in-the-world is a radical rejection of what we have called the *representational theory* (p. 300), the central claim of which is that we are directly or immediately acquainted only with ideas in the mind. If Heidegger is right, what we are directly and immediately acquainted with are functionally understood items in the world around us.
†Compare the anti-atomistic remarks of the later Wittgenstein, pp. 592–593.

this understanding consist? Most basically, I understand a hammer when I know how to hammer with it—when I can use it to drive the nails into the boards. The Being of the hammer does not reveal itself to a disinterested observation of its appearance or to a scientific investigation of its weight and material properties. Its Being is manifest primarily and fundamentally in a skill I have, particularly when I actualize this skill in actually hammering. That is how the hammer shows itself to be what it is. Hammers are understood in virtue of a kind of "know-how," not (primarily) by way of a "theory of hammers." Its being a hammer reveals itself to my *circumspective concern*—to my care-full involvements with it in the projects I am engaged in. Heidegger calls this kind of Being "readiness-to-hand."

Tools, gear, and equipment in general have this kind of Being. And dealing with the ready-to-hand is the most fundamental mode of our Being-in-the-world. On all sides we find it, if we only have eyes to look. It is easy to miss, because it is so "close" to us, almost too familiar to notice. But our skillful coping with nearly everything we encounter during a day's dealings is a matter of encountering over and over again the ready-to-hand. Our fundamental mode of understanding is not theoretical or scientific, but practical. We *understand how* to drive a car, use a fork, put on a pair of pants, open a can. And we manifest that understanding in actually driving, hammering, using the computer, combing our hair, and so on. The Being of Dasein is in this primordial sense a Being-in-the-world.

It cannot be emphasized too much that this concernful dealing with the ready-to-hand is *basic*. If Heidegger is right about this, the question of whether there "really" are hammers and cars and cans simply cannot arise. Philosophers have thought this is a real problem only because they have missed the Being of Dasein as Being-in-the-world and Dasein's relation to the ready-to-hand.

We are making some progress, but we do not yet know what it is to be a world. A clue can be derived from the fact that the ready-to-hand never comes alone, but always in a context of references and assignments to other entities. The hammer is to pound the nails; there would be no nails if there were no boards to join; the boards are shaped the way they are to build a house; houses are for sheltering and for dwelling in. All these things are meaningful together—or not at all. Each has the structure of an in-order-to. But if we pay close attention to this phenomenon of interlocking in-order-to's, we can see that three other things are also manifest.

1. Though we do not usually pay attention to the hammer directly—what we are involved in is *the work,* and the hammer is used "transparently"—the work involves *making use of something* for a purpose. Consider a cobbler making shoes.

> In the work there is also a reference or assignment to 'materials': the work is dependent on leather, thread, needles, and the like. Leather, moreover, is produced from hides. These are taken from animals, which someone else has raised. . . . Hammer, tongs, and needle, refer in themselves to steel, iron, metal, mineral, wood, in that they consist of these. In equipment that is used, 'Nature' is discovered along with it by that use—the 'Nature' we find in natural products. (*BT,* 100)

As Heidegger is careful to point out, the "nature" that presents itself in this way is nature as a resource: "the wood is a forest of timber, the mountain a quarry of rock; the river is water-power, the wind is wind 'in the sails'" (*BT,* 100). This nature is part of the world of equipment "in" which Dasein essentially is. So it is not quite the "nature" of the scientist (to which we will come shortly). Along with the ready-to-hand Being of equipment, then, there is revealed the world of nature.

2. Other entities having the same kind of being as Dasein are also manifest. I, after all, did not make the hammer I pound with, nor did I manufacture the nails, nor did I shape the boards I join with them. They did not just "happen," either. These entities reveal that I am not alone in the world but live in the world with others who are like me.* This world, moreover, shows itself to be

---

* Just as the "external world" problem seems like a pseudoproblem from Heidegger's point of view, the same is true of the problem of "other minds." It just doesn't arise!

a *public* world. Hammers are mass produced; they are designed specifically so that *anyone* can hammer with them. The instruments in a car are intentionally designed so that the *average person* can easily read them. It would be a big mistake (we will soon see just how big) to understand Heidegger as saying that each Dasein lives in his own little world. Far from it. While we can quite properly speak of the chicken farmer's world, or the magazine publisher's world, or the cyclist's world, these are not fundamental. Each is carved out of the larger public world. These smaller worlds are not the world in which Dasein most fundamentally dwells; that world is the one and only public world. The Being of Dasein is Being-in-*the*-world. And this is a world I have in common with others.

3.   There is a third phenomenon that is evident together with the ready-to-hand: Heidegger calls it a "for-the-sake-of-which." Let's go back to the hammer. The hammer has its Being as equipment; it is ready-to-hand for hammering. As we have seen, there is a whole series of references or assignments in which the hammer is involved: it is essentially related to nails, which "refer" to boards, which "point" toward building houses. Does this set of functional relations have a terminus? Is there a point to it? Does it come to an end somewhere? Is there anything *for the sake of which* this whole set of relations exists? Yes. The totality of these involvements

> goes back ultimately to a "towards-which" in which there is *no* further involvement: this "towards-which" is not an entity with the kind of Being that belongs to what is ready-to-hand within a world; it is rather an entity whose Being is defined as Being-in-the-world, and to whose state of Being, worldhood itself belongs. . . . The primary 'toward-which' is a "for-the-sake-of-which". But the 'for-the-sake-of-which' always pertains to the Being of *Dasein,* for which in its Being, that very Being is essentially an issue. (*BT,* 116–17)

Dasein, concerned for its own Being, understands the possibility that it might freeze in the winter and provides for itself a house. It is in terms of the possibilities of Dasein's Being that the entire set of

functional relations attains its structure and Being. We get the image of an immensely complicated, crisscrossing network of functional assignments in which all the entities in the world are caught up and have their Being. This network is anchored in the Being of Dasein, that Being for whom its own Being is a matter of concern and whose Being has the structure of Being-in-the-world.

It is important to note that *the world* is not an entity; nor is it a collection of entities; nor is it a totality of facts, as the early Wittgenstein thinks.* Heidegger's thought is as far removed from the atomism of the *Tractatus* as you can imagine. It is only within the context of the world that something can *be* a hammer. The world is a prior whole, presupposed by the Being of the ready-to-hand; it is not the *sum* of lots and lots of things, each of which might equally well exist alone. There would be no hammers in a world without nails to drive; there would be no nails without boards to join; there would be no boards without houses to build; and there would be none of these entities without Dasein—that for-the-sake-of-which they all exist and whose mode of Being is Being-in-the-world.

But if we are clear about what the world is *not,* we are still not clear about what it is. The world in which Dasein has its Being is one of those all-too-familiar, too-close-to-be-observed phenomena. The world is not, for instance, the earth. It would sound very odd indeed to talk about Being-in-the-earth (as though one lived underground). Nor is the world the same as the universe. (Christians talk of the "sins of the world," but "sins of the universe" makes no sense at all.) What, then, is this familiar, but strange, phenomenon of the world?

Though our immediate focus is usually on the things *in* the world, Heidegger suggests that there are certain experiences in which the phenomenon of the world itself—the *worldhood* of the world—comes to the fore. Consider working with a lever, trying to move a large and heavy box. What is manifest is the work, the project—to get *this* over *there*—and in a subsidiary (but not explicitly focused) way, the lever. Suddenly the lever breaks. It

---

* See the discussion of the first sentences of the *Tractatus,* pp. 554 and 557–558.

is no longer ready-to-hand. We could, in fact, call it unready-to-hand. It takes on the character of *conspicuousness*. Whereas we had hardly noticed the lever before, just using it in that familiar transparent way, suddenly it announces itself, forces itself into awareness.

Two things happen. For one thing, "pure presence-at-hand announces itself in such [damaged] equipment" (*BT*, 103). There occurs a transition to another mode of Being. The functionality that defined the lever *as* a lever vanishes; the item is disconnected from that series of references and involvements that made it be—as a lever. It no longer *is* a lever. It just *lies there*. We no longer seize hold of it in that familiar way to use in our project. It is no longer alongside us in our work. Rather, it stands over against us. We observe it, stare at it. It has become an *object*. It now *is* merely *present-at-hand*.

Heidegger allows that in the course of our everyday lives, this moment of pure presence-at-handedness may not last very long; the item soon takes up a new place in our system of functional involvements, with the meaning of "to-be-fixed" or "to-be-discarded." But this glimpse into the presence-at-hand is a revelation of another whole mode of Being: a realm of pure objects, suitable for contemplation and scientific investigation. It is important to note that in some sense, it is the same entity as before; however, its *mode of Being* changes. Now it is just an *object, a substance with properties.** Revealed in this way, it can be a theme for investigation by the natural sciences. In fact, *nature*—in the sense dealt with by modern physics—now first makes its appearance. This is not nature as a resource, as part of the equipment character of the world; it is nature disconnected from Dasein's concern—a sheer presence.

Along with the stripping away of functional characteristics, something else takes place in the transition to presence-at-hand. Every tool has a "place," almost in an Aristotelian sense.* If you have "misplaced" your hammer, there are certain places you will look for it and certain places you won't; you won't look in the oven. There is a "region" in which it "belongs."

> In the 'physical' assertion that 'the hammer is heavy' we *overlook* not only the tool-character of the entity we encounter, but also something that belongs to any ready-to-hand equipment: its place. Its place becomes a matter of indifference. This does not mean that what is present-at-hand loses its 'location' altogether. But its place becomes a spatio-temporal position, a 'world-point,' which is in no way distinguished from any other. (*BT*, 413)

Heidegger is describing (1) the existential genesis of those infinite spaces whose "silence" so frightens Pascal[†] and (2) the *origin* of that objectifying way of understanding the world that has so dominated our tradition. The important thing to note is that the present-at-hand is not primordial, or basic. The objects of natural science have their Being in a *modification* of the more fundamental entities that are ready-to-hand. Our tradition since Plato and Aristotle, but especially since Descartes, has assumed (without proof, Heidegger insists) that the basic mode of Being for the things of the world is just this objectified presence-at-hand, in which things are available for perceiving and theorizing about, independent of their role as equipment in the world. Suppose *you* are asked, for example, "What is there—*really*?" You are likely to answer in terms of the entities described by physical science: rocks and trees and electrons and such. But that answer is, Heidegger believes, precisely backwards. The most basic mode of Being for the entities we encounter in the world is Being-ready-to-hand; objects as there for disinterested scientific inquiry ride piggyback on that.

This claim has its bite in the notion that no matter how much of the world we "objectify," we always, necessarily, do so on a background of

---

* Recall that the "substance/property" concept is one of the categories of Kant, one of the fundamental ways that objects can—*must*—be. See p. 386. Heidegger is here claiming that this mode of being is a derivative one; it belongs to the present-at-hand, which is a modification of the more basic ready-to-hand. What is fundamental is not the *object,* but the *tool*.

---

* See the discussion of the ancient idea that things have a "natural place" and of how "space" comes to supplant "place" as a basic concept in seventeenth-century science (p. 287).
[†] See p. 287.

circumspective concern, of practices that involve the ready-to-hand. Dasein cannot, if Heidegger is right, totally objectify itself. Yet, that is just the way our tradition has treated Dasein—as an *object* with *properties* of a certain sort (distinctive properties, perhaps, but an object nonetheless). That is why we tend to think that explanations of a *scientific* sort can be given for human behavior: explanations in terms of conditioning, or complexes, or drives, or peer "pressure," or any number of other analogues to explanation in physical science. And that is why the question of the meaning of Being is so obscure to us; in assimilating our own Being to that of the present-at-hand, we have lost the sense of what it is to *exist*. Since existence is our own mode of Being, that mode of Being about which we are concerned, of which we necessarily have some understanding, a misunderstanding here turns everything topsy-turvy. It is no wonder that clarifying the meaning of Being is so difficult a task.

But we still have not clarified the meaning of "the world." What is it to be a world? That is the second thing that shows up in those experiences where tools go wrong in some way. When the lever breaks, not only does the present-at-hand light up, but the whole network of relations in which it was transparently embedded now comes into view. When the lever gets disconnected from this network and just lies there, the network itself becomes visible. Part of it is disturbed and we notice that it has been there all the time! The *worldhood of the world* is constituted by this system of references, within which Dasein and the ready-to-hand have their Being. To be a world, in other words, is to be a structure within which entities *are* and have their meaning.* This entire network of in-order-to's and toward-which's and for-the-sake-of's—

that is the phenomenon of the world. So the world is neither a thing, nor an entity, nor a collection of entities. It is that wherein entities have their Being, whether that Being is existence, readiness-to-hand, or presence-at-hand.

You should now have a fairly clear understanding of that basic *existential,* that most fundamental characteristic of Dasein: that Dasein is Being-in-the-world.

The "Who" of Dasein

Who is Dasein?

That may sound like a strange question, and in fact it is. Not because the term "Dasein" is a strange one, but because the answer seems so straightforward. If Dasein is in each case "mine," then it would seem that, in my case anyway, the answer would be *I myself,* this *person* named Norman Melchert, this *individual,* this *self* or *subject; I* am who Dasein is in this case. And each of you should be able to answer in the same way. What could be more obvious?

But Heidegger thinks this easy and familiar answer covers up or disguises the ontological reality. To talk of self or subject is to fall prey to the temptation to suppose that I am a *thing,* a kind of "soul substance" (perhaps in the way Descartes thinks). But the *Being* of Dasein in its everydayness is not lighted up by this kind of answer; rather, it is hidden.* This question is then in order: Who is Dasein as it exists in its averageness? The answer Heidegger gives to this question is extraordinary.

---

*Heidegger's conception of "the world" is something like that "scaffolding of the world" that the early Wittgenstein thinks logic provides. (See p. 561.) The enormous difference, of course, is that Wittgenstein's scaffolding supports only sheer meaningless facts— what Heidegger would call the present-at-hand—whereas the worldhood of the world is rich in functionality, usefulness, meaning. But it is interesting to note a correspondence between Heidegger's claim that the phenomenon of the world is usually "too close" to us to be observed and the *Tractatus* claim that this logical structure "cannot be said," but must be "shown."

*Hume rejects the "soul substance" of Descartes (pp. 360–362), as does Hobbes in quite a different way (p. 335). And we can interpret Kant and Hegel as denying that a person is an object; a person, they would say, is subject! (See pp. 395 and 428). But Heidegger thinks that nonetheless—and despite Kant's explicit denial—they all are implicitly using the category of *substance* to characterize the subject; in doing so, they assimilate the Being of Dasein to that of the present-at-hand, and they one and all miss the ontological character of Dasein's Being—its *existence.* Heidegger agrees with Kierkegaard in thinking of the Self as a *task,* not something *given.* That is part of what it means that Dasein's own Being is an *issue* for it; how it is to be constituted is a matter for *decision.* See pp. 448 and 456.

It could be that the "who" of everyday Dasein just is *not* the "I myself." (*BT*, 150)

Heidegger's phenomenological answer to the question about the "who" of Dasein in everydayness is *das Man*. This phrase is based on an ordinary German term that occurs in contexts like "Man sagt," which can be rendered as "One says," or "It is said that," or perhaps as "They say." While in the detergent aisle of the supermarket one day, I heard one woman say to another, "I think I'll try this; they say that's good." You might ask, Who is this "they"? If you had put this question to her, she probably wouldn't have been able to tell you.*

So Heidegger finds that Dasein in its average everydayness is this "They" or "the One."† But what does that mean? We have already seen that *Others* are "given" along with the ready-to-hand (e.g., with this shirt, which was cut and sewn in a factory somewhere.) And if our account is to be phenomenologically adequate, it must record the fact that Others are encountered as themselves Being-in-the-world. The Others, too, *exist* with that same concernful Being-in-the-world as I do.

Moreover, the existence of Others like me is not something that has to come as the conclusion of an argument, as the old problem of "other minds" suggests. I do not first start with *myself* and then conclude on the basis of similarity between observable aspects of myself and Others that they must be persons, too.‡ That would not be an accurate description of my experience of Others.

---

*The translators of *Being and Time* render "das Man" as "the They." Hubert Dreyfus argues in an unpublished commentary that it is much better to bring it into English as "the One" (*Being-in-the-World: A Commentary on Heidegger's Being and Time, Division I*, June 1988). I will sometimes use one locution, sometimes the other.
†Dreyfus argues convincingly that Heidegger does not always distinguish clearly two facets of his own account of "the One": a positive function Dreyfus calls "conformity" or "Falling-in-with," and a negative function he calls "conformism" or "Falling-away-from." The latter, but not the former, correlates with Dasein in the mode of *inauthentic existence*. We will try to keep these aspects distinct.
‡To proceed in this way would be to assume that I *first* have an ontologically adequate grasp of myself and *thereafter* extend this understanding to others. But that is just the (very Cartesian) assumption that Heidegger says we cannot make.

By 'Others' we do not mean everyone else but me—those over against whom the "I" stands out. They are rather those from whom, for the most part, one does *not* distinguish oneself—those among whom one is too. . . . The world of Dasein is a *with-world*. Being-in is *Being-with* Others. Their Being-in-themselves within-the-world is *Dasein-with*. (*BT*, 154–55)

Being-with is, like Being-in-the-world, an *existential*—one of the characteristics that defines Dasein's Being. This means that Dasein could not exist without Others, any more than it could exist without the world. It is part of Dasein's very *Being* to be with-Others-in-the-world. This is true even when Dasein is alone or neglects the Others or is indifferent to them. The anchorite in the cave is *with* Others, if only in the mode of seeking to avoid them. The anchorite carries the Others with her into the cave in her ability to speak a language, to think, to meditate in the way she does; this "carrying with" is what it means to say that Being-with is an *existential*.

The discovery of Being-with is an important step. But it does not yet get us clearly to the "who" of Dasein. There is a clue, however, in the phrase, "those from whom . . . one does *not* distinguish oneself." We could paradoxically put it this way: One is, oneself, one of the Others. In fact, Heidegger tells us, we are so much one of the "they" that we are constantly concerned lest we differ too much from them.

> In one's concern with what one has taken hold of, whether with, for, or against, the Others, there is constant care as to the way one differs from them, whether that difference is merely one that is to be evened out, whether one's own Dasein has lagged behind the Others and wants to catch up in relation to them, or whether one's Dasein already has some priority over them and sets out to keep them suppressed. The care about the distance between them is disturbing to Being-with-one-another, though this disturbance is one that is hidden from it. (*BT*, 163–64)

We can think of this as the existential foundation for the familiar phenomenon of "keeping up with the Joneses." Heidegger calls it *distantiality* (still another of those invented words!); he uses this term to signify the constant concern of Dasein that it might get too far away from the norm—from what "they say," or what "one does." (Compare: "One just doesn't *do* that!") Either one doesn't want too large a "distance" to open up between oneself and the Others, or one takes care to preserve a certain "appropriate distance."

Heidegger suggests that this phenomenon is "hidden" from Dasein. And, indeed, I think that is so. When I have suggested to young people that an enormous part of their lives is governed by norms they participate in but are hardly aware of, I usually get a lot of resistance. They all want to think of themselves as unique, self-made individuals! But we all hold our forks the same way, a way different from that of the English; and we North Americans all stand roughly the same distance from others when we converse with them, a distance farther away than Latin Americans stand. If you spell "existence" as "existance," I correct you. And so on. We do as *they* do. When someone strays, they are brought back in line, usually so gently that it is scarcely noticed, but forcefully if necessary. Sociologists tell us that this establishment and enforcement of norms is one of the principal functions of gossip.

> . . . this distantiality which belongs to Being-with, is such that Dasein, as everyday Being-with-one-another, stands in *subjection* to Others. It itself *is* not; its Being has been taken away by the Others. Dasein's everyday possibilities of Being are for the Others to dispose of as they please. These Others, moreover, are not *definite* Others. On the contrary, any Other can represent them. What is decisive is just that inconspicuous domination by Others which has already been taken over unawares from Dasein as Being-with. One belongs to the Others oneself and enhances their power. . . . The "who" is not this one, not that one, not oneself, not some people, and not the sum of them all. The 'who' is the neuter, *the "they"* [the One]. . . .
>
> We take pleasure and enjoy ourselves as *they* take pleasure; we read, see, and judge about literature and art as *they* see and judge; likewise we shrink back from the 'great mass' as *they* shrink back; we find 'shocking' what *they* find shocking. The "they" [the

One], which is nothing definite, and which all are, though not as the sum, prescribes the kind of Being of everydayness. (*BT*, 164)

Let's take one of these "they" phenomena from everydayness and examine it: consider the "proper" distance to stand from someone you are talking with. Social scientists will tell you that there is a "norm" here based on your cultural background. You almost certainly behave according to your cultural norm, and you are uncomfortable if it is violated. Is this something you *decided*? Certainly not. What is its ground, its reason, its justification—its *logos*? There really doesn't seem to be any. Is there a Platonic Form governing this matter? No. Is it "natural"? No, though it feels natural to us, just as other distances feel natural to people of other cultures. Where does it come from, this "naturalness"—this "rightness," even—that we are uncomfortable violating? Can there be any other answer than "that is what we do?" * This is how it is done, how *One* does it. That is all the foundation it has!

Along with *distantiality*, the phenomenon of *averageness* is an existential characteristic of the One. And this involves a kind of *leveling down*, in which every kind of uniqueness, oddness, or priority is smoothed out as much as possible. We noted the *public* character of the world as manifest in ready-to-hand items. Now we see that the world is a common, public world in another sense, too. The "way things are done" is set by the One, not by each Dasein privately for itself. The world of the One is a *public* world from the start. It is into that world, moreover, that Dasein comes from the very beginning; it is the One that shapes it and makes Dasein's "who" what it is. We are all *das Man*. In a striking phrase, Heidegger puts it this way:

> Everyone is the other, and no one is himself. (*BT*, 165)

The public character of the world of the One— the world of everyday Dasein (our world)—has an interesting consequence.

---

* Compare the later Wittgenstein, pp. 588, 590, and 593.

. . . it deprives the particular Dasein of its answerability. The "they" . . . can be answerable for everything most easily, because it is not someone who needs to vouch for anything. It 'was' always the "they" who did it, and yet it can be said that it has been 'no one'. . . .

Thus the particular Dasein in its everydayness is *disburdened* by the "they." (*BT,* 165)

Who is responsible for the way everyday life goes? No one. It is just the way One does it. Dasein conforms to this *way of Being;* Dasein *Falls-in-with-it.* Notice that this is not—so far—something for which Dasein is to *blame;* distantiality and averageness are *existentials;* that is, they are aspects of the very *essence* of Dasein's existence. It couldn't be otherwise for Dasein. And isn't this fortunate? To have to bear the burden of responsibility for the whole of the way one lives would be too much; the "they" is there to help out. In its average everydayness, Dasein does not feel this burden because

the "*they*", which supplies the answer to the question of the "*who*" of everyday Dasein, is the "*nobody*" to whom every Dasein has already surrendered itself in Being-among-one-another. (*BT,* 165–66)

It is important to note that Heidegger distinguishes three modes in which Dasein can relate itself to itself: **inauthenticity, authenticity,** and an undifferentiated mode, which is neither. We have so far been trying to describe the undifferentiated mode of Dasein's existence, though the eagerness with which Dasein accepts the "disburdening" is a hint of what inauthenticity amounts to. As a being for whom its own Being is always at issue, Dasein is always facing the *decision* between existing inauthentically or authentically; it always exists predominantly in one mode or the other. We will explore these modes more fully, but we can now say that authentic existence is not a grasping of some nature or essence of oneself quite different from the "they-self"; it is, rather, a matter of coming to terms with the fact that this is what one is and that one is *no more than this.* And inauthentic existence is a way of hiding this truth from oneself. Existing as "the One" is not yet inauthentic.

But "the One" constantly presents to Dasein the possibility of evading the disquieting aspects of *having to Be the being that it is* by fleeing into the security of what "they say." Thus the One is both a constitutive factor in Dasein and a temptation to inauthenticity.

For now, though, we can see that the answer to the question about the "who" of Dasein is this: in its average everydayness, Dasein exists in the mode of "the One." Dasein (you and I in our way of existing) belongs to "the They."

Modes of Disclosure

What makes Dasein seem a promising entity to analyze, given that the meaning of Being is our quarry, is the fact that Dasein's own Being is an issue for it. That means that Dasein has an understanding of its own Being, though it is not explicitly worked out. But what sort of understanding is this? In what ways is Dasein already *always* disclosed to itself? Think of a dense and dark forest, and in the midst of it imagine a clearing. The clearing opens up a space within which flowers and trees can appear; in fact, it is the clearing that is the condition for anything at all being visible. And now, with this analogy in mind, let us ask, Is there such a clearing in the *world?* Does Dasein exist in such a clearing? Not exactly, Heidegger answers. Rather, he wants to say, Dasein *is* such a clearing.*

. . . *as* Being-in-the-world it is cleared in itself, not through any other entity, but in such a way that it *is* itself the clearing. . . . Dasein brings its "there" along with it. If it lacks its "there", it is not factically the

---

*The German word here translated as "clearing" is "Lichtung." It is important that the word comes from the word for light—"Licht." Dasein is in itself the "light of nature" (Descartes, *Meditation III*), the condition for uncovering the truth. Compare also Augustine on the interior illumination of the soul (p. 224) and Plato on the Image of the Sun (p. 120). What Augustine attributes to the Interior Teacher (Christ) and Plato to the Form of the Good, Heidegger takes to be the very essence of Dasein itself—that it is *there.*

entity which is essentially Dasein; indeed, it is not this entity at all. *Dasein is its disclosedness.* (*BT,* 171)

A human being that was not in itself this kind of openness to beings and to Being would not yet be a Dasein; such a human would, perhaps, be a corpse. In any case, it would not be "there." Disclosedness is part of the existential constitution of Dasein. And that is what we now have to bring more clearly to light.

Heidegger discusses this "thereness" of Dasein under three headings: **attunement,** understanding, and discourse.* These are very rich pages in *Being and Time,* and we must be content with omitting much. But it is essential to grasp something of these modes of disclosure.

Attunement

We are sometimes asked, "How are you doing? The surprising thing is that we can always answer. And in answering, we report our *mood.* We say, "Fine," or "Awful—I think I failed the calculus exam." Heidegger holds that moods don't *just happen;* they are not just meaningless present-at-hand items we undergo, the way our heart sometimes beats faster and sometimes slower. Moods are *cognitive.* They are disclosive. But what do they disclose? They reveal how we are coping with this business of having to exist, that is, how we are bearing the burden of having to be here. Dasein is "attuned" to its own Being.

Moreover, moods are not experienced as private states or feelings, independent of the world out there. Suppose you are in a bad mood, that (as we say) you got out of bed on the wrong side

_____

* The term I am bringing into English as "attunement" (following Dreyfus) is *Befindlichkeit.* There is no very good equivalent; the translators of *Being and Time* translates it as "state-of-mind." But that plays right into the hands of Heidegger's opponents in the conversation who interpret the modes of disclosure as "states" belonging to a present-at-hand entity—for example, as properties of something like Descartes' mind-substance. It is such "subjectivism" that Heidegger is combating through and through. A commentator suggests "situatedness," which captures part of it but misses the experiential feel of the thing.

this morning. Where, phenomenologically speaking, does this mood reveal itself? In your head, while the world goes on its sunny way? Not at all. *Nothing,* you are likely to say, is going right. *Everything* seems to be against you. Your *world* is dark. And why should it not be so, if your Being is indeed Being-in-the-world? Moods are pervasive, coloring everything. Suppose you have been watching a horror movie on a video all alone, late at night. Thereafter, every creak in the house, every hoot of an owl, and every gust of wind in the trees takes on an ominous quality. You anxiously check the locks and make sure the windows are closed. The *world* is now a scary place! How are you now bearing the burden of having to be there? Not very well.

Dasein never exists without a mood. Even the flat, calm, easygoing character of an average day is a mood. Dasein *is,* remember, its disclosedness. In revealing its "thereness," Dasein's mood discloses how Dasein is attuned to its world. In this disclosure is revealed a further aspect of Dasein's Being: **thrownness.** We find ourselves "thrown" into our Being-in-the-world in the following sense. None of us chose to be born. Nor did we decide to be born in the twentieth century, rather than the thirteenth. Nor were we consulted about whether we would be American or Chinese or Mexican. Nor if we preferred being male or female. Nor black nor white nor any other color. Nor to be born to just *these* parents in just *that* town with just *those* relatives and neighbors, with a certain very specific kind of housing, transportation, and tools at hand. (Lucy says to Snoopy: "You've been a dog all your life, haven't you? I've often wondered what made you decide to become a dog." Snoopy, lying on his doghouse roof, replies, "I was fooled by the job description." But that is a joke, isn't it? It *belongs* in the comics!) We just *find ourselves* in existence—in a world of a particular sort, having one language rather than another and one characteristic way of looking at things, rather than another. We are, as Heidegger says, "delivered over" to our "there," to our world (*BT,* 174).

We could put this idea in another way: *Who* we are is a very particular sort of *One;* there is no help for it, for we are "thrown" into one "they" rather than another. Even if we eventually reject certain features of this One, as characteristically happens when human beings mature, we do so drawing on the resources available in *this* world; we cannot make use, for instance, of the psychological and technological discoveries of the twenty-third century. We are *thrown* into the world.

This thrownness is a fact. It is a fact about our Being. So it is an *ontological* fact. Heidegger uses two words for facts. Ordinary facts (that the kiwi is a bird native to New Zealand, for instance, or that this book is written in English, or that I am five feet, ten inches tall) he calls *factual*. Facts about things present-at-hand, for instance, are factual. Ontological facts about Dasein, facts about us not as beings, but about our Being (or *way* of Being), he calls *factical*. Our being a "clearing," for instance, is factical; our Being-in-the world is factical; our thrownness is part of our **facticity**. In attempting a "fundamental ontology" of Dasein, then, Heidegger is investigating its facticity: the facts about its Being. The facticity of our being thrown is one of the things that moods reveal.

A phenomenologist could go through mood after mood and display the character of each as revealing an aspect of Dasein's Being. But Heidegger focuses on one mood in particular, which he thinks has far-reaching implications. Let us sketch his analysis of *anxiety.*

Like all moods, anxiety is cognitively significant; that is, it discloses something. Anxiety is rather like fear; but it would be a big mistake to confuse them. Fear discloses the fearful: some particular threat to a future possibility of Dasein (the charging bull, the assassin relentlessly hunting one down). Anxiety, by contrast, reveals a very general feature of Dasein's Being. Anxiety is directed, not to a particular threatening entity, but to something more fundamental and far-reaching.

> . . . *that in the face of which one has anxiety is Being-in-the-world as such.* (BT, 230)

What is Being-in-the-world? We already know; it is the most basic existential characteristic of Da-

sein. So what Dasein is anxious-in-the-face-of is *itself!* Heidegger is suggesting that anxiety reveals in a peculiarly conspicuous way Dasein's having-to-Be. Ordinarily, average Dasein goes along "absorbed" in the world of its concern, engaged in projects that seem unquestionably to have a point and meaning. But if we remember that the self of everyday Dasein is *the One,* we can see that these projects are those set down by the public world; they have their meaning dictated by the "they." And normally Dasein does not notice this. In its average everydayness, Dasein is delivered over to Being-in-the-public-world-of-already-assigned-significances. Dasein has "fallen-in" with the world of what "One says," what "One does and doesn't do." *

Anxiety, Heidegger suggests, is unique among moods because it is a disclosure of that world *as such.* Unlike fear, in which some entity *within the world* is apprehended as possibly detrimental, the "object" of anxiety is no *thing.* If a person suffering from anxiety is asked what she is afraid of, she replies, "Nothing." And that, Heidegger says, is exactly right; nothing *in the world* is the object of this mood. Rather, that whole system of assignments and references that makes up the worldhood of the world becomes present and *stands over against one.* No longer caught up in it, Dasein beholds it as something alien to itself. Dasein catches sight of itself as Being-engaged in this now alien world of the One. And it shudders.

> In anxiety what is environmentally ready-to-hand sinks away, and so, in general, do entities within-the-world. The 'world' can offer nothing more, and neither can the Dasein-with of Others. Anxiety thus takes away from Dasein the possibility of understanding itself, as it falls, in terms of the 'world' and the way things have been publicly interpreted. Anxiety throws Dasein back upon that which it is anxious about—its authentic potentiality-for-Being-in-the-world. Anxiety individualizes Dasein. . . .
>
> Anxiety makes manifest in Dasein its *Being to-*

---

* It is important to remember that this feature is an *existential*; it is not something Dasein could be without. So it is not something to *blame* Dasein for or to *regret.*

wards its ownmost potentiality-for-Being—that is, its *Being-free* for the freedom of choosing itself and taking hold of itself. (*BT,* 232)

The meaningfulness of the world slips away. Significance vaporizes. The world doesn't exactly become meaningless; it is still *the world* (i.e., a set of in-order-to's). But in anxiety one is detached from it; it means nothing to the particular Dasein that is gripped by anxiety. One can still see others going through the motions, but it seems absurd.* Anxiety distances us from our ordinary everyday *Being-in*. It makes clear that how I am to be is a matter of *choice*—that the responsibility lies squarely with *me*. As Heidegger says, anxiety "individualizes." It separates us out from the One.

Wrenched out of the familiar "falling-in" with the way of the world, Dasein experiences itself as *not-at-home-in-the-world*. Yet, it is essentially nothing but Being-in-the-world! Dasein has no other reality; it cannot repair to its own "substance" or enjoy its own "essence" apart from the world. "Just be *yourself*," we are often advised. But, if Heidegger is right, there is no one for us to be apart from the world of the One! In anxiety, then, Dasein is made aware of that fact, but in the mode of not being at home in it. There is no home but that home, yet, anxiously, we are homeless.†

On the one hand, anxiety reveals with penetrating clarity the nature of Dasein's Being. But on the other hand, it provides a powerful motivation for Dasein to hide itself from itself—to flee back into the comfortable, familiar, well-ordered, meaningful world of the One, to avoid the risky business of taking up responsibility for one's own Being. That is why Heidegger says that Dasein is anxious about its "authentic potentiality-for-Being-in-the-world." Anxiety presents Dasein with the clear choice between existing authentically or inauthentically. The temptation is to flee back into the world, to be reabsorbed in it, to shut one's eyes to the fact that a *decision* about one's way of life is called for. The temptation is to think that our lives are as antecedently well ordered as the career of a hammer—that the meaning of life is *given* and doesn't have to be *forged*. To flee back into the predecided life of the One would "disburden" Dasein and quiet anxiety. But such fleeing on the part of Dasein would be "falling-away-from" itself, the *inauthentic* kind of **falling**.* Falling-away from oneself is the same as falling-prey-to the One. So Dasein "tranquilizes" itself in the familiar world of significance, fleeing *away from* its oneness and its not-at-homeness *into* the world of the One; thus it disguises from itself its true Being (that its Being is an *issue*). We crave a world in which we can say, "I had no choice." And behold, in the world of the One, all crucial decisions are already made, dictated by the norms of what One does and doesn't do. The possibilities open to Dasein are "disposed of" beforehand. One's life is *settled*. And anxiety is covered up.

Moods, then, are cognitively significant; they always tell us something about ourselves and, in particular, about our Being. Among the moods, anxiety most clearly reveals the Being of Dasein—that it is thrown-Being-in-the-world-of-the-One. And in doing so, it both distances Dasein from that Being and provides a motivation for falling back into that world in an inauthentic way.

---

* This is a word that I don't believe Heidegger uses in this context. But it plays a large role in the thought of French existentialist thinkers, such as Sartre and Camus. See, for instance, Sartre's novel *Nausea* and Camus' *The Myth of Sisyphus* and *The Stranger*. Heidegger does not like Sartre's version of existentialism; it essentially preserves rather than overcomes Cartesian dualism, he maintains. But the Heideggerian influence in these thinkers is strong.

† The German word here is "Unheimlichkeit," literally "not-at-homeness." The translators of *Being and Time* bring it into English as "uncanniness." It is perhaps this same sense of homelessness that Augustine has in mind when he prays, "Our hearts find no peace until they rest in you" (p. 241). Unlike Augustine, Heidegger cannot believe that there is a home for us *beyond* the world.

---

* Remember that there are two kinds of "falling": *falling-in-with* is one of the essential characteristics of Dasein, an *existential*. Dasein's "who" is invariably and inevitably the *One*. The second kind of falling, *falling-away-from*, is Dasein's fleeing from the anxious realization of its own essential homelessness into the illusory security that the life of the One seems to offer. Such fleeing is the mark of *inauthentic* existence, of not appropriating the Being that is *one's own*. Heidegger does not always distinguish the two kinds of falling as clearly as one might wish, though there is plenty of support in the text for the distinction.

Understanding

In one way or another, Dasein is always "attuned" to its world. But every attunement carries with it an understanding of that world (and every understanding has its mood); understanding, Heidegger says, is *equiprimordial* with attunement (meaning that they come together and that neither can be derived from the other). We have already met "understanding," of course. Dasein from the beginning has been held to be that being who—simply by virtue of Being—has an understanding of its Being. To be "there," in fact, *is* to understand. But this is hard to—understand. Let us see if we can do so.

We can begin in a very familiar way by examining what we mean when we say that Jane understands carburetors. We mean that she is competent with respect to carburetors, that she can adjust, tune, and repair them. It need not be that Jane could write a book about carburetors; perhaps she couldn't. But if you are having carburetor troubles, Jane is the one for you. She really *understands* carburetors! Now it is crucial to note that *possibility* or *potentiality* is involved in this kind of understanding. Jane can do more than just describe the current present-at-hand state of your carburetor; she can see *what's wrong* with it. And this means that she has in view a potential state of the device that is different from its current state; a possibility that it might function properly. And she has the *know-how* to produce that state. Jane's understanding is a matter of being able to bring it from a condition of not working well to one of satisfactory performance, a possibility not now realized.

This notion of possibility is also involved in the existential understanding that belongs to Dasein. For what does Dasein essentially understand? Itself, in its own Being. Suppose someone (God, maybe) had a list of everything factually true of you at this moment: every hair on your head, the state of every neuron in your brain, and every thought and feeling. Would this list tell us who you are? It would not. It wouldn't, even if it listed every fact about you since you were born. Why not? Because you, as a case of Dasein, are not something present-at-hand, a mere collection of

facts; you are essentially *what you can be.* You are a certain "potentiality-for-Being," to use Heidegger's language. Unless I understand your *possibilities*, I will not understand you.

> . . . Dasein is constantly 'more' than it factually is, supposing that one might want to make an inventory of it as something-at-hand and list the contents of its Being. . . . But Dasein is never more than it factually is, for to its facticity its potentiality-for-Being belongs essentially. (*BT*, 185)

But now let's shift the perspective. Rather than thinking of what would be required for a third party to understand you, think about what is needed for you to understand yourself. Here is the somewhat startling answer: Nothing—beyond your Being-there. To exist *is* to understand.* Understanding (as an *existential*) is having competence over one's Being; that is not something added on "by way of an extra" (*BT*, 183). That is what it is to exist. And this understanding is an understanding of possibility. Right now, at this very moment, you *are* a certain understanding of your possibilities (e.g., the possibility of continuing to read this chapter, of underlining this phrase, of going to the refrigerator for a cold drink, of calling a friend, of becoming an engineer or accountant, perhaps of dropping out of school and bumming around the world). You exist these potentialities in your every thought and movement. And this understanding, which you *are,* is not something that you need to conceptualize or explicitly think about. It just is a certain *competence* with respect to your Being that you cannot help manifesting.

How is it that understanding is a basic part of Dasein, not something added to it? Understanding has the structure of *projection.* We are always projecting ourselves into possibilities. Again, we must be careful not to think of this as a matter of reflecting on possibilities, of reviewing or deliberating, or of having them "in mind." It is more primordial

---

*This is quite compatible, of course, with your *misunderstanding* yourself; a misunderstanding is a kind of understanding. This is why inauthentic existence is one of your possibilities.

than that. To understand a chair, for instance, is to be prepared to sit in it rather than wear it. To understand oneself as a student is to *project* oneself into potentially mastering Chinese or statistics or into the possibility of being a college graduate. Understanding oneself as a student *permeates* one's Being. To exist in a specific situation *is* to have an understanding (or a misunderstanding) of the promise or menace of what is impending. Understanding in this fundamental sense is a matter of our *Being*. It is an aspect of what it means to *exist*. Since we are what we *can be,* possibility is even more fundamental to our Being than the actuality of the facts about us. And these possibilities are not something external to our Being. They are possibilities that we *are*.

This understanding, as a kind of competence with respect to the potentialities of our Being, is always there; just because it is always there, however, it tends to be tacit. But it can be developed more explicitly; it then takes the form of *interpretation*. Interpretation is not something different from understanding; it is understanding itself come to fruition. Consider the light switch in your room, something you understand very well in one sense; you operate with it in such a familiar way that you scarcely notice it; you probably couldn't tell me what its color is. But suppose one day it fails to function. Now its "place" in the functional ordering of the world is disturbed; you had all along been taking its role as equipment for granted—that is, understanding it implicitly. But now it comes to the fore, and you understand it explicitly—*as* a device to transmit electricity. This "as" structure is already implicit in your everyday and familiar understanding. But now it is expressed; it becomes explicit in an *interpretation*. Interpretation always lays bare "the structure of *something as something*" (*BT*, 189).

The fact that interpretation (whether of a device, a text, the meaning of someone's action, and so on) is always founded on a prior understanding has an important implication for Heidegger. There is no way we can disengage ourselves from our Being-in-the-world sufficiently to guarantee a completely "objective" view of something. Every interpretation *always* takes something for granted;

it is worked out on some background that is not itself available for inspection and decision. That does not mean that truth is unavailable to Dasein. But it does mean that Dasein is involved in a kind of circle it cannot get out of.* Interpreting is understanding x as y—for example, the switch *as a* device for controlling the flow of electricity. But interpretation just makes explicit that prior understanding of it *as* a switch in the first place. That understanding is a matter of having a certain competence with respect to it. Such competent understanding is a matter of (largely unreflective) projection, of ways of behaving toward what *could be*. And all this exists only on the background of our Being-in-the-world in general, which involves understanding the potentialities of such equipment as light switches.

This circle is usually called **the hermeneutic circle;** all interpretation is caught up in what is understood beforehand. It is not a vicious circle, Heidegger maintains.[†] But it is one that should be recognized.

If the basic conditions which make interpretation possible are to be fulfilled, this must . . . be done by

---

*It is interesting to compare this point with the pragmatist claim that we must give up the quest for certainty. See Peirce's triangle example on p. 527; the image of sailors on a ship, p. 530; and the summary of Dewey's view of experience, pp. 540–541. Heidegger is here combating the desire of Descartes to find an Archimedean point from which to view the world; there is, Heidegger claims, no "view from nowhere." We can also think of it as an argument against Hume's motto (taken from Newton) to frame no hypotheses (see pp. 347–351). If framing hypotheses is a matter of bringing a certain understanding *to* a situation, then we cannot help framing hypotheses—just as Kant thinks there is no getting around the *a priori* structures that make knowledge possible. There is some justice in viewing the history of modern philosophy as a conversation between the rationalists, the empiricists, and the pragmatists. In this (oversimplified) schema, Heidegger would line up with the pragmatists.

[†]Note that Heidegger grants one of the fundamental claims of the skeptic: The structure of our knowledge does involve a circle. He thinks this isn't damaging because Dasein, as he conceives it, does not have to *break* into the clearing (e.g., by means of some *criterion*); Dasein is already the clearing, the revealing of Being. This doesn't mean, of course, that Dasein always knows the truth; the One and individual Dasein can conspire to cover it up. For the relevance of this circle to skeptical claims, see the discussion of Sextus Empiricus, p. 200. This same problem comes up in Plato and Aristotle. See pp. 119–121, and 154–155.

not failing to recognize beforehand the essential conditions under which it can be performed. What is decisive is not to get out of the circle, but to come into it in the right way. (*BT,* 194–95)

"The right way" is to come without illusions (that is, without imagining that one can get a kind of "bare" look at the object of interpretation) and to be as clear and explicit as possible about what one is bringing to the interpretive task. Part of Heidegger's conviction is that this background can never be made *completely* explicit.* For it is this background that Dasein *is.*

Let us summarize. Understanding, like attunement, is an *existential.* There is no Being-there that does not involve understanding. The primordial mode of understanding is a kind of know-how or competence with respect to things, particularly with respect to Dasein's own Being. This is largely implicit, but it can be spelled out in an interpretation. It is just such an interpretation that Heidegger is striving to construct with respect to the meaning of Dasein's Being and ultimately for the meaning of Being in general.

Discourse

Because the world of Dasein is a world of significations (in-order-to's, toward-which's, and for-the-sake-of's, to put it in Heideggerese), Dasein exists in an *articulated* world; like a turkey, it has "joints" at which it may be carved. The hammer is distinct from the nails but is *for* pounding them into the boards, which are a third articulated item. In understanding how to use a hammer, Dasein displays a primordial understanding of this articulation. As

we have seen, this primitive kind of understanding can be made explicit in interpretation. And now we must add that interpretation itself is a phenomenon *in-the-world* only in terms of *discourse.*

Discourse, Heidegger says, is equiprimordial with attunement and understanding. (Again, this means that while it cannot be reduced to either of them, it is equally basic.) Discourse, too, is an *existential.* It is an essential characteristic of Dasein. There is no Dasein that doesn't *talk.** In talk, or discourse, the articulations of the world of Dasein are expressed in *language.* Moreover, we talk *with one another,* so discourse essentially involves Being-*with.* Discourse involves communication.

> Discoursing or talking is the way in which we articulate 'significantly' the intelligibility of Being-in-the-world. Being-with belongs to Being-in-the-world, which in every case maintains itself in some definite way of concernful Being-with-one-another: Such Being-with-one-another is discursive as assenting or refusing, as demanding or warning, as pronouncing, consulting, or interceding, as 'making assertions,' and as talking in the way of 'giving a talk'. (*BT,* 204)†

Again, Heidegger warns against a misunderstanding.

> Communication is never anything like a conveying of experiences, such as opinions or wishes, from the interior of one subject into the interior of another. Dasein-with is already essentially manifest in a co-state-of-mind [co-attunement] and a co-understanding. In discourse Being-with becomes 'explicitly' *shared;* that is to say, it *is* already, but it is unshared as something that has not been taken hold of and appropriated. (*BT,* 205)

This remark should be understood as part of Heidegger's continuing polemic against the Cartesian

---

*Hubert Dreyfus is the most notable (though not the only) person to apply this point to artificial intelligence. It shows, he believes, that the work in traditional artificial intelligence was bound to fail because it was based on the assumption that all the rules by which an intelligent system operates could be made explicit and operate on items that are context-free (i.e., not in-a-world). If Heidegger is right, this is not true of us and is very likely not true for any system that has more than strictly limited capabilities. You might look at Dreyfus' book, *What Computers Can't Do* (New York: Harper and Row, 1972) and the book he wrote with his brother Stuart (a computer engineer), *Mind over Machine* (New York: Macmillan Co., The Free Press, 1985).

---

*What about newborn babies, you ask? The answer seems to be that while they are clearly human, they are not a case of Dasein. They are not (yet) *there* in that way characteristic of Dasein. As they are socialized, Dasein slowly dawns in them.

†Compare what Wittgenstein says about the ways we use language (p. 581). Heidegger, like the later Wittgenstein, is convinced that philosophy has often been led astray by supposing that *assertion* has first place in discourse.

picture of the isolated subject shut up within the walls of the mind and forced to find some way to "convey" a message across an empty space to another such subject. As Being-with, we already live in a common world with others—the public world of equipment and its structural articulation. In discourse we "take hold" of this common legacy and express it in language.

Falling-Away

With the analysis of the modes of disclosure, the general shape of Heidegger's fundamental ontology is coming into view. Dasein is

- Being-in-the-world
- Being-with-others
- Falling-in-with the One
- Thrown
- A Clearing, manifesting itself in attunement, understanding, and discourse

We also know that Dasein has the potentiality for existing in either an authentic or an inauthentic fashion. We need to understand these alternatives more clearly. Let us begin by discussing inauthenticity.

Dasein *is* Being-in-the-world and as such "falls-in-with" the "others" who constitute "the One." Dasein has no secret, private essence *out of which* it could fall; nor is Dasein initially "innocent," later falling into sin. As long as we are talking about the first kind of falling—falling-in-with—questions of innocence or guilt are not yet in order. This kind of falling is a constitutive, ontological characteristic of what it is to be Dasein.*

---

* Despite Heidegger's protestations, some theologians suggest that we might have here the basis for an interpretation of what the Christian tradition has called "original sin." If there is no "pure" essence of Dasein to be corrupted in the first place, and if—as we will shortly see—the One which becomes the "who" of Dasein is itself inauthentic, how could Dasein *not* be "conceived and born in sin"? Rudolph Bultmann and Paul Tillich are among the theologians who have been strongly influenced by Heidegger. For Augustine on original sin, see pp. 234–235.

In discussing anxiety, we noted that Dasein is tempted to flee its anxious homelessness and *lose itself* in the tranquilizing security of the public world. But Heidegger now wants to go a step farther and claim that simply Being-in-the-world is itself *tempting*. For the world is, after all, the world of the One. And to understand why this might by its very nature tempt Dasein toward inauthenticity, we need to understand the modes of disclosure characteristic of the One. How does *One* understand? How are "they" attuned to their Being? What sort of discourse is Dasein thrown into as it takes up its Being-in-the-world?

Idle Talk

As we have seen, discourse has its Being in language, which expresses the articulations making up the world. Discourse is essentially revealing, disclosing. It opens up the world. But in average everydayness, discourse tends toward being just idle talk.

> We do not so much understand the entities which are talked about; we already are listening only to what is said-in-the-talk as such. What is said-in-the-talk gets understood; but what the talk is about is understood only approximately and superficially. (*BT*, 212)

This is something you can test for yourself. Listen carefully to the conversations that go on among your acquaintances; see how much of their "everyday" talk is just a matter of latching on to "what-is-said" as such, without any deep commitment to the subject matter being discussed or to the truth about it. How much of it is just chatter? Or an attempt to impose opinions on others? How much is what Wittgenstein calls "just *gassing*"? *

> And because this discoursing has lost its primary relationship-of-Being towards the entity talked about, or else has never achieved such a relationship, it does not communicate in such a way as to let this entity be appropriated in a primordial manner, but communicates rather by following the route of *gossiping*

---

* See pp. 562, 571, and 586.

and *passing the word along.* What is said-in-the-talk as such, spreads in wider circles and takes on an authoritative character. Things are so because one says so.

The groundlessness of idle talk is no obstacle to its becoming public; instead it encourages this. Idle talk is the possibility of understanding everything without previously making the thing one's own. (*BT,* 212–13)

It is into the idle talk of the One that Dasein is thrown, when it is thrown into the world.

This way in which things have been interpreted in idle talk has already established itself in Dasein. There are many things with which we first become acquainted in this way, and there is not a little which never gets beyond such an average understanding. This everyday way in which things have been interpreted is one into which Dasein has grown in the first instance, with never a possibility of extrication. In it, out of it, and against it, all genuine understanding, interpreting, and communicating, all re-discovering and appropriating anew, are performed. (*BT,* 213)

Discourse is an existential; it is one of the essential characteristics of Dasein. Dasein is a talking entity. But when Dasein falls-in-with the others in its world, as it must, it also falls-in with this degenerate form of discourse. Note that there is no possibility of extricating ourselves from idle talk. It is the milieu in which we exist. The best we can do is to struggle against it—from within it—toward "genuine understanding." But as long as we remain inauthentically content with what-is-said, idle talk will cover over the meaning of Being, including the meaning of our own Being. That is why Heidegger can say, "Being-in-the-world is in itself tempting" (*BT,* 221).

Curiosity

Dasein, we have said, is in its very Being a "clearing" in the midst of the world. It is a clearing because *understanding* is an aspect of its essence. But in its average everydayness, understanding, too, tends to become shallow and disconnected from Being. As long as we are absorbed in our work,

hammering away on the roof, our understanding is engaged in the project. But when we take a rest, understanding idles. And then it becomes *curiosity.* Curiosity is a concern just to see—but not in order to understand what one sees.

It seeks novelty only in order to leap from it anew to another novelty. In this kind of seeing, that which is an issue for care does not lie in grasping something and being knowingly in the truth; it lies rather in its possibilities of abandoning itself to the world. Therefore curiosity is characterized by a specific way of *not tarrying* alongside what is closest. Consequently it does not seek the leisure of tarrying observantly, but rather seeks restlessness and the excitement of continual novelty and changing encounters. In not tarrying, curiosity is concerned with the constant possibility of *distraction.* Curiosity has nothing to do with observing entities and marvelling at them. . . .* To be amazed to the point of not understanding is something in which it has no interest. Rather it concerns itself with a kind of knowing, but just in order to have known. (*BT,* 216–17)

One is reminded of those folks who visit the Grand Canyon primarily to bring back slides to show their friends. Curiosity and idle talk, Heidegger says, reinforce each other; "*either* of these ways-to-be drags the other one with it" (*BT,* 217). You can see why this is so. If one never tarries anywhere, one's understanding is bound to be expressed in idle talk about what one has "seen." Together, Heidegger wryly remarks, they are supposed to guarantee a "life" which is genuinely "lively."

Ambiguity

Because of the predominance of idle talk and curiosity, ambiguity pervades Dasein's Being-in-the-world. It

soon becomes impossible to decide what is disclosed in a genuine understanding, and what is not. . . .

Everything looks as if it were genuinely under-

---

*At this point Heidegger makes a reference to Aristotle's remark that all philosophy begins in wonder (p. 160). You should also review the "rotation method" from the first part of Kierkegaard's *Either/Or* (p. 443).

stood, genuinely taken hold of, genuinely spoken, though at bottom it is not; or else it does not look so, and yet at bottom it is. (*BT*, 217)

Genuine understanding of something is, of course, difficult. It takes time, patience, and careful attention. But in a day when the results of the most mathematically sophisticated physics are reported in the daily paper in a way that is supposed to inform the average person, who can tell what is truly understood and what is not? Since understanding is the "light of nature" in which beings and Being are "cleared," and since understanding is essential to the very Being of Dasein, a deadly ambiguity seeps into Dasein's existence.

Dasein, in its average everydayness, is *the One*. But the average everydayness of the One is characterized by idle talk, curiosity, and ambiguity. It follows that Dasein

has mostly the character of Being-lost in the publicness of the "they". Dasein has, in the first instance, fallen away from itself as an authentic potentiality for Being its Self, and has fallen into the 'world'. "Fallenness" into the 'world' means an absorption in Being-with-one-another, in so far as the latter is guided by idle talk, curiosity, and ambiguity. (*BT*, 220)

In falling-in-with the way of the world, Dasein tends to fall-away-from itself. While it is important to keep these two notions distinct, one gets the definite impression that Heidegger believes the first invariably brings the second with it. Dasein falls away from itself by failing to grasp its own Being clearly—with understanding. It understands itself the way "they" understand. It even takes its moods, its way of being attuned, from the One—what matters to Dasein is what "they say" matters. Dasein does not decisively seize itself for itself; it lets itself float, lost in the interpretations of the public "they." It is this not being *one's own*, belonging only to the One, that is the heart of inauthenticity. And we all *are* inauthentic in this way.

This idea is driven home by a further reflection about *thrownness*. To this point, we have talked about being "thrown" into the world as if it were an event that happened to us once, at birth. But

Heidegger maintains that we are constantly being thrown into the world.

Thrownness is neither a 'fact that is finished' nor a Fact that is settled. Dasein's facticity is such that *as long as* it is what it is, Dasein remains in the throw, and is sucked into the turbulence of the "they's" inauthenticity. (*BT*, 223)

Dasein remains "in the throw" as long as it *is*. We are constantly being thrown into the world, and the world is always the world of the One. This has important implications for what *authentic* existence might be.

. . . *authentic* existence is not something which floats above falling everydayness; existentially, it is only a modified way in which such everydayness is seized upon. (*BT*, 224)

But we will return to that shortly.

Care

Heidegger's interpretation of the ontology of Dasein is rich and complex. We have explored quite a number of the *existentials*, or "categories" that define its way of Being. At this point, Heidegger asks whether this multiplicity of concepts is founded in a deeper unity. He thinks he can point to a unifying ontological concept, in the light of which all the rest make sense.

The simplified, single phenomenon that lies at the root of Dasein's Being, Heidegger tells us, is *Care*. Care is understood as the ontological structure that makes possible Dasein's everyday *concerns* for its projects, its *solicitude* for Others, even its *willing* and *wishing*. In typical Heideggerian fashion, Care is spelled out as

- Being-ahead-of-itself by projecting toward its possibilities, while
- Being-in-the-world, and
- Being engaged with entities encountered within-the-world.

(This kind of talk should now be making some sense to you; go over these phrases carefully, making sure that it is not simply "idle talk" to you.)

It is important to note that Care is not some special "ontic" attitude that Dasein might occasionally display. Care is the *Being* of Dasein: without care, no Being-there. Care is manifest in all understanding, from the intensely practical to the most purely theoretical. It is present in attunement and in all discourse. Dasein is not fundamentally the *rational animal*, not basically the *ego cogito*, not primarily a *knower*. What is most fundamental to Dasein's Being is caring: Dasein is the being for whom things *matter*.* And that brings us right back to the very beginning, where we noted that Dasein is that being for whom its own Being is *an issue*.

Heidegger supports this interpretation of the unity of Dasein's Being by quoting an old Latin fable about the creation of human beings by the gods:

> Once when 'Care' was crossing a river, she saw some clay; she thoughtfully took up a piece and began to shape it. While she was meditating on what she had made, Jupiter came by. 'Care' asked him to give it spirit, and this he gladly granted. But when she wanted her name to be bestowed upon it, he forbade this, and demanded that it be given his name instead. While 'Care' and Jupiter were disputing, Earth arose and desired that her own name be conferred on the creature, since she had furnished it with part of her body. They asked Saturn to be their arbiter, and he made the following decision, which seemed a just one: 'Since you, Jupiter, have given its spirit, you shall receive that spirit at its death; and since you, Earth, have given its body, you shall receive its body. But since 'Care' first shaped this creature, she shall possess it as long as it lives.' (*BT*, 242)

Not long ago, my wife was recovering from a severe case of flu. Sitting on the sofa in the living room and looking about, she said, "I must be alive; I'm beginning to care that the house is a mess." Heidegger would have liked that.

We have in Care, then, a single, unitary, simple foundation for all the complexities we have so far discovered in the Being of Dasein—and for those still to come. But before we fill in the final bits of the picture, we need to pause a moment to think about *truth*.

Truth

According to the Western philosophical tradition, truth belongs to what is said, to assertions or judgments.* The tradition develops this notion into the idea that in true judgments there is a "correspondence" between the assertion and what it is about; in a similar way, Saint Thomas talks about an "adequation" of the intellect to reality, and others about an "agreement." Heidegger does not want to claim these views are mistaken, exactly. But he does think they are misleadingly formulated and shallow. The problem is one we have met before in our analysis of everydayness: the items involved (assertion and object) are conceived by the tradition as items present-at-hand, when this is not their mode of Being at all.

To mistake their mode of Being makes for insoluble problems; what, after all, *is* it for the assertion "Corn grows in the Midwest" to *agree* with fields of corn in Iowa? As marks on this page, that sentence doesn't seem related at all to what grows around Iowa City. So the tradition feels compelled to *supplement* that present-at-hand item with some mental state (an idea, a concept, an intention, a significant content). But this presents three further problems: (1) Such states are also conceived as something present-at-hand; they just have a different "locus" (in the subject). But is that really their mode of Being? (2) How is the *mental state* related to the *marks on the page*? and (3) Doesn't the same

---

* Some years ago, the rock group Queen recorded a song in which this phrase was repeated: "Nothing really matters." Is this an argument against Heidegger's claim that Care is the essence of Dasein? Not at all. It if were *true* that nothing really mattered, Queen would not bother to sing it in that poignant and nostalgic way they do. They *care* that "nothing matters," thereby proving that something *does* matter.

---

* See Aristotle's incomparable definition of truth, p. 149.

question arise with regard to those mental states: What is it for *them* to "agree" with reality?

In addition, we always have this nagging problem: How could we ever *tell* if our judgments correspond to their objects? *

What is needed, Heidegger is certain, is attention to the *Being* of truth. What mode of Being does truth have? In developing an ontology of truth, Heidegger thinks we can bypass these traditional puzzles and answer the old problem posed so poignantly (or was it cynically?) by Pilate: "What is truth?" (John 18:38).

We already have the clue to untangle this mess. For we know that Dasein *is*, in its very Being, disclosure. In attunement, understanding, and discourse, Dasein *dis*-covers itself, others, the world of equipment, nature, and the present-at-hand. To "be there" is to *uncover* entities.

> To say that an assertion "*is true*" signifies that it uncovers the entity as it is in itself. Such an assertion asserts, points out, 'lets' the entity 'be seen' . . . in its uncoveredness. The *Being-true (truth)* of the assertion must be understood as *Being-uncovering. (BT, 261)*

When I say that a picture is askew (supposing that it is), what I say is true. But its being true is not a matter of two present-at-hand items (my saying and the angle of the picture) having some sort of relation holding between them. It is a matter of my actually uncovering it *as it is*. That my assertion is true is demonstrated when I look at the picture; what I have "put forward in the assertion (namely the entity itself) shows itself *as that very same thing*" (*BT,* 261). What the perceiving confirms is that the assertion is indeed an *uncovering;* it is what it purports to be.

Heidegger does not think of this notion as casting away the traditional view of truth. Rather, he says, thinking of truth as *uncovering* is a way of giv-

---

*This, you will recall, was one of the major motivations leading Kant to his Copernican revolution, in which the problem is "solved" by trying to show that objects are (partially) *constructs* by the judging mind. See pp. 377–378. Representation is a crucial issue in current cognitive science and work in artificial intelligence.

ing that view an ontologically adequate foundation. In fact, he believes that one can detect this view of truth in the earliest pronouncements of the Greeks; only later, with Plato and Aristotle, did the notion of assertions and things "corresponding" come to prominence. This was, in Heidegger's eyes, *not* an advance.

> . . . the ultimate business of philosophy is to preserve the *force of the most elemental words* in which Dasein expresses itself, and to keep the common understanding from leveling them off to that unintelligibility which functions in turn as a source of pseudo-problems. (*BT,* 262)

The "classical" view of truth as a correspondence between two independently existing items is just such a "leveling off" of the primordial phenomenon of uncovering, and it leads to the expected "pseudo-problems."

Being-true, then, is Being-uncovering. It is Dasein that uncovers entities by virtue of Being that clearing, that disclosedness, which comes along with Being-in-the-world understandingly. So Being-true is a way of Being for Dasein.

> *Dasein is 'in the truth.'* This assertion has meaning ontologically. It does not purport to say that ontically Dasein is introduced 'to all the truth' either always or just in every case, but rather that the disclosedness of its ownmost Beings belongs to its existential constitution. (*BT,* 263)

If this sounds too optimistic to be true, remember that Dasein is also falling-away-from itself into the world of the One, where idle talk, curiosity, and ambiguity dominate. So Dasein, while essentially "in the truth" in the sense that it is disclosive in its very Being, is also in "untruth." And in fact, since we are "thrown" into the world of the One, it is untruth that is "closer" to us than truth. In our everydayness

> entities look as if. . . . That is, they have, in a certain way, been uncovered already, and yet they are still disguised.
>
> Truth (uncoveredness) is something that must

always first be wrested from entities. Entities get snatched out of their hiddenness. The factical uncoveredness of anything is always, as it were, a kind of *robbery*. Is it accidental that when the Greeks express themselves as to the essence of truth they use a *privative* expression . . . [a-letheia]? When Dasein so expresses itself, does not a primordial understanding of its own Being thus make itself known—the understanding . . . that Being-in-untruth makes up an essential characteristic of Being-in-the-world? (*BT*, 265)

Remember that in idle talk one tends to listen only to what-is-said. This mode of One's communication in average everydayness covers over phenomena ("disguises" them) while still revealing something. A genuine insight must, after all, be communicated in assertions. But soon the assertions begin to wear out and be taken for granted and only half-understood. They suffer the leveling characteristic of the world of what "they say." As what "they say," the assertions become "what everyone knows" and take on the character first of the ready-to-hand (instruments we can use), and eventually of the present-at-hand. At that point the classical view of correspondence takes over. But if a genuine disclosure is to take place, Dasein must force its way through this everydayness and uncover the phenomenon itself—for itself. This happens in scientific revolutions and (as we will see) in art.

Heidegger finds it significant that the Greek word for truth begins with *a* ("not") and that the middle part of the word *lethe* is the same as the word for forgetfulness. (Lethe is the river in Hades whose water causes those who drink it to forget the past.) So truth is *not-forgetting,* an idea suggesting that what is uncovered is something that was previously forgotten, covered over, hidden.* And Heidegger's view of Dasein as falling (into the world of the One and away from itself) accounts for just such a phenomenon. That is why there is something *violent* about the quest for truth; it is

---

*Perhaps this meaning of the word is connected with Socrates' view that coming to know the truth is a matter of "recollecting" what we once knew in a time before our birth but have since forgotten. See p. 98.

like, he says, robbery. For Dasein must penetrate the fog that rises up around the One—to which fog, remember, each Dasein is also contributing—to "wrest" the truth from entities. Truth is difficult to achieve.

This view of truth as an *existential,* as an essential aspect of Dasein's Being, has interesting consequences for the problem of relativism. Heidegger thinks it enables him to stake out a middle ground between the sophists, skeptics, and relativists on the one hand and the absolutists who talk of eternal truth on the other.

> *'There is'* truth only in so far as Dasein is and so long as Dasein is. Entities are uncovered only *when* Dasein *is;* and only as long as Dasein *is,* are they disclosed. Newton's laws, the principle of contradiction, any truth whatever—these are true only as long as Dasein *is.* Before there was any Dasein, there was no truth; nor will there be any after Dasein is no more. For in such a case truth as disclosedness, uncovering, and uncoveredness, *cannot* be. Before Newton's laws were discovered, they were not 'true'; it does not follow that they were false, or even that they would become false if ontically no discoveredness were any longer possible. . . .
>
> To say that before Newton his laws were neither true nor false, cannot signify that before him there were no such entities as have been uncovered and pointed out by those laws. Through Newton the laws became true; and with them, entities became accessible in themselves to Dasein. Once entities have been uncovered, they show themselves precisely as entities which beforehand already were. Such uncovering is the kind of Being which belongs to 'truth'. (*BT*, 269)

Because Dasein is "in the truth," the uncovering of entities *as they really are in themselves* is a possibility. This possibility, of course, depends on Dasein-like beings: no Dasein, no truth—that is, no uncovering of entities. All truth, as Heidegger says, "*is relative to Dasein's Being*" (*BT*, 270). In a sense, Protagoras was right in saying, "of all things, the measure is man." * But does this mean that truth is *subjective* in the sense that it depends on what a

---

*See p. 41.

given Dasein happens to think? Not at all. For Dasein, in uncovering entities, comes "face to face with the entities themselves" (*BT,* 270). It is true, of course, that each Dasein is "thrown" into a certain language and culture; and each language and culture already has a certain understanding of entities and Being embedded in it. This understanding is always a mixture of truth and untruth. But the possibility of genuine uncovering is given with Dasein's Being; nothing in principle stands between Dasein and the truth.

Moreover, although truth exists only in conjunction with Dasein (so that there are no eternal truths unless Dasein always existed), what is uncovered is uncovered as *already having been there.* So Heidegger is not an idealist who claims that entities are constructions on the part of a subject. The world is revealed as having antedated the emergence of Dasein. But it is revealed only *to* Dasein. Newton's laws *became* true (i.e., dis-covered) in Newton's day; but what these laws tell us, they tell us about those entities that also existed ages before Newton lived.*

Death

In spite of the extensive analysis we have been following, Heidegger is not satisfied that he has explored all the dimensions of Dasein's Being. In particular, it is not clear that we have an understanding of the *totality* of Dasein. Nor has much been said about the character of *authenticity.* So these topics remain. We will first explore the idea of totality.

Is it even possible to understand Dasein *as a whole*? We have seen that Dasein's existence is characterized by projection toward possibilities: at every stage, Dasein is what it is *not yet;* there are always potentialities-for-Being that are yet unrealized. As Heidegger now puts it, this means that there is always "something *still outstanding,*" something "*still to be settled*" with respect to Dasein's Being (*BT,* 279). Can that be brought into our understanding in a way that will give us an interpretation of Dasein as a totality? This obviously brings us to the topic of the *end* of Dasein: to death. It is death that makes Dasein a *whole.* But how is death to be understood?

It seems I cannot experience my own death, since to do so I would have to live through it—and then I wouldn't be dead.*

> When Dasein reaches its wholeness in death, it simultaneously loses the Being of its "there." By its transition to no-longer-Dasein, it gets lifted right out of the possibility of experiencing this transition and of understanding it as something experienced. (*BT,* 281)

Death must be understood in terms of the Being of Dasein; that is, we must understand it in the light of that unitary phenomenon of Dasein's Being: Care. Dasein's death is not just its end in a physical or biological sense. Death, as a *possibility* for Dasein, is something that, in a queer sense, Dasein *lives.* Care, after all, means Dasein's Being-ahead-of-itself in an understanding of possibilities. Dasein *is* its possibilities. And among those possibilities is the possibility that Dasein will die. This is, in fact, a strange possibility, because it is one that Dasein is *bound* to realize. Unlike other possibilities, this is one about which Dasein has no choice. As Heidegger puts it, death is "not to be outstripped" (*BT,* 294).† We are *thrown* into this possibility, with never a chance of extrication.

One of the aspects of Dasein, however, is *falling.*

---

* There are difficult passages where Heidegger says that although *entities* are not dependent upon Dasein, *Being* is. So, he thinks, Being and truth always come together. This is hard to understand; what it means must depend upon the general solution to the question of the meaning of Being.

* There are reported cases, of course, of people who "died" and came back to tell about it. They often tell of experiences they had while they were "dead." But what Heidegger would surely say about these cases is that they are not cases of death but something else. They are not death, because the persons involved did not lose their "Being-there."

† One of my own professors used to say in his raspy voice, "As soon as a man is born, he is old enough to die."

And in falling-away-from itself into the world of the "they," Dasein exists this possibility of death in the inauthentic mode of fleeing-in-the-face-of-it. Everydayness, in various ways, covers over this possibility. The One hides from Dasein the fact that *it* must die. How does it do this? By interpreting death as a mishap, an event, as something present-at-hand—but not yet!

> Death gets passed off as always something 'actual'; its character as a possibility gets concealed. . . . By such ambiguity, Dasein puts itself in the position of losing itself in the "they" as regards a distinctive potentiality-for-Being which belongs to Dasein's ownmost self. The "they" gives its approval, and aggravates the *temptation* to cover up from oneself one's ownmost Being-towards-death. This evasive concealment in the face of death dominates everydayness so stubbornly that, in Being with one another, the 'neighbors' often still keep talking the 'dying person' into the belief that he will escape death and soon return to the tranquillized everydayness of the world of his concern. Such 'solicitude' is meant to 'console' him. . . . In this manner the "they" provides a *constant tranquillization about death*. At bottom, however, this is a tranquillization not only for him who is 'dying' but just as much for those who 'console' him. (*BT*, 297–98)

Everydayness transforms death from one's ownmost possibility into an event which is distant and then says it is nothing to be *afraid* of. But in so tranquilizing Dasein, it closes off the *anxiety* a genuine appropriation of this possibility generates.* Dasein's fleeing in the face of death takes the form of evasion. Our Being is a *Being-towards-death,* but everydayness *alienates Dasein from this Being.* This is one of the modes in which Dasein is in "untruth," since no matter how the One tranquilizes and evades and alienates, Dasein—each of us—will die.

So, our ontological interpretation of Dasein *can* get hold of Dasein as-a-whole; Dasein's Being is a Being-towards-death, in which Dasein's death is understood as a possibility that in each moment is

a defining characteristic of Dasein. Dasein's Being (as a potentiality-for-Being) in a way encompasses its death. Any adequate interpretation of Dasein will necessarily have grasped Dasein's death. Being-towards-death, too, is an *existential.*

The evasion and alienation from oneself typical of absorption in the "they" is a form of inauthentic existence. Is, then, an authentic appropriation of death possible? We know what it would be like. There would be no evasion, no explaining away, no misinterpreting of the mode of Being of death. Death would be steadily apprehended as a possibility of Dasein's Being—not in brooding over it or thinking about it, but existing in every moment in the *anticipation* of death.

> Being-towards-death is the anticipation of a potentiality-for-Being of that entity whose kind of Being is anticipation itself. In the anticipatory revealing of this potentiality-for-Being, Dasein discloses itself to itself as regards its uttermost possibility. (*BT*, 307)

This authentic anticipation of death wrenches Dasein away from the One. It *individualizes* Dasein, brings each Dasein before a possibility that belongs to it alone: it says, "I must die." It forces the realization that one is *finite* and so lights up all the possibilities that lie between the present and death. They, too, are uniquely *mine.* Anticipation grasps both the certainty of death and the uncertainty about when it will come. We are certain to die, but we know not when. Anticipation is a mode of understanding; in anticipation of death, Dasein authentically understands itself as a finite, limited whole. This understanding of itself on the part of Dasein is accompanied by an attunement. (Remember that every understanding has its mood, every mood an understanding.) The mood that accompanies anticipation is *anxiety.* Again, anxiety is displayed as the mood in which Dasein comes face to face with itself—and *doesn't* flee.

> We may now summarize our characterization of authentic Being-towards-death as we have projected it existentially: *anticipation reveals to Dasein its lostness in the they-self, and brings it face to face with the pos-*

---

* See again the contrast between fear and anxiety, pp. 613–614.

sibility of being itself, primarily unsupported by concernful solicitude, but of being itself, rather in an impassioned freedom towards death—a freedom which has been released from the illusions of the "they" and which is factical, certain of itself, and anxious. (BT, 311)

Because anticipation releases us from bondage to the interpretations of the One and puts us "in the truth," we are "freed" to *Be ourselves* as a whole—but only as Being-towards-death. Any evasion casts us back into the "they" and inauthenticity.

Conscience, Guilt, and Resoluteness

Authentic existence is now our theme. But there is a problem. Dasein is caught up in the life of the One, living wholly by what "they say." Remember that there is no private essence to Dasein, no "interior" self with contents of its own. In everydayness, Dasein acquiesces in the way "they" understand its possibilities; it goes-along with the mood and understanding and discourse of the One; it has not "taken hold" of itself. How then does Dasein know there is anything *but* the life of the "they-self"? How does it become *aware* that it is not being *itself* but is fleeing itself by falling-into-the-world inauthentically? What resources does Dasein have to enable it to come to itself in authentic existence?

> . . . because Dasein is *lost* in the "they," it must first *find* itself. In order to find *itself* at all, it must be 'shown' to itself in its possible authenticity. In terms of its possibility, Dasein is already a potentiality-for-Being-its-Self, but it needs to have this potentiality attested. (BT, 313)

What is it that can "show" Dasein to *itself* as a possibly authentic Self? What "attests" to this possibility? The voice of *conscience*, Heidegger says (BT, 313). But we have to be careful here, as elsewhere, not to interpret this "voice" in the way it is ordinarily understood. By now we should be sufficiently on guard: conscience, like understanding, attunement, and discourse, has an everyday form

that hides as much as it discloses. And, in any case, what we are looking for is the *existential ground* on the basis of which ordinary experiences of conscience are *possible*.

So conscience in this existential or ontological sense is not to be identified with that nagging little voice that occasionally tells us we have done something wrong or that warns us not to do what we might like to do. The deep sense of conscience must have the same sort of Being as Dasein; it is not occasional, but constant. It is, moreover, a mode of disclosure, in which something is presented to be understood. So we need an interpretation of this phenomenon that makes clear where this "voiceless voice" comes from, to whom it is addressed, and what it "says."

In the mode of average everydayness, Heidegger says, Dasein is constantly listening. But it "listens away" from itself and hears only the voice of the "they." As a result, it "fails to hear" itself. As we have seen, Dasein *is* the One; each of us is one of "the others" (from whom, for the most part, we do not distinguish ourselves); and this indefinite One is what generally determines how life goes in the world.

Conscience is a "call" to this One (who we are). So conscience is a call to oneself in the mode of the One and is a mode of discourse. But it is a wordless discourse; it does not chastise you for lying, for example. Yet, like all discourse, it has a content. But it doesn't convey information; it is more like a *summons*.

> *What* does the conscience call to him to whom it appeals? Taken strictly, nothing. The call asserts nothing, gives no information about world-events, has nothing to tell. Least of all does it try to set going a 'soliloquy' in the Self to which it has appealed. 'Nothing' gets called to this Self, but it has been *summoned* to itself—that is, to its ownmost potentiality-for-Being. (BT, 318)

As we have seen, Dasein *is* just such a potentiality-for-Being. That is what *existing* is—having certain possibilities in the mode of already-understandingly-being-them. And existence is the essence of

Dasein. But this Being of Dasein is hidden to itself as long as it is governed by the "they." What conscience does is to disclose Dasein to itself as such a potentiality for being. Conscience requires that Dasein *choose* among possibilities. So conscience "calls Dasein forth to its possibilities" (*BT,* 319). In effect, it says, "You cannot hide behind the 'they' any longer; *you* are responsible for your existence!" (In putting words in the mouth of conscience, I am of course falsifying somewhat Heidegger's insistence that the call is "wordless," but not in a damaging way, I hope.)

We now know to whom the call of conscience is addressed: to Dasein in its everydayness. And we know what the call "says": *you must become yourself!* * The call, then, summons inauthentic Dasein to take hold of itself, to take itself over, and in so doing to be itself authentically. But who is doing the calling?

> *In conscience Dasein calls itself.* (*BT,* 320)

Well, we might have known! Still, that is not exactly clear. How can Dasein call itself in this way? If it is Dasein to whom the call comes, how can it be Dasein that is doing the calling? Indeed, as Heidegger acknowledges, the call typically seems to come from *beyond* oneself. It seems to be

> something which *we ourselves* have neither planned for nor prepared for nor voluntarily performed, nor have we ever done so. 'It' calls, against our expectations and even against our will. On the other hand, the call undoubtedly does not come from someone else who is with me in the world. The call comes *from* me and yet *from beyond me.* (*BT,* 320)

This seems phenomenologically accurate; it is the basis, Heidegger suggests, for interpretations of the call as the voice of God or for attempts to give a sociological or biological interpretation of conscience. None of these will do, however, since these causal accounts all try to locate conscience in *something*—that is, in something present-at-

---

* Compare Nietzsche, p. 511 and Kierkegaard, pp. 453–455.

hand. And the call has to have the kind of Being of Dasein.

The puzzle can be solved if we recall the not-at-homeness that is revealed in the mood of anxiety. Anxiety, you will remember, individualizes Dasein, pulls it out of the "they," and makes clear that it is its own *having to be.* In anxiety, Dasein feels alienated from the world of the One, yet recognizes that it has no other home. It comes to understand itself as *thrown into existence.* With this contrast between Dasein as *at home in the world on terms set out by the "they"* and Dasein as *cast out of that familiar home* we can solve the problem. The "it" that calls is "uncanny" Dasein in its mode of not-being-at-home-in-the-world; and "it" calls to Dasein in the mode of the "they," summoning it *to itself.*

And now we can also see why authentic existence is not a wholly different kind of existence than inauthentic but just a modified way in which such everydayness is seized upon. To exist authentically is to take responsibility for the self that one is. And that is inevitably, inextricably, and for as long as one lives, the self that has been (and is being) shaped by the particular "they" into which one has been "thrown." There is no "true self" other than this.

Conscience, then, is a call: a summons. It summons Dasein, lost in the "they," to take up responsibility for itself. It is true that you are not responsible for yourself "from the bottom up," so to speak; you are not responsible for how and where you were "thrown" into existence. But in authentic existence you shoulder the burden. The authentic self does not excuse itself, blaming parents, society, or circumstance for its shortcomings. Authentic Dasein *makes itself responsible;* it says, "Yes, this is who I am, who I have been; and this is who I will become."

Conscience summons Dasein to Be itself, to turn away from the rationalizations and self-deceptions of the "they." It summons lost Dasein back to its thrownness and forth into existence—into an understanding that projects itself into the peculiar possibilities of its own future. The summons issues from Dasein itself. And Dasein hears the verdict: Guilty. Why "guilty"? Because Dasein, in fleeing itself into the world of the "they," has not been what it is now called to; Dasein has not been *itself*. Yet we are not summoned to a kind of wallowing around in self-recrimination; we are to realize our essence—that is, for the first time truly to *exist*.

The existential interpretation of conscience, then, is what "attests" to inauthentic Dasein that there is another possibility and calls it to exist authentically by taking over this having-to-be-itself into which it has been thrown. Dasein takes it over in a certain *understanding* of its own authentic possibilities, in the *mood* of anxiety (since the tranquilizing "they" is set aside), and with a reticence that answers to the wordless *discourse* of conscience. There is nothing to be said; there is everything to be done.

> This distinctive and authentic disclosedness, which is attested in Dasein itself by its conscience—*this reticent self-projection upon one's ownmost Being-guilty, in which one is ready for anxiety*—we call "resoluteness." . . .
>
> In resoluteness we have now arrived at that truth of Dasein which is most primordial because it is *authentic*. (*BT*, 343)

Resoluteness is the term for authentic Being-in-the-world. To be resolute is to *be oneself*. In resoluteness, Dasein exists in that disclosedness which puts it "in the truth." But since what Dasein grasps in the understanding of resoluteness is its own Being-guilty, it understands that in truth it has been, and perhaps will soon again be, "in untruth." *

We can put the results of the last two sections together in the following way. In *anticipation,* authentic Dasein grasps and does not hide its Being-toward-death. In answering the call of conscience, Dasein sets aside the temptations of the One and *resolutely* takes up the burden of Being-itself as thrown, existing, falling, guilty Being-in-the-world. But in resolutely Being-itself, a finite whole, Dasein must anticipate its death. And anticipation, for its part, is not a kind of free-floating imagina-

tion, but a way of Being that has come to itself and has become transparent to itself. So anticipation and resoluteness, if understood deeply enough, imply each other.

In **anticipatory resoluteness,** Dasein comes at last authentically to itself.

We don't often hear Heidegger speak of "joy." But in the section where he discusses anticipatory resoluteness, he writes:

> Along with the sober anxiety which brings us face to face with our individualized potentiality-for-Being, there goes an unshakable joy in this possibility. (*BT*, 358)

Temporality as the Meaning of Care

Imagine that you know a secret and are *very* sure that Peter doesn't know it. But on Thursday afternoon he makes an extremely puzzling remark. At first you can't figure out what his remark *means;* nor (which is not the same) what it *means* that Peter made the remark. But as you think about it, you realize that he must know the secret, too. Only on that background does his remark make any sense. What Peter said is *intelligible* only on that assumption. It is that background—Peter knowing the secret—that made it *possible* for him to say what he did.

This example brings us to Heidegger's sense of *meaning*. This is, of course, an everyday example, and Heidegger's interest is directed to the meaning of Being. That is the fox we have been hunting through all these hills and dales and twisty paths. It is for the sake of uncovering the meaning of Being that Heidegger engages in the analysis of Dasein. But so far we have asked, What is the meaning of *Dasein's* Being? In particular, we have been asking, What is the meaning of everydayness? In asking this, we have been constructing an *ontology*. This ontology (the *existentials*) serves as a background against which the phenomena of average everydayness become *intelligible*. We can now say that it is the articulated structure of Care

---

* See pp. 623–624.

that makes everyday Dasein *possible*. And we can summarize this structure:

- Existence (Being-ahead-of-itself-in projecting possibilities)
- Facticity (thrownness into-the-world and to-ward-death)
- Falling (in-with-the-Others and away-from-itself)

Taken together as a totality, these features define Care as the essence of Dasein's Being. But have we reached rock bottom with the concept of Care? Or can we ask once again, What is the *meaning of Care*? At this point, we need to pay explicit attention to meaning. Heidegger's discussions of meaning are difficult. Here is an example:

> What are we seeking ontologically with the meaning of care? What does "*meaning*" signify? . . . meaning is that wherein the understandability of something maintains itself—even that of something which does not come into view explicitly and thematically. "Meaning" signifies the "upon-which" of a primary projection in terms of which something can be conceived in its possibility as that which it is. Projecting discloses possibilities—that is to say, it discloses the sort of thing that makes possible. (*BT*, 370–71)

That is hard to understand. But if you think back to our example, you should be able to grasp it. What does it *mean* that Peter makes this remark? To uncover the meaning of the remark, we "project" his remark on a background (or larger context) that makes it understandable—that is, that Peter knows the secret. This background is that "upon which" we project Peter's remark. In this larger context, Peter's remark makes perfect sense; it is meaningful. So meaning is "that wherein the understandability" of the remark "maintains itself."

Moreover, it seems that only if Peter knows the secret is it *possible* for him to say what he does. So "projecting discloses possibilities"—the "sort of thing that makes possible." It is Peter's know-

ing the secret that makes possible his saying what he does.

Here is another analogy. Some think that human life is meaningful only if it is projected on a larger background, perhaps of immortality or divine purposes. In that context life has, perhaps, the meaning of a *test*. Without such a background, they say, life is meaningless—pointless. The meaningfulness of life is possible only if it is embedded in a larger context. Whether this is so is an interesting question we will not directly address (though Heidegger's views are relevant to an answer). But the sense of meaning is the same as the one in Heidegger's question about the meaning of Care—and, ultimately, of the meaning of Being.

So if we are now asking about the meaning of Care, we are asking about a deeper background, or larger context, in the light of which the phenomenon of Care becomes intelligible. We are asking about that upon which Care can be projected to make it understandable and to show it as possible. Is there a still more fundamental (more primordial) structure to Dasein's Being that makes possible existence, facticity, and falling? That is the question.

We are still not ready for the general question about the meaning of Being. But what can be said about the meaning of Care? Heidegger takes as his clue the Being of Dasein when it is most "true," or most itself: authentic existence. (This is legitimate, since the other modes of Dasein's Being have been displayed as a falling-away from this truth; even though inauthentic everydayness is the mode of Being that is "closest" to us, it is nonetheless *ontologically* derivative.) We have seen authentic existence spelled out in terms of anticipatory resoluteness. Anticipatory resoluteness, for its part, is

> Being towards one's ownmost, distinctive, potentiality-for-Being. (*BT*, 372)

What makes this "Being towards" possible? Time—and in particular, the future.

For anticipatory resoluteness to be *possible,* it must be that Dasein is in itself, in its very Being, *futural*—temporal. This doesn't mean that Dasein is "located" in time, any more than Dasein's Being-in-the-world means that Dasein is "located" in an objective space.* Dasein is "futural" in that it *comes towards itself* in that projecting of possibilities that defines existence. Dasein is always ahead-of-itself-in-time.

We have seen that anticipatory resoluteness also fastens onto itself as Being-guilty. Dasein takes over its facticity—makes its thrownness its own—by taking responsibility for itself.

> But taking over thrownness signifies *being* Dasein authentically *as it already was*. . . . Only in so far as Dasein *is* as an "I-*am*-as-having-been", can Dasein come towards itself futurally in such a way that it comes *back*. Anticipation of one's uttermost and ownmost possibility is coming back understandingly to one's ownmost "been." Only so far as it is futural can Dasein *be* authentically as having been. The character of "having been" arises, in a certain way, from the future. (*BT*, 373)

You "are" your possibilities. But what these possibilities are depends on what you have been. You can only project yourself authentically into the future by "coming back" to yourself as having been something.

What does it mean, though, that this "having been" itself arises from the future? That seems strange. I think we can understand Heidegger's thought here in this way. What you have been (and now are, as a result) is not just a set of dead facts. These facts take life and meaning from your projects. You are now, let us say, a college student; as each moment slips away, this is something you have been. But *have you been* preparing for a job? Or *have you been* learning to understand yourself? Or laying a foundation for a scholarly life? Or inching up the ladder of monetary reward? Four people who answer these questions differently might have taken exactly the same courses and read exactly the same books to this point. But the *meaning* of what they have done is radically different; it is projected against a different background (and notice that each background essen-

tially makes reference to the future!). Because the meaning of what they have done is different, what they "have been" is also different. The difference is defined by the different futures they project. That is how the character of "having been" arises from the future.* We can now see that since it is futural, Dasein also essentially has a past. But once again we must be careful. This is an *existential* past, not one that is composed of moments that have added up and then dropped away into nothingness. It is a past that one constantly *is*.

Finally, anticipatory resoluteness plants one firmly in the current situation. It does not live in daydreams or fantasy; it is not lost in nostalgia. Authentic Dasein resolutely takes action in the light of an attuned understanding of its potentialities and its having been. It encounters what *has presence* by *making present* the entities that define its situation and dealing with them. An unblinkered, clear, disclosive *sight* of what is present is essential to Dasein's authentic appropriation of itself.

> Only as the *Present* in the sense of making present, can resoluteness be what it is: namely, letting itself be encountered undisguisedly by that which it seizes upon in taking action. (*BT*, 374)

Those who live in illusion do not act decisively and effectively, because they do not "make present" the entities about them; they veil them over and hide them, fantasize and misunderstand them.[†] Authentic "making present" is the existential meaning of the Present as a mode of temporality. This present is not a neutral "now," through a series of which a life must pass. It is not just the knife-edge dividing future from past. It is the rich activity of

---

*Review the discussion of Being-in on p. 603.

*For reasons like this, Sartre claims that we are *radically free* and that any kind of causal determination of our actions is ruled out. If what we have been depends on what it means, and if what it means depends on what we project ourselves to be in the future, then there is no neutral causal description "at-hand" to serve as a basis for deterministic laws. If Heidegger is right, there is no call for the reconciliation projects of Hume and Kant, since the kind of causal determinism with which freedom needs to be reconciled cannot even gain a foothold. But is he right? (See pp. 362–364 for Hume and pp. 395–398 for Kant.)

[†] Compare Kierkegaard on despair, pp. 453–455.

authentic dealing with things by *making-present* the things that are, in the light of our potentialities and what we have been.

And now we can say that

Temporality reveals itself as the meaning of authentic care. (BT, 374)

So that "upon which" Care becomes intelligible is the structure of temporality. Temporality involves projecting into the future, coming back to one's past, and making present. It is important to note that this structure is not itself an entity; it is not a thing or a being. Most importantly, it is not like an empty container in which temporal items can be placed.* Temporality is the most fundamental structure of Dasein's Being-there. Dasein is essentially temporal and essentially *finite*, since authentic Dasein anticipates its end in death. Time, in the sense of existential temporality, is the framework within which something like Care is possible. Time is, to put it in Heidegger's terms, the *horizon* of Dasein's Being. Just as whatever is visible to you now is within the horizon, the framework of temporality defines the horizon for Dasein. All the features of Dasein's Being we have examined are possible only against this background.

Heidegger's analysis of Dasein is now virtually complete. Not much needs to be said about birth as the beginning of Dasein, except that between birth and death Dasein "stretches itself along" (*BT*, 423). One gets the image of a rubber band fastened down at birth and stretching out towards the future. Dasein is at any moment not just what it is *then*, but also what it has been and will be. This "connectedness" of Dasein in its stretching along Heidegger calls *historicality*. And he thinks the proper understanding of that phenomenon—enlightened by the entire analysis of the Being of Dasein—is essential to the proper writing of "history." These are interesting matters, but we will

stop here and turn to the big question for which all this has been preliminary: the question about the meaning of Being.

The Priority of Being

I write about the thought of the later Heidegger with some caution. If you thought things were difficult to this point, try to read some of the later essays, which contain sentences one can read over and over with hardly a glimmer of an idea of what they might mean.* Part of the difficulty, too, is that Heidegger's thought undergoes some development from the early 1930s until the time near his death in 1976, but he almost never acknowledges that it does. Moreover, he looks back to *Being and Time* and reinterprets some of the things he said there— but without admitting that this is what he is doing. He says over and over that the understanding of the *question* is the most important thing and stresses the tentativeness of his formulations. And he uses the same terms in somewhat different ways in different periods, again without telling us that this is what he is doing.

But throughout he insists that he is always trying to say the same thing: to give expression in language to the *meaning of Being*. And he maintains that what he is trying to say is very *simple*. It is its simplicity, in fact, that is the cause of so much obscurity. He even suggests occasionally that the proper way to express what he wants to say is through *silence*.† Yet he writes a great deal, struggling again and again to put it in words. Certain lines of thought do stand out with some clarity, and I will try to give you some idea of how the problem about the meaning of Being fares after the period of *Being and Time*.

---

*Clock time, or ordinary everyday time, which looks rather like this, is the result of a kind of "leveling off" of this rich existential temporality. It gets a kind of objectivity in much the same way that present-at-hand items do: by abstracting away the meaningfulness of Dasein's Being-in-time.

---

*Consider the last sentence in a lecture called "The Turning": "May world in its worlding be the nearest of all nearing that nears, as it brings the truth of Being near to man's essence, and so gives man to belong to the disclosing bringing-to-pass that is a bringing into its own." This work can be found in *The Question Concerning Technology: Heidegger's Critique of the Modern Age*, translated by William Lovitt (New York: Harper and Row, 1977).
†Compare Wittgenstein on the unsayable, pp. 567–568.

I will simplify all this drastically and focus on one central theme. We are reminded of this theme in an image that Heidegger borrows from Descartes, the image of philosophy as a tree.* The roots of the tree, Descartes says, are metaphysics, the trunk is physics, and all the other sciences are the branches.

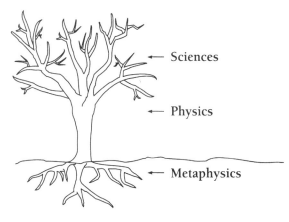

← Sciences

← Physics

← Metaphysics

Heidegger accepts this image. But what he wants to ask about (and has been asking about since the first page of *Being and Time*) is the *ground* in which the roots are sunk. Metaphysics is concerned with *beings, entities, substances, things*. It wants to know what kinds of entities there are and whether there is an ultimate explanation for them (perhaps in God, the "highest being"). Metaphysics is more general than the special sciences and goes deeper. Each science deals with a certain *kind* of being and orders it, describe it, and gives an account of how and why it changes. Biology deals with living things, for example, history with historical things; metaphysics, by contrast, deals with things or substances in general. But everywhere, in science and in metaphysics alike, beings (entities) are the focus of attention.

Beings always appear, says Heidegger, in the light of *Being*. Amoeba *are*, and biology can tell us a lot about them; but biology does not tell us what it means for amoeba to *be*. A mountain *is*, and geology can explain how it came to have the shape it

has; but geology does not explain what it is for a mountain to *be*. It may be that Platonic Forms *are*, that Aristotelian substances *are*, that Augustine's God *is*, that Cartesian minds *are*, that Hobbesian matter *is*, that the Hegelian subject-Spirit *is*, and so on, throughout the history of the great conversation. What makes all these entities available for investigation and understanding (if they are) is that they *are*. But if Heidegger is right, in no case has a metaphysician directly approached the question of *what that means*. What does it *mean* for something—anything—to *Be*? This, he thinks, is the question he alone first asks.

Note again that *this* question is not answered by an appeal to God or a first cause understood as the highest being. If such a first cause *is*, the very same question applies to it. What does it mean for God to *Be*? As we have seen, the published parts of *Being and Time* are devoted to what Heidegger calls "fundamental ontology," an analysis of that peculiar entity whose very mode of Being involves an understanding of what that means—even if that understanding is inadequate and distorted. A quick review of the results will be useful.

*   *Temporality* makes possible
*   *Care,* which is the essence of
*   *Dasein,* which is a
*   *Clearing,* in the light of which there come to presence
*   *Beings* (Dasein itself, the ready-to-hand, and the present-at-hand, each of which has a mode of
*   *Being* (Care, Functionality, Objectness).

Temporality (primordial time) is the meaning of Dasein's Being—that is, the deepest structure in Dasein through which everything else is seen to make sense. By projecting itself into future possibilities while being firmly anchored in the past of its thrownness, Dasein makes present the situation in which it acts and stretches itself along, caringly, in time. The published parts of *Being and Time* end with the suggestion that this primordial temporality might be the horizon for understanding Being itself. So time might be not only the meaning of Dasein's Being, but also of Being in general. And the title of the book makes one think that this is how the unpublished part would have gone.

Now what's wrong with this? Why does Heidegger not follow out this lead and publish the rest of what he had planned to write? What causes this "turn" in his thinking? I think the answer must be that the pattern in this thinking makes Being too dependent on Dasein. And there are two things wrong with this.

1. It is too subjective. Throughout *Being and Time*, Heidegger struggles against subjectivism in philosophy, against the idea that Being is somehow dependent on the subject. The whole analysis of Dasein as a clearing and as Being-in-the-world is designed to show that the terror of being trapped inside our own minds is a "put-up job," the solipsistic consequence of a mistaken starting point. Dasein is *in its very essence* beyond itself, transcendent, *in* the world among entities. But now at the end it suddenly looks as though subjectivism has not been escaped at all. If the meaning of Being is time and if time is a structure of Dasein's Being, then it seems obvious that Being itself is dependent on Dasein's understanding of it.

2. It is too *metaphysical*. Dasein is after all a being, one entity among others. And if Being itself is dependent on Dasein, then it seems the metaphysical pattern of trying to find a ground for Being *in some entity* is repeating itself in Heidegger's thought. And this is intolerable! His objection to traditional metaphysics is that it neglects Being by concentrating on beings, searching *among beings* for a ground or first principle that accounts for them. In a way, this outcome of *Being and Time* is even worse. Traditional metaphysics, in Heidegger's view, is *oblivious* of the question about Being. He, by contrast, devoting all his intellectual energies to clarify the meaning of Being, has fallen directly into the metaphysical trap.

So a new direction is called for. It is not that the work done in *Being and Time* has to be repudiated, but that it all gets transposed into a new key. Without exactly taking anything back, everything is transformed. Let me try to say how. Dasein is no longer thought of as fundamental in the project to discern the meaning of Being, so the notion of a "fundamental ontology" disappears. The term "Dasein" itself tends to give way to the term "man," or "human being." And the human being now is thought of not as "a clearing," but as one element in a clearing that is now called *the truth of Being*. The other elements of the truth of Being are variously identified but always involve time and Being itself. The idea in *Being and Time* that truth is a kind of "robbery," that it has to be "wrested" resolutely out of its hiddenness, is replaced by the notion that truth is a gift we need only receive. The Open, the Clearing, the Unhiddenness of Being is not something we have to create, just to recognize (not that this is easy). And the initiative is not with us; it is on the side of Being, which "sends" to us various ways of unveiling itself. These various "sendings" of Being constitute historical epochs, which are defined by the understanding of Being they have. And what "they say," the opinion of the faceless "one," is replaced by the very particular and specific understanding of Being in an epoch—for example, in our day. Authentic existence, too, is transformed; the focus is not on the anxious individual who has to appropriate the self in anticipatory resoluteness, but on Being, which graciously "calls" or offers itself. And the thought is that if this call could be accepted, the very essence of the human being might alter. The key throughout is that the priority and the initiative shift from the human being to Being.

But we need to fill in at least some of the details that constitute this "turn." A good place to start is Heidegger's understanding of the present age. It is an age dominated, he says, by science and technology. This is a kind of truism, but Heidegger understands this in a peculiar way, one we need to grasp.

We often think of technology as a matter of instruments we can use for one purpose or another. Sometimes we hear that technology in itself is "neutral" and can be used for either good or evil, just as a poison may be used to kill disease-infested rats or one's wealthy aunt Matilda. That is not a mistaken way to think about technology, but, Heidegger claims, it is shallow. It may be "correct," but is it "true"? Does it disclose the *essence* of technology? Today we are battling many ills brought on by technology: air and water pollution, the population explosion, the extinction of species, the depletion of the ozone layer, waste disposal, the threat of nuclear war. But we tend to think that we can master them: what we need is more and better technology! So we equip our cars with catalytic converters and spend much money on antiballistic missile systems. We think we can *master* technology by devising technological "fixes" for technological problems.

But what, Heidegger asks, if the essence of technology is not this business of devising means to desired ends? What if technology is fundamentally something quite different? What if technology is basically a way of revealing, of bringing forth, of unconcealing? What if technology were a "place"— a clearing—where *truth* happens?

And so in fact it is. What is distinctive about *modern* technology is that it does not just use means that nature supplies, as the windmill makes use of the wind. What it does is *store up* energy in a way the older technology could not. It is

> a challenging, which puts to nature the unreasonable demand that it supply energy which can be extracted and stored as such.
> . . . a tract of land is challenged in the hauling out of coal and ore. The earth now reveals itself as a coal mining district, the soil as a mineral deposit. . . . Agriculture is now the mechanized food industry. Air is now set upon to yield nitrogen, the earth to yield ore, ore to yield uranium, for example; uranium is set upon to yield atomic energy, which can be released either for destruction or for peaceful use. (*QCT,* 296)[2]

Technology reveals *everything* as what Heidegger calls the **standing-reserve.** What is characteristic of this mode of openness is that everything presents itself as something to be "set upon" and "ordered" and "stored" for *use.* He gives a particular example.

> The hydroelectric plant is set into the current of the Rhine. It sets the Rhine to supplying its hydraulic pressure, which then sets the turbines turning. This

turning sets those machines in motion whose thrust sets going the electric current for which the long-distance power station and its network of cables are set up to dispatch electricity. In the context of the interlocking processes pertaining to the orderly disposition of electrical energy, even the Rhine itself appears to be something at our command. . . . What the river is now, namely a water-power supplier, derives from the essence of the power station. In order that we may even remotely consider the monstrousness that reigns here, let us ponder for a moment the contrast that is spoken by the two titles: "The Rhine," as dammed up into the *power* works, and "The Rhine," as uttered by the *art* work, in Hölderlin's hymn by that name. But, it will be replied, the Rhine is still a river in the landscape, is it not? Perhaps. But how? In no other way than as an object on call for inspection by a tour group ordered there by the vacation industry. (*QCT,* 297)

What is "monstrous" about this is not that the Rhine supplies power, but that whatever we behold presents itself as "standing reserve," something to be mastered and ordered, to be unlocked and exposed, to be set upon and challenged to provide "the maximum yield at the minimum expense" (*QCT,* 297). What the Rhine *is,* within this mode of revealing, is *defined* by the possibility of damming it up for power. Imagine a lovely valley being "challenged," "set upon," to supply lots for subdivisions for suburban housing. This valley is "standing-reserve" for development. If we were to use the terminology from *Being and Time,* we could say that this is just the way "One" sees it or that this is how "they" now experience the world.*

But putting it that way makes it seem as though this way of experiencing the world is in our control, as though we can simply change it if we wish to. Heidegger does not believe this is so.

> Who accomplishes the challenging setting upon through which what we call the real is revealed as standing-reserve? Obviously, man. To what extent is man capable of such a revealing? Man can, indeed, conceive, fashion, and carry through this or that in one way or another. But man does not have control

---

*Review the discussion of Dasein as "the One," pp. 608–611.

over unconcealment itself, in which at any given time the real shows itself or withdraws.

Wherever man opens his eyes and ears, unlocks his heart, and gives himself over to meditating and striving, shaping and working, entreating and thanking, he finds himself everywhere already brought into the unconcealed. The unconcealment of the unconcealed has already come to pass whenever it calls man forth into the modes of revealing allotted to him. (QCT, 299–300)

I cannot decide to "unconceal" the real; nor can you; nor can we together. Nor can we simply decide to reveal it in a new and different way. That is not something in our power. As soon as we meditate or strive, shape or work, ask or thank, as soon as we do anything at all we are *already* within the clearing of unconcealment. (This corresponds to Dasein's being "in the truth" in *Being and Time*.) A certain "mode of revealing" has been "allotted" to us. We have not *decided* to see things in this technologically relevant way; that is the way they *present* themselves to us. The origins of a revealing are not more in our control than the thrownness of Dasein.

Heidegger calls this challenging of nature that orders it as the storehouse of standing-reserve **enframing.** Enframing is a mode of disclosure, of revealing the real. It reveals the real as orderable for use. Enframing, while itself nothing technological in the ordinary sense, is the *essence* or *meaning* of technology. It is what makes ordinary technology possible. If you recall our discussion of "meaning," you can see that to call enframing the meaning of technology is to say that enframing is "that wherein the understandability of [technology] maintains itself" (*BT*, 370). We live in a technological world in precisely this sense: that everything in it is revealed as standing-reserve. This is *our* meaning for Being.

It has not always been so, of course. Other epochs have experienced the world differently. And this fact suggests that the "revealing" characteristic of our time, enframing, hides as much as it discloses. We are "in untruth" as well as in the truth. What accounts for the different ways in which Being presents (and hides) itself in different

ages? Heidegger's answer is that there is *no explanation* for this. Whatever explanations we have already presuppose a certain revealing of reality; they are internal to a mode of grasping Being. In our case, explanations have the scientific/technological character they do because they are internal to enframing. They *express* our fundamental relation to reality, so they cannot *explain* it.*

Enframing is our *destiny*. We are ourselves "challenged forth" to order things in the mode of standing-reserve. This *comes* to us; we do not invent it. It is *given* to us. It is "too late" to ask whether we should or should not approach reality this way. The Greeks did not *decide* to experience reality as *physis*, a kind of production (Aristotle's actualization of potentialities), a *bringing forth* of things into appearance—as opposed to *challenging forth*. It was not up to the Medievals to understand reality as the creation of almighty God; this way of experiencing things seemed so natural that it was hard to imagine it could be otherwise. Nor was it the conscious decision of those early Moderns who applied calculation to nature to experience the world as a world of *objects*. These ways of unconcealing are "sent" to us; we participate in them without ever having them totally in our power. And no *reason* can be given for the shifts from one mode of revealing to another.

Heidegger uses the word "monstrous" in his description of the Rhine as a power source. We need to say a bit more about this. Any "destining" of a mode of revealing brings along with it a *danger*. Within a given revealing, much that is correct may be asserted; however, the danger is that "in the midst of all that is correct, the true will withdraw" (*QCT*, 308). With respect to enframing, this danger is intensified; in fact, Heidegger thinks enframing is so dangerous that it is worthy of being called "the supreme danger" (*QCT*, 308). What is this danger?

---

*Compare the later Wittgenstein's remarks about justification coming to an end and about the "spade turning" on "what I do." See pp. 588 and 593. Heidegger sees a kind of "history of Being" in the successive modes of its being revealed. This reminds us of Hegel—except that there is no dialectical necessity posited for the shifts.

This danger attests itself to us in two ways. As soon as what is unconcealed no longer concerns man even as object, but exclusively as standing-reserve, and man in the midst of objectlessness is nothing but the orderer of the standing-reserve, then he comes to the very brink of a precipitous fall, that is, he comes to the point where he himself will have to be taken as standing-reserve. Meanwhile, man, precisely as the one so threatened, exalts himself to the posture of lord of the earth. In this way the illusion comes to prevail that everything man encounters exists only insofar as it is his construct. This illusion gives rise in turn to one final delusion: it seems as though man everywhere and always encounters only himself. Heisenberg has with complete correctness pointed out that the real must present itself to contemporary man in this way. *In truth, however, precisely nowhere does man today any longer encounter himself, i.e., his essence.* . . .

Thus, the challenging-enframing not only conceals a former way of revealing, bringing-forth, but it conceals revealing itself and with it that wherein unconcealment, i.e., truth, comes to pass. (QCT, 308–9)

We are back again to the forgetfulness of Being with which *Being and Time* begins, but now it is in a different guise. The danger in enframing is twofold, Heidegger tells us.

1. We ourselves may be taken simply as standing-reserve, to be ordered forth for use.* But as we relate to ourselves in this technological/scientific way, we miss what is peculiar to us: our essence, our Being-open (what Heidegger earlier calls Dasein). Heidegger goes as far as to say that *nowhere* do we today encounter ourselves in this essence. Enframing is a drastic and extreme mode of *hiding* our Being from ourselves.

2. Since everything looks like material-for-use ordered by our science and technology, it seems we *nowhere* can get beyond ourselves: again, subjectivism triumphs! And this, Heidegger consis-

---

*Compare Kant's distinction between persons and things, and his second formulation of the categorical imperative: that rational beings must never be used as means only, but always treated as an end. (See p. 407.) Enframing human beings means taking them to be available as standing-reserve for use, not respecting them as persons.

tently holds, is a "delusion." Enframing exalts man to the position of "lord of the earth" and so *misses* the phenomenon of enframing as itself a mode of revealing—as a way the truth of Being is made manifest. We are plunged so deep in enframing that it is difficult for us to realize that this is what we are doing. Again we "forget" our Being and the fact that other modes of revealing are possible.

Enframing blocks the shining-forth and holding sway of truth. The destining that sends into ordering is consequently the extreme danger. What is dangerous is not technology. Technology is not demonic; but its essence is mysterious. The essence of technology, as a destining of revealing, is the danger. . . .

The rule of enframing threatens man with the possibility that it could be denied to him to enter into a more original revealing and hence to experience the call of a more primal truth. (QCT, 309)

Heidegger is not purely negative about science and technology. For one thing, it *is* a way in which entities become "unhidden." He allows that results in the sciences may be "correct." For another, the technological/scientific way of understanding reality is, he thinks, the legitimate heir of the entire Western philosophical tradition. Philosophy has always been, in Heidegger's view, fundamentally metaphysics. As the individual sciences mature and separate from their mother, as they set up business on their own (or, to use Descartes' image, as the branches of the tree flourish), they take over the task of telling us what entities there are in reality. *This* job can now be done *better* by the scientist in the laboratory than by the metaphysician in an armchair. As Heidegger tells us more than once, philosophy as metaphysics is *finished*. And we are left with enframing, which is the way we have been granted to understand what there is.

So technology and its companion, modern science, have a positive role to play. They constitute the "extreme danger," however, in what we might call their "imperialism": in the claim that there is no other way to reveal reality than this. Remember, this is *our* way of experiencing the world, one we cannot simply step out of, any more than the authentic individual of *Being and Time* has a private reality into which she can repair to "be herself," leaving behind the world of the "One."

But now Heidegger quotes the poet Hölderlin.

But where danger is, grows
The saving power also. (*QCT*, 310)

As the *extreme* danger, enframing seems to close off all modes of revealing but itself. But if we can just concentrate our attention on enframing's *being a revealing* we may catch sight of *its coming to presence*. This attempt to let Being *Be* and to express it in language Heidegger calls *thinking*. This may not seem very illuminating, since we imagine that thinking is something we all do every day. But he (typically) understands thinking in a very particular and peculiar way. Thinking is *recalling Being out of its hiddenness*. It is through this kind of thinking that we may come to understand ourselves as part of that "constellation" in which modes of revealing are "sent" or "granted" to humans, in which beings are lighted up in their becoming *present*. Philosophy and metaphysics, then, must be *replaced* by thinking. And thinking must *supplement* enframing.

And yet this way of putting it is still too subjective. It makes it seem as though this "turning" toward the presence of things is something that is up to us. It makes it seem as though we can just *decide* to think. But even this turning is a granting we cannot manage by ourselves; it is one we can at most be ready for.*

We can ask, though, where we might look for such a revealing of the Being of things and ourselves. Heidegger has two answers to this question: in the thinking of the thinker and in poetry and art. We cannot discuss his understanding of art in detail here. But it is significant, he thinks, that the Greek word for art is *techne*. In the "technology" of the artist, however, what is produced is not something for use, to be stored and transformed and used up. What is produced is a *work*. A work *stands there*. In and through the work, a *world* opens up; and a world is (roughly) the way things present themselves. So art, too, is a mode of unveiling, revealing, unconcealing. But it is not a challenging, a forcing, an imposing and mastering of things. Rather, it *lets things appear* as they are. And in being a *work*—that is, something that has been *worked* into being—it reveals its *presencing* of the world in a way that enframing finds hard to do.

Art is a

"letting happen of the advent of the truth of beings, . . . the setting-into-work of truth. (*OWA*, 184)[3]

Art "opens up a world" (*OWA*, 169); it *lets the truth happen*. It is truth setting *itself* into the work to reveal a world. Art, moreover, is not concerned (or should not be concerned) with the beautiful, which is just a by-product. In the form of a Greek temple, or in Hölderlin's poetry, art unveils the Being of things. Art is a matter of truth.

But again, we must be careful. For great art is no more a matter for individual decision than any mode of revealing is. Notice that art is understood as the setting-*itself*-into-work of truth. Art is not entirely in the control of the artist, any more than we are in control of enframing. Talk of the "muses" may be an expression of this idea. The work is *given* to the artist, and through the artist to us. Art, too, is a gift, a granting of unveiledness that the human cannot be the master of.

We have spoken again and again of a "sending" or a "destining" of a "gift" that must be received and cannot be forced, invented, or created. Every mode of revealing, Heidegger holds, has this character. Let us now, at the end of our consideration, ask, Who does the sending? From whom is this gift received? In asking this question, we approach the clearest answer Heidegger has given as to the *meaning of Being*. Here is his most explicit statement.

From the dawn of Western-European thinking until today, Being means the same as presencing. . . . Being is determined as presence by time.[4]

---

*You might like to compare the contrast between the early and the late Heidegger (between anticipatory resoluteness and receptive openness) with the contrast between Pelagius and Augustine. See pp. 240–241. There are also obvious echoes of Plato's Myth of the Cave, in which what is required is a *turning* away from shadows toward the light of the sun (pp. 122–124).

Again, Heidegger reminds us that we must not think of Being as a *thing* (or entity). Nor is time a *thing*. Nor is it strictly correct to say that Being *is*.* What there *is* are things: this book is, the sun is, your sister is. Being is what these entities *have*. But to say that they have it suggests again that it is a *thing*, like the purse or credit card that you have, or a property they might have or lack, like being brown or heavy. But neither of these can be right. See how hard it is to say what Heidegger wants to express!

Being is not what is present. Being, he tells us, is the *presencing* of things. The notion of "presencing" seems clearly to involve time. Presencing is "making-present" or (better) "letting-be-present." But it would be a mistake, too, to think that Being—presencing—is itself temporal. What is temporal (in time) are entities: this book, the sun, your sister. These things begin, are present for a while, and end. Entities (beings) have a past, a present, and a future.

Nor is time something temporal. Time does not "have" a past, a present, and a future—though my car does. Nor is it strictly correct to say of time that it *is*. Entities *are*. But entities are—*in time*.

Entities *are* precisely in their *presencing*. And presencing is being-present. And being-present is one mode of temporality, or time. So it is *Being* and *Time*, or *Time* and *Being*, after all—but without the priority given to Dasein! And yet presencing must involve that which is open to and receives it; Being involves humans. You can see how Heidegger is struggling to clarify and understand in an authentic way the relations of Being, beings, humans (or Dasein), and time. As he sees it, each one involves the others.†

We have seen that entities are present in one mode of revealing or another; currently, the mode is scientific/technological, what Heidegger calls enframing. This is how things *present themselves* now to us. This is something not in our control; it

is "sent" to us. And we asked, Who does the sending? And now we can see two possible answers: either Being or time.

But neither is adequate, Heidegger thinks. To think of either Being or time as the "giver" of the gift of Being, of presencing, is to turn them back into entities. And that is precisely the wrong way to think. Better, he thinks, is the German phrase *es gibt*. Literally, this means "it gives," but a more idiomatic translation is "there is." So we can say that "it gives Being" or "there is time." There is no "sender" of the gift of Being, if by "sender" we mean "thing that sends." To suppose there is would be to ground Being in *a* being—precisely the error that metaphysics has made all these centuries. We must just acknowledge that "there is time" and "there is Being."

But that acknowledgement is hidden from us under the domination of enframing. Intent on control and mastery of entities, even thinking of human beings as part of the standing-reserve, we pass right over the mystery and wonder of their *presence*. Were we to "turn" from our preoccupation with "challenging" and "setting-upon," this would be an event—perhaps the event of events! It would be the "gathering together" of Being as presencing, of time as the horizon within which presencing occurs, and of man. This would be the true clearing, in which Being and time are *appropriated* by man, and by which man could come into his true essence as the entity that is *open to Being*. Heidegger calls this the *event of appropriation*.

If this were to occur, human beings would no longer think of themselves as lords of the earth, but as guardians or shepherds of Being. They would take it as their responsibility to preserve and protect Being, recognizing that *presencing* is a gift they cannot master or control. We are not, Heidegger says, the masters of Being but its "neighbors."

In the age of enframing, where everything is understood as standing-reserve, there is no "room" for God. (Or perhaps even God is thought of as "standing-reserve," a kind of public utility that can be used to gain satisfaction for one's desires; one

---

* It is interesting to compare here what Plato says about the Form of the Good as "beyond being." See p. 121.

† Compare again Augustine on time, pp. 230–233.

often gets this impression from the television evangelists).* Heidegger does not talk much about God. He thinks of the present time as

> the time of the gods that have fled *and* of the god that is coming.[5]

And he is clear that he does not regard Being as God or a god. But in the event of appropriation, where a man opens up to the mystery of presencing, there is also uncovered the "space" in which God (or "the god," as he sometimes says, echoing Socrates), might become meaningful again. He speaks of this as the sphere of "the holy" and suggests that this is what the poet is apt to reveal.

> Only from the truth of Being can the essence of the holy be thought. Only from the essence of the holy can the essence of divinity be thought. Only in the light of the essence of divinity can it be thought and said what the word "God" is to signify. Or must we not first be able to understand and hear these words carefully if we as men, i.e., as existing beings, are to have the privilege of experiencing a relation of God to man? How, then, is the man of the present epoch even to be able to ask seriously and firmly whether God approaches or withdraws when man omits the primary step of thinking deeply in the one dimension where this question can be asked: that is, the dimension of the holy, which, even as dimension, remains closed unless the openness of Being is cleared and in its clearing is close to man.† Perhaps the distinction of this age consists in the fact that the dimension of grace has been closed. Perhaps this is its unique dis-grace.[6]

We await the event of appropriation, a gracious new gift of "sending," a mode of revealing in which Being is not forgotten or hidden, in which man appropriates what is "given," namely, Being as presence. In this *truth of Being,* this disclosedness, people will come to themselves not by force or resolute willing, but in simply *letting Being be.* If this should take place, we will be transformed as we experience

> the marvel of all marvels; that what-is is.[7]

Basic Questions

1. Indicate the difference between Being and beings. Why does Heidegger say that Being is not *a* being?
2. Why does Heidegger choose *us* as the beings to "interrogate" in his quest for the meaning of Being? And why does he designate us with the term "Dasein"?
3. What does it mean to say that Dasein exists? And what will an existential analysis provide for us?
4. How will a fundamental ontology help in the quest for the meaning of Being?
5. Why does Heidegger recommend we begin our search by examining Dasein's average everydayness? And why is phenomenology the appropriate method?
6. What is hermeneutics? And why must our phenomenology of existence be hermeneutical?
7. How does the notion of Dasein's Being-in-the-world undercut the philosophical tradition about the nature of the self or subject? What does it mean to be in-the-world? And why is epistemology not fundamental?
8. Contrast, using an example, the ready-to-hand with the present-at-hand. Which is basic?
9. What is the world? Contrast Heidegger's answer with that of Wittgenstein's *Tractatus.*
10. What does it mean to say that Dasein is (in its average everydayness) the One? Explain in terms of distantiality and averageness.
11. Explain how the One is both an existential (i.e., is essential to or constitutive of Dasein) and a temptation to inauthenticity.
12. What do moods reveal? How are they related to what Heidegger calls thrownness?
13. What does anxiety reveal? How is it related to responsibility? To inauthenticity?
14. In what way is possibility or potentiality involved in Dasein's understanding of itself?

---

* Compare Augustine on the contrast between use and enjoyment, pp. 241–242, and Socrates on "trading-skill" religion.
† One way to understand Heidegger is to see him addressing a question very similar to the one Kierkegaard thinks is *preliminary* to the question of what it is to be a Christian. See p. 458. You might also compare the "dimension of the holy" to what Wittgenstein calls *the mystical* (p. 567).

15. Explain why understanding is necessarily involved in the hermeneutic circle. Does this have any implications for how certain you should feel about your opinions?

16. Explain idle talk, curiosity, and ambiguity as inauthentic modes of Dasein's Being.

17. What does it mean to say that Care is the Being of Dasein?

18. What is it for an assertion to be-true? Why does Heidegger think that this ontological understanding of truth recovers a meaning that goes deeper than correspondence between a sentence and a state of affairs?

19. Why is a consideration of death necessary if we are to understand Dasein as a totality? Why is Being-towards-death one of the existentials?

20. How does average everydayness manage to "tranquilize" itself about death? Contrast with an authentic appropriation of death.

21. In what way does the call of conscience call Dasein to itself? Relate this to authenticity, responsibility, and guilt.

22. "Temporality reveals itself as the meaning of authentic care." Explain.

23. How does Heidegger conceive that metaphysics is related to the special sciences? To Being?

24. What is the essence of technology, according to Heidegger? In what sense is seeing the world technologically not in our control?

25. In what sense is enframing the "heir" to traditional metaphysics? Why does Heidegger think of enframing as the "supreme danger"?

26. How does Heidegger conceive the relations between art and truth?

27. What is the meaning of Being? How are Being, time, and humans related in presencing?

28. What does it mean that we humans are the "shepherds" or "neighbors" of Being?

For Further Thought

1. Contrast the notion of "world" in the early Wittgenstein and Heidegger. Which do you think is the more basic notion? Why?

2. Write a short story in which the main character exemplifies some aspects of inauthenticity as Heidegger understands that notion.

Notes

1. Quotations from Martin Heidegger's *Being and Time,* trans. John Macquarrie and Edward Robinson (Oxford: Basil Blackwell, 1967), are cited in the text using the abbreviation *BT.*

2. Quotations from Martin Heidegger, *The Question Concerning Technology,* trans. William Lovitt, in *Basic Writings,* ed. David Farrell Krell (New York: Harper and Row, 1977), are cited in the text using the abbreviation *QCT.*

3. Quotations from Martin Heidegger, *The Origin of the Work of Art,* trans. Albert Hofstadler, in *Basic Writings,* are cited in the text using the abbreviation *OWA.*

4. Martin Heidegger, *On Time and Being,* trans. Joan Stambough (New York: Harper and Row, 1972), 2.

5. Martin Heidegger, *Hölderlin and the Essence of Poetry,* trans. Douglas Scott, in *Existence and Being,* ed. Werner Brock (Chicago: Henry Regnery Company, 1949), 289.

6. Martin Heidegger, *Letter on Humanism,* trans. Edgar Lohner, in *Philosophy in the Twentieth Century,* v. 2, ed. William Barrett and Henry D. Aiken (New York: Random House, 1962), 294.

7. Martin Heidegger, "Postscript to *What is Metaphysics?*" in *Existence and Being,* 355.

Afterword

We have come to the end of our survey of Western philosophy. But have we come to the end of philosophy? Although Wittgenstein and Heidegger suggest that philosophy as we have known it is over, the great conversation still seems to be flourishing. As always, it is stimulated both by changes in the world outside itself and by internal developments. Here I want simply to set down a few notes from a philosophy watcher, indicating some interesting things currently happening, hoping to convince you that philosophy is not just its history—that it is *not* all in the past. The situation is somewhat chaotic, as always; only from a later historical perspective could someone say with any assurance what it all means. Remember Hegel's owl. So here are a few impressions.

1. The development of the computer has provided a dramatic new stimulus for thinking about the mind. Here we have a model of something that is clearly a machine but may hold the promise of being genuinely intelligent. This prospect obviously has implications for the quarrel between Descartes and Hobbes about the nature of mind. Philosophers are engaged in fruitful conversations with psychologists, computer scientists, linguists, and neuroscientists in what may become a new discipline: cognitive science. It may be too soon to promise a unified science of the mind, but the work in this area is the most exciting since the heady days of Hume and Kant.

2. The activity in practical, or applied, ethics has been intense. The stimulus of new technologies in medicine and the worries about nuclear war, poverty and starvation, the environment and shady business practices, together with those seemingly intractable problems of abortion and capital punishment, have led to much interesting work. Philosophers not only write books and articles, but also serve on hospital ethics committees, lead seminars on business ethics, and even serve as aides in Congress.

3. Historical and sociological studies of the history of science have raised this question: To what extent—if at all—can we regard the deliverances of the sciences as "objective"? Perhaps (this is the most radical suggestion) they are ideological through and through, governed in their choice of problems and favored solutions by social values they are loath to acknowledge. Perhaps physics is just another kind of literature that tells us more about its creators than about the world! Naturally, this view is not without its critics. And voices in this part of the conversation are sometimes less than calm and measured.

4. Feminist critics have raised worries about the degree to which moral theories have been shaped by male values. Do the Kantian and utilitarian emphases on rules and universality, for instance, reflect the fact that these theories were devised by men living in a world of male dominance? What does this "ethics of impartiality" have to say about the more intimate spheres of personal and family relationships? Should these, too, be governed by a moral law that applies universally? Or would this be the death of them and of something precious to us that makes our lives worth-

while? Have the values of caring and nourishing been unduly neglected by our tradition?

5.   The fact that we now live in a "global village," where very different cultural, religious, and philosophical assumptions confront each other daily, is expanding the context in which we ask philosophical questions. This book is a history of *Western* philosophy; one might think that it is oblivious to those broader contexts. But, as Heidegger urges, unless we understand our own tradition in some depth, we will be shallow and unpromising partners in the broader conversation between East and West. We can look to an intensification of the conversation on this front.

6.   The old antagonism between the relativists and the objectivists seems no nearer resolution. Currently, the sophists seem to be on the ascendant, and devotees of Socrates on the defensive. But many are struggling to see whether there may be a way to acknowledge a truth in relativism without giving up the Socratic quest altogether.*

We can hardly say that Kant's four questions

---

*For a look at the current state of the argument about relativism, see Norman Melchert, *Who's to Say?: A Dialogue on Relativism* (Indianapolis: Hackett Publishing Co., 1994).

have been settled to everyone's satisfaction. We are still asking and must continue to ask

1.   What can we know?
2.   What ought we to do?
3.   For what can we hope?
4.   What is man?

And as to the fourth question, if using the term "man" in just this way now makes us somewhat uncomfortable, we acknowledge one result of how the conversation has gone recently.

Philosophy isn't everything. Daniel Dennett has said that if the unexamined life is not worth living, the overexamined life is nothing to write home about, either (*Elbow Room: The Varieties of Free Will Worth Wanting* [Oxford: Clarendon Press, 1984], 87). But philosophy has the peculiar characteristic of being inescapable for us all. And so we should try to do it with something approaching Aristotelian "excellence" to the extent possible for each of us, remembering what my own German professor once said: "Whether you will philosophize or won't philosophize, you *must* philosophize."

Glossary

a posteriori   A term applied primarily to statements, but also to ideas or concepts; knowledge of the *a posteriori* is derived from (comes *after*) experience (for example, "Trees have leaves").

a priori   A term applied primarily to statements, but also to ideas or concepts, that can be known *prior to* and independently of appeal to experience (for example, "Two and three are five," or "All bodies are extended").

absolute knowledge   A term in Hegel's philosophy designating the state of consciousness when everything "other" has been brought into itself and Spirit knows itself to be all of reality.

alienation   Hegelian term appropriated by Marx to describe the loss of oneself and control over what properly belongs to oneself in capitalist social structures. One's work and the products of one's labor, for instance, are made "alien" to oneself and belong to another. Existentialism stresses the general feeling of alienation among modern human beings.

analytic   A term applied to statements the denial of which is a contradiction (for example, "All bachelors are unmarried").

anticipatory resoluteness   Heideggerian term for authentically facing the fact that one is destined for death.

appearance   The way things present themselves to us, often contrasted with the way they really are (for example, the oar in water appears bent but is really straight). Kant holds that all we can ever come to know is how **things-in-themselves** *appear* to our senses and understanding; appearance is the realm of **phenomena** versus **noumena**.

argument   A set of statements, some of which (the premises) function as reasons to accept another (the conclusion).

atomism   From a Greek word meaning "uncuttable"; the ancient Greek view of Democritus and others that all of reality is composed of tiny indivisible bits and the void (or empty space). See also **logical atomism**.

attunement   In Heidegger's thought, the term for a mode of disclosure that manifests itself in a mood; for example, the mood of anxiety discloses Dasein's not-being-at-home in the world of its ordinary concern. See **Dasein**.

authenticity   Being oneself, taking responsibility for oneself in accepting the burden of having to "be here"—that is, thrown into this particular existence with just these possibilities (Heidegger).

autonomy   Self-rule or giving the law to oneself, as opposed to heteronomy or being under the control of another. A key principle in Kant's **ethics**.

Being   The fundamental concept of **metaphysics**. Doctrines of **categories** such as those of Aristotle and Kant attempt to set forth the most general ways that things can *be*. The meaning of Being is the object of Heidegger's quest.

Being-in-the world   The most general characteristic of **Dasein**, according to Heidegger; more fundamental than knowing, it is being engaged in the use of gear or equipment in a world functionally organized.

categorical imperative   The key principle in Kant's moral theory, bidding us always to act in such a way that the maxim (principle) of our action could be universally applied.

categories   Very general concepts describing the basic

modes of being. Aristotle distinguishes ten, including "substance," "quantity," and "quality." Kant lists twelve, the most important of which are "substance" and "causality."

causation   What accounts for the occurrence or character of something. Aristotle distinguishes four kinds of cause: material, formal, efficient, and final. According to most recent theories, influenced by Hume, causation is a relationship between events where the first is regularly or lawfully related to the second.

compatibilism   The view that human liberty (or freedom of the will) can coexist with determinism—the universal **causation** of all events. Classic sources are Hobbes and Hume.

convention   The Sophists contrast what is true by nature (*physis*) with what is true by convention or agreement (*nomos*) among humans. The latter, but not the former, can also be changed by human decision.

correspondence   A view of truth; a statement is said to be true provided that it "corresponds" with what it is about—that is, it *says* that reality is such and such, and reality *is in fact* such and such.

criterion   A mark or standard by which something is known. The "problem of the criterion" is posed by skeptics who ask by what criterion we can tell that we know something and, if an answer is given, by what criterion we know that this is the correct criterion.

Dasein   Heidegger's term for the way of being that is characteristic of humans. Literally meaning "Being there," it designates that way to be in which one's own **Being** is a matter of concern.

determinism   The view that there is a causal condition for every event, without exception, sufficient to produce that event just as it is. The philosophical relevance of determinism lies particularly in relation to human action.

dialectic   A term of many meanings. For Socrates, it is a progression of questions and answers, driving toward less inadequate opinions. For Plato, it is the sort of reasoning that moves from **Forms** to more basic Forms, and at last to the Form of the Good. For Hegel, it is the progress of both thought and reality by the reconciliation of opposites and the generation of new opposites. Marxists apply the Hegelian doctrine to the world of material production.

dogmatism   A term applied by philosophers to the holding of views for no adequate reason.

dualism   The metaphysical view that there are two basically different kinds of things in reality; the most common dualism is that of mind and body, as in Descartes, for instance.

empiricism   The view that all knowledge of facts must be derived from sense experience; a rejection of the view that any knowledge of nature is innate or constructable by reasoning alone. Exemplified by Hume and the **logical positivists**.

enframing   Heidegger's term for the technological understanding of **Being** as **standing-reserve**, where everything is "set upon" to produce the maximum yield at minimum expense. Enframing is the essence or *meaning* of technology.

entelechy   A goal or end residing within a thing, guiding its development from potentiality to the actuality of its **essence** (Aristotle).

epiphenomenalism   The view that consciousness is an effect of physical happenings in the body but has no causal powers itself. It is just "along for the ride."

epistemology   Theory of knowledge, addressing the questions of what knowledge is, whether we have any, what its objects may be, and how we can reliably get more.

essence   That set of properties which makes each thing uniquely the kind of thing that it is.

esthetic   Kierkegaard's term for the style of life that aims at avoiding boredom and keeping things interesting; the pursuit of pleasurable experiences. Esthetics (also spelled "aesthetics") is the theory of art and of the experience of the beautiful or sublime.

ethics   The study of good and evil, right and wrong, moral rules, virtues, and the good life; their status, meaning, and justification.

existentialism   The philosophy that focuses on what it means to exist in the way human beings do—usually stressing choice, risk, and freedom. Kierkegaard is a main figure, as is Heidegger.

facticity   The way of Being of **Dasein** (Heidegger). One aspect of our facticity, for instance, is our **Being-in-the world**; another is our **thrownness**—simply finding ourselves in existence in some particular way.

fallibilism   The view expressed by Peirce, and earlier by Xenophanes, that though we may know the truth in certain cases, perhaps in many cases, we can never be certain that we do.

falling Heideggerian term for the phenomenon of being defined by others. **Dasein** inevitably *falls-in-with* what "they" say and tends strongly to *fall-away-from* itself.

family resemblance Wittgenstein's term for the way many of our concepts get their meaning. There is no set of necessary and sufficient conditions for an item to be a *game*, for instance, only overlapping and crisscrossing resemblances among instances of things we call games.

Forms Those ideal realities Plato takes to be both the objects of knowledge and the source of the derived reality of the sensible world: the Square Itself, for instance, and the Forms of Justice and the Good.

free spirit A term used by certain late nineteenth-century thinkers, such as Nietzsche, to symbolize their freedom from the inherited tradition—particularly the religious tradition.

great chain of being The view that reality is stretched between God (or the One) and nothingness, with each kind of thing possessing its own degree of being and goodness. Found in Plotinus and Augustine; widespread for many centuries.

hedonism The view that pleasure is the sole objective of motivation (psychological hedonism) or that it is the only thing good in itself (ethical hedonism).

hermeneutic circle The idea that any interpretation takes something for granted; for example, understanding part of a text presupposes an understanding of the whole, and vice versa. Every understanding lights up its objects only against a background that cannot at the same time be brought into the light. It follows that complete objectivity is impossible.

hubris A Greek word meaning arrogance or excessive self-confidence, particularly of mortals in relation to the gods.

idealism The view that objects exist only relative to a subject that perceives or knows them. There are many forms; in Hegel's *absolute idealism*, for instance, mind or Spirit (the Absolute) is the only ultimate reality, everything else having only a relative reality.

inauthenticity Heidegger's word for Dasein's fleeing from itself into the average everyday world of what "they" say and do; not being oneself.

induction A method of reasoning that infers from a series of single cases to a new case or to a law or general principle concerning all such cases.

innate ideas Ideas that any mature individual can acquire independently of experience. Defended in different ways by Plato and Descartes, attacked by the empiricists.

instrumentalism Dewey's term for his own philosophy, according to which all our intellectual constructions (concepts, laws, theories) have the status of tools for solving problems.

language-games Comparing words to pieces in a game such as chess. What defines a rook are the rules according to which it moves; what characterizes a word are the jobs it does in those activities and forms of life in which it has its "home." Language is a game we play with words (the later Wittgenstein).

light of nature Descartes' term for reason, in the light of which things can appear so clear and distinct that they cannot possibly be doubted.

logical atomism A view expressed by the early Wittgenstein, in which language is thought of as a logical calculus built up from simple unanalyzable elements called names. Names stand for simple objects, which are the substance of the world.

logical positivism A twentieth-century version of **empiricism** that stresses the **tautological** nature of logic and mathematics, together with the criterion of **verifiability** for factual statements; if they are not verifiable by sense experience, the statements are not meaningful.

logical truth Truths that are true by virtue of logic alone. Wittgenstein explains logical truths as **tautologies**.

logos Greek term meaning word, utterance, rationale, argument, structure. In Heraclitus, the ordering principle of the world; in the Gospel of John, that according to which all things were made and which became incarnate in Jesus.

materialism The view that the fundamental reality is matter, as understood by the sciences—primarily physics. Mind or spirit has no independent reality.

metaphysics The discipline that studies being as such, its kinds and character, often set out in a doctrine of **categories**. Also called by some "first philosophy."

monism The metaphysical view that there is only one basic kind of reality; materialism is one kind of monism, Hegelian idealism another.

naturalism A view that locates human beings wholly within nature and takes the results of the natural and human sciences to be our best idea of what there is; since Darwin, naturalists in philosophy insist that the human world is a product of the nonpurposive process of evolution.

nihilism   The view that nothing really matters, that distinctions of value have no grounding in the nature of things; what threatens, according to Nietzsche, when God dies.

noumena   Kant's term for things as they are in themselves, quite independently of how they may appear to us; he believes they are unknowable. Contrasted with **phenomena** or **appearance**.

nous   Greek term usually translated as "mind." In Aristotle, *nous* is the active and purely formal principle that engages in thinking and contemplation; he argues that *nous* is more than just the form of a living body; it is a reality in its own right and is eternal.

objective spirit   That realm in which Spirit expresses itself externally, giving rationality to institutions, law, and culture (Hegel).

Ockham's razor   A principle stated by William of Ockham demanding parsimony in the postulation of entities for the purpose of explanation; often formulated as "Do not multiply entities beyond necessity."

One, the   1. In Plotinus and Neoplatonic thought, the source from which the rest of reality emanates. 2. A translation of Heidegger's term "das Man," designating **Dasein** as not differentiated from "the others," the crowd, the anonymous many who dictate how life goes and what it means.

ontic   Heidegger's term for the realm of ordinary and scientific facts; contrasted with **ontological**.

ontological   1. Having to do with **being**, with what there is in the most general sense. 2. In Heidegger, having to do with that deep structure of **Dasein's Being** which makes possible the **ontic** facts about average everydayness; disclosed in *fundamental ontology*.

ontological argument   An argument for God's existence that proceeds solely from an idea of what God is, from his **essence**. Different versions found in Anselm and Descartes; criticized by Aquinas and Kant.

phenomena   What appears, just as it appears. In Kant, contrasted with **noumena**. The object of study by **phenomenology**.

phenomenology   The attempt to describe what appears to consciousness; a science of consciousness; its structures, contents, and objects. In Hegel and later in Husserl and Heidegger.

pictorial form   What a picture and the pictured have in common that allows the first to picture the second (early Wittgenstein).

possible experience   In Kant, a term designating the extent to which sensibility and understanding can reach, structured as they are by the *a priori* intuitions of space and time, together with the *a priori* concepts or **categories**.

possible state of affairs   In early Wittgenstein, the way in which objects could relate to each other to constitute a fact.

pragmatism   A view developed by Peirce, James, and Dewey in which all of our intellectual life is understood in relation to our practical interests. What a concept means, for instance, depends wholly on the practical effects of the object of our concept.

present-at-hand   A Heideggerian term for things understood as bereft of their usual functional relation to our interests and concerns; what "objective" science takes as its object. A modification of our usual relation to things as **ready-to-hand**.

primary qualities   In Galileo and other early Moderns, qualities which a thing actually has—for example, size, shape, location—and which account for or explain certain effects in us (**secondary qualities**), such as sweetness, redness, warmth.

rational psychology   Kant's term for that discipline which attempts to gain knowledge of the self or soul in nonempirical ways, relying on rational argument alone; Kant thinks it an illusion that rational psychology produces knowledge.

rationalism   The philosophical stance that is distrustful of the senses, relying only on reason and rational argument to deliver the truth (Parmenides and Descartes).

ready-to-hand   Heidegger's term for the mode of **Being** of the things that are most familiar to **Dasein**; gear or equipment in its functional relation to Dasein's concerns.

realism   A term of many meanings; central is the contention that reality is both logically and casually independent of even the best human beliefs and theories.

relativism   A term of many meanings; central is the view that there are no objective standards of good or bad to be discovered and that no objective knowledge of reality is possible; all standards and knowledge claims are valid only relative to times, individuals, or cultures.

representational theory   The view that our access to reality is limited to our perceptions and ideas, which function as representations of things beyond themselves; a problem associated with this theory is how we can ever know that there are things beyond these representations.

rhetoric   The art of persuasive speaking developed and taught by the **Sophists** in ancient Greece, whose aim was to show how a persuasive *logos* could be constructed on each side of a controversial issue.

secondary qualities   Those qualities, such as taste and color, produced in us by the **primary qualities** of objects—size, shape, and so on.

semantics   Study of word-world relationships; how words relate to what they are about.

sense-certainty   What is left if we subtract from sensory experience all interpretation in terms of concepts, for example, the sheet blueness we experience when we look at a clear sky; the immediate; where Hegel thinks philosophy must start, though it is forced to go from there.

showing   Contrasted in Wittgenstein's early philosophy with *saying*; logic, for instance, shows itself in every bit of language; a proposition *shows* (displays) its sense, and it *says* that this is how things stand.

skepticism   The view that for every claim to know, reason can be given to doubt it; the skeptic suspends judgment about reality (Sextus Empiricus, Montaigne). Descartes uses skeptical arguments to try to find something that cannot be doubted.

social contract   The theory that government finds its justification in an agreement or contract either among individuals or between individuals and a sovereign power (Hobbes and others).

solipsism   The view, which must be stated in the first person, that only I exist; the worry about solipsism motivates Descartes to try to prove the existence of God.

Sophist   From a Greek word meaning "wise one." The Sophists were teachers in ancient Greece who taught many things to ambitious young men but specialized in **rhetoric**.

standing-reserve   Heidegger's term for the way **Being** is apprehended in a technological society—as entities ready for rational ordering, stockpiling, and use.

Stoicism   The view that happiness and freedom is at hand for the asking if we but distinguish clearly what properly belongs to ourselves and what is beyond our power, limiting our desires to the former and thus keeping our wills in harmony with nature.

substance   What is fundamental and can exist independently; that which has or underlies its qualities. There is disagreement about what is substantial, Plato taking it to be the **Forms**, Aristotle the individual things of our experience. Some philosophers (for example, Spinoza) argue that there is but *one* substance, God.

syllogism   An **argument** of two premises and a conclusion composed of categorical subject-predicate statements; the argument contains just three terms, each of which appears in just two of the statements (Aristotle).

synthetic   A term applied to statements the denial of which is not contradictory; according to Kant, in a synthetic statement the predicate is not "contained" in the subject but adds something to it (for example, "Mount Cook is the highest mountain in New Zealand").

tautology   A statement the truth table for which contains only *T*s. Wittgenstein uses the concept to explain the nature of logical truth and the laws of logic.

teleology   Purposiveness or goal-directedness; a teleological explanation for some fact is an explanation in terms of what it is or what end it serves.

theodicy   The justification of the ways of God to man, especially in relation to the problem of evil: What would justify an all-powerful, wise, and good God in creating a world containing so many evils?

things-in-themselves   In Kantian philosophy, things as they are quite independent of our apprehension of them, of the way they appear to us; **noumena**. Things-in-themselves are unknowable.

Third Man   Term for a problem with Plato's **Forms**: we seem to be forced into an infinite regress of Forms to account for the similarity of two men.

thrownness   Heideggerian term for **Dasein's** simply finding itself in existence under certain conditions, without ever having a choice about that.

transcendental   Term for the conditions on the side of the subject that make knowing or doing possible. Kant's critical philosophy is a transcendental investigation; it asks about the *a priori* conditions for experience and action in general.

utilitarianism   Moral philosophy that takes consequences as the criteria for the moral evaluation of action; of two alternative actions open to one, it is right to choose that one that will produce the best consequences for all concerned—for example, the most pleasure or happiness.

validity   A term for logical goodness in deductive arguments; an **argument** is valid whenever, if the premises are true, it is not possible for the conclusion to be false. An argument can be valid, however, even if the premises are false.

verifiability principle   The rule adopted by the **logical positivists** to determine meaningfulness in factual statements; if no sense experience can count in favor of the truth of a statement (can verify it at least to some degree), it is declared meaningless, since meaning is said to consist in such verifiability.

Credits

Text Credits

Extracts from Hegel, *Reason in History*, translated by Robert S. Hartman, reprinted with permission of Simon & Schuster. Copyright 1953 by The Bobbs Merrill Company; renewal copyright © 1981 by Rita S. Hartman.

Extracts from Wittgenstein, *Philosophical Investigation,* translated by G.E.M. Anscombe, reprinted with permission of Simon & Schuster. Copyright 1953 by The Bobbs Merrill Company; renewal copyright © 1981.

Extracts from Augustine, *On Free Choice of the Will,* translated by Benjamin & Hackstaff, reprinted with permission of Simon & Schuster. Copyright © 1985 by Macmillan Publishing Company; © 1964.

Extracts from Augustine, *On Christian Doctrine,* translated by D.W. Robertson, Jr., reprinted with permission of Simon & Schuster. Copyright © 1985 by Macmillan Publishing Company; © 1958.

Extracts from Epicurus, *Letters, Principle Doctrines and Vatican Sayings,* translated by Russell Geer, reprinted with permission of Simon & Schuster. Copyright © 1985 by Macmillan Publishing Company; © 1964.

Extracts from Ludwig Wittgenstein, *On Certainty,* copyright © 1969 by Basil Blackwell.

Extracts from *The Influence of Darwinism on Philosophy,* pp. 3–14, in *John Dewey: The Middle Works, 1899–1924, Vol. 4: 1907–1909* (Carbondale: Southern Illinois University Press, 1977) © 1977 by Southern Illinois University Press, by permission of Southern Illinois University Press.

Extracts from Martin Heidegger, *Being and Time,* copyright © 1962 by Basil Blackwell.

Extracts from Martin Heidegger, *Basic Writings,* copyright © 1977 by Harper & Row Publishers Inc. Copyright © 1977 by David Farrell Krell. Reprinted by permission of HarperCollins Publishers Inc.

Extracts from John Mansley Robinson, *An Introduction to Early Greek Philosophy,* copyright © 1968 by Houghton Mifflin Company. Used with permission.

Extracts from W.K.C. Guthrie, *The Greeks and Their Gods,* copyright © 1950 by Methuen & Company.

Extracts from Ludwig Wittgenstein, *Tractatus Logico-Philosophicus,* copyright © 1961 by Routledge & Kegan Paul Ltd.

Extracts from Plato, *Symposium,* copyright © 1935 by Michael Joyce.

Extracts from David Hume, *A Treatise of Human Nature,* edited by L.A. Selby-Bigge, second edition revised by P.H. Nidditch, 1978. Copyright © 1967 by Oxford University Press.

Extracts from Hegel, *Phenomenology of Spirit,* translated by A.V. Miller, copyright © 1977 by Oxford University Press.

Extracts from *Hegel's Philosophy of Right,* translated by T.M. Knox, copyright © 1952 by Oxford University Press.

Extracts from Plato, *Gorgias,* copyright © 1953 by W.D. Woodhead, published by Thomas Nelson and Sons Ltd, 1953.

Extracts from Saint Augustine, *The City of God,* translated by Henry Bettenson (Penguin Classics, 1972), copyright © 1972 by Henry Bettenson. Reproduced by permission of Penguin Books Ltd.

Extracts from Saint Augustine, *Confessions,* translated by R.S. Pine-Coffin (Penguin Classics, 1961), copyright © 1961 by R.S. Pine-Coffin. Reproduced by permission of Penguin Books Ltd.

Extracts from Hesiod, "Theogony," as found in *Hesiod and Theognis,* translated by Dorothea Wender (Penguin Classics, 1973), copyright © 1973 by Dorothea Wender. Reproduced by permission of Penguin Books Ltd.

Extracts from Thucydides, *The Peloponnesian War,* translated by Rex Warner (Penguin Classics, 1954), copyright © 1954 by Rex Warner. Reproduced by permission of Penguin Books Ltd.

Photography Credits

INDEX

For readers using the two-volume set of *The Great Conversation,* page numbers 1–332 refer to material in Volume I: *Pre-Socratics through Descartes* and 269–640 refer to material in Volume II: *Descartes through Heidegger.*